BEHAVIOR AND MEDICINE

Dedicated to
Dr. Raymond J. Corsini
the best of my teachers
– DW

To Larry, Emma, and Ben, who gave up so many
evenings of family time so I could work on this book.
– MS

BEHAVIOR AND MEDICINE

FOURTH EDITION

Editors:
DANNY WEDDING, PhD, MPH
Director, Missouri Institute of Mental Health
Saint Louis, Missouri
Professor of Psychiatry
University of Missouri – Columbia School of Medicine
Columbia, Missouri

MARGARET L. STUBER, MD
Jane and Marc Nathanson Professor of Psychiatry
Semel Institute for Neuroscience and Human Behavior
David Geffen School of Medicine
University of California – Los Angeles
Los Angeles, California

Library of Congress Cataloguing-in-Publication Data

is available via the Library of Congress Marc Database
under the LC Control Number 2006920396

Canadian Cataloguing in Publication Data

Behavior and medicine / editors, Danny Wedding, Margaret L.Stuber. — 4th ed.
Includes bibliographical references and index.
ISBN 0-88937-305-1.
Medicine and psychology—Textbooks.   2.Sick—Psychology—Textbooks.
3.Health behavior—Textbooks.
I.Wedding, Danny   II. Stuber, Margaret L., 1953–

R726.5.B45   2006   155.9'16   C2006-900192-8

© 2006 by Hogrefe & Huber Publishers

PUBLISHING OFFICES
USA: Hogrefe & Huber Publishers, 875 Massachusetts Avenue, 7th Floor,
              Cambridge, MA 02139
              Tel. (866) 823-4726, Fax (617) 354-6875, E-mail info@hhpub.com
Europe: Hogrefe & Huber Publishers, Rohnsweg 25, 37085 Göttingen, Germany
              Tel. +49 551 49609-0, Fax +49 551 49609-88, E-mail hhpub@hogrefe.de

SALES AND DISTRIBUTION
USA: Hogrefe & Huber Publishers, Customer Service Department, 30 Amberwood
              Parkway, Ashland, OH 44805, Tel. (800) 228-3749, Fax (419) 281-6883
              E-mail custserv@hhpub.com
Europe: Hogrefe & Huber Publishers, Rohnsweg 25, 37085 Göttingen, Germany
              Tel. +49 551 49609-0, Fax +49 551 49609-88, E-mail hhpub@hogrefe.de

OTHER OFFICES
Canada: Hogrefe & Huber Publishers, 1543 Bayview Avenue, Toronto, Ontario, M4G 3B5
Switzerland: Hogrefe & Huber Publishers, Länggass-Strasse 76, CH-3000 Bern 9

Hogrefe & Huber Publishers
Incorporated and registered in the State of Washington, USA, and in Göttingen, Lower Saxony, Germany

The Editors have undertaken every effort to identify those holding rights in the literary and art works cited in this volume and to obtain their permission for this use. If you should be aware of any additional rights not covered by the credits given, please contact the publisher at one of the addresses given on this page.

Printed and bound in the USA
ISBN 0-88937-305-1

Cover design: Daniel Kleimenhagen, Designer AGD

Foreword

Despite our booming economy, we still face a health-care crisis in the United States. There are at least 45 million people in this country who have no health insurance, while millions more have inadequate insurance. Without access to affordable health insurance, millions of Americans will postpone care and will not be able to afford preventive care. Furthermore, without a regular doctor, many Americans will postpone visiting a physician until their situation becomes critical, and then they will be forced to seek out health care in hospital emergency rooms, further exacerbating our nation's problem with escalating health-care costs.

Our problems with the uninsured and health-care financing stand in marked contrast to the fact that we have, *at the very same time,* the finest health-care delivery system in the world and that we provide the best medical care money can buy—for those who have the money to buy it. Our leadership in medical research and development is unquestioned; the National Institutes of Health are the finest research institutions in the world; our physicians and nurses receive superb educations; and it is common for ill citizens of other countries to come to the United States seeking the best available medical care.

How can these two sets of facts be reconciled? How can it be that we know so much, spend so much, and still acknowledge that a child born in Bulgaria has a better chance of living to see his or her first birthday than a child born two miles from the nation's capitol?

In part, the answer lies in our failure to realize that the health-care problems we face in this country are at their core *behavioral* rather than medical. Our infant mortality statistics are inextricably linked to behavioral problems such as drug abuse and teenage pregnancy and to societal problems such as poverty and ignorance, whereas our lower longevity rates are linked to still other behaviors such as high-fat dietary habits, sedentary living, smoking, and excessive alcohol consumption. Unfortunately, the traditional education of medical, dental, and nursing students has ignored the salience of these relationships, and students have learned little about health and behavior links or about their own ability to alter patient behavior.

I am delighted that *Behavior and Medicine* addresses these issues head on, and I believe this book has the potential to change the thinking and the practice habits of a generation of health professionals. It repeatedly makes the point that the challenges of the future lie more in chronic care than in acute care and that the most significant power of the physician or other health-care provider may lie not in technologic expertise but in his or her capacity to act as a *behavioral change agent* and as a catalyst to get patients to modify a variety of self-injurious behaviors.

Drs. Wedding and Stuber and their contributors have made an important contribution to the medical world with *Behavior and Medicine.* The artwork has been carefully and judiciously selected, the poems are moving, and the epigraphs are poignant. But, of course, the message is far more important than the packaging, and the message is clear: Physicians, nurses, and other health professionals can enhance their understanding of the conditions they encounter by more fully understanding the patients they treat and by appreciating the magnitude and significance of the cultural, social, economic, and political networks in which patient behaviors occur. Both students and practitioners will find that *Behavior and Medicine* is a fine place to start cultivating that understanding.

Tom Daschle

Foreword

I agree wholeheartedly with Tom Daschle's perception about the paradox of the brilliance of American medicine's scientific and clinical achievements and technology and the simultaneous fact that, for most key health indices, the citizens of at least 20 nations are healthier than Americans! At the same time medical sciences have deciphered the genetic code, imaged the brain changing as it functions, showed that psychotherapy affects brain physiology, identified some basic biochemistry of learning, and turned HIV infection – for those properly treated – from a death sentence into a somewhat controllable chronic illness, 18,000 Americans die annually due to lack of health insurance, between 44,000 and 98,000 die annually because of medical errors, and the boundary between medicine and industry becomes progressively more porous, to the point where some observers (and doctors) view medicine not only as a learned, altruistic profession but also as a business. And I couldn't agree more with Tom Daschle's point that much of the problem is behavioral – reflecting the behavior of patients and families, health-care professionals, industries, communities, and the social and economic system.

The media comment hourly on these problems, the population is affected continually, and influential medical education-related organizations like the Institute of Medicine (IOM) and the Accreditation Council of Graduate Medical Education (ACGME) have studied the situation and published strong recommendations concerning behavior in medical education. In its 2004 report, *Improving Medical Education: Enhancing the Behavioral and Social Science Content of Medical School Curricula*, the IOM states unequivocally that, "Approximately half of all causes of morbidity and mortality in the United States are linked to behavioral and social factors." It recommends that "Medical students should be provided with an integrated curriculum in the behavioral and social sciences throughout the 4 years of medical school" and recommends that medical students demonstrate competency in the following domains:

- Mind-body interactions in health and disease
- Patient behavior
- Physician role and behavior
- Physician-patient interactions
- Social and cultural issues in health care, and
- Health policy and economics

The IOM also recommends that the National Institutes of Heath (NIH) or private foundations provide considerable funding for U.S. medical school demonstration projects in behavioral and social science, and for career development awards to produce leaders in the behavioral and social sciences in medical schools, and for the U.S. Medical Licensing Examination (USMLE) to increase behavioral and social science content on its certifying examinations.

These topics also play a central role in education of resident physicians in all medical specialties. The ACGME, which accredits residency programs, requires that all residents be certified as competent in behavioral areas strongly related to the IOM's "domains," including "systems-based practice, as manifested by actions that demonstrate an awareness and responsiveness to the larger context and system for health care"; "interpersonal and communication skills that result in effective information exchange and teaming with patients, their families and other health professionals"; "professionalism, as manifested through a commitment to carrying out professional responsibilities, adherence to ethical principles, and sensitivity to a diverse patient population"; and "medical knowledge about established and evolving biomedical, clinical and cognate (e.g., epidemiological and social-behavioral) sciences and the application of this knowledge to patient care."

Drs. Wedding, Stuber and colleagues have addressed these topics wonderfully in this new book, the chapters of which respond to the IOM's "domains" and are highly relevant to ACGME core competencies. I have read, cover to cover, each of the previous three editions of Danny Wedding's *Behavior in Medicine*, and I am an admiring fan of Dr. Wedding and of the series.

Like its predecessors, this edition is written crystal clearly, and it is a very enjoyable up-to-date "read" filled with wise recommendations and precious information. Its chapters on interviewing and on difficult patients provide numerous helpful examples of patient-doctor dialog with explanations, very useful in preparing for the commonly asked USMLE "what do you say to the patient" test items. The chapter on cultural competence is down-to-earth and practical. The chapter on medical student culture will strike home for many readers. The one on medical humanities is interesting and instructive and, as in the previous editions, the literary quotes and artwork give the book a unique texture and aesthetic dimension. All the authors are experts and fine writers.

Frederick S. Sierles, MD
Professor and Director of Medical Student Education
in Psychiatry and Behavioral Sciences
Rosalind Franklin University of Medicine and Science

Preface

I have been pleased and gratified with the enthusiastic reception of the first three editions of *Behavior and Medicine*. The book has been read by tens of thousands of medical students, and most of these former students are now practicing medicine. One likes to think that the clinical practice of these students will be influenced by the book, and that patient care will be a little more humane, a little more gentle, and perhaps a little more effective because some of the ideas in *Behavior and Medicine* took root.

I'm especially honored to have Dr. Margaret Stuber, the Jane and Marc Nathanson Professor of Psychiatry and Biobehavioral Sciences at UCLA, as my co-editor for this edition. Dr. Stuber is a child psychiatrist with an international reputation who has focused her time in medical education since 1991. Dr. Stuber shares my passion for convincing medical students that understanding human behavior is absolutely critical to their future practice, and she brings experience and training in the design and writing of board examinations. I don't believe I could have picked a better collaborator for this edition.

Hogrefe & Huber publish both in the U.S. and internationally, and they are able to market *Behavior and Medicine* to relevant groups of students around the world. Many medical schools in non-English speaking countries use English language texts, and *all* physicians need to be conversant with the basic principles of behavioral science covered in *Behavior and Medicine*. We're proud that *Behavior and Medicine* has been used to educate medical students in Canada, Great Britain, Australia, New Zealand, South Africa, Thailand, Scandinavia, and dozens of other countries as well as the original target group—medical students preparing to take the United States Medical Licensing Examination.

I have also been pleased with the warm reception *Behavior and Medicine* has received in a number of health professions outside of medicine. Although the book clearly targets medical students and has the avowed aim of helping these students pass the behavioral science portion of the USMLE, professors in training programs in nursing, dentistry, public health, social work, and psychology have adopted the book and found its content germane to their students. In addition, a number of physician assistant training programs have used *Behavior and Medicine* as a core text.

The 4th edition has been explicitly designed to reflect the pedagogical and content recommendations made by the Institute of Medicine in their seminal 2004 publication *Improving Medical Education: Enhancing the Behavioral and Social Science Content of Medical School Curricula*. Dr. Stuber and I believe this is a critically important monograph: Every chapter in the book relates in one way or another to the recommendations in the IOM report, and we have worked hard to ensure that *Behavior and Medicine* addresses each of the priority areas addressed by the Institute of Medicine.

All of the sample questions at the end of the book, designed to help students prepare for the Behavioral Science questions on the National Boards, have been updated and revised to reflect the new USMLE format. Dr. Stuber has spent hundreds of hours preparing these questions, and we believe they offer a useful preview of the kind of behavioral science questions that will be encountered on the USMLE. The student who reads the book and reviews the sample questions should have little trouble with the Behavioral Science section of the USMLE examination; in fact, one of my most gratifying personal rewards as an editor and a medical educator has been the numerous students who have reported that they "aced" the Behavioral Science section of the USMLE after studying *Behavior and Medicine*.

In order to make the book as useful as possible for USMLE review, we have highlighted all **key words, names,** and **phrases** by putting them in bold type, and we have emphasized all the *key concepts* that I think are likely to show up on the USMLE by putting them in italics. Thus, a student who does not have time to read each chapter (and, regrettably, this may include all too many medical students) can still prepare for class examinations and the Behavioral Science portions of the USMLE by reviewing the bold and italicized text. This is not an ideal situation, but we have taught medical students long enough to realize it is both pragmatic and necessary.

We also have worked hard to make this new edition *clinically relevant*, and almost all chapters include a Case Study illustrating the application of the principles being discussed. Every case draws on the clinical experience of the authors and illustrates how the principles of the chapter can be applied in a clinical setting.

Multiple interlocking themes link each chapter in the fourth edition. One theme is the simultaneous *poignancy and beauty of the transitions of life*. As children we were filled with awe and fascination; later we worked through the turmoil of adolescence; still later we each trembled at the touch of a lover. Some of us will be fortunate enough to grow old with someone we care about deeply. All of us will die. Those students who take time to appreciate the majesty of this unfolding will be better physicians and more effective healers.

A second theme of the book is the *salience of the sense of self*. Every cell in the body changes with age and time, but a continuing awareness of self, a continuity of personal identity, significantly shapes and influences our behavior.

A third theme is reflected in the title of *Behavior and Medicine*. Morbidity and mortality are profoundly affected by how we behave; what we eat, drink, and smoke; whom we choose as our sexual partners; how often we exercise; and whether we take medicines as prescribed. Most people are aware of the factors affecting their health and yet continue to engage in maladaptive and harmful behavior. Only the most naive health-care provider sees his or her job as simply telling patients how they *should* behave.

A fourth theme, reflected especially in the section of the book dealing with medical economics, is that *the U.S. health-care system is inefficient, inequitable, and inadequate*. As practitioners, we have witnessed first hand how the corporatization of health care and the rise of for-profit medicine has changed the way health care is delivered and financed in the United States. I am ashamed to live in a wealthy country that stands alone among developed nations in not providing health care for all of her citizens.

A final theme of the book is the *brevity of life and the certainty of death*. The art and poems that illustrate every chapter in the book often portray scenes or descriptions of death. Paradoxically, awareness and acceptance of death can make life richer, fuller, and more meaningful.

It has been profoundly rewarding for me to have a role in the education of several thousand medical students. I hope I have affected their lives; they have clearly shaped mine.

Danny Wedding
Saint Louis, Missouri

ACKNOWLEDGMENTS

One of the pleasures in editing a book is the brief opportunity to thank the many people who contribute to it.

We especially appreciate the chapter authors who were patient with our frequent queries and multiple revisions of their work. Every contributor is a seasoned medical educator, and all are prominent authorities in their respective fields.

The book continues to reflect the values and priorities set by the book's original advisory board. The members of the advisory board and their original university affiliations were John E. Carr, PhD (University of Washington), Ivan N. Mensh, PhD (University of California at Los Angeles), Sidney A. Orgel, PhD (SUNY, Health Sciences Center at Syracuse), Edward P. Sheridan, PhD (Northwestern University), James M. Turnbull, MD (East Tennessee University), and Stuart C. Yudofsky, MD (University of Chicago).

We benefited tremendously from comments made by our colleagues in the Association of Directors of Medical School Education in Psychiatry (ADMSEP), the Association of Psychologists in Academic Health Centers (APAHC), and the Association for the Behavioral Sciences and Medical Education (ABSAME). Many of these individuals use *Behavior and Medicine* as a text, and a significant number are chapter authors in the current edition. These colleagues made dozens of helpful suggestions that have been incorporated in this new edition.

Rob Dimbleby, our editor at Hogrefe & Huber, has become a wonderful friend and valued collaborator. We truly appreciate his support, good judgment, clear thinking, and consistent good humor.

Vicki Eichhorn did more than anyone else to help with the fourth edition. She is an extraordinary assistant, and Danny Wedding would not be half as productive without her. We especially appreciate the extra efforts she took to ensure that we met the production deadlines set by Hogrefe & Huber. Vicki lead a small army of support staff at the Missouri Institute of Mental Health (MIMH) who cheerfully pitched in with the numerous administrative tasks associated with publication of the new edition.

Danny Wedding   **Margaret Stuber**
danny.wedding@mimh.edu   mstuber@mednet.ucla.edu

Contributors

Jack B. Amiel
Summer Intern
Foundation for Psychocultural Research-UCLA
Center for Culture, Brain, and Development
Los Angeles, California

Adam Arechiga, DrPH, PsyD, CHES
Fellow
University of California-Los Angeles
School of Medicine
Center for Human Nutrition
Los Angeles, California

E. Andrew Balas, MD, PhD
Dean & Professor
College of Health Sciences
Old Dominion University
Norfolk, Virginia

Pamela J. Beasley, MD
Director, Pediatric Psychiatry Service
Children's Hospital Boston
Harvard Medical School
Boston, Massachusetts

Deborah Bendell Estroff, PhD
Professor
Fielding Graduate University
Clinical Professor
David Geffen School of Medicine at UCLA
Los Angeles, California

Jonathan Bergman, MD
Department of Urology
David Geffen School of Medicine at UCLA
Los Angeles, California

Pilar Bernal, MD
Assistant Professor
Kaiser Permanente
Stanford University
Palo Alto, California

Laurence A. Bradley, PhD
Division of Clinical Immunology & Rheumatology
University of Alabama at Birmingham
Birmingham, Alabama

Marc Brodsky, MD
Assistant Clinical Professor
UCLA Center for East-West Medicine
Department of Medicine
David Geffen School of Medicine at UCLA
Los Angeles, California

Howard Brody, MD, PhD
Professor
Department of Family Practice
Michigan State University
East Lansing, Michigan

George R. Brown, MD
Professor of Psychiatry
Chief of Psychiatry
James H. Quillen VA Medical Center
Professor and Associate Chairman
Department of Psychiatry
East Tennessee State University
Johnson City, Tennessee

Brenda Bursch, PhD
Associate Professor, Psychiatry & Biobehavioral
Sciences, and Pediatrics
David Geffen School of Medicine at UCLA
Clinical Director, Pediatric Psychiatry
Consultation-Liaison Service
Los Angeles, California

John E. Carr, PhD, ABPP
Professor Emeritus
Department of Psychiatry & Behavioral Sciences,
and Psychology
Seattle, Washington

Salvador Ceniceros, MD
Department of Psychiatry
James H. Quillen VA Medical Center
East Tennessee State University
Johnson City, Tennessee

Steven Cody, PhD
Professor
Department of Psychiatry & Behavioral Medicine
Joan C. Edwards School of Medicine
Marshall University
Huntington, West Virginia

Carol C. Donley, PhD
Andrews Chair in Biomedical Humanities
Co-Director
Center for Literature and Medicine
Hiram College
Hiram, OH

Randall Espinoza, MD, MPH
Associate Clinical Professor and Vice Chief of Staff
Department of Psychiatry and Biobehavioral Sciences
Medical Director, Clinical Geriatric Psychiatry Team
Initiative and ECT Program
Semel Institute for Neuroscience and Human Behavior
at UCLA
Los Angeles, California

David Feinberg, MD, MBA
Associate Professor of Clinical Psychiatry
Semel Institute for Neuroscience and Human Behavior
David Geffen School of Medicine at UCLA
Los Angeles, California

Iris Cohen Fineberg, PhD, MSW, LCSW
General Internal Medicine and Health Services Research
David Geffen School of Medicine at UCLA
Los Angeles, California

Donald M. Hilty, MD
Associate Professor of Clinical Psychiatry
Department of Psychiatry and Behavioral Sciences
University of California, Davis
Sacramento, California

Ka-Kit Hui, MD, FACP
Professor and Director
UCLA Center for East-West Medicine
Department of Medicine
David Geffen School of Medicine at UCLA
Los Angeles, California

Martin Kohn, PhD
Co-Director
Center for Literature and Medicine
Hiram College
Hiram, OH
SAGES Fellow
Case Western Reserve University
Cleveland, OH

Peter Kunstadter, PhD
Adjunct Professor and Research Anthropologist
Department of Medical Anthropology, History,
and Social Medicine
Institute for Health Policy Studies
University of California, San Francisco
Department of Family & Community Medicine
UCSF-Fresno Medical Education Program
University of California
San Francisco, California

Joseph D. LaBarbera, PhD
Associate Professor
Department of Psychiatry
Vanderbilt University
School of Medicine
Nashville, Tennessee

Russell F. Lim, MD
Associate Clinical Professor
Director of Diversity Education and Training
Department of Psychiatry and Behavioral Sciences
University of California, Davis
School of Medicine
Davis, California

John C. Linton, PhD
Associate Professor and Chief Psychologist
Department of Behavioral Medicine
West Virginia University Health Sciences Center
Charleston, West Virginia

Francis G. Lu, MD
Professor of Clinical Psychiatry
Department of Psychiatry
San Francisco General Hospital
San Francisco, California

Gregory Makoul, PhD
Associate Professor and Director
Program in Communication and Medicine
Northwestern University Feinberg School of Medicine
Chicago, Illinois

J. Randy Mervis, MD
Associate Clinical Professor of Psychiatry and
Biobehavioral Sciences
David Geffen School of Medicine at UCLA
Chief, Geropsychiatry Consultation Services
Greater Los Angeles Veterans Affairs Health System,
Sepulveda Campus
Los Angeles, California

Thomas F. Newton, MD
Professor
Department of Psychiatry and Biobehavioral Sciences
David Geffen School of Medicine at UCLA
Los Angeles, California

Barry Nurcombe, MD
Emeritus Professor of Child and Adolescent Psychiatry
The University of Queensland
Queensland, Australia

Jeannine Rahimian, MD, MBA
Assistant Clinical Professor
Department of Obstetrics and Gynecology
David Geffen School of Medicine at UCLA
Los Angeles, California

John E. Ruark, MD, FACP
Clinical Assistant Professor of Psychiatry
Stanford University School of Medicine
Stanford, California

Steven C. Schlozman, MD
Staff Child Psychiatrist, Massachusetts General Hospital,
Boston, MA
Associate Director, Medical Student Education in
Psychiatry, Harvard Medical School
Associate Director, Child and Adolescent Psychiatry
Residency, MGH/McLean Program in Child Psychiatry
Instructor in Psychiatry, Harvard Medical School
Lecturer in Education, Harvard Graduate School
of Education
Cambridge, Massachusetts

Daniel J. Siegel, MD
Associate Clinical Professor
David Geffen School of Medicine at UCLA
Co-Director, Mindful Awareness Research Center
Psychiatry and Biobehavioral Sciences
Semel Institute for Neuroscience and Human Behavior
Los Angeles, California

Alex W. Siegel
Summer Intern
Foundation for Psychocultural Research-UCLA
Center for Culture, Brain, and Development
Los Angeles, California

David M. Snyder, MD, FAAP
Medical Director
Assessment Center for Children
Exceptional Parents Unlimited
Fresno, CA
Associate Clinical Professor
Department of Pediatrics
UCSF School of Medicine
Madera, California

Margaret L. Stuber, MD
Jane and Marc Nathanson Professor of Psychiatry
Semel Institute for Neuroscience and Human Behavior
David Geffen School of Medicine at UCLA
Los Angeles, California

Harsh K. Trivedi, MD
Fellow, Child and Adolescent Psychiatry
Children's Hospital Boston
Harvard Medical School
Boston, Massachusetts

Sharon K. Turnbull, BSN, MPH, PhD
Johnson City, Tennessee

Fredric W. Wolf, PhD
Professor and Chair
Department of Medical Education and Biomedical
Informatics
School of Medicine
University of Washington
Seattle, Washington

Peter B. Zeldow, PhD
Department of Psychiatry
Feinberg School of Medicine
Northwestern University Medical School
Chicago, Illinois

Poetry Credits

The following poems are reproduced with permission of the respective rights holders.

Chapter	Poem	Permission
Section I (p. 2)	*How to be a Poet*	Copyright © 2005 by Wendell Berry from *Given*. Reprinted by permission of Shoemaker & Hoard Publishers.
Chapter 1 (p. 3)	*Brain* by John Stone	From *In All This Rain* © 1980, Louisiana State University. Reprinted by permission.
Chapter 1 (p. 19)	*Seizure* by Jeanne Murray Walker	From *Poetry* (1986). Used with permission.
Chapter 3 (p. 33)	*Only Stars* by Duncan Darbishire	Used with permission.
Chapter 3 (p. 41)	*Emily Drowned* by Darbishire	Used with permission.
Chapter 4 (p. 51)	*The Discovery of Sex* by Debra Spencer	From *Pomegranate*. © Hummingbird Press. Reprinted by permission
Chapter 5 (p. 66)	*The Pleasures of Old Age*	From *Against Romance* by Michael Blumenthal, copyright © 1987 by Michael Blumenthal. Used by permission of Viking Penguin, a division of Penguin Group (USA) Inc.
Chapter 5 (p. 72)	*The Wages of Mercy*	From *Saying the World* by Peter Pereira. Copper Canyon Press (2003). Reprinted by permission.
Chapter 6 (p. 87)	*What Matters*	From *Saying the World* by Peter Pereira. Copper Canyon Press (2003). Reprinted by permission.
Chapter 7 (p. 98)	*Knitted Glove* by Jack Coulehan	Used with permission.
Section II (p. 110)	*Doctors' Row*	From *Collected Poems,* Oxford University Press, copyright © 1970 by Conrad Aiken. Reprinted by permission of Brandt and Hochman Literary Agents, Inc.
Chapter 8 (p. 121)	*He Makes a House Call* by John Stone	From *In All This Rain* © 1980, Louisiana State University. Reprinted by permission.
Chapter 9 (p. 130)	*Two Suffering Men*	Used with permission.
Chapter 12 (p. 157)	*Unrequited Love* by Elizabeth Bartlett	Used with permission.
Chapter 12 (p. 162)	*The Boy Who Played with Dolls*	From *Saying the World* by Peter Pereira. Copper Canyon Press (2003). Reprinted by permission.
Section III (p. 166)	*A Scab*	From *Collected Poems* 1953–1993 by John Updike, copyright © 1993 by John Updike. Used by permission of Alfred A. Knopf, A division of Random House, Inc.
Section IV (p. 188)	*What the Doctor Said* by Raymond Carver	From *A New Path to the Waterfall,* copyright © 1989 by Tess Gallagher. Reprinted by permission of International Creative Management, Inc.
Chapter 15 (p. 190)	*Patients* by U.A. Fanthorpe	Used with permission
Chapter 16 (p. 203)	*But Her Eyes Spoke Another Language* by Duncan Darbishire	Used with permission.
Chapter 21 (p. 264)	*Rock of Ages* by Jack Coulehan	Used with permission.
Section V (p. 270)	*The Hands* by John Stone	From *Renaming the Streets* © 1985, Louisiana State University. Reprinted by permission.
Section VI (p. 302)	*Coda* by Samuel Stearns	Used with permission.
Chapter 25 (p. 313)	*Murmur*	From *Saying the World* by Peter Pereira. Copper Canyon Press (2003). Reprinted by permission
Chapter 26 (p. 326)	*Peau D'Orange* by Marcia Lynch	Used with permission.

Contents

PART 1: MIND-BODY INTERACTIONS IN HEALTH AND DISEASE

PART 2: PATIENT BEHAVIOR

PART 3: THE PHYSICIAN'S ROLE

PART 4: PHYSICIAN-PATIENT INTERACTIONS

PART 5: SOCIAL AND CULTURAL ISSUES IN HEALTH CARE

PART 6: HEALTH POLICY AND ECONOMICS

PART 7: APPENDICES

PART 1
MIND-BODY INTERACTIONS
IN HEALTH AND DISEASE

How To Be a Poet
(to remind myself)

Make a place to sit down.
Sit down. Be quiet.
You must depend upon
affection, reading, knowledge,
skill—more of each
than you have—inspiration,
work, growing older, patience,
for patience joins time
to eternity. Any readers
who like your work,
doubt their judgment.

Breathe with unconditional breath
the unconditioned air.
Shun electric wire.
Communicate slowly. Live
a three-dimensioned life;
stay away from screens.
Stay away from anything
that obscures the place it is in.
There are no unsacred places;
There are only sacred places
And desecrated places.

WENDELL BERRY

1 Mind, Brain, and Behavior

Daniel J. Siegel, Alex W. Siegel, & Jack B. Amiel

BRAIN
is
most like
a priest
who revels in
the body's feast
and says
too much
and asks
how long
and sings his own
electric song
until he totters
on his shelf
and as he falls
forgives himself.

JOHN STONE

INTRODUCTION

What does a professional in the art of healing need to know about the science of the brain and the nature of the mind? How does knowledge about the brain and its influence on behavior enrich clinical practice? Why should a practitioner who works with others to help alleviate their suffering invest the time and energy into understanding the brain and behavior when there are so many other details to learn about illness and treatment? The simple answer to each of these questions is that in order to understand how to treat people, we need to understand how patients experience their illness, their encounter with you, and their behaviors that may support a path toward healing. At the heart of a person's inner experience and outer behavior is the mind.

One dictionary definition states that the mind is "considered as a subjectively perceived, functional entity, based ultimately upon physical processes but with complex processes of its own: It governs the total organism and its interaction with the environment." The mind is often viewed as synonymous with the psyche, the soul, the spirit, and the intellect. From this perspective, the mind is not distinguished from the "heart," and thoughts are not separated from feelings. In this chapter we will explore the ways in which we can view the mind as the core of a person's evolving identity. The ways in which that person responds in an interview, a diagnostic test, or a discussion about potential illnesses, and his or her specific attitude and approach to treatment are each a function of that person's mind.

The mind is a process that regulates the flow of energy and information. Your mind is taking in the information of these words at the moment you read them. You are investing energy in the reading of this sentence, and the layers of information processing beneath your awareness are making linkages to ideas and facts you've thought of in the past. In fact, most of the flow of energy and information—the essence of our minds—is beneath our awareness. Mental activity, such as feeling and thinking, can enter conscious awareness and subsequently be shared with both our own conscious mind and with other people. When the important feelings and thoughts in our nonconscious mental lives remain out of the spotlight of conscious attention, out of our awareness, they can still influence our decisions, reactions, and behaviors.

In this chapter we'll be offering you a way to think about the mind at the center of human experience. The benefit for you in reading through this chapter will be that you'll gain a new view of others' minds, and perhaps even your own. Because of the necessary brevity of this discussion, only major concepts will be highlighted. If you are interested in further reading you may find the works cited in the Suggested Readings to be an excellent way to learn more about this fascinating topic.

> The separation of psychology from the premises of biology is purely artificial, because the human psyche lives in indissoluble union with the body.
>
> C.G. JUNG

BRAIN AND MIND

You can see from the definition given above that the mind has the interesting quality of being "based ultimately upon physical processes" but that it also has "complex processes of its own." The mind is a subjective entity, meaning that we each experience within us the process of mind that may not be wholly available to objective, and especially quantitative, analysis. The reason we need to pay attention to subjective mental life is that objective research shows us that physical health is directly related to mental well-being. The subjective nature of the mind, and the mind's well-being, are in fact some of the most important contributors to physiological well-being. For example, studies have quantitatively proven that how you focus your attention during a medical treatment, such as "light therapy" for psoriasis, has a profound impact on the outcome of medical interventions. People who practice a form of being aware in the present moment, called **mindful attention**, have been shown to have improved immune function. The focus of attention literally means how you regulate the flow of information in your, i.e., how you regulate your mind. Therefore, mental life directly affects medical states—such as those of the heart, immune system, and lungs.

You may be wondering how a "subjective entity" such as the mind can affect the physical processes of the cardiovascular system or the activity of the immune system. One way to explore this relationship between mental function and physiology is to take a look at the connection between the information and energy flow of the mind and the physical activity of the brain.

Many disciplines of science are concerned with understanding the mind. One of those fields is the fascinating area of neuroscience, the study of the structure and function of the nervous system. Branches of this field study specific aspects of neural functioning, such as how the activity of the brain gives rise to thinking, emotion, attention, social relationships, memory, and even moral decision-making. Taken as a whole, the field of neuroscience has been exploding with new insights into the correlation between the brain's function and internal mental processes affecting the outward expression of behaviors. The numerous and expanding insights into brain-mind correlations have direct relevance for the clinical practitioner.

Neural Activity Correlates with Specific Mental Processes

While science demonstrates correlations between activity in the brain and the subjective experience of the mind, we can only say at this point that these are associational findings. In other words, *neural activity in one area of the brain correlates directly with mental activity of a certain type.* Here's one example: When you look at a picture of, say, the Golden Gate Bridge, we know that the posterior part of your brain, in the occipital lobe of the neocortex, will become active. You may already know that that back part of your brain has been called the **visual cortex** because of this association. We even know that if you *remember* the visual scene of the Golden Gate Bridge, that same area of the cortex will be activated. In fact, remembering anything you've seen will activate that posterior region. But here's a new finding that puts a slight twist on what we should call that area. It's been known for some time that blind people use the occipital cortex to process what they feel with their fingers, including the raised letters of Braille. Recently a study examined the brain function of people who volunteered to be blindfolded for 5 days, using their fingers to feel their way around the controlled environment in which they lived during that period of time. Without the input of their optic nerves during that sightless period, the input from their fingers became dominant in influencing the activity of their occipital lobes, and their occipital lobes were activated whenever they touched something with their fingers.

What does this mean? This study proves that *the brain is an ever-changing, dynamic organ that is extremely responsive to experience.* Also, as this study reveals, the precious information-processing real estate of the brain is open to "the most competitive bidder." In the study just described, the now dominant input from the fingers to sense the spatial world came to be "processed" in the occipital lobe. In fact, some researchers have suggested that the visual cortex be renamed the "spatial cortex." For us, the important issue is that our five senses directly shape the neural architecture and function of the brain.

The overly simplistic view that the mind is "just the activity of the brain" can mislead us into reductionistic thinking and unhelpful conclusions. Our minds can be understood in the example given to create an image of the spatial world and will harness any neural machinery necessary to create that three-dimensional perspective. In fact, a range of studies has demonstrated that how we harness the flow of energy and information—how our minds function—can directly shape the connections in the brain.

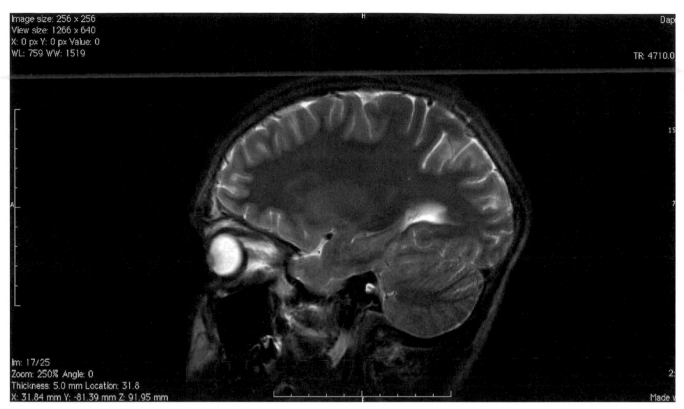

FIGURE 1.1 Advances in imaging technology offer an extraordinary opportunity to relate brain morphology with behavioral functioning

Some people even believe that the mind "uses the brain" to create whatever it needs. In this chapter, we embrace this open dimension of the associational and bidirectional influence of mind-brain relationships.

Mental Experience Occurs as Neurons Become Active

Mental processes occur when neurons fire. Whenever you think of "experience," try translating that into the idea of "neural firing in the brain"—that is, every time you have an experience there is specific activity occurring in your brain, meaning that specific clusters of neurons are becoming active. The benefit of this thinking is that it helps you understand how the mind works. The firing of neurons can lead to a cascade of associated firings because the brain is an intricate, interwoven set of web-like neural circuits. Specific regions in the brain are devoted to specific forms of mental processing, such as spatial perception for the occipital regions, as we discussed earlier. Knowing a bit about brain anatomy can, therefore, inform us about the architecture of our mental lives. The more we can understand the underlying structure and function of our internal, mental lives the more we can understand ourselves and patients. In fact, studies of the doctor-patient relationship reveals that such an understanding of others' minds, called

empathy, is one of the most important factors in determining the extent to which clinicians can help others with their difficulties.

To understand the mind in a deeper way, we are turning toward the brain for scientifically based insights that can build our capacities to be empathically sensitive to the subjective lives of others. Here we are starting with the principle that mental processes emerge as neurons fire in specific areas of the brain. What does "neural firing" really mean? Recall that the basic cell of the nervous system is the neuron. This long spindly cell reaches out to other neurons to connect at the space called a synapse. Synaptic junctions are generally at the receiving neurons' cell body or dendrite. The electrical current, known as an action potential, passing down the length of the neuron, leads to the release of neurotransmitters from the presynaptic neuron to influence the firing of the postsynaptic neuron. Ultimately the summation of the excitatory vs. inhibitory transmitters at the synaptic cleft will determine if the downstream (postsynaptic) neuron will in turn send an action potential down its membrane to influence further neural firing.

Here are the numbers that illuminate the fascinating complexity of the whole process. *The average neuron in your brain is connected directly to about ten thousand other neurons. The estimated twenty to one hundred billion neurons in your brain allow for trillions of connections in a spider-web of soft neural tissue in your skull.*

Neurons that Fire Together, Wire Together

Before this seems too overwhelming, remember that there are several principles that make this intricate anatomy actually quite understandable, interesting, and relevant for clinical practice. One of these is our third general principle: *Neurons that fire together, wire together.* Described long ago, this underlying property of the nervous system has now been explored in great detail. The "linkages" among neurons, the synaptic connections interweaving numerous neurons to each other, is what we mean by the saying that "neurons wire together." The first part of the principle, "Neurons that fire together," means that when we have an experience the brain becomes activated in various regions. When neurons are activated at a given time, the connections among those simultaneously active neurons are strengthened. This is why if you've had an experience (remember, "neural firing patterns activated") say, of hearing a certain song when you've felt very happy, in the future you are likely to have the same feeling (neural firing of joy) when you hear that same song (neural firing in response to the sounds of the music). This is how learning and memory work. Neurons that fire together at one time are more likely to fire together in the future because the synaptic connections that link them together have become strengthened as a result of the experience.

In fact, it is this synaptic connecting that shapes the architecture of the brain, making each of us unique. Even identical twins will have subtle differences between their brains that are created by the unique experiences that shape those synaptic connections that directly influence how the mind emerges from the activity of the brain. Our inner mental life, a life of thoughts, feelings, and memories, is directly shaped by how our neurons connect with each other—which in turn has been directly shaped by our experiences. In addition, our external behavior is directly shaped by the synaptic connections within our skulls. In short, the brain shapes both our minds and our behavior.

> Future generations, paying tribute to the medical advances of our time, will say: "Strange that they never seemed to realize that the real causes of ill-health were to be found largely in the mind."
>
> LORD PLATT
> Professor of Medicine, Manchester, UK
> *British Medical Journal*

The Mind Can Shape the Connections in the Brain

The fascinating relationship between brain and mind goes even deeper than the one-way street of the brain leading to

Head Stripped From Top to Show Ventricles and Cranial Nerves *J. Dryander (1573).* Courtesy of the National Library of Medicine. *Brain size and cranial capacity have not been demonstrated to be meaningfully related to intelligence in humans.*

mental activity and behavioral output. A fourth principle reveals the bidirectionality of mental process and neural firing: *The mind shapes the connections in the brain.* Recall that the mind is the regulation of energy and information flow. Also consider the fact that the mind has "processes of its own," beyond the physical processes of the brain from which it emerges. Researchers have clearly established the mind's power to shape neural firing patterns.

Try this out: Think of what you had for dinner last night. Now try to imagine—using visual imagery—what you'll have for dinner tonight. In this simple exercise, you have chosen (with a little suggestion from these words, but ultimately of your own volition) to use your mind in ways that involve aspects of memory and visualization in your occipital region. Now consider this question: Did your mind make your brain become active in these areas, or did your brain activate and then your mind followed afterwards? The force of mental power to activate the brain gives us a profoundly important insight into how our minds can directly shape the physical state of our bodies. In this exercise, the information flowing from these printed words to your eyes directly influenced your mind—the flow of energy and information within you.

It is helpful in life and in clinical work to realize that a person's "mental will" and "intention" are mental processes that can shape how neurons fire. In turn, how neurons fire shapes how they alter their connections with each other. As those neural connections change, the patterns of the mind—ways of thinking, feeling, and behaving—can change. In other words, the mind directly shapes the physical properties of the brain, which in turn alter how our bodies, including the brain, function. These somatic and neural changes in turn can directly influence how our minds function, and how we feel and how we interact with others.

Consciousness Permits Choice and Change

This raises a fifth and final principle for this section. *With consciousness comes the possibility of choice and change.* Neural connections in the brain allow for certain patterns of thinking, feeling, and behaving to be enacted. In the course of normal living, these mental activities are often on "automatic pilot," and are likely shaped largely by the neural connections that then directly influence mental processes. With conscious awareness, however, something new appears to enter this otherwise automatic self-fulfilling brain prophecy. With focal attention—with the focusing of awareness onto a process—the power of the mind can be engaged to actually alter old habits of behaving, emotionally responding, and thinking. With consciousness there is the possibility to "wake up" and change old patterns. With practice in living *intentionally,* these new mentally activated neural firings can create the changed neural wiring that will make these new patterns of mind more likely to occur, even automatically. In other words, what initially required deliberate conscious attention to change old patterns can become a new and less energy-consuming set of behaviors in the future. This is the essence of new learning.

EXPERIENCE AND GENES SHAPE THE BRAIN: RELATIONSHIPS, CULTURE, AND LIFELONG DEVELOPMENT

As you've seen in our earlier discussion, experience not only involves neural firing, but it also shapes neural connections. This may come as a surprise to many who thought that solely genes dictate the structure of the brain. The fact is that both genes and experience shape the brain's structural properties—the ways that neurons

are synaptically connected to each other. About a third of our genes directly determine neural connections, and another one sixth indirectly influence synaptic connections. That's one half of our genome influencing neural architecture. In the womb, genes play a major role in shaping the basic foundation of the brain. Even after birth, genes continue to influence how our neurons link up to one another. However, both the environment in the womb and our experiences after birth influence the synaptic linkages within our brains. When a baby is born, the distinct neural patterns emerging from these prebirth influences contribute to what is called our innate **temperament**. These constitutional patterns of responding and perceiving can make some of us shy and others outgoing. Some may be quite sensitive to stimuli and become overwhelmed easily, while others thrive with intense sounds and sights.

As we grow our temperamental features interact with our experiences in shaping the person that we become. One of the earliest types of experiences that shape us is our relationship with our caregivers. Known as **attachment**, these early child-caregiver experiences are thought to directly shape the circuitry of the brain responsible for how the child comes to regulate his emotions, govern his thoughts, and engage with other people. But while early attachment is extremely important, *the brain proves to be open to change throughout the lifespan.* Understanding the impact of early life experiences on how you grew up has scientifically been proven to be an important aspect of how the mind can "wake up" and *not* repeat unhelpful learned patterns from the past. These attachment studies resulted in two important findings: (1) It is never too late to make sense of one's early life experiences and become the person one may truly want to be, and (2) without such understanding, individuals often live on "automatic pilot" and repeat suboptimal ways of relating to others within their personal and professional lives.

Given that the brain continues to make new connections and possibly even grow new neurons throughout the lifespan, *each of us can use the power of our mind to alter the connections in our brains.* The experiences we continue to have within the specific culture in which we live can continue to shape how our brains are changing in response to experience. Becoming aware of the impact of these cultural and personal experiences on our continually changing brains can help us understand the ways in which our external environment shapes our internal world.

Becoming aware of ourselves and waking up means becoming conscious of the power of the mind to make choices that may have previously been considered impossible. Neither our genes nor our early life experiences permanently restrict our minds. The key for clinicians is learning how to teach patients scientifically grounded facts about of how central the mind is in shaping its own pathway.

CENTRAL ORGANIZING PRINCIPLES

Self-Regulation

These are powerful ideas that are not easily taken in and understood by either professionals or patients. Fortunately there are a few central principles that can help organize these ideas about brain, mind, behavior, experience, and physiology. One of these principles has to do with *self-regulation*. In physiology we learn about the process of **homeostasis**, how the body maintains its various systems in balance for optimal functioning. Whether it is the renal system, the cardiovascular system, or the respiratory system, we can examine how homeostasis is maintained to achieve a state of health and well-being. Whenever a system is stressed, homeostasis is challenged. Some stressors lead to high-energy processes that strive to regain homeostasis; other stressors can lead to overwhelming imbalance and devastation that can cause a massive shutting down of normal functioning and even death without intensive intervention.

The brain also functions as a self-regulatory system that achieves balance by using a number of domains of functioning. In the simplest terms, the brain moves toward neural homeostasis by alternately using internal and external components. An internal component of the nervous system would include the synaptic connections in the brain itself, or the level of firing in particular regions. An external component of the nervous system would involve input from the environment, such as altering the signals being received from other people. For example, a newborn who is overwhelmed with stimuli from the external environment will fall asleep in order to maintain balance. Some have used the term **allostasis** to refer to how the person achieves stability through adaptive variability. In other words, the mind can utilize its different internal and interpersonal capacities to alter its functioning in order to maintain equilibrium in the long-run. Homeostasis of the body parallels equilibrium of the mind. The concept of **self-regulation** implies that this equilibrium is achieved by altering internal elements, such as how you think or feel, and external interpersonal elements, such as the people you communicate with during a stressful period. Self-regulation in our social lives entails modifying both individual and relational elements to achieve equilibrium.

Out of the Balanced Flow: Chaos or Rigidity

Our brain achieves balance by directing the flow of energy and information within its neural firing patterns to optimize functioning. One way to describe this neural equilib-rium is to use the metaphor of a river. Each bank represents the extreme poles of brain balance: one bank is a state of chaos, the other bank is a state of rigidity. Down the middle between rigidity and chaos flows the river of well-being, which can be defined as harmony. In this harmonious state, one is flexible, adaptive, coherent, energized, and stable. The acronym **FACES** can be used to remember these five qualities of neural equilibrium and mental well-being.

The neurons encased in the skull achieve equilibrium through a process called **neural integration**. Integration means the linking together of differentiated components into a functional whole. Neural integration is what the brain naturally strives to do. When a brain is integrated, it is able to achieve the most flexible, adaptive, and stable states of functioning, the "FACES" flow of the mind and brain that occurs when information and energy are flowing in a harmonious manner. When the brain cannot achieve such integration, a person can experience states of either chaos or rigidity. The brain may become inflexible, mal-adaptive, incoherent, depleted of energy, and unstable. You may notice such a stressed neural or mental system in your self or others by observing how internal mental processes, such as thoughts or feelings, or external behaviors, such as reactions to others, occur in response to the extremes of rigidity or of chaos.

As a general starting point, this central organizing principle of self-regulation emerging from the brain's natural drive toward integration helps us see when the everyday challenges of life become overwhelming and when stress has produced a mental pathway that is rigid or chaotic. As a professional, the river metaphor can help you understand how you, your colleagues, or your patients may be adapting to life's daily challenges to neural homeostasis and mental well-being.

THE BRAIN IN THE PALM OF YOUR HAND

We've now seen that behavior emanates from the neural firing patterns of the brain and other areas of the nervous system in creating the mind. Mental processes emerge from the firing patterns of particular clusters of neurons. Knowing a bit about these neural regions can be helpful in getting a sense of the relationships between brain and behavior. We've explored the notion that mental well-being and neural equilibrium flow like a harmonious, coherent river with rigidity and chaos on either side. This river of well-being includes being flexible, adaptive, coherent, energized, and stable. In this flow, however, there are twists and turns as the body attempts to integrate its differentiated components to achieve these pathways. As we explore the different regions of the brain, keep in mind that this neural integration involves how differentiated, specialized areas are brought together as a functional whole. This is what neural integration is—the ways that the brain links disparate areas together as a functional whole. When integration is achieved, equilibrium is possible and that state of a coherent and harmonious mind can occur. When integration is impaired, the mind moves into rigid or chaotic states that are not adaptive.

The Nonverbal Right Hemisphere

One way that we can see the nature of how the overall mental system functions is through examining the emotional state of a person. Emotions involve subjective internal feelings, physiological changes in the body, and often, but not always, nonverbal communication. Nonverbal expressions include eye contact, facial expressions, tone of voice, gestures, posture, timing, and intensity of responses. You can remember these seven nonverbal signals by pointing to your eyes, circling your face, pointing to your voice box, gesturing with your hands, pointing to your body, and then pointing to your watch. Interestingly, *these nonverbal expressions are both sent and received by the nonverbal right hemisphere of your brain*. In contrast, words are most often sent and received by your left hemisphere, the seat of logic and linear thinking. The right hemisphere, however, appears to be more closely linked to our emotional limbic areas that register autobiographical memory and receive an

integrated map of the body, including input from the heart and intestines.

The Subcortical Brainstem and Limbic Regions

In addition to having two halves of the brain that are separated in the cortex and the limbic areas but are connected via the corpus callosum, we also have other regions worth knowing a bit about. If you put your thumb in the middle of your palm and fold your fingers over the top, you'll have a pretty handy model of the brain and a useful way to visualize some major brain regions. Your wrist is the representation of the spinal cord coming up your back and connecting to the brain at the base of the skull. The first of three major areas we'll be examining in this model is the brainstem, located in the middle of the palm of your hand. The brainstem carries out basic physiological regulation functions, such as heart rhythms and sleep-wake cycles. The brainstem is also responsible for the survival reflexes of fight, flight, or freeze in reaction to threat. The next major region is represented by your thumb and is the limbic area. (Ideally we'd have two thumbs, a left and right limbic area). In this region are the areas of the brain responsible for generating emotion, motivation, the appraisal of the meaning of experiences, and attachment relationships. Evolved in our mammalian heritage, these limbic areas include the **amygdala**, responsible for the fear response, and

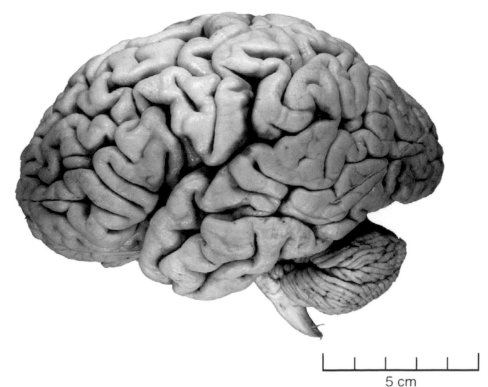

FIGURE 1.2 The Human Brain. Courtesy of the University of Wisconsin-Madison Brain Collection. *Few of us pause to reflect on the majesty of the human brain, or the extent to which it is an integral part of what we call the self.*

5 cm

the **hippocampus**, which is involved in certain forms of memory.

The Cortex

If you fold your fingers over the limbic thumb area, you'll find the location of the **cortex**, which also developed during our journey into mammalian life. This "outer bark" of the brain is in general responsible for complex representations, such as perception and thinking. In general, the posterior lobes of the cortex carry out perception. The frontal lobes, located from the second-to-last knuckles to your fingertips, represent the regions responsible for motor action and planning as well as more complex thinking and reasoning. The front-most part of this area is represented from your last knuckles down to your fingernails and is called the prefrontal cortex. As you'll see, the prefrontal cortex is important for many functions relevant for understanding the connections among mind, brain, and behavior.

The Prefrontal Cortex

The prefrontal cortex can be divided into two areas: a side part and a middle part. Naturally the whole brain could be divided ultimately into at least one hundred billion parts, the neurons in the brain. But the brain's numerous neurons are clustered into groupings that work together as differentiated regions that carry out specialized functions. As we've seen, the brain strives toward integration of these differentiated areas. The prefrontal regions' anatomic location actually makes them quite important in connecting separate areas to each other. The side part, called the **dorsal lateral prefrontal cortex**, is important in creating working memory. Acting like the "chalkboard of the mind," this side region links its activity with other activated areas to create the experience of conscious awareness. When we say "put [something] in the front of your mind," we are inviting the dorsal lateral prefrontal cortex to link its activity with whatever that something is, whether an abstract thought or a bodily sensation.

The middle part of the prefrontal cortex is also in a unique position to integrate widely separated areas into a functional whole. Take a look at where the middle two fingernail regions rest in your hand-model of the brain. Notice how this middle prefrontal cortex area "touches everything" just as this area of the brain links the brainstem, limbic areas, and cortex into a functional whole. As we'll see below, this area also links the input of the body and the input from the social world, binding together somatic, cerebral, and social functions into an integrated process.

The middle part of the prefrontal cortex consists of the regions called the **orbitofrontal cortex**, located just behind the eyes, the **anterior cingulate**, just behind it, and the **medial prefrontal cortex** behind the forehead. Together, these three regions carry out very important integrative functions. Here is a list of nine functions mediated by the middle prefrontal regions extracted from the research literature on the human brain:

1. *Bodily Regulation:* This area regulates the two branches of the autonomic nervous system, and it keeps the sympathetic ("accelerator") and parasympathetic ("brakes") branches in balance.
2. *Attuned Communication:* When we lock eyes with someone and align our own state of mind with another person, this resonant state involves the activation of the middle prefrontal cortex.
3. *Emotional Balance:* The lower limbic areas generating emotion are able to achieve enough arousal for creating meaning in life but are kept from becoming excessively aroused and disabling a person's information processing. This is achieved by the inhibitory action of the fibers from the middle prefrontal regions, which extend to the limbic areas such as the amygdala.
4. *Response Flexibility:* Our ability to take in multiple channels of stimuli and pause before acting long enough to choose from a range of adaptive responses is mediated by this region.
5. *Empathy:* Putting yourself in the mental perspective of another person, seeing through another's eyes, involves middle prefrontal activity.
6. *Self-Knowing Awareness:* Having the capacity to reflect on your past, link it to the present, and anticipate and plan for the future are middle prefrontal activities.
7. *Extinction of Fear:* Recent studies have revealed that the middle prefrontal region sends **GABA** (the inhibitory neurotransmitter **gamma amino butyric acid**) fibers downward to the fear-generating amygdala to inhibit the amygdala-generated fear response.
8. *Intuition:* The input of our body's organs, such as the physiological state of the intestines and heart, find their way to the middle prefrontal regions. These organs appear to have neural processors surrounding them that act as a kind of "peripheral brain" in which our gut and heart's responses actually process information about the social and personal worlds. Intuition may involve paying attention to these important nonverbal sources of knowledge.
9. *Morality:* Studies of individuals with damage to the middle prefrontal region reveal that moral reasoning appears to be processed via the integrative circuitry of this region. When the prefrontal cortex is damaged, people may become amoral, no longer able to consider the larger good for others when thinking through a problem.

CASE EXAMPLE: Neurobiology and Personality
Phineas Gage (1848)

Phineas Gage's medial prefrontal and orbitofrontal cortex were irrevocably damaged when an explosive charge he was setting detonated and blasted an iron pole, 3 feet in length and 2 inches in diameter, through his face and up through the front of his skull. Miraculously, Gage survived, and after a lengthy recovery period he was able to resume a normal life.

The accident rendered Gage a changed man. Once described as "a most efficient and capable foreman" who possessed "a well-balanced mind" and who was perceived by all who knew him as a "shrewd, smart businessman, very persistent in executing all his plans of operation," Gage was reduced to existing in a state described by his closest friends as "fitful, irrelevant, often indulging in the grossest of profanity." He was furthermore "impatient of advice when it conflicts with his own personal desires—devising many plans of future operation which are no sooner arranged than abandoned." John Harlow, the physician documenting the case, described Gage as behaving like " an ill-tempered child, giving expression to an endless succession of strong emotions."

These Victorian descriptions of behavior may differ from ours but they are surprisingly illuminating. What they show is that at least six of the nine functions mediated by the middle prefrontal cortices are implicated in Gage's behavioral changes.

Behavior that is "fitful" and "irrelevant" clearly shows damage to the functions of *attuned communication* and *response flexibility*. The

adjective "profane" points us at an impaired sense of *morality* and *empathy*, while the "impatience of advice" suggests a failure of *emotional balance* and *self-knowing awareness*. Clearly Gage could no longer see himself in an objective, rational way. It seems that the once capable future-planner and decision-maker was now given to making decisions that varied depending upon his emotional state. Gage's ability to perceive himself, and to project that perception of self into the future, were heavily compromised.

All the descriptions are indicative of poor self-control, reduced emotional regulation, and a lack of empathy for social constraints and the feelings of others. They demonstrate the importance of the frontal region's control over the emotions and desires that originate in the limbic areas.

With the destruction of Gage's neural structures we are able to define by their absence the importance of the role they play in mediating and integrating our emotional lives with our social behavior. Though we don't know the nature of Gage's internal narrative, the destruction of the frontal cortex and inhibitory fibers explains why Gage was no longer able to control and regulate his emotions and why he would behave "like an ill-tempered child." That ill-tempered child died over 100 years ago, but we are still learning from him. This case and other like it combined with recent brain imaging studies point to the important role of the prefrontal areas in the creation of personality. These prefrontal regions play an important role in integrating many regions of the brain and in this way bring together the processing of emotional, social, and bodily inputs in the creation of patterns of perception, thinking, and behavior that we call personality.

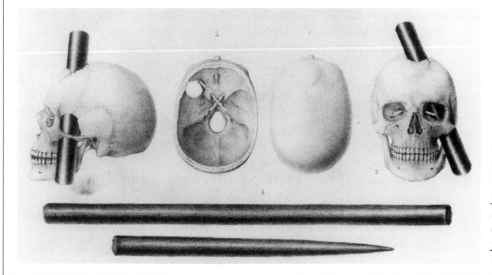

Phineas Gage Experienced One of the Best-Documented Cases of Open Head Injury *Gage lived for some years after his injury, but his personality altered, presumably because of the effects of his injury on frontal lobe functions.* Courtesy of the National Library of Medicine.

The High Road and the Low Road

The nine functions carried out via the integrative fibers of the middle prefrontal regions reveal that our brains are involved in linking together bodily, social, and mental processes into one set of integrated functions. As the case of Phineas Gage reveals, neurological damage to this region may result in impairment of a range of these functions. In addition, it appears that under conditions of emotional

stress many people may be at risk of moving from this integrated, "higher mode" or high road of functioning in which these nine processes are intact to a nonintegrated, "lower mode" or low road of functioning in which some or all of these processes may be temporarily impaired. You can picture this movement from the high road to the low road in your hand model by taking your hand-brain and lifting up your cortical fingers to expose the thumb-limbic areas. With intense emotion it may be possible to flood the middle prefrontal cortex and temporarily disable the integrative fibers of this region from performing their important functions. In such a lower mode of processing, the brain produces a rigid or chaotic state of mind. This temporary "flipping your lid" can involve any or all of the following: loss of regulation of bodily functions, disconnection from others, emotional imbalance causing rigid shutting down or chaotic flooding, inflexible knee-jerk reflexes instead of adaptive thoughtful responses, loss of empathy for others, lack of insight, return of deep fears, being out of touch with intuition, and amoral behavior.

Temporarily losing our coherent minds when our brains become nonintegrated can be both confusing and frightening to ourselves and to those around us. Understanding the emotional triggers that activate such low-road states can be an important step in making sense of such sudden shifts in an otherwise well-functioning individual. Whether it happens in yourself, your colleagues, or your patients, seeing the human aspect of such common lower mode activities can be an important step in bringing compassion to the experience. Each of us can lose our minds; what is important is to make the repair with others that is necessary to reestablish an open, trusting connection. Such repair is one of the key ingredients to healthy relationships of all sorts, from friendships or child-parent attachments to the relationship between patient and doctor.

In addition to repairing relationships that may have been affected by low-road experiences, it is also important to try to understand the triggers that may have caused them in the first place. Examining the experiences of the person in the hours and days before the event may be important to establish a background state of mind of the person. Trying to determine the trigger is akin to finding the "straw that broke the camel's back," the final piece of an emotional puzzle that destroyed the middle prefrontal area's ability to cope. Often, triggers are related to the context of what was occurring in a person's life and relationships. Feeling frustrated, misunderstood, threatened, or ignored are common emotional states that may trigger low-road states. Sometimes these emotional states are related to things from the past stored in various forms of memory. We'll turn now to learning about how the brain remembers to understand more about brain-behavior relationships.

THE NATURE OF MEMORY

The Brain is an Association Organ

Memory is the way an experience changes the probability of how our brains function in the future. There are many layers of memory that are important for a health-care professional to understand in order to help patients with their present difficulties. Memory will directly shape how a patient comes to you with their current problems. Memory will also influence how they take what you offer them and use it in the future. In many ways, memory links a person's past, present, and future together into one integrated process. Your role as a health-care provider will be more effective if you understand how to help your patients integrate these three time dimensions of their lives into one process that will offer them the best chance of living a healthy lifestyle, accepting clinical recommendations, and following through with interventions that influence their well-being.

Memory is how our minds are altered by experience. Each time we have an experience, neurons fire. When neurons become active, the synaptic connections among those firing can be strengthened. New synapses can form, or old ones can be made stronger. Other aspects of synaptic change can include alterations in the neurotransmitters released and changes in the receptors in the membrane at the post-synaptic receiving end. These changes are the ways in which experience alters the structure and function of the brain.

We now are also learning that the brain throughout the lifespan appears to be able to grow new neurons in response to new experiences. Studied primarily in the hippocampus, these new neurons are created by the continual division of stem cells in the brain. Stem cells are uncommitted cells that divide into a stem cell and daughter cell. The stem cell continues the stem line; the daughter cell under the right conditions of new forms of stimulation can grow over the next few months into a fully integrated cell of the brain. This cellular growth is called **neurogenesis**, and it is another way in which experience alters brain structure and function.

Overall, the process through which experience alters brain structure is called **neural plasticity**. This exciting area of study enables us to deepen our understanding of how experiences can positively change the way in which a person will behave in the future based on what happened in the past. Understanding some of what we know now about neural plasticity can help you as a professional optimize the nature of your interaction with a patient to try to help them remember your clinical recommendations.

Before we turn to the layers of memory, let's outline briefly how neural plasticity is thought to occur. When the action potential flows down the axonal membrane leading to release of neurotransmitter at the synaptic junction that links that neuron to other neurons' dendrites and cell bodies, something very special occurs. Neuronal firing can lead to the activation of the genetic material in the nucleus of the presynaptic neuron. With the unraveling of DNA, the transcription into RNA, and finally the translation into protein at the ribosomes in the cytoplasm, new protein building blocks for cellular growth can occur. Proteins are an essential component of long term changes in neuronal connections Research into neural plasticity uses inhibitors of transcription, translation, and protein synthesis to demonstrate their essential role in memory processes. Memory is all about how new associations among neurons are made based on earlier firing patterns.

Short- and Long-Term Memory

When we are aware of something in the moment we can link the activity in our brains to the side part of our prefrontal cortex and have the mental experience of something being in "our mind's eye" or on the "chalkboard of our mind." In this moment of awareness we can have short-term memory for the things upon which we are focusing our attention. This **short-term memory** may last less than a minute without further rehearsal and does not involve DNA transcription, RNA translation or protein synthesis. Such short-term memory appears to involve a temporary functional associational enhancement, likely via neurotransmitter release and neural firing processes. Temporary alterations in synaptic strengths are established through functional changes in the neurotransmitter properties among related neuronal groups for a transient time during this short-term recall. There are no long-term structural changes associated with the firing patterns of short-term memory. With this moment-to-moment awareness we pay attention to sensory, bodily, and mental activity that can be recalled seconds or even minutes later. We can be aware of our senses bringing in information from the outside world or our **interoception** bringing in data from our body. We can also become aware of our self-reflection enabling us to focus on our minds' thoughts, feelings, or memories.

Short-term memory is also called immediate memory or working memory; it enables us to deal with a limited number of items. The classic number of **seven plus or minus two** is thought to be the range of items that can be dealt with effectively in this working memory state. Imagine looking up a phone number to call a restaurant to order lunch. You remember the phone number (usually seven digits) long enough to dial the number and order your salad or sandwich, but then you soon forget the number if it isn't one you'll repeatedly use. Short-term recall is helpful, but cluttering our minds with details we no longer need would make us dysfunctional. *Forgetting is an essential function of the mind for proper mental health.* When elements on our chalkboard of working or immediate memory are sorted through and categorized and chunked together, they can then be stored in a more long-term form that does require translation, transcription, and protein synthesis. However, if a patient is in a state of high arousal and distress, elements in working memory may not be processed into long-term storage. Excessive anxiety and fear can shut down the normal capacity to integrate elements of short-term working memory into the long-term memory.

Long-term memory always involves gene activation and protein production to alter the structural connections among neurons. As the healthy brain is open to change across the lifespan, memory can continue to occur in a long-term manner if the mind of the person continues to take on new experiences that promote neural plasticity. Optimal levels of arousal are needed to make this new learning into long-term memory occur. Too little arousal, such as with boredom and understimulation, can lead to impaired memory integration into long-term storage. Excess arousal in states of distress and shock can also impair long-term processing. This provides a way of understanding the familiar clinical situation in which a patient does not process "what the doctor says." If the information being given is potentially quite important, the state of distress that is created may directly impair the patient's capacity to hold on to details of the diagnosis and treatment. They may recall the first few words you say about the diagnosis, but the other things you've discussed that were not written down may disappear because the DNA, RNA, and protein synthesis processes were impaired by the rising state of arousal at that moment.

Being open to creating new connections, keeping neuroplasticity alive and engaged with new experiences are important for all of us as we age. New approaches to keeping the mind young involve mental exercises that stimulate the brain in new ways. The neurobiology of this makes sense: Our brains are designed to change their neural connections if they are challenged with new stimulation. We can decide to take on these new challenges with our minds that purposefully stimulate our brains to grow new connections over the lifespan. Novel experiences should be engaging and lead to optimal arousal: they should not be too stressful, but not boring either. In many ways this flow toward optimal arousal is the same as that which we've discussed for mental well-being. Boredom and understimulation are similar to the state of rigidity; anxiety and excess stimulation are akin to the state of chaos. Optimal learning and memory, as with optimal mental well-being, flow down the river of coherence and harmony between those two extremes of rigidity and chaos.

There is an optimal amount of challenge that goes along with healthy neural plasticity. If experiences are routine and dull, the brain will not become aroused in any meaningful way and neural plasticity will not be activated. If the individual becomes flooded with anxiety in situations that are too new and feel overwhelming, then the flood of **adrenaline** and the stress hormone **cortisol** will contribute to the shutting down of optimal neural plasticity. Optimal brain changes occur during moderate amounts of brain arousal. Too little or too much arousal does not promote healthy forms of remembering.

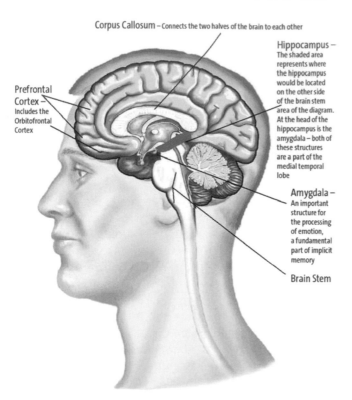

Corpus Callosum – Connects the two halves of the brain to each other

Hippocampus – The shaded area represents where the hippocampus would be located on the other side of the brain stem area of the diagram. At the head of the hippocampus is the amygdala – both of these structures are a part of the medial temporal lobe

Prefrontal Cortex – Includes the Orbitofrontal Cortex

Amygdala – An important structure for the processing of emotion, a fundamental part of implicit memory

Brain Stem

FIGURE 1.3 Diagram of the human brain looking from the middle toward the right side. Some key structures involved in memory are noted, including the amygdala (implicit emotional memory processing), the hippocampus (explicit memory), and the orbitofrontal cortex (explicit autobiographical memory processing). Coherent life stories may involve integration across the hemispheres via the corpus callosum. From *Parenting from the Inside Out* by Daniel J. Siegel and Mary Hartzell. Copyright © 2003 by Daniel J. Siegel and Mary Hartzell. Used by permission of Jeremy P. Tarcher, an imprint of Penguin Group (USA) Inc.

Encoding, Storage, and Retrieval

With optimal learning, short-term memory transitions into long-term encoding and storage with the gene activation and protein synthesis that enables neuronal connections to change. **Encoding** is the initial firing of neurons and the stimulation of new connections. **Storage** is the way that new neuronal linkages structurally can create the potential for new firing patterns by the activation of newly associated groups of neurons in the future. *Storage is a probability function, not a photo-copy machine.* The conditions at time of recall will shape the nature of *retrieval*, which is the re-activation of associations of neuronal groups similar—but never identical—to the groups associated during the encoding process.

Imagine telling a patient that she potentially has a serious, life-threatening illness. The interaction with you during that conversation will have a great impact on how that discussion is "remembered." If the patient is very anxious to begin with and your interaction with her is matter-of-fact and not emotionally tuned-in to her anxiety, her state

of flooding is likely to increase and may lead to either a difficulty remembering what you said in the long-term or to the association of excessive fear and a sense of being left alone with the potential diagnosis. Being alone at a time of great stress is itself stress-increasing. Comfort comes from feeling that one is with another person. For the patient, feeling understood by you and knowing that you understand the patient's feelings will greatly reduce anxiety and fear. With this feeling of connection and comfort, the patient will be in a better position not only to feel better, but also to engage the physiological mechanisms of memory necessary to enable encoding and storage of the important things you have to say at that time.

Approaching the interaction as a form of new learning can help you optimize the clinical experience for your patient. Being aware of a patient's internal state and being concerned about his or her diagnosis is essential if your patient is going to feel understood and comforted by you. Once that feeling of security with you is established, discussions about the technical issues involved in the medical work-up can occur without hyperarousal. Recall that memory is optimized when the person is in the mid-range of arousal, not bored or flooded. *It is up to you as a medical professional to become sensitive to the internal state of your patient to best help him or her remember the important communications between the two of you about crucial medical issues.*

This discussion of memory clearly highlights the importance of medical professionals understanding their essential role in paying attention to the internal mental state of their patients. One word we commonly use for this internal state is **emotion**. Though emotion has many definitions in science, for medical practice we can say that the patients' emotional states will directly influence how they remember their interactions with you. How you pay attention to their emotional states will directly shape the outcome of the patient-doctor relationship. The emotional states that directly shape neural plasticity can be understood and then approached in ways that optimize learning and memory. We'll turn now to emotion and interpersonal relationships to deepen our insights into this important dimension of brain and behavior.

Implicit and Explicit Memory

Memory can be divided into two types—implicit and explicit—that dramatically influence the way information is perceived and processed in the brain. **Implicit memory** is available throughout the lifespan and perhaps even prenatally. Implicit memory includes the domains of emotion, perception, motor response, and likely also bodily sensation. In addition, implicit memory includes the generalizations the brain creates as summations of repeated

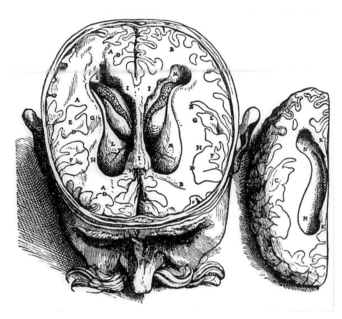

Horizontal View of the Brain Exposing the Lateral Ventricles *(De Human Corporis Frabrica) Andres Vesalius.* Courtesy of the National Library of Medicine.

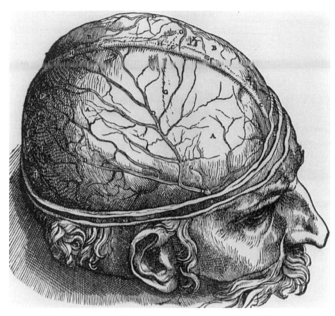

Head With Scalp Exposed to Show Dura Mater and Middle Cerebral Artery *Andres Vesalius (1543).* Courtesy of the National Library of Medicine.

experiences, called mental models, or **schema. Priming,** the way the mind is readied to respond in a certain fashion, is also a product of implicit processing. Implicit memory differs greatly from common preconceptions of "memory" in that it does not create a feeling of something being recalled from the past. Interestingly, implicit memory does not require conscious, focal attention to be encoded. Implicit memory is encoded whenever these specific domains of neural firing, from perceptions to motor action, are activated. This initial implicit encoding causes new synapses to be formed that will guide subsequent responses to a similar input. Therefore, these subsequent responses are influenced by the implicit memory formed after the initial encoding without the individual's awareness that something from the past is influencing his behavior. For example, you know not to touch fire because you know that it will burn you—even if you can't remember a specific time when you were burned by fire. This implicit "knowing" is probably the result of an experience you had as a young child when you touched a fire and experienced pain or were told not to touch the fire. The pain was immediately perceived and processed in your brain, creating an implicit association between fire and pain to protect you from a similar experience in the future. Implicit memories do not require the hippocampus to be activated, so patients with damage to the medial temporal lobes that house the hippocampus will still be able to both encode and retrieve implicit memories.

Explicit memory becomes available in the second year of life as the hippocampus is thought to mature after that time. Explicit memory includes the two domains of **factual (semantic) memory** and **episodic (autobiographical)**

CASE EXAMPLE: Impaired Explicit Memory Encoding

Damage to the medial temporal regions (including the hippocampus) yields severe amnesia. There are two types of amnesia—retrograde and anterograde. Retrograde amnesia refers to the inability to recall explicit memories encoded prior to the damage. Anterograde amnesia is the inability to form new explicit memories following the damage. There is a story told in the annals of neurology that clearly illustrates the difference between implicit and explicit memory and demonstrates anterograde amnesia. There was a patient who suffered bilateral damage to his medial temporal lobes (including the hippocampus). Thus, he had impaired explicit memory and could not form new short- or long-term memories. The doctor came into the room where the patient was waiting, introduced himself, and offered a handshake. The patient greeted the doctor and gladly shook his hand. The doctor then left the room for a few minutes and returned with a pin hidden in the palm of his hand. He introduced himself to the patient (who had no explicit recollection of ever meeting the doctor, likely experiencing only a vague feeling of familiarity from his implicit memory) and offered a handshake. Once again, the patient greeted the doctor and gladly shook his hand, but recoiled in pain after being pricked by the pin. The doctor apologized and left the room. The doctor came back a few minutes later (with no pin), introduced himself for the third time, and offered a handshake. Even though the patient had no explicit memory of being pricked by the prior handshake, the patient refused to shake the doctor's hand and could not explain why. The patient had an implicit memory that associated the handshake with the pain of being pricked that gave him a feeling of danger when the doctor offered his hand. This illustrates the patient's intact ability to form implicit memories even after severe hippocampal damage that impaired explicit memory encoding.

memory. When you recall an explicit fact or a sense of the self in the past, you have the internal sensation that a memory is being recalled. Explicit memory requires conscious and focused attention to be encoded. Explicit memories are formed by the creation of new synapses after a conscious experience is processed via the hippocampus. For short- and long-term explicit memory retrieval, the hippocampus also must be activated for recollection to occur. Neither short- or long-term memories are in and of themselves permanent. However, these long-term memories have the potential to become permanent through **consolidation**. While long-term memory requires the focused attention of the hippocampus for retrieval, consolidated (permanent) memory does not. Thus, consolidated memories, such as your name or date of birth, can be recalled even if the hippocampus is damaged or removed.

WHAT IS EMOTION?

Emotion as a Form of Integration

Emotion is a profoundly important part of human life. The science of emotion can involve a range of academic disciplines that explore the ways different cultures promote the communication of internal states to one another, how an individual develops within social relationships across the lifespan, or how the brain integrates its functioning with the bodily and social processes that are fundamental to its organization. Whether the scientist is from anthropology, psychology, or neurobiology, it is fascinating that each of them studying emotion uses the concept of integration. Though specific definitions of "emotion" may differ, each field of science examining this sometimes elusive process of emotion highlights the fundamentally integrative role emotion plays in the developmental, social, mental, or somatic life of the person.

Recall that integration means the linking together of separate elements of a system into a functional whole. In this way we can say that emotion may be a way of describing how a system is becoming integrated. When we are emotionally close to others, our minds are integrated with them. When we feel emotionally understood, others see our minds in a clear and authentic fashion. When we feel emotionally whole, often many pieces of our life are "falling into place" or becoming a coherent, integrated whole. Emotional well-being often emerges when we integrate the various dimensions of our lives, including the social, somatic, and mental aspects of our experiences across our life's path.

Categorical Emotion

There are two practical ways we describe emotion. One common way is in what are called **categorical emotions,** which Charles Darwin described in the late 1800s. These are the universally perceived categories of sadness, anger, fear, disgust, surprise, happiness, and shame. Other categories have later been described with a huge variety of these internal states that become integrated to the point that they can be expressed externally as classic facial expressions. Most cultures have names for these categories, and hence they are called "universal." We are also learning that each of these categories of emotion has a physiological finger print, a characteristic profile of cardiovascular activity that correlates with specific patterns of nonverbal expressions.

Primary Emotion

One important dimension of emotion can be seen before the person is aroused to the level of having a categorical emotion communicated on the face or through tone of voice as one of the universal expressions. The dimension of emotion that occurs before categories of emotion arise can be called *primary emotion.* Primary emotion is the way that the internal state of our brains and bodies are organizing their functioning to shape some very important aspects of our internal worlds.

Here is one way to describe this fundamental nature of the subjective quality of our ongoing internal mental state. First we orient our attention to a particular internal or external stimulus. This **initial orientation** directs the energy and information flow of our minds, and, thus, is a first step in creating mental life. Next we appraise the object of our attention as either good or bad. Should we get closer to it if it is good or move away from it if it is bad? This is called **appraisal** and is exactly what our limbic, emotion-generating brain areas are designed to do. After initial orientation and appraisal there is a rapid **elaboration of arousal** that continues to govern the flow of energy and information processing. As arousal is elaborated it channels neuronal firing in specific directions and, thus, shapes the nature of our internal mental state.

Primary emotion occurs all the time. We orient our attention, appraise the meaning of events, and respond depending on those appraisals. Orientation, appraisal, and arousal are the primary elements of the internal "emotional state" that continually shapes our subjective mental state of mind. We become aware of others' primary emotional states by their focus of attention and by their nonverbal expressions. Those nonverbal expressions we discussed earlier reveal the internal, primary emotions of the individual. *As a medical professional, being aware of the importance of these nonverbal*

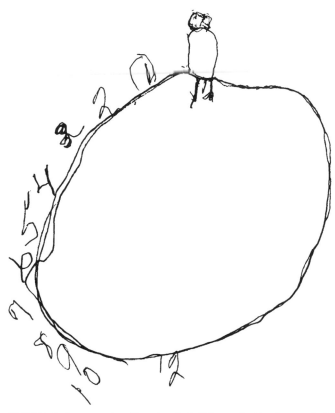

FIGURE 1.4 An example of hemineglect. When asked to draw a clock, this patient ignored the right half of space.

signals such as eye contact, facial expression, and tone of voice can enable you to "tune-in" to the primary emotional state of your patient. It is this moment-to-moment "attunement" to your patients' states that will enable you to get a glimpse into their internal world. In turn, when your patients experience that you are tuned-in to their internal mental life, they will feel comforted and secure with their connection to you as their physician.

Why is being aware of another's primary or categorical emotional states important? Relationships between clinician and patient (or between spouses, friends, or children and their parents) that involve a respectful attitude and sensitivity to the internal subject emotional state of the other person are those that promote well-being in both individuals. This respect begins with a sense that the internal subjective experience of another person is important. People feel cared about and respected. The subjective mental life of another person is different from yours, but it is worthy of being understood and embraced for its uniqueness and importance. *Being sensitive to the internal state of another means focusing your mind on the nonverbal signals of the other person and thinking about what these may mean.* An excessive state of arousal and an appraisal of some communication from you as being negative can greatly impair memory and how a patient will respond to your suggestions. Being aware of these internal reactions in the patient can help you tune-in to their concerns in a sensitive and

respectful manner. You may be pleasantly surprised at how direct and helpful an awareness of emotional communication can be.

LEFT MEETS RIGHT

To enhance the patient-physician relationship, it is important to understand how brain, mind, and behavior work together. We've seen how the internal state of activation of the brain shapes the subjective experience of mind. How you pay respect and attention to this internal mental state can make a crucial difference in the outcome of the doctor-patient relationship. Your mental state and the mental state of your patient are shaped by the location of activations in each of your brains. One very general way to describe these locations of neuronal firings is in the separation of the two halves of the brain. Though some writers have taken the science beyond reasonable boundaries and dichotomized whole societies as either "right-brained" or "left-brained," it is nevertheless a biological reality over millions of years of evolution that our nervous systems are asymmetric, and left is different from right. Knowing these neurobiological asymmetries can greatly aid your understanding of your own and your patients' mental life. As you'll see in this brief overview, knowing distinctive regions of the brain can help you be more sensitive to your patients' and your own internal mental states.

During *in utero* development, the lower brainstem structures give rise to asymmetric limbic regions. After birth, these subcortical asymmetries in turn influence the development of the right and left cortex in very different ways. The right hemisphere develops earlier than the left, being more active in both its growth and neural firing during the first 2 to 3 years of life. After that time, the child goes through cyclical alternating periods of dominance in growth and activity of the left and the right hemisphere of the brain.

The Right Mode of Processing

The right and left hemispheres have somewhat different anatomical connections. *The right hemisphere appears to have cortical columns that are more horizontally integrated with each other, meaning that there is more cross-modal integration.* The cortex is divided into vertically arranged columns of roughly six cell layers in thickness. These columns specialize in processing certain "modes" of mental activities, such as vision or hearing. With more horizontal integration across these vertical columns, there is a cross-modality integration that creates a different kind of wholeness to the way the right hemisphere processes information. This integrated state results in processing across various forms of perceptual input, enabling the right hemisphere to create holistic, visuospatial representations. The right hemisphere also specializes in having an integrated map of the whole body, the capacity to send and receive nonverbal signals, and it stores representations of autobiographical memory. Because of the right cortex's more direct neural connections to the limbic areas, the right hemisphere also specializes in more direct, intense, and raw affective or emotional experience.

For this reason it also appears that the right hemisphere specializes in the process of *emotional resonance* in which our internal affective and physiological states are directly influenced by what we see in another person. These important nonverbal emotional processes make the right hemisphere an important component of the experience of **empathy** or putting ourselves in the mental experience of another person. Some neurologists are now referring to the right side of our brains as the seat of our social and emotional selves.

The Left Mode of Processing

The left hemisphere in contrast seems to have cortical columns that are more vertically integrated. This lends the left hemisphere a specialization in what is called "digital processing" (compared to the "analogical processing" of the right side) in which information is handled in a very vertically refined, yes-no, on-off, manner. *Language, linear processing, logic,* and *literal thinking* are the four-L's of the Left hemisphere. We use linguistic language to both understand with our left hemispheres and to communicate with others. The left loves linearity and predictability, and your left hemisphere is currently highly active as you read this long, linear, linguistic sentence. One word follows the next and then the next. The logic of the left is called **syllogistic reasoning**, and is the way we (our left hemispheres) search for cause-effect relationships in the world around us, and within us.

When we encounter others, both our hemispheres are important in becoming active in the communication that will occur. No one mode or side is better than the other. However, the two modes are quite different. Sometimes we may move toward over-use of one and exclusion of the other at times of stress, or just out of habit. For example, if we become overwhelmed with a patient's serious diagnosis, our left hemisphere may attempt to take over communication and shut down our empathy for the patient's pain. Brief adaptations like "leaning to the left" may be quite natural and temporarily helpful to reduce overwhelming emotional reactions. However, prolonged exclusion of the right hemisphere from interactions with our patients, or with

our friends or even our selves, can lead to serious problems in those professional and personal relationships. Our own sense of vitality and well-being can become seriously compromised if we do not find a way to integrate the two sides of our experience.

> To appreciate the limits of your personal control of your behavior, try the following experiment:
> 1. While sitting at your desk, lift your right foot off the floor and make clockwise circles with it.
> 2. Now, while doing this, draw the number "6" in the air with your right hand. Your foot will change direction.

The Importance of Integrating Right and Left

Bringing the right and the left hemispheres of our brains together is an important first step. Patients may also become overly dominant in one side or another in response to what you may say to them. For example, someone who is flooded with fear may be processing mainly with the right side of his brain. He may need to use self-talk and logic to help him after he feels that you are open and trying to understand him. But bringing in his left hemisphere is not done for the purpose of shutting off his emotions. Rather, it is to bring him into an integrated state of balance, so that he can be aware of his emotions and help regulate them in a more helpful manner. As studies have shown, naming an internal affective state helps the whole system come into balance.

At other times patients may be so terrified that they shut-off their right hemisphere's functioning, or at least their awareness of the input of the right mode of processing. In this condition you may sense that a patient is quite distant from his or her autobiographical recollections and is "living" in a very logical, linear, linguistic, and literal internal mental world. In this state, the patient may seem disconnected and defended. It is important not to flood the patient with right hemisphere activation, but your awareness of their defended state should be noted in your own mind and gentle support should be offered to ease the patient's reconnection with the emotions being processed in a nonverbal way in the right hemisphere.

In many ways we use our left hemisphere's language to communicate with the left hemisphere of another person. We use the nonverbal language of our right cortices to relate to the right hemisphere of someone else. Feeling connected to our doctors involves both what they say to us in words and how they reveal their connection to our own internal states by way of their nonverbal signals. *Your facial expressions, eye contact, tone of voice, gestures, posture, and the timing and intensity of your responses are the direct route to connecting your right hemisphere to that of your patient.*

SEIZURE

I gave you what I could when you were born,
salt water to rock you,
your half of nine month's meat,
miles of finished veins,
and all the blood I had to spare.

And then I said, this is the last time
I divide myself in half, the last time
I lie down in danger and rise bereft,
the last time I give up half my blood.

Fifteen months later, when I walked into your room
your mobile of the sun, moon,
and stars was tilting
while your lips twisted,
while you arched your back.

Your fingers groped for something in the air.
Your arms and legs flailed like broken wings.
Your breath was a load too heavy
for your throat to heave into your lungs.
You beat yourself into a daze against your crib.

We slapped your feet,
we flared the lights,
we doused you in a tub of lukewarm water.
But your black eyes rolled.
You had gone somewhere
and left behind a shape of bluish skin,
a counterfeit of you.

                              It was then,
before the red wail of the police car,
before the IV's, before the medicine
dropped into you like angels, before you woke
to a clear brow, to your own funny rising voice,

it was then that I would have struck the bargain,
all my blood
for your small shaking.
I would have called us even.

JEANNE MURRAY WALKER

When these nonverbal signals from you reflect openness and caring about the internal, often right hemisphere, states of your patient, he will feel secure and comforted. A new discovery has illuminated some of the basic mechanisms of this compassionate and empathic connection we can make with each other.

NEURONS THAT MIRROR OTHER MINDS

The Mirror Neuron System

In the mid-1990s a system of neurons was discovered, first in monkeys and later in humans, called the **mirror neuron system**. These neurons reveal how our brains are profoundly social and can focus on the internal mental state of another individual. In many ways the doctor-patient relationship may be shaped by the automatic processes that the mirror neuron system creates.

The first discovery of mirror neurons occurred serendipitously when a researcher studying a single-neuron's activity found that that neuron being studied became active in response to both eating a peanut and observing another person eating a peanut. No, these are not peanut neurons, but they are a system of neurons that showed us a number of profound aspects of our brain's functional neuroanatomy. First of all, this study revealed that *motor action and perception are integrated processes*. In the cortex, the posterior perceptual regions are indeed linked by axonal fibers that connect the perceptual columns to the frontal motor regions of the cortex. But these motor-perceptual neural systems did not just fire off at any perception: Mirror neurons only became active with the observation of an act with intention.

If a woman in front of you lifted her hand to her mouth, you'd have no idea what she was about to do. You couldn't detect her intention and you would not be able to anticipate the outcome of her action. However, if she held a cup of water in her hand, you'd be able to detect what the likely goal of her action of lifting was, and you'd anticipate she'd drink from the cup. Mirror neurons reveal a summation and learning process in the brain that detects intentional acts. In this way the mirror neuron system reveals how the brain makes maps of the internal intentional state of another person's mind.

Detecting Intention and Creating Emotional Resonance

The profound implication of this finding is that beyond just encoding neural maps of perceptions or motor actions, *the brain appears to create maps of others' minds.* Some researchers have taken this extremely exciting and revolutionary finding and explored how the mirror neuron system is involved in emotional resonance and empathy.

Our mirror neurons enable us to observe an intentional act in someone else and then prime or ready our brains to carry out that same act. When others yawn or drink a cup of water, we yawn or get thirsty. In addition to priming our brains for action, mirror neurons also prime our brains for emotional resonance and empathy. We observe another's nonverbal expressions of their internal state and our own internal state is directly shaped by what we perceive. If you see sadness on another person's face your brain will activate circuitry that creates a sad affective texture in your brain, and the somatic responses in your heart, lungs, intestines, and musculature will reflect that sadness. In other words, your feelings and your bodily state will be shaped directly by what you sense in another person. This is called **emotional resonance.**

Mirroring as the Gateway of Empathy

The next step in the story comes when we use the prefrontal part of our neocortex, the part behind our eyes and forehead, to create the mechanisms of empathy. *Empathy means imagining the internal mental state of another person.* When the middle prefrontal cortex takes the step of "looking inward" at its own limbic and somatic states, we call this **interoception.** Next the prefrontal region *interprets* interoceptive data to surmise what the self is experiencing in that moment. Am I feeling sad? Am I frightened? Do I feel relieved? These are all the types of questions your prefrontal cortex may mediate before it takes the next step of *attribution* in which it attributes these internal states to the person you are observing.

The benefit of this capacity to have emotional resonance, and then the interoception, interpretation, and attribution of empathy, is that emotional resonance allows us to understand both ourselves and others. With such insight and empathy, life can make sense, relationships can feel profoundly rewarding, and people can be helped to heal.

As a clinical professional, though, the mirror neuron mechanisms reveal how there is a risk to emotional resonance. Without awareness it is possible that the automatic emotional resonance process may create in you the same affective states of distress of your patients, and this experience can become overwhelming. One term used to describe this process is **secondary traumatization.** Fortunately with consciousness of this important healing process, the healer can also be helped. By putting these internal states of your affective feelings and your body's responses "out in the

open," you can successfully deal with your internal responses in a way that is helpful to both you and conducive to your efforts to have a healthy doctor-patient relationship.

Knowing that your internal state will be shaped by your patient's enables you to take steps to (1) make your emotional resonance a part of your awareness—becoming conscious of how you feel and what your body is sensing; and (2) to examine how this interoceptive data can be consciously interpreted and then used in a positive way to understand your patients. *At first this may be an effortful process, but soon, as with any learned skill, this empathic intelligence will become more automatic.* The exciting news is that the more you come to be open to these often nonverbal internal processes, the more you'll come to understand your self. In addition you'll find that your work with patients becomes more rewarding and that their relationship with you will become more deeply healing.

THE ROLE OF SUBJECTIVE EXPERIENCE IN CLINICAL PRACTICE

The Stories of Our Lives

Ultimately the movement toward well-being likely involves helping patients adapt by integrating the wholeness of their social, mental, and somatic selves. Linking the two halves of the brain is one step in bringing this integrated state of wellness into being. Often we must first start with our selves in learning what this integrated left-right connection feels like. One way to feel that sense of wholeness is in helping the stories of our lives become coherent—i.e., making sense of our life experiences.

As the left side of our brain has a drive to use language to tell the linear story of the events of our lives, many authors see the left hemisphere as the narrative drive for our species to tell stories. But when we realize that the autobiographical details of our lives are stored in the right hemisphere along with the affective meaning and texture of our internal and interpersonal lives, then it becomes clear that to tell a coherent and meaningful story of our lives we must come to integrate the left and the right sides of the brain. This is how we deepen our self-understanding.

In your own life it may be helpful to reflect to yourself, in a journal, or with close friends, on how the events of your own life have brought you to where you are now in your life's journey. When you come to understand yourself in this open and coherent way, you may find that nonverbal memories in the form of pictures and sensations in your mind become activated and then sorted through by the linguistic, logical, linear processing of your left hemisphere. As you come to put words to the previously word-less images in your head, you may find, as many studies have shown, that there is deep sense of harmony that emerges in your mind. Research has also shown that telling your life story can improve your immune function and physiological well-being.

Making sense of your own mind and creating a coherent story of your life enables you to have an openness to the events of your life that promotes a sense of well-being. In addition, such a receptive state of awareness in your own mind creates an openness to others' experiences that promotes well-being within relationships. As you find your way to helping patients deal with their suffering and the challenges in their life, such an openness will enable them to feel deeply comforted and to have the strength to face their difficulties with you as their care provider.

Mental coherence will also create an openness in you that will help you be attuned to your own mental and somatic state of being. You'll be able to remain compassionate to your own needs for rest and relaxation in the exciting and challenging work of helping others in need. By taking care of yourself and being attuned to your own needs, you can serve as a model for how your patients can come to learn to take care of their own needs as well.

SUMMARY

In this chapter we've been exploring how to integrate the objective findings of science into a deeper understanding of the subjective nature of mental life. By turning to the brain, we've been able to understand different aspects of how neural functioning creates memory, learning, emotion, and the nature of our communication with others.

One of the important principles from this perspective is that the subjective essence of the mind is objectively the most important dimension of how we communicate with each other. Also, because the brain is a profoundly social organ of the body, *interpersonal relationships and the communication patterns that shape them directly influence neural functioning.* When the brain functions optimally, the mind becomes coherent and the body-proper can adapt to stress is a more effective manner. In this way the doctor-patient relationship that places the subjective experience of the patient at the top of the priority list of "things to pay attention to" will be the most likely to be optimally supportive and helpful to the patient.

We now have objective, scientifically established data that the subjective nature of our lives is one of the most essential dimensions of health and healing. This is a tremendously exciting time, and one in which we can integrate this scientific importance of subjectivity into our daily lives with our patients—and with our selves.

CASE STUDY

Ms. Smith is a 30-year old business school student who comes to the university medical clinic with a complaint of pain in her arm and jaw. She has finished her first semester of graduate school and is now embarking with four other students on a new business venture involving novel approaches to selling software on the internet. You perform a physical exam that appears normal as does her EKG and chest X-Ray. Her vital signs and basic lab work are normal, and there is no family history of early cardiac disease or psychiatric illness such as panic disorder.

After further questioning, you find that Ms. Smith has recently felt quite anxious. She has had difficulty falling asleep and awakens frequently during the night. In the office she denies other symptoms of depression, such as loss of appetite or energy, negative mood or preoccupations with feelings of guilt or sadness. Ms. Smith also reveals that she "is afraid of falling flat on [her] face" if she tries something new. There is insufficient evidence to suggest cardiac disease, but something about this patient's statement feels important.

You ask Ms. Smith to say what comes to her mind about "falling on her face," and she immediately begins to experience an intensification of pain in her arm. She then grasps her jaw and tells you she feels pain there as well. You ask her to say more about this pain, noting that she does not appear to be in acute cardiac distress, and she tells you that she feels as if she has fallen down. On further questioning you find that when Ms. Smith was in preschool learning to ride a tricycle, she had hit a rock and fallen on her face, fracturing her arm and breaking two of her front teeth. Knowing about the nature of trauma and implicit memory, you realize that this may be an example of blocked integration of this implicit form of somatosensory memory with Ms. Smith's larger narrative of her life. With overwhelming events, the hippocampus may be blocked from integrating the basic elements of implicit memory into its explicit autobiographical form.

When implicit memory is not integrated into the higher forms of factual and autobiographical explicit memory, it is often reactivated without an individual being aware that something is being accessed from the past. The "meaning" of that early traumatic event is not only that this patient feels pain implicitly without recognizing its origins in the past, but also that there is a general "theme" that is extracted from that event–i.e., trying anything new is fraught with danger. In reflecting on this issue and later writing in her journal about the tricycle accident and her fear of attempting anything new, Ms. Smith's anxiety and sleep disturbances are abated. She is now able to place within her conscious awareness a narrative reflection on how an earlier frightening event led her to fear exploring new experiences in her life. Nine months later she reports that she remains symptom free and that her business venture was a success.

SUGGESTED READINGS

Beer, J.S., Shimamura, A.P., & Knight, R.T. (2004). Frontal lobe contributions to executive control of cognitive and social behavior. In M.S. Gazzaniga (Ed.), *The cognitive neurosciences III* (pp. 1091–1104). Cambridge, MA: MIT Press.
A very helpful chapter that provides an overview of how our frontal lobes help to create the fundamental thinking and interpersonal nature of our human lives.

Cozolino, L. (2006). *The neuroscience of relationships*. New York: Norton.
This text provides an excellent overview of the neural circuitry underlying our interpersonal relationships, from attachment to our everyday encounters with other people.

Damasio, A. (1994). *Descartes' error: Emotion, reason, and the human brain*. New York: Grosset/Putnam.
A classic text creatively integrating the history of Phineas Gage with modern neurology in exploring how damage to the prefrontal cortex alters personality.

Davidson, R.J. (2004). The neurobiology of personality and personality disorders (2nd ed.). In D.S. Charney & E.J. Nester (Eds.), *Neurobiology of mental illness* (pp. 1062–1075). Oxford: Oxford University Press.
This textbook chapter describes the neural underpinnings of personality and is embedded in an overall resource book that is on the cutting edge of the neurobiology of psychiatric disorders.

Macrae, C.N., Heatherton, T.F., & Kelley, W.M. (2004). A self less ordinary: The medial prefrontal cortex and you. In M.S. Gazzaniga (Ed.), *The Cognitive Neurosciences III*. Cambridge, MA: MIT Press.
This chapter offers an exciting view of the middle aspect of the prefrontal cortex that appears to play a central role in the organization of personality. The chapter is a part of a huge volume exploring the wide range of topics within the large field of cognitive neuroscience with excellent chapters summarizing the latest in research in this important academic area.

Schore, A.N. (2003). *Affect regulation and the repair of the self*. New York: Norton.
For those interested in an in-depth analysis of how early trauma can be repaired by psychotherapy and other healing relationships, this book provides a view into the complexities of the brain that may underlie how we move toward mental health.

Siegel, D.J. (1999). *The developing mind: How relationships and the brain interact to shape who we are*. New York: Guilford.
This book offers an overview of the field of interpersonal neurobiology, exploring the nature of memory, emotion, and attachment and providing insights into how making sense of one's life can help promote integration within the brain and a more adaptive and flexible way of living.

Siegel, D.J. (2006). *Mindsight*. New York: Bantam Random House.
This book explores the interpersonal and neurobiological nature of insight and empathy, focusing on how individuals can promote both in their own lives to foster well-being in themselves and those with whom they interact.

2 Families, Relationships, and Health

Margaret L. Stuber

> Happy families are all alike; every unhappy family is unhappy in its own way.
>
> LEO TOLSTOY
> *Anna Karenina*

Much of the focus of medical student education is on the patient or the doctor-patient interaction. However, treatment of medical illness requires that physicians look beyond the individual patient to the social context in which patients exist. The social context will determine aspects of health behavior, including how a patient expresses symptoms, who comes to the office or hospital with the patient, and how decisions are made about treatment. It is the social network that helps patients cope with illness, and which supplies the instrumental assistance that determines whether or not a patient can function at home or on the job. The social network in turn is influenced by a patient's medical diagnosis, treatment decisions, and the way the patient responds to illness and treatment.

This chapter will explore the impact of a social support network on the doctor-patient interaction, the patient's health, and treatment decisions, as well as the impact of illness on the family and social network. Discussion and case examples will illustrate how physicians can use this knowledge to plan treatment and increase patient adherence.

WHAT IS A SOCIAL NETWORK?

A social network is the community of people upon whom one can rely for emotional and physical (instrumental) support. Traditional sources of a social network include the nuclear and extended family, the school or work community, the religious community, and the neighborhood. Each of these groups shares some common beliefs, values, and experiences that lead them to help one another. Examples of community support would include helping a neighbor "raise" a barn, bringing food when a member of your religious community is sick, or giving a classmate a school assignment from a day they missed school. Within this type of community everyone knows everyone else, sometimes more than a member may have wished. This is the kind of village that could be counted on to raise a child.

Changes in the family and community in the United States over the past 50 years have altered many aspects of the social network. The two-parent family with an at-home mother is no longer the norm. Extended families living in the same house—or even in the same town—are increasingly uncommon. Family size in the United States has decreased to an average of just over two children per household. People are less likely to stay in one job for the duration of their career, making it less usual for families to raise their children entirely in one neighborhood. All

---

CASE EXAMPLE

A 22-year-old college student volunteered to serve as a living-related donor to his sister for a partial liver transplant. During his interview with the doctor to determine his eligibility to donate, one of his brothers asked to come into the office. The brother addressed the prospective donor, saying that this was not his decision to make. Given that the proposed procedure would endanger his life to save that of his sister, the family felt that this was a family decision, and needed to be discussed as such. The doctor explained that according to U.S. law, this was a decision the young man could make independently. However, she encouraged the young man to discuss the decision with his family before finalizing the donation.

of these changes reduce the stability, size, and availability of social networks.

Despite these changes, social networks continue to exist and have a strong impact on individuals. This is particularly true for people who move to the United States from other countries. Although the size of their social network is diminished, with much of the extended family far away, family and community remain important, and their role may be enhanced because of the family's isolation from its cultural base. Conflicts between the expectations of the country of origin and the adopted country are common, and often difficult to communicate.

HOW FAMILIES AND FRIENDS ALTER DIAGNOSIS AND TREATMENT DECISIONS

Patients make decisions within a social network. These decisions can include how patients respond to preventative care, and whether or not their symptoms are serious enough to justify a visit a doctor. For example, the difficulty involved in following a low fat, low salt or low carbohydrate diet will differ tremendously depending on whether or not the family usually eats a lot of cheese, highly flavored food, or a rice-based diet. If the physician makes recommendations to the patient, but not to the person who is preparing the meals, it is unlikely the physician's advice will be followed. Similarly, even if the person who needs the diet is the person cooking, that does not necessarily mean that she is the person who determines what the family eats. It is difficult for a family to have multiple different meals for the family. Thus, if one person is to really follow a prescribed diet, it is often necessary for the rest of the family to adhere to the same diet.

Seeking care for symptoms may seem like a personal decision. However, if the patient is the primary wage-earner, or does not usually have access to the family car, or is responsible for care of multiple children, symptoms may be ignored for the sake of the family. For example, *a clinic to treat women with HIV found that the best way to get women to come in was to offer medical care for their children* at the same clinic. The mothers were much more likely to seek medical care for their children than to seek out care for their own problems.

Unfortunately, medical treatment is often complex and expensive. It requires organization to make and keep appointments, fill prescriptions, and cope with insurance and bills. Children and the elderly generally must rely on other family members to perform these tasks, but illness can make it difficult for even normally independent adults to take care of the dozens of details associated with health care. Chaotic or multiproblem families are less likely to successfully carry out these tasks. As one pediatric nurse noted, *you know a family is in trouble if having a child diagnosed with cancer is not the worst thing that ever happened to the family*.

Migrant Mother *Dorothea Lange (1936).* Courtesy of the Library of Congress, Washington, D.C. *Poverty is a significant stressor for families.*

HOW FAMILIES AND FRIENDS HELP PATIENTS COPE

Social support has repeatedly been found to be a significant, independent predictor of emotional well-being in adults and children with chronic or acute illness or injury. These studies have looked at a range of illnesses including adolescents with severe burns, children with cancer, and adults with heart disease. The evidence is clear: *People who have extended and available social support networks, consisting of friends and/or family members, are less anxious, and are less likely to become depressed or develop posttraumatic stress disorder.* One very large study of psychiatric symptoms in response to highly stressful events found that individuals with more support from friends had less psychiatric morbidity after death or serious illness in the family at a 3-year follow-up. Another study showed that the emotional outcome of adolescents with significant burns was more significantly correlated with their social support network than with the size or location of the burn.

HOW FAMILIES AND FRIENDS HELP PATIENTS RECOVER FROM ILLNESS

A famous study of women with metastatic breast cancer was a model for a series of investigations into the utility of social support in decreasing both psychiatric and medical morbidity and mortality. This Stanford study found that *women who participated in a structured support group lived longer than matched comparisons.* Replications have sought to explain the mechanism and identify the "active ingredient" of the intervention; however, these studies have produced mixed results. One explanation for the effect of group therapy on longevity is that the groups reduced isolation and helplessness, which in turn reduced the physical stress response, which facilitated healing and/or immune response. Other investigators have seen an improved immune response in cancer patients who were involved in psychoeducational support groups. However, not all support groups are equally effective in benefiting participants.

This variability may result because the type of interactions between the patient and the social support network influence the usefulness of the network. Studies of individuals with schizophrenia, depression, and bipolar affective disorder, for example, have found that patients with these serious mental illnesses can be harmed if the social network is very emotionally involved with the patient but is not supportive. *Patients living with family members who were deeply involved but were highly critical of the patient suffered more* *relapses and required more medication than patients whose family members were less involved and less critical.*

At the simplest level, social support can make it easier or harder to follow treatment recommendations, which in turn greatly influences morbidity and mortality. Adolescents are a classic example, as this is an age when any treatment that alters one's appearance is extremely poorly tolerated because of social pressure. A teenager may really mean it when she says she would rather die than lose all her hair. Likewise, young children may be humiliated if they need to go to the nurse for medications during the day at school, as it sets them apart from the other students. Women may delay seeking care for obvious breast masses because of the social (or marital) pressure to keep the discovery of a lump private or to ensure that their breasts remain intact. Although few patients actually say they would rather die than lose a breast, this sadly occurs all too often.

The Child's Bath (1893) *Mary Cassatt, 1844–1926.* Oil on canvas, 100 × 66 cm. Robert A. Waller Fund. © The Art Institute of Chicago. *Even well-intentioned parents often fail to follow treatment recommendations for their children.*

HOW FAMILIES AND FRIENDS ARE AFFECTED BY ILLNESS

Lengths of stay in hospitals have shortened dramatically over the past 10 to 20 years. Although this is partially a result of improved medications and the awareness that long convalescent periods are not always desirable, it is also based on the sometimes mistaken belief that uncomplicated recovery can occur safely at home. Given the tremendous expense of each day spent in a hospital, patients are frequently sent home within 24 hours of an uncomplicated delivery, a cardiac catheterization, and even a mastectomy. The assumption behind such discharges is that the patient will have someone who can drive them home, help them with activities of daily living, and be alert for any complications that might arise. However, this is not always the case. Elderly patients may have a spouse at home who is willing, but who is equally old and in frail health, and simply unable to help the patient get to the toilet or bath. Adults who live alone may not have any friends or family who can take off work to care for them. Children may have families of their own and already be stressed coping with school, work, and childcare. In each of these cases, one or two crises can generally be handled. However, when care becomes a chronic need, the financial and emotional toll can be overwhelming to all concerned.

A recent study of adolescents living with parents who had AIDS and a study of the emotional well-being of teens whose parents had died provided insight into the impact of chronic illness on family members. Both of these studies revealed that *adolescents were more emotionally distressed during the period of chronic illness than they were after the death of the parent.* The teens reported much more uncertainty and instability in their living situation during the time of illness than after the parental death. Similar findings have been reported for children who lost a parent to cancer—the disruption of school, living situations, and activities was even more distressing than the grief related to the death of a parent.

For parents of a child who is seriously injured or has a life-threatening illness, a sense of helplessness and horror can lead to both acute and long-term symptoms of traumatic stress. Acute symptoms include nightmares, hypervigilance, and numbing or avoidance of reminders. All of these can be understood as normal or even adaptive responses to a terrible event. However, these symptoms also can become chronic, and lead to clinical distress or reduced function. This is more likely when the parent is anxious even before the event, when the event is perceived by the parent as likely to result in death of the child, or when the treatment is perceived by the parent as very stressful. It is important to remember that *symptoms are dependent on the perception of the individual,* and not on what is seen by the physician as the "objective" threat. For example, studies have found no significant correlation between the perceptions of patients

The Family *Egon Schiele (1918). Österreichische Galerie Belvedere, Vienna. Psychoanalysts believe that the fundamental structure of personality is established in the first few years of life.*

and physicians as to the life-threat or treatment intensity for childhood cancer. The correlation between the perception of life-threat between parents and physicians is statistically significant, but not high enough to suggest they are actually assessing the same factors.

The **resilience** of families is another critically important variable affecting health. For example, one study of resilient mothers with spinal cord injuries compared with healthy mothers found no difference in the individual adjustment, attitudes toward their parents, self-esteem, gender roles, or family functioning. Even patients and caregivers who experience a medical diagnosis and treatment as traumatic may report that there were some positive consequences as a result of the experience. *Studies over the past 20 years have found that patients with HIV, childhood cancer survivors, and caregivers of Alzheimer's patients have reported changes in how they look at what is important in their lives, and an increased appreciation for interpersonal relationships.* This has resulted in the study of what is called "posttraumatic growth," which is further described below.

THE ROLE OF THE RELIGIOUS COMMUNITY AND SPIRITUAL BELIEF IN HEALTH

Most of the population of the United States reports a belief in a higher power or God, and the power of religion and spiritual belief has been a topic of growing interest in the medical community. As research has become more sophisticated, it has become clear that there are at least two separate factors that mediate the impact of religion or spirituality on health. One is the religious community. The other is personal faith. Each is considered below.

A **religious community** is a group of people who are joined by a common set of beliefs. This can be a formal church, temple, or mosque, with written expectations of the faithful, or a less formal group such as a prayer group, or practitioners of a form of yoga. This may be a group one is born into, or a group that one joins. *The power of the group results from providing a sense of community and a meeting place for whatever rituals are special to that community.* Membership in the community provides a clear sense of one's role and often instructs members in how to properly deal with difficult issues. For example, many religious groups provide guidelines as to how to deal with death and grief, and support one another through these difficult transitions. For those who are comfortable with the traditions of their religious community, these traditions are reassuring and provide social support at difficult times. However, for those who are estranged from the traditions of their communities, or who straddle two communities (such as second-generation Americans or those who marry outside their own community of believers), the community can add stress to an already difficult situation.

The strength of support from the religious community is generally measured with questions such as

- Are you a member of an organized religion?
- Do you go to religious services? How often?
- Do you get emotional support from your religious organization?
- Do you get physical support from your religious organization, such as food, transportation, or money?

The religious community provides support similar to that of an extended family. One example is The Church of the Latter Day Saints, or Mormon Church, which is well-known for the support they provide for members who are seriously ill. Food, lodging, and visitors can be arranged for family members who are caring for a patient, even when care is provided at a hospital far from the patient's home.

Personal faith may be shared with others, but is essentially a private sense of meaning or purpose. The faith may be consistent with an established doctrine or dogma, but it is perceived as being individually experienced. *The strength of personal faith is independent of the degree of participation in a religious community*, although some people with personal faith will also attend religious services. The support it provides is not physical or instrumental, but entirely emotional or spiritual.

The language of inquiry about faith can be tricky. When asked if they are "religious," many people assume the question has to do with an organized or formal religious set of beliefs. They may say they are spiritual, but not religious, or that they are religious, but not observant. Similarly, people may say they are religious, and really be referring to a set of beliefs with which they were raised, but which are no longer of personal importance.

Personal faith is generally measured by questions such as

- How important is your faith or spirituality in your daily life?
- Do you get strength or support from your faith?
- Is prayer or a spiritual practice a part of your daily life?

Some individuals experience illness as a test of their faith, and believe they became ill because their faith was insufficient. This may take the form of a belief that faith will heal them, or that failure to recover is evidence of insufficient faith. This viewpoint is classically represented in the **Church of Christ, Scientist**, where traditional medication and physicians are seen as unnecessary to those of faith. However, some variation on this idea is present in many other belief systems. Likewise, the belief that illness is sent as a trial or punishment that must be endured is challenging for physicians who must balance their desire to help the patient with respect for the patient's personal values and beliefs.

Traumatic events can sometimes reveal or even create a stronger sense of personal faith. **Posttraumatic growth** refers to an increased sense of meaning or purpose after a traumatic event. People sometimes report that the traumatic event they experienced resulted in the destruction of their usual assumptions about how the world worked, and that out of the ashes, a new and stronger faith was born. This may include a change in their formal religious faith, or a reorganizing of their values and priorities. The term is generally used for relatively permanent changes. Posttraumatic growth has been reported by patients, spouses, parents, and adult children who have dealt with a variety of medical issues, including childhood cancer, HIV, prostate cancer, Alzheimer's disease, and heart disease.

CASE EXAMPLE

A woman was distraught over the diagnosis of cancer for her oldest son. It was not until one of the medical team was able to talk with her alone that it became clear that the woman was overcome with guilt. She believed that God was taking her son away from her as punishment for a sexual affair that occurred early in her marriage. She could not share this with anyone in her family or her church, effectively removing all social support from her at a time of crisis in her life.

HOW TO WORK WITH FAMILIES AND COMMUNITIES

Pediatricians learn early that they are never only working with one patient. Since the child is not the decision-maker, at least one parent is always involved. *A wise pediatrician involves both parents whenever possible, and is always aware of which parent makes which decisions.* Obviously when parents are divorced, a determination must be made as to which parent makes medical decisions. However, even in cases in which the parents are happily married to each other, one parent often takes on primary responsibility for getting the child to a clinic or staying with them at the hospital. Relying on that parent to communicate everything is a tremendous burden for the parent, and excludes the other parent from a full understanding of the medical situation.

Similarly, geriatricians are usually careful to assess the support network of their patients as part of the assessment of activities of daily living. The participation of the patient's spouse, adult children, siblings, or even neighbors or grandchildren may be necessary for decision-making and ensuring adherence with complex regimens of medication and other treatment. The wise physician determines who the key players are, and keeps them informed and involved by including them in clinic visits and telephoning them about new developments. This is somewhat more complex with adults than with minors, as any such communication can only be done with the permission of the patient, unless the patient is not competent to make medical decisions. It can be time-consuming to determine who else should be involved, and to communicate with them. However, the cost in time and success of treatment can be significant if this is not done. *The stress of visiting a doctor makes it difficult for even organized patients to keep track of their own questions, as well as the doctor's answers and instructions.* A friend or relative can help the patient remember what has been said. Possibly more important, involvement of the friend or relative reduces the likelihood that they will sabotage the treatment plan through disagreeing with treatment recommendations or unwittingly supporting the patient's resistance.

Young and middle-aged adults generally handle most of their medical care by themselves. However, *the importance of the immediate and extended family and social support system can be enormous.* The spouse may be the true decision-maker in some families, or the patient may feel unable to make decisions that would affect the family without first discussing the decision with the family. Some families may even prefer that all medical information be conveyed to someone other than the patient. This is only legally permissible if the patient requests that information be handled in this way, and this situation is usually very difficult for the physician. It is important to recognize that shielding patients from information is usually done out of a belief

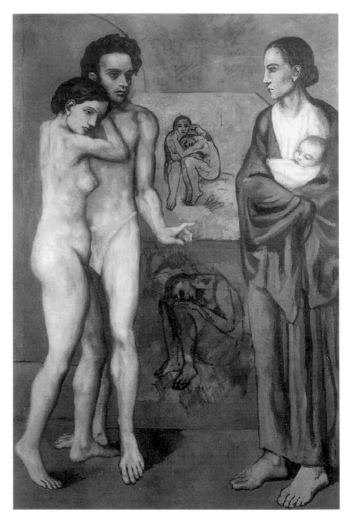

La Vie (1903) *Pablo Picasso,* Spanish, 1881–1973. Oil on canvas, 196.5 × 129.2 cm. The Cleveland Museum of Art, 2003. Gift of the Hanna Fund, 1945.24. © 2001 Estate of Pablo Picasso / Artists Rights Society (ARS) New York. *Picasso's La Vie is one of his most enigmatic paintings. The standing male originally was a self-portrait; Picasso later changed the picture to portray his friend Carlos Casagemas who had committed suicide in 1901. The embracing couple in the top painting appears to pay homage to Gauguin, the crouching figure in the lower painting is reminiscent of Van Gogh's Sorrow, a lithograph of the unhappy prostitute he lived with in Amsterdam. The painting is allegorical and leaves the viewer thinking about the life cycle, sexuality, the complexity of relationships, and human suffering. All four of these themes are reflected in* Behavior and Medicine, *and physicians must deal with all of these problems in their daily practice.*

that too much information will compromise the health of the patient by removing hope or causing anxiety. Physicians generally feel more comfortable with this approach when it involves pediatric patients rather than adults. However, the same principals apply in either case. This approach reduces open communication within the family, and it creates dependency in the patient. In families in which this is the norm, this may be well tolerated. In others, this can lead to isolation and anxiety for the patient, who can tell others are upset, but are not discussing why.

In situations in which communication occurs with a family member rather than directly with a patient, the physician must carefully choose which family members to involve, and this must not be done without the permission of the patients except in extreme circumstances. The classic situation that arises in pediatrics is with adolescents. Although parents may be the medical decision-makers, vital information may be missed if the entire history and exam is done with the parent in the room. *Adolescents should not be expected to be comfortable asking questions or giving personal information in front of their parents, particularly when the discussion deals with sex or drugs.* On the other hand, parents *do* need to give permission for medical treatment. How much parents need to be involved in decisions about treatment related to sexuality and drugs varies from state to state. Some states have parental notification laws regarding abortion, for example. All states require reporting of sexual abuse or physical abuse of minors. Although these laws require reporting a suspicion of child abuse to the police, the nonoffending parent would usually also have to be informed.

SUMMARY

Physicians never treat patients in isolation from their families and community. Understanding how a social network influences the patient's perspective, and how the network can be used to support health and healing, is extremely useful. A wise doctor knows how to work with the beliefs and social supports to provide the best medical care possible.

CASE STUDY

A 7-year-old girl is diagnosed with acute lymphoblastic leukemia. She is the only child of her parents, who are observant Roman Catholics. The girl is very anxious, and wants her mother with her for all procedures. However, the mother is very difficult for the staff to manage, arguing with them about who she will allow to perform procedures on her daughter. A private conversation with the mother reveals that she feels very angry with God about this illness. She had miscarried twins 2 years earlier, and now is beginning to feel that she is cursed. Her husband is coping with their daughter's illness by working long hours, and spending all of his free time at Mass and prayer meetings. Their marriage is deteriorating, as her whole life is dedicated to dealing with her daughter and the doctors, and her faith is shattered.

Some 7 years later, the now 14-year-old daughter comes in with her mother for a check-up. She has successfully navigated 2 years of treatment, a later relapse, and a bone marrow transplant. Her parents are divorced, and her father has remarried and has two other children. When the adolescent is seen alone she says her primary goal is to have some other focus in her life than cancer. She begs the doctor to get her mother off her back, so she can be a "normal" teenager. A separate meeting with the mother reveals that she also sees the cancer episode as finally over. However, she finds she does not know what to do with her life now. She has put all of her energy into fighting for her daughter's life. She has left the church, has no hobbies, works at a boring job, and has no friends. She eventually accepts a referral to a psychiatrist, who helps her focus on creating a life for herself, which includes, but is not dependent on, her daughter.

SUGGESTED READINGS

Alexander, C.J., Hwang, K., & Sipski, M.L. (2002). Mothers with spinal cord injuries: Impact on marital, family, and children's adjustment. *Archives of Physical Medicine and Rehabilitation, 83*, 24–30.
This study found that spinal cord injury in mothers does not appear to affect their children adversely in terms of individual adjustment, attitudes toward their parents, self-esteem, gender roles, and family functioning.

Koenig, H.G., McCollough, M.E., & Larson, D.B. (2001). *Handbook of religion and health.* New York: Oxford University Press.
This book reviews studies examining how people who are physically ill can use religious beliefs and practices to relieve stress, retain a sense of control, and maintain hope and their sense of meaning and purpose in life. The authors examine the current evidence that religious involvement helps those with serious and disabling medical illness to cope better and experience psychological growth from their negative health experiences, rather than be defeated or overcome by them.

Manne, S., Ostroff, J., Winkel, G., Goldstein, L., Fox, K., & Grana, G. (2004). Posttraumatic growth after breast cancer: Patient, partner, and couple perspectives. *Psychosomatic Medicine, 66*, 442–454.
This study had 162 women with breast cancer and their partners complete surveys assessing posttraumatic growth, cognitive and emotional processing, and marital satisfaction at three time points spaced 9 months apart. They found that posttraumatic growth increased for both partners during this period.

Schor, E.L. (2003). American Academy of Pediatrics Task Force on the Family. *Pediatrics, 6*, 1541–1571.
This report summarizes the essential role of the family in the practice of pediatrics, and provides guidelines on how best to work with families as a pediatrician.

3 Birth, Childhood, and Adolescence

Harsh K. Trivedi & Pamela J. Beasley

> Your children are not your children. They are the sons and daughters of Life's longing for itself.
>
> KHALIL GIBRAN
> *The Prophet*

The life of a child from birth through adolescence is marked by enormous personal and interpersonal growth. The many "firsts" that occur, such as saying "mama" for the first time or taking the first few steps, mark the achievement of numerous developmental milestones. However, the fascinating interplay between a child's genes and his or her environment can create significant variability in the rate and extent of development. For example, a child with a genetic trajectory for normal motor ability may not sit up until 11 months of age when raised in a neglectful environment with poor nutrition. More commonly, the findings are less dramatic and parents will ask questions such as, "Our older daughter started talking at 10 months, but our son is nearly a year old and only says a few words. Is that normal?" It is critical to understand normal child development as a foundation upon which to better appreciate areas of potential concern.

Beyond the inherent variability of development across different children, there is the additional complexity of development occurring along multiple lines within each child. Studying a group of first graders, one quickly notices that there are significant differences in motor development as seen in the way they hold their pencils and work on fine motor tasks. In addition, if you study one particular child from the group, he or she may be developmentally on track for motor development, but may have mild cognitive delays. This creates the need for a structured method by which to study development.

Children can be studied from the perspective of gross motor, fine motor, language, cognitive, social, or myriad other developmental lines. At any given time, a clinical snapshot can be taken of a child to study where he or she stands along different developmental lines. Children can often be at different levels of development depending upon which line is being assessed. A clinically important factor to keep in mind is that many children may appear at age level on most developmental tasks and initially only exhibit a delay along one particular line of development. If left untreated, this delay has the potential to affect development along other lines over time. For example, consider the child with age-appropriate cognitive and visual-motor development, but who has motor speech delay. If this motor articulation problem is not addressed in the child with speech delay, the development of language and socialization skills may be hindered.

It is also important to consider how the same developmental delay may manifest differently based upon the child's age and developmental stage. The child with speech delay may express poor frustration tolerance as a toddler, may be quite shy and anxious during latency, and may become irritable and withdrawn during adolescence. This complexity of variable presentations during development combined with the intertwining of progress among the different developmental lines makes systematic study of the child even more important.

As one takes clinical snapshots of different children, it is important to understand normal development for various age groups in order to distinguish what is clinically significant. For example, ask yourself the question, what should a child entering elementary school be able to do? The linking of important periods of life with developmental milestones will make it easier to remember what most children are able to do at a particular age.

When potentially troublesome areas are found, early intervention is key as a delay in treatment may further hamper other lines of development. Also, children can be remarkably resilient in making developmental gains once the issue

TABLE 3.1 Overview of development across structural theories and developmental lines.

	Birth	1yo	2yo	3yo	5yo	7yo	11yo	18yo
Structural Theories								
Freud's Psychosexual Stages	Oral		Anal	Phallic	Latency		Adolescence	
Erikson's Psychosocial Stages	Trust v. Mistrust		Autonomy v. Shame & Doubt	Initiative v. Guilt	Industry v. Inferiority		Ego Identity v. Role Diffusion	
Piaget's Cognitive Stages	Sensorimotor			Pre-Operational		Concrete	Formal	
Developmental Lines*								
Gross Motor	Head Steady Sit No Support Roll Over	Walks Stands	Jumps	Balance on 1 Foot Hops	Heel to Toe Walk Balance on each Foot 6 Seconds			
Fine Motor	Follow to Midline Pass Cube Grasps Rattle Pincer Grasp	Tower 2 Cubes	Vertical Line	Copy a Circle Copy a Cross	Copy a Square Copy a Triangle			
Speech and Language	Coos Babbles	"Mama, Dada" 1-3 words	2-3 Word Phrases	Sentences	Name 4 Colors Define 7 words			
Social	Regards Face Social Smile	Wave Bye-Bye Imitate Activities	Put on Clothing Name Friend	Play Card Games				

* Adapted from the Denver II, DA Form 5694, 1988

is addressed, but it is important to act before children are so delayed that their global functioning is affected. Finding out that a child in the seventh grade has oppositional behavior and school refusal because he has an undiagnosed learning disorder and is tormented about being "stupid" by classmates is a grave disservice to that child. Even when the learning disorder issues are addressed, the damage to the child's self-esteem and long history of poor social interactions with peers may leave lasting problems that are harder to correct.

Lastly, just as children can present with different symptomatology based upon their developmental stage, it is important to remember that the intervention must be developmentally appropriate to be most effective. When planning treatment for a child with speech delay, the intervention will be different for a 2-year-old, a 6-year-old, or an adolescent.

OVERVIEW OF DEVELOPMENT

The information in this chapter is presented by age groups to facilitate understanding the whole child from multiple perspectives. When studying development, it is important to keep an eye on the development of the entire child and to extrapolate how one particular delay may be affecting multiple areas of a child's functioning. Table 3.1 presents an overview of development, listing major developmental

theories and milestones from birth to 18 years of age to provide the "big picture" as you explore this topic in greater depth. Rather than memorizing which stage comes after Erikson's stage of Autonomy vs. Shame and Doubt, it is more helpful to be able to put the information in context and to understand how the successful resolution of that stage can help guide further development. Specifically, it is important to keep interrelating the various developmental lines and structural theories to decipher how these different aspects of development intertwine to allow a particular child to reach age-appropriate developmental milestones.

Developmental Lines

Development can be studied from the perspective of tracking a particular domain over time. For example, how does gross motor function develop from birth through adolescence? By following the attainment of successive milestones among many children, a population-based standard distribution is created which plots the range of variability in the development of each milestone. Based upon this data, the concept of "normal" refers to those children who fall within two standard deviations of the mean. Domains commonly studied include gross motor, fine motor, language, and social abilities.

ONLY STARS

This evening there are only stars—
Roland is born and I delivered him.
One hour ago my apprehensive hands
slid his body down onto a towel,
cut his cord and wrapped him in a sheet.
For one quick moment I held my child
and he blended with my half-crooked arm
as if he had been held that way forever.
This evening there are only stars.

This evening there are only stars
and one small human is made half from me
and half from his adoring mother.
He is of the morning dew and unaware
that I am of the afternoon and see into the night.
We all come from the same drumming darkness,
take the light of one brief life
and then return into the blackness whence we came.
But, though we are ephemeral, we have
a galaxy which fires us from within—
this evening there are only stars.

DUNCAN DARBISHIRE

You may give them your love but not your thoughts.
For they have their own thoughts.
You may house their bodies but not their souls,
For their souls dwell in the house of tomorrow, which you cannot visit, not even in your dreams.

KHALIL GIBRAN
The Prophet

Structural Theories of Development

Development can also be studied by examining how the attainment of certain skills allows for the progressive learning of new ones. The structural theories introduce the concept that there is some formation or reorganization of the mind that allows further progression of development.

Many different theories have been formulated to explain development. The major theories that will be covered in this chapter include Freud's Theory of Psychosexual Development, Erikson's Theory of Psychosocial Development, Piaget's Theory of Cognitive Development, Mahler's Theory of Separation-Individuation, and Bowlby's Attachment Theory. Each theory uses different labels occurring at different age ranges to demarcate the various stages. For this chapter, children will be described using developmental snapshots at specific age groups. The goal is to understand the child by incorporating the multiple developmental lines and structural theories in order to gain a more complete view of the child from multiple perspectives.

Sigmund Freud's Phases of Psychosexual Development

Freud developed *psychoanalytic theory*, a body of hypotheses concerning mental functioning and personality development. One of Freud's most important contributions was the concept of the *unconscious*, which refers to thoughts and motives that exist outside a person's awareness and have the capacity to influence thoughts and actions. Freud's psychoanalytic treatment used the process of *free association* (the patient says everything that comes to mind) to bring unconscious material into conscious awareness.

Freud also introduced the concept of *drives*, instinctual urges that produce a state of psychic excitation or tension, that impel the individual to activity. The two major drives, sexual and aggressive, are each associated with psychic energy. The psychic energy associated with the sexual drive is termed *libido*.

Freud's theory of psychosexual development describes the sequential manifestations of the sexual drive from infancy onward. He postulated that developmental stages progressed as the child's focus of *libidinal energy* shifted to different erotic areas (Table 3.2). The child's goal during each stage is to experience the pleasure that comes from that area while attempting to lessen pain. Resolution of conflict involved in each of these stages allows the individual to move toward achieving normal adult functioning. Through this theory, Freud stressed the importance that development in childhood, including that which occurs during infancy, has on the grown adult.

In 1915, Freud published his *Three Essays on the Theory of Sexuality* in which the mouth, anus, and genitalia were

TABLE 3.2 Phases of Freud's theory of psychosexual development

Phase	Age (Years)
Oral	Birth to 1
Anal	1 to 3
Phallic	3 to 5
Latency	5 to 11
Genital	11 to 18

described as foci for *libidinal energy*. He also added a period of decreased sexual interest, termed *latency*, which continues until the onset of puberty. Despite more recent work that has shown significant psychosexual activity during the latency phase, Freud's theory of psychosexual phases is a helpful tool in understanding development.

Erik Erikson's Stages of Psychosocial Development

Erikson focused more on the interplay between biology and society as it influences psychosocial development. In contrast to Freud, he stressed the importance of childhood events and experiences during adulthood. He presented the *epigenetic principle* that states that development occurs sequentially through eight stages over the course of a lifetime. Each stage has two possible outcomes, one positive (healthy) and the other negative (unhealthy), and builds upon the progress made in the previous stage. If a stage is not satisfactorily resolved, then the person is unable to achieve a new and higher level of functioning (Table 3.3).

TABLE 3.3 Stages of Erikson's theory of psychosocial development

Stage	Age (Years)
Basic Trust vs. Mistrust	Birth to 1
Autonomy vs. Shame and Doubt	1 to 3
Initiative vs. Guilt	3 to 5
Industry vs. Inferiority	5 to 11
Ego Identity vs. Role Diffusion	11 to 21
Intimacy vs. Isolation	21 to 40
Generativity vs. Stagnation	40 to 60
Ego Integrity vs. Despair	over 60

As our society changes, the relative age spans for each of the stages may shift as well. For example, as people live longer and retire later in life, the generativity vs. stagnation stage may become prolonged and the ego integrity vs. despair stage may be delayed.

The adolescent mind is essentially a mind of the moratorium, a psychosocial stage between childhood and adulthood, and between the morality learned by the child and the ethics developed by the adult.

ERIK ERIKSON
Childhood and Society

TABLE 3.4 Stages of Piaget's theory of cognitive development

Stage	Age (Years)
Sensorimotor	Birth–2
Preoperational thought	2–7
Concrete operations	7–11
Formal operations	11–18

Jean Piaget's Stages of Cognitive Development

Piaget studied children's thoughts and behavior to derive his theory of cognitive development. He theorized that intellectual functions were fundamentally at the core of personality formation and provided for the coordinated progression of development along all spheres. Like Freud and Erikson, he expressed that future stages are dependent upon properly negotiated previous stages. However, although the stages occur sequentially, they rely on the maturation of the nervous system and on life experiences to determine their rate of progress (Table 3.4).

Piaget also introduced the concept that *assimilation* and *accommodation* were necessary tools for cognitive development. Assimilation is defined as the ability to fit an experience with an existing cognitive structure. Consider a child who turns on a switch at home and understands that by turning the switch he caused the lights to turn on. By assimilation, he can then correlate that turning on a switch at his grandparents' home may also cause the lights to turn on. Accommodation, however, is the process of adapting the existing cognitive structure to new experiences. For example, when faced with an object at a tall height, a child uses accommodation to figure out that the baseball bat he usually uses to hit balls can also be used as an implement to reach tall objects.

John Bowlby's Attachment Theory

Bowlby's *attachment theory* incorporated his psychoanalytic understanding of child development with evolutionary theory to postulate a genetic basis for infant attachment to caregivers. He described attachment as "a warm, intimate, and continuous relationship with the mother in which both find satisfaction and enjoyment." Bowlby theorized that attachment behaviors promote nearness to the attachment figure so that dangers can be avoided. Early attachment behaviors include crying, smiling, and cooing. Later attachment behaviors include verbalizing and nonverbal signaling; these behaviors persist throughout life. Bowlby described three stages of attachment (Table 3.5). During

TABLE 3.5 Stages of Bowlby's attachment theory

Stage	Age
Preattachment	Birth–8–10 weeks
Attachment in the Making	8–10 weeks–6 months
Clear-Cut Attachment	6 months–end of life

the *preattachment* stage (birth to 8–10 weeks), the baby orients to the caregiver, follows her with his eyes over a 180-degree range, and turns toward her voice; however, the infant does not discriminate among caregivers in this stage. In the second stage, the *attachment in the making* stage (8–10 weeks to 6 months), the infant becomes attached to one or more figures in his or her environment. In these first two stages, as long as the infant's needs are being satisfied, separation from a particular person does not induce distress. In the *clear cut attachment* stage (6 months to end of life), the infant is distressed by separation from the caregiver and stops crying and clings upon her return.

Margaret Mahler's Theory of Separation-Individuation

Mahler studied the separation-individuation process between mother and child from birth to 3 years of age (Table 3.6). The *normal autistic phase* (birth to 4 weeks) refers to a state of half-sleep, half-wake during which the major task is to achieve homeostatic equilibrium with the environment. In the *normal symbiotic phase* (3–4 weeks to 4–5 months), the infant has a vague awareness of the mother, but still functions as if he and the caretaker were in a state of undifferentiation or fusion. Mahler identified four subphases of separation-individuation. The first subphase, *differentiation* (5 to 10 months), describes the process of "hatching from the autistic shell" as the infant develops a more alert sensorium. "Stranger anxiety" develops at this time, and is most prominent around 8 months. The sec-

A Boy is Beaten Because He Broke a Jar *Francisco José de Goya (circa 1800).* Courtesy of the National Library of Medicine. *Parents frequently use punishment to control the behavior of their children, but reinforcement is more effective in the long run.*

ond subphase, *practicing* (10 to 16 months), is marked by upright locomotion and using mother as "home base." Separation anxiety typically develops around this time. During the third subphase, *rapprochement* (16 to 24 months), the infant becomes more aware of himself as separate from the mother, and a sense of identity is consolidated. Two characteristic patterns of behavior emerge: shadowing of the mother and running from her. These *rapprochement crises* are ultimately resolved as the child experiences gratification from doing things for himself. The fourth subphase of separation-individuation is termed *consolidation and object constancy,* and refers to the child's internalization of the mother as stable and reliable. This allows the child to tolerate separations from the mother because he knows she will return.

TABLE 3.6 Mahler's phases of separation-individuation

Stage	Age
Normal Autistic Phase	Birth to 4 weeks
Normal Symbiotic Phase	3–4 weeks to 4–5 months
Separation-individuation proper: subphases	
Differentiation	5 to 10 months
Practicing	10 to 16 months
Rapprochement	16 to 24 months
Consolidation and object constancy	24 to 36 months

> It is as natural to die as to be born; and to a little infant, perhaps, the one is as painful as the other.
>
> SIR FRANCIS BACON
> *Essays*

DEVELOPMENTAL SNAPSHOTS

Infancy (Birth to 18 Months)

The average newborn weighs between 7 and 7.5 pounds, and measures 19–21 inches in length. Growth occurs at a faster rate during the first year of life than at any subsequent period until the onset of puberty. An infant will normally grow between 10 and 12 inches within the first year of life, and height at age 2 will be about 50% of mature adult height. Weight gain is approximately an ounce a day for the first few months of life. Birth weight is doubled by 4 months of age, tripled by the end of the first year, and quadrupled by age 2. The average infant gains 14 pounds in the first year of life.

A newborn child is born in a state of complete dependency for survival and must rely on parents and caretakers for all aspects of basic care. The child has poor sensory function and only minimal control over limb movements. Vocalizations and other communicative skills are lacking. Because of the child's inability to self-soothe and the need for immediate responses from caregivers, eye gaze, head turning, and sucking are used to indicate preference.

The major developmental tasks in these first months of life involve the formation of a secure attachment, regulation of the sleep-wake cycle, and creation of a feeding pattern. The ability of the child and parents to resolve these issues is often dependent upon the child's temperament. *Temperament* refers to a set of inborn traits that organize the child's approach to the world. The child's personality will be determined by the interaction of these individual differences in behavioral style with the environment. Chess and Thomas identified nine temperamental traits of infants (Table 3.7) that correlate to a stratification of temperament into "easy," "difficult," and "slow to warm up." The concept of temperament is helpful as it incorporates the role of the child in these early interactions and influences the "goodness of fit" between child and caregiver. It stresses that there needs to be a match between the child's temperament and the caregiver's parenting style in order to improve functioning and to avoid behavioral and emotional problems.

TABLE 3.7 Chess and Thomas' nine behavioral dimensions for temperament

Activity Level
Rhythmicity
Approach or Withdrawal
Adaptability
Intensity of Reaction
Threshold of Responsiveness
Quality of Mood
Distractibility
Attention Span and Persistence

By the second month of life, the child becomes more interactive with parents and develops a social smile. This is followed by the ability to examine and reach for objects in the midline by 3 months, rolling over by 4 months, and being able to hold the head up and coo (produce long vowel sounds in musical fashion) soon after. These activities provide positive reinforcement for parents who in turn respond with additional attention and affectionate behavior toward the child.

During this time, Erikson's *Basic Trust vs. Mistrust* stage (birth to 1 year) comes into play, as infants learn whether their needs are being met. The availability of a supportive and responsive parent allows the formation of a secure attachment and a sense of basic trust. Inconsistent parenting leads to mistrust and feelings of despair in the child. Bowlby found that the lack of a secure attachment with the caregiver could negatively impact the child's emotional and intellectual development. He found that three stages exist during mother-infant separation. Initially, the child protests and cries for the caregiver. This is followed by despair when the child believes that the caregiver will not return. With continued separation, detachment occurs as the child loses emotional connection to the caregiver.

> A smart mother makes often a better diagnosis than a poor doctor.
>
> AUGUST BIER
> German professor of surgery

At 6 months, the child can sit unsupported, lift a cup, and transfer objects. At 9 months, the child develops a *pincer grasp* (uses thumb to help grasp tiny objects), pulls self to standing, says "mama" or "dada," and plays interpersonal games like "peek-a-boo." The ability to manipulate objects with better motor control allows the child to place objects in his or her mouth. As the child successfully maneuvers different objects, he or she achieves a sense of mastery, which creates an increased desire for autonomy (e.g., feeding self). The child's focusing of libidinal and aggressive energy toward oral pleasure zones is explained by Freud's *Oral Phase* (birth to 1 year). The child is receiving oral gratification from the act of nursing while attempting to control aggressive urges to bite, chew, or spit. The child works to develop trust in the caregiver. A child who adequately resolves these conflicts develops the ability to give and receive from others, trust others, and experience self-reliance. A child with poor resolution of this stage may exhibit dependent features, low self-esteem, envy, and jealousy.

Piaget's *Sensorimotor Stage* (birth to 2 years) refers to the development of sensory awareness, which allows the child to gain better control over motor functions. As the child receives sensory input, his or her motor system responds in a stereotyped, reflexive way. As this happens again and again, the child gradually becomes aware of this stimulus-response loop. Piaget's theory refers to this stimulus-response awareness as a *schema*. Later, as the child's interaction with the environment increases, he or she develops specific *schemas* (mental categories of information) about different objects and experiences. Each of these schemas is built upon to construct more complex *schemata*. The schemata then serve as reference points for the actions of assimilation and accommodation, which enable further progression of development.

> At every step the child should be allowed to meet the real experiences of life; the thorns should never be plucked from his roses.
>
> ELLEN KEY
> *The Century of the Child*

By 9 months, object permanence forms as the child becomes aware that objects continue to exist even when they can no longer be seen. This leads to stranger anxiety in which children find it hard to separate from parents and will protest if left with strangers. Mary Ainsworth developed the "Strange Situation" research project to assess the quality of infant-parent attachment in 1–2-year-olds. In this attachment paradigm, infants were observed across episodes of increasing stress (a series of separations from and reunions with their mothers). Ainsworth identified three distinct types of attachment in these infants. *Securely attached* children were able to use their mother as a base for exploration of toys and the environment, were active in seeking contact with her, and were reassured after making contact with her. Children with *anxious/resistant attachment* were unable to use the mother as a base for exploration, were not readily comforted by contact with her, and mixed contact seeking with anger. Infants with *anxious/avoidant attachments* withheld contact with the mother and ignored or avoided her following separation. Ainsworth believed that a caregiver's consistent responsiveness to the infant's needs leads to secure attachment. Insensitive care leads to the resistant pattern of attachment, and indifferent or rejecting care leads to the avoidant pattern of attachment. Ainsworth showed that the interaction between infant and caregiver during this early attachment period significantly influences both the child's current and future behavior.

By 12 months of age the child can walk independently, stack blocks, and speak 3–4 words. By 15 months, the child can creep upstairs, walk backwards, and scribble by imitation. Play during infancy is primarily solitary (playing alone) or parallel (playing beside other children without interacting).

CASE EXAMPLE

Jennifer is a 15-month-old Caucasian female who presented to her pediatrician with malnutrition and poor weight gain. Jennifer's visits to her pediatrician had been sporadic since birth, and on this visit her height and weight were noted to be below the 5th percentile.

Jennifer was admitted to the hospital for evaluation. A thorough medical workup failed to reveal an underlying physical cause for her malnutrition and poor weight gain. In the hospital, Jennifer responded rapidly to adequate feeding, and began gaining weight almost immediately.

Jennifer had no prior history of medical problems and no prior hospitalizations. She was the product of a normal full-term pregnancy, the youngest of four children, and lived with her mother. Mother was 25 years old and had completed high school. She was unemployed, and reported that she had been dealing with a number of stressors including her boyfriend moving out of the home, limited financial resources, and the recent death of her parents in an automobile accident. She endorsed symptoms of severe depression and anxiety, and reported being unable to get out of bed on some days. Mother denied the use of alcohol or illicit drugs.

On examination, Jennifer was a cachectic appearing infant who was below the 5th percentile for height and weight, and in the 25th percentile for head circumference. She avoided eye contact, appeared to be disinterested in her surroundings, and resisted cuddling. She was able to sit alone, but was unable to walk. Mother described Jennifer as an irritable baby who cried frequently and awakened often during sleep. She reported that Jennifer had not yet spoken, and that she rarely smiled. Mother admitted feeling overwhelmed with Jennifer's care and often relegated it to Jennifer's 10-year-old sister.

The medical team requested a psychiatry consult to assess the mother's emotional functioning and a social work consult to assess Jennifer's social environment. The psychiatrist reported that Jennifer's mother met criteria for a severe depressive disorder as well as an anxiety disorder, and recommended treatment with medication and psychotherapy. The social worker reported that the mother had a history of domestic violence and was socially isolated, and that her level of poverty prevented her from providing her children with adequate nutrition.

The consensus of the medical team was that Jennifer met criteria for *failure to thrive*, a multifactorial syndrome characterized by weight gain deceleration, linear growth delay, and developmental delays. In Jennifer's case, weight gain and growth delays were thought to be the result of inadequate caloric intake, while her developmental delays were likely the result of emotional and socioeconomic deprivation. Because Jennifer's mother was so incapacitated by her depression and anxiety, the team decided to file a report with the state's Department of Social Services (DSS).

Together with DSS, the medical team developed a treatment plan that included referring the mother for treatment of her psychiatric disorders as well as for parenting classes, making a referral for early intervention services for Jennifer, and making arrangements for visiting nurses to go to the home to assist the mother in developing a feeding schedule for Jennifer. DSS was also able to make arrangements for daycare for the three other children, and assisted Jennifer's mother in setting up an appointment with a career counselor.

The development of a sense of self is a critical developmental task.

Toddler (18 Months to 36 Months)

By the age of 18 months, the child has an improved sense of balance and a steadier gait. This improvement in motor skills leads to the ability to run and climb stairs. Cognitive development has also progressed allowing the child to solve problems in new ways. For example, instead of crying for a parent when a ball has rolled under the sofa and out of reach, the child can now use a stick to get it.

This added functional ability gives rise to Erikson's stage of *Autonomy vs. Shame and Doubt* (1 to 3 years). In this stage, the child faces the urge to explore the environment further as well as to develop greater anal sphincter control. In attempting these tasks, the child relies on basic trust to deal with the distress of being separated from parents and of having a bowel or bladder accident. Shame and doubt occur when a child is unable to achieve autonomy in these functions.

At 18 months, Mahler's *rapprochement* stage of separation-individuation occurs as the child's increasing awareness of helplessness and dependence leads to greater anxiety over separation from the caregiver. The child may test the waters by slowly moving away from the caregiver a short distance and then returning for additional support and reassurance. As the level of comfort increases and anxiety decreases, the distance from the caregiver also increases.

A *transitional object* assists the child in making the transition from complete dependence on the caregiver to independence. First described by Winnicott, the transitional object may take the form of a blanket, pillow, or stuffed toy. These objects remind the child of the caregiver and serve a soothing function while the child is falling asleep, or during times of stress or separation from the caregiver. Attachment to a transitional object is a normal and healthy phase in the development of a toddler.

Children at 18 months have a vocabulary of 15 words, which increases to 100 words by 24 months. The newly emerging language development marked by this exponential increase in vocabulary signifies the end of Piaget's sensorimotor stage and the beginning of his *Preoperational Stage* (2 years to 7 years). During this stage, children continue to function at a prelogical state, i.e., they are not yet able to use logical processes to arrive at conclusions. Piaget's experiment on conservation of mass illustrates this point. Children are asked to transfer water between two glasses that are shaped differently but hold the same amount of water. When asked which glass holds more water, children with prelogical thinking will pick the longer, taller glass despite seeing the same amount of water being exchanged back and forth.

The emergence of symbolic play and magical thinking influences the child's interactions in new situations. As opposed to play in the sensorimotor stage where little attention is paid to the toy's intended purpose, the child now understands the functional use of toys, and can even use them to represent other things. For example, a doll can be the mean mommy who gives time-outs for misbehaving. Magical thinking can be troublesome as a blurred sense of reality testing in conjunction with prelogical thinking can make many things seem plausible. For example, children

---

CASE EXAMPLE

Sam was a 2- and- one-half-year-old boy who was referred for a developmental evaluation by his pediatrician because of concerns about language delay. Sam was the product of a normal pregnancy and delivery and lived with his parents and 5-year-old sister. Parents described that Sam had been a very fussy baby who was difficult to soothe and who often seemed to be "in a world of his own." Sam had never exhibited stranger anxiety, and had shown only mild interest in the social games of infancy such as peek-a-boo and pat-a-cake. He did not seem to take comfort in being held, and in fact would stiffen when his parents picked him up. Sam had no interest in pretend play or social interactions, and seemed happiest when sitting by himself lining his crayons from end to end. He had always exhibited very poor eye contact.

The parents described Sam as a "rigid" child, who was very sensitive to sounds and food textures and who insisted on the same routine every day. He would have severe behavioral outbursts if his routine was changed or when asked to try new foods. Sam's motor development had been normal, although he exhibited repetitive motor behaviors such as hand flapping when excited. Parents reported that his vocabulary consisted of only several words, however, he did appear to have an age-appropriate understanding of language.

Sam had no history of medical problems and took no medications. There was no family history of medical or psychiatric disorders. A comprehensive medical workup, which included a hearing test, EEG, CT scan, genetic screening, and chromosomal analysis, was negative.

On the basis of Sam's disturbances in social interaction, language, and communication, as well as his restricted, repetitive, and stereotyped patterns of behavior, the diagnosis of autism was made. Sam was enrolled in an intensive multidisciplinary treatment program that included speech and language therapy, occupational therapy, and behavioral therapy, as well as training in social skills.

CASE EXAMPLE

Tommy was a 5-year-old boy who was referred by his pediatrician for psychiatric evaluation of "severe behavioral disturbance." Tommy had recently entered kindergarten, and was on the verge of being expelled for obstreperous behavior. His mother related that at a recent school conference, the teacher stated that Tommy "never sat still" and was constantly in motion throughout the day. In addition, she reported that Tommy talked incessantly and frequently blurted out answers to questions before hearing the entire question. He had difficulty waiting for his turn in classroom activities, and was disliked by the other children because of his inability to play cooperatively. The teacher also reported that Tommy was unable to sustain attention on anything for more than a few minutes, was easily distracted, and never listened to anything she said. Mother reported that the teacher called her almost every day because Tommy wouldn't follow simple routines and had difficulty playing with peers. He was sent to the "time-out corner" almost every day.

Mother described similar behaviors at home. She reported that Tommy had always been a very active and curious child who was constantly "on the go." Recently Tommy had started referring to himself as a "bad boy," and his mother worried that all of the negative interactions at school were affecting his self-esteem. He had no prior history of medical or psychiatric problems, and there was no family history of medical or psychiatric disorders. Tommy was on no medications. A complete medical workup to rule out a physical cause for his behavioral problems had recently been performed and was negative.

On evaluation, Tommy was a well-developed, well-nourished boy who appeared his stated age. He initially sat quietly in a chair next to his mother for several minutes, however he soon had difficulty sitting still and began to fidget. He walked to the toy chest and began to take out all of toys and place them on the floor without playing with any of them. He threw a ball across the room and nearly hit the window. For the remainder of the examination, Tommy displayed hyperactive and impulsive behavior.

On the basis of Tommy's history as well as medical and psychiatric evaluations, the diagnosis of Attention Deficit Hyperactivity Disorder, combined type, was made. A comprehensive treatment plan was developed which included behavioral therapy, social skills training, family therapy, school consultation, and parent training. The decision was made to hold off on pharmacotherapy (e.g., a trial of stimulant medication). Tommy responded well to this treatment regimen, with significant reduction in symptoms of hyperactivity and impulsivity, and improved relationships with parents, peers, and teacher.

---

may fear sitting on a toilet for fear of getting swallowed down the drain.

At this time, greater sphincter control and erotic sensations in the anal area lead to Freud's *Anal Phase* (1 year to 3 years). This is a period marked by the need to separate and develop autonomy from the caregiver while obtaining greater bodily control and a capacity for speech and symbol formation. The child's sense of autonomy is combined with ambivalent feelings about separating from the caregiver while acquiring new skills. This ambivalence may be expressed by holding in or letting out feces during a bowel movement, or by needy and clingy behaviors.

Preschooler (3 Years to 5 Years)

The child's rate of growth slows during the preschool years. The average preschooler can be expected to gain 5–6 pounds annually until age 6, and grow 2–3 inches in height per year. In addition, the preschool child experiences fur-

ther improvement in gait and balance. The ability to throw, catch, and kick balls is seen in the common games of this age. Bowel and bladder control have developed by 30 months of age on average, with girls achieving control before boys. Vocabulary continues to grow to nearly 2,000 words by age 5. Preschoolers now speak in sentences, use proper grammar, and use speech to express emotions instead of acting them out.

EMILY DROWNED

She asked me, aching-eyed.
I nodded. She sighed.
A twenty second silence followed,
Intense, explosive, hollowed
From the echo of the vaulted ceiling.
Charged with growing feeling
She screamed, "Oh! No. Oh! No,"
   and sank her nails
   into her husband's shoulder.
He, not much older,
Comforted her in vain
And stemmed his agony with a taut drawn rein.

A policeman came in haunting blue.
I left the parents to their loneliness
   and walked out through
The hall. In the grey street
My reluctant feet
   threw shattering steps upon the tar.
   We stopped.
The officer lifted the tailgate
Of his van and I heard him grate
His teeth. There, on a tartan rug, lay
Emily—three yesterday—

Pale and cold, she unmoving,
   I, so moved, I nearly cried.
I had to touch her skin
   to certify her death.
I raised her eyelids. My misted breath
Dulled the already dull complexion of her eyes.
   She was dead.
I nodded to the officer and whispered, "She's
dead,"
And thought of my own small daughter
Asleep at home in bed.
   Emily had drowned in two feet of water
In the field behind
Her house. The weather signed
The sadness of the evening
With a bereaving
Winter shower.

I had to return to the parents
   who would sob for hour
On hour in each other's arms.
Gone were the infant charms
That dressed their home;
They cried together, but alone.

DUNCAN DARBISHIRE

There is also a shift from primarily parallel play at age 2 to cooperative play by age 4. During cooperative play, children must balance their egocentrism with the wishes of the group or playmate. To deal with this new form of interaction, rules are seen as absolute with guilt assigned for bad outcomes regardless of the other child's intention. Behavioral limits are progressively internalized such that by age 5 the child can internally regulate what is considered appropriate behavior.

These skills are essential for success in the classroom. The ability to internalize limits and self-soothe helps the child to control behavior and emotions when away from his or her parents. Internalized images of trusted adults allow the child to experience comfort and security during times of separation and stress.

Children in this age group continue in Piaget's *Preoperational Stage* until 7 years of age, as described previously. Thinking is characterized by *egocentrism*, in which the child experiences every event in reference to him or herself. For example, the child may believe that night comes to make him sleep or that rain falls to keep him inside. Children of this age also believe they can alter reality by their thoughts or wishes *(magical thinking)*.

In Erikson's stage of *Initiative vs. Guilt* (3 years to 5 years), the child's basic task is to develop a sense of initiative and competence. He or she will develop a positive sense of self and ambition if allowed to initiate meaningful motor and intellectual activities and explore the environment. If children are made to feel inadequate about their interests they may emerge from this stage with a sense of guilt over self-initiated activity. During this stage, the child also experiences sexual impulses toward the parent of the opposite sex, which leads to fantasies of competing with the same-sex parent for a special relationship with the opposite sex parent. For example, a girl in this stage may become very jealous of her mother holding father's hand, or a boy may insist on taking a photo with

---

MEMORY TIP The "Bottom" Line

WET has three letters and most children should gain bladder control shortly AFTER age 3.

MESS has four letters and most children should gain bowel control shortly BEFORE age 4.

mother alone to the exclusion of his father. By the end of this stage, the child's conscience has developed, which leads to the moral sense of right and wrong. The child has learned that aggressive impulses can be expressed in constructive ways, such as through play and sports.

Freud's *Phallic Phase* (3 years to 5 years) presents his views of this process. Children at this age are aware of the physical differences between boys and girls. Their focus is shifted toward the genitalia and play during this time is characterized by activities that reflect curiosity about the body's sexual functions. The child has strong libidinal and aggressive urges, which establish the *oedipal complex*. In the oedipal complex, the child seeks a relationship with the opposite sex parent and has aggressive urges to get rid of the same sex parent. In boys, this leads to *castration anxiety*, in which the fear of father cutting off his penis leads to repression of sexual interest in mother. Children can become very possessive of the opposite sex parent with hostility toward the same sex parent during this time. This conflict is played out through fantasies and dreams, ultimately leading to resolution of the oedipal complex.

School Age (5 to 12 Years)

Increases in height and weight during the school-age years are gradual and steady compared with the earlier years and adolescence. Between the ages of 6 and 12, the average child will grow 2–2.5 inches and gain 3–6 pounds a year. The average 6-year-old child is approximately 3.5 feet tall and weighs about 40 pounds. By 12 years of age, the average child is almost 5 feet tall and weighs approximately 80 pounds. Growth rates in boys and girls are similar until about age 9, when girls begin to grow more rapidly.

By 5 years of age, children no longer experience magical thinking and are better able to separate fantasy from reality. They are able to apply rules, to understand alternate points of view, and to sustain attention over 45 minutes for class. They can tolerate the increased demands from school as they begin the first grade. Children develop self-esteem as they learn to gauge their performance in class. They look for positive praise from teachers outside of the home (e.g., teachers and coaches) and focus on accomplishment. The irrational fears of the preschool child are replaced with more realistic concerns about everyday life, such as school failure and peer rejection. Children may cope with these fears by identifying with superheroes who are seen as invincible.

The beginning of school brings Erikson's stage of *Industry vs. Inferiority* (6 to 12 years) to the forefront as the child seeks mastery at school. The level of success a child experiences at school will impact self-esteem as he or she looks for praise beyond what is experienced from parents. If the

Father's Day card from Jeremy Wedding, age 9. *Parents typically cherish the cards and handmade gifts they receive from their children.*

CASE EXAMPLE

Amy was a 10-year-old girl who was brought to her pediatrician's office for evaluation of persistent abdominal pain and vomiting of 4 weeks duration. The symptoms began during winter vacation, occurred on a daily basis, and were constant and severe. The abdominal pain and vomiting were worse in the mornings, and gradually subsided over the course of the day. Amy did not experience her symptoms over the weekends. She had been unable to attend school for the past month, and her mother was considering making arrangements for home tutoring. A complete medical workup performed recently showed no evidence of physical disease to account for the symptoms. Amy lived with her parents and younger brother, and was in the 5th grade. She had no history of medical or psychiatric disorders, and took no medications. Her family history was significant for anxiety in Amy's mother and maternal grandmother.

Amy's pediatrician recommended a psychiatric evaluation to assess for an emotional contribution to her symptoms. The psychiatric evaluation revealed that Amy had functioned extremely well in school until this year, when her grades had dropped significantly. Amy reported that she had trouble concentrating on her schoolwork because "I just don't get it most of the time." She reported that her classmates made fun of her for being stupid and that her teacher was constantly reminding her to "stop daydreaming and get to work." Just prior to winter vacation, her group of girlfriends had "ditched" her, leaving her to eat lunch alone each day. Amy endorsed symptoms of mild depression including insomnia, decreased energy, and low self-esteem.

The psychiatrist recommended that Amy undergo psychoeducational testing, which revealed a learning disorder. In addition, Amy met criteria for a depressive disorder and school phobia. The treatment plan included returning to school with implementation of remedial educational services, social skills training, and psychotherapy aimed at treating depression and improving self-esteem.

Golden Days *Balthus (1945).* Hirshhorn Museum and Sculpture Garden, Smithsonian Institution, Washington D.C., Gift of Joseph H. Hirshhorn, 1966. Copyright © 2001, Artists Rights Society, Inc. (ARS), New York/ADAGP, Paris. *This provocative painting captures the twin themes of emerging sexuality and preoccupation with self. Preoccupation with personal appearance is common in teens; in adults it can suggest the presence of a narcissistic personality disorder.*

child feels competent in academic and social interactions, he or she will develop a sense of industry or confidence. If the child is unsuccessful in these areas he or she will develop a sense of inferiority.

Piaget's Preoperational Stage continues until age 7 when the stage of *Concrete Operations* begins. The word *operations* refers to the logical principles (rules) we use to solve problems. During this time, the child's reasoning and conceptual skills develop, and thinking becomes more organized and logical. As abstract thought is lacking or very limited, school-age children are consumed by a need to follow or to conform to rules. With concrete operations in effect, the child is now able to *conserve* number, length, and liquid volume. Conservation refers to the idea that a quantity remains the same despite changes in appearance.

The child now enters Freud's *Latency Phase*. Although Freud postulated this to be a time of diminished sexual drive with disappearance of observable sexual behavior, children at this age do indeed engage in sexual play including masturbation.

During this phase the child begins to identify with the same sex parent and may imitate his or her behavior. There is an incorporation of more of the beliefs and values of the culture, and the child learns to distinguish between acceptable and unacceptable behaviors in society. During this phase, children tend to seek playmates of the same sex. They are interested in joint play, and make friendships on the basis of shared interests or experiences. Boys tend to engage in aggressive and competitive play, while girls tend to engage in cooperative games such as hopscotch, jump rope, and "Simon says."

Children spend their days in school, where they must adjust to separation from parents, negotiate new relationships with teachers and peers, and begin the process of structured learning.

Adolescence (13 Years to 18 Years)

Adolescence is the period of transition from childhood to adulthood. It is characterized by rapid growth, changes in physical appearance, and sexual development. *Puberty* refers to the period of adolescence that results in sexual maturation, while *adolescence* refers to the time from onset of puberty to the beginning of adulthood. The adolescent *"growth spurt"* begins with the onset of adolescence and refers to changes in height, weight, and body proportions. It typically begins earlier in girls than boys, and lasts about 4 and one half years. The adolescent growth spurt is accompanied by sexual maturation.

Sexual maturation in girls begins with breast bud development between 8 and 13 years of age, followed by a spurt in height, pubic hair development, and finally onset of menses between 10 and 15 years of age. In boys, testicular enlargement begins at age 9, accompanied by changes in voice tone and sexual interest. Ejaculation occurs for first time during masturbation or sleep (see Figures 3.1, 3.2, and 3.3).

Adolescents are acutely aware of the changes taking place in their bodies (see Figures 3.1, 3.2, and 3.3). The timing of maturation can play an important role in the adolescent's perception of himself or herself. For example, early maturing boys tend to be respected by peers and treated

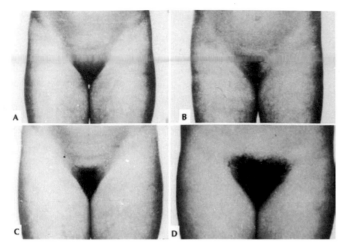

FIGURE 3.1 Pubic hair development in females. A, Sparse, lightly pigmented, straight along medial border of labia. B, Darker, beginning to curl, increased amount. C, Coarse, curly, abundant among but less than adult. D, Adult female triangle, spread to medial surface of thighs. The preadolescent has no pubic hair development. Adapted from Johnson TR, Moore WM, Jeffries JE (Eds.), *Children are different: Developmental physiology* (2nd ed.), 1978. Used with permission.

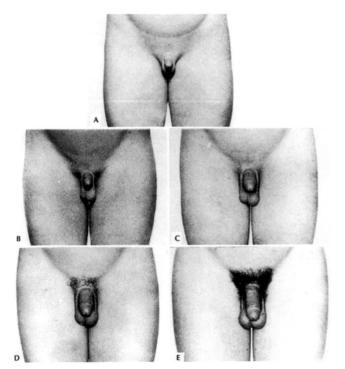

FIGURE 3.2 Penis and testes/scrotum development in males. A, Penis, testes, and scrotum preadolescent. B, Enlargement of scrotum and testes, texture alteration; scrotal sac reddens; penis usually does not enlarge. C, Further growth of testes and scrotum; penis enlarges and becomes longer. D, Continued growth of testes and scrotum; scrotum becomes darker; penis becomes longer; glans and breadth increase in size. E, Adult size and shape. Adapted from Johnson TR, Moore WM, Jeffries JE (Eds.), *Children are different: Developmental physiology* (2nd ed.), 1978. Used with permission.

more like adults. They may become involved with girls sooner and have more confidence in boy-girl relations than late maturing boys. Overall, early maturing boys tend to be more poised and self-confident than late maturing boys. Early maturing girls, on the other hand, often feel different from and may be teased by their peers. Tobin-Richards and colleagues found that seventh grade girls who perceive their rate of development to be similar to their peers had higher self-esteem than late maturing girls.

Adolescents may start dating, engage in homosexual experimentation, and spend less time with same sex peers. They question and analyze extensively and may have more strained relations with family. Freud's *Genital Phase* (12–18 years) begins with the physiological changes associated

---

CASE EXAMPLE

Jay is a 16-year-old boy who presented to his pediatrician's office for a routine checkup. His mother told the pediatrician of her concerns, which included recent school suspension because of oppositional behavior and lack of respect for authority. She reported that Jay seemed to have a "very short fuse" lately, that he'd "sleep all day if he could," and that his irritability and sullen moods had made family life "impossible."

In the interview, Jay described his mood as "always bored" and noted that he was unhappy with his life. He described fatigue, lack of energy, irritability, and hypersomnia, while exhibiting a sad affect. Jay reported sometimes "thinking about" suicide; however, he denied any intent to harm himself. He reported a 6-month history of marijuana use with occasional binge drinking. The rest of his physical exam was benign.

Jay's mother reported a family history significant for depression in Jay's father and paternal aunt. There was a history of current psychosocial stressors including Jay's girlfriend's recent move across the country and parental conflicts related to his mother's recent acceptance into law school. He had been an honor roll student until this year, when his grades dropped to C's and D's. For the past 6 months he had seemed easily distracted in class and had been exhibiting increasing levels of oppositional behavior at school.

His pediatrician thought that Jay met the criteria for major depressive disorder and substance use disorder. Jay was referred for a psychiatric evaluation that confirmed these diagnoses. He was started on a multimodal treatment regimen, which included individual psychotherapy directed at helping Jay come to terms with his recent loss as well as addressing his marijuana and alcohol abuse. Family therapy was initiated to address and resolve intrafamilial conflicts related to his mother's new career aspirations. Pharmacotherapy with an SSRI antidepressant was initiated upon his symptom severity and his positive family history of depression. Psychoeducational testing was performed and revealed a learning disability for which remedial services were instituted. Within several months, Jay's symptoms of depression had significantly improved, as well as his school performance and his relationship with his family.

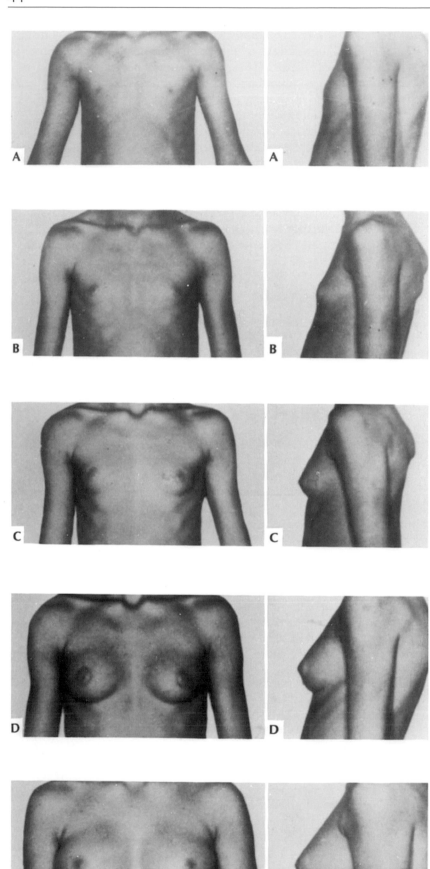

FIGURE 3.3 Maturational sequence in girls. A, Preadolescent. B, Breast and papilla elevated as small mound; areolar diameter increased. C, Breast and areola enlarged; no contour separation. D, Areola and papilla form secondary mound. E, Mature; nipple projects areolar part of general breast contour. Adapted from Johnson TR, Moore WM, Jeffries JE (Eds.), *Children are different: Developmental physiology* (2nd ed.), 1978. Used with permission.

Adolescence *Gerald Leslie Brockhurst (1932). Etching on wove paper. Gift of Cloud Wampler, 1963. Courtesy of the Syracuse University Art Collection, Syracuse, N.Y. Sexual awakening is a critical part of the adolescent's development.*

Healthy identity develops with successful resolution of the previous three psychosocial stages and identification with healthy parents or other important adults. Failure to successfully negotiate this stage leads to role diffusion (identity confusion) in which the adolescent questions his place in the world and does not have a firm sense of self. This may lead to depression and behavioral problems such as running away, abusing substances, or joining gangs or cults in order to develop a sense of identity.

SUMMARY

The development of children from birth through adolescence illustrates the fascinating interplay between genes and the environment. Children are born with a biological trajectory, which is influenced by the nature of their experiences and their environment. A systemic method for studying development will aid in the thorough and thoughtful evaluation of children and adolescents. Early detection of developmental delays will allow for course correction before a child's global functioning is affected. Most importantly, timely and developmentally appropriate interventions can lead to lifelong improvements in the life of that child.

CASE STUDY

Matthew is a 15 year-old boy with a history of Crohn's disease, admitted to the hospital for evaluation of abdominal pain and diarrhea. Matthew was diagnosed with Crohn's disease at age 5, and has a history of multiple hospitalizations over the past 10 years. Matthew reports that he had been experiencing severe abdominal pain and bloody diarrhea for the past 3 days. He appears sad as he describes his frustration with his illness and multiple hospitalizations, and states "sometimes I wish I could go to sleep forever."

On evaluation, Matthew says that he is "tired of dealing" with his chronic illness. He has missed many weeks of school over the years, and often felt "left behind" both academically and socially. He reports that he is embarrassed by his short stature and delayed pubertal development, and describes being frequently teased by peers. For the past year he has been experiencing frequent sad and irritable moods, decreased interest in activities, diminished ability to concentrate on his schoolwork, insomnia, feelings of worthlessness and hopelessness, and thoughts that life isn't worth living.

Matthew's parents describe him as a temperamentally shy, quiet, and somewhat anxious child. His gross motor, fine motor and language development have been normal, but he has always been a small child with delayed physical

with puberty. During this final phase of psychosexual development, there is a renewed interest and pleasure derived from excretory activity. In addition, masturbation takes place and is engaged in much more frequently at this time than during the anal stage. Initially, the adolescent seeks associations with same sex peers; however, as this phase progresses, he or she begins to form relationships with opposite sex peers. The primary objectives of this phase are the development of a sense of identity and self-reliance with less dependence on parents, which will allow the transition to adult roles and responsibilities.

Piaget's stage of *Formal Operations* marks the ability to use abstract concepts, consider real and hypothetical events, solve problems systematically, and use logic and deductive reasoning. This ability to consider different possibilities and what *might* occur often leads to idealism and grandiosity, as well as interest in politics, religion, ethics, and philosophy.

During Erikson's stage of *Identity vs. Role Diffusion* (12 to 20 years), the primary task of the adolescent is to develop a sense of identity with respect to self and society in order to avoid role confusion (lack of a clear identity).

development due to his illness. Parents describe Matthew as a bright child who had done well in school until 8th grade. At that point Matthew began to refuse to go to school, complaining of frequent teasing by peers and not understanding the coursework. Six months ago he was started on home schooling. Matthew reports that when he thinks about returning to school, he experiences palpitations and feelings of severe anxiety. Parents are worried that Matthew's chronic illness had affected his self-esteem, and that he might be depressed.

Matthew's medications include Prednisone 10 mg bid and Zantac 150 mg bid. Matthew has no history of psychiatric illness or treatment. His family history is significant for anxiety and depression in his mother and paternal aunt. Matthew lives at home with his parents and 10 year-old sister, and reports getting along well with his family. Matthew denied the use of alcohol or illicit substances.

On mental status examination, Matthew presents as a thin male with short stature who appears several years younger than his stated age. He speaks softly, is cooperative with the interview, and exhibits poor eye contact. He is alert and oriented to person, place and date. Intellectual functioning is within normal limits. Matthew reports his mood as being "frustrated," and he exhibits a sad and withdrawn affect throughout the interview. There is no evidence of psychosis. Matthew reports having frequent thoughts that life wasn't worth living, however denies having any plans to harm himself.

Matthew is exhibiting symptoms consistent with severe depression and school phobia. Biological contributions include his chronic medical illness and family history of anxiety and depression, in conjunction with a shy and anxious temperament. Chronic steroids are likely contributing to his mood disturbance, as well as to his delayed physical development. Frequent hospitalizations have led to multiple school absences, with academic difficulties and rejection by peers at a time in adolescent development when feeling part of a peer group is critical. Treatment recommendations include antidepressant medication in conjunction with specific individual therapy targeting coping with his illness, and developing strategies to improve peer relations, in preparation for Matthew's gradual return to a full schedule at school.

This case illustrates how a stressor affecting one area of development (i.e., chronic illness leading to delayed physical maturation) may lead to delays in other domains of development (i.e., social, academic and emotional). It also highlights the complex interplay among the biological, psychological and social variables that contribute to healthy development of the child and adolescent.

SUGGESTED READINGS

The suggested readings include classical readings on the topic of development, which form the basis of studying the topic in greater detail. In addition, there are two overview chapters listed which will further explain development in greater depth from a child mental health and medical perspective.

Ainsworth, M.D., Blehar, M.C., Waters, E., & Wall, S. (1978). *Patterns of attachment: A psychological study of the strange situation.* Hillsdale, NJ: Erlbaum.

Discusses the "strange situation" and provides a rich description of the behavior of children in relation to attachment theory.

Bowlby, J. (1967). Attachment. In *Attachment and loss*, (Vol. 1). New York: Basic Books.

Presents Bowlby's attachment theory and provides a context for understanding the stages that are proposed.

Chess, S., & Thomas, A. (1986). *Temperament in clinical practice.* New York: Guilford.

Presents the original work of Chess and Thomas on the influence of temperament and goodness of fit on the interaction between parent and child.

Erikson, E. (1959). *Identity and the life cycle.* New York: International University Press.

Describes Erikson's stages in greater detail and allows for a more comprehensive understanding of development beyond adolescence into old age.

Freud, S. (1953). Three essays on the theory of sexuality. In J. Strachey (Ed.), *The standard edition of the complete psychological works of Sigmund Freud*, (Vol. 7). London: Hogarth Press.

Presents Freud's seminal work in the field of psychosexual development. A classical reading that continues to foster thought regarding development as well as to stir discussion.

Lewis, M. (2004). Overview of development from infancy through adolescence. In J.M. Weiner & M.K. Dulcan (Eds.), *Textbook of child and adolescent psychiatry* (pp. 13–44). Arlington, VA: American Psychiatric Publishing, Inc.

This chapter provides a more in-depth analysis of development that child and adolescent psychiatrists use during clinical evaluations of children. It also reviews the fundamental theories and their influence on understanding development.

Needleman, R.D. (2004). Growth and development. In R.E. Behrman, R.M. Kliegman, & H.B. Jenson (Eds.), *Nelson textbook of pediatrics* (17th ed., pp. 23–66). Philadelphia: Saunders.

This section of the textbook provides an overview of development along successive age groups from a medical model of development. It provides additional information on the interplay of genetic disorders and medical illnesses on the progression of development.

Piaget, J. (1962). The stages of the intellectual development of the child. *Bulletin of the Menninger Clinic, 26*(3), 120–145.

Presents Piaget's work on the cognitive development of children.

4 Early Adulthood and the Middle Years

Joseph D. LaBarbera, Sharon Turnbull, & Barry Nurcombe

In youth you find out what you care to do and who you care to be ... In young adulthood you learn who you care to be with ... In adulthood you learn to know what and whom you can take care of.

ERIC ERIKSON
Dimensions of a New Identity

Only recently has a developmental perspective been applied to adults. A barrier in doing so is the great variability that characterizes the lives of adults, compared to those of younger people. For example, while the vast majority of 10-year-old children in the United States may be spending much of their time in school or playing with peers, the life patterns of adults are more diverse: Adults work at various jobs or not at all, some are married and some not, and some have children while others don't. That multiplicity of roles and activities complicates our ability to generalize about adult development.

Until the late nineteenth century, there was little appreciation of the factors that contribute to change in young people, much less adults; children were viewed at that time largely as unformed grown-ups. Freud's work, which emphasized the role of unconscious conflict in early psychological development, altered that, but psychoanalysis had little to say about the developmental stages and challenges associated with adulthood. Much later, after initial work on children, Erickson turned his attention to adult development. *Erikson suggested that the key developmental task of young adulthood is to achieve a capacity for **intimacy**.* A person who can sustain intimacy is capable of close friendships and of giving and receiving love in a sexual relationship. Such a person is also able to join in solidarity with his or her comrades when their values or interests are threatened by outside forces. On the other hand, the person who is incapable of intimacy is likely to become isolated and self-absorbed, with cold, stereotyped relationships, unable to join others in

common cause. *Mid-adulthood for Erikson involves a resolution of the issue of **generativity**.* This refers to an individual's ability to contribute in various contexts, as for example through reproduction and childrearing and through investment in work. Thus, embedded in Erikson's work is the idea that people change, often in predictable ways, throughout their entire life span, that adults are not the same at 65 years as at 25 years, and that understanding adulthood demands more than an appreciation for the events—career choices, marriage, parenting—that people typically experience.

Several authors have described a key task of adulthood as *emancipation from the family of origin*. As an infant, one had to separate and individuate from the mother as a step toward mastering the tasks ahead, such as attending school and establishing relationships outside the family. So too does the young adult need to branch out on his or her own, this time more completely, as parents are left behind. The task of leaving the adolescent world may require one to modify or terminate adolescent relationships, reappraise values and interests, and clarify aspirations. Entrance to college facilitates disengagement from the old and assumption of the new. For the person who seeks out separation too early, paradoxically there may be too little genuine internal separation; conversely, one whose emotional separation is delayed may ultimately reject the "old ways" more completely than he or she would otherwise have done.

On entering adulthood one is faced with conflicting demands. One must maintain hard-won independence and keep options open, exploring the world and considering potential occupations, workmates, lovers, and friends. The same person must create a consistent life structure, avoiding chronic rootlessness. The expansiveness of adolescence gives way to adult commitment. In the end, most young adults will willingly give up part of their hard-won autonomy for the promise of satisfaction in work and love.

There are several fairly predictable crises or challenges of middle age. The heady dreams of young adulthood must

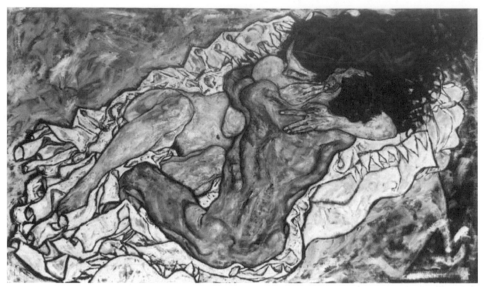

Embrace *Egon Schiele (1917).* Österreichische Galerie Belvedere, Vienna. *Loving someone deeply and well is a fundamental parameter of mental health.*

often be abandoned in the face of the knowledge that time and energy are running out. In the best of cases these youthful dreams are replaced by an enjoyment of life as it is and by the anticipation of what it can realistically become. For some, the dreams of marriage and parenthood must be forsaken. Others find that their careers stall, with expected promotions going to younger coworkers. Still others succeed financially in mid-life but find they have little enthusiasm for their work or its rewards. Some sense the beginnings of physical and sexual decline or experience the death of romance through familiarity, and their marriages falter. Financial concerns and problems preoccupy many during the middle years. Although worrying about saving for their own retirement, the middle- aged may also be concerned with financing children's college education and weddings and the launching of their careers. Children leave home, and parents, mentors, and friends die.

The concept of **"midlife crisis"** was coined by Jacques (1965), and popularized in the 1960s and 1970s by Levinson's *Seasons of a Man's Life* and Sheehy's *Passages*. It referred to the frustration and impatience in the middle-aged person who might, therefore, make sudden and dramatic life adjustments, as for example quitting a job, buying a sports car, or getting a divorce. While such patterns of behavior undoubtedly take place, the results of a large-scale study of the functioning of people in midlife (Brim, Ryff, & Kessler, 2002) have suggested that *the midlife crisis is exaggerated in its frequency.* Most middle-aged adults are guided by "psychological turning points," involving their recognition of their limitations, as for example the politician who realizes she will never attain a major office or the executive who sees he will forever be merely a middle-manager. Such awareness prompts frequent but minor adjustments in attitude and behavior, obviating the pressure for an ultimate "crisis." Furthermore, the midlife crisis, when it does occur, tends to be an affliction of the affluent; rosy

illusions are easier to sustain into middle age if one is shielded from unpleasant realities such as poverty.

MARRIAGE

Those who have reflected on the tasks of early adulthood have emphasized the importance of establishing intimate relationships. It is critical that, to affirm independence from the family of origin, the individual establish a mature relationship that recapitulates the closeness of a family. *Vaillant (1977) noted that those who have a stable marriage before age 30 and remain married until age 50 have the most favorable outcomes and are the best adjusted.* Successful marriage serves to facilitate autonomy from parents by replacing them as the primary sources of gratification. However, it is important that a new marriage not merely replicate the roles of parent and child. Levinson (1978) observed that the success of a marriage will be determined by several factors including conscious and unconscious needs relating to self-worth, intellectual stimulation, and the influence or pressures of family members and peers. Naturally, the degree to which spouses are able to react to each other, especially over time, contributes to success or failure. Because few people stay the same over decades, a strong commitment is required to deal with differences and misunderstandings; failure to do so will weaken or even break the bond. Also critically important to the success of marriage is the ability to adjust over time to the changing needs, attitudes, and concerns of one's spouse. The husband or wife at ages 25 and 60 is a very different person.

Marriage, even during young adulthood, seems to traverse distinct phases. Several authors have described an initial idealization, the earliest years bringing the highest level of satisfaction. What follows is typically a period of disenchantment. The experience of intense romantic love does not endure; once spent, it can leave the participants disillusioned. A renewed commitment may be required at that time, one based on factors that are more realistic than was the case initially. Those who are capable of doing so with a minimum of ambivalence will have the most successful marriages.

Levinson (1978) made the point that those who marry between adolescence and young adulthood have special problems with their relationships. A young man in that position is likely to view his wife, and a young woman her husband, as a powerful parenting figure. Such concerns are of less relevance for later marriages. Older people are capable of making choices less connected to parental pressures and "ghosts," and more in line with their true life goals and preferences. In other words, their spouses are partners rather than parents.

The early years of family life, filled with promise, enthusiasm, and shared enjoyment in the challenge of parenting, do not end abruptly. However, many of the middle aged suddenly confront the financial burden of parenting, worry about relating to in-laws and relatives, and feel the impact of growing children on their sexual and marital relationships. The couple who either has opted not to have children or has been unable to have them faces somewhat different challenges. Their lives are filled with the need to balance careers, social responsibilities, and hobbies. Frequently, career demands may be so great that the partners fail to pay sufficient attention to each other's personal needs for attention and support, and they become entangled in tensions arising over changing needs for dependence or independence in the relationship.

Issues confronting the midlife marriage include:

1. *Establishing boundaries:* Defining the extent to which family, such as in-laws, and friends impinge on family activities and decisions.
2. *Coping with careers and finances:* Dealing with the issues of dual career family, changes in work status (promotion, unemployment, and job satisfaction), financial competition between spouses, and the control of money.
3. *Parenting:* Deciding how many children to have and when to have them; allocating responsibility for child care; surviving the stresses of parenting; helping (or pushing) children into adulthood; and adapting to the empty nest.
4. *Sex and romance:* Finding time and energy for sex and intimacy; adjusting to the effects of aging on normal sexual functioning; overcoming sexual dysfunction; preventing or surviving infidelity.
5. *Facing chronic illness, disability, or both:* Shifting the nature and extent of the partners' responsibilities; seeking support from health-care professionals, friends, and community; adjusting to shifts in power and dependen-

cy needs; and dealing with depression and changes in self-image.

Women's employment, especially when career oriented, slightly decreases the likelihood of marriage. The rise in divorce rates has been linked with the increased participation of women in the work force, although it is unclear which is cause and which is effect; that is, whether women seek employment in response to a troubled marriage or whether the stress of the wife's employment contributes to marital failure. The risk of separation or divorce increases with the amount of the woman's income. In spite of the negative association between women's employment and marital stability, *general satisfaction with life, mental and physical health, and satisfaction with work are consistently found to be higher in women employed outside the home.*

Not to be overlooked is the impact of children on married adults both young and middle-aged. Marriage requires intimacy and sharing. Habits, cherished ways of doing things, and traditions are established by adults and shaped by their own personalities and expectations. However, the arrival of a child complicates matters, and sometimes results in disillusionment. Children *do* affect marital satisfaction, often for the better, but sometimes for the worse.

Rearing children inevitably consumes a large share of a married couple's financial, emotional, and temporal resources. Parents must learn to balance limit setting and parental control with a willingness to give up authoritative control while the child accepts and demonstrates the ability to handle increasing responsibility for his or her own behavior. The development of self-discipline is the long-term goal. In many situations a fatigued parent will settle for immediate peace rather than confront a child in the interest of his or her long-term development. In other families, firmness slips into domination and results in forcing parental will on the child, leading to rebelliousness. *Successful parents temper their firmness with flexibility and have enough humility to acknowledge when they are wrong.* Highly successful adults often attribute their effectiveness to the influence of their parents. They report parental characteristics such as firmness (as opposed to permissiveness or rigidity), direction without dictation, rules that made sense, high expectations, and mutual trust and respect. Although as children and teenagers they occasionally rebelled against their parents' demands and values, the rebellion was generally verbal and rarely took the form of acting out or destruction.

The recent trend toward postponement of marriage and parenting has produced a new class of middle-aged parents with young children. Although little research is available concerning the "older" parent of young children, some trends are obvious. These parents are likely to have greater maturity and experience on which to draw, for example, although this is offset by a decline in the total energy available for parenting and the possible sense of loss and sacrifice that a couple may experience after having grown ac-

Drought Refugees from Oklahoma Camping on the Road *Dorothea Lange (1936). Courtesy of the Library of Congress, Washington, D.C. One of the most demanding challenges of young adulthood may be meeting your family's health-care needs with a limited income.*

customed to the relative freedom, independence, and wealth they enjoyed as a childless couple. Most parents in their middle years, however, follow the traditional pattern and confront the issues of raising adolescents and coping with an "empty nest" during the middle years.

Eventually children leave home, and the nuclear family is reduced to the parents alone. Child-rearing is over, and the nest is empty. The change, although often a hoped-for relief, is not always easy. Much of the success in negotiating this transition is determined by whether husband and wife have accomplished the tasks of parenthood, how they have grown, how well they have maintained their marital relationship, and how they take up their new roles as a childless couple. Traditionally women, especially those who have stayed at home to raise the children, are most at risk of developing the **empty nest syndrome**, a personal crisis marked by depression and loss of identity. Working mothers and fathers may suffer profoundly as well, although men are less likely to articulate their feelings of loss or seek professional help in dealing with those feelings.

MARITAL PROBLEMS

Although the highest divorce rates occur during young adulthood, approximately half of the first marriages of those in their third decade of life also end in divorce. *Most*

who divorce eventually remarry, although women are less likely to do so. Middle-aged adults are much quicker to marry their second spouses than are the younger divorced. *About half of these marriages will falter, resulting in a second divorce. However, remarried couples are no less satisfied with their marriages than are first-married couples.* The equal satisfaction and stability of first and second marriages might represent a simple unwillingness to repeat the highly traumatic experience of divorce, but it seems more likely that this statistic represents true gains. Given the myriad complexities and potential for conflict inherent in second marriages (with their constellations of former spouse, stepchildren, and additional financial burdens), maturity and cooperation are necessary.

Divorce is frequently linked with **infidelity**. *It is estimated that 60% to 75% of husbands have been unfaithful to their wives and that 30% to 50% of wives have had affairs.* Considering the frequency with which couples divorce, it is perhaps easy to trivialize the event and to overlook the personal disruption associated with it. Divorce poses challenges on several levels. It involves psychological loss, as partners are compelled to give up completely their love objects and roles as wife and husband. That grieving process sometimes takes years. A couple must negotiate the legal system which, even in this era of no-fault divorce in many states, frequently provokes antagonism and distress. The two, especially the wife, frequently suffer severe financial loss and lowered standards of living. Divorced couples must reconfigure their social networks. Those with children often parent them without a partner.

Coping with the causes and effects of infidelity is an important task for many married individuals. *The intense shock, anger, and depression that result from learning of a partner's betrayal require resolution, either through the rebuilding of the relationship or through its dissolution.* Several life events or stressors that are likely to precipitate sexual infidelity have been identified. These risk factors exist when *either* partner is experiencing one of the following:

1. Selection or initiation of a new career
2. Expansion or success at work
3. Changing jobs
4. Traveling extensively alone
5. Depression linked with failure
6. Monotony or fatigue produced by dull overwork
7. Retirement

Additional risk factors exist when the *couple* is having experiences such as:

1. Pregnancy or the birth of a child
2. Young children demanding attention
3. Bereavement from the death of a parent, sibling, child, or friend

4. Emotional crisis such as an accident or illness
5. Children leaving home
6. Stressful changes such as moving, buying a home, or undergoing a major change in lifestyle

Traditionally women were responsible for caring about and working on relationships. Although research has shown that men benefit from marriage even more than their wives, they are often less attuned to the need for emotional connectedness. Not surprisingly then, it is often the women who overfunctions in the relationship, struggling for change, however, ineffectually. A **systems model of family functioning** (Lerner, 1989) is useful in understanding the problems that often beset marriages during the middle years. The **overfunctioner** focuses much emotional energy, such as anger, strategizing, or worry, on the other or on the relationship, attempting to change or blame the other. Meanwhile, the other partner typically **underfunctions**, avoiding the experience of intensity by distancing or withdrawing from the partner or from a particular issue. Underfunctioning seriously impedes the relationship, resulting in discontent and a diminished ability to cope with the inevitable crises and transitions of the middle years. Successful marriages involve the coupling of two individuals "expressing strength and vulnerability, weakness and competence, in a balanced way" (Lerner, 1989).

The **triangulation of relationships** is another concept that is useful for understanding family interaction. It refers to an attempt to deflect emotional energy or anxiety about important issues between the partners onto a third party. The third party can be a child, in-law, or, very frequently, an extramarital affair. In essence, *triangles allow direct confrontation to be avoided and thereby stabilize, at least temporarily, the relationship.* Emotionally intense and conflictual relationships often represent disguised problems in the primary, or couple relationship. The child-focused triangle, for example, is common. The previously reliable teenager may rebel against family rules when the parent's level of stress as a result of a grandparent's death becomes unbearable, thus triggering the father's fury and the mother's overprotectiveness and allowing the parents to avoid having to experience their grief. According to Lerner (1989)

> Whenever adults are not actively working to identify and solve their own problems, children may volunteer to deflect, detour, and act out adult issues in most imaginative ways. Indeed, children tend to inherit *whatever* psychological problems we choose not to attend to.

The Discovery of Sex

We try to be discreet standing in the dark
hallway by the front door. He gets his hands
up inside the front of my shirt and I put mine
down inside the back of his jeans. We are crazy
for skin, each other's skin, warm silky skin.
Our tongues are in each other's mouths,
where they belong, home at last. At first

we hope my mother won't see us, but later we
don't care,
we forget her. Suddenly she makes a noise
like a game show alarm and says Hey! Stop that!
and we put our hands out where she can see them.
Our mouths stay pressed together, though, and
when she isn't looking anymore our hands go
back inside each other's clothes. We could

go where no one can see us, but we are
good kids, from good families, trying to have
as much discreet sex as possible with my mother
and father
four feet away watching strangers kiss on TV,
my mother and father who once did as we are doing,
something we can't imagine because we know

that before we put our mouths together, before
the back seat of his parents' car where our skins
finally become one—before us, these things
were unknown! Our parents look on in disbelief
as we pioneer delights they thought only they knew
before those delights gave them us.

Years later, still we try to be discreet, standing
in the kitchen now where we think she can't see us. I
slip my hands down inside the back of his jeans
and he gets his up under the front of my shirt.
We open our mouths to kiss and suddenly Hey! Hey!
says our daughter, glaring from the kitchen doorway.
Get a room! she says, as we put our hands
out where she can see them.

DEBRA SPENCER

> One can live magnificently in this world, if one knows how to work and how to love, to work for the person one loves, and to love one's work.
>
> LEO TOLSTOY

BEING SINGLE

Marriage rates have dropped to a record low. Postponement of marriage, divorce, and cohabitation have resulted in what some call a "postmarital society." It should be noted that for many, being single is a matter of choice, a preferred state. Also, among those usually counted as single are members of homosexual couples whose long-term, committed relationships closely resemble marriages but who are not allowed that legal sanction. The common perception of America as a country of couples forces single adults into a second-class status that is more likely to affect women than men. *As a result of disparate death rates favoring women and customary marriage of older men to younger women, the number of single men of the same age or older who are available for marriage is not sufficient and decreases with each decade of life.* The likelihood of marriage or remarriage drops drastically as a woman ages.

Clearly a number of issues and challenges face the single middle-aged adult, particularly the woman. Some women postpone marriage to complete their education and advance their careers and, when entering their 30s, hear the ticking of the biological clock only to discover that "all the good men are already taken." Dreams of eventual marriage and children may be shattered. Other obvious victims of recent social changes are the men and women in their 40s and 50s who entered marriages years before with a clear understanding of what was expected of them, only to find later that they must now make serious adjustments. Most tragic, perhaps, is the displaced homemaker who cultivated only the skills of wife and mother and then was suddenly made vulnerable by divorce or widowhood and found herself unprepared to provide for her income. Blumstein and Schwartz (1983) summarized displaced homemakers:

> They actually have fewer resources and less confidence than they did 20 years before. Not only must they enter a new and inhospitable world of work, with few of the necessary qualifications, they must also face a romantic or sexual marketplace for which they are unprepared.

WORK

Work cannot be considered effectively in isolation; if so, we could refer simply to the various stages of career, namely, the preparatory stage involving education and training, the point at which the individual is committed to a particular line of work, and so forth. However, career development is intimately intertwined with the individual's development as a person. Work interacts with identity. Work determines how we live, compels us to select different traits for further development, determines and maintains status, and undergirds our values. Levinson (1978) has described the typical person in his or her 20s as poor in self-reflection but fairly skilled when it comes to performing tasks, careful at following rules, anxious for promotion, and willing to accept "the system." The typical 25-year-old is determined to "make the grade" and, by contrast, not particularly concerned with psychological conflicts about success. The individual must identify an occupational "dream" and set goals to achieve that dream. This process may be marked by conflict and uncertainty, which can be inhibited or suppressed; if so, such feelings may appear full-blown later on in life. **Mentor relationships** are also forged during this period. The mentor plays the role of a teacher who takes a special interest in enhancing the younger individual's skill. The mentor plays other roles as well, sponsoring the young adult's career, inducting him or her into the social scene, and serving as an exemplar. Mentor relationships are intense and may be difficult to terminate at the end of early adulthood when guidance is no longer needed. Thus, abrupt or painful terminations of these relationships may occur.

Career choices during the early 20s are often characterized by ambivalence. The 25-year-old may feel uncomfortable with any choice, because choice brings a narrowing of the opportunity and freedom which, as an adolescent, were hard won. However, successful choices involve single-mindedness, and choose the person must. Although a commitment made too early may be regretted, one made too late places the individual at a distinct disadvantage. One cannot always delay a career choice until one is ready.

Career choices made during the 20s often amount to a merely preliminary definition of interests and values; reconsideration often takes place toward the end of the 20s or early 30s. Thus, the person in the early 30s enters a period of settling down, which amounts to establishing a second life structure. At this point there may be a redoubling of investment in career and a desire to realize youthful goals and ambitions. There are often two main tasks during the early 30s period. First, one must establish a niche in

> The great majority of us are required to live a life of constant, systematic duplicity. Your health is bound to be affected if, day after day, you say the opposite of what you feel, if you grovel before what you dislike and rejoice at what brings you nothing but misfortune …
>
> BORIS PASTERNAK
> *Dr. Zhivago*

physician may be promoted to medical school dean, a position requiring vastly different social and occupational skills.

Note that the emphasis in the previous discussion is on the experience of men. Studies of early adulthood, like development in general, have been primarily male-centered. The lives of women during early adulthood have been relatively ignored. Recent studies have begun to redress this imbalance. Gilligan's (1982) work emphasized fundamental differences between men and women from the standpoint of career development. Women, she claims, tend to value caring and sensitivity over autonomy. Success on the job, including financial success, may be less critical to the psychological well-being of women. *Although Levinson and Vaillant believe that work is the central developmental concern of men, Gilligan underscored that for women nurturance and attachment may be just as critical, if not more so.* Gilligan also discusses the female sense of morality, which arises from an emphasis on need and inclusion rather than the balancing of claims. Mercer and her colleagues (1989) have reflected on transitions in women's lives, including those of early adulthood. They made the point that, in general, women's transitions are more varied than those of men. Women may or may not elect to work outside the home, as almost all men do or at least attempt to do.

In any case, the early adult years involve emancipation from the family for women as well as men. A woman enters college, marriage, or the workplace during this period, and dependence on others turns into reliance on others, such as husband and coworkers. A few women may, in Levinson's terms, follow a life dream, but many do not. Some return to their dreams in middle age, seeking professional training or artistic fulfillment delayed by the responsibilities of the child care. The leveling phase during the end of the 20s is a time when many women change their earlier life pattern, confirming their commitment to family as opposed to work, or vice versa.

Work and career occupy much of the attention of the middle aged, as well as the young adult. What once was a stimulating test of the ability to succeed can become a tedious routine undertaken only to provide the necessary paycheck. The ambitious aggressiveness that characterized the early working years may give way to a "don't make waves" attitude and a preference for the tried and true methods of the past. Unsure that he or she can keep abreast

Heavy the Oar to Him Who is Tired, Heavy the Coat, Heavy the Sea *(1929) Ivan Le Lorraine Albright, 1897–1983.* Oil on canvas, 135.3 × 86.4 cm. Gift of Mr. and Mrs. Earle Ludgin, 1959. Copyright © The Art Institute of Chicago. All rights reserved. *Work can be viewed as a blessing or a curse. Read Ernest Hemingway's* The Old Man and the Sea *for an example of someone whose life is defined by his work.*

one's chosen area, a "project" of some sort that sets one apart from coworkers. A second task is to advance or make it in the system as reflected by an enhancement of social rank, income, and power. Toward the end of the 30s, the young adult can "become his or her own person," a senior member, capable of speaking with real authority within the organization. Such a sequence of events does not always lead to success, because there are always other, less fortunate, consequences of development. Aside from advancing consistently within the newly defined life structure, one might fail in pursuing one's dream. Other people break out of the mold and rewrite their life script. For some, success leads to a dramatic change in life structure. For example, a

> "When you come to a patient's house, you should ask him what sort of pains he has, what caused them, how many days he has been ill, whether the bowels are working, and what sort of food he eats." So says Hippocrates in his work *Affections.* I may venture to add one more question: What occupation does he follow?
>
> BERNARDINO RAMAZZINI
> *Diseases of Workers* (circa 1700)

of new advances, the middle-aged worker may begin to focus on issues of job security and pensions and hesitate to take risks. *Research suggests that the most satisfactory transition occurs when the role of ambitious "young turk" is exchanged for that of a mentor who "passes the torch" to the young, fostering their professional growth and guiding their careers.* In contrast, women who return to school or work after their children are older often find themselves invigorated by the new challenges of the workplace. They may, however, find little support or encouragement from husbands who have already established successful records in the workplace and who are currently in the process of beginning to disengage from the world of work.

Losing a job can be a major stressor in midlife. Many employees who are fired or laid off eventually find other positions; however, a Labor Department study found that only 20% of those retrained under a federal program for dislocated workers got a job paying at least 80% of their former position's salary or wages. Other workers, faced with the possibility of termination, elect to take early retirement for which they may be emotionally and financially unprepared. In short, their expectations that hard work and years of loyal service would guarantee secure employment or that a college education or years of experience would secure managerial positions have proved naive.

> I have now no relief but in action. I am becoming incapable of rest. I am quite confident I should rust, break, and die if I spared myself. Much better to die doing.
>
> CHARLES DICKENS (who died of heart disease thought to have been exacerbated by his work habits)

ADAPTING TO CHANGES IN HEALTH

Whether it is greeted with mild apprehension or outright panic, the recognition of physical decline and eventual mortality faces each of us in the middle years. Some react to the first signs of aging with a hypochondriacal preoccupation with changes in body appearance, functions, and sensations. Others embark on self-improvement programs of diet and exercise, and still others valiantly attempt to modify self-destructive behaviors such as smoking or drinking. Concerns about health, physical attractiveness, fitness, and mortality surface frequently in both the healthy and the ill.

Contrary to the expectations of many, the middle years are not marked by illness. In a study by Verbrugge (1986) the number of days on which people noticed health problems (symptoms requiring rest, absence from work, self-medication, visits to a physician, or hospitalization) was not higher in the middle-aged group than in the younger. In fact, 78% of middle-aged women and 79% of middle-aged

men reported their overall health as being good or excellent.

Although good health is the norm, chronic illnesses often make their initial appearance during the middle years. Development of a chronic illness can involve threats not only to life and physical well-being but to self-image, social and occupational functioning, and emotional equilibrium. For a satisfactory adjustment to chronic illness, the middle-aged adult must undertake several adaptive tasks:

1. Changing harmful behaviors and modifying his or her lifestyle.
2. Tolerating and accepting loss of body parts, functions, or potential; compensating or replacing if possible.
3. Maintaining self-image and a sense of worth.
4. Maintaining satisfaction in relationships with family, friends, and health-care providers; accepting a realistic degree of dependence.
5. Maintaining emotional equilibrium and a positive outlook in the face of depression, fear, anxiety, and anger, which are normal responses to threat and loss.

Coping with the psychological demands of a chronic illness is challenging at any stage of the life cycle. For the middle aged it intensifies the evaluation of life, personal worth, goals, and values. Successfully managed, the crisis of a chronic illness may even accelerate progress through the introspective developmental tasks of the middle years.

SUMMARY

Adult psychological development is a recent area of study; developmentalists have traditionally focused on earlier stages. Erik Erickson suggested that the primary developmental task of early adulthood involves achievement of the capacity for intimacy, and for middle adulthood, generativity or the ability to contribute to the welfare of others. Moving into the adult world, one separates from the family of origin, yet is pressed to make new commitments, including those to a spouse. The success and gratification derived from married life is determined by many factors, including the age of the couple at the time of marriage, the duration of the marital relationship, the presence or absence of children, and the response of the participants to the children eventually leaving home. Marriages falter when spouses are unable to adjust to demands that change over time or when conflictual issues are not effectively identified or addressed. Young adults are pressed not only to find mates, but also to decide on careers, even when not entirely prepared to do so. During early and middle adulthood good physical health is the norm, although chronic illness does often make its introduction during this time.

CASE STUDY

Sue Clifton, a 34-year-old patient in your family practice, brings her 14-year-old daughter to your office for diagnosis and treatment of a strep throat. You are shocked by how tired and thin Sue appears. You recall that she has generally been in good health, seeking help only for minor, episodic illnesses. You express your concern, and she responds, "I'm just stressed out right now, but everything's fine. I started back to school in September, and I plan to go into nursing. It's stressful, but I love it." You congratulate her but encourage her to come in for a physical examination because she hasn't had one in more than 2 years.

When you next see Mrs. Clifton, what possibilities will you want to explore?
On her return visit you note that Sue has lost 13 kg without dieting since her last visit 14 months ago. Your review of systems and physical does not reveal any problem, although you must wait on laboratory results to rule out anemia and thyroid disease. Sue admits she feels tired much of the time, but she attributes her fatigue to a "sleep shortage" since she studies late into the night after the family retires. She states that she is smoking a lot more now and drinking coffee almost continuously. She admits to frequently skipping meals.

Your feeling of unease, that you may be missing something important, persists. What other areas of inquiry should you pursue?
You remember that Sue's husband, John, is a machinist you once treated for a gastric ulcer. You recall being concerned that he was a moderately heavy drinker. You ask, "Is John being supportive of your going back to school?" She responds, "Who are you kidding ... he's the main reason I'm doing this. The shop has cut him back to part time and he could be a big help around the house, but all he does is hang out with his buddies and drink beer." You wish her luck with her finals and tell her that you'll be in touch when you get her laboratory results.

What directions should you be considering regarding future discussions with the patient?
Stress management training, nutritional planning (with or without supplementation), and referral for marital/personal counseling or support groups should all spring to mind.

SUGGESTED READINGS

Brim, O.G., Ryff, C.D., & Kessler, R. (Eds.). (2004). *How healthy are we: A national study of well-being in midlife*. Chicago: University of Chicago Press.
This reports results from a large scale study sponsored by the MacArthur Foundation on the functioning of people in midlife.

Gilligan, C. (1982). *In a different voice: Psychological theory in women's development*. Cambridge, MA: Harvard University Press.
This book attempts to redress the imbalance in developmental theories which have been built on observations of men's as opposed to women's lives.

Krantzler, M., & Krantzler, P.B. (1992). *The seven marriages of your marriage*. New York: HarperCollins.
Offers numerous examples, case histories, and self-help techniques to sustain and enrich couple relationships. The authors identify seven stages of midlife development and address the challenges to the relationship that reflect the couple's changing lives and needs. It is suitable reading for patients.

Lerner, H.G. (1989). *The dance of intimacy*. New York: Harper & Row.
Based on the author's interpretation and application of Bowen's theory of family systems, this book focuses on intimate relationships. Case studies illustrate how we get in (and out) of trouble with the most important people in our lives.

Levinson, D.J. (1978). *The seasons of a man's life*. New York: Ballantine Books.
This is a longitudinal study of men resulting in detailed description of adult developmental stages, with an emphasis on occupational success and failure.

Mercer, R.T., Nichols, E.G., & Doyle, G.C. (1989). *Transitions in a woman's life: Major life events in developmental context*. New York: Springer.
This developmental study of the life trajectories of women underscores the importance of nonnormative or unexpected life events such as illness, divorce, and death of loved ones.

Vaillant, G.E. (1977). *Adaptation to life*. New York: Little, Brown.
A landmark longitudinal study investigating ways in which some men cope effectively with variations in their lives while others cope badly or not at all.

5 Old Age

Randall Espinoza & Randy Mervis

> Like a morning dream, life becomes more and more bright the longer we live, and the reason of everything appears more clear. What has puzzled us before seems less mysterious, and the crooked paths look straighter as we approach the end.
>
> JEAN PAUL RICHTER

WHO IS OLD?

The later stages of life can be positive and fulfilling, replete with rich experiences, fond memories, and expressions of gratitude, happiness, and love. Relationships spanning decades alongside new connections add to the vibrancy and color of the lives of older persons. However, mystery, myths, and misconceptions about the aging process abound. In contrast to the common belief that a person's later years are uniformly fraught with disease and decline, in fact the vast majority of older persons continue to function proficiently and sufficiently. Indeed, *the heterogeneity of many aspects of individuals increases with aging, as a result not only of intrinsic genetic and biologic variation, but also as a result of the variety and multitude of experiences, exposures, and challenges encountered and lived.* Changes in culture and sociological mores have also evolved over time so that expectations of living into one's later years healthier, still capable and independent are more common. This chapter discusses and describes the biopsychosocial aspects of aging in twenty-first century America.

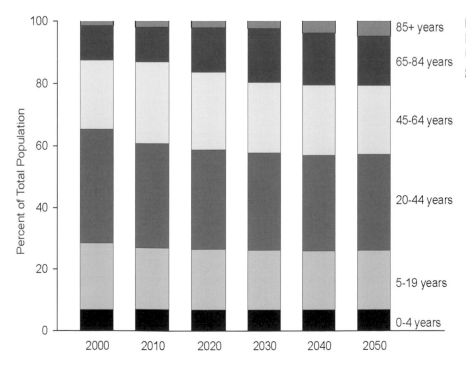

FIGURE 5.1 Projected change in age of the population of the United States 2000–2050 (Source US Census Bureau, 2004. http://www.census.gov/ipc/www/usinterimproj)

Aging of the Population

America is graying. The 2000 U. S. census indicated that there were presently about 34.9 million Americans, or just about 13% of the total population, over the age of 65 years. *In 2010 the first of the baby boomers will begin to turn 65,* adding over the next few decades an additional 76 million older individuals. By 2030, people over age 65 will comprise about one fifth of the total population, or about 70 million citizens, nearly double the number of today.

However, the elderly are not a monolithic group, and there are significant changes in the size and growth rate among the **young-old** (persons between 65 to 74 years), the **middle-old** (persons between 75 to 84 years) and the **oldest-old** (persons age 85 and greater). Compared to the 1900

census, the young-old group in 2000 was 8 times larger, the middle-old group was 16 times larger, and the oldest-old group was 31 times larger. In fact, *the oldest-old group is growing the fastest* (see Figure 5.2). By 2050, there will be over 800,000 individuals in the United States older than 100 years of age. These increases in life expectancy are the result of gains both at birth and at age 65 years. A child born in 1996 could expect to live 76.1 years, or about 29 years longer than a child born in 1900. The gains in life expectancy at age 65 are even more remarkable. Between 1900 and 1960, life expectancy at age 65 increased by 2.4 years, but since 1960, life expectancy has increased by 3.4 years, or by 140% in less than 40 years.

While age 65 is usually considered the beginning of old age, it is important to keep in mind that the demarcation

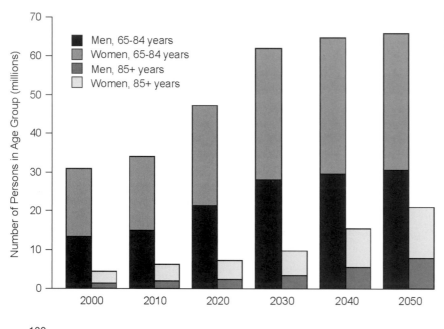

FIGURE 5.2 Projected growth of the older population of the United States by age and sex: 2000–2050 (Source: U.S. Census Bureau, 2004, http://www.census.gov/ipc/www/usinterimproj/).

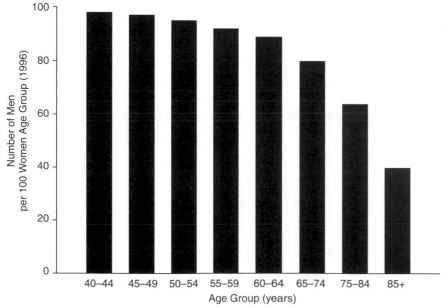

FIGURE 5.3 Number of men per 100 women by age group.

between middle age and older age at 65 years is arbitrary and reflects social legislation of the early part of last century. *Age by itself is often an inaccurate indicator of a person's underlying physical, cognitive, and mental capability and sense of well-being.*

Gender Differences

Men and women in the U.S. do not share uniformly in these gains in life expectancy (see Figure 5.3). In general, women maintain a slight advantage in life expectancy earlier in life, but by age 50 the differences in life expectancy begin to more noticeably diverge and rapidly accelerate in the eighth and ninth decades of life so that *by age 85 or greater there are only 40 men for every 100 women.* Much of the difference is the result of higher male mortality from heart disease, lung cancer, industrial and motor vehicle accidents, and violence.

Socioeconomic Status

Income and other economic factors bear upon the quality and extent of life of the older person. For example, *increased income results in higher life expectancy.* Having wealth and status positively affects means and access to health care. Wealthier individuals typically are able to maintain health and to treat illness. Being poor has the opposite effects. After children, the elderly have some of the highest poverty rates in America. People who were poor throughout early and adult life typically become even poorer in later life. However, many others, because of rising health-care costs, retirement and loss of income, and dwindling investments face impoverishment only after becoming old. *While by numbers the vast majority of the poor are white, a greater proportion of ethnic and racial minority elderly are poor and their poverty is more severe.* Additionally, women of all racial and ethnic groups, and especially the oldest-old, are particularly susceptible to impoverishment.

NORMAL CHANGES WITH AGING

As related earlier, myths and misconceptions abound about aging. Distinctions in the past were often not made between **normalcy**, i.e., a biomedical notion of what is observed in the absence of disease, and **normality**, i.e., a statistical notion of what is usual or typical for a group. Thus, previous concepts of the effects of aging were confounded by the lack of control for the underlying effects of disease, contributing to the erroneous belief that aging and disease were synonymous. Current modern notions view normal aging in broader nonpathological terms that cover life satisfaction and morale, survival and good health. Normal aging encompasses not just physical health and absence of disease but also behavioral competence, psychological well-being, perceived quality of life, and a person's objec-

> To resist the frigidity of old age, one must combine the body, the mind, and the heart—and to keep them in parallel vigor, one must exercise, study, and love.
>
> KARL VON BONSTETTEN

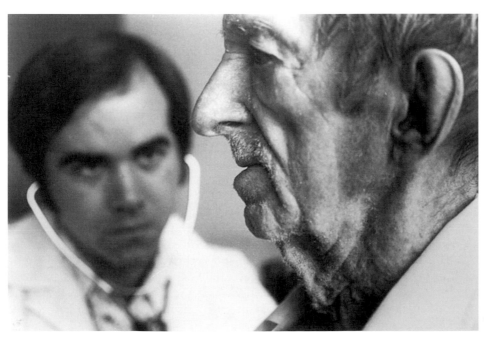

Young Doctor Courtesy of the National Institute on Aging. *Young physicians often feel uncomfortable counseling patients older than themselves.*

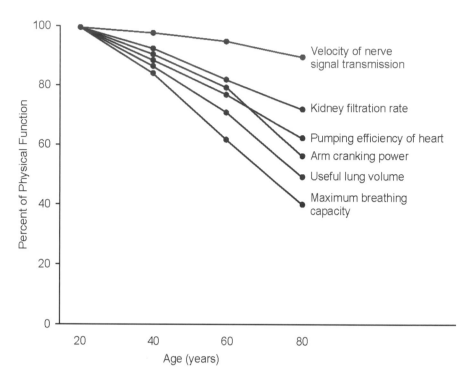

FIGURE 5.4 Average declines in bodily functions with increasing age for sedentary individuals. Source: Modified from Weg (1983) and Spirduso (1995).

tive environment. The body retains a tremendous capacity for resilience, especially if given the appropriate time, care, and support to recover and heal. Along these lines, there are several ways to conceptualize processes and groups of aging.

Concepts of Aging

One distinction describes groups according to usual aging and successful aging. Applying to the vast majority of people, **usual aging** describes the aging of individuals who have one or more medical conditions that become prevalent in later life. Here extrinsic factors heighten the effects of intrinsic aging processes. **Successful aging**, in contrast, appears to apply solely to a small select group of individuals who do exceedingly well physically, mentally, and cognitively into their latter years with many living active and full lives into their 90s and 100s and experiencing very little illness. Here extrinsic factors counteract intrinsic aging factors such that there is minimal or no functional loss.

Another distinction is between primary and secondary aging. **Primary aging** refers to those processes that appear to be most highly regulated or expressed by genetic influences. People may have better health outcomes and preserved health due to inheritance of "good" genes, or conversely, may be more susceptible to disease or effects of degeneration due to inheritance of "bad" genes. **Secondary aging** refers to processes that are not influenced directly by genetics, and includes results from accidents, injuries or

traumas, the cumulative effects of life-long habits like smoking and heavy drinking (negative) or exercise and healthy diet (positive), the effects from environmental exposure, e.g., from toxins and smog, and finally, behaviors that are modulated by sociocultural beliefs, e.g., ageism.

In the end what matters to most people is to achieve **optimal aging**, which means continuing to function at the highest possible level despite the inevitable limitations that growing older brings, or getting the best of what is possible for as long as possible across physical, cognitive, psychological and social domains.

Physical and Physiologic Changes

In general, a person experiences changes in all body parts and bodily functions over a lifetime with most of these changes beginning in early adulthood. Body parts vary naturally in the extent and pace of change with illness and disease influencing the type, degree and rate of change. However, changes in a body part may not relate to a similar change in body function. Visible physical changes of aging include gray hair, loss of teeth and hair, wrinkled skin, elongation of ears and nose, postural changes and loss of height. Other changes are loss of muscle mass and subcutaneous fat and declining eyesight and hearing. Importantly, not everyone experiences all of these changes or experiences them at the same rate. The physiologic changes in bodily functions have been well described (see Figure 5.4.)

A physician shown at two points in his life journey.

> Old places and old persons in their turn, when spirit dwells in them, have an intrinsic vitality of which youth is incapable; precisely the balance and wisdom that comes from long perspectives and broad foundations.
>
> GEORGE SANTAYANA

Brain and Intellectual Changes

Common alterations in brain structure found in aging include brain atrophy manifested by a decrease in brain volume and an increase in cerebrospinal fluid volume, ventricular enlargement, and decreases in the density of gray and white matter. Deep white matter changes are of varying significance and various patterns and frequencies exist in an aging brain. Cerebral metabolic rates of glucose and oxygen utilization seem stable but cerebral blood flow diminishes, although the data are contradictory. The usual pattern of frontal cerebral blood flow being greater than parietal cerebral blood flow is lost with aging. Finally, there are age-related decrements in various neurotransmitter receptor-binding sites across several brain regions. *However, underlying structural brain changes in aging do not necessarily result in loss of mental and cognitive capacity and function.*

Despite these structural, morphologic, and functional brain alterations, cognitive and neuropsychological abilities appear to vary with age, and sometimes don't change at all. For example, *primary and tertiary memory appear better preserved in older adults in contrast to secondary memory which manifests with difficulties in encoding and retrieval processing.* Additionally, older adults remain capable of learning and benefit from encoding strategies, from longer exposure to the stimulus that is to be remembered, and from techniques to enhance motivation. Cognitive abilities that remain stable include attention span, every day communication skills, lexical, phonological and syntactic knowledge, discourse comprehension and simple visual perception. Interestingly, studies suggest that some abilities such as judgment, accuracy and general knowledge may actually increase with age. However, abilities that appear to decline with age include selective attention, cognitive flexibility, ability to shift cognitive sets, naming of objects, verbal fluency, more complex visuoconstructive skills and logical analysis. **Crystallized intelligence**, which is the result of experience, tends to increase throughout life in healthy and active persons. In contrast, **fluid intelligence**, being more biologically determined, may be more susceptible to decline with age. Nonetheless, the mental and intellectual capabilities of older individuals, in the absence of medical or neurological disease, remain relatively intact with only minor deficits described that are usually not functionally or socially impairing. For example, while reaction time studies show a loss of speed of response in the central nervous system with age, if older persons have enough time on tests, they function as well and accurately as younger persons. *Assessments of cognitive and mental capacity must take account of health status as poor health can adversely affect cognitive performance.* In general, with good physical health, adequate education, and intellectual stimulation, older persons do not appear to decline in intellectual abilities.

HEALTH PROMOTION AND PREVENTION

Activities and behaviors that promote healthy living and disease prevention are receiving increasing attention.

Maintaining an active lifestyle throughout adult and later life with regular, and preferably vigorous, exercise results in lower risks for heart disease, some types of cancer, and dementia. Also, maintaining a productive mental life by reading, delving into novel subject areas, and actively learning new skills are all associated with better overall health outcomes for a variety of medical conditions and with a lower risk of development of a cognitive disorder. Likewise, maintaining social connections and having extensive social supports through networks of friends and family result in increased life satisfaction, lower prevalence of depression and better overall health status and quality of life.

ADAPTATIONS TO AGING

> For age is opportunity no less than youth itself, though in another dress, and as the evening twilight fades away, the sky is filled with stars, invisible by day.
>
> HENRY WADSWORTH LONGFELLOW

Cultural Attitudes and Ageism

An individual's encounter with the final stages of life reflects sociocultural biases and internal cumulative life experience. The elderly inevitably face multiple changes and losses. However, an individual's encounter with the final stages of life also reflects sociocultural biases and internal cumulative life experience.

The physiologic changes of aging described previously are accompanied by transitions in roles in society, families, and work and in various interpersonal relationships. In a society fearful of the aging process, an older person dealing with end of life issues may become isolated and shamed and left feeling unwanted and unneeded. Focused on youth, athleticism and a rapid pace, modern American society often devalues the older person. Perceived more as taxing or slowing the quick rush of modern times, the elderly sometimes are not valued for their sagacity and wisdom. **Ageism** is discrimination against a person based on age. Many aspects of current culture manifest ageism from jokes about dentures and adult diapers to negative portrayals of the elderly in movies, commercials and novels as doddering, dim-witted, or incompetent individuals. However, the baby boomers, a youth oriented generation born between 1946 and 1964, are now entering the early stages of older age. By sheer numbers, this large group, which represents about 28% of the U.S. population, may change traditional stereotypes of aging. This cohort particularly appears deeply invested in maintaining health, physical image, and high levels of activity and of independence.

> That time of year thou mayest in me behold
> When yellow leaves, or none, or few, do hang,
> Upon these boughs which shake against the cold,
> Bare ruined choirs where late the sweet birds sang.
>
> WILLIAM SHAKESPEARE
> *Sonnet 73*

Life Transitions

Family Relationships Across the Life Cycle

For the elderly, the importance of family cannot be overstated. Greater longevity allows individuals to experience more marriages, divorces, and more complex and blended family structures. Increased longevity has led to an increase in "beanpole" families, characterized by more generations with fewer members in each generation. Their children may have their own families with extended familial relationships. This change in structure may provide opportunities for rich family interactions with closer relationships, or simply for more complex conflicts, disagreements and family discord. More relationships potentially subject the older person to more important losses. The elderly experience the death of their parents, often of their own siblings, and of many other important relatives who may have been central figures in their lives since youth. If older persons have not yet lost their parents, they face the frequently daunting task of taking care of them physically and financially. Some studies note that *a 60-year-old has a 44% chance of having and caring for an elderly parent.* Centenarian parents are often cared for by their retired children who are themselves in their 70s and 80s. Spouses may provide the most important relationship, as they are an older person's emotional and social support system representing security and comfort. Marital roles change over the years, however, and if not successfully transitioned, resentment and breakdowns in communication, sometimes expressed in verbal or physical altercations, may ensue. *At the beginning of the twentieth century most marriages, on average, lasted 28 years until the death of a spouse. One hundred years later marriages may last 45 years or more until the death of one of the partners.*

New diverse family structures present challenges in the interactions within and across generations. Children with alternative life styles may be a source of pride or shame for the elderly. Financial pressures may at times force older children in their 40s, 50s and even 60s to return to their parents' homes. Family members living together once again may recreate old dysfunctional dynamics or present new problems as aging parents and their children confront reversed caretaking roles. Caregiving and caretaking are mistakenly construed as reversed parenting with elderly parents being treated inappropriately, dismissively, or disrespectfully.

Nursing Home Room Courtesy of the National Institute on Aging. *Many people desire a simpler and more stable life-style as they grow older.*

> It is not by muscle, speed, or physical dexterity that great things are achieved, but by reflection, force of character, and judgement; in these qualities old age is usually not only not poorer, but is even richer.
>
> CICERO
> *On Old Age*

Retirement

Nearly two million people retire in the United States every year. Longevity has changed retirement patterns, and *today an individual can expect to live one quarter of life in retirement.* Planning and preparation for retirement can facilitate a successful transition to a new life stage, but a lack of such planning can create hardships across generations. Beginning new hobbies and cultivating new interests should not be left until retirement. Some elderly continue to work as a source of enjoyment and of supplemental income, while many are forced to retire or are subtly eased out of their careers. Retirement can bring a focus on one's health and financial status. Social Security benefits were not intended to be the sole source of secure retirement income to retirees. Yet in 1998, according to the Social Security Administration, 16% of Social Security recipients received 100% of their income from this source and another 45% received between 50–90% of their income from Social Security alone. Thus, many elderly are living at poverty levels, and must continue to work or to seek additional employment to make ends meet. There are now proposals to change the present form of Social Security and to increase the age of eligibility for full benefits, which would reduce projected deficits in the Social Security Trust Fund, but which would have the greatest adverse impact on low income workers who are less able to save, have greater healthcare needs, and are often not able to work into their later years. Sadly, a financially safe and comfortable retirement may not be an option for many. Mounting financial pressures have left many low-income elderly having to choose between medications, other essential medical treatments, food, or shelter. Not surprisingly, a higher economic status at retirement is associated with more positive health outcomes and more satisfaction.

Successful retirements are not totally dependent on health and financial matters, however. Making creative use of time influences quality of life to a great degree. There are many physiological and psychological benefits the retiree gains from leisure activities and volunteer work. Leisure activities such as gardening, dancing, and traveling add a sense of fun and entertainment while enhancing the quality of retirement. Membership in volunteer associations and volunteer work allow the elderly to share their expertise and skills while continuing to contribute to society. While it has been estimated that 40% of the elderly do some form of volunteer work, elderly women are more likely to volunteer their time. Much of the volunteer activity done by the American Red Cross is by retirees who continue to share their skills and compassion while working with those in need. Other types of volunteer work include tutoring, helping religious organizations, raising money for charities or social and political causes, handiwork, office work, and hospital work. Helping others in need provides a way to achieve a sense of purpose and greater life satisfaction, which can significantly enhance retirement years.

Housing

Our homes provide a refuge of security and safety, and for the elderly, the form and structure of their living situations may change significantly. There are many types of housing arrangements for the elderly. More than 21 million people over the age of 65 live in their own homes. Nearly 80% of the elderly own their homes and about 50% have owned their homes for more than 25 years. Moving to a smaller residence after a spouse's death or as a result of financial need may be very difficult. On the other hand, voluntarily downsizing to a smaller residence can bring a sense of relief by lessening financial obligations and reducing worry about the physical burden of the upkeep in an aging house. Most elderly prefer independent living with options ranging from condominiums to cooperative apartments. Elder Cottage Housing Opportunity (ECHO), Accessory Units, and "Granny Flats" refer to housing arrangements where seniors share a single family home, a separate apartment, or a rental unit on a single family lot with another person or family. There are also age-segregated retirement communities, senior housing developments and retirement hotels, and mobile homes and recreation vehicles that are all available at various costs. For those needing assistance in their living arrangements, Continuing Care Retirement Communities (CCRCs) allow individuals and couples to enjoy independent living in apartments until they need further help or a change in the level or intensity of care. Short- and long-term nursing care is often available on site as needed. **Assisted living** is for those elderly who do not need nursing home care but who desire a facility where housing and meals are provided along with help with everyday living activities and transportation. Board and care homes are usually located in a private home setting where rooms, meals, and supervision are provided for a monthly fee.

Institutionalization

The majority of those over the age of 65 do not live in nursing homes, and according to the 2000 U.S. Census Bureau, only 5% of elderly above age 65 do. However, the rates of admission to nursing homes go up with age; for example, *almost 50% of those elderly older than age of 95 live in nursing homes*. Entering a nursing home has many ramifications. Families and spouses often feel as though they have failed their loved one, and family dynamic issues surrounding the decision for nursing home placement can be difficult and painful. However, *caregivers who attempt to provide total care for their family members have high rates of morbidity and mortality*, as they often neglect their own health and succumb to stress. The transition to a nursing home is

Portrait of an Old Man and a Young Boy *Domenico Ghirlandaio (ca. 1490). Courtesy of the Musée du Louvre, Paris. Grandparents are often influential role models in the lives of children. (Could you diagnose the old man's rosacea?)*

difficult but the care received in this setting is usually more successful and less stressful for both patient and family. The nursing home can never be the same as home, nor can the care delivered be the same as that from a devoted family member. However, now an entire cadre of nursing home staff provides the care formerly delivered by one or two family members, which results in an enhanced quality of life for all. Concerns about abuse, neglect, or exploitation by nursing home personnel are real, but state and federal regulations and guidelines help ensure the safety and quality of care.

There are high rates of psychiatric disorders in nursing homes. Although healthy community-dwelling elderly have lower rates of depression, *between 25% and 50% of elderly patients residing in nursing homes have or will develop clinical depression*. Nearly two thirds of elderly patients in nursing homes exhibit some element of dementia. One of the issues confronting society is where the demented patient who exhibits problematic neurobehavioral symptoms should be placed. These patients are not appropriate for acute adult psychiatric units, where they are at risk of being abused or injured, but remain a danger to themselves and/or to others

> Tumours destroy man in a unique and appalling way, as flesh of his own flesh, which has somehow been rendered proliferative, rampant, predatory and ungovernable
>
> FRANCIS PEYTON ROUS
> *Dictionary of Medical Eponyms*

in a conventional nursing home setting. Currently, there are not enough dedicated and locked dementia facilities capable of managing this growing population of often physically robust but cognitively impaired patients who are no longer capable of controlling their behavior or of navigating an environment safely and unsupervised.

Finally, for terminally ill patients, **hospices** and **palliative care settings** and programs are now increasingly available for use by patients and families to help them through the final days, weeks, or months of life. These programs aim to maintain dignity and compassion in the experience of death and in the dying process. In the year 2000, about 2.4 million Americans died and nearly 600,000 received hospice care. Eighty percent of these patients were over the age of 65. These settings promote and foster comprehensive and compassionate care in hopes of avoiding another acute futile hospitalization, another abrupt change of surroundings, or introduction of new providers who are not familiar with the patient and family, and another traumatic experience and further stress.

Driving

Driving represents independence, freedom, and personal power in our society. Curtailing or discontinuing unfettered access to an automobile can represent a significant social and psychological loss for an older person. Compounding the difficulty of this transition, *older persons with cognitive deficits and impaired realty testing often cannot make an accurate assessment of their driving competence.* The challenge of identifying and removing the impaired and incompetent older driver before a tragedy strikes confronts many states, and there is no national standard or law for evaluating or reporting an older individual who is no longer fit to operate an automobile. The role of the physician or health-care provider is not to determine driving competency, which is the purview and obligation of the state licensing agency or department of motor vehicles, but is to identify those persons who may be unsafe to drive as the result of a physical, mental, or cognitive disorder that might hinder safe operation of a vehicle. Tactics employed by states legislatures and state licensing departments to standardize evaluation of the older drivers include more frequent evaluations beyond a certain age and more comprehensive physical, visual, and cognitive assessments.

THE PLEASURES OF OLD AGE

When my grandmother Lisette turned ninety-nine,
all she could think of was men—
how they would enter her room during the night
from the vast mixer of the mind, wild
with desire, drunk with a desperate love
for only her. All day she sat, spectacle-less,
over romance magazines, until, at night,
she could dream them back into her arms,
those beautiful men, and, when morning came,
rise from her immaculate bed, pink
with the glow of the newly deflowered,
to enter the world again. All over our island
that was Manhattan, bachelors sprouted like
      dandelions
in the field of her hungers—Baruch Oestrich, stifled
by shyness at eighty-eight, for whom she would
      primp for hours;
Hugo Marx, a youthful seventy-seven, but too
      tired to notice;
Walter Hass, a sprightly eighty, who had sat shiva
for his wife for thirty years. Afternoons,
like a young girl dateless at prom time,
she would wait by the phone, sure that deliverance
would come in the voice of some stranger, resolved
that her double digitry would grow centuried
in a whirl of romance. I don't know what she
      was thinking
that day, when she fell from the top of the stairs
to die at the bottom, but I like to imagine
it was of who would enter her room that night,
and of her great joy in beautiful men—
how she had trembled for them once,
how she would gladly tremble for them again,
even now.

MICHAEL BLUMENTHAL

Sexuality

Physiological and psychological changes may affect sexuality in the later stages of life. These changes occur in the context of a society that does not promote or accept sexuality in the elderly, and sexual expression at this stage is either ignored or, more often, ridiculed. This bias is reflected in the paucity of studies looking at sexuality in the elderly. Physiological changes may make sex less spontaneous or carefree for the elderly, but clearly, *the yearning for closeness, sexual pleasure, and sexual release are still part of the lives of older persons.* Issues of love and intimacy, homosexuality, and masturbation remain important parts of the daily lives of many elderly people. Increasingly, research in the area of human sexuality in the elderly supports the notion of "use it or lose it," meaning that *those who maintain active sex lives as they age can expect to remain so and to derive pleasure from sexual activity long into the latter stages of life.* An unusual but possible concern is sexual exploitation of the cognitively impaired individual in an institutional setting. These problems are often not addressed or discussed, although there is increasing evidence for their occurrence as more people become cognitively impaired while remaining physically and sexually robust.

COPING WITH LOSS

A series of changes and losses accompanies aging. Erik Erikson, a noted psychologist, wrote of eight stages of personality development from birth to death. Each life stage had a conflict that had to be resolved for successful completion. Postulated to occur in the last decades of life, the final stage of development involves the struggle between **ego integrity and despair** in the face of death. Integrity occurs when a person accepts life's accomplishments and accepts death as inevitable. Those persons who have the ability to accept life's joys and pains in perspective and

> **The Wisdom of JOHN F. KENNEDY, 1917–1963**
> **US President**
>
> A medical revolution has extended the life of our elder citizens without providing the dignity and security those later years deserve.
>
> We cannot afford to postpone any longer a reversal in our approach to mental affliction. For too long the shabby treatment of the many millions of the mentally disabled in custodial institutions and many millions more now in communities needing help has been justified on grounds of inadequate funds, further studies and future promises.
>
> A proud and resourceful nation can no longer ask its older people to live in constant fear of a serious illness for which adequate funds are not available. We owe them the right of dignity in sickness as well as in health.

with resolve have an easier time accepting death. Those living in despair view life as misspent and are full of regrets. They fear death as an unacceptable aspect of life.

Shame is a universal human emotion that occurs throughout the life cycle and that may become more pronounced in the aged. The stigma of ageism and existential issues inherent in the aging process form the basis for shame in the elderly. Shame is a painful emotion resulting from an awareness of inadequacy or guilt. Thus, shame in later life is the reaction felt to multiple losses and deviations in appearance, status, role, and ability from the idealized youthful, healthy, and powerful "self." Society also shames individuals about diseases and frailty, both of which happen more in older age. Shame in these circumstances becomes more intense when the elderly person feels invisible or is treated with rejection, impatience, disrespect, and derision. Patients may experience physical or psychological limitations as defects or inadequacies that threaten treasured images of the self such as youth, beauty, strength, stamina, dexterity, self-control, independence, and mental competence. Some conditions and treatments may further jeopardize self-image; e.g., loss of hair and weight, mastectomies, and erectile dysfunction from cancer treatment or surgeries are degrading to patients. *Reactions to shame can take many forms and are often masked by anger, sadness, depression, or noncompliance.*

Physical Health

Many people as part of the aging process will develop a chronic illness, which often begins in the mid 50s. Most elderly patients learn to live with one or more chronic illnesses for the rest of their lives. Degenerative musculoskeletal diseases, loss or decline in primary sensory function (vision/hearing/taste), gastrointestinal conditions like ulcers or acid reflux, cardiovascular diseases, endocrinologic disorders like diabetes and hypothyroidism, genitourinary problems like incontinence, urgency, or prostate enlargement, and several cancers, some benign and some not, commonly present in older age. These changes and decrements in function, while common, may precipitate a psychiatric disorder as the elderly person attempts to cope with these losses and signs of degeneration. In addition, chronic health neglect and poor hygiene begin to show detrimental cumulative effects as the person ages. Lifelong smoking, drinking, substance abuse, lack of exercise, poor dental hygiene, and poor eating habits often take years to affect gross health, and with the onset of older age, these behaviors begin to harm the physical and mental condition of an older person. Unfortunately, making significant changes in poor lifelong habits is frequently difficult to achieve.

Aging Scholar Courtesy of the National Institute on Aging. *Although some individuals experience cognitive decline with aging, the more common experience is to remain intellectually active and alert.*

Cognitive Functioning

The public is now aware of Alzheimer's disease, and many eldcrly are understandably concerned and afraid of losing their cognitive abilities. Former President Ronald Reagan's announcement of his diagnosis and the subsequent media coverage of his illness over the years highlighted the ravages of this disease. The fear of developing dementia when an occasional memory lapse occurs, such as misplacing keys or being unable to remember a person's name, can lead to increased anxiety and depression. *A single or occasional lapse rarely signifies a dementia process, and without other evidence, the older individual should be reassured and counseled about some of the natural but normal cognitive changes with aging.* Conversely, anxiety and depressive disorders may affect an older person's abilities, and clearly, these need to be addressed. Perhaps surprisingly, many elderly are reluctant to participate in a cognitive assessment. Some may even become insulted when asked to answer questions about their cognitive state. Others may fear that their deficits will be exposed or that they will be ridiculed for appearing stupid or dumb. Finally, some elderly are concerned that poor test results will have some adverse effect on their ability to remain independent. Therefore, evaluation of cognition should be performed with sensitivity to the potential issues uncovered and involved. If diagnosed with a cognitive disorder, an individual may respond in a variety of ways. Common responses are denial that test results are correct or that memory problems are significant, and projection that others are mistaken or that others are having difficulties coping. Confrontation of denial is often met with

further resistance because of impairment of insight, termed **anosognosia**, and lack of judgment, both of which may accompany cognitive loss. On the other hand, some elderly are keenly aware of their problems and cognitive struggles, and become anxious and depressed. *Approximately 25% of patients with early stage Alzheimer's disease present with symptoms of depression that should be treated.* A cognitive disorder in the elder head of household will impact all family members. The necessary changes in family structure and responsibilities for decisions will create new challenges as shifts in family dynamics and power differentials add caregiver burden and stress.

Competency

Independence and the ability to make decisions is an important and defining characteristic of being an adult. Losing the ability to make decisions about one's health care, finances, and legal matters is a serious infringement of the basic rights of an adult individual. The task of assessing whether to deny a person their rights cannot be taken lightly. Confusion surrounds the difference between the terms capacity and competency, which are often used interchangeably, if imprecisely. **Capacity** refers to the ability or inability of an individual to make decisions, whether concerning medical, financial, or legal matters of estate or of person, and is a conclusion reached usually after a medical or clinical evaluation. **Competency**, on the other hand, is a legal definition and reflects the decision of the state about a person as adjudicated by a court or judge who hears evidence concerning the proposed question and who incorporates the findings of a professional evaluator such as a physician, psychologist, religious arbiter or attorney. Thus, the terms are not entirely synonymous.

Competency assessments should focus on the specific decision or task that is being questioned, since incompetence or competence in one area may not predict or correlate with ability in another. Typical concerns arise when an older adult with a possible cognitive, medical, or psychiatric illness that impacts decision-making is changing or writing a will, signing a contract, distributing property, or considering a potentially dangerous or experimental medical treatment or procedure. In truth, any time an older patient is making or considering a choice on any matter, competency is a factor.

Legal authorities and forensic experts use several processes for determining competency. Essentially, to be legally valid, any decision made by an individual must be voluntary, informed, and competent. Voluntary decisions are freely given and not the result of coercion, threat, or undue influence. Additionally, the person must evidence a choice either explicitly in writing or by speech, or implicitly by actions and behaviors. The decision must also be informed, which entails, for medical decisions, disclosure of the condition being treated and indication(s) for treatment, discussion and description of the recommended intervention or treatment, review of the risks, benefits, and side effects of the recommended treatment, disclosure of alternative therapies including doing nothing at all, and the consequences of those choices. The clinician should assess for understanding of the information presented and *ask the patient to repeat and describe the discussion in her own words.* In short, the clinician must determine if the older person has the ability to assimilate relevant facts, and if the person appreciates or rationally understands his or her own situation as it relates to medical circumstances. For older patients with cognitive impairment or serious medical or psychiatric illness, information may have to be presented multiple times or in multiple formats. Importantly, the state of competency can vary over time, e.g., during delirium or during a period of grave illness in which a patient was not able to make decisions or to participate in discussion. Conversely, with dementia, other cognitive disorders, and pervasive unremitting psychiatric conditions, cognitive abilities may be so impaired that competency will never be regained, a situation that may lead to guardianship or conservatorship where a court formally appoints and charges another person with the responsibility and authority to make all medical, financial, and/or legal decisions.

Standardized tools may help facilitate the evaluation of competency, but these need to be used in conjunction with a thorough clinical evaluation that might entail a complete medical history, review of medications, physical and psychiatric evaluations, and laboratory tests. A diag-

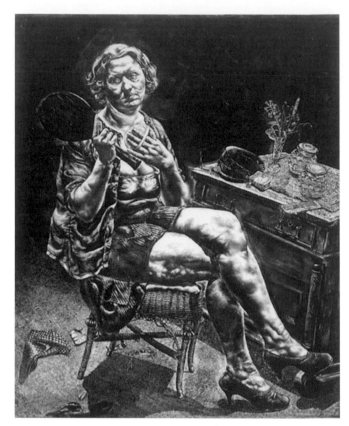

Into the World There Came a Soul Called Ida (The Lord in His Heaven and I in My Room Below) *(1929/1930) Ivan Le Lorraine Albright, 1897–1983 .* Oil on canvas, 142.9 × 119.2 cm. Gift of Ivan Albright, 1977. Copyright © The Art Institute of Chicago. All rights reserved. *Physicians have to be able to deal with patients who present with somatic concerns related to fading beauty, declining physical prowess, and loneliness.*

nosis, if established, may impact the determination of the decision-making ability and guide further work-up. Finally, evaluation of family structure and social network and, at times, interviews of family members, caregivers, and friends are necessary for a complete competency assessment.

Separation and Death

Loss of loved ones, especially of a spouse or child, is devastating for most people. There are often changes in the survivor's social and financial situation. *The death of a spouse is associated with high rates of morbidity and mortality in previously healthy people.* Depression, anxiety, and insomnia are common psychiatric features of bereavement. Studies suggest that the stress of bereavement produces changes in the body's immune system creating negative health outcomes. Women generally adjust better than men do to the loss of a spouse, and males are much more likely to die within a year after being widowed. Widowhood is difficult, but in many cases, after the period of grief passes, survivors adjust and find that they can enjoy a sense of independence. Some elderly find new experiences and new relationships in the aftermath of the death of a spouse or partner. *The losses of parents and adult children can be extremely painful for the elderly. Having a strong social network of close and valued relationships with friends and family provides the best means of coping with these losses.* Early psychological treatment of complicated bereavement may prevent the development of clinical depression. Grief support groups available through pastoral counseling, hospice programs, or community organizations are helpful in providing or creating a sense of security and of sharing and are sources for new relationships. The role of spirituality and religion, for those who subscribe to these tenets and hold these beliefs, cannot be underestimated as a source of comfort, strength, and solace.

> You're only as young as the last time you changed your mind.
>
> TIMOTHY LEARY

MENTAL HEALTH AND ILLNESS

Psychiatric Assessment of the Older Adult

Psychiatric assessment of older individuals entails an evaluation and analysis of a person's thoughts, emotions, behaviors, and cognition. The presenting psychiatric symptoms must be analyzed comprehensively and placed in the appropriate medical and psychosocial contexts. Importantly, *psychiatric evaluation of the older individual must balance respect for personal autonomy, dignity and privacy with the need to gather information from a variety of collateral sources,* including spouses, partners, adult children, extended family and friends, and usually multiple providers. The older person is considered competent until proven otherwise and, except in an emergency, his or her permission must be sought to discuss their care and treatment with others. However, there may be cultural differences and sensitivities to observe, and ideally, the clinician should be aware of these at the outset. Lastly, some elderly persons may shun psychiatric evaluation because of the stigma of mental illness or show a tendency to express psychological difficulties as somatic complaints as a means to avoid the perception of character flaws or weaknesses.

Medical or neurologic comorbidity may also complicate the psychiatric evaluation of an older individual. Psychiatric symptoms by themselves are relatively nonspecific and may develop in practically any medical disorder. That is, *medical conditions may present with psychiatric symptoms,* e.g., pancreatic cancer or hypothyroidism presenting with depressed mood, and conversely, *psychiatric disorders may present with medical symptoms,* e.g., clinical depression presenting with weight loss or panic disorder with chest pain. Medications, over-the-counter drugs, herbal remedies, and supplements may cause an alteration in cognition, thinking, emotion, or behavior as the result of drug side effects, drug-drug or drug-supplement interactions, or toxicities. A careful, systematic, and comprehensive approach is necessary when evaluating an elderly patient, and includes query for past medical and neurologic history, review of medication lists, family medical and psychiatric history, social history, and review of systems. The physical examination focuses on acute processes and must include at least an elemental neurologic examination (cranial nerves, reflexes, and motor exam). The **mental status exam**, which starts when the patient enters the room, continues throughout the interview, and incorporates observation of the interaction between patient and interviewer as well as between patient and environment, should specifically assess for suicidality, psychosis, and impaired thinking.

An older person may be experiencing an exacerbation of a preexisting psychiatric disorder, present since earlier in life, or may be developing a psychiatric disorder for the first time only later in life. The former group is said to have an early-onset disorder and the latter to have a late-onset disorder. Patients with early-onset disorders have positive psychiatric histories, although details may be sketchy or hard to corroborate, as well as higher genetic or biological load with positive family histories of mental disorders. Patients with early-onset disorders, in general, tend to have overall poorer physical health in later life compared to their peers without any prior psychiatric history. In contrast, patients with late-onset disorders typically have negative past and family psychiatric histories and carry a lower genetic or biological load. Late-onset psychiatric disorders appear to be associated with the development or worsening of an underlying medical or neurological condition. Many of the same conditions found earlier in life can develop later in life, although the likelihood, risk, and prevalence of disorders are different.

Psychiatric Disorders in Later Life

Anxiety Disorders

Anxiety disorders are among the most common yet poorly recognized and diagnosed mental conditions in later life. While *de novo* anxiety disorders are relatively rare in elderly persons, many patients live decades without accurate identification. These patients in particular are at high risk for self-medication with or abuse of alcohol, of prescription drugs such as benzodiazepines or opiates, or of over-the-counter

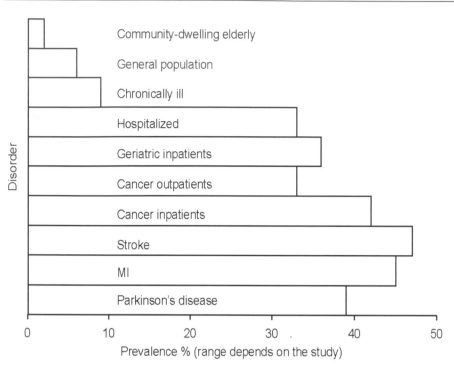

FIGURE 5.5 Prevalence of depressive disorders in various patient groups and populations.

sedatives and pain relievers. Often, these patients are only identified because of an alcohol-related or medication-induced medical problem or withdrawal syndrome. However, it is important to appreciate that anxiety may be a normal response to a stressful life event or serious medical problem. Only when anxiety symptoms become too overwhelming, interfere with daily functioning, or impair health or safety is psychiatric evaluation or intervention needed. Finally, anxiety may be a component of a variety of medical conditions or a manifestation of drug side-effect or drug toxicity.

Mood Disorders

Mood disorders are common in the elderly population, albeit at a lower prevalence than generally thought. Mood disorders include unipolar and bipolar depression, dysthymia, subsyndromal depression, substance-induced depression, and mood disorder as a result of general medical conditions. In fact, *in community-dwelling, healthy, elderly the prevalence of clinical depression is only about one third the rate of the general adult population. However, the prevalence rates of depression increase across more medically ill populations and in various medical settings* (see Figure 5).

Depression should be recognized because it is a diagnosable and treatable condition. Unfortunately, studies continue to show that *depression in the elderly remains under recognized, misdiagnosed, and both poorly and less intensely treated.* Many older persons, their families, or health-care providers may also show therapeutic nihilism and attempt to explain away the reasons for depression. However, an untreated mood disorder is associated with poorer medical and psychiatric outcomes. Depression in later life is associated with lower quality of life, prolonged suffering, more disability, increased health-care utilization and costs, and increased morbidity and mortality. Psychiatric consequences of late life depression include mental health related disability, increased risk of substance abuse, and increased risk of suicide.

Diagnosis of depression or any mood disorder in the medically ill elderly patient may be particularly difficult due to the overlap of many physical complaints with the symptoms of depression. Evaluation for the psychological symptoms of depression such as depressed mood or sadness, **anhedonia** or loss of interests, feelings of guilt or worthlessness, or suicidal ideation, or of behavioral equivalents such as crying, social regression, or withdrawal can increase the specificity of diagnosis. Neurovegetative symptoms like sleep disturbance, loss of appetite or weight, psychomotor retardation, or fatigue are less specific for depression in medically ill elderly, but may be considered attributable to depression if these worsen or covary with mood. An older person with depression may develop severe cognitive impairment and appear demented. These patients may be either in the prodrome of a dementia syndrome or at higher risk of subsequently converting to a dementia syndrome, and in any case merit particularly close attention. Screening instruments are available for use in the elderly population and include the **Geriatric Depression Scale**, which is available in several item and language versions and is validated across different settings, and the **Cornell Scale for Depression in Dementia**. However, *the gold standard for diagnosis of depression remains a thorough clinical interview.*

Psychotic Disorders

Primary psychotic disorders in the elderly include schizophrenia, schizoaffective disorder, and delusional disorder. However, symptoms of psychosis may manifest in other psychiatric conditions such as major depression, substance-induced intoxication and withdrawal states, and cognitive disorders such as dementia or delirium. Since DSM-IV, there is no longer an age specification for schizophrenia onset, although interestingly, it appears that older women may be at higher risk. Elderly patients with late-onset schizophrenia, whose illness typically begins after age 60, tend to have positive symptoms like paranoid delusions or hallucinations, while negative symptoms, like alogia and apathy, and disorganized states occur, in general, less frequently in older groups compared to younger adults and compared to those elderly with early-onset disorder. The original assumption that all patients with early-onset schizophrenia suffered unrelenting cognitive deterioration, i.e., **dementia praecox**, is likely wrong, and some patients remain remarkably stable over a lifetime. Late-onset schizophrenia, also termed **paraphrenia**, may be more common in women and in patients with primary sensory (vision and hearing) impairment, and is marked by predominance of paranoid symptoms and less bizarre ideation. *De novo psychotic symptoms in later life may be a manifestation of underlying central nervous system disease such as dementia, other neurodegenerative disorders like Parkinson's or Huntington's diseases, stroke, inflammatory processes, infection, primary or metastatic cancer, seizure disorder, or trauma.*

Substance Abuse and Dependence Disorders

Substance abuse and dependence disorders in the elderly remain poorly understood, appreciated, and studied. The elderly may abuse alcohol, prescription drugs like opiates and benzodiazepines, or over-the-counter drugs and supplements. As in younger populations, *substance abuse in the elderly significantly increases the risk for medical and psychiatric morbidity and mortality.* Prevalence estimates of the extent of substance abuse in older populations are difficult to ascertain for a variety of reasons. For example, identification of problem drinking in older patients is challenging because alcoholism may be a hidden condition, diagnostic criteria developed for younger populations may not apply to older groups, and physicians may be reluctant to make a diagnosis in an older adult. While most problem drinkers began in early life, about one third to one half of older people developed a problem with alcohol only later in life. Periods of high risk include the time around the death of a spouse or companion, stresses around illness, loss of function or life transitions, and development of clinical depression. Additionally, many elderly may minimize or conceal their extent of alcohol or drug use. Elderly patients with multiple conditions may visit multiple providers and obtain multiple prescriptions.

The elderly are more prone to the toxic effects of alcohol and drugs. As a result of the physiologic changes of aging, older people have higher blood levels of alcohol and drugs, and manifest toxic effects more readily, e.g., confusion, disorientation, memory loss, poor motor coordination, unsteady gait, and more falls. Chronic alcohol use is associated with poor nutritional status and with vitamin and protein deficiencies, which may lead to peripheral and central nervous systems disorders like motor palsies, neuropathies, Wernicke's encephalopathy, or Korsakoff's psychosis. Consequences of alcoholism and unsupervised or inappropriate drug use are serious, leading possibly to early deaths. In the elderly, drug-alcohol interactions and withdrawal syndromes from central nervous system depressants can be lethal.

Cognitive Disorders

With the increasing elderly population, dementias and other cognitive disorders are now major problems confronting the United States. *Current estimates of the number of Americans with dementia number around 4 million, and by 2020 the number may reach 11 to 14 million.* **Dementia** refers to a variety of acquired conditions that involve impairments across multiple domains, usually including a primary deficit in memory function. These deficits develop for the first time in adulthood or later and impair functioning in daily life, work, or social relationships. **Amnesia**, in contrast, refers to dysfunction only in the domain of memory that can occur any time in life. While age by itself is not synonymous with dementia, *aging is the greatest risk factor for development of dementia* with incidence and prevalence rates increasing rapidly with age. Diagnostic schemas are predicated upon descriptions of presenting symptoms, clinical course of illness, and increasingly, an understanding of epidemiology, risk factors, and neurogenetics. Dementias are either primary or secondary. **Primary dementias** are further classified as cortical or subcortical. The prototypic primary neurodegenerative dementia is Alzheimer's Disease, which is also the most common form of dementia in later life. The second most common dementia syndrome is **vascular dementia**, which actually is comprised of several subtypes. Although the primary presenting symptoms of dementia involve memory loss and at least one or more neuropsychological impairments, many patients will also develop psychiatric symptoms such as depression, anxiety, psychosis, personality changes, or behavioral disturbances.

Delirium is another important cognitive disorder that occurs more frequently in the elderly population. Delirium if unrecognized may lead to death. Delirium, also called altered mental status or acute confusional state, usually presents closely to an acute medical insult such as myocardial infarction, pneumonia, stroke, metabolic derangement, systemic infection, or drug toxicity or withdrawal syndrome, although *frequently the cause of delirium is multifactorial*, meaning that a single definitive etiology may not be found. Delirium presents with impaired consciousness and attention deficits and may include psychiatric symptoms and behavioral disturbances. *Risk factors for delirium include older age, serious medical illness, multiple active illnesses, use of multiple drugs, and preexisting cognitive or psychiatric disorder*. In contrast to dementia, delirium develops quickly over hours to days, fluctuates throughout the course of the day, and if the underlying cause is identified and treated, will usually reverse. Elderly delirious patients are very difficult to manage and treat because of the many possible etiologies involved. Elderly delirious patients are also prone to neglect, dehydration, aspiration pneumonia, poor nutrition, deconditioning, pressure sores, and strangulation from entanglement in intravenous lines and monitoring equipment. A sitter or family member is ideal to have at the patient's bedside to provide reassurance and calming and obviates the need for restraints and the excessive use of sedatives or tranquilizers.

Psychiatric Intervention

Psychotherapy

When Sigmund Freud, the father of psychoanalysis, was himself 68 years of age, he described those over the age of 50 as unsuitable for individual psychotherapy because he thought that older individuals, given a set character structure, no longer had the capacity or motivation for change and that the duration of treatment required to produce change portended an interminable therapy. It is interesting that Freud completed the majority of his work and prolific writings on psychoanalytic theory and treatment after the age of 50. However, his dismissal of insight-oriented therapy for older adults led to a long period of neglect and of limited study of this age group. *Over the past two decades renewed interest and research from several studies indicate that several forms of psychotherapy can be as effective as pharmacotherapy in treating several types of depression in the elderly patient, and more importantly, the combination of both modalities has better outcomes than when either is used alone.* There is, however, a striking disparity between the estimated need for mental health care of the elderly and the availability of privately and publicly funded services and providers. Older adults are much more likely to be treated in primary care settings rather than in mental health settings. Many fear dependency and mockery when seeking help for mental problems. They may also fear appearing weak and needy if they see a mental health-care provider, as it is perceived to be more acceptable to seek medical or physical care. Talk therapy focuses on exposing and confronting disavowed feeling states, whereas medical care offers treatments aimed at curing physical suf-

THE WAGES OF MERCY

The medics tell me he's been ten years
in the nursing home, dwindling
the past few weeks, refusing to eat,
asking only for his Winstons
and to be left alone.
Tonight when he spiked a fever,
and quickly became unresponsive,
with no family, no friends
to contact, the nurses asked
he be brought here, to the Emergency Room,
the open hands of strangers.

His color is awful. He's barely breathing.
I wonder for a moment what all
the commotion is about,
nurses frantically starting IVs
and drawing blood and
placing EKG electrodes;
it's only death—
as if we hadn't seen death before.

I shine a penlight into vacant
eyes, touch his heaving chest
and abdomen with the bell
of my stethoscope, listening
to the pneumonia crackle and pop.

The nurses ask what I want to do,
as if we must do something, anything.

I stroke a lock of matted hair
away from the old man's brow,
order a liter of saline and
some oxygen, biding time with comfort
as I sit at his bedside,
rifle through his voluminous chart.

Cardiac monitors beep and whir,
keeping guard with the syncopated melody.

The telephone rings three times, then stops.

PETER PEREIRA

fering. Psychological issues represent a problem of self-image, whereas medical treatment displaces perceived injury of self onto an isolated body part. A shame response is possible in both milieus, but it is in the psychiatric setting where a patient may feel more vulnerable or exposed, and understandably avoids going to see a psychiatrist or therapist. Previously considered negative indicators for successful psychotherapy, may, in fact, be positive predictors of success. As people age and face a limited future, they have less time for, less use of, and less patience for counterproductive coping and poor interpersonal strategies. In the hands of a skilled therapist, the urgency for change may speed the therapeutic process; in addition, *the elderly bring to therapy a lifetime of experience, which can be used productively to explore dynamics and achieve resolutions.*

Besides psychodynamic or insight-oriented psychotherapy, several other forms of therapy are effective and available for use in older populations. Cognitive-behavioral, interpersonal and brief psychodynamic therapy studies show efficacy in the elderly. Beyond individual modalities, couples, family, and group therapy are variations to consider. The latter may be especially useful for caregivers. Groups provide the opportunity for sharing experiences, giving and receiving support, and social interaction. Groups for demented patients focus on improving memory and enhancing cognitive skills through music and art therapy, life reminiscing, and motor skills training and physical activity.

Somatic Treatment of the Older Patient

Compared to younger groups, elderly patients use more medications. Americans older than 65 years fill an average of 13 prescriptions per year, which is twice the national average and three times the average of individuals younger than 65 years. In general, the number of prescribed medications increases with age but so does the number of nonprescription over-the-counter (OTC) medications used. Nearly two-thirds of elderly patients report routine use of OTC medications. Somatic therapies in geriatric psychiatry consist of psychopharmacologic interventions and electroconvulsive therapy (ECT). When used appropriately and for the conditions indicated, both psychotropic medications and ECT are safe and effective in older patients. All treatments work best when matched to the disorder for which efficacy is demonstrated.

Unfortunately, studies of psychotropic drug use in the elderly show inappropriate use of many classes of medications. For example, in the recent past *elderly patients residing in skilled nursing facilities were frequently overmedicated, primarily for behavioral reasons, despite the fact that psychotropics, mainly antipsychotics and benzodiazepines, show limited efficacy for these purposes and cause untoward and serious side effects.* Other studies show that many elderly patients are reluctant to take psychotropic drugs because of fear or misunderstanding of their purpose and because

of the stigma associated with having a mental condition. Finally, other studies suggest that elderly patients are less intensely treated for their mental disorders in health-care settings, causing unnecessarily prolonged suffering and increased disability. For ECT, the matter is similar. ECT, the most effective treatment for depression, especially psychotic depression, carries an immense stigma. In fact, *ECT has low morbidity and mortality rates, and recent studies suggest that older age may be a positive predictor of response.*

Managing and treating an older patient can be very challenging. Increasing numbers of medical problems, both acute and chronic, make older patients less responsive to treatment for a variety of reasons. Comorbid medical burden is a predictor of poorer response to acute psychotropic treatment, limits the choices of potential medications, may limit the extent of response, and may leave the patient with greater residual symptoms and increased functional impairment. Additionally, medical conditions may be chronic or progressive, implying a high risk of intercurrent illnesses, interruptions in treatment, and need for frequent review and adjustments. More medical burden may make patients less tolerant to treatment as a result of less physiological reserve, less functional capacity, and a lower threshold for decompensation. Finally, *with increasing number of medications there is a higher risk for medication errors, inappropriate drug prescribing, drug-drug or drug-OTC interactions, and medication noncompliance because of complex drug schedules, drug interruptions, and cost.*

With an increased likelihood of more medical comorbidity and of being on several medications or supplements, an older patient may be at greater risk for an adverse outcome from a psychotropic drug. Alterations in pharmacokinetics and pharmacodynamics with aging increase the risk for an untoward or idiosyncratic drug reaction. **Pharmacokinetics** describes what the body does to the drug, i.e., absorption, distribution, metabolism, and excretion. Changes in aging can affect each one of these areas. **Pharmacodynamics** involves what the drug does to the body,

---

TABLE 5.1 Aging and pharmacodynamics

- Central nervous system: sedation, confusion, disorientation, memory impairment, delirium, agitation, mood and perceptual disturbances, headache
- Cardiovascular: hypotension, orthostasis, cardiac conduction abnormalities (arrhythmias, QTc prolongation)
- Gastrointestinal: nausea, vomiting, appetite changes, abdominal cramps, loose stool
- Peripheral anticholinergic effects: blurred vision, dry mouth, constipation, urinary retention
- Motor effects: tremor, impaired gait, increased body sway, falls, extrapyramidal system effects
- Other: sexual dysfunction; metabolic, endocrinologic, and electrolyte disturbances

i.e., side effects, toxicity, and withdrawal reactions. Changes in body and brain receptor sensitivity and receptor availability with aging account for many of these effects and presentations. Common aging and pharmacodynamic effects are listed in Table 5.1.

General principles for use of psychotropic agents in an older person include matching the right drug to the right disorder, having clear target symptoms at the outset, and monitoring for improvement, lack of response, or deterioration. All are clearly important to successful management. Additionally, *the starting dose is lower, typically about one fourth to one half of the younger adult initial dose.* Adjustments continue gradually, made every 3–5 days as tolerated, being certain to reach the usual therapeutic range. Some side effects may not be evident in the beginning and only develop after the drug accumulates in the body. Medications continue until the patient reaches remission or maximal improvement. Whether to maintain a medication depends upon the disorder being treated and the patient's history of relapse and stability. Some patients may require chronic treatment.

Hospital and Day Programs

Adult day care is a newer option for elderly patients who prefer to remain in their homes, but who need or could benefit from a range of services, including medical, rehabilitation, occupational, and social activities. Senior centers and day programs coordinate many of these services and also help prevent social isolation. These programs provide respite for caregivers, allowing them a chance to recharge, relieve stress, return to work, or to take care of other daily needs and routine tasks like marketing, shopping, or banking. Many of these programs are run by charitable or religious organizations and may be free or relatively inexpensive and others may be covered by insurance. Families can also receive grants and other funds from social agencies or government programs to help defray costs.

Suicide

Considering the many losses that the elderly experience, it is not surprising that this group has very high suicide rates. *Although the elderly make up about 13% of the population they comprise 25% of the annual suicides in the United States. Men account for 80% of the elderly suicides and approximately 85% will use a firearm, a very lethal means of suicide.* Suicide rates are the highest for older white males and elderly African-American males have lower rates of suicide. Risk factors for suicide include a history of divorce or loss of a spouse, poor or failing health, a history of alcohol or substance abuse, a history of major depression, social isolation, and having access to firearms.

There are many reasons an elderly person may want to end his or her life. Some possible reasons include multiple losses of loved ones, chronic illness, and poorly controlled pain. An older person may also fear becoming a burden on his or her family. Not uncommonly, an older person may want to end his life because of worry that an inheritance intended for family will be spent instead on mounting medical expenses. The fear of losing cognitive and physical abilities to make, execute, and control decisions is another common precipitant of suicidal thinking. Indeed, suicide provides the ultimate act of control over how life ends, avoiding the unknown and uncertainty of death. Finally, suicide may be viewed as the only realistic means of ending uncontrollable and unremitting pain.

Physician-assisted suicide (PAS) is a social and political subject being debated in this country and around the world. Physician-assisted suicide was recently legalized in the Netherlands, and approximately 2% of deaths in the Netherlands result from PAS. The experience there shows that over 85% who request PAS change their wishes when provided adequate pain medications and when given counseling and pharmacologic treatments for depression. Thus, clearly the majority of people who are interested in this option are suffering unnecessarily from untreated pain and depression.

As opposed to PAS, **passive euthanasia** entails the withholding or withdrawing medical treatment in the terminally ill. The recent and very contentious case of Terri Schiavo, a Florida woman in a chronic vegetative state for many years, is one example. Her husband wanted to honor her unwritten wish that she not be sustained by medical means, specifically by a feeding tube. Many social, legal, and emotional issues were debated and the eventual decision, after lengthy and dramatic court and political actions, was to withdraw her feeding tube. Questions of the "right to die" and the definition of **brain death** became front and center. Court litigation and treatment decision controversies are avoidable if individuals specify in writing what future treatment preferences are and note these in a **living will** or an **advanced life directive**. *Many patients and families find the topic hard to confront and broach, but the problem is made harder when clinicians unknowingly collude by avoiding discussion of these serious matters.* Importantly, the elderly should be encouraged to complete an advanced life directive or living will while they are still cognitively capable. Completion of these documents is a way to initiate a dialog about end of life issues. Fears about death and dying can then be openly addressed and relieved by proactive discussion of a frightening topic.

> To know how to grow old is the master-work of wisdom, and one of the most difficult chapters in the great art of living.
>
> HENRI AMIEL
> *Journal Intime*

Elder Abuse

Physical frailty and cognitive impairment may make the elderly more dependent on families and others, which possibly exposes them to abuse. Elder abuse occurs in many forms including physical or sexual abuse, psychological abuse, financial exploitation, medical abuse, and general neglect. The abuse can occur in any setting. These abuses may be the continuation of a lifelong pattern of abuse from a spouse or family member. Often, elder abuse stems from the breakdown of normal boundaries, as children or others assume caregiving roles, for which they are untrained, and experience caregiver stress, especially while attempting to maintain their previous lives and schedules.

Caregiver stress is a well-recognized risk factor for any type of abuse. As with other types of mistreatment and cruelty within the family or in professional settings, elder abuse may be subtle and difficult to detect. The victim frequently is fearful of reporting actions to authorities or others. The majority of states have laws protecting the elderly and have made reporting elder abuse mandatory if the suspicion arises. Worsening, relapse, or recurrence of an older person's underlying psychiatric condition, or development of new problem behaviors may be warning signs of abuse. Other signs include repeated trips to emergency rooms with evidence of recent trauma, and illnesses and wounds that do not respond to treatment. Financial exploitation and undue influence over an elderly person who is no longer competent is, sadly, not uncommon. These patients lack the means and the insight to recognize that their persons or estates are being victimized. Physicians and health-care providers must take the responsibility and execute the duty of identifying, protecting, and advocating for vulnerable older patients who are dependent, scared, and defenseless. Legal authorities, social services, and other governmental agencies such as Adult Protective Services should be contacted to provide further evaluation and protection.

> I like spring, but it is too young. I like summer, but it is too proud. So I like best of all autumn, because its tone is mellower, its colors are richer, and it is tinged with a little sorrow. Its golden richness speaks not of the innocence of spring, nor the power of summer, but of the mellowness and kindly wisdom of approaching age. It knows the limitations of life and its content.
>
> LIN YÜ-TANG

SUMMARY

The elderly are the most rapidly growing segment of the U.S. population and there are multiple social and eco-

nomic forces confronting this growing population. Gerontology is the study of the elderly and the aging process itself, and covers the social, psychological, and biological aspects of aging. Geriatrics is the branch of medicine that studies the diseases, disorders, and syndromes that occur in later life. Importantly, research funding for both the basic and clinical sciences of aging is increasing. Geriatric subspecialty training occurs formally in medicine, psychiatry, and family medicine, but many other specialties increasingly recognize the value and importance of this unique group of individuals. The clinical practice of geriatrics includes and integrates many disciplines across health care, involving professionals from medicine, nursing, social work, rehabilitation and occupational therapy, dietary and nutritional services, dentistry, pharmacy, psychologists, chaplains, and others. Treatment and management of the elderly encompasses legal, ethical, moral, medical, psychological, and even political issues. As this age group grows, interest in caring for, understanding, and treating the elderly also grows. Working with the elderly provides for an immensely rich and gratifying experience, and promises to be an area of immense health-care need for the foreseeable future.

CASE STUDY

Part I. Over the past 6 months Mrs. Mary Jones, who is 74, has become more forgetful and irritable. She was an attorney and considering a judgeship, but instead retired early about 20 years ago to care for an ailing husband. She gradually lost contact with many colleagues and professional friends. Her husband died last year after a long illness. She was the primary caregiver until 2 years ago when he went to a skilled nursing facility because she was unable to manage him at home after he suffered a fall and broke his hip. She blames herself for his demise and subsequent death, believing she could have done more, and she is angry at herself for ever agreeing to his placement at her children's urging.

Shortly after her husband's death, Mrs. Jones experienced a mild heart attack and her recovery was complicated by pneumonia. After a brief stay in a rehabilitation facility she moved, at her children's behest, from New York City to Los Angeles where she lives in her own apartment close to her daughter and grandchildren. During an office visit her daughter reports that she is worried that her mother, previously a bright and energetic woman, now appears lost, confused, and mentally dull.

Q1. What losses must she confront? Are there concerns about competency? What are useful courses of action to take?
Her life changed dramatically both in the short and long term. She gave up a professional practice and retired not

because she was ready to, but instead, to care for an ailing spouse. She no longer had the stimulation of complex work in a field that provided prestige and intellectual challenge and she also lost contact with friends who supported her professional identity. Additionally, Mrs. Jones, after experiencing a prolonged period of caregiver stress, lost her spouse, is grieving, and must adjust to widowhood. She is at high risk for complicated bereavement or depression. She feels she failed as a caregiver having placed her husband in a nursing home where he died. She wonders if she were pressured into the choice of placement.

Concerns about problems with competency are difficult to discern. The patient recently had to make various types of decisions, e.g., the care and placement of her husband, type and extent of medical treatment she received after a heart attack and her own placement in a rehabilitation facility, and relocation to a different city to receive more help and support from an adult daughter. Apparently, she made most decisions voluntarily, and although she may have been influenced by her family, there is no evidence that her choices resulted in worse outcomes medically, legally, or financially, caused anyone immediate danger or harm, or were made under threat or coercion. In the absence of any other evidence she must be presumed competent. Nonetheless, keep in mind that competency may vary over time and addresses specific questions or situations that must be assessed individually. If there is a specific concern, a clinical evaluation would strive to assess her **capacity** to make informed decisions, which could then be used to make a determination of her **competency** to manage a specific medical, legal, or financial affair.

However, she also has significant medical problems that may have been neglected as she focused more on her husband's ailments and nursing home placement. Caregivers often experience worse health outcomes, as they neglect their own health problems, or suffer physical setbacks because of the added burden of stress. She requires a thorough clinical medical evaluation including medical history, assessment of functional capability and of other psychiatric symptoms, review of prescribed medication and over-the-counter supplements, and reviews of psychiatric history, family history, substance abuse history, and of general systems. Furthermore, a physical exam assesses for acute medical processes and includes both an elemental neurologic exam and a mental status exam. Pertinent laboratory studies should be checked.

Part II. On clinical interview Mrs. Jones reports that she has hypothyroidism and hypertension. She relays that she forgot to fill her prescriptions and has not taken any medication for about 2 weeks. She complains of cold intolerance, constipation, and fatigue. As you discuss the need to treat her medical problems, she appears to fall asleep. You tell her daughter that a careful physical exam, vital sign check, and basic labs are needed. She agrees to let her moth-

er be examined and tested. The patient's blood pressure is low despite not taking any medications, but her temperature is mildly elevated. Her exam reveals no emergent medical process and is otherwise unremarkable. Her laboratory studies reveal several problems. Her urinalysis shows evidence of a serious urinary tract infection and a complete blood count shows a mild leukocytosis with a left shift. Her thyroid stimulating hormone level result is also mildly elevated.

When awakened and told of her problems, Mrs. Jones agrees to be admitted to hospital, where her infection is quickly treated with antibiotics and her low blood pressure stabilized after fluid hydration. She resumes her usual medications. On the day of discharge you notice the patient is quietly crying as she looks out the window. She says, "my life is falling apart," and complains that her thinking is "not right," as she has never before forgotten to take her medications. She worries that she has Alzheimer's, and she does not want to end up in a nursing home like her husband. Upon further questioning, Mrs. Jones reveals that she regrets moving to Los Angeles. She misses her church, her few close friends, and her home of 40 years. She resents not being able to drive since she sold her car. She complains of not sleeping well and feels bored, but she is worried that with all her recent health problems she is becoming a burden to her family. She says, "life would be easier if I weren't around to cause trouble."

Her daughter, while sympathetic, is also clearly frustrated. She has a young family at home and struggles to keep everything on schedule. Her brothers are not helping with their mother's care as they said they would. She discouraged her mother from driving in Los Angeles, as she is worried that she will have an accident. Since she has durable power of attorney, she instructs you to tell her mother that she can no longer drive. The apartment does not appear to be working out, but there is no room at her house. She wants her mother to move to senior retirement housing where she can meet other people.

Q2. What issues and problems should be explored now? What approaches, treatments, or resources could be useful at this point? What is her prognosis?

Mrs. Jones does not seem to be handling the move from New York to Los Angeles well. She also appears to be struggling with the transition from independent living at home to an apartment and misses the independence of having an automobile. Her health setback raises worries about other potential losses and she raises the fear of dementia and of nursing home placement. Her daughter may have her hands full with a young family and she receives limited help from her brothers, so family tensions may be running high. Her daughter is experiencing her own level of caregiver burden and stress, and while thinking she is coming up with solutions and recommendations, she may be overstepping her bounds of authority and role by insisting that her mother not drive and that her mother move to another living arrangement.

While not a crisis per se, the situation presents several needs and areas of concern to prioritize. First and foremost is the issue of patient safety, which has medical, psychiatric, and social components. One question is whether the patient is capable of being managed as an outpatient, which requires that she be able on her own or with additional supervision to attend to her basic needs. Her medical problems appear stable but do require consistent taking of medication and regular medical follow-up. Her understanding of this should be confirmed. If warranted, a visiting nurse can stop by and assess the home for safety and patient compliance. However, given the patient's despair and distress, the question of depression must be formally assessed prior to her discharge. A psychiatric consultation in hospital or soon after could be useful. If she is actively suicidal, outpatient management may not be possible without adequate supervision and follow-up. Options to review with the patient and family include inpatient psychiatric hospitalization, medication for depression, and psychotherapy to help her through unresolved bereavement and grief over the losses of her spouse, independence, home, and self-image. The family can also benefit from counseling to help adjust to their new roles and responsibilities. In particular, the family must appreciate that, absent a determination of incapability or finding of incompetence, their mother must be offered an opportunity to make choices and to participate in her own care. Finally, the patient and family may benefit from referral to social work to explore community, hospital day, and senior center programs.

Late-life depression is quite treatable as long as it is identified. While Mrs. Jones has many reasons to be depressed and several of her medical problems presented with symptoms similar to those of depression, she persists with complaints and sadness even after medical care. Her worries about cognitive dysfunction are very common, especially with the lapses demonstrated. She and the family should be reassured that there were other explanations for her confusion and memory complaints and that a thorough medical review, exam, and laboratory screen revealed no evidence for another cause. Thus, dementia appears unlikely. With adequate treatment and monitoring, once her depression improves and she settles into a new and normal routine, she can expect to live life happily, enjoying her grandchildren, learning new hobbies, volunteering, and making new friends.

SUGGESTED READINGS

Butler, R.N., Lewis, M.I., & Sunderland, T. (1998). *Aging and mental health: Positive psychosocial and biomedical approaches* (5th ed.). Boston, MA: Allyn and Bacon.
This book provides a clear overview of evaluation and interventions for mental health issues presenting in aging patients.

Coffey, C.E., & Cummings, J.L. (2000). *The American Psychiatric Press textbook of geriatric neuropsychiatry* (2nd ed.). Washington, DC: American Psychiatric Press.
This textbook, edited by two prominent experts in neuropsychiatry of the elderly, provides a comprehensive overview of current knowledge in this area.

Hayslip, B., & Panek, P.E. (2002). *Adult development and aging* (3rd ed.). Malabar, FL: Krieger.
This book provides an excellent overview of aging from a developmental rather than pathological perspective.

Sadavoy, J., Jarvik, L.F., Grossberg, G.T., & Meyers, B.S. (2004). *Comprehensive textbook of geriatric psychiatry* (3rd ed.). New York: Norton.
Edited by leaders in geriatric psychiatry, this book provides a detailed guide to the current research, evaluations, and interventions in the field.

6 Death, Dying, and Grief

John E. Ruark

> Death has to be waiting at the end of the ride before you truly see the earth, and feel your heart, and love the world.
>
> JEAN ANOUILH
>
> The right to happiness is fundamental.
> We live so little time and die alone.
>
> BERTOLT BRECHT

Less than a century ago physicians had little to offer beyond simple supportive care for most life-threatening medical conditions, and the processes that caused human illness, suffering, and death were largely mysterious. Most of the physician's art consisted of comfort and palliation in the face of disease processes that would run their courses regardless of the efforts of those attempting to treat them. *In all but the most recent history of medicine, physicians have regarded death less as an opponent to be ceaselessly fought than as a colleague to be welcomed*—a humane and kindly collaborator who could place a final limit on human suffering. Nineteenth century medical texts even referred to pneumonia as "the old man's friend" that brought a relatively painless end to lives that had lost their quality.

Times have changed to an amazing degree. At present it is only at the literal end of life that medicine has no life-extending treatment to offer. From relatively simple interventions, such as antibiotics, diuretics, corticosteroids, and pressors, through transplant technologies involving every vital organ system outside the central nervous system, to mechanical devices replacing (at least temporarily) all of the nonnervous vital functions, it is almost always possible to buy some additional amount of life until the actual moment of total body failure. However, the quality of the life so purchased, and the cost paid in suffering, human effort, and money to achieve it, must be questioned. Our plane-tary resources are rapidly becoming insufficient to provide even the most basic needs for one third of the earth's inhabitants, and people are more aware of the trade-off between quality and quantity of life. We can no longer thoughtlessly do whatever is technically possible to address every pathophysiological problem for every patient. This chapter addresses some basic facts about death, dying, and grieving to assist physicians in dealing more thoughtfully and appropriately with issues surrounding death.

DEATH AT THE BEGINNING OF THE TWENTY-FIRST CENTURY

Life Expectancy

At the beginning of the twentieth century the life expectancy from birth for the average American was about 49 years. *Advances in public health and medical technology have since increased life expectancy to 77.4 years in 2002, when women lived 79.9 years, and men 74.7.* Such advances spawn the hope that eventually we may vanquish death totally. However, life expectancy from age 75 years increased only 3 years during the last century, and normal deteriorations in important body functions threaten life by the mid-eighties. In the absence of such fundamental breakthroughs as the resetting of a genetically programmed "aging clock," *even with optimal medical care we can hope for a life span of only 85 years, with a standard deviation of about 5 years.*

> A good physician appreciates the difference between postponing death and prolonging the act of dying.
>
> "MINERVA"
> Contemporary British medical columnist (*BMJ*)

In the depth of his heart he knew he was dying, but not only was he not accustomed to the thought, he simply did not and could not grasp it.

The syllogism he had learnt from Kiezewetter's Logic: "Caius is a man, men are mortal, therefore Caius is mortal," had always seemed to him correct as applied to Caius, but certainly not as applied to himself. That Caius—man in the abstract—was mortal, was perfectly correct, but he was not Caius, not an abstract man, but a creature quite, quite separate from all others. He had been little Vanya, with a mamma and a papa, with Mitya and Volodyn, with the toys, a coachman and a nurse, afterwards with Katenka and with all the joys, griefs, and delights of childhood, boyhood, and youth. What did Caius know of the smell of that striped leather ball Vanya had been so fond of? Had Caius kissed his mother's hand like that, and did the silk of her dress rustle so for Caius? Had he rioted like that at school when the pastry was bad? Had Caius been in love like that? Could Caius preside at a session as he did? "Caius really was mortal, and it was right for him to die; but for me, little Vanya, Ivan Ilyich, with all my thoughts and emotions, it's altogether a different matter. It cannot be that I ought to die. That would be too terrible."

LEO TOLSTOY
The Death of Ivan Ilyich and Other Stories

Advances in preventive medicine and new treatments for conditions currently disabling the elderly are likely to result in a **compression of morbidity** into the last few years of most people's lives in the next century.

Many patients think that life is virtually over once they are in their sixties. However, *the average 65-year-old woman can expect to live another 19.5 years and the average 65-year-old man another 16.6 years.* Although early death causes a large reduction in the life expectancy from birth, adult patients can expect far more life than simple examination of total life expectancies might indicate. The physician's advice to elderly patients should reflect this reality, especially since the "use it or lose it" dictum has been so well demonstrated in medical practice. We should encourage the elderly to maintain active lives as long as possible and to plan for much longer lives than simple life expectancies from birth would indicate.

Location of Death

In 1900, more than 80% of people died in their homes, and a large fraction of those dying in institutions had tuberculosis, a disease for which isolation was the only known public health measure. *The opposite is now the case, with more than 80% of people dying in institutional settings.* Although the **hospice movement** and the extreme costs of institutional care are motivating some persons toward dying at home, most Americans can expect to die in an institution. This is

one reason that the attitudes and efforts of health-care personnel have such a critical effect on the dying process.

Any human service involving an institution requires a compromise between values dictated by the well-being of the individual served and values dictated by the requirements of the service institution. This inherent conflict of interest is most evident in institutions providing care to the critically and terminally ill. Federal and third-party funding seldom suffices to support optimal care, and many of these institutions, especially those providing chronic care, have significant limitations in number, training, and quality of staff. Thus, it is not surprising that a majority of patients would prefer to die at home rather than in an institutional setting. If physicians work to promote their patients' interests above those of the institution, they can have a profound impact on the experience of dying patients and their families.

Definition of Death

The definition of death is surprisingly unclear. Before the last few centuries, death was defined by the absence of the most obvious evidence of life: breathing. The fundamental nature of the **pulmonary definition** of death is apparent in such phrases as his or her "last gasp" or "the patient has expired." The **pulmonary definition** of death was more widely used than the **cardiac definition,** because the pulse is slightly harder to observe than respiration; however, with the evolution of the stethoscope, emphasis shifted to auscultation of the heart as the final arbiter of the presence or absence of life. The development of the electrocardiogram led the determination of death even further into the technological era. The ability to artificially maintain cardiopulmonary function shifted the focus to a **neurological definition,** and the electroencephalogram became the ultimate criterion of death. The concept of "brain death" became particularly critical with the evolution of transplant technologies enabling the replacement of hearts and lungs. Currently a presidential commission has set uniform criteria for the definition of death that are listed in Table 6.1.

TABLE 6.1 Criteria for establishing death

1. Unreceptivity and unresponsiveness, even to intensely painful stimuli
2. No movement or spontaneous respiration for 3 minutes after being removed from a respirator
3. Complete absence of reflexes, both deep tendon and central
4. A flat electroencephalogram for at least 10 minutes of technically adequate recording, without response to noise or painful stimuli
5. All of the above tests repeated in 24 hours with no change
6. No history of hypothermia or use of central nervous system depressants before onset of coma

> What is the worst of woes that wait on age?
> What stamps the wrinkle deeper on the brow?
> To view each loved one blotted from life's page
> And be alone on earth, as I am now.
>
> BYRON
> *Childe Harold*

Although the neurological definition of death has been useful, it is far from perfect. It is not uncommon for disruptions of circulation or oxygenation of the brain to destroy large areas of the cerebral cortex while preserving function in the midbrain and brain stem. These types of patients do not meet the criteria in Table 6.1, but meaningful life clearly has ended. This situation illustrates the need for an expansion of the concept of brain death into a more realistic **neocortical definition**, because it is well-established that *most of the functions that give life meaning depend on the integrity of the neocortex.* As demonstrated by the recent **Schiavo case**, this issue remains fraught with controversy, though more for political and religious than medical reasons.

Causes of Death

An examination of the principal causes of death in 1900 compared with 2002 reveals some interesting trends. In 1900 the three leading causes of death were influenza and pneumonia, tuberculosis, and gastroenteritis (accounting for 31.4% of all deaths), followed by cardiovascular disease (14.2%). In 2002 cardiovascular disease was the leading cause of death, responsible for 28% of all deaths, followed by cancer (23%) and stroke (7%). At the turn of the century *infectious* disease was the most likely killer; currently, even in the era of AIDS, *degenerative* diseases end most lives. *Advances in public health, antisepsis, and antibiotics have resulted in a situation in which infectious diseases kill primarily persons with compromised immune systems, the elderly, or the chronically ill.* The resulting increased life span has brought us to the limits of the circulatory system, and its failures account for half of all current deaths. Modern death is much more likely to result from chronic wear and tear or abuse of the body than from an acute attack by an external pathogen.

It is disturbing to note that **suicide** is included in the list of the top 11 causes of death. It is also ironic that the danger of dying by gunshot is far greater in modern America than it was in the Wild West. It is particularly troublesome to discover that suicide is the third leading cause of death among Americans 15 to 24-years-old, accounting for 12% of deaths in that group. Health professionals should be particularly careful in investigating depression in young patients, and *physicians must openly and diligently pursue suicidal thoughts or plans when evaluating a distraught young*

That Which I Should Have Done I Did Not Do *(1931–1941) Ivan Le Lorraine Albright, 1897–1983.* Oil on canvas, 246.4 × 91.4 cm, Mary and Leigh Block Charitable Fund, 1955. Copyright © The Art Institute of Chicago. All rights reserved. *Physicians can encourage family members to express love and deal with unresolved family issues while there is still time.*

person. Threats or gestures should be taken seriously, and errors should be made on the side of being overly conservative to ensure the safety of such individuals.

DYING

Thoughts and Fears About Death

We think about death in three sharply divided ways: impersonal, interpersonal, and intrapersonal. The **impersonal** death is the death of the stranger, whose death does not touch us personally. We can read the reports of casualties from wars or natural disasters without paralyzing horror because our minds do not allow these deaths to become real. We refuse to consider seriously the possibility that events this horrible could happen to us. The terrorist attacks of September 11, 2001 have challenged this defense for many Americans.

When we lose someone who matters to us, we shift to the **interpersonal** manner of thinking about death. When myriad experiences with another individual are part of the fabric of our lives, the loss of that person constitutes a disruption of some part of ourselves. The degree to which each loss affects us parallels the importance of the deceased person's role in our lives.

Patients and families who have lost a loved one often feel alienated by the perceived impersonal attitude of professionals. This is unfortunate and ironic, because most people who enter the health-care field do so because people *matter* to them. We do ourselves and our patients a service when we can clearly communicate this caring. *Contrary to the advice of some authors, I believe physicians, nurses, and other health-care providers should strive to make each death with which they are closely involved an interpersonal rather than an impersonal one.* The necessary delicate balance involves letting each death be personal enough so that we can be emotionally connected to patients and families but not so personal that our professional judgment is compromised. The ability to strike this balance consistently is one of the characteristics of truly gifted practitioners. Patients and families recognize and respond to our personal involvement, as recognized over a century ago by William Osler, who said "Patients don't care how much you know until they know how much you care."

> The whole of his life had prepared Podduyev for living, not for dying.
>
> ALEXANDER SOLZHENITSYN
> *Cancer Ward*

The concept of **intrapersonal death** is perhaps the most crucial concept for health professionals to grasp. The available evidence suggests that *death anxiety is significantly higher in those who choose a career in medicine than in others who choose similarly intellectually challenging fields.* Particularly for physicians, the thought of confronting our own mortality may be overwhelming, and the belief that "knowledge is power" may have unconsciously motivated many of us to seek careers in a field that fosters the illusion of power over death. Perhaps this accounts for the frequency with which physicians collude with or even press for inappropriate persistence in efforts to cure obviously terminal conditions. It also may lead to the tendency toward emotional aloofness around critical illness that patients find alienating. Those of us who care for patients confronting death are ethically bound to face the issue of our own death and to achieve enough internal peace that we are confident that our own anxiety is not affecting patient care.

The Dying Process

Since the publication of Kübler-Ross's book *On Death and Dying,* popular attention has been increasingly focused on issues surrounding death. This work, along with Waugh's *The Loved One* and Mitford's *The American Way of Death,* made death an acceptable topic of conversation and study in the 1960s. Kübler-Ross's work should be required reading for anyone entering a health profession, and it remains worthwhile reading for all educated adults.

One of the key concepts Kübler-Ross introduced was that of **stages of dying**. Although she presented them with appropriate disclaimers as to the unpredictability of their order or importance in any particular case, her stages have become more of a law than she intended. These stages are as follows:
1. Denial
2. Anger
3. Bargaining
4. Depression
5. Acceptance

Kübler-Ross's first stage of dying is denial. **Denial** is a primary primitive defense mechanism and is a predictable reaction to sudden overwhelming news of any sort. Patients or family members may manifest this response in ways ranging from shocked rejection of the physician's "verdict" to complete repression of any memory of the conversation in which they were confronted with the likelihood of death. Most patients seem to experience such responses fairly often during a terminal illness. *It is not useful to challenge the patient each time denial occurs; in fact, the response may be adaptive, and sometimes a few moments or hours of denial affords a vital respite from an overwhelmingly negative reality.* It is only when denial becomes *dysfunctional,* when it leads to poor decisions or family problems, that it requires confrontation. When such problems arise, careful exploration of the inner logic motivating denial will often be valuable to patients by enabling their emotional adaptation to impending death.

Anger, the second of Kübler-Ross's stages, is as ubiquitous as denial among terminal patients. It is an equally natural response to the threat against personal integrity posed by our own critical illness or that of a loved one. Unfortunately, it is also an emotion with which few of us are comfortable (either in ourselves or in others), and health professionals receive little training in managing anger. *The key to handling patients' or family members' anger successfully in terminal care settings is simple: Let it be.* If anger is viewed as the individual's natural response to unmet needs for protection or nurturance, we can see that the critically ill have a right to be angry. We should assume that our patients' anger is valid, regardless of the inappropriateness with which it is expressed. Clinicians will be most effective if they remain nondefensive while conducting thoughtful inquiry into how they might more fully meet the needs of patients and families.

> One cannot help a man to come to accept his impending death if he remains in severe pain, one cannot give spiritual counsel to a woman who is vomiting, or help a wife and children say their good-byes to a father who is so drugged that he cannot respond.
>
> MARY BAINES
> Palliative care physician

Bargaining, the third of Kübler-Ross's stages, consists of an effort to retain at least the illusion of control in a situation in which one is powerless. Manifestations range from vows to survive only until a personal landmark or anniversary, such as a graduation, to deals with physicians to accept treatments only under certain circumstances. *The physician who can accept bargains that do not substantially compromise patient care can ameliorate the sense of powerlessness that inevitably accompanies life-threatening illnesses.*

The fourth of Kübler-Ross's stages is **depression,** which is as universal among terminal patients as denial and anger. Any psychologically healthy individual is bound to experience depression at times during the course of a terminal illness. However, *the clinician must distinguish between this normal mood variation and a more serious clinical depression that demands medical intervention.* The latter is characterized by **neurovegetative symptoms,** which are disturbances of the functions necessary to maintain life and requires pharmacological intervention as the standard of care. However, disturbances of sleep, appetite, and libido are difficult to assess in critically ill patients, especially in the hospital. It is somewhat easier to assess **anhedonia** (the inability to experience pleasure from usually pleasurable stimuli) and **psychomotor retardation** (especially increased speech latency). Special care must be taken when using any psychoactive chemical in patients with complicated medical conditions.

In my clinical practice with dying patients, I am too often dismayed by the degree to which physicians and medical institutions seem to forget that the limited moments left are precious. Given how destructive untreated clinical depression can be to quality of life, it is particularly important to treat this condition in terminally ill patients.

Kübler-Ross's final stage is **acceptance** of death. She points out that *most patients fail to achieve a truly clearheaded acceptance of their death.* What appears to be a state of acceptance is often a combination of exhaustion and advancing organic brain dysfunction. A sense of resignation that death must be preferable to persisting in a painful and futile struggle is common as vital energy wanes and death approaches. This is not to say that certain rare patients cannot uplift everyone around them with the nobility and serenity with which they face their own deaths.

Weisman has addressed the issue of coping with dying by defining his own phases of dying. His phases roughly parallel those of Kübler-Ross and include:

1. **Existential plight** at the confrontation of an individual's own mortality
2. **Mitigation and accommodation** of an individual's illness and its treatments
3. **Decline and deterioration** of an individual's physical and mental abilities as the illness advances
4. **Preterminality and terminality** in which waning physical powers increasingly dictate quality of life

> But when all usefulness is over, when one is assured of an unavoidable and imminent death, it is the simplest of human rights to choose a quick and easy death in place of a slow and horrible one.
>
> CHARLOTTE PERKINS STETSON GILMAN
> US writer on social and economic subjects

My experience involves many thousands of hours of contact with dying patients over the last 28 years. I have found that *most individuals alternate between denial and acceptance of their conditions.* The tenor of each person's reaction to the first revelation of a life-threatening condition tends to be repeated with subsequent recurrences or exacerbations of the illness. Furthermore, the historical reactions of a patient to losses or threats earlier in life provide valuable clues as to how that individual will cope with the challenge of a life-threatening illness.

> Euthanasia is a long, smooth-sounding word, and it conceals its danger as long, smooth words do, but the danger is there, nevertheless.
>
> PEARL S. BUCK
> *The Child Who Never Grew*

Protecting Patient Rights During Terminal Illness

When patients become terminally ill, particularly if they are not medically sophisticated, issues of **informed consent** and the protection of individual rights become particularly critical. Since many professionals are unaware of the exact rights their patients have, it is important to summarize relevant portions of the **Patient's Bill of Rights**, as promulgated by the American Hospital Association and enacted into law in most states.

The most important patient right is the right to receive *considerate and respectful care.* If this right is thoughtfully maintained, all of the others follow directly from it. The second right is to receive *information about the illness,* its treatment, and its likely outcome, in a language patients can understand. The third right involves *informed consent;* patients are entitled to information about proposed treatments or procedures, their potential risks and benefits, and the risks and benefits of reasonable alternative treatments, including no treatment at all. The fourth right is the right to *active participation in decisions* regarding medical care, including the right to refuse any or all treatments. The last right is the right to *transfer all of the previously mentioned rights* to a legal surrogate if an individual should become incompetent to make decisions for himself or herself. If these rights are thoughtfully preserved, it is hard to go too

> I take it that no man is educated who has never dallied with the thought of suicide.
>
> WILLIAM JAMES
> US psychologist

far wrong.

Health-care professionals can provide invaluable support for patients and families as they deal with terminal illness. The primary way in which we can be helpful is by actively supporting patients or their legal surrogates in exercising authority over their medical care. *Physicians should regard themselves as consultants employed to advise patients of their options regarding medical problems; they can assume authority only after it is explicitly granted.* We are also wise to reconfirm major decisions periodically even when we have been given authority to decide.

Support is also possible through communication. Physicians are responsible not only for attempting to communicate but also for ensuring that the communication necessary to foster optimal decision-making takes place. Important discussions should be held in a private, comfortable environment. We should anticipate that the stress of the situation may impair reasoning, and simple language is often adequate and usually more effective. Expression of questions and feel-

> Medicine cures the man who is fated not to die.
>
> Chinese proverb

ings should be actively encouraged, because many people are intimidated by physicians and hospitals. Given the multicultural complexity of many patient care settings, clinicians must learn to take culture and ethnicity effectively into account in order to achieve adequate communication. Patients or surrogates should be asked periodically to summarize what they have heard so the professional can check the accuracy of communication and correct any misconceptions. Finally, professionals should make specific efforts to sharpen their communication skills. These skills are crucial to medical practice, but they are seldom systematically taught.

The final principle in the protection of the rights of patients in medical crises is the important concept of **proportionality**. Proportional treatment is that which, *in the view of the patient,* has a reasonable chance of providing benefits that outweigh its attendant burdens. *Although the issue of costs and benefits is present throughout medical practice, it is especially significant in the context of life-threatening illness.* The intensity of interventions required to treat many serious conditions is great enough that quality of life, if not life itself, can be significantly endangered by treatment. It is vital that patients, not professionals or family members, ultimately answer these difficult questions. *Physicians tend to be invested in fighting and curing disease, and family members tend to be invested in anything that offers hope of holding on to their loved ones. These forces militate against the best interests of the patient in many critical-care settings.* Thus, the explicit early determination and ongoing review of each patient's views about proportionality are vital to optimal management of life-threatening conditions. Physicians must be candid in presenting realistic assessments of likely benefits and costs of proposed interventions. Previous decisions must be reassessed with major clinical changes, because each patient's willingness to fight can change with advancing debilitation or realization of the limited likelihood of an absolute cure. In short, *physicians should seek to prolong useful living as defined by the patient.* Medical intervention not guided by this principle may serve only to prolong the dying process, which is generally undignified and painful for all involved.

The recent **Terri Schiavo** case highlights a few important issues surrounding the end of life. First of all, the absence of any legally recognized documentation expressing her wishes, termed an "advanced directive," set up a potential for the unfortunate events that followed. Second, the lack of a professionally guided process between her loved ones toward achieving consensus about her wishes and who was empowered to represent her made the resulting conflict almost inevitable. Most critical-care facilities have trained

The Wisdom of WILLIAM SHAKESPEARE, 1564–1616

Our remedies oft in ourselves do lie,
Which we ascribe to heaven.
All's Well That Ends Well

Last scene of all,
That ends this strange eventful history,
Is second childishness and mere oblivion,
Sans teeth, sans eye, sans taste, sans everything.
As You Like It

By medicine life may be prolonged, yet death will seize the doctor too.
Cymbeline

To sleep–perchance to dream: ay, there's the rub!
For in that sleep of death what dreams may come.
When we have shuffled off this mortal coil.
Must give us pause.
Hamlet

It is not strange that desire should so many years outlive performance?
Henry IV, Part II

It provokes the desire, but it takes away the performance. Therefore much drink may be said to be an equivocator with lechery.
Macbeth

Macduff was from his mother's womb
Untimely ripp'd.
Macbeth

personnel who can be called in to facilitate a humane negotiation that can avoid such fiascoes.

GRIEF AND MOURNING

Human life consists of a never-ending process of coming into and out of relationship with everything in our world. The possessions we hoard, the youth we covet, the food, water, and air we consume, and even the molecules that compose us are with us only transiently. This is most poignantly true of the people we love. Those who master efficient and effective ways to gracefully let go of that which they are losing are enabled to find renewed vitality in new attachments. Grief and mourning are the natural emotional healing mechanisms that restore our ability to enjoy life after any serious loss.

The loss of a loved one constitutes the greatest challenge to human coping that most of us face short of, perhaps, our

own death. The psychological processes that lead to eventual resolution of bereavement are vital to mental and emotional health and the resumption of useful functioning. These processes begin with **grief**, which we define as a *clinical syndrome* characterizing the acute psychological and physiological reaction of human beings to significant losses. It is useful to regard grief as the initial phase of a more global phenomenon of **mourning**, defined as a complex *intrapsychic process* in which a person withdraws attachment from a lost object and works through the emotional pain and injury of that loss.

Although grief and mourning are eloquently described in literature dating at least as far back as Homer, systematic attempts at understanding these processes began in 1917 with Sigmund Freud, who posited that grief required an investment of emotional energy (**libido**) in the lost object. Mental health and intrapsychic stability could not be restored until this attachment was withdrawn, an inherently painful process. Uncomplicated mourning proceeds when the reality of the loss is increasingly accepted and the bereaved person is gradually able to let go of memories and expectations attached to the deceased person. Pathological grief occurs when the bereaved person is unable to fully comprehend or work through the loss.

Bowlby explained grief and mourning in terms of a phenomenon he called **attachment behavior**, that is, any behavior that results in attaining or retaining closeness to a preferred individual. Many of the most intense human emotions arise as a result of the formation, maintenance, and disruption of these bonds ("falling in love," "being in love," and "mourning"). Thus, **separation anxiety** may be the basis of grief and leads to efforts to regain the lost object. Rage and frustration are likely to persist among mourners until emotional nurturance becomes available through new attachments to replace what was lost.

More psychologically mature defense mechanisms, such as **identification**, that provide a link to the lost loved one may bring comfort during the process of reattachment to a new object. We see identification in action when bereaved persons wear clothing or adopt mannerisms belonging to the deceased. More primitive defense mechanisms, such as **introjection** (the wholesale enactment of traits of a lost loved one), may cause problems because new sources of emotional attachment can be unconsciously regarded as threats to the life of the internalized lost person. An extreme cinematic example of introjection would be the character of Norman Bates in Alfred Hitchcock's *Psycho*. Persons who have experienced

Body and mind, like man and wife, do not always agree to die together.

CHARLES CALEB COLTON
English clergyman, sportsman, author and suicide
Lacon

difficulties with attachments and losses can be anticipated to continue to have problems of this sort with each new mourning process, and they are likely to require professional assistance to cope with the period of mourning.

Grief

Erich Lindemann conducted a systematic examination of acute grief in his study of the survivors of the Coconut Grove fire in Boston, and his description of the acute grief syndrome remains a classic. Common symptoms of grief Lindemann observed included sensations of somatic distress that came in waves at least hourly, tightness in the throat, choking, shortness of breath, sighing, sensations of abdominal emptiness, muscular weakness, and intense emotional distress best characterized as **psychic pain**. The syndrome also included a sense of unreality, gastrointestinal complaints, preoccupation with the deceased, emotional distance from others, guilt, irritability, and anger. *Lindemann concluded that the five basic pathognomonic symptoms of grief included somatic distress, preoccupation with the deceased, guilt, hostility, and the loss of habitual patterns of conduct.* He observed that within 4 to 6 weeks, given optimal emotional support, the acute grief reaction could be settled for most people; however, this adjustment required the resolution of the conflict between the desire to remain attached to the lost person and reality testing that confirmed the loss.

Practicing health professionals need to appreciate that human beings are innately endowed with the resources necessary to negotiate all of the expectable traumas of life, including grief and mourning. Barring psychological de-

I am not mad: this hair I tear is mine;
My name is Constance; I was Jeffrey's wife;
Young Arthur is my son, and he is lost:
I am not mad: I would to heaven I were!
For then, 'tis like I should forget myself:
O, if I could, what grief should I forget!
Preach some philosophy to make me mad,
And thou shalt be canonized, cardinal;
For being not mad but sensible of grief,
My reasonable part produces reason
How I may be deliver'd of these woes,
And teaches me to kill or hang myself:
If I were mad, I should forget my son,
Or madly think a babe of clouts were he:
I am not mad; too well, too well I feel
The different plague of each calamity.

WILLIAM SHAKESPEARE
King John
Act III, Scene IV

velopmental injuries, such as the sort of childhood physical or psychological abuse or deprivation that often accompanies personality disorders, most people are able to resolve acute grief if they have adequate emotional support. Such support involves validation of the strong primary emotions (anger, grief, terror) of the acutely bereaved and avoidance of psychochemical suppression of these feelings, even when they are disruptive to routine medical practice.

Health professionals are likely to be the targets of free-floating anger associated with normal grief. If we can nondefensively accept this rage, reflecting only how frustrating it must be for the bereaved to encounter how little power we actually have over death, we can continue to meet the needs of our patients and ourselves. The healthiest message we can send to the majority of patients encountering acute grief and mourning is that we are there to support them in the completion of a normal process that requires them to experience many uncomfortable feelings. Patients should be encouraged to rely on both professional and proven nonprofessional sources of emotional support to get them through this difficult period.

Mourning

John Bowlby divides the mourning process into three phases that occur after the resolution of the acute grief reaction. These phases parallel the reactions of the dying described by Kübler-Ross and Weisman; in many ways the dying person is simply mourning the loss of the whole world. Bowlby's first phase is **protest**, a period characterized by spontaneous reactions of disbelief focused on the deceased. Bereaved persons may cling tenaciously to thoughts of the deceased and may direct strong anger or despair toward the deceased and others. Particular anger may focus on those who encourage the bereaved to let go of the deceased and to resume normal life. This anger may disrupt important relationships at exactly the worst time, resulting in dangerous isolation for mourners.

Bowlby's initial phase of protest is followed by a period of **despair**. This period is usually precipitated by the intuitive realization that the deceased person is indeed lost. Free-floating anxiety and depression tend to overwhelm any compulsive activity that may have allowed the bereaved person to tolerate the previous reactions. Indeed, it may be that this disintegration, marking the abandonment of patterns centering on the deceased, is a necessary prelude to the development of new and more viable structures leading to eventual resolution of the loss.

The final phase of mourning that Bowlby characterizes is **detachment**. In this phase the personality of the bereaved is reorganized in such a way that the emotions that previously focused on the deceased are reoriented toward other people or activities. This process eventually leads to the res-

So death, the most terrifying of ills, is nothing to us, since so long as we exist, death is not with us; but when death comes, then we do not exist. It does not then concern either the living or the dead, since for the former it is not, and the latter are no more.

EPICURUS
Greek philosopher

olution of serious interpersonal losses, and the bereaved individual is able to resume a more satisfying life.

Parkes studied the process of normal bereavement and reached a number of important conclusions. He observed that the usual period of protest lasts a few months and usually resolves, in the absence of grief pathology, within the course of the first year. He also observed that inhibited feelings associated with grief and mourning tend to be more intense and difficult to manage when they finally surface. Loneliness, sadness, anger, despair, and reactive depression constitute natural and appropriate responses to any serious loss. Those who do not experience these emotions may be ignoring a vital biological imperative and may be exposed to far-reaching and potentially devastating consequences.

Physician consultations, physical illnesses, hospitalizations, and physiological abnormalities all increase significantly during bereavement. Furthermore, increased mortality has been demonstrated in many instances, sometimes exceeding the mortality rates of age- and health-matched nonbereaved cohorts by a factor of five or more. Parkes summed up these findings in his poignant description of the **broken heart phenomenon**, observing that *heart disease caused three fourths of bereavement-associated early mortality.*

In conclusion, it is clear from the literature that widowers and widows are more likely than their cohorts to seek medical help and that they are at greater risk for physical illness and death during the year after their loss. Not surprisingly, many studies reveal that the bereaved are also at greater risk for psychiatric illness.

Grief Pathology

Pathological variants of normal grief are quite common in medical practice. These variations include absence of grief, delayed grief, dysfunctional denial, the "manic escape," dysfunctional hostility, and clinical depression.

*The **absence of grief** phenomenon is particularly prevalent in death-denying cultures such as our own.* The grieving and mourning processes are inherently painful, and many people are reluctant to engage fully in them. This resistance is overcome in many cultures by institutionalized rituals surrounding death, and modern American culture is strikingly deficient in such supportive structures. Bereaved individu-

als should be supported in resisting social pressures that compel them to go on with life as if nothing had happened; however, many people in our culture continue to believe a person is "handling it well" if he or she is not making others uncomfortable by overt manifestations of distress.

Professionals should be alert to the absence of the signs of acute grief described previously, and gentle inquiries should be made within a few weeks if it appears that a bereaved person is not grieving. Many times the inquiry itself triggers a flood of emotion, but if not, counseling may be necessary. The main therapy for the absence of grief is the provision of a safe, supportive context in which bereaved persons are encouraged to express their sadness, despair, fear, and rage. Expert psychotherapy is required in the presence of more severe psychopathology, because supportive counseling alone is unlikely to be adequate.

The second most common form of grief pathology is **dysfunctional denial**. Although some denial is probably necessary for dealing with any catastrophic stress, dysfunctional denial interferes significantly with normal human function-

WHAT MATTERS
— for Eric

The nurse drifts in, checks
the level of the morphine drip.
We let our eyes wander to you
to the windowsill of poinsettias
framing the snowbound city below.
From the sink of white porcelain
to the field of white that covers
your body, uncomfortable in our comforting
because there is nothing more
for us to do now but attend.
We close our eyes, listen to you breathe.
Pause when you pause, linger over each
exhalation as if it were your last.
That you circled the world as a merchant
marine, spent seven years in a monastery,
raised show dogs and exotic birds,
no longer seems important.
What matters is now, this moment.
How quiet your room has become,
only the sound of the winter sun
streaming through the panes of glass.
We kiss your face, squeeze your hand;
hang on before we let go.

PETER PEREIRA

How do I help someone grieve?

Grieving is active. It is *work*. It requires remembering repetitively experiences shared with the dead person, over a long period of time; *talking about* and *expressing* the mixed emotional ties-particularly the anger, remorse, and sadness, perhaps, even relief-until the devastating potency of the loss is neutralized.

The most important balm a counselor can offer is presence and concern. *You are facilitating the grieving process by being there:* by listening, nonjudgmentally, and by reassuring the bereaved persons that they are not "going crazy." You can affirm that the acute pain they are experiencing is grief in process, and that it will not last forever.

1. Encourage the saying of goodbyes at the bedside, before death, whenever possible.
2. Encourage active participation in the care of the person dying, in being present at the moment of death, and even in preparing the body for burial. There is great solace in knowing "I was there and I did all that I could."
3. Encourage involvement with the mourning rituals of funeral, eulogy, celebration, and memorial services. Such rites provide outlets for the expression of sorrow and help delineate the grieving process. Viewing the dead body helps one accept the fact of death. Unveilings and anniversary rites also mark the progress of grief.
4. Listen, nonjudgmentally, realizing, as Samuel Coleridge's Ancient Mariner reminds us, that the albatross of grief falls off with retelling the story. Encourage reminiscences, the painful as well as the positive, and expression of the hostile, angry, and negative feelings that seem so incompatible with the genuine love for the dying or dead person. Again, offer reassurance that such ambivalence is normal.
5. Monitor your own feelings. You are not immune to sadness, anxiety, or the need to express personal concern. Your reactions are conditioned by your own experiences with earlier losses and by your ability to handle hostile reactions from those you are counseling: friend, patient, client, student, or family member.
6. Be informed about self-help support groups such as "Candlelighters," "Living with Cancer," "Sibs with Cancer," "People with AIDS," "Widow-to-Widow" and bereavement programs sponsored by churches, hospitals, hospices, and civic organizations in your community. Such groups assist in answering practical questions, in understanding feelings, in providing networks, and in enabling participants to reach out to others as they gain mastery in their own personal experiences.
7. Know when referral is necessary. You are in a good position to detect unresolved and complicated grief and pathological mourning and, when you suspect a severe problem, you should enlist additional psychotherapeutic help.

Grief is not a disease. It is love not wanting to let go. It can be likened to a "blow" or a cut in which the wound gradually heals. For a while, one is acutely vulnerable, physically and emotionally. Though grief can be temporarily disabling, working through it ultimately brings strength. Colin Murray Parkes sums it up nicely in his book, *Bereavement*, reminding us just as broken bones may knit together more strongly, so the experience of grieving can strengthen or mature those who have previously been shielded from misfortune: "The pain of grief is just as much a part of life as the joy of love; it is, perhaps, the price we pay for love, the cost of commitment. To ignore this fact ... is to put on emotional blinders which leave us unprepared for the losses that will inevitably occur in our own lives and unprepared to help others to cope with the losses in theirs."

---

ing. Both intrapersonal and environmental forces may conspire to encourage bereaved persons to deny the seriousness, or even the existence, of a major loss. Manifestations of dysfunctional denial range from reluctance to participate in rituals surrounding a death, to refusal to devote time or energy to the grieving process, to frank delusions that the death has not occurred. Gentle exploration of the patient's thoughts and feelings about the deceased is the most effective therapeutic approach. As this painstaking exploration proceeds, most patients without severe psychopathology are able to restore reality testing and move on with their grief.

A third type of grief pathology is termed the **manic escape**, characterized by the classic "merry widow," and marked by frenetic activity, often accompanied by an inappropriately cheerful demeanor. It may represent an attempt to regain at least the illusion of power over an overwhelming situation. The brittle quality of this defense is unmistakable and leaves the observer feeling that the bereaved would crumble if the defense was challenged. Therapy in-

volves gentle exploration of the loss and reflection of the feeling of powerlessness underlying the defense. Frequently exploration of the loss of control opens up more complex esteem and control issues relating to the deceased and the bereaved person's family of origin.

The next common grief pathology is **dysfunctional hostility**. Here again the term "dysfunctional" reflects the observation that significant hostility is normal in grief and mourning, and is pathological only when it interferes with essential functioning. In fact, *acknowledging and working through anger are two of the most important tasks in grief work*. However, when anger is poorly managed, it can drive away potential sources of support at exactly the wrong time. The anger in the grieving process is frustrating because its target is the deceased person, and yet most people have difficulty allowing their anger to consciously center on the deceased, so their rage is apt to be displaced toward less threatening targets. Given the negative associations most bereaved persons have with the failure of medical care to save their loved one, it is not surprising that physicians and nurses are particularly likely to come under fire in these situations. The key for therapy is validation of the rage, even when its manifestations are inappropriate and harmful. However, firm limits must be compassionately set against abusive expressions of rage, since they endanger patient care by alienating caregivers and increasing risk of professional burnout. Patients typically feel guilty about their irrational outbursts and seldom need chiding. The physician can give overt permission for anger directed at the caregivers or the deceased, and safe physical outlets can be encouraged for aggressive feelings.

Clinical depression is the final manifestation of grief pathology to be discussed. *The importance of a therapeutic alliance in treating clinical depression cannot be overemphasized.* All the medications for depression are fraught with side effects that often manifest most strongly before therapeutic benefits appear, and many of them are lethal in the hands of a suicidal patient. Frequently, the conviction that their physician is a competent, collaborative ally is sufficient to carry patients through the few weeks when the side effects of medication may offset the therapeutic benefits experienced from antidepressants.

Many of the grief pathologies described can be prevented if professionals encourage patients and families to support expression of the strong, often negative emotions of grief. Ongoing caring and contact initiated by the professional can often minimize pathological grief. However, it is usually the patient's support network that offers the greatest solace and comfort, and professionals should actively support this important safety net.

SUMMARY

In this chapter we have examined the inescapable medical reality of death from a variety of perspectives relevant to physicians in training. We began with a survey of the facts of death—when, where, and how it takes place for our patients (and for us!). Then we turned to the dying process, including how people think about it and fear it. Next we focused on the rights of patients during life-threatening illness and how physicians can and should act to safeguard these rights. Finally, we reviewed normal and pathological variants of the grief and mourning processes whereby people are enabled to recover from significant losses. If this material is incorporated and applied to interactions with patients facing death, the result will be a more humane and optimal experience for all concerned.

> Education never ends, Watson. It is a series of lessons with the greatest for the last.
>
> ARTHUR CONAN DOYLE
> *The Adventure of the Red Circle*

CASE STUDY

Mr. B was a 41-year-old married computer consultant with one preschool child who was referred for psychiatric evaluation by his hematologist during hospitalization for treatment of an acute myelogenous leukemia of ominous prognosis. The purpose of the referral was to assess for possible depression and to provide psychological support during a very arduous course of therapy. When I was called, Mr. B had been in the hospital for more than 4 weeks longer than expected because of complications that occurred when blood clots caused a series of intracardiac catheter failures. During the week before my consultation, the nurses and Mrs. B had observed Mr. B to become lethargic, less cooperative with vital self-care procedures, and alternatively withdrawn and uncharacteristically irritable.

After standard infection control procedures (scrubbing, gowning, gloving, and masking), I entered Mr. B's darkened room and introduced myself. I found a thin, tall, completely hairless man resting flat on his back in bed, who greeted me with reserve and apparent wariness. I asked him if he knew why I was there, and he said, "I guess they all think I'm crazy." I asked him what *he* thought, and he said, "I think I'm sick to death of this prison and everyone and everything connected with it." When I responded that based on what I had read in his chart I thought he would be more likely to be crazy if he *didn't* feel that way, he perceptibly relaxed and became more engaged in our conversation.

Can you determine which Kübler-Ross stage best describes this patient? How should a physician respond? What would happen if you confronted this patient and told him his anger was inappropriate?

In the next hour, Mr. B recounted with increasing energy his frustrations around this illness that had derailed what he termed his "perfect yuppie life." He focused a disproportionate wrath on minor technical errors by nurses, house officers, and surgical consultants, to which he inaccurately attributed the complications that had prolonged his hospitalization. I observed that it must be highly disturbing to have his life entrusted to people who demonstrated that they could make mistakes; he must feel even more out of control of a situation that makes most people feel extremely powerless. Once again an accurate **empathic reflection**, coupled with my failure to "rise to the bait" by defending the staff, caused a palpable increase in his energy and sense of engagement in our conversation. The foundation for a therapeutic alliance between us had been formed by my demonstration that I could find a sensible way to "be on his side" even when he was being critical of my friends and colleagues.

Mr. B and I explored the specific areas of his medical evaluation and treatment over which he felt the least control. Most of these centered around confusing or inadequate information which did not enable him to understand what was going on and why. Because I was familiar with his unit and the treatments and procedures it employed and had read his chart carefully, I was able to explain most of his concerns to his satisfaction and to refer him to specific persons for answers to the questions that exceeded my expertise.

This patient is potentially depressed. What symptoms will you want to assess before making a diagnosis?

We then moved on to examine issues more specific to the evaluation of depression: his personal and family psychiatric and medical histories and the details of his symptomatic response to his leukemia and its treatments. It became clear that although his sleep and appetite had been typically compromised during his hospitalization, Mr. B's enjoyment of his toddler son had persisted. He visibly brightened as he showed me pictures of his son and described their daily telephone conversations (which were the limit of their contacts because of infection control procedures). Likewise, he admitted that his interest in sex had persisted, and on direct inquiry, he admitted concerns that nurses might accidentally interrupt him while he was masturbating or when he and his wife were "cuddling." Finally, the increase in his animation and the enthusiasm with which he spoke during our conversation was inconsistent with a clinical depression. Thus, I was comfortable reassuring Mr. B's physicians that he would probably not benefit from a trial of antidepressants at that time.

Is sexual intimacy appropriate in a hospital? Would it be therapeutic in this case? Would you feel differently if the visitor was the patient's girlfriend rather than his wife?

Toward the end of our initial consultation, Mr. B responded with enthusiasm to my suggestion that I visit him every few days to help him deal with his situation on an ongoing basis. In these visits, in addition to providing a safe environment in which he could ventilate his frustrations and fears, we focused on areas of his treatment that he *could* control. These included my visits, which we decided would be left up to him to request (and which I always took pains to conduct at prearranged appointment times to support the belief that his time was as valuable as mine). Because his mental status could fluctuate at times as a result of infections, medications, or metabolic abnormalities, we always wrote down any specific plans or questions he wanted to pursue so that he would be more likely to remember them.

I continued to meet with Mr. B and his wife periodically throughout the remainder of his initial hospitalization and his subsequent bone marrow transplant. We also met in my office during times when he was out of the hospital, and on one occasion I mediated a conflict between Mr. B's mother and Mrs. B regarding the manner in which they were sharing the responsibility of supporting him in the hospital. As this patient's condition worsened, our therapeutic alliance enabled me to be helpful through each of the harrowing complications and medical decisions he and his wife had to face before his death.

SUGGESTED READINGS

Bertman, S.L. (1991). *Facing death: Images, insights, and interventions.* New York: Hemisphere.
This is a remarkable little book full of images, poems, and literary vignettes used by the author in her teaching and counseling as Director of the Program in Medical Humanities at the University of Massachusetts Medical Center.

Fries, J., & Crapo. L. (1981). *Vitality and aging.* San Francisco: Freeman.
Two distinguished geriatricians take a scholarly and practical look at the realities of life during advancing age.

Gonda, T. (1989). Death, dying, and bereavement. In H.I. Kaplan & B.J. Sadock (Eds.), *Comprehensive textbook of psychiatry,* (pp. 1339–1351). Baltimore: Williams & Wilkins.
One of the giants of modern thanatology in his last publication before his own death provides a coherent and accessible summary of the field.

Gonda, T., & Ruark J. (1984). *Dying dignified: The health professional's guide to care.* Reading, MA: Addison-Wesley.
This is a readable award-winning summary that applies theoretical concepts to the clinical realities of terminal care.

Kubler-Ross, E. (1969). *On death and dying.* New York: Macmillan.
This is a ground-breaking classic that first introduced America to the realities of death. The observations of this master clinician remain fresh, moving, and insightful.

Nuland, S. (1994). *How we die: Reflections on life's final chapter.* New York: Knopf.
A remarkable analysis of death written by a physician.

Psychiatric Annals. (1990). *20.*
This entire issue contains valuable updates by such leaders in thanatology as Parkes, Zisook, Schucter, and Rynearson. A concise review of the field by its key contributors.

Ruark, J., & Raffin, T. (1988). Initiating and withdrawing life support: Principles and practices in adult medicine. *New England Journal of Medicine, 318,* 25–30.
This position paper of the Stanford University Medical Ethics Committee garnered national attention as the first widely publicized guideline to ethical issues involved in life support. It remains a useful summary for practicing clinicians.

Spiegel, D. (1993). *Living beyond limits.* New York: Random House.
Based on voluminous research and clinical experience, this thorough and readable guide directed toward patients is also valuable for clinicians caring for those facing life-threatening illness.

7 Chronic Benign Pain

Laurence A. Bradley

> The greatest challenge of pain continues to be the patient who has received every known treatment yet continues to suffer.
>
> RONALD MELZACK and PATRICK D. WALL

THE CHALLENGE OF PAIN

Chronic benign pain is an important public health problem that produces enormous physical, emotional, and economic burdens for the patient, his or her family, and society. Precise epidemiological data for chronic pain are not available. However, the National Center for Health Statistics has reported that *80% (70 million) of all office visits to physicians each year in the United States are prompted by the experience of pain.*

In addition, approximately 11.7 million Americans are substantially impaired by pain, with 2.6 million temporarily disabled and 2.6 million permanently disabled by chronic pain. Indeed, chronic pain syndromes annually cost the country between $65 and $70 billion in lost work days, health-care costs, and payments for workers' compensation and litigation.

Chronic benign pain may be defined as any pain resulting from nonmalignant causes that is not alleviated by appropriate medical, pharmacotherapy, or surgical treatment. Since the early 1970s physicians have become increasingly aware that behavioral and psychological factors play an important role in the development and maintenance of chronic pain. *There is now widespread acceptance that physicians, behavioral scientists, and other health professionals must evaluate and treat chronic pain in an interdisciplinary manner to achieve optimal results.*

CONCEPTS OF PAIN

The International Association for the Study of Pain (IASP) has defined pain as "an unpleasant sensory and emotional experience associated with actual or potential tissue damage, or described in terms of such damage." This definition indicates that *pain is a subjective, personal experience that encompasses both sensory (e.g., pulling, burning, and aching) and emotional (e.g., anxiety and depression) qualities.* The definition also acknowledges that the intensity or aversiveness of the pain experienced by an individual is not necessarily related to the severity of tissue damage that person has incurred. There are some individuals who display unusual pain responses to very low levels of sensory input. For example, it is not surprising that patients with unilateral, end-stage **osteoarthritis** of the knee show very low thresholds for pain in response to pressure stimulation of the affected knee. It is unusual, however, that these patients also display low pressure pain thresholds in the healthy contralateral knee (i.e., mirror-image pain). In contrast, there are individuals with extensive tissue damage who report very low levels of pain, especially during exposure to highly stressful events. A brief review of the neural events involved in pain signalling and the inhibition of pain will aid our understanding of the factors that contribute to variations in pain perception among people as well as within the same individuals.

Classical View of Pain Signaling

Figures 7.1a and 7.1b illustrate the major neural events involved in pain signaling under usual conditions. Noxious sensory stimuli, such as heat, cold, or mechanical pressure, may activate nerve receptors and initiate the transmission of signals along afferent A-δ and C fibers to the dorsal horns of the spinal cord. These signals then excite second-

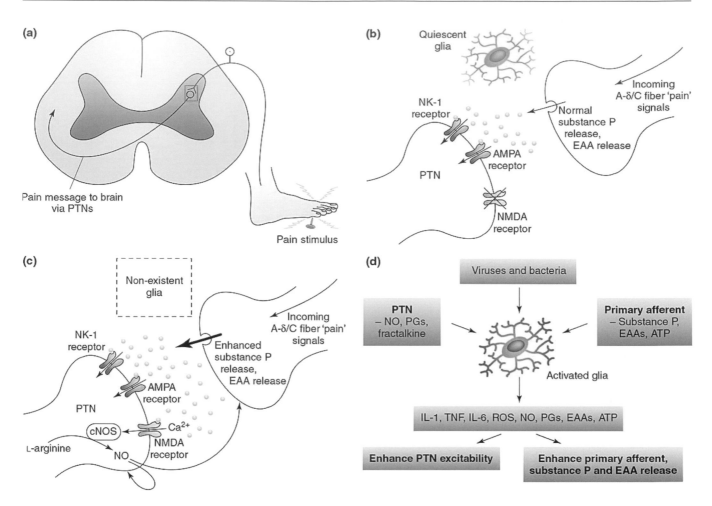

FIGURE 7.1 Illustrations of (A, B) classical view of pain signaling; (C) classical view of pathologic pain evoked by central sensitization; and (D) current view of pathologic pain. Note: EAA = excitatory amino acids; AMPA = alpha-amino-3-hydroxy-5-methylisoxazole-4-proprionic acid; PTN = second-order pain transmission neutron; ROS = reactive oxygen species; IL = interleukin; NOS = nitric oxide synthase; TNF = tumor necrosis factor. Reprinted from *Trends in Neurosciences* 24, Watkins LR, Milligan ED, Maier SF, Glial activation: a driving force for pathological pain, 450–455. Copyright © 2001, with permission from Elsevier.

ary neurons in the spinal dorsal horns through the release of several neurotransmitters. The main excitatory transmitter from the afferent fibers is glutamate, which acts on postsynaptic N-methyl-D-aspartate (NMDA) receptors of dorsal horn neurons. Other excitatory molecules include substance P and neurokinin A (NK), both of which act on postsynaptic NK receptors of the dorsal horn neurons, as well as calcitonin gene-related peptide (CGRP), nerve growth factor (NGF), and dynorphin A. The signals generated by the dorsal horn neurons are then transmitted to several brain regions (e.g., thalamus, somatosensory cortex, and limbic system) via their axons.

However, several factors may inhibit the transmission of these signals to the brain as well as the cortical and subcortical functions that process this input. These include descending input from brain stem sites to the spinal dorsal horns, environmental events (e.g., exposure to stressors), as well as physiological (e.g., genotype, neuroendocrine, and autonomic nervous system activity), cognitive (attention to

sensory events, memories of previous painful events), and affective (e.g., anxiety, depression) factors. Figure 7.2 illustrates the interactions between factors that promote and inhibit pain signaling and, thus, contribute to our perceptions and behavioral expressions of pain. These interactions also influence the stress-regulation functions of the central nervous system (CNS) including hypothalamic-pituitary-adrenal (HPA) axis activity, immune function, and the release of endorphins as well as proinflammatory and antiinflammatory cytokines in peripheral soft tissues and the CNS.

CNS Plasticity and Abnormal Pain Sensitivity

Some conditions characterized by chronic pain are produced both by pain signalling following tissue damage as

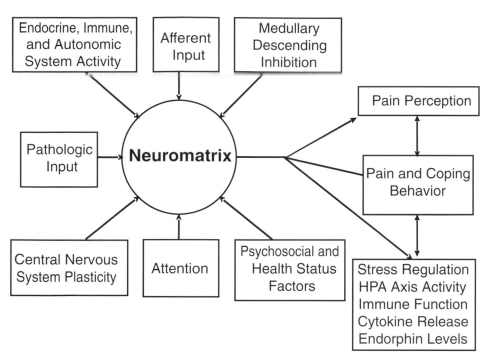

FIGURE 7.2 Model of the physiological and psychosocial factors that influence pain signaling and pain inhibition

well as by CNS plasticity, or persistent alterations in the function of neural pathways involved in pain transmission or inhibition. One important example of these alterations is termed **central sensitization**. This phenomenon is associated with several neuropathic pain syndromes conditions such as diabetic neuropathy and postherpetic neuralgia. Figure 7.1c shows that intense or prolonged nociceptive input from A-δ and C afferents may sufficiently depolarize the dorsal horn neurons that Mg^{2+} exits NMDA-linked ion channels. This is followed by an influx of extracellular Ca^{2+} and production of nitric oxide (NO), which diffuses out of the dorsal horn neurons. NO, in turn, promotes the exaggerated release of excitatory amino acids and substance P from presynaptic afferent terminals and causes the dorsal horn neurons to become hyperexcitable. As a consequence, low intensity stimulation of the skin or deep muscle tissue generates high levels of sensory input to the brain and the perception of intense and unpleasant pain. The pain associated with central sensitization may be diminished by treatment interventions that either reduce sensory input from A-δ and C afferents or enhance pain inhibitory functions of the CNS. For example, after recovery from total joint replacement surgery, persons with unilateral knee osteoarthritis experience substantial reductions in pain in the affected knee as well as elimination of abnormal pain sensitivity in the contralateral healthy knee. In addition, antidepressant medications that block reuptake of serotonin and norepinephrine frequently produce substantial reductions in pain associated with diabetic neuropathy or postherpetic neuralgia. Nevertheless, *there are a large number of chronic pain syndromes that are difficult to treat because we do not have interventions that will effectively reduce noxious sen-*

sory input or we do not completely understand the factors that generate this input (Kosek & Oderberg, 2002).

Recent evidence indicates that dorsal horn glia cells also play a role in producing and maintaining abnormal pain sensitivity. Figure 7.1d shows that synapses within the central nervous system are encapsulated by glia cells that normally do not respond to noxious sensory input. However, following the initiation of central sensitization, spinal glia cells may be activated by a wide array of factors that contribute to abnormal pain sensitivity such as immune activation within the spinal cord, substance P, excitatory amino acids, NO, and prostaglandins (PGs). Once activated, glia cells release several proinflammatory cytokines (e.g., TNF-α, IL-6, IL-1) and excitatory amino acids that, in turn, (1) further increase the release of excitatory amino acids and substance P from the A-δ and C afferents that synapse in the dorsal horn and (2) enhance the hyper-excitability of the dorsal horn neurons, Recent evidence also suggests that activated glia release neuroexcitatory substances in response to morphine, thereby opposing its analgesic effects. This phenomenon contributes to development of opioid tolerance and tolerance-related enhancement of pain (Watkins et al., 2005).

Inhibition of Pain Signaling

It was noted earlier that an array of biological, cognitive, affective, and environmental factors may inhibit pain signalling and the experience of pain. We already have described the beneficial effects of removing the source of noxious sensory input (e.g., total joint replacement) and the use of certain classes of antidepressant medications for patients with chronic pain associated with central sensitization. *It also is possible, however, to alter pain perception and behavior using psychosocial interventions.* For example, *hypnotic suggestions concerning alterations in the intensity or aversiveness of pain produced by noxious stimuli in the laboratory evoke reliable changes in pain perception and in cerebral blood flow in brain regions that process sensory input evoked by pain signaling* (Rainville et al., 1997). Other psychosocial interventions that alter pain responses include training in adaptive coping strategies, such as deep muscle relaxation, which reduce pain intensity ratings and the frequency of pain behaviors (e.g., guarded movement) among patients with rheumatoid arthritis (RA) or osteoarthritis (Bradley et al., 1987; Keefe et al., 1990).

It is not true that suffering ennobles the character; happiness does that sometimes, but suffering, for the most part, makes men petty and vindictive.

W. SOMERSET MAUGHAM
The Moon and Sixpence

Pain Behavior in Patients with Chronic Pain

Although it is essential to understand the array of physiological, cognitive, affective, and environmental factors that influence pain signaling and pain inhibition, we usually cannot observe the effects of these factors outside of the laboratory setting. Therefore, clinical assessment of pain experienced by our patients requires the observation and recording of verbal and motor behaviors that indicate they are experiencing pain. Box 7.1 provides examples of several common pain behaviors. It is possible to record and quantify these pain behaviors both in the laboratory and in clinical practice using (1) patients' responses to standardized rating scales of the intensity or unpleasantness of pain, (2) video recordings of patient behavior evoked by standardized motor tasks (e.g., walking, rising from a chair, lifting, etc.), and (3) patients' daily recordings in paper or electronic diaries of their pain experiences and occurrence of psychosocial or environmental events (e.g., altered mood, stressors) that may influence their pain experiences.

It is important for physicians and patients to understand that *although the treatment of acute pain generally is directed toward eliminating pain signaling and painful experiences, it may not be possible to consistently produce substantial reductions in pain intensity among patients with some chronic pain syndromes. The treatment of chronic pain, then, often must focus on reducing pain behavior or increasing healthy behavior (e.g., return to work) despite limitations in our ability to substantially reduce the subjective experience of pain .* For example, when patients seek care from a physician for persistent, diffuse, musculoskeletal pain, the physician usually

---

BOX 7.1 Verbal and nonverbal pain behaviors

Verbal
Moaning
Complaints of pain
Yelling
Sighing

Nonverbal
Taking analgesic medication
Guarded movement
Grimacing
Absence from work

---

performs a physical examination, orders various laboratory and imaging procedures, or requests consultation from other medical specialists to identify and eventually eliminate the source of pain signaling. The physician also may prescribe rest and analgesic medication to reduce the patient's subjective perceptions of pain during the diagnostic process. It is assumed, then, that once the source of noxious sensory input is eliminated, the patient's pain perceptions will disappear and further treatment will be unnecessary.

Unfortunately, many persons seen for medical care with persistent, diffuse, musculoskeletal pain never receive precise diagnoses or effective treatment. Others may have a condition diagnosed as **fibromyalgia**, a rheumatologic disorder that primarily affects women and is characterized by widespread aching, exquisite tenderness at specific body sites, low pain thresholds, high levels of functional disability, disturbed sleep, and the absence of laboratory evidence of an inflammatory process. This condition currently is not well understood and cannot be treated reliably, although amitriptyline, duloxetine, and pregabalin as well as aerobic fitness training have been shown to reduce pain in controlled clinical trials. Thus, the pain usually remains chronic. Moreover, during the long diagnostic process and trials of various treatments for the pain, great opportunity exists for psychological and social factors to influence the patient's pain behavior (e.g., frequency of physician visits, medication usage). These factors may include episodes of sexual or physical abuse, the experience of anxiety and depression, as well as the environmental consequences that follow pain behavior.

Abuse and Other Psychosocial Stressors

Much greater information is available regarding the medical and psychological consequences of sexual and physical abuse in women than in men because the frequency of abuse among women sampled from the community and those who seek medical treatment ranges from 20% to 76%, whereas the frequency of abuse among men ranges from 6% to 17%. It has been found that *abused women are significant-*

ly more likely than nonabused women to experience chronic pain, display low thresholds for pain, use the health-care system, and report high levels of physical disability and symptoms of psychiatric disorders. These relationships have been found among individuals with both medically unexplained conditions, such as irritable bowel syndrome or fibromyalgia, and those with chronic pain syndromes in which the pathophysiology is well understood (e.g., gastroesophageal reflux disease). The associations among abuse, chronic pain, and other dimensions of health status in men currently are not known (Scarinci et al., 1994).

Some investigators have examined the extent to which abuse or other psychosocial stressors may be risk factors for the development of chronic pain. A community-based study in the New York metropolitan area revealed that, although women reported a significant increase in painful musculoskeletal symptoms in the first 6 months following the World Trade Center attacks, there was not a significant increase in frequency of onset of fibromyalgia-like symptoms. In contrast, several prospective studies of onset of chronic musculoskeletal pain in the workplace indicate that both the occurrence of physical injury and psychosocial factors contribute to the development of persistent widespread pain. For example, a study of nearly 900 newly employed workers over a 2-year period revealed that several physical maneuvers that might cause tissue damage as well as psychosocial factors were associated with the onset of widespread body pain (Harkness et al., 2004). The physical maneuvers included lifting more than 24 pounds with both hands, pulling more than 56 pounds, and prolonged working with hands at or above shoulder level. The psychosocial factors included low job satisfaction, low social support, and monotonous work.

Anxiety, Depression, and Environmental Consequences

It is generally accepted that anxiety tends to magnify individuals' perceptions of pain. It also is well known that depression often accompanies chronic pain and that depression is positively associated with the pain intensity ratings of chronic pain patients. To understand the relationship between pain behavior and its environmental consequences, it is important to remember that *pain behavior may be considered to be either a response to noxious stimulation or an operant that is shaped by environmental contingencies.* Examples of respondent pain behavior include reflexively withdrawing one's finger from a hot stove or wincing and grimacing after falling on a hard surface. However, other pain behaviors, such as verbally complaining, taking analgesic medication, and lying in bed, are complex operants influenced by environmental contingencies. Indeed, *the longer that subjective perceptions of pain persist, the more likely it becomes that pain behaviors are being governed by the principles of operant conditioning.*

> **BOX 7.2** Environmental reinforcers for pain behavior
>
> *Positive*
> Massaging the patient
> Asking the patient how he or she can be helped
> Giving analgesic or sedating medication to the patient
>
> *Negative*
> Taking over unpleasant chores from the patient
> Granting the patient sick leave from aversive work
> Recommending reduced social or sexual contacts with a spouse in a dysfunctional marriage

Box 7.2 shows that the environmental consequences of pain behavior may include **positive reinforcement** such as nurturant attention from family members and the mood alterations produced by ingesting narcotic or sedating medications. Pain behavior also may be followed by **negative reinforcement** such as permission to stay home from work or to refrain from performing strenuous household tasks. Moreover, individuals may not receive positive reinforcement after displays of healthy behavior. For example, individuals with persistent pain may want to try to resume some of their usual activities but can be discouraged by physicians or family members from doing so. Thus, because of the consequences that follow pain and healthy behavior, patients may learn to display excessive or dramatic levels of pain behavior regardless of their subjective perceptions of pain intensity and unpleasantness and whether or not pain signaling occurs. The operant model of pain behavior also suggests that the actions of physicians that are appropriate for patients with acute pain (e.g., prescribing medication or releasing them from work duties) may contribute to the development and maintenance of chronic pain behavior and suffering. Therefore, *a major focus of treatment of chronic pain usually is the modification of patients' displays of pain behavior rather than the complete elimination of the subjective perceptions of pain or pain signaling.*

The role of physicians in the development and maintenance of chronic pain was demonstrated in an experiment performed by Wilbert Fordyce and his colleagues at the University of Washington (Fordyce, 1976). This study compared patients with acute back pain who were encouraged by their physicians to take analgesic medication and limit physical activity in response to increases in their pain perceptions with a similar group of patients who were instructed by physicians to take a fixed amount of medication and perform physical activity at specific times each day regardless of the intensity of pain they may experience. The former patients reported greater functional disability, pain, and health-care service usage at a 1-year follow-up assessment. Similar findings were reported in a study investigating prescription of bed rest for patients with acute back pain. These investigations indicate that a primary focus on minimizing pain *perception* actually can lead to prolonged and excessive displays of pain *behavior*. In contrast, setting limits on the display of pain behavior regardless of the patients' subjective perceptions of pain can lead to better recovery from acute pain episodes.

> It is by poultices, not by words, that pain is ended, although pain is, by words, both eased and diminished.
>
> PETRARCH, 1359

ASSESSMENT OF CHRONIC PAIN

Optimal evaluation of patients with chronic pain requires cooperation among physicians, psychologists, and other health professionals such as physical and occupational therapists. The physician's evaluation varies as a function of his or her specialty training and the patient's problems. However, the evaluation always includes some form of physical examination, a behavioral interview, and psychological assessment procedures. The physical examination is not discussed here.

Behavioral Interview

The interview portion of the evaluation should generally involve both the patient and the spouse or some other family member. It is helpful to begin by explaining that the purpose of the interview is to determine how the pain has affected the patient's life and what factors may influence the pain. The physician can then determine the patient's and the spouse's perceptions of the cause and future consequences of the patient's pain problems. Patients and their families often believe that pain implies ongoing or worsening tissue damage and that physical activity will exacerbate the physical damage that has occurred. For example, one of my patients interpreted a computed tomography (CT) scan finding of a bulge at L4–5 as a life-threatening spinal tumor. The patient's reluctance to increase his activity level and the spouse's anger toward previous physicians for their refusal to help her husband were understandable. Reassurance, education, and reinterpretation of the CT scan findings were helpful in changing their attitudes and behavior.

At this point it may be useful to continue the interview process with the patient and spouse separately to obtain independent responses to the same questions. If the patient and spouse are interviewed together, it is helpful to encourage the spouse to contribute his or her thoughts during the interview, even if a question is not directed specifically to the spouse.

The behavioral interview consists of five important objectives. **First,** it is necessary to *evaluate the patient's daily activities* by determining the following:

1. How the patient typically spends his or her time during the day
2. Which activities the patient has performed more or less frequently since the onset of pain
3. Whether any activities have been eliminated since the onset of pain

It also is important to assess the degree to which the patient has enjoyed his or her current activities, as well as those that have been eliminated. If the patient has eliminated several pleasurable activities, it may be possible to use these activities as goals in future treatment. However, if the elimination of certain activities has brought positive consequences for the patient, there is evidence that operant factors are influencing the patient's pain behavior. It is also important to note any inconsistencies in activities with similar physical demands that have been altered because of pain. For example, if a male patient reports that he is unable to work as a store clerk but continues to serve as an umpire for his son's Little League baseball games, it may well be that pain behavior has been negatively reinforced by release from work duties.

The **second** behavioral objective is to *identify the events that reliably precede exacerbations in the patient's pain perceptions and pain behavior, as well as the events that reliably follow these exacerbations*. This can be accomplished in part by observing the patient and spouse together during the interview. Do certain interview topics elicit increases in the patient's pain behavior such as grimacing, shifting body positions, rubbing, or sighing? Does the presence of the spouse appear to be associated with change in the frequency of the patient's pain behavior? How does the spouse respond to the patient's display of pain behavior during the interview? It must be remembered, however, that the display of frequent or dramatic pain behavior alone does not imply that the patient's pain is highly influenced by reinforcements. Several studies of patients with low back pain and RA have shown that medical and disease severity factors are the primary predictors of pain behavior frequency. Nevertheless, the *environmental context* within which pain behaviors occur can provide insight concerning the functional significance of these behaviors.

In addition to observing behavior during the interview, the physician should ask the patient and spouse how others know when the patient is experiencing high levels of pain and how they respond to these increases. Do certain situations or tasks seem to be closely associated with severe pain? Do family members or friends provide positive reinforcement for pain behavior by increasing their attention or nurturance (e.g., massaging the patient's back or bringing the patient analgesic medication)? If persons do respond in a solicitous manner, it is likely that pain behavior is being maintained in part by reinforcement. It is essential to remember that negative reinforcement also may influence pain behavior. In a troubled marriage, for example, reduced interactions with the spouse or children after the display of pain behavior might be rewarding to the patient.

In addition to determining the events that influence pain behavior, physicians should attend to the events that reliably precede and follow the patient's attempts to engage in relatively healthy behavior (e.g., exercise, social activities, and household tasks). Positive responses from family members after healthy behavior tend to increase the frequency with which such behavior is displayed. However, spouses and other family members often do not respond positively to healthy behavior because they fear that patients may hurt themselves or increase their pain. Patients also are frequently reluctant to engage in healthy behavior because they share their family members' fears of injury or pain. Moreover, if healthy behavior is followed by increases in pain caused by poor physical conditioning or overexertion, encouragement from family members probably will not be rewarding.

The **third** objective of the behavioral interview is to *determine the extent to which the patient may exacerbate his or her suffering.* For example, a patient may report that since the onset of pain, he or she has restricted or eliminated certain activities or body movements because of an expectation of increased pain. This **avoidance behavior** may represent the beginning of a vicious cycle of increased pain and inactivity (Figure 7.3). That is, avoidance behavior and inactivity are negatively reinforced by allowing the patient to prevent or reduce increases in his or her subjective pain perceptions. Prolonged inactivity or avoidance behavior may lead to decreased physical strength, decreased energy,

or distorted gait. This deconditioning, in turn, will lead to increased pain if healthy activities are attempted. At the same time, long periods of inactivity tend to contribute to depression, social withdrawal, and overconcern with somatic perceptions and pain.

A small number of patients try to engage in high levels of activity until their perceptions of pain intensity become severe. These individuals often appear to be good patients because they tend not to complain excessively. However, if physicians listen carefully to the descriptions of their patients' daily activities, they often sense a desperate quality in these activities. Indeed, if these patients are not taught to better regulate their behavior, their attempts to distract themselves from pain through excessive activity tend to become ineffective. As their distraction efforts become increasingly ineffective, they usually experience depression because they find it difficult to accept that they cannot behave exactly as they did before the onset of pain.

The **fourth** objective of the behavioral interview is to *evaluate the degree to which the patient is experiencing depression or other psychological disturbances.* Thus, the physician should note whether the patient has experienced any change in mood or outlook on life since the onset of pain and whether the patient has experienced vegetative signs of depression such as sleep disturbance, change in eating habits, or decreased libido. However, physicians must be careful in evaluating depression because these vegetative signs may also be produced by the experience of chronic pain or excessive use of narcotic analgesics. In addition, questions regarding sexual behavior frequently lead both men and women to report changes in sexual functioning (e.g., difficulty in achieving or maintaining erections, decreased vaginal lubrication, or dyspareunia) and sexual desire. It should be noted, however, that some illnesses, such as many of the rheuma-

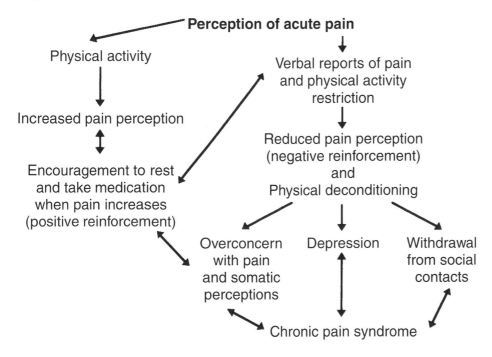

FIGURE 7.3 Illustration of the process through which perceptions of acute pain may lead to a chronic pain syndrome. Pain complaints and activity restriction are followed by both positive and negative reinforcement. This may lead to physical deconditioning, depression, social withdrawal, and somatic overconcern associated with chronic pain syndromes.

tological disorders, tend to be associated with sexual difficulties as a result of pain and restricted movement produced by joint destruction and inflammation.

Anxiety disorders also are highly prevalent among chronic pain patients. These usually take the form of generalized anxiety disorders, panic disorders, or phobias. As with depressive symptoms, however, indicators of anxiety such as muscle tension and sleep disturbance may result from chronic pain alone.

The physician must be sensitive to signs of cognitive dysfunction such as confusion, memory difficulties, distractibility, and language difficulties. Another potential indicator of cognitive dysfunction is the presence of a spouse or family member who frequently corrects the patient's responses or answers questions for the patient. Indeed, it has been demonstrated that patients with chronic pain with histories of major or minor head and neck injuries show greater difficulties in sustained attention and rapid problem-solving ability than patients with chronic pain without head and neck injuries. Inappropriate use of medication must always initially be ruled out as a cause of patients' cognitive difficulties. Nevertheless, identification of and instruction in coping with cognitive dysfunction can reduce disability and psychological distress among patients.

The **fifth** objective of the interview is to *determine if any relatives or friends in the family suffer from chronic pain or disabilities similar to those of the patient.* Careful questioning often reveals that the patient spends a considerable amount of time with relatives or friends who also have chronic pain problems. Thus, the patient may have a great deal of opportunity to learn maladaptive pain behavior by observing others.

Psychological Assessment Procedures

The following psychological assessment procedures may be used to supplement the information obtained during a behavioral interview:

1. Self-report measures of affective disturbance
2. Structured psychiatric interviews
3. Self-report measures of pain perceptions
4. Direct observation of overt motor behaviors
5. Self-monitored behavioral observations
6. Self-reports of functional disability
7. Measurement of psychophysiological responses

Self-Report Measures of Affective Disturbance

Although anxiety and depression are evaluated during the behavioral interview, most physicians and psychologists supplement their observations by administering standardized measures of affective disturbance to chronic pain pa-

THE KNITTED GLOVE

You come into my office wearing a blue
knitted glove with a ribbon at the wrist.
You remove the glove slowly, painfully
and dump out the contents, a worthless hand.
What a specimen! It looks much like a regular
hand,
warm, pliable, soft. You can move the fingers.

If it's not one thing, it's another.
Last month the fire in your hips had you down,
or up mincing across the room with a cane.
When I ask about the hips today, you pass
them off
so I can't tell if only your pain
or the memory is gone. Your knitted hand
is the long and short of it. Pain doesn't exist
in the past any more than this morning does.

This thing, the name for your solitary days,
for the hips, the hand, for the walk of your eyes
away from mine, this thing is coyote, the trickster.
I want to call, come out, you son of a dog!
and wrestle that thing to the ground for you,
I want to take its neck between my hands.
But in this world I don't know how to find
the bastard, so we sit. We talk about the pain.

JACK COULEHAN

tients. The most commonly used psychological assessment instrument is the **Minnesota Multiphasic Personality Inventory** (MMPI) (see Chapter 18 for a description of this instrument). Interpretation of chronic pain patients' responses to the MMPI, however, is complicated by the fact that several items on the Hypochondriasis, Depression, Hysteria, and Schizophrenia scales are typically answered in a pathological fashion because the items describe experiences associated with chronic illness and affective disturbance. For example, a significantly greater number of patients with RA relative to age-matched control subjects respond false to the item, "I do not tire quickly." A false response to this item contributes to scores on the Hypochondriasis and Depression scales; however, false responses also are associated with relatively low grip strength (a measure of RA disease activity) evaluated with a hand dynamometer.

Given the problems associated with the use of the MMPI, some health-care professionals have begun to employ several other psychological assessment instruments with chronic pain patients. These instruments include the **Multidimensional Pain Inventory**, the **Millon Behavioral Health Inventory**, and the **Symptom Checklist-90**. However, no evidence exists that any of the alternative instruments have greater clinical use with chronic pain patients than the MMPI.

Structured Psychiatric Interviews

There are several advantages associated with the use of structured psychiatric interviews for patients with chronic pain. For example, these interviews may be used to identify psychiatric disorders (e.g., panic disorder) that may alter pain perception. Thus, appropriate pharmacologic or behavioral treatments for these disorders also may produce reductions in the subjective pain experiences of the patients. The psychiatric interview also may allow one to identify patients who have mixed symptoms of anxiety and depression that do not meet all diagnostic criteria for specific psychiatric disorders but that nevertheless place them at risk for more severe somatic complaints, as well as for mood and anxiety disorders, when they are exposed to substantial life stresses. Finally, *the use of a structured psychiatric interview often allows one to enhance rapport with patients because it tends to communicate that the physician is interested in a wide variety of symptoms and life problems.* As a consequence, physicians usually may pose questions regarding emotionally charged issues, such as sexual and

> I commenced inhaling the ether before the operation was commenced and continued it until the operation was over. I did not feel the slightest pain from the operation and could not believe the tumor was removed until it was shown to me.
>
> JAMES VENABLE
> *Account by first ether patient who underwent public demonstration of ether at the Massachusetts General Hospital, 16 October 1846*

physical abuse, during the psychiatric interview without threatening their relationships with the patients.

The two structured psychiatric interviews used most frequently with chronic pain patients are the **Diagnostic Interview Schedule** (DIS) and the **Structured Clinical Interview for DSM-IV** (SCID). Both interviews provide reliable and valid diagnoses based on the *Diagnostic and Statistical Manual of Mental Disorders,* fourth edition, of the American Psychiatric Association. The DIS is a highly structured interview that may be administered verbally or by computer software. In contrast, the SCID may be administered only verbally because it allows the physician to supplement the structured interview with (1) additional questions to clarify differential diagnosis; (2) challenges to inconsistencies in patients' responses; or (3) ancillary information drawn from hospital records, family members, or other clinical staff. This supplemental information is particularly useful because the DIS decision tree procedure occasionally may produce diagnoses that do not appear to be consistent with clinical impressions.

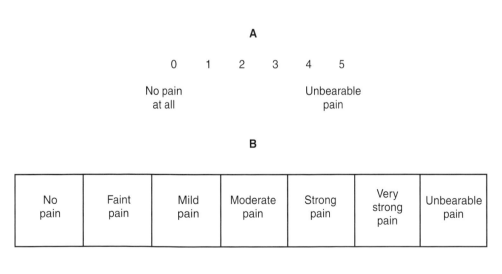

FIGURE 7.4 Several commonly used self-report measures of pain perceptions: (A) numerical category scale; (B) verbal category scale; and (C) visual analog scale.

Hour beginning	Sitting Major activity	Time	Walking or standing Major activity	Time	Reclining Activity	Time	Medications Type	Amount	Absence 0	1	Pain 2	3	4	Unbearable 5
Midnight	watching TV	30	in kitchen	10	in bed	20	Darvocet	2 tablets				●		
1:00					sleep	60								
2:00						60								
3:00						60								
4:00	reading	30	in bathroom	5	sleep	25	Darvocet	2 tablets			●			
5:00						60								
6:00						60								
7:00	eating/reading	40	in bathroom/kitchen	20						●				
8:00	car/desk	40	walking to work	20						●				
9:00	at desk	55	break	5			Aspirin	2 tablets			●			
10:00	at desk	60									●			
11:00	at desk/meeting	50	walking	10							●			
noon	lunch	30	walking	10	resting	20				●				
1:00	at desk	40	talking with friends	20						●				
2:00	at desk	60										●		
3:00	at desk	55	break	5			Darvocet	2 tablets				●		
4:00	at desk/car	30	grocery shopping	30							●			
5:00			" & in kitchen	60							●			
6:00	watching TV	30	in kitchen	30							●			
7:00	eating	40	cleaning up	20							●			
8:00	reading paper	20	walking	40						●				
9:00	on phone	30			resting/TV	30				●				
10:00	sewing	50	ironing	10							●			
11:00					sleep	60	Elavil	50 mg		●				

FIGURE 7.7 Behavioral self-monitoring diary completed over a 24-hour period.

of health-care staff members and patients and it allows for continuous recording of a wide variety of behaviors in the patient's home or work environments. It is customary to ask a patient to complete diary recordings for 1 or 2 weeks. When the diary is returned, it is possible to compute the time spent by the patient each day in activity that involves sitting, standing or walking, or reclining. Because the diary requires the patient to record pain intensity level and medication intake every walking hour, it also is possible to examine the relationships among the patient's activity levels, pain perceptions, and medication consumption. These relationships can then be discussed with the patient to maintain or improve rapport and the patient's motivation for treatment. Moreover, the relationships among activity, pain perceptions, and medication usage can be used to guide treatment decisions. Use of additional diaries periodically during treatment also provides a record of the patient's progress and indicators for modifying the patient's treatment regimen.

Despite the advantages associated with self-monitoring, there are two important **drawbacks.** First, some patients find it difficult to maintain hourly recordings of their behavior and attempt to complete their diaries in a retrospective fashion (the error that can be present in retrospective recordings will become apparent if you attempt to reconstruct on an hourly basis the activities you performed yesterday). One approach to resolving this problem involves the use of hand-held devices similar to personal digital assistants. These devices may be programmed to cue patients to record ratings of their pain, mood, sleep quality, and events such as stressors at random intervals throughout the day. Given that the devices will only accept ratings made in conjunction with a cue, the problems associated with retrospective recording rarely occur.

The second drawback associated with the use of written and electronic diaries is that some patients produce inaccurate recordings because of their need to impress their physician, impaired cognitive functioning secondary to depression, narcotic medication dependence, or traumatic head-neck injury. If possible, patients' diary recordings should be periodically validated with unobtrusive observations of their behavior or with medication checks.

Self-Reports of Functional Ability

Clinicians and investigators recently have become interested in obtaining patients' ratings of their abilities to perform various activities of daily living. The **Sickness Impact Profile**, or SIP, has been used most frequently with chronic pain patients. One of the most positive features of the SIP is that it provides a profile of patient functioning in several areas (e.g., ambulation, mobility, and body care) that provide targets for behavioral intervention. Both the original 136-item form of the SIP and a shortened 24-item version of the instrument have been shown to be valid and sensitive to change.

The **Short-Form Health Survey** (SF-36) is a 36-item measure that, similar to the SIP, provides measures of both the physical and psychosocial dimensions of functional ability and quality of life. The SF-36 has been used with a wide variety of patient populations and is the most frequently used measure of quality of life in the medical and public health literature.

Other measures of functional ability include the the Multidimensional Pain Inventory, the Health Assessment Questionnaire, and the Arthritis Impact Measurement Scales. The **Multidimensional Pain Inventory** is a particularly useful adjunct to the behavioral interview because one portion of this instrument evaluates patients' perceptions of family members' responses to displays of pain behavior. Either the Health Assessment Questionnaire or the Arthritis Impact Measurement Scales should always be used in the evaluation of persons with RA because of the consistent finding that *low levels of functional ability are associated with 5-year survival rates of 50% or less among RA patients.* This relationship between functional ability and mortality in RA cannot be explained by age, duration of disease, disease activity measures, type of pharmacological therapy, educational level, smoking, or other diseases such as cardiovascular disease or peptic ulcer.

Measurement of Psychophysiological Responses

The assessment of psychophysiological responses represents an attempt to find objective evidence of the experience of pain. However, *no one has demonstrated a specific psychophysiological response that covaries reliably with subjective reports of pain or one that is free from the effects of extraneous factors such as expectations, attention, or subtle postural changes.*

Despite this difficulty, several psychophysiological responses are routinely evaluated in the assessment of chronic pain patients. **Electromyographic (EMG) activity**, for example, is frequently assessed among patients with low back pain or headaches. It generally has been assumed that many patients with low back pain restrict their spinal motion and other movements and thereby increase their paraspinal muscle tension levels for prolonged periods. This produces a vicious cycle in which normal activities of daily living evoke increased muscle pain, which leads to further restriction of motion. These patients need reliable and accurate measurement of paraspinal EMG levels and treatments such as EMG biofeedback or relaxation training to reduce their abnormally high EMG levels. A similar rationale has been used to explain the cause of tension headaches and to justify the use of biofeedback or frontal EMG levels as a treatment for this disorder.

These assumptions have been challenged by several recent findings. First, recent reviews of the literature concerning the psychophysiology of chronic back pain and headaches have revealed important inconsistencies across many of the research studies with regard to diagnostic criteria, control groups, psychophysiological recording procedures, and data analyses. Second, most of the relatively sophisticated studies that have been performed have found little evidence that either patients with back pain or tension headache differ from healthy control subjects in resting EMG levels. Finally, recent evidence regarding the relationship between EMG levels and pain has not supported the original assumptions regarding the cause of pain. For example, it has been reported that unlike pain-free normal subjects, patients with chronic low back pain tend to produce abnormal EMG patterns (e.g., asymmetry of right and left paraspinal EMG levels) during both static and dynamic activities. Similarly, several investigators have found differences in EMG activity patterns during flexion-extension movements between LBP patients and normal control subjects. Moreover, *it has been found consistently that actual biofeedback-mediated reductions in frontal EMG activity are neither necessary nor sufficient for amelioration of headache pain.*

Technological advances have made it possible to perform ambulatory monitoring of some psychophysiological responses as patients engage in daily activities in their home and work environments. For example, it is possible to monitor intracsophageal pH levels for up to 24 hours among persons who are suspected to suffer from **gastroesophageal reflux disease** (GERD). These pH-monitoring devices also permit patients to record periods of chest pain, meals, and sleep so that their physicians may examine relationships among pain perceptions, eating behavior, reductions in lower gastroesophageal sphincter pressure associated with reclining, and changes in pH level. This technology has greatly improved physicians' abilities to diagnose and treat GERD before patients develop ulcerations of esophageal tissue. However, similar to EMG activity, it has been shown that changes in pH levels do not always correspond with changes in patients' pain perceptions. Indeed, recent evidence indicates that chronically anxious patients with GERD tend to report greater symptom severity during prolonged stress in the laboratory despite the fact that intraesophageal pH levels do not increase with stress. It may be that when these patients are exposed to long periods of stress, afferent information is modulated by cortical activity so that low intensity stimuli originating in the esophagus are perceived as reflux symptoms. Moreover, central factors such as anxiety or stress responses also may contribute to the inconsistent associations between psychophysiological measures and symptom reports among other patient populations.

Positive associations between psychophysiological responses and pain perceptions have been found among patients with **myofascial pain syndromes**. Several myofascial pain syndromes may affect the head, neck, and back. However, all of the syndromes are characterized by the presence of at least one **trigger point**. These trigger points are self-sustaining, hyperirritable foci in skeletal muscle or its associated fascia that refer pain, tenderness, and autonomic changes to distant locations in patterns specific for each muscle. Trigger points may be identified by manual palpation, but more precise measurement is possible with the use of a **pressure algometer**. A typical pressure algometer consists of a hand-held scale with a 1 cm, circular, rubber-covered tip that is pressed into the skin until the patient reports pain. The scale records the force required for the patient to reach his or her threshold for perceiving pain. Pressure algometers have been found to produce reliable and valid measurements that are sensitive to change after passive stretching and fluorimethane spraying of trigger points.

Optimal evaluation of patients with chronic pain requires an interdisciplinary effort among physicians, psychologists, and other health professionals. In addition to the physical examination and related diagnostic procedures, the evaluation should include a behavioral interview and assessment of affective disturbance, pain perceptions, and functional ability. The physician in many cases should obtain direct or self-monitored measures of pain behavior and measures of psychophysiological responses. Multidimensional evaluation of chronic pain allows the treatment team to tailor interventions specific to patients' needs and provides multiple criteria for assessing the outcome of treatment.

BEHAVIORAL TREATMENT OF CHRONIC PAIN

The three major behavioral treatments for chronic pain are contingency management, biofeedback training, and self-management or cognitive-behavioral therapy. **Contingency management** is a form of operant conditioning; the goal of this treatment is to achieve sufficient control over the patient's environment so that reinforcement is withdrawn from pain behaviors, reinforcement is made contingent on well behaviors (e.g., increases in activity level), and persons in the home environment are trained to reinforce the display of healthy behavior and to withdraw reinforcement on the display of pain behavior.

For example, one published case study has described the management of a 68-year-old man's chronic groin and testicular pain. The pain management protocol included the following practices:

1. Physical therapy twice daily
2. Self-monitoring of physical therapy performance
3. Home practice of prescribed exercises
4. Instructions to the treatment staff to ignore all pain behaviors and to orally praise the patient for maintaining

his self-monitored observations and for improvements in physical function
5. Making rest periods and whirlpool baths contingent on completion of prescribed exercise activities rather than upon reports of pain.

At a 3-month follow-up assessment the patient reported that pain was completely absent, sleep and appetite had improved, and the only medication he took was an antidepressant. It should be noted, however, that contingency management programs tend to be very expensive because of the large amounts of effort and time that treatment staff must devote to controlling the patient's environment, which usually is an inpatient facility dedicated to the management of pain. As a consequence, insurance coverage for contingency management programs is becoming increasingly rare.

Biofeedback training is an outpatient procedure that involves monitoring and amplifying specific psychophysiological responses (e.g., EMG level). The response is then "fed back" to the patient in the form of a visual or auditory signal. With the aid of this feedback, the patient may be trained to develop an increased awareness of the psychophysiological response, achieve voluntary control of the response, and use the newly acquired control in the home or work environment to reduce pain. *For biofeedback training to be effective, however, the patient must actively participate in treatment and assume responsibility for developing the coping skills necessary for improvement.* One EMG biofeedback training program described in the literature was developed for college students with muscle contraction headaches. Training was administered during seven, 50-minute, biweekly sessions. Students also were urged to practice their newly learned skills at home when they were free of headaches and at the initial signs of headache activity. It was shown that relative to a waiting-list control condition (students who were assessed but not treated until after completion of the study) and a credible attention-placebo condition ("pseudomeditation"), EMG biofeedback training produced significant reductions in EMG and headache activity.

Self-management or cognitive-behavioral treatment interventions also are delivered almost exclusively on an outpatient basis. These interventions are based on the premise that patients' expectations influence their emotional and behavioral reactions to life events. Therefore, it is critical for physicians to help their patients believe that they can learn the skills necessary to control pain and other forms of disability. This objective is accomplished through self-management interventions that usually include multiple treatments such as education, teaching coping skills and progressive muscle relaxation training, practice in communicating effectively with family members and health-care providers, and provision of positive reinforcement for appropriate coping behavior. Patients are encouraged to take responsibility for managing their pain and disabilities with their newly learned skills and to attribute their successes to their own efforts.

Several investigators have developed **cognitive-behavioral treatment protocols** for patients with RA. One particularly effective protocol included five individual thermal biofeedback training sessions and 10 weekly small group meetings with patients and their spouses. These meetings included education, relaxation training, and instruction in devising behavioral strategies for coping with the consequences of RA and the use of self-reinforcement for their coping efforts. It was found that the cognitive-behavioral treatment, relative to a no-treatment and an attention-placebo control condition (patients given attention and solicitude but no active treatment), produced significant reductions in pain behavior and anxiety at posttreatment. However, only about one third of the RA patients were able to maintain their improvements at a 1-year follow-up assessment.

The preceding studies suggest that the three behavioral treatments for chronic pain share many principles and intervention techniques. For example, patients who are treated with contingency management or self-management interventions receive reinforcement from therapists or treatment staff for the reduction of pain behavior and increases in healthy behavior. Patients who are treated with biofeedback are reinforced by visual or auditory displays of control of psychophysiological responses and by verbal praise from their therapists. Indeed, it has been suggested that all current behavioral therapies for chronic pain share three underlying principles. First, *patients are taught that pain is both a physiological and psychological event;* thus, patients may acknowledge the potential benefits of participating actively in a behaviorally oriented rather than a medical treatment for their pain. Second, *patients learn new cognitive and behavioral skills* for pain control and strengthen these skills by practicing and by using other pain control strategies they already have mastered. These skills may include reduction of EMG levels, better pacing of rest and activity, and developing increased physical strength as a function of exercise. Finally, all therapies devote attention to helping *patients apply their newly learned skills* in their home and work environments and to maintaining their improvements after the termination of treatment.

An additional shared attribute of behavioral therapies for chronic pain is that they all require substantial professional time and expense. Thus, it may be more beneficial to channel limited resources toward the prevention of chronic pain. For example, evidence suggests that the way physicians treat patients with acute pain will influence the probability that these patients will have chronic problems. One investigation has examined the effectiveness of a secondary prevention program for nurses with back injuries who were deemed to be at risk for developing chronic pain. The intervention included 5 weeks of intensive physical therapy and cognitive-behavioral therapy. It was found that the intervention, relative to a waiting-list control condition, produced significant improvements in pain behavior, psychological distress, sleep quality, and work absenteeism because of pain. Most of these results were maintained at an 18-month follow-up. This follow-up also showed that the preventive intervention produced substantial economic savings for the nurses' employers. It appears then that effective treatment should be provided to patients before their pain problems become chronic. Moreover, future research may demonstrate that preventive interventions with workers are even more effective when they are provided before the onset of painful injuries.

SUMMARY

Behavioral assessment is necessary to understand fully the factors that contribute to the development and maintenance of chronic benign pain. Given that patients with chronic pain have failed to respond to appropriate medical or surgical treatment, behavioral treatment usually represents the only intervention likely to reduce the suffering of these patients. The empathic physician who employs behavioral treatment methods for these patients—or who refers to practitioners who do—can often significantly improve the lives of patients with chronic benign pain. However, behavioral interventions are time consuming and expensive and a great need exists for both primary and secondary preventive interventions to ease the burden that chronic pain places on individuals, their families, and society.

CASE STUDY

S.R. is a 37-year-old woman who has been referred to you by her local physician for evaluation of widespread musculoskeletal pain. She experiences the pain above and below the waist, as well as in her hands and feet and lower back area. She also reports frequent headaches and lower abdominal pain that is relieved with defecation. S.R. has experienced this pain for 30 months. The pain initially was localized in the lower back area after a complete hysterectomy but has since "spread" throughout her body. She has been told by her local physician that she suffers from chronic fatigue syndrome and has been found to have elevated Epstein-Barr virus viral capsid antibody titer. The patient's past medical history is noncontributory although she did suffer from childhood asthma. Since the onset of pain, the patient, who is 170 cm tall, has had considerable weight gain, to 103 kg. A rheumatoid factor and antinuclear antibody titer performed locally before referral were both less than 1:40. The test result for human immunodeficiency virus type I was negative. However, the erythrocyte sedimentation rate (ESR) was 36 mm/h, which is slightly elevated. Finally, computed axial tomography scans of the brain, which were performed to help evaluate her reports of headaches, were negative. The patient's current medicines include nabumetone (Relafen), 500 mg qam with meals; hydrocodone bitartrate (Lortab), 7.5 mg bid; Estrace hormone; fluoxetine (Prozac) 20 mg qam; amitriptyline (Elavil), 50 mg bid; and alprazolam (Xanax), 0.25 mg prn. Despite the large number of analgesic and psychotropic medications, the patient reports that her sleep is quite disturbed.

S.R. is married with two children. She worked as an elementary schoolteacher until 1 year ago when the pain became so severe she requested a leave of absence. During the past 30 months, she and her husband have had serious marital difficulties, culminating in an affair between the husband and a woman coworker. S.R. reported to her physician at this time that she was so depressed she could understand why people might try to kill themselves. This affair has ended, and the patient and her husband are receiving marital counseling through their church.

Blood pressure is 126/78 mm Hg, pulse rate is 92 beats per minute, weight is 103 kg, and temperature is 36° C. Lungs and heart are normal, abdomen is obese, and skin is normal. The patient's joints are normal with no swelling, tenderness, or pain. However, there is considerable pain between the joints and especially in the upper arms, neck, shoulder area, and on the medial aspect of the lower extremities between the knees and ankles. Palpation of the tender points associated with fibromyalgia reveals that the patient meets criteria for this disorder.

Are there any additional laboratory tests or referrals to other specialists that are warranted? Are there any psychological or environmental factors that might influence the patient's pain perceptions or behavior? How could this patient's pain be best treated?

Discussion

At this point, it is difficult to evaluate the possible importance of the elevated ESR and Epstein-Barr virus titer because there is a relatively high base rate for positive findings on these tests. The ESR should be re-evaluated in 3 months to determine if it remains elevated. The abdominal pain that is relieved by defecation suggests that the patient may suffer from irritable bowel syndrome, a functional gastroenterological disorder that is frequently found among persons with fibromyalgia. One should question the patient regarding her bowel habits. If she reports altered bowel function and has not had a recent sigmoidoscopic examination, she should be referred to a gastroenterologist for further evaluation.

The patient's absence from work, marital difficulties, and discussion of suicide with her local physician suggest

that she also should be referred to a psychologist or psychiatrist experienced in the assessment of chronic pain. On referral, the Diagnostic Interview Schedule shows that the patient currently meets the classification criteria for panic disorder, major depressive episode, and major depression, recurrent episodes (which began at age 33). In addition, the patient previously has met criteria for bulimia nervosa, which began at age 25 and of which the most recent symptoms were present at age 33. S.R. reports frequent pain during intercourse with her husband for which no underlying pathophysiology has been found. However, there is no history of sexual or physical abuse.

The behavioral interview and psychometric testing reveal that the patient reports high levels of pain on the McGill Pain Questionnaire. The Sickness Impact Profile shows that the patient reports great difficulty in performing a wide variety of daily activities. In addition, her displays of disability and pain behaviors often are followed by reinforcing responses from her husband (e.g., provision of pain medication). It appears, then, that S.R.'s disabilities, in part, represent learned behaviors. Indeed, one might speculate that the husband's solicitous responses to S.R.'s pain behavior may represent an attempt to relieve feelings of guilt regarding his extramarital affair.

Given the large number of psychological and social factors associated with the patient's pain, S.R. should be referred as an outpatient for self-management therapy at the medical center's pain clinic. The goals of this referral are to:

1. Reduce the patient's use of analgesic medication and initiate a less complex and more effective regimen of psychotropic medication for her panic disorder and depression.
2. Reduce the patient's pain behaviors and disability and increase her healthy behavior with a program of physical reconditioning, reduction of spouse reinforcement of pain behavior, and increasing spouse and self-reinforcement for healthy behavior.
3. Coordinate this treatment with marital therapy provided by the church to ensure that the patient and her husband do not receive conflicting therapeutic instruction.

SUGGESTED READINGS

Bradley, L.A., & McKendree-Smith, N.L. (2002). Central nervous system mechanisms of pain in fibromyalgia and other musculoskeletal disorders: Behavioral and psychologic treatment approaches. *Current Opinions in Rheumatism, 14*, 45–51.
This paper reviews the efficacy of psychological and behavioral pain management interventions that have been evaluated in randomized, controlled trials for patients with rheumatoid arthritis (RA),

osteoarthritis (OA), and fibromyalgia (FM). Using published criteria for empirically validated interventions, it is concluded that cognitive-behavioral therapies and the Arthritis Self-Management Program represent well-established treatments for patients with RA and OA. There currently are no psychological or behavioral interventions that can be considered as well-established treatments for persons with FM.

Bradley, L.A., Young, L.D., Anderson, K.O., Turner, R.A., Agudelo, C.A., McDaniel, L.K., Pisko, E.J., Semble, E.L., & Morgan, T.M. (1987). Effects of psychological therapy on pain behavior of rheumatoid arthritis patients. *Arthritis and Rheumatology, 30,* 1105–1114.

This is a particularly well-designed evaluation of a self-management intervention for patients with RA. The intervention, relative to a placebo treatment and standard medical care, produced significant reductions in pain behavior and disease activity.

Campbell, T.S., Hughes, J.W., Girdler, S.S., Maixner, W., & Sherwood, A. (2004). Relationship of ethnicity, gender, and ambulatory blood pressure to pain sensitivity: Effects of individualized pain rating scales. *Journal of Pain, 5,* 183–191.

This investigation provides evidence that ethnic group differences in responses to verbal pain rating scales may be caused, in part, by systematic ethnic or cultural differences in perceived intensity of pain communicated by words commonly used in the English language.

Fordyce, W.E. (1976). *Behavioral methods for chronic pain and illness.* St. Louis, MO: Mosby.

This is a classic text that provides detailed descriptions of learning processes that influence pain behavior and the contingency management approach to treating patients with chronic pain.

Harkness. E.F., Macfarlane, G.J., Nahit, E., Silman, A.J., & McBeth, J. (2004). Mechanical injury and psychosocial factors in the work place predict the onset of widespread body pain: A 2-year prospective study among cohorts of newly employed workers. *Arthritis and Rheumatism, 50,* 1655–1664.

This prospective investigation provides strong evidence that both mechanical injury and psychosocial factors, such as low social support and monotonous job duties, contribute to the prediction of persistent widespread pain among newly injured workers.

Keefe, F.J., & Block, A.R. (1982). Development of an observation method for assessing pain behavior in chronic low back pain patients. *Behavior Therapy, 13,* 363–375.

This provides a detailed description of the first standardized protocol for measuring pain behavior among patients with chronic low back pain.

Keefe, F.J., & Van Horn, Y. (1993). Cognitive-behavioral treatment of rheumatoid arthritis pain: Maintaining treatment gains. *Arthritis Care and Research, 6,* 213–222.

This is an excellent discussion of the problems encountered in helping patients maintain their improvements after termination of self-management interventions. It also provides a model for interventions that may prevent relapse of maladaptive cognition and behavior among patients with RA.

Kosek, E., & Oderberg, G. (2000). Lack of pressure pain modulation by heterotopic noxious conditioning stimulation in patients with painful osteoarthritis before, but not following, surgical pain relief. *Pain, 88,* 69–78.

This investigation demonstrates the presence of mirror-image pain sensitivity in the healthy knees of patients with end-stage, unilateral knee osteoarthritis. The abnormal pain sensitivity resolves after recovery from total joint replacement surgery. These findings indicate that abnormal pain responses associated with central sensitization dissipate after the source of sensory input to the spinal dorsal horns is eliminated.

Linton, S.J., Bradley, L.A., Jensen, I., Spangfort, E., & Sundell, L. (1989). The secondary prevention of low back pain: A controlled study with follow-up. *Pain, 36,* 197–207.

This presents one of the first controlled studies of a self-management intervention for the prevention of chronic pain among workers with recent back injuries.

Rainville, P., Duncan, G.H., Price, D.D., Carrier, B., & Bushnell, M.C. (1997). Pain affect encoded in human anterior cingulate but not somatosensory cortex. *Science. 277,* 968–971.

This study provided the first evidence that hypnotic suggestions may be used to alter individuals' perceptions of the unpleasantness or intensity of a stimulus as well as cerebral blood flow in brain structures involved in processing sensory input related to the intensity and unpleasantness dimensions of pain.

Scarinci, I.C., McDonald-Haile, J., Bradley, L.A., & Richter, J.E. (1994). Altered pain perception and psychosocial features among women with gastrointestinal disorders and history of abuse: A preliminary model. *American Journal of Medicine, 97,* 108–118.

This study demonstrates that sexual/physical abuse among women with painful gastrointestinal disorders is associated with low pain thresholds, poor coping strategies, and high levels of psychiatric illness, environmental stress, and disability. The authors propose an explanatory model that integrates these findings in an effort to better understand the high health-care system utilization displayed by women who have been abused.

Watkins, L.R., Milligan, E.D., & Maier, S.F. (2001). Glial activation: A driving force for pathological pain. *Trends in Neuroscience, 24,* 450–455.

This is a superb review of the evidence that central sensitization evokes activation of glial cells that release proinflammatory cytokines and other agents that enhance pain signaling in the spinal dorsal horns and thereby contribute to pathological pain states.

Watkins, L.R., Hutchinson, M.R., Johnston, I.N., & Maier, S.F. (2005). Glia: Novel counterregulators of opioid analgesia. *Trends in Neuroscience, 28* 661–669.

This review summarizes the evidence that activated spinal glial cells release neuroexcitatory substances in response to morphine, thereby opposing its effects. This suggests that development of agents for controlling glial activation could increase the clinical utility of analgesic drugs.

DOCTOR'S ROW

Snow falls on the cars in Doctors' Row and hoods
the headlights;
snow piles on the brownstone steps, the basement
deadlights;
fills up the letters and names and brass degrees
on the bright brass plates, and the bright brass holes
for keys.

Snow hides, as if on purpose, the rows of bells
which open the doors to separate cells and hells:
to the waiting-rooms, where the famous prepare for
headlines,
and humbler citizens for their humbler deadlines.

And in and out, and out and in, they go,
the lamentable devotees of Doctors' Row;
silent and circumspect—indeed, liturgical;
their cries and prayers prescribed, their penance surgical.

No one complains—no one presumes to shriek—
the walls are very thick, and the voices weak.
Or the cries are whisked away in noiseless cabs,
while nurse, in the alley, empties a pail of swabs.

Miserable street!—through which your sweetheart hurries,
lowers her chin, as the snow-cloud stings and flurries;
thinks of the flower-stall, by the church, where you

wait like a clock, for two, for half-past two;
thinks of the roses banked on the steps in snow,
of god in heaven, and the world above, below;
widens her vision beyond the storm, her sight
the infinite rings of an immense delight;

all to be lived and loved—O glorious All!
Eastward or westward, Plato's turning wall;
the sky's blue streets swept clean of silent birds
for an audience of gods, and superwords.

CONRAD AIKEN

8

Stress and Illness

John E. Carr*

We are simply not accustomed to the conceptual handling of complex entities where many factors, all vital, maintain a balance. The human body is one such entity, and disease . . . can be viewed as any persistent harmful disturbance of its equilibrium.

ALASTAIR CUNNINGHAM

Illness, injury, and disease are byproducts of the individual's efforts to adapt to the challenge of survival (allostatic load), and are the result of interactions with the environment, and failures of the body's systems of maintenance and defense (e.g., cardiac arrest, renal failure). However, disease and illness also occur as the result of the body's "successful" adaptive response to challenge and threat. In other words, under certain conditions, the body's attempts to "cure" may be worse than the disease.

Charles Darwin provided compelling evidence that individuals and species develop adaptive mechanisms and characteristics to facilitate survival. Natural selection over successive generations ensured that individual's with the capability to *learn from experience* would be more likely to survive and to genetically pass on that capability. **Claude Bernard**, a contemporary of Darwin, theorized that there was a system of adaptive responses that evolved in all species in order to maintain a constant internal state, the **milieu interieur**, despite changes in the external environment. This process by which adaptive efforts maintained temperature, electrolyte and fluid balance, blood pressure, waste removal, etc., was subsequently referred to as **homeostasis** by the physiologist, **Walter Cannon**. According to Cannon this system of adaptive responses, like the evolution of anatomical characteristics, evolved as a result of natural selection. While lower order organisms existed within their supportive and nurturing milieu, higher order organisms, in order to achieve independence from their environment, had to develop "life-support" systems that they could carry with them, i.e., circulatory, respiratory, digestive, and waste elimination systems. All of these systems had to be maintained in homeostatic balance and their responses to stress conditions coordinated. The organism's adaptive response to threat from the environment triggered a set of physiologic reactions, which Cannon labeled the **"fight or flight" response**, the goal of which was to mobilize the individual's resources in order to optimize ability to successfully meet any challenge to survival.

BOX 8.1 Functions of the stress response

- The rapid provision of energy in the form of glucose, proteins, fats and oxygen,
- Delivery via increased heart rate, blood pressure, and respiration,
- Blood flow that is redirected away from the periphery (to decrease risk of bleeding if injured), away from the kidneys (to conserve water), and the digestive system (not immediately needed), to the brain, muscles, and heart where it is most needed, and
- A temporary hold on long-term restorative and maintenance body functions such as digestion, growth, and reproduction to conserve resources for the emergency.

These adaptive responses enable the individual to meet emergencies by reducing the risk of bleeding, hypoglycemia, asphyxiation, circulatory collapse, emotional distress, and other threats to survival.

Cannon's most significant contribution was that he was able to show that these mechanisms for the maintenance

* The author wishes to acknowledge the support, review, and helpful suggestions of Dr. Richard C. Veith, Professor and Chair, Psychiatry and Behavioral Sciences, University of Washington School of Medicine.

of homeostasis and coordination of the **fight or flight response** were mediated by a remarkably complex collaboration between the nervous and endocrine systems.

Bernard and Cannon concentrated on the internal or homeostatic state and the mechanisms by which it was maintained. *It remained for* **Hans Selye** *to focus upon the nature of* **homeostatic challenge** *and its relationship to disease and illness.* Selye labeled these environmental threats and challenges as "**stress**," invoking a concept familiar to engineers and physicists but foreign to medicine. However, it was a definition that for the first time accurately reflected the strain, impact, implications, and process of interaction between the organism and the environment (Canon had actually used the term **stress** much earlier but Selye claimed credit for its introduction). Selye observed that stress appeared to trigger a "nonspecific" or uniform response on the part of the organism, regardless of the nature of the triggering stimulus. However, subsequent research has shown that the response is not uniform but varies in response to the intensity and nature of the stressor as well as its perception or appraisal by the individual.

Selye was among the first researchers to note that the body's response to stress, designed to heal, could cause disease and illness under prolonged or chronic stress conditions. Confronted with a stressor condition, the body initiated a complex adaptive response which Selye described as the **General Adaptation Syndrome** (GAS):

BOX 8.2 Stages of the General Adaptation Syndrome

- Alarm, the initial response of the body to the stressor;
- Resistance, or the mobilization of defenses and adaptive responses. However, if stress is prolonged, then there is a stage of ...
- Exhaustion, or the collapse of adaptive responses. It was this stage, Selye asserted, that resulted in gastrointestinal ulcers, immune and other system failures, and even death.

Selye observed that not all stress was bad; that in fact some conditions, which he labeled **eustress,** *could be beneficial, and that the stress condition could be an opportunity for adaptive learning.* Researchers began to recognize that stress is more than just an external environmental event, that *any* condition of change or challenge that causes tension or strain was stressful. Further, moderate challenge appeared to represent the best option for stimulating adaptive change and providing an incentive for learning, cognitive growth, and the development of novel solutions. Too little challenge may be boring and go unnoticed. Too much challenge may be overwhelming, harmful, traumatic, and potentially fatal. Finally, events are not intrinsically stressful but rather stress is "in the eye of the beholder," i.e., events that are highly stressful for one person may have little significance for another person.

Selye's definition of stress varied over his lifetime, fluctuating between stress as an external causal event, stress as a stereotyped pattern of response, and stress as a condition of strain or tension. The latter more closely approximates a valid definition of stress in health care yet the prevailing medical view continued to define stress as an external environmental event. Richard Lazarus and Susan Folkman proposed a broader stress model in an attempt to explain the role that the individual's cognitive processes played in the interaction between the individual and the environment. The impact of a stressor condition was determined or mediated by the individual's ability to **appraise**, to evaluate and assign meaning to the stressor based on past experience and learning; the individual's **vulnerability** and the individuals' **coping efforts.** The complexity of the stress phenomenon, however, warrants further elaboration of this model.

(1) **Vulnerabilities** represent not only physical or social limitations but biologic, cognitive, and behavioral limitations as well. A patient may be genetically vulnerable to sickle cell anemia, cognitively vulnerable to chronic depression, or behaviorally vulnerable to lung cancer from smoking. (2) **Appraisal** represents the cognitive process by which the individual interprets, assigns personal meaning to, or defines the stressor condition and its severity. This is obviously a byproduct of culture, past experience, and learning, all of which influence conceptualization and perception. (3) **Coping skills** include the individual's behavioral skills, cognitive strategies and expectations, as well as motivated effort in managing the stressor conditions. (4) **Social support** includes the reassurance, encouragement, validation, guidance, assistance, and bonds that bolster or can be called upon by the individual, and (5) **Resources** include not only the material supports that facilitate the individual's coping efforts (e.g., financial assets), but also the intrinsic as well as extrinsic incentives (opportunities, options), and cognitive as well as biologic resources (e.g., intelligence, creativity, health, personality characteristics) that are potentially instrumental in the individual's adaptive efforts.

Stress is a condition of change, strain, or disequilibrium that can result from diverse biologic, behavioral, cognitive, sociocultural, or environmental challenges to homeostasis or the status quo. These challenges, which can occur within any or all of these domains, constitute stressor conditions which, in turn, can impact or interact with all other domains (see Figure 8.1). The growth and development of the individual involves the accumulation, through learning and experience, of biologic functions; behavioral skills; cognitive knowledge and problem solving abilities; sociocultural beliefs, mores, and expectations; and coping responses to environmental challenges. Thus, an event in any one of these domains can be a source of challenge triggering responses to this challenge in all other domains. Like a giant balloon, the individual's experience may be pushed at one point only to respond at every other point. As can be seen, this is a far more comprehensive view of the role of stress in health care than the traditional concept of stress as an external event and "stress-related diseases" as a small, idiosyncratic group of disorders. It more accurately reflects the reality of the nature of stress and its role in the etiology of disease and illness. Any condition, whether it be behavioral, cognitive, sociocultural, environmental, or biologic, that challenges the organism or effects a departure from normal functioning (homeostasis) constitutes a stressor condition and can contribute to, i.e., predetermine or precipitate, disease and illness. In these terms, therefore, *all diseases and illnesses are "stress related" since they represent the impact of conditions that effect a departure from normal functioning.*

THE BIOLOGICAL BASIS OF THE STRESS RESPONSE

Incoming sensory information is collected by the limbic system and then forwarded to the association areas of the cortex for analysis. If the incoming information is appraised or interpreted to indicate a novel, threatening, or homeostatically challenging situation, a signal is sent to the hypothalamus, which immediately activates various neuroendocrine effector systems. Sympathetic Nervous System (SNS) pathways leading from the hypothalamus serve to immediately arouse and mobilize the organism by effecting rapid physiologic changes including altered blood flow, cardiac function, salivation, dilation of the pupils of the eyes, decreased kidney excretion, increased salivation and sweating, as well as other glandular activities. SNS activity is mediated by the release of norepinephrine at sympathetic nerve endings, which binds to receptors on smooth muscle and secretory cells. However, this SNS-activated response, while immediate, is short lived. In order to provide a more sustained response, the nervous system calls upon the endocrine and circulatory system. SNS impulses from the hypothalamus stimulate the adrenal medulla, which secretes catecholamines, mainly epinephrine, into the blood stream. Using the circulatory system, the epinephrine is transported throughout the body to select receptor sites in target glands, organs, and other structures, thus, serving to amplify and prolong the earlier direct and rapid SNS activation. The secretion of epinephrine into the blood stream has the same effect as direct SNS activation but provides a 20–30 second delay in onset and a 10-fold increase in the duration of the effect, thereby making a more sustained and sensitive response possible.

While the hypothalamus is triggering the rapid release of epinephrine and norepinephrine via the SNS, it is also pouring a variety of hormones into the blood stream. These **releasing hormones** converge on the pituitary where they stimulate select cells to release further hormones that, in turn, will travel through the blood stream to activate distant target glands. For example, the hormone **corticotrophin releasing factor** (CRF) travels to the pituitary where it stimulates cells to release **adrenocorticotrophic hormone** (ACTH), which in turn travels via the blood stream to the adrenal cortex where it stimulates the secretion of cortisol, a glucocorticoid, into the bloodstream. This **glucocorticoid response** has far reaching effects designed to take fuel out of storage and distribute it to select muscles and tissues. This is accomplished via (1) the inhibition of protein synthesis and the acceleration of protein catabolism, (2) increased glycerol and free fatty acid release leading to increased glucose production from protein and glycerol, and (3) decreased peripheral glucose metabolism in muscle and fat tissue providing added glucose to fuel the central nervous system. The glucocorticoids also play a key role in inhibiting or shutting down various systems during the emergency.

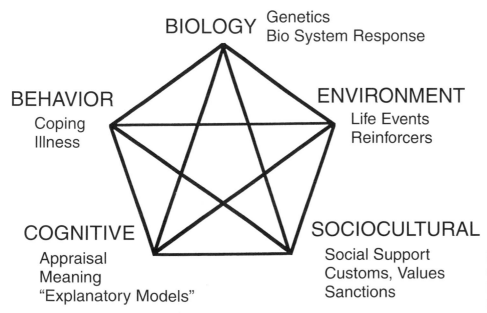

FIGURE 8.1 Interacting domains of variables that contribute to health and illness. Note that stress in one domain can affect a response in other domains.

In response to acute stress conditions, releasing hormones in the hypothalamus also stimulate the release of **vasopressin** from the pituitary, which helps to store water for emergencies, effect an increase in the retention of sodium by the kidney, and, thus, help to sustain blood pressure. The release of growth hormone affects bone growth, the development of muscle mass, and free fatty acid and glucose levels in the blood via the production of insulin in the pancreas. Thyroid hormones increase metabolism, heart rate, heart contractility, peripheral vascular resistance, blood pressure, and sensitivity to catecholamines (e.g., epinephrine). Gonadotropic hormones promote estrogen, progesterone, and testosterone secretion. All of these responses are designed to enable the individual to successfully adapt to acute or relatively short-term stress conditions. However, humans have been and are increasingly subject to more complex, prolonged, and, therefore, chronic stressor conditions. As a result, *these stress responses, when sustained, can reach a point of diminishing returns and begin to inflict damage rather than restore the various "life support systems" of the organism.* Since virtually all diseases and illnesses are "stress related" a review of such disorders would constitute the entire curriculum of clinical medicine. However, the following sections provide clinical examples from each of the organ systems of the etiologic impact of stress conditions.

Growth Disorders

Growth begins with cell division. All cells in the body contain the same genetic information in the form of DNA, a code that provides instructions for protein construction and cell growth. When the cell divides, the DNA is copied. If a mistake occurs during this process, resulting in the creation of an aberrant cell (a wrong amino acid or protein), a regulatory gene called P53 within the cell recognizes the error and stops further cell division until the error is re-

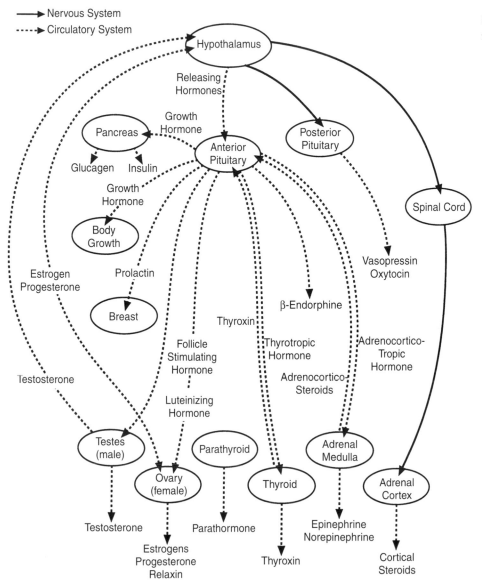

FIGURE 8.2 Schematic of neuroendocrine system responses to stress.

paired. If the error cannot be repaired, P53 causes the cell to self-destruct. Cells also contain molecular time clocks called **telomeres** attached to their DNA strands, which predetermine the number of cell divisions. When the cell reaches the end of its predetermined number of cell divisions, it stops dividing and dies. The constituents of the dead cells are then recycled for further use. *This programmed cell death or* **apoptosis** *(Greek for "fallen leaves") is essential to normal growth and development.* For example, as fingers develop in the embryo, the residual fin webbing between them must die and be recycled into new tissue growth. This process of DNA repair and restoration is another of the body's systems of maintenance, in this case at the cellular level. It is automatic and continuous, repairing damage and correcting growth errors.

While growth is largely determined by genetic predisposition, it is influenced by challenge. This is a good example of the "moderation in all things" principle, especially at the physiologic level. The hypothalamic-pituitary-adrenocortical system appears to be responsive to novel stimuli, and short-term or moderate stress has been shown to stimulate growth hormone secretion for a time. There is even some evidence to suggest that some stressors can enhance growth while others may impede growth. Thus, we would anticipate that organisms in moderately challenging or stimulating environments would likely experience optimal pituitary secretions of growth hormone resulting in bone growth, cell division, and the directing of nutrients into tissue growth. Under chronic stress conditions, however, there is an inhibition of growth hormone release. This appears to be in part attributable to SNS arousal (recall that in emergency situations, some functions like growth are put on hold). It is also partly the result of the presence of excess blood levels of glucocorticoids, which block secretion of growth hormone, reduce the sensitivity of target cells, and block the synthesis of new proteins and new DNA in dividing cells.

Recall also that stress can block digestion, disrupt metabolism, and thereby limit nutrition, which can influence growth. The diversion of nutrients away from growing tissue to fuel peripheral muscle, heart, and brain, if prolonged as in chronic stress, can have a decided impact on growth. As glucocorticoids course through the blood stream, halting long-term projects to provide all available energy for the emergency, they block the rebuilding of bone and the dietary uptake of calcium. Thus, *chronic stress can lead to a deterioration of bone mass*, an especially critical problem for older adults where bone replacement is not keeping up with bone reabsorption, increasing the risk of **osteoporosis**.

Immune System Disorders

The immune system is the "security system" of the body. As with all security systems, its job is to make sure that

> Stress is not necessarily bad for you: it is also the spice of life, for any emotion, any activity, causes stress.
>
> HANS SELYE
> *The Spice of Life*

organisms or agents that have no business in the body are not admitted. To accomplish this mission it must be able to identify and distinguish between alien and nonalien agents. It maintains a file of all admissible or acceptable agents, those who have "security clearance." It also keeps a file on all the "usual suspects," agents that do not have clearance and are in fact known to be dangerous to the body. Profiles of suspicious characters are developed to enable the immune system to spot suspects.

Since the immune system must function throughout the body, it relies upon the circulatory system and circulatory-borne hormones for communication. When an "invader" is detected, the immune system sets into motion an aggressive system of defenses composed of lymphocytes and monocytes (white blood cells). **Lymphocytes** are made up of B-cells that mature in the bone marrow and promote antibody production, and T-cells that mature in the thymus and promote cell-mediated immunity. Lymphocytes have receptors for a range of neurotransmitters that enable them to "monitor" and respond to the diverse stress response and recovery mechanisms of the body.

When an infectious invader is detected by a monocyte called a **macrophage**, it immediately activates the immune system response. B-cells produce antibodies that bind to the invading agent, immobilize it, and target it for destruction. The macrophage releases interleukin-1 to stimulate the T-helper cell activity. The T-helper cell in turn releases interleukin-2, which triggers the proliferation of T-killer cells, which attack and destroy the foreign agent. In addition, the T-helper cell also secretes B-cell growth factor, which promotes the proliferation of B-cells. Suppressor T-cells modulate the immune response by blocking helper T-cell activity.

Like all security systems, the immune system can be breached. Some invading agents become quite adept at impersonating cells that have "security clearance," thereby gaining admission to the body. Human Immunodeficiency Virus (**HIV**) breaches the security of the immune system by taking on the identifying characteristics of T-helper cells. The HIV penetrates the T-helper cell and alters its DNA through the action of an enzyme (RNA) enabling the HIV to take over the T-helper cell genes and produce other HIV genes. If the T-helper cell dies, the HIV simply moves on to another T-helper cell and repeats the process. HIV also infects macrophages, using them as transport to move about through the body. HIV infection results in a decrease in T-helper cells and low T-helper to T-suppressor cell ratio resulting in a reduced T-cell response to antigen activation. This leaves the individual susceptible to a wide range of opportunistic infections. **HIV** is transmitted by direct contact with fluids that contain HIV T-helper cells. Although blood, saline, tears, semen, mucous, breast milk, and vaginal secretions may contain HIV cells, transmission of the virus primarily occurs via blood to blood contact through hypodermic needles or transfusions, or is sexually transmitted through semen or vaginal secretions, or by passage of the infection from mother to newborn.

The immune system can also make mistakes. Sometimes the immune system can be overzealous, denying clearance or even targeting for destruction its own organs or tissue resulting in hyperactive immune system disorders or autoimmune disorders like **multiple sclerosis, pernicious anemia, rheumatoid arthritis, juvenile diabetes,** or certain **allergies.** Thus, the effect of chronic stress on the immune system is to either suppress or reduce its effectiveness as a defense against invaders or heighten its effectiveness to the extent that it begins to attack its host body. We have already seen that individuals are exposed to differential patterns and frequencies of stressors, that there are individual differences in genetically programmed resistance, vulnerabilities, resources, and the appraisal of what is a stressor. These variations influence the magnitude and the frequency of the individual's stress response, which, in turn, determines immune system effectiveness in resisting various diseases. Hence, although immune system suppression in response to stressor conditions has been associated with increased susceptibility to infectious disease (Cohen & Williamson, 1991), immune system response cannot be easily predicted—in some cases increasing in response to stress, in other cases being suppressed in response to stress. In general, mild acute stress, via SNS arousal, facilitates activation of the immune system enhancing its effectiveness. However, in cases of severe or chronic stress, continued SNS activation triggers the release of large cumulative quantities of glucocorticoids into the bloodstream effecting a suppression of the immune system, presumably to inhibit the immune system from overreacting and initiating an autoimmune condition.

It is important to understand that the stress-immune system-disease relationship is not linear. As we have already seen, a biologic response (e.g., the immune system) to any stressor does not occur in a vacuum but impacts and is accompanied by responses in each of the other domains, i.e., behavioral, cognitive, sociocultural, and environmental. Hence, the degree and nature of the stressor effect is modulated by the individual's appraisal of the stressor based upon past experience, coping skills, vulnerabilities (cognitive, behavioral, biologic, sociocultural), and resources (sociocultural, biologic, behavioral, cognitive, environmental). To the extent that these variables differ, the effectiveness of the immune system and the outcome of its efforts to protect the organism may be altered.

Autoimmune Diseases

There are two kinds of autoimmune diseases, organ specific and nonorgan specific. In organ specific diseases only one type of tissue is damaged by the immune system. The antigenic immune response focuses upon this tissue, like the thyroid in **Hashimoto's thyroiditis** or the myelin sheath surrounding the nerve cells of the central nervous system in **multiple sclerosis.** In nonorgan specific diseases the antigen may be universal, i.e., a part of every cell, as in **systemic lupus erythematosus** (SLE) or some forms of **rheumatoid arthritis.** In SLE the antigen appears to be part of the nucleus of every cell including the DNA, resulting in multiple manifestations such as inflammation of the joints, fever, skin eruptions, renal involvement, cardiopulmonary abnormalities, and lymph node involvement. Onset appears to be precipitated by a viral infection in a genetically predisposed individual. **Rheumatoid arthritis** is manifested primarily by inflammation and subsequent destruction of the peripheral joints, but systemic manifestations also include hematological, pulmonary, neurological, and cardiovascular abnormalities as well as fever, fatigue, and muscle weakness. Antigenic challenge leading to the synthesis of rheumatoid factors appears to be precipitated by bacterial infection.

Cancer

Earlier we described the genetically programmed cell repair, death, and recycle functions that are essential to normal cell growth and tissue development. Exposure to chronic stress conditions impairs the ability of the cell to carry out these cell activities that are so essential to normal growth and development. Some cancer cells are able to produce a protein that prevents the telomere function of programmed cell death. The cell becomes immortal and rapid, seemingly endless, cell division occurs. Also, the regulatory gene P53 can be mutated by carcinogens (e.g., tobacco smoke, UV rays, toxic chemicals, aflatoxin) so that it can no longer correct cell division errors or program cell death.

It is generally agreed that chronic stress has the greatest effect on tumors that are viral in origin, and that while stress effects the development of these tumors it does not necessarily contribute to their origin. At the neurohormonal level, stress activates the SNS, which in turn stimulates the release of a number of hormones including epinephrine and norepinephrine, glucocorticoids, prolactin, and endogenous opioids. Circulating glucocorticoids appear to block the production and activation of T-cells and B-cells, the immune systems' weapons against invading tumor cells. Glucocorticoids also inadvertently aid **angiogenesis,** the process by which increased capillary growth provides nutrients to the tumor cells. In addition, in the individual under stress, the tumor increasingly robs the blood stream of glucose before it can get to its emergency destinations in the heart, muscle, and central nervous systems. Hence, stress not only effects the body's defenses against tumor growth but in some cases actually facilitates the development of tumors as a by-product of the stress response, another example of how the stress response can be maladaptive as well as adaptive.

> There is one ailment in the chest which has difficult and peculiar symptoms. It should be heeded, as it is neither free of danger nor particularly uncommon. Its localization, the patient's feeling of suffocation, and the anguish accompanying it, give reason for calling it angina pectoris.
>
> WILLIAM HEBERDEN
> English physician

Cardiovascular Disorders

SNS activation in response to an acute stressor effects the following changes in the cardiovascular system: (1) arterial constriction, (2) increased blood pressure and heart rate, (3) altered blood flow away from digestive track, kidneys, and skin and toward the brain and muscles, (4) decreased urine formation to conserve water and maintain blood volume, and (5) emptying of bladder to reduce weight. *These responses are the same regardless of whether the stressor is physical or psychosocial, "real," learned, or perceived.* These responses are also the same in chronic stress, except that there is increased risk of damage from the continued stress response. Sustained increased arterial pressure causes the blood vessel to lose its elasticity and rupture, especially at branch points. Fatty acids and glucose begin to collect in the ruptures clogging vessels and causing **atherosclerosis** or the accumulation of plaques. This clogging and narrowing of the vessels deprives the heart of blood, oxygen, and glucose, a condition called **myocardial ischemia**. If the deprivation is severe, death of the cells can occur resulting in an **infarct** or heart attack. If a normal heart is subjected to a stressor, the release of an endothelium-derived relaxant factor (EDRF) causes the coronary artery to dilate permitting increased blood flow of nutrients and oxygen. However, a heart suffering **myocardial ischemia** loses its ability to release EDRF and instead, when subjected to a stressor, releases serotonin. This causes the coronary artery to constrict rather than dilate resulting in pain or **angina**. In such cases the ingestion of nitroglycerin, which is an artificial EDRF, relaxes the arterial walls and relieves the angina.

Exposure to chronic stress increases risk of **ventricular fibrillation**. The chronically stressed heart muscle becomes increasingly sensitive to SNS activation that arrives at the heart in the form of two simultaneous signals. Under conditions of chronic stress, a sudden increase in the frequency or intensity of the stress (e.g., bad news or a surprise) may cause asynchronous SNS signals resulting in a disorganized heart response called **fibrillation**.

Hypertension is one of the most common cardiovascular problems a physician will encounter. It is usually defined as arterial pressures in excess of 140 mm Hg systolic pressure and 90 mm Hg diastolic pressure. Hypertension that is caused by a biologic dysfunction is called **secondary hypertension** and accounts for approximately 10% of hypertension cases. The remaining cases are generally associated with homeostatic changes in blood pressure resulting from adaptations to other stressor conditions and are called **essential hypertension**. The continuous SNS-activated adaptations of the cardiovascular system to chronic stress can result in a resetting of the homeostatic setpoint of the carotid sinus and the aortic baroreceptors leading the cardiovascular system to tolerate higher and higher pressures over time.

Some individuals carry a genetic predisposition for heightened cardiovascular reactivity to certain precipitating stress conditions. Cognitive, behavioral, sociocultural, and environmental stressor conditions interact with biologic conditions, including a genetic predisposition, and contribute to changes in blood pressure that can become a chronic health-care problem. The **Type A response pattern** is a cognitive and behavioral response pattern that influences how individuals respond to acute precipitating factors. It is more common among males and relatively rare among females. It involves increased sympatho-adrenomedullary reactivity to stressors and is associated with increased risk for coronary heart disease. This behavioral pattern involves an emotional rather than problem-solving approach to stressor conditions that challenge the individual's sense of mastery and is characterized by a cynical, angry, hostile response to these frustrating situations.

Spasm of the arterial vasculature associated with stressor-induced SNS activity can result in vasospastic disorders like migraine headache and Raynaud's disease. Classical **migraine headache** is generally preceded by a prodrome, or visual, auditory, aphasic, and/or gastrointestinal dysfunction. The most frequently manifested prodrome is a visual phenomenon that is a symptom of severe arterial constriction. However, the pain of the migraine headache results from the vasodilation that follows the original vasoconstriction. Migraine headache may be precipitated by diverse stressor conditions including situational stressors, depression, anxiety, hormones, barometric pressure, light, smoking, medications and foods. The vasoactive mechanism can be triggered by chemicals in certain foods like red wine and aged cheese (tyramine), chocolate (phenylethylamine), coffee and tea (caffeine), alcohol, and food additives (monosodium glutamate, nitrates, and nitrites). These foods may be perceived as antibodies precipitating an immune response that produces vasoconstriction and subsequent vasodilation. **Raynaud's disease** is a vasospastic disorder resulting from episodic vasoconstriction and cyanosis of the fingers and/or toes, generally in response to exposure to cold or other stressors. Vasodilatation following vasoconstriction can result in aching or throbbing pain in the extremities.

Metabolic Disorders

We have already seen that one of the emergency responses to stress involves taking energy generating nutrients out of storage while temporarily shutting down digestion and storage process. In the absence of stress, food is digested and energy in the form of fatty acids, glycerol, glucose, and amino acids is metabolized and stored in the more complex forms of triglycerides, glycogen, and proteins through the action of insulin. In response to acute stress, the secretion of glucocorticoids into the blood stream results in the inhibition of digestion, a decrease in insulin secretion, and a decrease in the transport of food into storage. Instead, the stress hormones, (glucocorticoids, glucagon, epinephrine, and norepinephrine), cause the complex foods in storage to be broken down into simple foods and poured into the blood stream for immediate delivery to the brain, heart, and target muscles. The effect of chronic stress is to cause this process to repeatedly turn on, then off, then on again, with the result that through these constant conversions, energy is wasted, i.e., the stored energy is gradually depleted since it is never quite replaced. Once fat stores are exhausted, the muscles begin to waste. This process is frequently seen in patients who, in response to cognitive or sociocultural stressors (e.g., perceptions of self as too fat or sociocultural sanctions for body type), attempt weight management through a variety of maladaptive behaviors or **eating disorders**. Individuals who limit food intake excessively and/or engage in excessive physical activity (e.g., running or aerobics), purging, self-induced vomiting, or laxative abuse with resultant weight below 85% of acceptable norms, and amenorrhea suffer from **anorexia nervosa**. Individuals who, in response to cognitive or sociocultural stressors engage in binge eating, whether accompanied by subsequent purging or nonpurging behaviors, suffer from **bulimia nervosa**.

While excess physical activity and limited food intake represent one form of risk, the sedentary and overindulgent patient runs a different kind of risk. Stored fat builds up to the point where fat cells are full and the fat cells refuse to respond to insulin. In addition, stress-induced release of glucocorticoids tend to make the cells less sensitive to insulin (recall that under stress, fat storage is temporarily shut down). The increased concentrations of glucose (hyperglycemia) and fat in the blood stream begin to clog up

blood vessels and organs, impeding the delivery of food and oxygen to tissues, reducing the efficiency of organs, and even increasing the risk of impaired vision by contributing to the development of cataracts. This process leads to adult onset diabetes or **Type II, noninsulin dependent diabetes mellitus** (NIDDM). Type II diabetes (NIDDM) is a result of a failure of cells to respond to insulin. It is triggered by an overabundance of food, which stimulates excessive insulin production by the pancreas. Tissues normally responsive to insulin become less sensitive, as if satiated by the excess of insulin. Meanwhile, the insulin producing cells in the pancreas soon become exhausted, leading to impaired insulin production. This insulin shortage can generally be augmented by diet and/or oral medication, which facilitate glucose metabolism. Aging, overweight individuals are especially at risk for developing Type II diabetes (NIDDM), which unless treated or prevented, can develop into a major health-care problems in later years. *Fifteen percent of people over 65 suffer from Type II diabetes (NIDDM). It increases the risk of mortality two-fold and triples the risk of heart disease in males. It is a leading cause of blindness and the seventh leading cause of death.*

In contrast to Type II diabetes or (NIDDM), which is the result of a failure of cells to respond to insulin, **Type I** or **insulin-dependent diabetes mellitus** (IDDM), is caused, in part, by a genetically influenced shortage of insulin. In individuals with this genetic predisposition, the onset of Type I diabetes (IDDM) may be triggered by a viral infection involving the pancreas. The infection activates the immune system, which may begin producing antibodies that attack the insulin producing beta cells of the pancreas resulting in insulin deficiency and elevated blood glucose levels (hyperglycemia), a major characteristic of Type I diabetes (IDDM).

Gastrointestinal Disorders

Esophageal reflux results from irritation of the mucosal lining of the esophagus by digestive acids. The disorder can be exacerbated by stressor conditions and occurs as the result of gastric acid being forced up from the stomach by air (belching) or nausea, but usually occurs after a meal and when the patient is lying down. The symptoms include a painful burning sensation in the upper chest, which can radiate into the arms or jaw and can be confused with pain resulting from a cardiovascular disorder (angina).

The strong stomach acids require the body to protect its own tissues from being digested. A number of mechanisms contributing to excess stomach acid and/or the failure of these defenses can result in the development of **ulcers**. The pathogenesis of gastric ulcer appears to depend upon a genetic vulnerability (e.g., thin stomach lining and/or SNS activation of the vagus causing gastric hypersecretion) in combination with a precipitating stress condition. Normally, a thick stomach lining, buffered by bicarbonate that is secreted to neutralize the acid, protects the stomach tissue. However, with increased stress, digestion is inhibited, as is maintenance of the thickness of the stomach lining and the production of bicarbonate buffering since they are no longer needed. Once the stress is ended, food consumption and digestion are resumed but now in a more vulnerable stomach. Thus, the ulcer is formed as a result of the recovery from stress rather than from its onset.

Ulcers can also develop as a byproduct of the body's other stress responses. Recall that in response to stress, digestion and blood flow to the digestive track are inhibited. This can lead to oxygen deprivation, reduced flushing of wastes and acid, and resulting tissue damage. Under nonstress conditions, the digestive track is usually repaired through the secretion of prostaglandin. In response to stress the increased glucocorticoids in the blood stream inhibit prostaglandin synthesis, reducing the body's ability to repair its digestive tract. Finally, *bacteria in the gut appear to play a far more important role in the development of **ulcers** than previously believed.* Resistant to stomach acids, some of these bacteria attack stomach walls weakened by other stress effects. In addition, *chronic stress-induced suppression of the immune system lowers the body's defenses against these bacteria.*

Further down the digestive tract, the small intestine, under normal conditions, has principle responsibility for extracting nutrients from the mechanically and chemically broken-down food. Once this is accomplished, the left-over waste passes on to the large intestine where, with water extracted, it is evacuated. In response to acute stress, digestion and motility in the small intestine stop, while motility in the large intestine speeds up to dispose of excess weighty waste materials that will only impede the organism in an emergency. Under conditions of chronic stress, however, this delicate synchronization can become uncoordinated and result in a number of GI disorders including **diarrhea**, **constipation**, and **irritable bowel syndrome**. If small intestine motility is too inhibited, the result will be constipation. If large intestine motility is overly activated, the result may be diarrhea.

Stressful events appear to be the precipitating factor in the majority of cases of children who develop encopresis or fecal incontinence after successful toilet training. Events such as the birth of a sibling, illness of a parent, starting school, or parental separation or divorce, are associated with increased incontinence. **Enuresis** or the involuntary discharge of urine (e.g., bed-wetting in children) exemplifies the complexity of interacting stressor conditions that can contribute to a disorder. **Primary enuresis** (never consistently dry for more than a week or two) has a genetic component and is largely attributable to developmental immaturity, or anatomic anomalies or urologic dysfunction. However, **secondary enuresis** (wetting after an extended period of dryness) is more likely to reflect the impact of environmental stressors (e.g., infection); biologic stressors (e.g., sleep apnea); or cognitive, behavioral, or sociocultural stressors such as familial disruption, social pressure, conflict, or anxiety.

Irritable Bowel Syndrome (IBS) appears to be a disorder of excessive, probably genetic, gastrointestinal vulnerability to stressor conditions. **IBS** is characterized by abdominal discomfort, bloating, belching, and flatulence in the absence of a disease or lesion. It may be accompanied by mucus in the stools, fecal urgency, nausea, loss of appetite, and sometimes even vomiting. **Ulcerative colitis** and **Crohn's disease** are disorders characterized by inflammation and ulceration of the lining of the colon and the small bowel. These disorders appear to result from a genetic vulnerability in the form of an overly sensitive SNS activation, which, when precipitated by exposure to chronic stress, triggers an immune system response and/or increased levels of enzymes that can dissolve the mucal lining in the GI tract. **Ulcerative colitis** involves inflammation and ulceration of the mucosa of the rectum and sigmoid colon while **Crohn's disease** involves mucosal inflammation and edema, and thickening and scarring of the small bowel wall, which can cause bowel obstruction. While Crohn's disease usually occurs in the lower part of the GI tract, it can occur anywhere from the esophagus to the rectum (Schwarz & Blanchard, 1990).

Reproduction and Sexual Disorders

Among the hypothalamus' many functions is the secretion of releasing hormones that stimulate pituitary secretion of **luteinizing hormone** (LH) and **follicle stimulating hormone** (FSH). These hormones, in turn, activate sperm production and testosterone release from the testes in males. In response to stress, however, these reproductive functions are inhibited. As we have already seen, stress induces the release of multiple hormones from the pituitary, among them adrenocorticotrophic hormone (ACTH) and endogenous opioids (endorphins). ACTH induces the release of glucocorticoids that, among many inhibitory functions, also blocks responsivity of the testes to LH, inhibiting the release of testosterone. Glucocorticoids also appear to block the effects of the hypothalamic releasing hormones and the pituitary release of LH, thereby shutting down the whole process at its source. Another pituitary hormone, prolactin, when released in response to stress, also decreases the sensitivity of the pituitary to the hypothalamic releasing hormone. All of these converging inhibitory actions impede reproductive capability through the reduction of testosterone in circulation and reduced sperm motility.

In emergency situations, sex and reproduction are not high priorities. Therefore, it will come as no surprise to learn that under stressful conditions tumescence is less likely to occur. The difficulty lies in the fact that penile erections, which are hemodynamic, require parasympathetic nervous system activation. But, as we have already seen, any stressor condition will induce SNS activation, thereby either inhibiting the erection altogether, producing **impotence**, or, having occurred, bringing it to a rather early conclusion, **premature ejaculation**. The physiologic aspect of this problem has led to the development of a number of medical and surgical treatments. However, the problem can have significant psychosocial origins and sequelae. *Having occurred, the erectile dysfunction itself becomes a new stressor condition that in turn has profound cognitive, behavioral, sociocultural, as well as biologic effects.* These can frequently be treated successfully and less invasively by cognitive-behavioral and interpersonal treatment approaches.

The effect of stress on the reproductive functions of females is no less complex. Pituitary hormones LH and FSH stimulate the ovaries to release estrogen and produce eggs. During the "luteal phase" of the menstrual cycle progesterone stimulates the uterine wall to receive the fertilized egg where it develops into the embryo. Under normal, non-stress conditions enzymes in the fat cells of the female normally enable her to convert the already small amounts of male hormone (androstenedione) in her blood stream into estrogen. However, in response to stress this conversion process is impeded. Fat cells are commandeered to provide emergency energy leaving insufficient enzyme to convert the male hormone. The resultant buildup of the male hormone reduces progesterone levels and inhibits the reproductive process resulting in **amenorrhea**, a condition sometimes seen in the excessive physical activity of athletes or from **anorexia nervosa**. This stress-induced lowering of the progesterone levels tends to combine with or amplify the already familiar glucocorticoid-induced reduction of the ability of the body to recalcify bone, contributing to **osteoporosis**. It also reduces the ability of the body to protect itself against **atherosclerosis**, or provide sufficient nutrition for uterine wall maturation in support of pregnancy. Among the more serious reproductive consequences of severe chronic stress is the activation of the SNS, which releases epinephrine and norepinephrine resulting in redirected blood flow away from the uterus. This increases risk of asphyxiation of the fetus via decreased blood pressure and heart rate, and can contribute to **spontaneous abortion**.

Respiratory Disorders

Under stressful conditions the rate of respiration increases in order to ready the body for action, increasing oxygen intake and decreasing levels of carbon dioxide. This emergency adaptation to stress, like all of the body's stress responses, can be readily conditioned to a wide range of stimulus or stress conditions. Hence, **hyperventilation** is a commonly observed symptom among many patients in response to stress conditions. **Bronchial asthma** is a more complex respiratory disorder where mucosal secretions and swellings increase and the muscles surrounding the bronchioles contract, resulting in difficulty in breathing. Generally precipitated by stressor conditions such as infections, allergies, cold air, tobacco smoke, or interpersonal and cognitive conflict situations (to which it can be conditioned), the inability to breath itself becomes an added stressor further exacerbating the stress response and often leading to a respiratory crisis.

Emphysema is a condition of abnormal enlargement of the air spaces resulting from a breakdown of the walls of the alveoli, the clusters of air spaces at the ends of the airways in the lungs. The walls lose their elasticity and, unable to be held open during expiration, tend to collapse making the transfer of oxygen into the blood stream increasingly difficult. Excessive smoking is clearly a major risk factor in the etiology of emphysema although other forms of air pollution, occupational fumes, and repeated lung infections also play a role.

Bronchitis is a respiratory disorder characterized by chronic inflammation of the cells lining the bronchial passages and generally associated with exposure to an infectious agent (viral or bacterial). The body's usual defense against invaders, the immune system, is weakened by chronic stress and, under such conditions, the body is left increasingly vulnerable to respiratory disorders like **bronchitis** or the more serious infectious pulmonary diseases such as **influenza** and **pneumonia**. The immune system plays a different role in disorders like **hay fever** or other respiratory **allergic reactions**. In these cases the body reacts with an exaggerated autoimmune response upon encountering the offending antigen (e.g., pollen, mold, dust, etc). The body's excessive response in the form of swelling mucal membranes, increased nasal discharge, nasal obstruction, and sneezing are familiar symptoms. *The symptoms are exacerbated by stressful conditions and can be readily conditioned to associated stressful stimuli.* Hence, it is not surprising to find that a patient's complaints of increasing allergic reactions can increase at a time when job, social, or family pressures have increased.

Musculoskeletal Disorders

In acute stress conditions the musculoskeletal system provides the mobility required by the body to adapt. SNS activation enables the musculature to respond immediately while blood flow is redirected to muscles in order to energize and nourish. However, under chronic stress conditions, sustained muscular activity can result in neuromuscular disorders. **Muscle strain** and **tendonitis** are common sequelae of excess demands on musculature during stress

HE MAKES A HOUSE CALL

Six, seven years ago
when you began to begin to faint
I painted your leg with iodine

threaded the artery
with the needle and then the tube
pumped your heart with dye enough

to see the valve
almost closed with stone.
We were both under pressure.

Today, in your garden,
kneeling under the sticky fig tree
for tomatoes

I keep remembering your blood.
Seven, it was. I was just
beginning to learn the heart

inside out.
Afterward, your surgery
and the precise valve of steel

and plastic that still pops and clicks
inside like a ping-pong ball.
I should try

chewing tobacco sometimes
if only to see how it tastes.
There is a trace of it at the corner.

of your leathery smile
which insists that I see inside
the house; someone named Bill I'm supposed
to know; the royal plastic soldier
whose body fills with whiskey
and marches on a music box

How Dry I Am;
the illuminated 3-D Christ who turns
into Mary from different angles;

the watery basement,
the pills you take, the ivy
that may grow around the ceiling

if it must. Here, you
are in charge of figs, beans,
tomatoes, life.

At the hospital, a thousand times
I have heard your heart valve open, close.
I know how clumsy it is.

But health is whatever works
and for as long. I keep thinking
of seven years without a faint

on my way to the car
loaded with vegetables
I keep thinking of seven years ago

when you bled in my hands like a saint.

JOHN STONE

conditions. **Tension headache** results from the muscles of the head and neck being kept in prolonged contraction. **Low back pain** is a common disorder resulting from contraction of the back muscles while attempting to hold the body erect. Sustained contraction without muscle movement causes blood flow to the muscle to decrease resulting in decreased nourishment, buildup of waste products, and exhaustion of the muscle with attendant pain. Repetition of this sequence can result in the acute low back pain becoming conditioned to associated stress situations resulting in **chronic pain.**

Pain

Among the organism's many emergency responses to threat or other sources of stress is its capacity for damage control. The nervous system provides a complex network of pain receptors throughout the body to keep the brain advised as to potential and actual damage to the organism. Pain signal transmission from the periphery to the central nervous system involves two types of neurons, **A-delta** and **C fibers.** *A-delta fibers transmit localized brief pain sensations rapidly while C fibers transmit diffuse, dull pain sensa-*

tions slowly. These neurons transmit signals and continue to do so as long as there is damage (pain) perceived at the peripheral damage site. According to the **gate control theory**, another type of neuron essentially "gates" or interrupts the pain signal. The reason for this simple but elegant system has to do with priorities in an emergency situation. For example, imagine you are preparing dinner and accidentally touch a hot burner. A sharp pain effects a reflex act of withdrawing your finger. The burn would generally continue as a sustained throbbing pain, but, at that moment the smoke alarm goes off because the chicken is aflame in the oven, the doorbell rings announcing your dinner guests, your partner screams from the bathroom that the hot water just ran out, the phone rings just as the disposal clogs and sewage backs up into the sink. Your throbbing finger is down near the bottom of your priority list right now and as you scurry about attending to the myriad crises you are totally oblivious to your burned finger. In effect, your nervous system, observing that you are otherwise preoccupied, cancels out the pain signal until such time that you are able to attend to it and take appropriate curative action. Obviously, the central nervous system exercises significant executive control over this mechanism.

Acute pain refers to SNS activation that is adaptive and in response to specific trauma or tissue injury. *Acute pain is relatively brief (under 6 months) while* **chronic pain** *lasts beyond 6 months, is no longer adaptive, increasingly involves cognitive, behavioral, sociocultural, and environmental factors (vs. biologic), and begins to impair other functions.* **Chronic recurrent pain** involves alternating pain and pain-free periods (e.g., migraine headaches). **Chronic progressive pain** involves continuous, increasingly intense pain, presumably from progressive diseases (e.g., cancer). **Chronic intractable pain** is continuous but varies in intensity. It generally has its origin in an acute pain episode but continues even though the original lesion has healed or physiological damage is no longer evidenced (e.g., low back pain). The acute pain episode impacts the patient's environment, sociocultural setting, behavior, and cognition. Patients with chronic intractable pain frequently evidence **pain behaviors** (e.g., moaning, grimacing, limping, immobility, impaired functioning, helplessness, depression, anxiety) in excess of what might be expected in light of their actual physical condition. The patient's cognitive view of self may shift from that of a competent, self-sufficient, independent, and healthy individual to that of an impaired, dependent, helpless, and hopeless individual. These cognitions and behaviors become conditioned to the acute pain and may be reinforced by attention from health-care professionals, family and friends, excused responsibilities from work, family, and community, or even financial compensation for a disability. Thus, changes in the patient, in response to the acute pain, elicit sociocultural and environmental responses that can reinforce and maintain the patient's pain condition, turning it into a chronic condition.

The body has other means for modulating pain in the face of stressful emergencies. Recall that in response to acute stress the hypothalamus releases multiple releasing hormones including **corticotrophic releasing factor** (CRF), which travels to the pituitary where it causes the release of **adrenocorticotrophic hormones** (ACTH) and **beta endorphin** (BE) in exactly equal amounts. As we have already seen, ACTH stimulates the release of a glucocorticoid from the adrenals and these hormones course about through the bloodstream effectively shutting down temporarily unneeded functions. Meantime, BE, an endogenous opioid, is also circulating, ready to provide its analgesic properties in case of injury, enabling the organism to continue functioning (fight or flight) unencumbered by pain. However, since ACTH and BE are released simultaneously by the same stressor and since they have exactly opposite effects (ACTH = arousal, BE = quiescence) and since they tend to occupy the same receptor sites, what keeps them from canceling each other out and generally creating chaos during the emergency? ACTH and BE are antagonistic. ACTH is relatively more vigorous and usually first on the scene at their mutual receptor sites. ACTH occupies the receptor, blocking BE's access to the receptor. But ACTH has a relatively short half life, decays, and is metabolized out of existence while BE, with a longer half life, eventually moves in and binds to the receptor. As a result, the organism has a chance to respond in an emergent fashion to the crises, then, the damage control parties move in to limit the effect while the organism concentrates on trying to cope and survive.

Sleep

Among the body's most important homeostatic functions is the restorative process of sleep. It is during sleep periods that the body's various maintenance systems "catch up" with repairs; replenish nutrients; haul out wastes; provide "R & R" (rest and relaxation) for muscles, organs, and the central nervous system; conserve energy; and consolidate learning. Sleep is a circadian rhythm that is influenced by changes in environmental lighting. As with all other sensory input, signals proceed to the hypothalamus, which activates the release of melatonin from the pineal gland. *Melatonin appears to aid the synchronization of various bodily rhythms, including the circadian and sleep cycles.* It is hypothesized that when fatigue factors in the blood stream reach a threshold level, "hypnogogic factors," probably peptides, are released from the hypothalamus. Brain functioning begins to slow down as evidenced by the shift from low-voltage high-frequency beta waves (13–40 Hz), to Alpha (8–13 Hz), to mixed slower frequencies. Gradually the voltage diminishes, there is a gradual reduction in alpha waves, the rate slows, and the individual enters Stage I sleep.

Stage II is characterized by continued slowing and theta waves (1–5 Hz), and Stage III by a progressive slowing to about 20–50% delta waves (0.5–3 Hz). Finally the individual enters Stage IV as Delta waves account for more than 50% of the waveform activity. As sleep progresses there is a sudden burst of rapid eye movement giving this final stage its name, REM sleep.

Symptoms of inadequate or deprived sleep include fatigue, irritability, lapses in task performance, misperceptions, inability to concentrate, and, with extended periods of sleep loss, even disorientation. These symptoms evidence not only the physical toll of sleep loss but also the cognitive or mental impairment. While some sleep disorders have been linked to immune system functioning (**narcolepsy**), and others to airway obstruction (**apnea**), most fall under the category of the **insomnias**, i.e., inadequate or abnormal night's sleep, which affects about 35% of the population. As with all other functions of the organism, sleep is vulnerable to the interfering or impeding effects of stressor conditions. These may include noisy or uncomfortable environments, drug, alcohol, or food consumption, behavioral stimuli like nocturnal myoclonus or restless legs, other medical conditions, jet lag, changes in work conditions, and various other stressor conditions resulting from other behavioral, cognitive, sociocultural, or environmental changes.

SUMMARY

Disease and illness are byproducts of challenges to the integrity of the body and its functions, of failures in its adaptive responses to these challenges, and indeed of the success of these adaptive responses, which, under conditions of excessive or sustained challenge (chronic stress), can result in serious damage and dysfunction. Stressor conditions may be biologic, behavioral, cognitive, sociocultural, or environmental in nature and can effect changes in any or all of these same domains, setting into motion a reverberating chain of homeostatic responses as the organism attempts to maintain stable and healthy functioning. In almost all cases, disease or illness begins with individual differences in vulnerability, which are determined by **diatheses** or predispositions that are cognitive, behavioral, social, and biological, as well as genetic. Given these multiple diatheses, certain stressor conditions can precipitate diseases or illnesses by overwhelming the body's adaptive responses or initiating responses that, while successful in meeting the initial challenge, exert a toll from the body resulting in eventual disorder. In this regard, therefore, *every change or challenge to which the organism is subjected constitutes a stressor condition; every response to these challenges constitutes a stress response; and every disease or disorder or illness is a "stress-related disorder."* If disease and illness are the result of an interaction of factors in biologic, behavioral, cognitive, sociocultural, and environmental domains, it follows that diagnosis must involve assessment of change in each of these domains, and treatment must involve interventions within all of these domains. Thus, *the physician who is attentive to only the biologic parameters of disease has ignored 80% of the relevant information required to accurately diagnose the disorder and successfully treat it.*

CASE STUDY

A 35-year-old mother experiences acute severe pain after attempting to lift her 10-year-old son. She is given a prescription for pain medication and instructed to take the medication *prn* (as needed). The patient is concerned that she will become addicted to the drug and decides to take it only when the pain becomes unbearable. She then takes the medication and experiences relief. Meanwhile, between medication doses, the increasing pain all but immobilizes her. She is unable to return to her job or attend to various tasks around the house. She complains increasingly about the pain as its intensity increases. She then again takes the medication and experiences relief. After several weeks the patient complains to her doctor that the pain seems to be getting more intense, and she is having to take more and more medication to find relief. Her family reports she is increasingly complaining about the pain. The physician realizes that she has been taking the medication on a "pain contingent" schedule, i.e., taking the medication only when she has severe acute pain. The pain relief experienced following taking the medication is reinforcing the behaviors that immediately precede relief, i.e., pain complaints and taking medication. In effect her pain behaviors and medication taking are being conditioned to the pain experience and as they continue to be reinforced, the pain behaviors and medication taking increase. This is an example of an **iatrogenic treatment effect**. The physician correctly instructs the patient to take the medication on a "time contingent" schedule, e.g., a dose every 4 hours, in order to maintain constant blood levels and prevent the pain from occurring. The pain behaviors decrease, pain medication use is stabilized, the patient gradually resumes previous activities, and eventually progressively reduces the medication use as the injured tissue heals.

SUGGESTED READINGS

Baum, A., Newman, S., Weinman, J., West, R., & McManus, C. (1997). *Cambridge handbook of psychology, health and medicine.* New York: Cambridge University Press.

Exceptionally comprehensive, detailed, and up-to-date encyclopedic presentation of behavioral health. An impressive collection of contributors cover every conceivable topic in the field. If it's not in this book; it probably isn't important.

Bernard, L., & Krupat, E. (1994). *Health psychology: Biopsychosocial factors in health and illness*. San Diego: Harcourt Brace.
A very readable presentation of the field of health psychology. Provides a basic description of the components in the biopsychosocial model and how they interact in affecting disease and response to treatment. Includes a good overview of key organ systems for the nonmedically trained.

Carr, J. (1998). Proposal for an integrated science curriculum medical education. *Teaching and Learning in Medicine, 10*(1), 3–7.
Presents a model for teaching how biological, behavioral, cognitive, sociocultural, and environmental factors interact in response to stress in producing disease, based on current research in behavioral medicine and health psychology.

Carr, J. (1996). Neuroendocrine and behavioral interaction in exposure treatment of phobic avoidance. *Clinical Psychology Review, 16*(1), 1–15.
Describes one of the biobehavioral mechanisms within the human stress response that helps to explain how individuals develop avoidant behavior as a survival strategy, and how they learn to accommodate to these stressful situations and overcome avoidant fear.

Everly, G.S., & Lating, J.M. (2002). *A clinical guide to the treatment of the human stress response*. New York: Plenum Press.
A comprehensive review of definitions and theories of stress, the mechanisms and contributions to disease of the humans stress response, the multiple factors that influence it, and the range of interventions used to modify its effects. Well-organized, packed with information, and easy to read.

Goldstein, D. (1994). Stress and science. In O. Cameron (Ed.), *Adrenergic dysfunction and psychobiology* (p. 179–236). Washington, DC: American Psychiatric Association.
An excellent review of the history of stress and the issues that have been critical in shaping research and the development of the concept. Focuses on the importance of homeostatic mechanisms in the organism's response to stressors. Offers an especially interesting discussion of the role played by stress in evolution.

Kandel, E., & Hawkins, R. (1993). The biological basis of learning and individuality. In *Mind and brain: Readings from Scientific American* (pp. 40–53). New York: WH Freeman.
A well written and easily understood review of the biologic mechanisms presumed to underlay human learning. Helps bridge the gap between neuroscience and psychology and provides a fascinating ex-

planation of how experience is sensed, recorded, filed, and retrieved for future use.

Lazarus, R., & Folkman, S. (1984). *Stress, appraisal, and coping*. New York: Springer Verlag.
One of the key works in the conceptualization of stress emphasizing the importance of past experience, learning, and cognition in determining the effectiveness of the individual's response to management of stress.

LeDoux, J. (2002). *Synaptic self*. New York: Viking Press.
A remarkable book that describes the neuroendocrine mechanisms underlying learning, cognition, behavior, and other adaptive stress-response systems. A must read for any who wish to understand biobehavioral interaction.

Plomin, R., & Hershberger, S. (1991). Genotype-environment interaction. In T. Wachs & R. Plomin (Eds.), *Conceptualization and measurement of organism-environment interaction* (pp. 29–43). Washington, DC: American Psychological Association.
An excellent discussion of the varieties of interactions that can occur between biologic predisposition and environmental challenge. Helps to illuminate the complexities of the nature-nurture question.

Robles, T., Glaser, R., & Kiecolt-Glaser, J. (2005). Out of balance: A new look at chronic stress, depression, and immunity. *Current Directions in Psychological Science, 14*(2), 111–115.
An excellent review of research relating stress and depression, and the mechanisms by which they contribute to a range of diseases via the influence of proinflammatory cytokines.

Sapolsky, R. (1998). *Why zebras don't get ulcers*. New York: WH Freeman.
An engaging description of what happens to people exposed to chronic stress. A delightful read that is difficult to put down. Filled with humor and anecdotes everyone can relate to, this book brings the concept of stress to a new level of understanding, and demonstrates that science can be taught without being boring or unintelligible. If you read only one book on stress, make it this one.

Turner-Cobb, J. (2005). Psychological and stress hormone correlates in early life: A key to HPA-axis dysregulation and normalization. *Stress, 8*(1), 47–57.
This review examines the stress-illness relationship and the possible influence of early childhood stress experiences on subsequent resistance and health.

Weinstock, M. (2005). The potential influence of maternal stress hormones on development and mental health of the offspring. *Brain Behavior and Immunity, 19*, 296–308.
Examines the effects of psychosocial stress on HPA-axis activity during pregnancy and its impact on fetal development and birth outcome.

9 Addictions

Thomas F. Newton

> There is something distasteful in the sight of a highly developed society being forced to divert great resources, both financial and intellectual, to the care of its own self-inflicted diseases. We can characterize these as diseases of choice—those which arise from excesses in its lifestyle or pollution of its environment.
>
> J. GOODFIELD
>
> Smoking . . . is a shocking thing, blowing smoke out of our mouths into other people's mouths, eyes and noses, and having the same done to us.
>
> SAMUEL JOHNSON

DEFINITIONS

The word "addiction" is an old term with many nuances and emotional connotations. These connotations likely contribute to contemporary difficulties with use of the word and with confusion surrounding the intrinsic concept. Originally, addiction referred to surrendering one's legal rights over to another. Subsequently, it took the broader meaning of submitting to the opinions of others rather than thinking for oneself. Finally, in the past century, it took on its present meaning, operative in the context of opiate dependence.

The definition of addiction currently used in the medical literature emphasizes a range of concepts with varying applicability depending on the drug class under discussion. Physical changes associated (in part) with prolonged drug exposure include **tolerance** and **withdrawal**, such as develops in alcohol or opiate dependence. Other aspects of the definition emphasize loss of control over use, the crowding out of other behaviors in favor of those associated with drug use, and continued use despite adverse consequences. The most widely used terminology and definitions regarding addiction disorders derives from the Diagnostic and

---

BOX 9.1 DSM-IV-TR definition of substance abuse

A maladaptive pattern of substance use leading to clinically significant impairment or distress, as manifested by one (or more) of the following, occurring within a 12-month period:
- Failure to fulfill major obligations
- Use when physically hazardous
- Recurrent legal problems
- Recurrent social or interpersonal problems

BOX 9.2 DSM-IV-TR definition of substance dependence

A maladaptive pattern of substance use, leading to clinically significant impairment or distress, as manifested by three (or more) of the following, occurring at any time in the same 12-month period:
1) Tolerance, as defined by either of the following:
   a. A need for markedly increased amounts of the substance to achieve intoxication or desired effect.
   b. Markedly diminished effect with continued use of the same amount of the substance.
2) Withdrawal, as manifested by either of the following:
   a. The characteristic withdrawal syndrome for the substance
   b. The same (or a closely related) substance is taken to relieve or avoid withdrawal symptoms.
3) The substance is often taken in larger amounts or over a longer period than was intended (loss of control).
4) There is a persistent desire or unsuccessful efforts to cut down or control substance use (loss of control).
5) A great deal of time is spent in activities necessary to obtain the substance, use the substance, or recover from its effects (preoccupation).
6) Important social, occupational, or recreational activities are given up or reduced because of substance use (continuation despite adverse consequences).
7) The substance use is continued despite knowledge of having a persistent or recurrent physical or psychological problem that is likely to have been caused or exacerbated by the substance (adverse consequences).

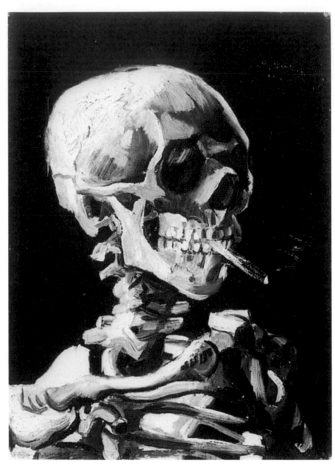

Skull of a Skeleton with Burning Cigarette *Vincent van Gogh (1886). van Gogh Foundation Museum, Amsterdam. The medical profession has played an important role in alerting the public to the addictive potential of nicotine and the lethality of tobacco.*

Statistical Manual of Mental Disorders (DSM-IV-TR). The DSM-IV-TR relies on the terms "dependence" to indicate conditions that approximate those typically referred to as addiction, while "abuse" is used to describe less severe levels of substance use or, in lay terms, is used to encompass the entire range of use of illegal drugs.

As is clear from the definition of dependence, neither dependence nor addiction refers to intermittent, occasional use of a medically stigmatized substance (e.g., tobacco) or of an illegal substance (e.g., cocaine). These behaviors may be foolish, dangerous, and may lead to addiction, but they are not addictions. **Substance abuse** refers to drug behaviors that produce adverse consequences without involving physical changes or loss of control.

> Drunkenness is temporary suicide: the happiness that it brings is merely negative, a momentary cessation of unhappiness.
>
> BERTRAND RUSSELL

PREVALENCE OF DRUG DEPENDENCE DISORDERS

Estimating the prevalence of drug dependence disorders depends on the definition used. Some cultures prefer more restrictive definitions, requiring severe pathology, whereas others may consider intermittent use of a proscribed substance sufficiently pathological so as to stigmatize it with the "addiction/dependence" appellation. In order to focus the discussion, material in this chapter will be limited to behaviors meeting the current DSM-IV-TR definition for dependence.

Drug dependence disorders are surprisingly common. In a classic study, 51.0% of survey respondents reported having used at least one drug at some time in their lives, and 15.4% had done so in the past 12 months. Of National Comorbidity Survey respondents, 7.5% (14.7% of lifetime users) were dependent at some time in their lives and 1.8% were dependent in the past 12 months. This estimate is similar to the Epidemiologic Catchment Area Study estimate of 5.1% among respondents in the age range 18 to 44 years, a comparison that matches the two other studies on year of assessment, age of risk, and cohort.

A recent survey of 5,692 people in selected households estimated that 3.8% of the English-speaking population of the United States 18-years-old and older met criteria for a substance use disorder in the 12 months prior to the interview. Similar surveys of non-English-speaking Hispanics and Asians are currently underway. Indeed, this estimate may understate the real prevalence, as people may be reluctant to reveal embarrassing information about themselves. Finally, this study used nonprofessional interviewers and this may affect the results, though correlations between findings from these interviews and from those performed by more thoroughly trained professionals are often quite good.

> First the man takes a drink, then the drink takes a drink, then the drink takes the man.
>
> Japanese Proverb

RISK FACTORS (GENETIC AND ENVIRONMENTAL) FOR ADDICTION DISORDERS

Both environmental and genetic factors contribute to addictions. The roles played by both factors are complex and have not been completely worked out. Complicating the picture, there are undoubtedly interactions between particular genetic vulnerabilities and other environmental factors. Twin studies are a classical means of parsing environmental and genetic contributions to behavior. *Twin studies have clearly documented a genetic predisposition for the development of addictions.* To some extent, factors influencing initiation of addictive behavior (e.g., initiation of smoking) can be distinguished from those contributing to the development of dependence. The former factors tend to be personal and environmental, whereas the latter have more genetic influence, though there are likely interactions between these factors as well.

Family studies have demonstrated that family members of subjects with substance use disorders had an eight-fold increase in the likelihood of having substance use disorders themselves. This enhanced risk appeared independent of other factors associated with the development of addiction, such as antisocial personality disorder or dependence on alcohol. To some extent, the tendency to develop dependence on a class of drug runs in families.

ioral effects of addictive drugs (such as drug seeking or drug self-administration). The neurotransmitter involved in this pathway is **dopamine**, which is why this particular neurochemical has been studied so extensively. More recently, investigators have demonstrated that the dopamine pathway may be relevant to a wide variety of behaviors in addition to those specific to addiction, and attention has shifted to other systems, including executive (cognitive), mood regulation, and stress systems. The exact contributions of each of these to the final common pathway of addiction remains a fertile area for future research. The neurobiology underlying the actions of individual drugs of abuse is reviewed in the following sections. Where applicable, treatment options are briefly mentioned. Further information regarding treatment options is available in standard texts (e.g., Galanter & Kleber, 1999).

NEUROBIOLOGY OF ADDICTION

The neurobiology of addiction shares some commonalities across drugs of abuse. *In general, these commonalities center on those brain regions associated with attribution of salience or prediction of reward.* These involve particular fibers originating in the ventral tegmental region of the brain stem and terminating in the nucleus accumbens of the striatum and the prefrontal cortex (the so-called **mesolimbic and mesocortical pathways**). The importance of these pathways has been demonstrated by lesion experiments, as either physical or chemical lesions can block relevant behav-

ALCOHOL

The mechanisms of action of alcohol are poorly understood. An early hypothesis focused on nonspecific interaction of ethanol with lipids. This cannot explain effects of alcohol at lower doses, where alcohol has clear reinforcing, anxiolytic, and euphoric effects. Instead, alcohol appears to affect protein subunits of multisubunit systems (GABA$_A$, NMDA, and nicotinic receptors). *The effects of alcohol on multiple systems may explain why under some conditions the effects of alcohol resemble those of stimulants, whereas under other conditions alcohol's effects resemble those of sedatives.*

The Drinkers *(1890) Vincent van Gogh, 1853–1890. Oil on canvas, 59.4 × 73.4 cm.* The Joseph Winterbotham Collection. Copyright © The Art Institute of Chicago. All rights reserved. *Both genetics and modeling influence a child's future drinking habits.*

> Drink no longer water, but use a little wine for thy stomach's sake and thine often infirmities.
>
> I TIMOTHY 5:23

GABA

This is the major inhibitory neurotransmitter system in the brain. Ethanol appears to potentiate effects of GABA, particularly via the $GABA_A$ subtype of the receptor. This may mediate acute effects, including impaired coordination, anxiolysis, and reinforcing effects. $GABA_A$ antagonists block some of the effects of alcohol, but not all of them.

NMDA

NMDA is one type of glutamatergic receptor, the major excitatory neurotransmitter system in the brain. Activation of NMDA appears critically important for learning, via long-term potentiation. Binding of glutamate + glycine depolarizes the cell and increases conductance for calcium ions, which activates several additional second messenger systems. Alcohol inhibits NMDA receptor function at low concentrations (10nM, 50 mg%, or 50 mg per 100cc plasma, or .05%). Alcohol also affects other glutamatergic receptor systems (AMPA). Overall, alcohol accentuates inhibitory neurotransmission via enhancing $GABA_A$ activation, and inhibits excitatory neurotransmission via inhibiting NMDA and AMPA glutamatergic systems. These effects may contribute to alcohol-induced memory impairments.

Serotonin

Moderate to high concentrations of ethanol (120 mg%) potentiate effects of serotonin at 5-HT3 receptor subtype and of nicotine at the nicotinic cholinergic receptor system. 5-HT3 receptors are located on dopamine (DA) cell bodies in the ventral tegmental region (VTA) and activation of these receptors facilitates mesolimbic neurotransmission. This is thought to contribute to the reinforcing effects of alcohol. 5-HT3 antagonists reduce this and may have a role in treatment of alcoholism.

Cannabinoids

Cannabinoids and ethanol can activate the same reward pathways, which could suggest endocannabinoid involvement in the rewarding effects of ethanol. For example, the high ethanol preference of young (6–10 weeks) mice is reduced by a cannabinoid receptor 1 (CB1) antagonist to levels observed in their CB1 knockout littermates or in old wild-type mice. In both of these, ethanol preference is unaffected by CB1 antagonists.

Chronic Neuroadaptations

Chronic alcohol exposure is associated with decreases in $GABA_A$ alpha-1 subunits and up-regulation of NMDA neurotransmission. *Abrupt cessation from heavy alcohol intake leads to a withdrawal syndrome, characterized by anxiety, sympathetic activation, and sleep disturbance.* When severe, it can lead to confusion, delirium, and seizures. This syndrome can be fatal if not treated.

Alcoholism is also characterized by range of nutritional deficiencies that may contribute to cognitive symptoms as well. For example, *chronic alcohol intake can lead to thiamine deficiency.* Glucose administration under conditions of thiamine deficiency can lead to neurologic dysfunction (e.g., Wernicke-Korsakoff Syndrome).

Acute management of physical dependence on alcohol involves reducing or blocking access to alcohol and requires addressing withdrawal symptoms and treating nutritional deficiencies. Therefore, **benzodiazepines** (which facilitate GABA neurotransmission) and nutrients specifically depleted in alcoholism (B12, folate, and thiamine) may be needed. Acute management of symptoms of physical dependence does not address the longer lasting neurobiological alterations underlying alcohol and drug dependence. These require behavioral treatment aimed at preventing relapse to drug use.

> There is in all men a demand for the superlative, so much so that the poor devil who has no other way of reaching it attains it by getting drunk.
>
> OLIVER WENDELL HOLMES, JR.

NEUROBIOLOGY OF OPIATES
Opioid Receptor Systems

Whether therapeutically used as medications (e.g., morphine, methadone) or abused as illicit drugs (e.g., heroin, opium) or as illicitly obtained medications (e.g., OxyContin, codeine), opiates activate Mu-opiate systems. These are part of a larger family, containing mu, delta, and kappa receptors. Agents acting at mu and delta receptors have similar analgesic, sedative, and euphoric effects; kappa activation produces dysphoria. Mu opioid receptors are located in many brain areas including cerebral cortex, striatum, hippocampus, locus coeruleus (primarily responsible for sedative, and euphoric effects), and the superficial laminae of the dorsal horn of the spinal cord (primarily responsible for analgesic effects). Mu binding onto GABA receptors in VTA reduces GABA actions. This disinhibits DA receptors, leading to enhanced DA release in the NAC. This appears responsible for reinforcing effects.

Chronic Neuroadaptations and Treatment

Chronic use produces a range of opponent processes characteristic of the opiate withdrawal syndrome. Symptoms include hyperalgesia, arousal, and dysphoria. These can last for several days following last use, and can serve as potent motivating factors in relapse. Treatment with opiate agonists such as methadone reduces withdrawal symptoms and allows focus on other activities of life.

Buprenorphine (compounded with or without naloxone) is unique because of its very high affinity for the mu receptor. Buprenorphine binds tightly to the mu receptor and dissociates slowly. Buprenorphine is a partial agonist at mu receptors. Increasing the dose does not increase the effect, and it can block effects of other opiates at higher doses. When compounded with **naloxone** (a nonspecific opiate antagonist), abuse liability is reduced because intravenous use of the combination produces withdrawal (a result of the naloxone). Oral or sublingual naloxone is very poorly absorbed (~10% oral bioavailability).

Buprenorphine is a promising "agonist" for opiate dependence, because it can treat the withdrawal syndrome and to some extent reduce effects of illicit opiate use. Management of symptoms of physical dependence does not address the longer lasting neurobiological alterations underlying dependence. These require behavioral treatment aimed at preventing relapse to drug use.

STIMULANTS (INCLUDING NICOTINE)

Stimulants covered here include cocaine base, cocaine hydrochloride, amphetamine and methamphetamine, and nicotine.

Cocaine

A coca leaf typically contains between 0.1 and 0.9 percent cocaine. Cocaine exists as the base (which is insoluble but which can be volatilized or "smoked"; also called "crack") and the salt (which is absorbed through membranes by "snorting"; also called powder). Cocaine produces euphoria lasting several minutes, though it has an elimination half-life of 1–3 hours. High-dose or chronic use can be associated with paranoia, which is occasionally severe and associated with other psychotic symptoms (e.g., hallucinations and delusions).

Methamphetamine

Use of methamphetamine (MA) produces many of the same problems that result from cocaine, but there are some aspects of MA-related disorders that appear specific to neurobiological consequences from MA. MA exposure is associated with more profound changes to dopamine and serotonin systems than manifest from cocaine use. Studies involving rats, guinea pigs, cats, and nonhuman primates have shown that high doses of MA permanently damage neuron cell-endings, though some regrowth may occur. Positron emission tomography (PET) scans of a monkey's brain after 10 days of use showed that dopamine production was significantly reduced for an entire year and that full recovery was not realized until 2 years later. The key ingredients for the necessary neurophysiological/neurochemical "healing" are ample amounts of time (6–12 months) and abstinence from MA use. This knowledge is likely to be relevant to research for MA treatment and development of treatment approaches. Over the past several years, the drug's low cost and easy availability have led to increasing use of methamphetamine. Use of cocaine appears stable or possibly declining slightly. This may be a result, in part, of increases in methamphetamine use.

Cocaine and amphetamines bind monoamine reuptake transporters and prolong action of DA, norepinephrine (NE), and serotonin (5-HT) in the synapse. Reinforcing effects require DA in the mesolimbic pathway (see above). Amphetamine and methamphetamine enter presynaptic neuron via transporter (reuptake pump) and produce release of DA, NE, and 5-HT. These compounds typically have more profound effects because they produce neurotransmitter release independent of neuronal firing, as is required of reuptake inhibitors such as cocaine.

To date, no medication treatment has been shown to reduce cocaine or methamphetamine use consistently in clinical trials. However, preliminary findings from two recent studies suggests that medications may be helpful, at least for some people. The medications **disulfiram** (which produces the familiar "antabuse" reaction to alcohol) and **modafinil** have both been associated with reduced cocaine use in small clinical trials. Disulfiram's mechanism of action may involve inhibition of the synthesis of norepinephrine (a neurotransmitter associated with stress responses) whereas modafinil mechanisms may involve fatigue reduction and cognitive enhancement.

Nicotine

Nicotine binds receptors located in many brain regions, including cortex, striatum, and limbic areas. Binding to receptors located on DA neurons in the ventral tegmentum is thought to lead to stimulation of DA release in the mesolimbic pathway. Stimulation of this pathway appears to produce nicotine's reinforcing effects. Chronic nicotine use (as is produced by cigarette smoking or smokeless tobacco use) also produces a withdrawal syndrome associated with irritability and poor concentration. This can contribute to relapse to nicotine use. *Treatment of the withdrawal syndrome using nicotine replacement therapy cuts relapse rates by half.* Bupropion treatment may also improve outcomes.

PSYCHOSOCIAL/BEHAVIORAL TREATMENTS

Several trials have evaluated the efficacy of several behavioral and cognitive behavioral treatments for stimulant use disorders. Treatment manuals have been empirically tested with stimulant-using populations, including manuals for cognitive-behavioral therapy and contingency management. At the present time, *cognitive behavioral treatment (CBT) and contingency management (CM) techniques have the strongest empirical support for application with stimulant users.* CBT emphasizes teaching relapse prevention techniques, education groups, social support groups, individual counseling, and urine and breath testing that is delivered in a structured manner in an outpatient setting over 2 to 4 months. The treatment is a directive, nonconfrontational approach that focuses on current issues and behavior change. CM emphasizes providing alternative reinforcers for abstinence, and has been implemented less frequently in treatment in nonresearch settings.

SUMMARY

Addiction refers to a maladaptive pattern of substance use leading to clinically significant adverse effects. Addictive disorders are relatively common, affecting a large proportion of the population at some point in time. Both environmental and genetic factors put one at risk for developing an addiction. Both factors also contribute to the tendency of addictive disorders to run in families.

The neurobiological substrates of addictions have received intensive study both in preclinical models and in clinical research. The mechanisms of action of alcohol, opi-

---

TWO SUFFERING MEN

I sat across, behind my desk,
and told him I thought
he might be alcoholic.
"I never been drunk," he said.
I made a note on the medical chart.

I could see him getting irked.
His liver sick;
his wife gone with the kids!
I made a note on the chart.

I saw him gaining rage.
He clenched his fists,
leaned forward,
his arms on the desk.
He held his breath
until he turned red,
then, sighing, fell back
in his chair and cried.

Breaking a long pause,
he asked, "You're telling me
I'm alcoholic? How in hell
would you know, in your
'pretty' white picturebook
middleclass hospital coat?"
His face suddenly tensed.
He pursed his lips
and lifted himself from the chair.
He stood tall, straight up,
bulging with pride
for all the ground-in years
of his laboring trade,
shouting,
"Stay out of my head.
Stay OUT of my head!"
and slammed the door behind him.

I longed to lower my eyes and cry.
But, from the bottom drawer
of my desk, just one small glass
of vodka and a chlorophyl candy
taste so damn good in the morning.

EUGENE HIRSCH

ates, stimulants, and nicotine involve many different neurotransmitters. Brain regions involved in the attribution of salience and the prediction of reward appear to be the most important ones, independent of the particular drug of abuse.

Medication treatments have been shown to improve outcomes among those with dependence on alcohol, opiates, and nicotine. Recent results suggest that specific medications may improve outcomes in cocaine dependence as well. Psychosocial treatments remain the mainstays of treatment. The best studied is cognitive behavioral treatment, which emphasizes learning skills important in prevention of relapse.

CASE STUDY

Mr. G is a 28-year-old man who was referred for treatment after twice presenting in the emergency room with a chief complaint that the "police are after me." It was evident at that time that he was intoxicated on some stimulant, and he was treated with low dose risperidone (2 mg), monitored, and discharged.

Mr. G. first saw a psychiatrist for attentional problems as a child. He was diagnosed with attention deficit disorder, but his parents did not want him to receive further treatment. Other substance use history includes cigarette smoking since age 14 and occasional alcohol use. He has tried heroin several times but did not develop dependence. He was otherwise healthy. His mother's brother and uncle had a history of alcohol use, and his father used cocaine 20 years ago. He completed high school and intermittently attended junior college. He lives by himself in an apartment, and has numerous friends and interests.

Mr. G. received cognitive behavioral treatment three times weekly. In these groups he learned about addiction and how it impacted his behavior, how events and people triggered drug use, and he learned time management techniques. He also attended cocaine anonymous groups and overall did fairly well. Two months after completing the treatment program he relapsed to cocaine use. He reentered the treatment program he had completed earlier. Two years later he continues to do well and has not used cocaine since.

SUGGESTED READINGS

Crabbe, J.C. (2002). Genetic contributions to addiction. *Annual Review of Psychology, 53*, 435–462.
  This article reviews the current research on the genetics of addiction, and how these interact with experience, such as trauma, to lead to physiological and behavioral change.

Galanter, M., & Kleber, H.D. (1999). *Textbook of substance abuse treatment*. Washington, DC: American Psychiatric Press.
  A basic and comprehensive guide to treatment of a variety of kinds of substance abuse and dependence

Goldstein, R.Z., & Volkow, N.D. (2002). Drug addiction and its underlying neurobiological basis: Neuroimaging evidence for the involvement of the frontal cortex. *American Journal of Psychiatry, 159*, 1642–1652.
  This article provides a good overview for those who are interested in reading more on the accumulating evidence for the neurobiological basis of drug addiction.

10 Psychodynamic Approaches to Human Behavior

Peter B. Zeldow

> Every man has some reminiscences which he would not tell to everyone, but only to his friends. He has others which he would not reveal even to his friends, but only to himself, and that in secret. But finally there are others which a man is even afraid to tell himself, and every decent man has a considerable number of such things stored away.
>
> FYODOR DOSTOYEVSKY
> *Notes from the Underground*
>
> All the art of analysis consists in saying a truth only when the other person is ready for it, has been prepared for it by an organic process of gradation and evolution.
>
> ANAÏS NIN
> *The Diary of Anaïs Nin*
>
> Every life is, more or less, a ruin among whose debris we have to discover what the person ought to have been.
>
> ORTEGA Y GASSET

For many people, psychoanalysis conveys the image of a patient lying on a couch, speaking endlessly (that is, session after session, and for many years) about dreams and sexual fantasies to a bearded and elderly psychoanalyst who remains relatively silent, except for an occasional oracular comment known as an interpretation. For those who have been superficially exposed to Freud in undergraduate psychology courses, psychoanalysis is both a largely discredited theory of personality and form of treatment for which there is little empirical justification.

Yet psychoanalytic theorizing and psychoanalytically influenced psychotherapy remain viable and continue, over a century after Freud's first publications, to have an influence not only in psychiatry and clinical psychology but in the arts and humanities in intellectual communities throughout the world. Contemporary psychoanalytic theory and practice have both changed dramatically since Freud's death in 1939 and can no longer be considered the work of a single man. They have evolved in many different directions, some of which represent radical departures from orthodox Freudian formulations. A very small sample of psychoanalytic theorists and concepts is provided in Box 10-1.

Another view of psychoanalytic theory, popular in some academic circles, considers it worthless because it is based on a biased sample (neurotic, middle class, nineteenth-century residents of Vienna) and because its concepts cannot be subjected to empirical testing. These criticisms are simplistic, and a rebuttal is beyond the scope of this chapter. Suffice to make the following comments. First the history of science suggests that those theories richest in explanatory power have often proved most difficult to study empirically. Newton's Second Law, for example, could not be demonstrated in a reliable, quantitative way for 100 years. Psychoanalytic theory is derived primarily from the experience of psychotherapy, and, in the eyes of those who have experienced it, provides a vocabulary and conceptual map for a set of experiences that are intense, highly personal, and otherwise hard to explain.

Furthermore, it is not true that all the theories of Freud and his followers are untestable. **Psychoanalytic hypotheses** may be difficult to subject to scientific scrutiny, but the same can be said about any psychological hypotheses involving complex phenomena and worthy of being tested. Psychoanalytic ideas have possibly inspired as much empirical research as any theory in the behavioral scienc-

BOX 10.1 Selected psychodynamic theorists

Sigmund Freud (1856–1939); Vienna; psychoanalysis	Creator of psychoanalysis as a theory, research method, and psychological treatment Psychosexual theory of development, emphasizing vicissitudes of biological drives through *oral, anal, phallic,* and, ultimately, *genital* stages
Carl Gustav Jung (1875–1961); Zurich; analytical psychology	Early disciple of Freud who disputed sexual nature of psychic energy, or *libido* Developed psychological types: *introverts* and *extroverts* Interested in spiritual crises of midlife Formulated theory of *archetype,* a universal, emotionally charged mythological image in the *collective unconscious*
Alfred Adler (1870–1937); Vienna; individual psychology	Early disciple of Freud who deemphasized sexual strivings in favor of *social interest:* "man is inclined towards the good" Emphasized conscious capabilities of humans Interested in effects of *birth order* and *earliest memory* Formulated theory of compensation for *organ inferiority*

Harry Stack Sullivan (1892–1949); New York and Washington, D.C.; interpersonal psychiatry	Eminent and influential American psychiatrist
	Defined the psychiatrist as an expert in interpersonal relations
	Formulated theories:
	    Anxiety results from threats to one's security
	    Self-system develops as guardian of security but limits personal growth
	    Good-Me remains conscious; Bad-Me is *dissociated*

Erik H. Erikson (1902–1994); Germany, Vienna, and United States; psychosocial theory of development	Emphasized *psychosocial* implications of Freud's psychosexual stages Extended developmental theory throughout adulthood (**Eight Ages of Man**) Wrote psychohistorical studies of Luther and Gandhi Developed concepts of *identity* and *identity crisis*
Donald Winnicott (1896–1971); Great Britain; object relations theory	*Transitional objects* such as blankets and teddy-bears, which soothe and comfort the child in its early efforts to separate from mother Capacity to be alone as a psychological achievement reflecting a cohesive self and successfully *internalized objects*
Margaret Mahler (1896–1985); United States; object relations theory	Central dimension of development from complete dependence (*symbiosis*) to differentiation of self (*separation-individuation*)
Heinz Kohut (1913–1981); Chicago; psychoanalytic self psychology	Emphasized *narcissistic* line of development from immature grandiosity and exhibitionism to more mature modes of self-enhancement Developed taxonomy of transferences classified according to type of experience patient is trying to recreate (*mirroring, idealizing, twinship*) Formulated theory of *selfobject,* defined as any object (person, thing, ideal) that lends sense of cohesion, strength, and harmony to self

es, and they have not always fared badly. Interested readers can consult Fisher and Greenberg (1996) or Westen's (2000) introductory psychology text for balanced discussions of the empirical status of contemporary psychoanalytic ideas.

My intention in what follows is to provide a clinically useful introduction to what I prefer to call the *psychodynamic* perspective on human behavior. As future physi-

cians and health-care professionals, most readers of this book will inevitably find themselves in clinical situations that will require them to empathize with patients, to understand patients' motivations and adaptations under stress, and to understand their own intensely personal reactions to their patients. I believe that psychodynamic formulations of human behavior often provide the most experientially useful roadmaps for clinical work.

PSYCHODYNAMIC ASSUMPTIONS

Unconscious Motivation

Any psychodynamic formulation of human behavior must include the notion that human lives are governed by internal forces of which they are unaware and that these forces, which may be images, thoughts, or feelings, are the primary determinants of who they are and what they do. Psychodynamic theorists emphasize the limits of self-report and self-awareness; they are more impressed with the human capacity for self-delusion as demonstrated in the following vignette.

A patient on a coronary care unit witnessed the fatal cardiac arrest of his roommate. Although the nursing staff expected that this would be traumatic for the patient, he denied any fright and eagerly accepted the staff's reassurance that he was not at similar risk. Only one seemingly minor event suggested that there was anything more to this situation: When patients were surveyed as to whether they would prefer single rooms or roommates should another hospitalization be required, all patients chose to have roommates, except for this patient and others who had witnessed cardiac arrests.

In this situation it is easy to see how the patient's denial of fear served to reassure him and maintain his psychological equilibrium. However, it is also difficult to believe that he was not terribly upset *at some level,* although the only evidence for this (his preference for a single room) is admittedly tenuous. Perhaps if the staff were to insist that he share a room, his protestations would increase and his anxiety would come closer to the surface.

There are strong objections to the notion of an unconscious among experimental psychologists, even though memory researchers accept the related notion of **implicit memory**. Can thoughts and feelings exist outside of awareness? If so, how can such repressed memories influence behavior? Still, many responsible clinicians have reported working with patients who have remembered events from their early lives that had long been forgotten. Such remembrances are often quite emotionally charged. It can be hard to avoid the conclusion that mental mechanisms had been at work to keep the memories out of awareness. At present, it is important to draw a distinction between a phenomenon (such as the apparent recovery of a memory) and the explanations that are proffered for it. Few psychologists would deny that there is much behavior that takes place without awareness. Whether the concepts of repression and unconscious motivation provide the best explanations of such phenomena is a question for further research.

Conflict

Psychodynamic formulations of human behavior begin with the inevitability of conflict, both intrapsychic and interpersonal. To speak of conflict in this way is simply to note that humans are complex organisms, capable of having incompatible goals and engaging in paradoxical actions.

Conflict can take many forms. There can be conflict between two impulses (love and hate); conflict between an impulse and a prohibition ("I want to kill" vs. "Thou shalt not kill"); conflict over a vocational choice (medicine vs. creative writing); or conflict over one's sexual identity ("Am I gay or am I straight?"). This is far from an exhaustive list. Furthermore, conflict can be experienced fully, partially, dimly, or not at all. In the psychodynamic perspective, conflict is considered to be the basis of most forms of functional (i.e., nonorganic) psychopathology.

It is easier to speak of psychological conflict if a hypothetical psychological structure is created, the parts of which may operate more or less smoothly (more or less conflictually). Such is the purpose served by Freud's heuristic division of the human personality into three components. **Id** is the repository of all biological urges and instincts, including hunger, thirst, and sexuality. Under most conditions, humans are unaware of its contents and functions. It is governed by the **pleasure principle**. This means that it attempts to avoid pain and obtain pleasure and cannot tolerate delay of gratification. The id is said to operate according to **primary process**, a primitive form of wishful and magical thinking. For example, if the organism is hungry, primary process provides a mental image of food, a wish fulfillment. Dreams and the hallucinations of psychotic patients are other examples of primary process thinking. Although they satisfy the id, such experiences do not enable the organism to deal with objective reality.

Ego develops to permit more effective transactions with the environment. In contrast to the id, the ego is governed by the **reality principle**, which aims to postpone gratification until an appropriate object is found. In other words, the ego will not accept a mental image of food or any wish-fulfilling fantasy. It operates according to **secondary process** thinking, which is basically synonymous with realistic thinking and problem solving. Ego functions include cognition (perceiving, remembering, speech and language, reality testing, attention, concentration, and judgment), interpersonal relations, voluntary movement, and defense mechanisms (discussed in this chapter). However, because the ego develops from the id, it is always beholden to it, and its various functions may be disrupted if the demands of the id are insufficiently addressed.

For humans to function effectively, they must learn not only to negotiate a balance between their bodily needs and the limitations of physical reality but also how to deal with the norms of society. The **superego** is the internal representation of the values, norms, and prohibitions of an individual's parents and society. It has two components: **conscience**, which both punishes the person for engaging in forbidden actions and thoughts and rewards morally acceptable conduct, and **ego-ideal**, which represents the moral perfection that humans strive for and never attain.

Intrapsychic conflict occurs when the demands of these three mental agencies are at odds. When id impulses threaten to become overwhelming, anxiety is generated. Anxiety, in this perspective, is a signal of impending danger. It may be experienced directly or may serve as a stimulus to new efforts by the ego to keep the id impulses unconscious. Some of these efforts of the ego to respond to signal anxiety are discussed in the section on defense mechanisms.

Developmental Perspective: The Past in the Present

A third assumption common to psychodynamic formulations is that the *events of the past, particularly the events of childhood, have a profound influence on our behavior as adults.* This influence appears in two distinct ways. First, humans are viewed as "repeating machines," playing out (as adults) crucial early experiences in an effort to master them and obtain the gratification that was unavailable in childhood. Second, modes of thinking characteristic of childhood remain with individuals as adults, unconscious and ready to be activated under appropriate conditions. Both of these influences are evident in the case study at the end of this chapter.

Respect for the Body

A fourth assumption inherent in most psychodynamic formulations is that *an individual's body plays a crucial role in personality development.* However controversial Freud's view that "anatomy is destiny" may be as an explanation of psychological differences between the sexes, two related points are clear. First, the anatomical differences between men and women are objects of no small interest to children, who notice the differences and wonder and fantasize about them. The possibility that these differences may have different consequences for boys and girls does not seem unreasonable. Certainly events such as menstruation, lactation, pregnancy, childbirth, and menopause are unique to the female life cycle and have profound effects on self-esteem and the ways in which needs and emotions are expressed. Anyone who has spent any time in a men's locker room knows that men, too, have some curious rituals (such as teasing each other about the size of their penises), which seem comprehensible only when some sort of genital anxiety is assumed. Second, all humans have to come to terms with their sexuality and their capacity to be hurtful and

destructive. The notion that psychoanalytic theorizing reduces everything to sex and aggression is caricature. It is equally ludicrous to pretend that characteristic ways of satisfying and inhibiting various bodily needs have nothing to do with the development of personality and psychopathology.

PSYCHODYNAMIC THEORIES OF DEVELOPMENT

When unconscious motivation is being considered, questions such as what precisely are the "contents" of the unconscious that motivate human beings and are the sources of conflict and inner divisiveness should be asked. In a consideration of the role of the past in the present, the aspects of human development that exert the most formidable influence and provide the greatest challenge should be determined. Unfortunately, psychoanalysts disagree considerably on these issues.

Freud's theory of psychosexual development represents an attempt to describe the path of the instincts through various erogenous zones and phases of childhood. Sexuality for Freud refers to a "primary, distinctively poignant pleasure experience" derived from the stimulation of an area of the body.

Sigmund Freud *(1856–1939).* Courtesy of the National Library of Medicine.

> The little girl likes to regard herself as what her father loves above all else; but the time comes when she has to endure a harsh punishment from him and she is cast out of her fool's paradise. The boy regards his mother as his own property; but he finds one day that she has transferred her love and solicitude to a new arrival.
>
> SIGMUND FREUD

Infantile sexuality has nothing but this sensual pleasure in common with the variety of experiences that we think of under the rubric of adult sexuality (or *genital sexuality*, to use Freud's terminology). During the **oral stage**, sucking, biting, and other oral activities are primary sources of pleasure. During the **anal stage**, at roughly age 2 to 3 years, pleasure is obtained through the expulsion and retention of excretion. During the next 2 or 3 years, in the **phallic stage**, the predominant erogenous zone is the genitalia. During the **latency period**, from 6 years to adolescence, drive activity presumably subsides. Only at the end of adolescence do we find psychosexual development culminating in sexuality as adults know it, with a capacity for orgasm and unambivalent, mutually gratifying relations with others. This so-called **genital stage** is not attained by all persons but represents the highest possible level of human development for Freud.

What is not apparent in so sketchy and abstract an account are the implications of this theory for personality development. Suffice to say that particular personality traits are associated with excessive gratification or deprivation at each stage. Problems at the oral stage, such as insufficient opportunity for oral gratification, can leave a legacy of pessimism, dependency, and excessive need for approval, as well as an inclination to eat, drink, and smoke excessively. Problems at the anal stage, such as toilet training that is too early or too severe, can result in compulsive neatness, stubbornness and defiance, ambivalence and indecisiveness, and stinginess. During the phallic phase, boys and girls must come to terms with their possessive love of the parent of the opposite sex and their murderous fantasies toward the same-sex parent. One purported outcome of difficulty in containing such feelings can be a lifelong pursuit of failure. In such a view, success is unconsciously equated with the gratification of the Oedipal fantasy and must be studiously avoided.

Several years ago a medical student came to see me after having failed an examination in one of his basic science courses. He had had no earlier academic difficulties during medical school and expressed the belief that he had unconsciously sabotaged his own performance. He explained that he was ambivalent about becoming a physician and that there were many unresolved tensions in his relationship with his father, an eminent physician-educator. He also reported that earlier in his life, he had failed to perform as well as expected in numerous important sports events. In retrospect, he thought that his history of underachievement was related to his relationship with his father, and he used the occasion of his academic difficulties to take a leave of absence from school to work out these problems in psychotherapy.

Erik Erikson has reformulated (some would say "sanitized") the psychosexual theory in psychosocial terms. For him the oral stage is the time at which a child ideally develops a basic sense of **trust vs. mistrust**, an outlook on life as essentially good, nourishing, and predictable, based on his or her early experiences with the mother. Similarly, the demand for bowel control that society imposes in the anal stage can leave a child with either a healthy sense of **autonomy**, rooted in mastery of his or her body, or a lifelong and pervasive sense of **shame and doubt**. Erikson spoke of the phallic stage in terms of **initiative vs. guilt** and defined the latency stage in terms of a child's sense of **industry** (i.e., learning the basic skills of society) **vs. inferiority**. He described adolescence as the time in which an individual establishes a firm sense of **identity** or becomes confused about his or her role in society. Erikson also made a major contribution by extending the notion of growth beyond adolescence. In contrast to Freud, he described adulthood not only as a stage for the playing out of infantile conflicts but as a series of new opportunities and dangers. The following are Erikson's developmental tasks of adulthood:

1. To develop a trusting and enduring relationship (**intimacy vs. isolation**)
2. To develop in midlife a concern with guiding the next generation (**generativity vs. stagnation**)
3. To develop in old age an acceptance of an individual's own life as a necessary and valued experience, lived with dignity (**ego integrity vs. despair**)

With such formulations, a clinician has a framework for evaluating the developmental progress of a patient at any stage of life.

Freud believed all behavior was ultimately in the service of, or an expression of, basic sexual and aggressive instincts. In contrast, a number of psychodynamic theorists have argued that the most significant lines of human growth and development concern self and **object relations** (objects are significant others or their intrapsychic representations). To these theorists, who have serious divergences of opinion among themselves, the understanding and treatment of psychopathology take very different forms from the traditional Freudian model. Mahler and Winnicott, two proponents of object relations theory, stress movement from the absolute dependence of the newborn to the independence and autonomy of the adult as the primary and lifelong developmental task. Development proceeds from a symbiotic fusion with the mother through various stages of partial differentiation of self and others toward a state of increased individuality and independence. The internalized images of others (or objects) in the infant (and the psychotic adult) are primitive, engulfing, devouring, and otherwise menacing. Only in maturity, when separation from the mother has been successfully achieved, is seen a capacity for empathy and for seeing others as they actually are and not as projections of an individual's primitive fantasies.

Even in maturity, there remains, more or less consciously, the eternal longing to lose separateness and be blissfully reunited with the "all-good, symbiotic mother." Ideally this is manifested in the capacity for loving and true intimacy. However, in persons who have failed to establish a firm sense of self and in those who, when under duress, find themselves losing this sense of separateness, love may become an attempt to recapture some of the primitive gratification characteristic of the earliest feelings of fusion with the maternal object. In such instances a desperate style of love relations may ensue wherein the lover is idealized, separations are intolerable, and rejection may be life threatening. The lover is not perceived in an accurate way as a separate person with strengths and imperfections but as the sole source of nurturance and need satisfaction. There is really no room for personal growth in such a relationship, and bitter disappointment is an inevitable consequence.

Kohut has been more concerned with the narcissistic line of development and the concomitant changes in the self as the individual moves from the grandiose and exhibitionistic fantasies of immature narcissism to the more realistic modes of action associated with healthy narcissism. He stresses that certain experiences (which he calls self-objects) are as vital to the developing self as are food and water to physical well-being. These experiences include the need to be confirmed and prized for who we are (the need for mirroring), and the need to look up to, admire, and feel a part of a source of calm infallibility and strength (the need for idealizing). In a child, these needs are expressed in unsocialized ways. As long as the child's caretakers provide a milieu in which such expressions are welcomed, the child will develop a healthy, self-assertive ambition and a viable set of values and ideals by which to live. If the child's needs are misconstrued, ignored, or disparaged, the child (and later the adult) will lack the internal sense of self that is so essential for psychological well-being. Lacking these emotional nutrients, such a person resorts to a variety of strained, desperate, and developmentally primitive measures to bolster a defective self. For example, if a parent continually responds to a child's *age-appropriate* expressions of aggression and sexuality with anger and contempt, it is difficult to imagine the child becoming an adult capable of expressing affection and assertiveness in a conflict-free way. Similarly, a drug addiction, which Freud might consider a direct attempt to satisfy oral cravings, would be seen by Kohut as an attempt to compensate for a defective self, the consequence of parental failure to provide the mirroring and calming functions so necessary for the child to learn to regulate his or her own feelings.

CLINICAL CONCEPTS AND APPLICATIONS

Defense Mechanisms

The concept of the defense mechanism was borrowed from immunology to describe the ways and means by which the ego wards off anxiety and controls unacceptable instinctual urges and unpleasant affects or emotions. The first systematic treatment of defense mechanisms was written in 1936 by Freud's daughter Anna Freud, an eminent child analyst. More recently, George Vaillant has introduced a classification of defenses based on the degree to which these mechanisms distort the perception of reality.

*The defense mechanism of **denial** is commonly seen in general medical practice.* It is a primitive defense wherein the facts or logical implications of external reality are refused recognition (denied) in favor of internally generated, wish-fulfilling fantasies. Denial involves a major distortion of reality and is common in healthy children until around age 5 years.

An example of denial is seen in the 50-year-old physician who ignores the classic signs and symptoms of an acute myocardial infarction and continues to clear his driveway of snow. Another is found in the woman who examines her breasts daily for lumps until she discovers one, ceases her self-examinations, and fails to report her findings to her physician. Denial in these examples is life threatening and clearly maladaptive. However, it can be adaptive at times: For example, a cardiac patient may refuse to accept that he or she has had a heart attack and appear incredibly cheerful and serene after admission to an intensive care unit.

Projection is another defense associated with considerable reality distortion. *In projection, an individual's own repressed (or unacceptable) impulses and desires are disowned and attributed to another person.* Most typical are projection of sexual and aggressive impulses, such as when, all evidence to the contrary, a patient is convinced that his or her physician is making sexual advances or that the physician is plotting with the nursing staff to have the patient killed. *Projection is the dominant defense mechanism employed by people with paranoid personality disorders.* It also plays a part in many prejudicial attitudes. When bigots assert that members of some minority group are all lazy, cheap, dirty, untrustworthy, immoral, etc., they are very likely projecting attributes that they need to disavow in themselves.

Regression is a partial return to an earlier stage of development and to more childish and childlike forms of behavior. Its purpose is to escape anxiety by returning to an earlier level of adjustment in which gratification was ensured. Like denial, regression is an extremely common response to severe and chronic illness and to hospitalization. Whenever confronted in clinical practice with a patient whose symptoms and incapacities are disproportionate to the physical disorder that underlies them, the clinician is probably dealing with a regressed patient. These are the patients who make insatiable demands on physicians and nurses, complain insistently, demand medication (and meetings with their lawyers), request special privileges, and accuse all those around them of indifference to their plight.

Regression is not necessarily a sign of psychiatric disturbance and short-lived reactions of the kind described here occur frequently. But when extended in time, such signs of emotional distress make it difficult for health providers to maintain their professional attitudes of equanimity and detached concern.

Regression can be precipitated by fatigue, drugs, chronic pain, stress, or any circumstance that deprives a patient of his or her autonomy. It is not uncommon to witness mildly regressive behavior in a group of students who have stayed up late to study the night before an examination. Psychoanalytic theories of creativity consider **regression in the service of the ego** to be one of the hallmarks of creativity. But when regression is prolonged and severe, it is associated with psychotic levels of functioning in which the ability to separate reality from fantasy is blurred.

Viederman (1974) uses the concept of regression to explain the behavior of patients on a renal transplant unit. He likens hemodialysis treatment to the mother-child relationship in two ways. First, the patient lives in a type of symbiotic fusion with the machine, and is attached to it by a plastic tube ... not too dissimilar to an umbilical connection. Patients readily enter into a love-hate relationship with this machine, which becomes both the preserver of their life and the tyrant that symbolizes the limitations of their freedom.

Second, because dietary and fluid limitations are severe, oral deprivation is a constant element in treatment. Viederman uses case material to demonstrate that successful adaptation to dialysis depends on the patient's ability to effect a partial regression to the stage of oral dependency, which in turn depends on a reasonably successful mother-child relationship during the patient's earliest years. The patient who, as a helpless child, was able to develop a hopeful and trusting relationship with his or her mother is more comfortable with the enforced dependency on the dialysis machine than the patient whose earliest years were characterized by less than adequate maternal care.

As one example of how psychoanalytic concepts can be studied and measured empirically, Lynne Braun and I (Zeldow & Braun, 1985) developed the BUMP Scale, a rating scale measure of regressive behavior (we called it Behavioral Upset) in medical patients. We found four distinct components to regressive behavior in hospitalized patients and discovered that a large minority (around 40%) manifest regressive symptoms of clinical proportion. The four factors of the BUMP Scale, along with representative items, appear in Box 10.2.

Fixation refers to a persistent inability to give up infantile or childish patterns of behavior for more mature ones and may occur because of either excessive deprivation or exces-

---

BOX 10.2 Dimensions of regression and sample items from the BUMP Scale*

I. **Regression proper**
   Clinging, needs reassurance
   Angry
   Uncooperative
   Complains
   Demanding
   Irritable

II. **Deteriorating relations with staff** (scored in opposite direction)
   Friendly
   Starts conversations
   Able to ask for help
   Accepts advice

III. **Depression/anxiety**
   Cries
   Looks worried
   Looks sad
   Says he or she is a burden to staff

IV. **Passivity/withdrawal**
   Refuses to speak
   Has to be reminded what to do
   Sleeps unless otherwise directed
   Passive

---

* Each item is rated by an observer on a five-point scale from "never" to "always." From Zeldow, P.B., & Braun, L. (1985). Measuring regression in hospitalized medical patients: The BUMP Scale. *General Hospital Psychiatry, 7*, 49–53. Used by permission.

---

sive gratification at the stage where development has ceased. When we say that a 40-year-old person has the mind of a 15-year-old person, we are implicitly saying that in some important ways (perhaps in capacity for intimate interpersonal relations), this person does not act as expected for someone of his or her chronological age. Various psychoanalytic theories emphasize different lines of human development (psychosexual, psychosocial, narcissistic), and an individual's progress can be stunted along any of these lines. For example, every human has a need for recognition, attention, and affirmation of worth. However, there are different ways of obtaining such so-called narcissistic gratifications at different points in time. A 4-year-old child who engages in blatantly exhibitionistic activity may be seeking such affirmation in an age-appropriate way. It may be the only way he or she knows. Adults should not feel that they have to outgrow such needs, but are expected to seek gratification in more mature ways. Recently a celebrity was quoted as saying that he loved his girlfriend because "she never makes demands on him." From a psychodynamic perspective, this is a rather selfish form of love. Mature people are not afraid of making demands on others, nor are they afraid of having demands made on them. Although it would not serve any purpose to say as much to the celebrity in question, his comment reflects a fixation at an immature level of psychosocial development.

It is somewhat inaccurate to speak of all the behaviors described herein as defense mechanisms. It is more accurate to describe them as having, among other things, *defensive aspects*. The "defense" of **identification** provides a good example. Identification is the psychological mechanism by which some traits or attributes of another individual are taken on as an individual's own (more or less permanently). This process is a major factor in the development of the superego, the moral dimension of personality. According to Freud, during the Oedipal phase, children relinquish their troubling attraction to the opposite-sex parent for fear of its consequences. By identifying with the parent of the same sex, the child is able to resolve this conflict. "Instead of replacing Daddy (or Mommy), I will become like him (her)." Such a resolution has its defensive side, to be sure, but it is also adaptive and plays a major role in personality development.

Identification is seen in its predominantly defensive aspects in pathological grief reactions–reactions to loss of a loved one in which the normal work of mourning, grieving, and truly accepting the loss is blocked. *For many people the death of a parent is a profoundly ambivalent experience.* At the same time an individual experiences acute pain and sadness, he or she may be more dimly aware of less admirable and more disturbing feelings: anger from being abandoned, relief if a long siege of suffering has ended or unconsciously wishing for the parent's death, and possibly guilt over such hostile wishes. Under such circumstances, normal grieving may be inhibited and identification can contribute to this process. For example, if the parent suffered a heart attack, the child may have chest pain. If the parent walked with a limp or spoke with a stutter, the child (even the adult child) may unintentionally adopt the same characteristic. In so doing, the child keeps the parent alive in a magical kind of way through identification. The new symptom also helps to distract the mourner from the pain of the loss.

A common variant is **identification with the aggressor** in which an individual masters the anxiety generated by being victimized through involuntary imitation. Anna Freud (1966) describes the case of a 6-year-old boy whom she interviewed shortly after he underwent a painful dental procedure:

> He was cross and unfriendly and vented his feelings on the things in my room. His first victim was a piece of India rubber ... Next he coveted a large ball of string ... When I refused to give him the whole ball, he took the knife again and secured a large piece ... Finally, he ... turned his attention to some pencils, and went on indefatigably sharpening them, breaking off the points, and sharpening them again.

As Anna Freud points out, this was not a literal impersonation of a dentist; rather, it was an identification with the dentist's aggression.

Concentration camp victims and terrorist hostages sometimes identify with their captors, taking on their characteristics and converting to their political points of view. Some medical educators have even described the occasional harsh treatment of medical students by residents as the result of a similar process. In these cases a resident who has been mistreated by an attending physician may be similarly abusive to a medical student clerk. Such an identification with the attending physician may temporarily reduce the hurt of his or her own mistreatment, but at the expense of the victim.

Repression refers to motivated forgetting, the process by which memories, feelings, and drives associated with painful and unacceptable impulses are excluded from consciousness. Repression is the basic defense mechanism, according to Freud. Only if repression fails or is incomplete do the other mechanisms come into play. Denial and repression are sometimes confused. Denial, however, is a reaction to external danger; repression always represents a struggle with internal (instinctual) stimuli. Repression must also be distinguished from suppression. Suppression reflects a voluntary or intentional effort at forgetting. It is as if the person knows the forgotten material is there but ignores it.

Suppression is considered to be one of the more mature defenses and has been shown empirically to correlate with various measures of adult mental health. I have always admired my wife's ability to use suppression appropriately. Once we were driving home from work on a Friday afternoon, and she was reviewing some stressful events that she fully anticipated would continue to preoccupy her during the next workweek. Because the weekend was on us, however, she declared that she would put it all out of her mind for now. It has always seemed to me that the emphasis on the volitional nature of suppression is not entirely accurate. My wife did successfully suppress the unpleasant thoughts about her work. But how many of us, having made the same declaration of intent, would be able to carry it out?

Reaction formation is the defense mechanism by which repressed motives are translated into their opposites. For instance, have you ever found yourself disliking someone who is overly kind and good? Much to your embarrassment you question the purity of their motives. Perhaps there is something to your intuitions. Unless this person qualifies for sainthood, a psychodynamic formulation of such behavior might involve a reaction formation against hostility: Repressive defenses were insufficient to keep hostile impulses from consciousness, so the defense of reaction formation is enlisted to aid in this effort by camouflaging the original aggressive intent of the behavior. In a reaction formation against dependency, a person who is unconsciously very needy often lives a life of exaggerated independence, refusing all help from others. In a reaction formation against sexual impulses, all sexual desires are repudiated. The individual takes up the cause of celibacy and lives a life of asceticism.

In all of the preceding examples it is fair to ask how an individual knows that these formulations are true or valid. *The psychodynamic clinician would point to the dreams and slips of the tongue (**parapraxes**) of the patient for evidence of the underlying impulse.* The patient's words (or associations) are another rich source of evidence. Excessive reliance on first-person pronouns and frequent allusions to power and status may reflect a narcissistic orientation. Themes of supply and demand and frequent use of food imagery may reflect an oral orientation. I was recently struck by a male patient's discussion of dating and its attendant risks. He constantly spoke of his fear of "sticking his neck out" and referred to singles bars as "butcher shops." Such imagery suggests castration anxiety to the psychodynamic clinician. Observations of how the individual in question handles unexpected life changes are another source of evidence. If an independent man were to sustain a minor injury and react with disproportionate emotion and distress, taking to his bed for the next 6 months, this would enhance our suspicion that dependent impulses lay beneath his pseudoindependence. With some regularity, the media treat the American public to scandalous revelations about the unconventional sexual preferences of some well-known sports figure, televangelist, politician, or entertainer. The psychodynamic clinician who is not surprised by such revelations is not a cynic and does not simply believe that base impulses alone underlie our noblest ideals. But such a clinician does know that human behavior has multiple determinants and that our bodies (including our sexual and aggressive impulses) cannot be ignored. Rare indeed is the individual who negotiates his or her childhood so smoothly that "no troops are left behind" to handle some problem on one or another path of development.

Isolation and **intellectualization** are two related defenses whose common purpose is to seal off feelings, or **affects**, to use a technical psychiatric term. *In isolation of affect, only the emotional component of an idea is repressed, whereas the cognitive component (or the idea itself) remains conscious.* People are often better off not experiencing the full extent of their emotional involvement in a situation. The capacity for logical thinking itself depends on isolation of affect. For physicians and other health professionals, isolation provides the distance and objectivity toward the suffering of patients that is needed to allow treatment to proceed. But if isolation is used too rigidly and pervasively, an individual is in danger of becoming unduly dispassionate and distant.

The distinctive feature of intellectualization is its "shift of emphasis from immediate inner and interpersonal conflict to abstract ideas and esoteric topics" (Schafer, 1954). When medical students enter the anatomy laboratory for the first time and begin to dissect cadavers, they must find ways to cope with the feelings of revulsion and disgust that are common reactions in the presence of the dead. By focusing intently and narrowly on the assigned anatomy lesson for the day, they are able to deflect many of these feelings in the service of learning. This is a perfectly acceptable use of intellectualization.

The following example illustrates a less adaptive use of intellectualization. An oncology resident had just informed a young man of approximately the same age as himself that he (the patient) had liver cancer. In response to questions from the patient concerning his prognosis and the alternative courses of treatment, the resident launched into a lengthy and technical discussion of "age-corrected mortality rates" and "double-blind clinical trials of chemotherapy." It is not difficult to appreciate the physician's anxiety. Nobody likes to be the bearer of bad news, and undoubtedly the similarity in age enhanced a troubling sense of identification with the patient that only compounded the problem. Unfortunately, the net result of such an abstract and intellectualized response was to increase the patient's anxiety level and to confuse him more about his prognosis and treatment. Were he to meet again with this resident, he might hesitate to express his deepest concerns or to ask the necessary questions. *Patients are often sensitive to the emotional states of their physicians and will go to great lengths to avoid burdening physicians (e.g., with difficult questions), even at the risk of jeopardizing their own care.*

Displacement involves redirecting an emotion from its original object to a more acceptable substitute. The emotion most commonly involved is anger. The classic example of displacement is the story of the milquetoast who comes home from the office where his boss has berated him mercilessly and displaces his pent-up aggression by yelling at his wife and kicking his dog.

Turning against the self is a special form of displacement in which impulses and fantasies directed at someone else are self-directed. It is a common feature in some depressed patients who have been provoked or wronged by another person but who do not display any overt anger. Instead, they grow increasingly depressed. Patients with postoperative complications and those who undergo painful procedures frequently become depressed through the use of this mechanism. These patients are angry and resentful toward their caretakers but do not express such feelings publicly for fear of jeopardizing these important relationships. Instead, they turn their rage on themselves. An individual can alleviate depressive symptoms that are generated in this way by giving the patient permission to turn the anger outward with assurance that such feelings will not alienate the hospital staff.

Undoing refers to a defense mechanism designed to negate or annul (undo) some unacceptable thought, wish, or actual transgression of the past. The neglectful parent who showers presents on his or her children and the underworld godfather who makes generous charitable donations may both be said to be engaged in undoing, that is, atoning for or attempting to counteract past misconduct. Undoing can become the predominant defense mechanism and virtually paralyze its victim, as illustrated in Carson's (1979) example:

Before going to school each day, a 13-year-old male went through an elaborate series of rituals that served no practical purpose. He checked his closet and checked under his bed exactly three times before leaving his room. On his way out of the house, he always straightened a picture on the living room wall until it looked just right. On his way to and from school, it was important to him to walk in definite pathways in relation to several telephone poles he passed. If he deviated from this routine, he became quite anxious. He was sexually inhibited, and experiencing guilt about masturbatory fantasies. His ritualistic behavior served the purpose of decreasing guilt and anxiety by magically undoing his unacceptable sexual fantasies and urges.

Sublimation may be understood as a relatively mature defense in which various instincts are displaced or converted into socially acceptable outlets. Normal sexual curiosity, for example, can become voyeurism under adverse circumstances. Under more favorable circumstances, the same impulse may be sublimated into an interest in photography. Similarly, a sadistic impulse to inflict pain can be sublimated into the socially acceptable and necessary practice of surgery. The surgeon can cut and hurt the patient in the service of a higher goal. Note that in both of these examples of sublimation, the infantile and sexual origins of these behaviors are nearly completely disguised.

Humor, altruism, suppression, and anticipation complete most lists of mature defenses.

Transference

Transference may be defined as "the attitudes, feelings, and fantasies which patient's experience with regard to their doctors, many of them arising, seemingly irrationally, from their own unconscious needs and psychological conflicts rather than from the actual circumstances of the relationship" (Nemiah, 1973). *The analysis of transference is the focal point of psychoanalytic treatment,* but our interest in it concerns its expression in a broader variety of health-care settings.

The physician-patient relationship is not entirely (or even primarily) rational. Patients attach all sorts of wishes, expectations, and sentiments to their physicians, the majority of which remain unknown to the physician. For example, when a patient is angry for having had to sit in the waiting room for 2 hours, this is not an inappropriate reaction and need not fall under the rubric of transference. But if this same patient were raised in a household with numerous siblings competing for the parents' attention and had to endure more than his or her share of delayed gratification, sitting in the waiting room might stir up all sorts of painful memories and associated feelings that,

whether conscious or not, would serve to intensify and color an otherwise legitimate resentment. Every interpersonal encounter has both realistic and transference components.

Transference is a double-edged sword. It can provide the physician (or any other health-care provider) with leverage in influencing a patient to comply with an unpleasant or inconvenient treatment regimen. It can also lead a patient to trust a physician long before he or she has an objective basis for such confidence.

A positive transference can help carry a patient through the anxieties that accompany most illnesses. I was once asked to see an elderly woman who was terrified of radiation treatment. She was upsetting her family and disrupting the nursing staff with her histrionic refusals. After a brief interview during which I simply allowed her to express her anxieties, she announced that I reminded her of her favorite grandson and promptly consented to the treatment.

Transference, whether positive or negative, can create great difficulties when it is not recognized and successfully managed. *The same transference that permits patients to imbue the physician with magical therapeutic powers also leads them to make impossible demands,* to rage when the physician disappoints them, to resent his or her authority, and to fear and rebel against the physician.

Melencolia I (Melancholy) *Albrecht Dürer (1514).* Courtesy of the National Library of Medicine.

Transference is basically a regressive phenomenon based on psychological factors and not on reality. For that reason, it is important not to take *personally* one patient's confession of undying love—just as it is important not to be offended by another patient's equally unjustified expressions of hatred and contempt. Such expressions must be acknowledged and understood, and the physician must help the patient separate reality and fantasy. To act on initial impulses in either of the preceding situations would disrupt the relationship with the patient and render the physician ineffective.

When such understandable but unprofessional feelings interfere with a physician's work, it is known as **countertransference.** Despite its exclusive reliance on male pronouns, I can find no better statement concerning the role of feelings in a clinician's professional life than the following by Nemiah:

> It would be unwise if not impossible for a doctor to avoid having any feelings for his patients. One cannot help at times being annoyed at a particularly hostile patient, pleased at praise that may not be entirely warranted, anxious and uneasy with some, warm and comfortable with others, charmed by the seductive behavior of an attractive woman, overcome by a feeling of helplessness in the face of hopeless situations. It is, however, of particular importance that the doctor have enough self-awareness to recognize how he is feeling. He must be able to judge whether his attitudes are really appropriate to the situation in which they arise, or whether they are a result of his countertransference. It is even more important that he be able to refrain from acting according to the dictates of his impulses and feelings, if such actions would conflict with the rationally determined goals of treatment. It is part of the physician's job to recognize the irrational in both himself and his patients; he must be able to provide the objectivity they lack, without losing his human warmth, understanding, and empathy.

SUMMARY

This chapter can only hint at the complexity and range of psychoanalytic ideas. My hope is that readers will find some of the ideas herein to be both thought-provoking and useful in understanding some of the less rational aspects of human behavior that one observes in patients and physicians as they cope with illness. The psychodynamic perspective may not provide the most scientifically rigorous approach to human behavior, but it offers a comprehensive conception of human concerns with room for all psychological phenomena. No other perspective is so successful at weaving together such disparate domains of experience: past and present, waking thought and dreaming, conscious and unconscious, will and compulsion, love and hate.

CASE STUDY

A third-year medical student began his clerkship year with a rotation in internal medicine. It soon became apparent to his supervisors that he overly identified with his patients, spending inordinate amounts of time engaging them in conversation, giving them false reassurances, and complaining to all who would listen that the nursing staff had been negligent in its duties. He was tactfully and justifiably confronted with his behavior by the chief resident, but his immediate reaction was a combination of resentment and denial. The next day he was temporarily overcome by feelings of depression and worthlessness, and he considered dropping out of medical school.

How can a psychodynamic perspective help you understand the student's behavior?
A psychiatric consultation revealed that this young man was the only son of a chronically depressed mother of four who rarely had sufficient energy or mental health to attend to her children's' needs. Over the course of his childhood, he and she established an unspoken arrangement, the essence of which required that he subordinate his own needs to hers in return for her approval. In other words, as long as he was a good little boy, uncomplaining and attentive, willing to listen to her lengthy complaints and to provide unrealistically optimistic feedback, he could avoid alienating her. His sisters coped with their mother's psychopathology in an entirely different way, by distancing themselves both physically and emotionally as best they could.

Repeated interviews with this student helped to delineate further the picture of an individual whose choice of vocation and whose characteristic ways of relating to patients could both be understood, in part, as efforts to win maternal approval by assuming the roles of healer, listener, and cheerleader. As an adult, he was still trying to master an impossibly complicated relationship with his mother. His perception of the nurses, too, was colored by his perception of his sisters as derelict in their responsibilities to their mother. To the degree that his concern for his patients was free of conflict, he was capable of being an unusually empathic physician. But to the degree that his self-esteem was at the mercy of his patients' well-being, he was at risk of impairment himself (Gabbard, 1985).

Childlike modes of thinking are most apparent in the student's denial and in his subsequent depressive reaction. He was unable to absorb criticism and keep it in perspective. Instead he exaggerated and overgeneralized, concluding on a flimsy evidential basis that he was no longer worthy of becoming a physician. This is an example of what is sometimes called *pars pro toto* **thinking** in which the part (in this case, one episode of problematic behavior) is mistaken for the whole (his worth as a person). Fortunately, a brief course of psychotherapy was sufficient to improve the student's morale and restore a mature perspective on the situation. He completed the clerkship (and the rest of medical school) uneventfully.

SUGGESTED READINGS

Fisher, S., & Greenberg, R.P. (1996). *Freud scientifically reappraised: Testing the theories and therapy*. New York: Wiley.
This book reviews the social science research conducted to prove or disprove some of Freud's most influential ideas, including the nature of dreams, the Oedipal complex, the origins of depression and paranoia, and the outcome of psychoanalytic treatment.

Gabbard, G.O. (1985). The role of compulsiveness in the normal physician. *Journal of the American Medical Association, 254*, 2926—2929.
An application of psychoanalytic thinking to the psychology of medical students and physicians, this article shows how personal traits can be adaptive or maladaptive in a physician depending on the uses to which they are put.

Mitchell, S.A. (2002). *Can love last? The fate of romance over time*. New York: Norton.
A thoughtful and optimistic book by a brilliant psychologist who demonstrates the relevance of contemporary psychoanalytic thinking to a subject of interest to us all.

Westen, D. (2001). *Psychology: Mind, brain, and culture*. New York: Wiley.
An excellent introductory psychology text with unusually good coverage of psychoanalytic perspectives.

Zeldow, P.B., & Braun, L. (1985). Measuring regression in hospitalized medical patients: The BUMP Scale. *General Hospital Psychiatry, 7*, 49–53.
This article demonstrates that psychoanalytic concepts can be measured and enriched by their measurement and offers an empirical basis for a typology of hateful patients.

11 Facilitating Health Behavior Change

Adam Arechiga

> Habit is habit, not to be flung out of the window but rather coaxed downstairs, one step at a time.
>
> MARK TWAIN
>
> The unfortunate thing about the world is that good habits are much easier to give up than bad ones.
>
> W. SOMERSET MAUGHAM
>
> My doctor told me to stop having intimate dinners for four. Unless there are three other people.
>
> ORSON WELLES

INTRODUCTION

With improvements in medical care, and the resultant aging of the population, chronic-care models have become an increasingly important component of medical care. Long-term problems affecting multiple organ systems, such as diabetes, hypertension, and obesity, are widespread

---

TABLE 11.1 Common lifestyle changes that health-care professionals advocate

- Eat a healthier diet (e.g., decrease sodium intake, increase consumption of fruits/vegetables)
- Increase physical activity
- Quit smoking
- Drink alcohol only in moderation
- Change medication or medication regimen
- Monitor blood glucose or blood pressure

Adapted from Rollnick, Mason, and Butler (1999)

---

and account for much of the utilization of health-care resources. Successful treatment and management of these problems require lifestyle modification on the part of the patient.

Physicians are responsible for the diagnosis and treatment of such chronic illnesses. They can also play a crucial role in facilitating behavior change on the part of the patient. Unfortunately, physicians often fail to take advantage of opportunities for effective interventions when they arise. The purpose of this chapter is to provide a basic understanding of effective ways to help patients begin the process of lifestyle change.

TRANSTHEORETICAL MODEL

In the past few years **the transtheoretical model** (TTM) of Prochaska and DiClamente has increasingly been used to understand and teach health behavior change, especially in the field of addictions. The TTM or **"stages of change"** theory is based on the idea that change occurs in well-defined, predictable stages or time periods, each of which is associated with specific tasks. These stages are defined as precontemplation, contemplation, preparation, action, maintenance, and termination.

Individuals in the **precontemplation** stage tend to resist change. They may use denial and place responsibility for their problems on factors such as genetic makeup, addiction, family, or society. They may lack information about their problem. They really have no intention to change their behavior any time soon.

Individuals in the **contemplation** stage acknowledge that they have a problem and have begun to consider some

TABLE 11.2 Recommended interventions for each stage of change

Stage of Change	Intervention Strategies
Precontemplation	Inquire about past attempts at behavior change Use patient-centered, empathic approach Discuss health problem Explore the "cons" to change
Contemplation	Discuss the history of the problem behavior Discuss health consequences of the behavior Discuss benefits of change Build self-confidence of change (self-efficacy)
Preparation	Match patient to appropriate behavior change model Refer to appropriate treatment provider Facilitate development of realistic goals
Action	Use standardized self-help materials Give support for health behavior change Problem solve for barriers to change Give relapse prevention training
Maintenance	Provide on-going support for lifestyle changes Give health feedback, emphasizing improvements Address "pros" of behavior change Discuss other related behavior change issues (e.g., possible negative consequences of change)

Adapted from Clark and Vickers (2003).

kind of behavior change. While many contemplators may consider taking action in the next 6 months, they may be far from doing so. Individuals can remain stuck in this stage for months or years.

Individuals in the **preparation** stage plan to take action in the next month and are making the final adjustments before they begin to change their behavior. While they may appear committed and ready to change their behavior, they may not have resolved their ambivalence toward change.

The **action** stage is where real behavior change begins. This stage requires the greatest commitment in terms of time and energy. Changes made during this stage are the most visible to others and, thus, receive the most recognition. The danger of this stage is that many health professionals equate action with change, ignoring the important preparation for action and the efforts to maintain the changes that follow action.

In the **maintenance** stage any gains achieved in the preceding stages need to be consolidated. *It is important to understand that change does not end in the action stage.* This stage requires a strong commitment to maintenance of the behavior change if relapse is to be avoided, and it can last from 6 months to a lifetime. Any program that promises

an easy change or a "quick fix" does not acknowledge that maintenance is a long, ongoing, and sometimes difficult task.

The **termination** stage is the final goal for anyone who is trying to change their behavior. Individuals who eventually reach this stage have complete confidence in their new or healthier behavior and do not fear relapse. The effort to maintain the new behavior from the previous stage is no longer present. *Many individuals might not reach this stage and will have to work at maintaining their healthier behavior(s) for the rest of their lives.*

While the progression through the stages of change appear linear in nature, in reality change more closely follows a spiral path. Individuals who have progressed to the action stage may suffer a setback and return to the contemplation or precontemplation stage. *Patients rarely work through each stage of change without some kind of setback or relapse.* The majority of people who are trying to change their behavior struggle for years to find an effective solution to their problems.

Death Awards Bacchus First Prize *Wood engraving after Thomas Nast (1870).* Courtesy of the National Library of Medicine. *Most of us will die sooner than necessary because of bad decisions we make about food, alcohol, and exercise.*

TABLE 11.3 Facilitating health behavior change

How not to do it	A better method
Doctor: Have you though about losing some weight?	*Doctor:* Have you thought about losing some weight?
Patient: Yes, many times, but I can't seem to manage. It's my one comfort, my eggs in the morning, my fried chicken at lunch. I'm stuck in the house so much these days.	*Patient:* Yes, many times, but I can't seem to manage. It's my one comfort, my eggs in the morning, my fried chicken at lunch. I'm stuck in the house so much these days.
Doctor: It would certainly help your blood pressure	*Doctor:* It's not easy.
Patient: I know, but what do I do when I really want my two eggs for breakfast? It's a family tradition. [sighs] I always get told to lose weight when I come here.	*Patient:* You can say that again!
Doctor: Have you thought about a gradual approach, like leaving out just one of the eggs for a while, and seeing what a difference it makes?	*Doctor:* Some people prefer to change their eating, others to get more exercise. Both can help with losing weight. How do you really feel at the moment?
Patient: Yes, but what sort of difference will that make?	*Patient:* I'm not sure. I always get told to lose weight when I come here.
Doctor: Over time, as you succeed with one thing, you can try another, and gradually your weight will come down.	*Doctor:* It's like we always know what's good for you, as if it's just a matter of going out there, and one, two, three, and you lose weight!
Patient: Not in my house. The temptations are everywhere, you should just see what's on the table to munch any time you want.	*Patient:* Exactly. I'm not sure I can change my eating right now. I used to get a lot more exercise, but life's changed and I've gotten lazy.
Doctor: Have you talked to your partner about leaving these off the table, just to make it easier for you?	*Doctor:* Well, I'm certainly not here to harass you. In fact, all I want to do is understand how you really feel, and whether there is some way you can keep your blood pressure down. Perhaps there isn't at the moment?
Patient: Yes, but ...	*Patient:* Well, I could think about ...

Adapted from Rollnick, Mason, and Butler (1999).

MOTIVATIONAL INTERVIEWING

Motivational interviewing, developed by Miller and Rollnick, is a therapeutic method or approach to enhancing behavior change in individuals. It is a directive, client-centered counseling style that is intended to help a client or patient become "unstuck" and to begin the process of changing a behavior. *It is not so much a set of techniques as a way of being with people.* Motivational Interviewing has four main principles that guide clinical interactions: (1) express empathy, (2) develop discrepancy, (3) roll with resistance, (4) support self-efficacy.

Express empathy. The foundation of motivational interviewing is a client-centered, empathic counseling style based on "acceptance." The counselor attempts to understand the client or patient's perspectives and feelings without judging, blaming, or criticizing. It should be noted that you can understand or accept a patient's perspective without endorsing or agreeing with it. Likewise, acceptance does not stop the counselor from expressing an opinion

different from the patient's. The interesting thing is that when you accept patients for who they are, it frees them to change. Conversely, if you adopt a nonaccepting attitude, it will typically halt the change process. The client or patient is not viewed as incapable of change, but rather as having become "stuck" through understandable psychological processes.

Develop discrepancy. Motivational interviewing is intentionally directive. It aims to resolve ambivalence toward positive health-behavior change, and gets patients unstuck and moving toward positive change. One way to do this is to *create and amplify any discrepancy between the patient's current behavior and their broader goals and values.* For example, a physician might note the discrepancy between a patient's current state of health vs. his/her desired state of health. The reality is that *many patients may already perceive such a discrepancy, but are ambivalent about changing their behavior.* The goal of the health provider is to make good use of the discrepancy, increasing and amplifying it until the patient becomes unstuck and

TABLE 11.4 Example of Questions to Elicit Change Talk

Disadvantages of the status quo
- What worries you about your current situation?
- What makes you think that you need to do something about your blood pressure [or weight]?
- What difficulties or hassles have you had in relation to your drug use?
- What do you think will happen if you don't change anything?

Advantages of change
- How would you like for things to be different?
- What would be the good things about losing weight?
- What would you like your life to be like 5 years from now?
- If you could make this change immediately, by magic, how might things be better for you?
- The fact that you're here indicates that at least part of you thinks it's time to do something. What are the main reasons you see for making a change?
- What would be the advantages of making this change?

Optimism about change
- What makes you think that if you did decide to make a change, you could do it?
- What encourages you that you can change if you want to?
- What do you think would work for you, if you decided to change?
- Have you ever made a significant change in your life before? How did you do it?
- How confident are you that you can make this change?
- What personal strengths do you have that will help you succeed?
- Who could offer you helpful support in making this change?

Intention to change
- What are you thinking about your weight [or other behavior] at this point?
- I can see that you're feeling stuck at this moment. What's going to have to change?
- What do you think you might do?
- How important is this to you? How much do you want to do this?
- What would you be willing to try?
- Of the options I've mentioned, which one sounds like it fits you best?
- Never mind the "how" for right now, what do you want to have happen?
- So what do you intend to do?

Adapted from Miller and Rollnick (2002).

is able to move toward change. This process is often facilitated by identifying and clarifying the patient's own goals and values that conflict with his or her current behavior. *It is imperative for the patient to present his or her own reasons for change and not feel coerced by the health professional.*

Roll with resistance. Resistance is to be expected and should not be directly opposed; instead, the physician or other healthcare provider should "flow" with the resistance. In motivational interviewing, reluctance and ambivalence toward change are noted and acknowledged as natural and understandable. The health provider's role is not to impose new views or goals, but to invite their patient to consider new information and new perspectives. Patients are invited to do what works best for them. This may involve turning a patient's question or problem back toward them ("Yes, but ..."). *When a health provider rolls with resistance they are actively involving the patient in the problem solving process.*

Support self-efficacy. One of the keys of behavior change is **self-efficacy**, which is a person's belief in his or her ability to change and/or meet goals. One goal of motivational interviewing is to enhance or increase the patient's confidence in his ability to achieve successful change. This can be accomplished by letting patients know that you *can* help them change vs. telling them that you as the health provider *will* change them. Self-efficacy may also be enhanced by looking at the success of others or building upon the patient's own past success.

> A person should not eat until his stomach is replete but should diminish his intake by approximately one fourth of satiation.
>
> MOSES BEN MAIMON (MAIMONIDES)
> *Mishneh Torah*

CLINICAL APPLICATIONS

Example of Motivational Interviewing Techniques Applied to Smoking Cessation

Introduce Topic and Assess Readiness for Change

- **Introduce topic**—Use open-ended, nonjudgmental question or comment to invite the patient to discuss smoking:
  "I'm interested in hearing you talk a little bit about your smoking."
  "I want to understand what it is like for you to be a smoker, please tell me about it."
  "How do you really feel about your smoking these days?"

- **Rate motivation**—Ask the patient to rate their motivation to quit smoking:
  "I'd like to have you rate for me, on a scale from 1 to 10, your current motivation to quit smoking. If 1 is not at all motivated to quit smoking and 10 is completely ready to quit smoking, what number are you right now?"

- **Rate confidence**—Ask the patient to rate their confidence to quit smoking:
  "Again on a scale from 1 to 10, how confident are you that you could be successful at quitting smoking if you decided you wanted to quit right now? If 1 is not at all confident that you could quit and stay quit, and 10 is absolutely confident that you could be successful, what number are you right now?"

Address Motivation and Confidence

- **Discuss motivation**—Elicit patients' self-statements about change by having them explain their motivation rating:
  "Why are you a ... ... and not a 1 on the scale?"
  "What would it take for you to move from a ... to a [higher number]?"

- **Weigh the pros and cons**—Explore with the patient both the benefits of change and the barriers to change:
  "What do you like about smoking?"
  "What concerns you about smoking?"
  "What are the roadblocks to quitting?"
  "What would you like about being a nonsmoker?"

Summarize both the pros and cons provided by the patient and then ask: "So where does that leave you now?"

- **Provide personal risk information**—Share nonjudgmental information about risk and/or objective data from medical evaluation, then ask the patient's opinion of this information (Avoid giving advice or attempting to shock or frighten the patient into change):
  "What do you think about these results?"
  "Would it be helpful for you if I gave you some information about the risks of smoking?"
  "What do you need to hear from me about this?"

- **Discuss Confidence**—Get the patient to make self-statements about his or her confidence to quit smoking by discussing their confidence rating:
  "Why are you a ... and not a 1?"
  "What would help you move from a ... to a [higher number]?"
  "What can I do to support you in moving up to a [higher number]?"

Offer Support and Make a Patient-Centered Plan

- Work with the patient to create a patient-centered plan that matches the patient's readiness to quit.
- Encourage the patient to consider what could work, rather than focus on what would not.
- Provide options (referral, nicotine replacement, patient education materials, etc.), but not direct advice.

TABLE 11.5 Recommendations for behavior change counseling

Frame plan to match patient's perceptions.
- It is important to assess the beliefs and concerns of the patient and to provide information based on this foundation. Remember that behavior change interventions need to be tailored to each patient's specific needs.

Fully inform patients of the purposes and expected effects of interventions and when to expect these effects.
- This will help limit discouragement when the patient cannot see immediate effects. If side effects are common, tell the patient what to expect specifically, and under what circumstances the intervention should be stopped.

Suggest small changes rather than large ones.
- Individuals experience success just by achieving a small goal; this will initiate a positive change.

Be specific.
- Explain the regime and rationale of the behavior change; it is often useful to write the regime down for the patient to take home.

It may be easier to add a new behavior rather than eliminate an established one.
- For example, it may be more effective to suggest that patients increase their physical activity rather than change their current dietary patterns.

Link new behaviors to old behaviors.
- For example, suggest using an exercise bike while watching television.

Use the power of your profession.
- Patients see physicians as health experts, so be sympathetic and supportive while giving a firm, definite message.

Get explicit commitments from the patient.
- Asking the patient how he plans to follow the recommendations encourages him to think about how to integrate a specific behavior into his daily schedule

Refer
- Sometimes it is not possible to counsel patients properly. Therefore, refer patients to behavioral specialists, nutritionists, or support groups to review the appropriate intervention.

Adapted from the *Guide to Clinical Preventive Services* (2nd ed., 1996).

- Ask patient to select the next step.
- Reinforce any movement toward making a change.
- Follow-up on subsequent visits.

TABLE 11.6 Examples of tailored intervention responses

Not Ready	Unsure	Ready
Goal: raise awareness	*Goal:* build motivation and confidence.	*Goal:* negotiate plan.
Major task: inform and encourage	*Major task:* explore ambivalence.	*Major task:* facilitate decision making.
Ask open-ended questions. "What would need to be different for you to consider making additional changes in your eating?" "You said you were a ... on the scale. What would have to happen for you to move from a ... to a ...?"	*Explore ambivalence.* "What are some of the things that you like (and dislike) about your current eating habits?" "What are some of the good (and not so good) things about changing your diet?"	*Identify change options.* "What do you think needs to change?" "What are your ideas for making a change?" "Which option makes the most sense to you?"
Respectfully acknowledge the patient's decisions. "I respect your decision to not make any new or additional changes in your eating."	*Look into the future.* "I think I can understand why you're unsure about making new or additional changes to your diet. Let's just take a moment and imagine that you decided to change. Why would you want to do this?"	*Help patient set a realistic and achievable short-term goal.*
Offer professional advice. "It should come as no surprise that my recommendation is for you to ... But, this is your decision. If you should decide to make some changes to your diet, I'm here to help you. Regardless, I would like to keep in touch."	*Refer to other teens.* "What do your friends like to eat?" "What would your friends think if you ate this way?"	*Develop a plan to eat healthier diet.*
	Ask about the next step. "Where does this leave you now?" (Let patient raise the topic of change)	*Summarize the plan.*

Example of Motivational Interviewing Techniques Applied to Adolescent Dietary Adherence

- **Establish Rapport**
  "How's it going?"

- **Opening Statement**
  "We have ... minutes to meet. So here is what I thought we might do:
  Hear how your new diet is going;
  Give you some information from your last diet recall and cholesterol values;
  Talk about what, if anything, you might change in your eating;
  How does that sound? Is there anything else you want to do?"

- **Assess Diet Adherence and Progress**
  "On a scale of 1–10, if 1 is not following the recommend-ed diet at all, and 10 is following the recommended diet all the time, what number are you at right now?"
  "Tell me more about the number you chose."
  "Why did you choose a ..., and not a 1?"
  "What times do you follow your diet, and when don't you?"
  "How are you feeling about the recommended diet?"
  "The last time we met, you were working on .... How has that been going?"

- **Give Feedback**
  Show patient test data.
  Compare participant results with normative data or other interpretive information.
  "This is where you stand compared to other teenagers."
  Elicit patient's response information.
  "What do you think of all this information?"
  Offer information about the meaning or significance of the results. (Note: only do this if the patient shows interest or asks questions about the information.)
  "Most teenagers who have cholesterol values around ..., are more likely to ...."

- **Assess Readiness to Change**
  "On a scale of 1–10, if 1 is not ready to make any new changes in your diet, and 10 is completely ready to make changes such as eating foods lower in saturated fat and cholesterol, what number are you at right now?"
  "Tell me more about the number that you chose."
  "What made you choose a ... instead of a 1?"

- **Tailored Intervention Approach** (See the following Case Study for an example of a tailored intervention)

- **Close the Encounter**
  Summarize the session.
  "Did I get it all?"
  Support self-efficacy.
  "I can tell that you are really trying and I know that you can do it. If this plan doesn't work so well, we can adapt it or change it so that you are successful."
  Arrange next appointment.

SUMMARY

Lifestyle change is a necessary step for patients with chronic illnesses. Unfortunately behavior change can be difficult. Health-care providers have an important role in facilitating this change in their patients. Two of the most relevant models for facilitating health behavior change are the **Transtheoretical Model** and **Motivational Interviewing**. The TTM posits that health behavior change occurs in distinct stages (precontemplation, contemplation, preparation, action, maintenance, and termination) each of which has its own tasks that need to be accomplished before an individual can effectively progress. Motivational Interviewing is a directive client-centered counseling approach that is used to get a patient "unstuck" and begin the process of behavior change. The four main principles of this approach are expressing empathy, developing discrepancy, rolling with resistance, and supporting self-efficacy. When used successfully, these models can help facilitate and foster behavior change in patients.

CASE STUDY

Mr. Brown is a 51-year-old accountant who has a number of health issues. He experiences fatigue, depression, and insomnia. He is concerned about his heart because of a family history of heart disease (his father died of a myocardial infarction at age 59). He is obese (BMI 34 kg/m^2), has hypertension, elevated cholesterol, and is sedentary. When given this feedback, Mr. Brown sighs and says that he has tried to lose weight in the past but that nothing has worked.

When you ask about his eating and exercise habits, he responds, "I work 80+ hours each week, eat when I can (usually out of the vending machines at work), and have no time to exercise."

What would be the best approach with this patient?

Mr. Brown is unsure about any health behavior change. If you confront this patient, it will most likely lead to denial and resistance. The best approach would be to start by establishing rapport and expressing empathy toward the difficulty of lifestyle change.

Open-ended questions, such as "Tell me more about your concerns of heart disease." "What are your thoughts about your weight?" and "What weight-loss methods have you tried in the past?" can help highlight past successes and failures in terms of lifestyle change. Questions such as these may also reveal the patient's readiness to change, and identify the pros and cons of such a change.

The main goal for this initial appointment might be to have Mr. Brown examine his problem behaviors more closely and to begin thinking about what would be necessary for him to change. At a following appointment it may be possible to present Mr. Brown with different lifestyle options that would positively affect his risk factors, and help him develop a plan of action once he had identified the behavior that he felt most comfortable attempting to change.

> Those who think they have not time for bodily exercise will sooner or later have to find time for illness.
>
> EDWARD STANLEY, EARL OF DERBY
> *The Conduct of Life—Address at Liverpool College*

SUGGESTED READINGS

Berg-Smith, S.M., Stevens, V.J., Brown, K.M., Van Horn, L., Gernhofer, N., Peters, E., Greenberg, R., Snetselaar, L., Ahrens, L., & Smith K. (1999). A brief motivational intervention to improve dietary adherence in adolescents. *Health Education Research, 14*, 399–410.
This article describes specific alterations in the motivational interviewing approach that are helpful when working with adolescents.

Clark, M.M., & Vickers, K.S. (2004). Counseling for health behavior change. In R.S. Lang & D.D. Hensrud (Eds.). *Clinical preventive medicine* (2nd ed., pp. 59–67). New York: AMA Press.
This chapter provides a basic outline of Motivational Interviewing as applied in a medical setting.

Miller, W.R., & Rollnick, S. (2002). *Motivational interviewing* (2nd ed.). New York: Guilford.
The authors and creators of Motivational Interviewing have written a book that explains their method of counseling for health behavior change. In addition to providing a detailed description of the foundation for Motivational Interviewing, they provide easy to follow examples of the clinical application of their counseling method.

Prochaska, J.O., Norcross, J.C., & DiClemente, C.C. (2002). *Changing for good*. New York: Quill.
This book explains the Transtheoretical Model of behavior change in a way that can be used with the lay public.

Rollnick, S., Mason, P., & Butler, C. (1999). *Health behavior change: A guide for practitioners*. London: Churchill Livingstone.
This book provides a more in-depth understanding of how motivational interviewing can be used in medical practice.

12 Human Sexuality

Jeannine Rahimian, Jonathan Bergman, George R. Brown, & Salvador Ceniceros

> I believe in the flesh and the appetites,
> Seeing, hearing, feeling are miracles
> And each part of me is a miracle.
>
> WALT WHITMAN
> *Song of Myself*

Sexual functioning is an important aspect of human life and interaction. However, sexual health is also highly susceptible to the effects of many illnesses and medications. For example, impotence is among the many problems faced by diabetics secondary to neuropathy and micro-vascular disease. The newer antidepressants may have few adverse effects, but a decrease in sexual desire causes many patients to stop taking these medications. The public's interest in enhancing sexual function is evident in the glut of advertising (including computer spam) for medications to help men with erectile dysfunction. One measure of the importance of sexual functioning in the United States is that most insurance plans will cover the cost of drugs for erectile dysfunction, despite their high cost. *Evaluation of sexual function is a critical part a physician's evaluation of patients, particularly when patients have illnesses or medications that are associated with sexual dysfunction.*

Despite its importance, it is estimated that only 35% of primary care physicians often or always take a sexual history as part of routine patient evaluations. The reasons given for this lack of attention to sexual health include time constraints, embarrassment, the belief that a sexual history is not relevant to the chief complaint, or the physician feeling ill-prepared. Medical schools are now more systematically addressing these issues, and medical students actively practice taking sexual histories to help them feel more prepared and less embarrassed. Questions that are tailored to the specific needs of the patient are highly relevant and not unduly time consuming.

This chapter will outline the types of questions that are best used for screening, describe how to determine when to ask more questions, and illustrate how to get specific information when it is needed. In addition, the chapter will address some simple interventions that a clinician can use to help patients who have problems with sexual function. Most such problems are relatively easily addressed, reducing yet another obstacle to asking questions about sexual function—a physician's sense of helplessness about doing anything helpful.

> Sex is not an antidote for loneliness, feelings of inadequacy, fear of aging, hostility, or an inability to form warm friendships.
>
> ISABEL P. ROBINAULT
> *Sex, Society and the Disabled*

THE SEXUAL HISTORY

The sexual history should be a part of a general assessment and would rarely be the first set of questions asked. *A physician should always establish rapport with a patient prior to asking personal questions about sexual health.* Once ready to ask the sexual questions, a transition statement can be helpful. For example, one might say:

Now I am going to ask some questions which may be a bit more personal. I ask these questions as a part of a total medical history. Your answers are confidential, and you don't need to answer any questions if you are uncomfortable.

Generally the patient will not be embarrassed as long as the doctor is matter-of-fact, sensitive, and nonjudgmental. *Sexual orientation or behavior should never be assumed, and the way questions are worded should provide permission to give honest responses.* For example, questions such as "how many partners have you had in the past year?" are more likely to elicit accurate information than questions about whether a patient has a girlfriend or boyfriend. Normalization of specific activities or problems may help patients feel more comfortable giving information that they may otherwise find embarrassing. For example, one might ask if the number of lifetime partners was "about 5, 10, 20, or more?" This gives permission for the patient to acknowledge it if he or she has had more than a few partners. Similarly, telling a diabetic patient that "many people with diabetes experience changes in sexual function" may ameliorate some of the patient's potential embarrassment.

Screening *questions for a sexual history should be included in the patient's initial evaluation*, as an important component of a comprehensive history and examination. Some relevant questions might include the following:

- Are you currently sexually active, or have you been in the past?
- Do you have sex with men, women, or both?
- Do you use contraception? If so, what type?
- Do you desire a pregnancy in the near future?
- How many partners have you had in the past month? In your lifetime?
- What type of sex activities do you participate in (oral, vaginal, anal, other)?
- Are you satisfied with your sexual functioning?
- Is there an area in which you would seek improvement?
- Do you have difficulty achieving orgasm or ejaculation?
- Do you ever have pain with intercourse?
- Do you use any toys or devices during sex?
- Have you ever been tested for a sexually transmitted infection (STI)? Have you ever had an STI?
- Have you ever been tested for HIV? Would you like to be tested today?
- What is your understanding of STI transmission, including HIV?
- Are you ever pressured into having sex when you do not want to?

In situations in which sexual dysfunction is suspected, open-ended questions such as "How can I help you?" or "What is the problem?" can be quite helpful. These can be followed with more specific questions after the patient has had an opportunity to explain the problem(s) as he or she perceives them. *Silence can be a powerful tool in taking a sexual history, and repetition of what the patient has said shows empathy and attentiveness to the patient's needs.*

> Venus found herself a goddess
> In a world controlled by gods,
> So she opened up her bodice
> And evened up the odds.
>
> HARVEY GRAHAM
> *A Doctor's London*

INTERVENTIONS

Once a problem has been identified, it is important to let the patient know that it is good that he or she shared this information. Following this, the physician can address the patient's concerns. Often the intervention is very simple, although in some cases consultation with an expert in sexual function is indicated. Jack Annon's **PLISSIT** model offers a graduated series of responses to sexual concerns raised by patients.

1. *Permission:* Most sexual concerns can be addressed with simple permission, such as assuring the patient that there is no "correct" position for intercourse, or explaining that problems with decreased libido can often be addressed by simply switching to a different antidepressant.
2. *Limited Information:* Sexual concerns that require more than permission are often handled with simple and limited information. For example, a woman with orgasmic problems may be "cured" with information about the role of clitoral stimulation in female orgasm, or a man with erectile dysfunction may need to be told that alcohol decreases sexual performance.
3. *Specific Suggestions:* The physician can provide suggestions specifically tailored to each patient's problems and desires. This may include prescriptions for medications for erectile dysfunction, or vaginal cream for painful intercourse. In some cases, this is the point at which a primary care physician would seek consultation from a specialist, such as a urologist or gynecologist.
4. *Intensive Treatment:* If the less intensive interventions are not sufficient, individualized therapy by a trained sex therapist or couples therapist is sometimes needed. The physician's recommendation that the patient get help can add significantly to the likelihood that the patient will follow through with treatment.

The remainder of the chapter will provide more details on what is known about "normal" and problematic sexual response. However, it is important to note that *the concept of "normal" or healthy sexual functioning is profoundly influenced by the time and culture in which the patient and physician are functioning.* For example, some sexual behaviors labeled as psychiatric disorders by the American Psychiat-

TABLE 12.1 Major physical changes occurring in the sexual response cycle	
Male	Female
Excitement (mechanism: vasocongestion) *Appearance of sex flush over neck, chest, face, torso, and genitals; increase in heart rate and blood pressure; increase in muscular tension*	
Erection of penis Swelling and elevation of testes	Clitoris increases in size Vaginal lubrication Inner two thirds of vagina lengthens and expands
Plateau (mechanism: vasocongestion) *Continuation of increases that began in excitement phase*	
Continued enlargement and elevation of testes Rotation of testes Secretion of a few drops of fluid from Cowper's gland	Clitoris retracts under hood Outer one third of vagina swells, forming the orgasmic platform
Orgasm (mechanism: neuromuscular) *Muscular contractions throughout the body; respiratory rate and pulse may double, and blood pressure may increase as much as 30%; vocalizations may occur*	
Contractions extending from testes to penis itself Three or four strong ejaculatory contractions occurring at 0.8-sec intervals, followed by two to four slower contractions of the anal sphincter	Muscular contractions (2-4/sec) beginning in outer one third of vagina followed by 3 to 15 contractions occurring at 0.8-sec intervals Uterine contractions
Resolution *Rapid reduction in vasocongestion occurs; respiration, pulse, and blood pressure return to normal; muscles relax*	
Gradual return of penis to its unstimulated state Testes descend and return to normal size	Clitoris, vagina, and external genitalia return to normal

ric Association 30 years ago are now considered to be within the range of "normal" behavior. Laws regarding sexual behavior differ by state within the United States. The powerful and intimate nature of sexuality leads it to be the focus of intense moral and spiritual debate throughout the world.

THE SPECTRUM OF SEXUAL RESPONSE

Prior to the work of **Masters and Johnson** in the 1960s, men and women were thought to be very different in their physiological sexual responses. However, the pioneering work of Masters and Johnson established that most of the physiologic changes during sexual response were similar for both sexes (Table 12.1). Masters and Johnson did report two dramatic differences between men and women: (1) male sexual functioning is characterized by a lengthy **resolution phase**, whereas many women are capable of experiencing multiple orgasms in a single sexual episode; and (2) male orgasms are punctuated by ejaculation, whereas female orgasms are not. More recent research has suggested that even these differences may not be universal, with some men capable of multiple orgasms and some women reporting ejaculation during orgasm.

Masters and Johnson proposed that the intensity of sexual response in men did not vary widely, but they did report a wide variety in the relative length of various sexual response phases (Figure 12.1). At one end of the spectrum is premature ejaculation, with a very rapid progression through the excitement and plateau phases, culminating in an abrupt orgasm much earlier than either the man or his partner wishes. At the other end of the spectrum, men and women can exhibit a pattern of greatly delayed or absent orgasm, often in the context of otherwise typical arousal and excitation.

Sexual Dysfunction in Men

Premature ejaculation is defined as ejaculation that occurs before it is desired, without reasonable control over the timing of ejaculation. There are many factors associated with this problem, which may occur more often in less experienced men. The prevalence of premature ejaculation is estimated at 30%. In practice, the term premature ejaculation is only

Women may experience a pattern that resembles the sexual response of men, i.e., multiple orgasms sufficiently far apart that they are experienced as separate events (pattern A). Women with less sexual experience may have a gradual and somewhat tenuous increase in arousal and a slow resolution phase (pattern B). Some women have an "escalating effect" with continued stimulation after orgasm, resulting in several orgasms each building on the intensity of the previous one (pattern C).

This variability in female response undoubtedly contributed to the notion that psychologically mature women obtain orgasm with men through vaginal stimulation by the penis rather than from clitoral stimulation. Masters and Johnson maintained that clitoral stimulation, direct or indirect, is the primary source of orgasmic stimulation and that the types of orgasmic response are physiologically indistinguishable. However, in contrast, at least three types of female orgasm have been identified by a small body of research:

1. **Vulvar orgasm** is characterized by contractions of the outer one third of the vagina as a result of coital or non-coital stimulation. No refractory period occurs with this type of orgasm.
2. **Uterine orgasm** is characterized by altered breathing distinguished by gasps and climaxing with an episode of involuntary holding of the breath that is exhaled at orgasm. This response is then followed by a refractory period characterized by deep relaxation and a feeling of satiation. This type of orgasm occurs during repeated deep stimulation involving deep thrusting.
3. **Blended orgasm** contains features of both vulvar and uterine orgasms, resulting from simultaneous stimulation of the clitoris and the vaginal wall.

There is little research on the sexual response disorders of women. Available data suggest that drugs and illnesses exert similar effects on sexual function in the same phase of the response cycle in men and women. For example, *about half of men taking serotonergic antidepressants experience delayed ejaculation and orgasm and a similar percentage of women experience treatment-emergent orgasmic difficulties.* Most disorders occur in both men and women, although certain disorders may be more prevalent or troublesome in one gender or the other. Men are more likely to seek professional advice than women with regards to sexual dysfunction. Women whose sexual arousal disorder involves a failure to lubricate may resort to self-help measures such as over-the-counter remedies with some success, thereby avoiding the need for professional help.

Recurrent or persistent genital pain experienced during or after sexual intercourse is called **dyspareunia**. Pain may be felt at the entrance to the vagina (the **introitus**) or deep in the vagina or pelvis, and can result from either physical or psychological problems. Women will often become con-cerned if they are evaluated by a physician and informed that there is nothing physically abnormal. However, although no anatomic abnormality may be present, physicians can often identify a physiological basis for sexual problems if they conduct a careful examination. For example, scars from previous episiotomies or from adhesions due to previous pelvic inflammatory disease may result in pain during intercourse. A vaginal infection or insufficient lubrication also may cause irritation and inflammation of the vaginal walls. Similarly, a dry, thinning vagina in a post-menopausal woman will often lead to dyspareunia.

Psychologically, sexually inexperienced women who were taught that men are insensitive and uncaring or that sex is to be tolerated but not enjoyed may expect pain, with their fear and anxiety leading to subsequent dyspareunia. The influence of sexual abuse or trauma on many women's sexuality cannot be overstated, especially given the high prevalence of these problems.

The involuntary contraction of the pubococcygeus muscles that surround the outer third of the vagina is termed **vaginismus**. Spasm of these muscles can interfere with coitus and can prevent penetration of the penis. *More than half of women with vaginismus also have a history of dyspareunia.* The majority of women with this disorder will contract their pubococcygeus muscles in response to anything inserted into the vagina (e.g., a finger, speculum, or tampon). These contractions of the pubococcygeus muscles are not under voluntary control. Attempts to penetrate the vagina can produce pain and associated anxiety. Some women avoid the possibility of such pain by avoiding all sexual encounters. Obtaining a thorough medical and psychological history is essential for these women, to discover whether rape or sexual abuse as a child has occurred. A history of either suggests psychotherapy may be required in addition to sex therapy.

Treatment of vaginismus is highly effective, with success rates reported at up to 100%, with no relapse at 5-year follow-up. Treatment should combine education, counseling, and behavioral exercises. Treatment begins with self-discovery, masturbation, and relaxation learned via exercises and audio tapes. The next step involves insertion of successively larger dilators into the vagina while controlling the pace of treatment. The exercises and insertion of dilators are then explained to the partner, who takes over the insertion, with the woman guiding her partner's hand. Sexual intercourse should not proceed until she feels ready. *The majority of unconsummated marriages result from vaginismus,* and many couples remain together for years without having sexual intercourse.

Societal attitudes toward female orgasm have changed markedly with time. In Victorian times, orgasm was considered abnormal and harmful, which is not the case today. This shift in cultural norms has produced increased emphasis on orgasm, and diagnostic precision, including development of appropriate differential diagnosis, must be applied before labeling a woman as anorgasmic. However, some women are simply unable to reach orgasm, despite adequate sexual stimulation. They may look forward to sex and experience a high level of sexual excitement, with vaginal swelling and lubrication, but still be unable to experience the release of orgasm.

Inhibited female orgasm is divided into two major subtypes: global and situational. **Global** or generalized orgasmic disorder refers to the inability to experience orgasm in all situations and with all partners. **Situational** orgasmic disorder refers to the ability to experience orgasm only in specific circumstances, e.g., during masturbation but not with intercourse, or with one partner but not another. The treatment for inhibited female orgasm consists of helping the patient progress through nine basic steps:

1. Self-examination.
2. Genital touching.
3. Identification of pleasurable areas.
4. Learning of masturbation (with or without assistance of a training film).
5. Experience of arousal from erotic pictures, stories, or fantasies.
6. Use of a vibrator.
7. Observation by a partner.
8. Participation by a partner.
9. Intercourse.

Hypoactive sexual desire disorders affect both sexes and may result from a wide variety of conditions, such as obsessive-compulsive personality traits or disorder, and **anhedonia** (a symptom of depression). Gender identity problems or specific sexual phobias may also contribute to lack of sexual desire. In addition, numerous physical conditions can result in low sexual desire. For example, diabetic women may have repeated yeast infections, leading to difficulty in lubrication and decreased sexual response. Psychiatric illness can also be an integral part of this form of sexual dysfunction. *Anxiety disorders, mood disorders, and substance abuse must be treated before or concomitant with treatment for hypoactive sexual desire.*

Deficiency in sexual desire is also strongly tied to the complexity of relationships. Some people are no longer attracted to their partners, or their partners may have poor sexual or communications skills. Power struggles between sexual partners may diminish sexual desire. Treatment is therefore difficult, given the multifactorial etiology of the problem. In these cases, the psychosocial aspects of the sexual problem have to be addressed, including development of verbal and nonverbal communication between the sexual partners, developing new ways of thinking about the relationship, and potentially increasing the frequency of sexual play.

Sexual aversion is a sexual desire disorder where the patient experiences an aversion to and avoidance of specific sexual activities, organs, or sexual content. These patients initially have a normal level of interest in sexual activities. However, if left untreated, their specific aversion may reduce libido, resulting in a difficult to treat desire disorder. In fact, the majority of patients who present for treatment already have reduced sexual desire. Aversion frequently occurs in conjunction with panic disorder and with sexual phobias. This extreme level of anxiety triggered by sexual activity can be connected to cases of sexual victimization, such as rape or abuse in childhood. Because many of the treatment techniques used in sex therapy may escalate these anxieties, these patients often seem unable to benefit from therapy. If the problem is recognized, the integration of anxiolytic medication and brief psychotherapy into overall treatment can increase the likelihood of success.

Nocturnal Arousal and Morning Sex

The sexual excitement and response that occur while a person sleeps are referred to as **nocturnal arousal.** *Many men and women experience multiple episodes of sexual excitement (erection with and without ejaculation in men and vaginal lubrication and clitoral enlargement in women) during rapid eye movement sleep.* The potential contribution of this response to reproductive success is unclear, although nocturnal arousal may provide adequate sexual outlet if waking sexual experience is diminished or absent.

One effect of nocturnal arousals is that males frequently have erections upon waking. For men who encounter difficulty having erections when awake, morning erections are vital to the clinical history and may also present an opportunity to engage in sexual activity. The interpretation of some women of morning erections as being caused by a reflex rather than a response to the sexual partner must be addressed if treatment is to be successful.

Effects of Aging on Sexual Function

Age affects the sexual function of both men and women. Men generally experience a gradual but steady decline in sexual functioning after the early twenties, with some potential decrease in drive as well. Women reach their sexual peak in their thirties or forties, with a gradual decline in their fifties. After age fifty, sexual performance in men and women declines in each successive decade. For women, the sentinel event in sexual decline is menopause. Reduced estrogen levels may lead to vaginal dryness and thinning, resulting in dyspareunia. The use of **water soluble lubrication** during intercourse is highly recommended, and hormone replacement therapy can be considered, although the benefits of the latter must be weighed against the medical risks associated with this treatment. The psychological ef-

Nearly 4 centuries ago, Shakespeare described the enduring quality of a commitment of love, despite the ravages of changing circumstance, fading beauty, or time.

Let me not to the marriage of true minds
Admit impediments. Love is not love
Which alters when it alteration finds,
Or bends with the remover to remove:
Oh, no! it is an ever-fixed mark,
That looks on tempests and is never shaken,
It is the star to every wandering bark,
Whose worth's unknown, although his height be taken.
Love's not Time's fool, though rosy lips and cheeks
Within his bending sickle's compass come;
Love alters not with his brief hours and weeks,
But bears it out even to the edge of doom.
If this be error and upon me proved,
I never writ, nor no man ever loved.

WILLIAM SHAKESPEARE
Sonnet 116

fect of menopause varies across different women, but potential feelings of decreased femininity must be addressed to maximize sexual function and pleasure.

*In men, the **refractory period** begins to lengthen at around 30 years of age, increasing yearly.* Typical refractory periods are 20–30 minutes in teenagers, and 3 hours to 3 days in 70-year-old men. Additional stimulation is typically required to achieve erections in older men. Men's partners should be made aware that this is a normal physiological response and does not represent decreased attraction toward the partner.

Women's higher life expectancy compared to men results in a disproportional number of elderly women without sexual partners. Widows and widowers who resume sexual activity after long periods of abstinence often experience considerable difficulty with sexual function and desire. Generally, however, *although sexual function declines with time, sexual interest typically remains constant later in life.* Large national surveys have shown that 75% of men and 58% of women in their seventies have a moderate to strong interest in sex. Eighty-one percent of married couples in their seventies are still sexually active, while 75% of unmarried men and 50% of unmarried women in their seventies remain sexually active. *It is, therefore, important to address sexual function in the elderly, as sexual desire is often substantial later in life.*

Sexual Pleasure: Masturbation

Masturbation is defined as self-stimulation for the purpose of sexual excitation and/or orgasm. Children may mastur-

bate because they enjoy the sensation. Adults may masturbate when they are lonely, tired, bored, or sexually aroused. Masturbation may help relieve sexual tension, stress, or anger, or may aid in initiation of sleep. Masturbation is typically accompanied by sexual fantasies, many of which will never be acted upon, providing a safe outlet for sexual desires. *Masturbation is a normal, healthy activity that enhances the quality of life of most individuals*; in some cases, however, it may dull the desire for interpersonal sexual interaction. Excessive masturbation is associated with several psychiatric disorders, although the majority of people who masturbate more frequently than twice per day do not have a psychiatric disorder.

Patterns of masturbatory activity can provide insight into sexual problems. For example, women who are anorgasmic rarely masturbate. Orgasm during masturbation but not during intercourse suggests a psychosocial etiology or a deficiency in the sexual interaction between a woman and her partner. Women with vaginal spasm often masturbate to orgasm without difficulty. Men with premature ejaculation may masturbate to release tension, not merely for pleasure. Men with delayed ejaculation may masturbate compulsively and become overly engaged in autostimulatory activity. Ideally, masturbation is an affirmation that an individual is worthy of pleasure. Sharing sexual experiences with other people is a matter of choice. Masturbation is a satisfactory sexual outlet for many individuals; however, for others it may not provide the emotional satisfaction of an interpersonal sexual relationship.

Sexual Fantasies

Sexual fantasies usually begin during early adolescence and decrease in middle age. Men report more frequent sexual fantasies than women, and these fantasies occur during both masturbation and intercourse. Fantasies can relieve monotony, increase arousal, and permit one to imagine behavior that would be unacceptable or undesirable in reality. People sometimes find fantasies intolerable, humiliating, or frightening. Men with sexual dysfunction may visualize another person making love to their partner; this second person is often who the dreamer wishes to be. Some individuals have violent fantasies, which may or may not be undesired, while others may have fantasies that involve humiliation or degradation. Most self-described heterosexuals have occasional same-sex fantasies.

Specific fantasies may precede a new romance or sexual encounter. Individuals who are contemplating an out-of-relationship affair may fantasize about the affair before it happens, and this may be a stressor for both partners. When the fantasy becomes ineffective, the likelihood of acting on the fantasy increases.

Hylas and the Nymphs *John W. Waterhouse (1896).* © Manchester City Galleries, Manchester, UK. *Fantasy is a natural and important part of our sexual being, and physicians frequently need to reassure patients that fantasies are harmless.*

Sexual Pleasure with a Partner

When combined with communication and guidance, exploration of each other's bodies can provide information on techniques that increase a partner's pleasure. Mutual masturbation provides an often satisfying alternative to intercourse, and mutual caressing of the breasts and genitals can be an enjoyable prelude to intercourse. Oral sex may also serve as a precursor or alternative to intercourse. **Fellatio** involves oral stimulation of the male genitals; **cunnilingus** refers to oral stimulation of the female genitals; **analingus** is oral stimulation of the anus; and **soixante-neuf** (French for **sixty-nine**) involves simultaneous fellatio and/or cunnilingus. The desirability of oral sex differs from person to person, although recent surveys of sexual behavior in U.S. teens suggests that this practice is becoming increasingly common and accepted among young people.

For many people, the anus, which is supplied by the same nerves and spatially related to the pelvic organs and muscles involved in sexual response, may be a source of sexual pleasure and eroticism. For other individuals, anal sex is not enjoyable because of association with defecation, rape, or prior painful attempts with rectal penetration. Some heterosexuals may be uncomfortable with the association of anal sex with male homosexuality. However, *anal sex forms part of the sexual repertoire of at least one fourth of the heterosexual population and at least three fourths of the male homosexual population.*

The risk of infection with the **human immunodeficiency virus (HIV)** and other **sexually transmitted infections (STIs)** is particularly high with anal sex because of the presence of delicate blood vessels in the anal-rectal region. For this reason, the use of a lubricated condom is recommended in all nonmonogamous relationships. In all cases, lubrication is recommended because of the lack of natural lu-

brication; in addition, the penis should be carefully washed after anal penetration before insertion into another body cavity.

While some primates use the rear entry position almost exclusively, humans use a wide variety of positions during intercourse. Different sexual positions allow exploration of a variety of methods of stimulation and also introduces novelty into the sexual experience. Face-to-face positions allow kissing and observation of the partner's facial expressions. Rear entry with the partners lying on their sides is the least physically demanding position, and it is recommended for those with medical problems that limit vigorous sexual activity. Masters and Johnson reported that a woman's excitement develops more rapidly and intensely when the woman is on top, which allows the man's hands to provide additional stimulation.

Sexual Orientation

Sexual orientation is defined as an erotic affinity and engagement in sexual activity with those of the opposite sex (heterosexuality), the same sex (homosexuality), or either sex (bisexuality). Homosexuals tend to have stronger spontaneous erotic feelings for members of the same sex, while heterosexuals tend to have stronger spontaneous erotic feelings for members of the opposite sex. Many individuals have the ability to become aroused by members of both sexes, although for most people arousal from one sex or the other predominates. *A sizable portion of people who self-describe as exclusively homosexual or heterosexual report the capacity to be sexually aroused by or to have engaged in sexual activity with members of both sexes.* A self-identified heterosexual has not necessarily had sex exclusively with members of the opposite sex, nor has a self-identified homosex-

THE BOY WHO PLAYED WITH DOLLS

remembers the family photograph
of him in shorts, knees pressed close,
the toes of his sandals touching.
A missing tooth makes an awkward smile
as he gazes into the camera,
wincing as if the flash has wounded him.
The two large dolls are naked,
hair shorn, arms and legs akimbo
as they dangle from his hands.
Even at five years old
he is too tall to hold them
so their feet like his
will touch the ground.
Years later, his mother will say:
You weren't a sissy, you were practicing
to be a doctor.

PETER PEREIRA

ual had sex exclusively with members of the same sex. People who engage in **situational homosexuality**, such as in a prison setting, do not typically persist in this behavior once they leave the restricted setting. They do not necessarily consider themselves homosexual, nor do they define their situational homosexual behaviors as gay sex. Fantasies may allow them to dissociate their actual partner from the envisioned partner.

The **Kinsey Report** estimated that approximately 5–10% of American men and 3–5% of women were homosexual. Kinsey and his colleagues reported that 37% of men and 14% of women had had homosexual experience to the point of orgasm before the age of 45, with 4% of men and 0.03% of women remaining exclusively homosexual. However, problems of definition, classification, and reporting hamper efforts to provide precise estimates. For example, is anyone who has engaged in same-sex activity homosexual? In 1994 The National Health and Social Life Survey found that 2.8% of men and 1.4% of women identify themselves as exclusively gay. Reports of voluntary same-gender sexual contact within the past year, however, range from 2%–15%, with a trend toward increased reporting of same-gender sexual activity over time when the same methodology is employed.

The prevalence of **bisexuality** is also difficult to estimate with accuracy. Bisexuality involves a tendency toward some combination of same-sex and opposite-sex sexual expression. Many individuals who consider themselves to be either heterosexual or homosexual are capable of being sexually aroused by members of both genders. One study in 1978 found that 52% of exclusively homosexual men and 77% of exclusively homosexual women had engaged in intercourse with a member of the opposite sex on at least one occasion. Although not precise, *estimates project that a small number (roughly 6%) of marriages involve one heterosexual and one homosexual spouse.* Comparable data do not exist for bisexual individuals. Additionally, it is estimated that 1% of marriages involve a homosexual man and homosexual woman in a marriage of convenience.

A considerable body of research has failed to provide definitive evidence of any specific biological or psychological basis for any sexual orientation. *An individual's sexual orientation appears to be deeply ingrained at an early age and is generally immutable.* Nevertheless, negative attitudes toward homosexuality and bisexuality still prevail across different societies and ethnicities. "Sexual preference" is a misnomer because it implies that individuals actively choose their sexual attraction, while the vast majority of research suggests that sexual attraction is not a choice. *In 1973, the American Psychiatric Association removed homosexuality from its list of recognized mental disorders,* largely based on the absence of evidence of any direct correlation between sexual orientation and mental disorder. However, when sexual orientation of any type leads to psychological distress or impairment, the psychiatric diagnosis of "Sexual Disorder Not Otherwise Specified" can be made.

Potential psychological differences between homosexuals and heterosexuals have not yet been completely elucidated. *Homosexual teenagers have a significantly higher rate of depression and suicide that their heterosexual peers,* although the cause of this disparity is clearly multifactorial. Early awareness of same-sex arousal may be accompanied by a sense of isolation from peers, possibly accompanied by either self-imposed social isolation or being ostracized by heterosexual peers. Differences in the parietal cortex of homosexuals and heterosexuals have recently been reported, as have varying responses to pheromones between the two groups. Many researchers believe that sexual orientation will eventually be explained exclusively on a genetic or hormonal basis. Previous teachings that homosexuality and bisexuality result from an early conflicted parent-child relationship are unfounded and speculative. The factors that contribute to the development of an individual's sexual orientation remain unknown.

Homosexuals and bisexuals tend to have different psychosocial support networks than their heterosexual peers. For both gays and lesbians, the presence of social support is positively related to good psychological adjustment. However, the rates of depression and substance abuse are still higher in the homosexual and bisexual population than it is in the heterosexual population.

PARAPHILIAS

Paraphilias, or deviant attractions, are consuming sexual fantasies or activities characterized by erotic exclusion of an adult partner and significant distress or dysfunction as a direct result of these fantasies or activities. It is inherently problematic to define any sexual behavior or fantasy as deviant or abnormal, given the wide array of normal human sexual interests. However, when sexual activities harm others, involve nonhuman objects in a way that erotically and emotionally excludes an adult partner, require the participation of animals or nonconsenting adults, or cause an individual significant distress or impairment, such activities are generally considered evidence of a psychiatric disorder rather than part of a healthy, varied sexual appetite. The fourth edition of the Diagnostic and Statistical Manual of Mental Disorders of the American Psychiatric Association explicitly requires a clinical significance criteria be met before a sexual activity can be labeled a disorder.

Individuals with one or more paraphilias (see Table 12.2) often spend considerable time, energy, and money

TABLE 12.2 Paraphilias described in DSM-IV	
Paraphilia	**Description**
Exhibitionism	The exposure of one's genitals to strangers
Fetishism	Sexual use of nonliving objects, such as underwear, shoes
Frotteurism	Touching and rubbing against a nonconsenting person
Pedophilia	Sexual activity with a prepubescent child by a person who is at least 16 years old and at least 5 years older than the child; including activities with children in an individual's own family (incest)
Sexual masochism	The act (real, not simulated) of being humiliated, beaten, bound, or otherwise made to suffer
Sexual sadism	The act (real, not simulated) in which the psychological of physical suffering (including humiliation) of the partner is sexually exciting
Transvestic fetishism	Dressing in the clothes of the opposite sex is required for sexual excitement
Voyeurism	Observing people who are disrobing, engaging in sexual activity, or naked, without their consent
Others	Paraphilias not already specified, such as telephone scatologia (obscene phone calls), necrophilia (sexual activity with corpses), zoophilia (with animals), partialism (exclusive focus on a specific body part), and klismaphilia, coprophilia, and urophilia (respectively, arousal from enemas, feces, and urine)

satisfying their all-consuming urges. For example, a voyeur may prowl the streets in search of unsuspecting persons disrobing or engaging in sexual activities that can be viewed through open curtains or telescopes. This may be time-consuming to the point of interfering with other life activities. **Pedophilia** involves sexual interaction of an adult with a child for sexual gratification. *These children are nonconsenting minors; even if they agree to the interaction, a power dynamic exists in which the child is not capable of knowledgeably consenting to the interaction.* Of note, pedophilia, much like rape, is now believed to be a crime of aggression, violence, and power, rather than a crime of sexual lust. That is, an adult male may molest a young boy not because the adult is a homosexual who is sexually attracted to the young boy, but as an expression of aggression. Many pedophiles desperately seek treatment. There have been several reports of suicide as an alternative to relapse, as the pedophile wants to avoid the future crime but does not trust him or her self to abstain.

The vast majority of paraphiles are men and since most never come to clinical attention, information about paraphilias has come from the minority of individuals who do seek treatment. These individuals typically have multiple paraphilias. *Contrary to public belief, effective treatment regimens do exist for a majority of paraphiles, including pedophiles.* The most successful treatments consist of multimodal approaches incorporating social skills training, group or individual psychotherapy, and antiandrogen medication (e.g., leuprolide acetate, medroxyprogesterone acetate, or cyproterone acetate).

HIV AND SEXUALITY

When the HIV epidemic began in the early 1980s, it was labeled a "gay disease." As evidence of transmission accumulated, it became clear that HIV could be transmitted through vaginal intercourse, anal intercourse, blood to blood contact (including intravenous drug use), and even oral intercourse. Today, *the worldwide rate of heterosexual transmission exceeds all other routes of infection.* In 1996, with the development of protease inhibitors and delineation of the **highly active antiretroviral therapy (HAART)** protocol, significant suppression of HIV replication, partial restoration of immunity, reduction of morbidity, and extension of lifespan was achieved. Projected life expectancy for individuals on HAART is believed to be greater than 10 years, although only preliminary data are available. However, because HIV is currently a noncurable and ultimately mortal disease, it has changed the way many individuals consider sexuality as related to sexually transmitted infections (STIs).

Several studies have found that approximately 70% of HIV-positive patients report one or more sexual problems.

A scab
is a beautiful thing—a coin
the body has minted, with an invisible motto:
in God We Trust.
Our body loves us,
and, even while the spirit drifts dreaming,
works at mending the damage that we do.

Close your eyes, knowing
that healing is a work of darkness,
that darkness is a gown of healing,
that the vessel of our tremulous venture is lifted
by tides we do not control.
Faith is health's requisite:
We have this fact in lieu
of better proof of le bon Dieu.

JOHN UPDIKE
Ode to Healing

13 Medical Student and Physician Well-Being

Margaret L. Stuber

> Let us emancipate the student, and give him time and opportunity for the cultivation of his mind, so that in his pupilage he shall not be a puppet in the hands of others, but rather a self-relying and reflecting being.
>
> SIR WILLIAM OSLER
>
> If you listen carefully to what patients say, they will often tell you not only what is wrong with them but also what is wrong with you.
>
> WALKER PERCY

Entrance into medical school is for many students the fulfillment of a long-held dream. The path to medical school always involves a great deal of effort. Often it also requires competition, and a drive to be the best. Once in medical school, however, students are expected to work and learn in teams and small groups. Personal best, rather than competition with peers, is encouraged—at least officially. The amount of information that must be mastered is overwhelming, as is the responsibility of making life or death decisions. It is often difficult for medical students, driven to care and to know, to cope with the significant pressures they encounter during medical school. Unfortunately, the result, too often, is depression or even suicide. *The chances of dying by suicide are higher for physicians than nonphysicians, particularly in women.* Male physicians have a rate of suicide that is 70% higher than that of male nonphysicians. Female physicians have a suicide rate 250% to 400% higher than female nonphysicians.

These increases in suicide are partly a result of the fact that doctors are more likely to actually die when making a suicide attempt; ironically, this results in part from their enhanced understanding of physiology and drugs. *These same data also reflect a greater prevalence of depression in physicians.* A recent study found as many as 25% of first- and second-year medical students were depressed. The researchers who conducted this study suggest that *although the rate of depression among entering medical students is similar to the general population, the prevalence increases over the course of medical school. The period of greatest distress is during the clinical rotations, usually in the third and fourth years.* Few of the physicians who died by suicide were receiving psychiatric treatment just before their death.

This chapter will examine what is needed to make the transition from college graduate to physician. It will also examine the factors that predict well-being as a physician, and the obstacles to achieving these goals. Unlike the other chapters in this book, which emphasize the context of clinical care or physician-patient interactions, this chapter will focus on you, and your own behavior.

> Nothing will sustain you more potently than the power to recognize in your humdrum routine…the true poetry of life—the poetry of the commonplace, of the ordinary man, of the toil worn woman, with their joys, their sorrows, and their griefs.
>
> SIR WILLIAM OSLER'S advice to medical students (circa 1905)

A NEW LANGUAGE AND A NEW ROLE

Even for students who have had in-depth training in some aspect of science, medical school requires learning a new and technical language. In the first 2 years this new learning involves learning numerous multisyllabic Latin terms for anatomy and various new uses of common words for pa-

Medical Students at Work on a Cadaver, 1890 From the collection of the Minnesota Historical Society, Minneapolis. *Human dissection is a unique learning experience that links every freshman medical student with previous generations of physicians.*

thology (e.g., "cheesy necrosis"). Clinical work brings an onslaught of abbreviations, many of which are used in different ways by different specialists (e.g., MS can refer to either multiple sclerosis or morphine sulfate).

Students are often amused or offended about having formal courses in which they are taught how to "interview" patients. Surely you know how to talk to people, be friendly, communicate information, and ask questions? Quickly however, it becomes apparent that *you are now expected to ask total strangers about intimate and often unpleasant topics in a way that would be considered totally inappropriate in any other context.* Conversations between doctor and patient commonly focus on topics such as diarrhea, vomit, blood, itching, bloating, and "discharge" from a variety of orifices. In many clinical situations, the physician must engage in a matter-of-fact conversation about whether someone has sexual interactions with men, women, or both, and about the details of those interactions. Obvious advice—often unwanted and unappreciated—has to be offered about the need to stop smoking, lose weight, or improve personal hygiene. These are precisely the things you have been taught *not* to talk about in polite society since early childhood, and so these interactions are naturally uncomfortable and often awkward.

Similarly, you are asked to notice and report details about people that polite people would overlook. You need to consider not only the smell of alcohol on someone's breath, but also the earthy odor of upper GI bleeding or Candida, and the sweet smell of ketosis. A person's gait, posture, and facial expression are all potentially important

data, to be noted, evaluated, and used. Slips of the tongue, restlessness, or confusion cannot be politely ignored, as one might socially. For many of you, this is a new, uncomfortable, and intrusive way of relating to others.

YOU CAN'T KNOW EVERYTHING

Medical school has been compared to drinking from a fire hose—the volume is high, the pressure intense, it is impossible to completely consume the product, and the experience is often less than completely satisfying. Although most medical schools have changed the ways they present material, genuinely trying to reduce the vast amount of minutia to memorize and the number of dense readings to plow through, *it is simply not possible to know, understand, and remember everything that is presented to you in medical school.*

The intense pressures of medical school are, to some extent, purposeful. You will never have the security of knowing you know all there is to know about your field. There will always be the need to look up some detail, or to seek new information, or seek out consultation. You will have to be able to say "I don't know, but I will find out" thousands of times throughout your career. *An important task in medical school and in your continuing medical education is to learn what you really do have to know, and figure out how to look up everything else.*

Sir William Osler Lecturing to Medical Students at Johns Hopkins Courtesy of the National Library of Medicine. *Master teachers have always been appreciated by medical students. Note that almost all of the students appear to be male.*

THE CULTURE OF MEDICINE

Professional schools, such as law and medicine, are action oriented. This is a very different orientation than other graduate schools in which contemplation and deliberation are highly valued. Obviously, the actions that are necessary are radically different for different specialties. Physicians such as those in the Emergency Department or Anesthesia must make instant decisions in acute situations, and rarely spend more than a few hours with a patient. In contrast, Family Medicine physicians engage in long-term planning aimed at health maintenance and illness prevention. Nonetheless, physicians are evaluated primarily on what they do or do not do for their patients. Since time is almost always at a premium, this creates a situation in which efficiency is highly valued.

Most inpatient medical teams in academic medical centers operate in a very hierarchical system. Each member of the team has a specific job or area of expertise and contributes to patient care, but one person ultimately is responsible for final decision-making. Decisions by consensus are rarely used; the process simply takes too long to be useful in this setting. Some teams, however, operate with a blend of these two systems, having differentiated responsibility for team members, and regular means of communication for coordination.

In medical school, interns and residents report to attending physicians, and medical students report to the interns and residents. This means that as a medical student you are at or near the bottom of this hierarchy. This stands in stark contrast to the rest of your life, when you have very

likely been one of the smartest of the members of every group, and a leader in many settings and situations. Indeed, you are in medical school training so that some day you can actually lead a medical team. This situation—the hierarchy, the time pressure, and your personal history—creates a perfect set up for misunderstandings, frustration, and power abuse.

> There is within medicine, somewhere beneath the pessimism and discouragement resulting from the disarray of the health-care system and its stupendous cost, an undercurrent of almost outrageous optimism about what may lie ahead for the treatment of human disease if we can only keep learning.
>
> LEWIS THOMAS (1979)

Other chapters in this book make the point that *you must understand the cultural and experiential world of a patient in order to effectively communicate and negotiate treatment.* This is also true in the culture of medicine. However, this does not mean that medical students should expect or accept that they will be abused by the attending physicians, residents, and nurses with whom they work. It is inevitable that your coworkers and teachers will occasionally be irritable, they may sometimes be rude, and some may make racial or sexual jokes that you believe to be in very bad taste. However, *you do not have to tolerate other physicians systematically degrading or insulting you, throwing things at you, or repeatedly making unwanted sexual ad-*

BOX 13.1 Attitudes that influence the happiness of medical students and physicians*

Path 1 These coping attitudes will not be very useful to you in medicine, in the long run.	*Path 2* These coping attitudes will lead to more long-term satisfactions and enjoyment in medicine.
The strong silent approach. Don't tell others what you are thinking.	Learn to listen to the feelings of others, and to share your own.
Success means good grades and, later, wealth and material goods.	That's okay, but it doesn't compare to enjoying your work and people.
Your needs must take a second place to more important things in life.	You must fill your own needs at the same time you are accomplishing your other goals.
Your worth depends on what you accomplish. When you don't accomplish as much as others or as much as you can, you are basically inadequate.	There is a source of self-worth that cannot be measured by your accomplishments, that is non-negotiable and fundamental.
Mistakes are the result of ignorance, apathy, carelessness, and general basic worthlessness.	Mistakes aren't exactly okay, but they are a fact of life, even in medicine. Mistakes are your chief source of wisdom. Learn from them and don't make them twice. Perfectionism leads to burnout.
Criticism is a demonstration to the world of your inadequacy. Defend, justify, explain, and attack!	Criticism isn't exactly pleasant, but get used to the idea that it doesn't imply inadequacy. Learn to use it.
You are helpless in a world that controls your behavior.	You are in charge of what you do; it's no use blaming anyone else. What you do is up to you.
When you are feeling overwhelmed, lonely, anxious, depressed, and can't study, it is up to you to "snap out of it." Be strong, work hard, and keep a stiff upper lip. It's just a matter of willpower.	There is nothing wrong with you; everyone has trouble coping and could use some help. It may be embarrassing to find that you don't know everything yet. A sense of self-worth that keeps you from getting help may lead to real trouble.
Results are more important than people. (Type A behavior is goal oriented.)	People are more important than results. (Type B behavior is "process" oriented.)
Thinking is the highest function.	There is more to you than thinking. Don't let your feelings and intuition atrophy; don't become an intellectual nerd.

* From *Coping in Medical School* by Bernhard Virshup. Copyright © 1985, 1981 by Berhard B. Virshup. Used by permission of W.W. Norton & Company, Inc.

---

vances. All medical schools have systems in place to deal with such problems. So why do they still happen? It is a two-fold problem. First, medical students are very reluctant to say anything, to the perpetrators or to anyone else, knowing that students are vulnerable. The residents and attending physicians write student evaluations, and can make life very difficult. However, the administration can only act if there is evidence of repeated or outrageous offenses. Second, in some settings, particularly those that are very high-stress or time-sensitive, it is considered acceptable to abuse medical students, interns, and residents. In some areas, such as Pediatrics, verbal abuse of students appears to be rare, whereas in others, such as Surgery, it appears to be far more frequent. Medical school deans, department chairs, and administrators are working hard to change this aspect of these cultures. However, as with all cultural change, this will take time.

So what do you do in the meantime if you feel you are being abused? A few basic guidelines follow:

1. First, take a deep breath, and make sure you are not taking something out of context or personally when it was not meant that way.
2. Calmly let the person know that this was uncomfortable for you, and why.
3. Wait for a response. If there is an acknowledgment or apology, great! If not, but the behavior is not repeated, no further action is needed unless the abusive behavior is then directed at someone else.
4. If the response is only further abuse, or the abuse is repeated despite acknowledgment or apology, seek help. Help is available from the medical school ombudsman's office, the Student Affairs Office, or the Chair of the course or clerkship.

ASKING FOR ACADEMIC HELP

Everyone who is accepted to medical school has the academic ability to complete medical school. Those who have such serious academic difficulty in medical school that they do not graduate generally do so because they were not willing or able to ask for help when they needed it.

"My family/friends need me." Medical students are smart and hard-working people, and their family and friends admire and count on them—sometimes too much. However, medical school is a full-time job. It may have been possible to run the family business while in college, or you may have always been the one that all of your family depended on to make important decisions or to host all family events. Medical school is much less flexible about absences than undergraduate school. You may be expected to be in the hospital by 5 a. m., each morning to round on your patients. Being pulled in too many directions can cause serious problems for a medical student.

> This is all very fine, but it won't do—Anatomy—Botany—Nonsense! Sir, I know an old woman in Covent Garden who understands botany better, and as for anatomy, my butcher can dissect a joint full and well; no young man, all that is stuff; you must go to the bedside, it is there alone you can learn disease.
>
> THOMAS SYDENHAM

"I have always been able to do it, and I will be able to do this too." Some medical students have overcome significant obstacles on their way to medical school. They may come from families with few financial resources, or limited educational background. They may have had medical or psychological problems to cope with, or learning disabilities to overcome. They may have dealt with tragedy or violence. The fact that these students made it to medical school is a testimony to their hard work, determination, and intelligence. They deserve to be proud of their accomplishments. It is, therefore, a terrible loss when such students do not avail themselves of any supports they need once in medical school. All too often a student will refuse to meet with anyone after they fail an exam or course, thinking that all that is needed is to work harder. It is not until a pattern has emerged, and the student is forced to agree to an evaluation, that he or she is found to need a quieter test setting, different study approaches, or help in coping with anxiety. Medical schools are required to supply accommodation to any otherwise capable student for any documented learning disability or sensory impairment—but only if the student requests such accommodation. It is up to you as a student to request the evaluation and accommodations.

"I can't let anyone know that I can't do it." Although most students have worked hard to get to medical school and are there because they want to be, some are not. Some students are in medical school because that is what their parents expected or demanded, and many of those students are not sure they want to be there. Other students are convinced they are not capable of succeeding academically. These students experience embarrassment and shame when they encounter academic difficulty, and it often feels like they have let their friends and family down. These students often find it difficult to admit that they need help.

ASKING FOR NONACADEMIC HELP

Academic difficulty is not the only reason students do not graduate from medical school. For some students, the work load and the sense of never knowing enough can precipitate or uncover depression or anxiety. Trouble sleeping, difficulty concentrating, or not having enough energy to get to class or the hospital can exacerbate a situation that already felt overwhelming. Although help is available, it is often resisted. This is understandable: If you are having trouble functioning on your surgery rotation, the last thing you may want to do is to ask for time off to see a counselor. A less short-term assessment, however, shows that *it is far better to deal with such responses earlier rather than later.* The time lost when a student fails a course or clerkship is much more consequential and costly than any time invested in solving a problem before it gets out of hand.

> The physician himself, if sick, actually calls in another physician, knowing that he cannot reason correctly if required to judge his own condition while suffering.
>
> ARISTOTLE
> *De Republica*

Substance abuse, suicidal ideation, depression, and anxiety are much more wide-spread among medical students and physicians than is commonly believed, especially given how bright and accomplished medical students are. It is important for you to understand that *these problems are generally quite treatable*—if the individual seeks help. However, studies of medical students have found that less than 25% of those who were clinically depressed used mental health services. Barriers students most frequently cited included lack of time, lack of confidentiality, stigma, cost, fear of documentation on academic records, and fear of unwanted intervention.

All medical schools are required to have confidential counseling services, and these services include access to medications, addiction counseling, and psychotherapy.

ing." *You will be a better and more interesting person, but also a better and more sensitive physician, if your time is not spent solely with your patients and your journals.*

Different people find different ways to relax. Some physicians are uncomfortable when they have unscheduled time, and if this applies to you, you may need to have your weekends and vacations very structured. Other people are happy spending all of their free time with other people, while still others have a genuine need to spend some time alone. Getting to know what works for you is an important step in taking care of yourself.

5. Sleep

The amount and timing of sleep needed is different for different people, and these needs change as a person ages. What is true for all is that some amount of restful sleep is essential for well-being, and most of us do not get as much sleep as our bodies need. This means it is important to understand and respect your own personal needs, and watch how these needs change over time. *Teenagers and people in their twenties often have an internal diurnal pattern that makes it easiest for them to concentrate and work at night*, and difficult to function effectively in the early morning. This pattern changes over the years, until by the age of 60 or 70 the early morning is the most active time for the majority of people. Most people need approximately 8 hours of sleep a night. However, some adults do very well on 6 or even 4 hours, while others really need 9 or 10 hours.

> Today's trainees have different values and demand a more balances lifestyle than those who believed the only thing wrong with every other night-call was that you missed half the good cases.
>
> H. SANFEY
> Contemporary US surgeon, University of Virginia
> *British Journal of Surgery*

Probably more important than the amount of sleep is what interferes with sleep. Coffee and other caffeine-containing drinks are an integral part of the culture in the United States, and they have become an expected part of medical culture. However, these beverages can have a significant effect on sleep, particularly when they are used to artificially induce alertness when the body is exhausted. Alcohol is especially likely to affect sleep patterns. *Often used as a relaxant, alcohol is actually disruptive to sleep.* Although a drink may help induce sleep, it also interferes with deep sleep, leads to wakening during the night, and interferes with restful sleep. Similarly, because of their ready access to sedatives, physicians often use drugs to induce sleep. The dangers of this are obvious, and yet the temptation is strong.

SUMMARY

In choosing to become a physician, you are starting on your way to a life which promises to be challenging and rewarding, intellectually and emotionally. Learning to handle the new language, culture, and stresses of the world of medicine can be as difficult as learning anatomy and the physical examination. A realistic approach to medical school, which allows one to ask for help and includes some relaxation, will provide an excellent preparation for a long and satisfying career.

CASE STUDY

A first-year medical student failed an important Anatomy examination in the first semester of medical school. She told the course director that she had an anxiety attack, but she reported that she was now fine, did not need treatment, and only requested an opportunity to retake the exam. However, the next semester she fails a midterm. When she is asked to see the course chair, she acknowledges that she has been extremely anxious, and she has had difficulty concentrating when she tries to study. She reluctantly agrees to go to Student Health. A counselor at the Student Health Center learns that she is the first one in her family to ever go to college, much less graduate school. Her family is very proud of her, but cannot be very emotionally supportive, as they do not understand the pressures and demands of medical school. She also feels conflicted because her family is experiencing financial distress, and she feels she should be working and supporting her family. She is trained in relaxation skills, and she is given medication for an underlying depression that has never been treated. However, it is the counseling about her professional goals and her obligation to the family that are ultimately the most helpful.

SUGGESTED READINGS

Epstein, R.M., & Hundert, E.M. (2002). Defining and assessing professional competence. *JAMA, 287*, 226–35.
    This article reviews the expectations now made of medical students, including those having to do with professionalism, and how these are assessed.

Hampton, T. (2005). Experts address risk of physician suicide. *JAMA, 294*, 1189–1191.
    This article reviews a recent report from a group of experts in medicine, health insurance, and physician licensing convened to identify those factors that discourage physicians from seeking treatment for depression.

Rosenthal, J.M., & Okie, S. (2005). White coat, mood indigo—depression in medical school. *New England Journal of Medicine, 353*, 1085–1088.
    This recent article outlines the incidence and probable causes of depression in medical school, as well as the obstacles to treatment, and what some schools are doing to address this.

14 Working with Other Professionals, Organizations, and Communities

Iris Cohen Fineberg

Collaboration is central to the practice of medicine, whether in the setting of a hospital, clinic, or private office. However, collaboration requires working *with* other people rather than simply *beside* them. The degree to which care is effective is influenced by the quality of relationship that providers have with other professionals, organizations that serve patients, and the communities in which patients and families reside. *Learning to work with others in providing care for patients is an important skill that, like other skills, requires attention and thoughtful consideration in order to be successful.* If done well, it will positively affect both the quality of care and one's satisfaction with work. This chapter will discuss the value of professional collaboration, models of collaboration, elements and attitudes of effective collaboration, and the importance of culture. The information about working with other professionals applies to working with organizations and communities, but additional considerations for the latter two situations are also addressed.

WORKING WITH OTHER PROFESSIONALS

Health care involves professionals from many different disciplines. Although the biomedical model traditionally centers on the physician, many others provide critical components of each patient's care. Examples of professionals with whom physicians interact regularly in the hospital setting include nurses, social workers, clergy, physical therapists, occupational therapists, nutritionists, and pharmacists. Medical staff may also have regular contact with other hospital staff such as phlebotomists and radiation technologists. Very frequently, physicians need to work with other physicians from different specialties who offer their expertise as consultants or collaborating providers. Whether one is working with a professional from within medicine or from a different discipline, the goal should be to work *with* the other person rather than simply alongside him or her.

VALUE OF COLLABORATION

Necessity

There is a practical need for collaboration in medicine, as no profession works in a complete vacuum. If a patient is going to receive high quality medical care, the expertise and cooperation of many people must occur: prescriptions require the involvement of pharmacists, and medical tests are administered by people trained in specific procedures and related technology. In addition, medical specialists are often consulted to assist in the evaluation or care of a patient, creating a set of multiple physicians who must work together effectively to serve one patient. It is important to be able to work and communicate with many types of professionals in order to provide coordinated and effective care to patients; in fact, *patients' experience of care is highly affected by the collaborative skills of the physician who is coordinating the care.* A physician's success in working with other professionals will directly influence whether a patient feels care is cohesive and safe or is fragmented and potentially harmful.

Complexity of the Human Experience

In addition to being a practical necessity, collaboration is a natural consequence of the complexity of contemporary life, and medical care has to be responsive to the variegated needs of human beings. A person coming to see a doctor for a medical problem comes with a life history, and the patient does not leave that history behind when he or she becomes a patient. The patient comes from a family; has a personal history; and needs to pay bills, work, and socialize. As a result, an entire team of professionals may be necessary to respond to the various needs of the patient. Basic needs, such as assistance with obtaining durable medical equipment or arranging home-based assistance with activities of daily living, may require the intervention of professionals such as case managers, home health nurses, physical therapists or occupational therapists. Emotional and psychological issues, such as anxiety, depression, or problems with alcohol, may affect the person's ability to cope with his or her medical problem or follow through with treatment recommendations. Referral to a mental health professional, such as a psychiatrist, psychologist, or social worker, may be an important component of a patient's overall care. Social and family issues, such as unemployment or domestic violence, may benefit from the expertise of a social worker or marriage and family therapist. Patients' circumstances when they arrive in the medical setting often require the services of diverse professionals who may assist with many aspects of life that intertwine with medicine but are simply beyond physicians' expertise.

Cohesive Care

Working with other professionals rather than simply alongside them offers the important advantage of a coordinated, united approach to patient and family care. *Patients and families are often anxious or distressed in the medical setting, and these feelings may be amplified by the involvement of numerous health-care professionals who are*

> It is owing to the doctors that there is so high a mortality in childbed.
>
> IGNAZ PHILIPP SEMMELWEIS
> *Aetiology, Concept and Prophylaxis of Childbed Fever*

each providing different information and interventions. Contradictory messages from different providers cause patients and families unnecessary confusion and distress that may be minimized or completely avoided through collaboration. Health-care professionals can offer consistent, united perspectives by working effectively with each other. Cohesive care for patients and families is one component of high quality care.

An additional advantage of cohesive care is sparing patients and families from exposure to and entanglement in staff conflict. *It is not unusual for professionals to disagree about plans of care, but this disagreement should be resolved prior to presenting information to patients and families.* If professionals disagree or experience conflict, patients and families should not have to bear the emotional burden of this conflict nor the confusion caused by unclear care plans. Coordination among professionals allows identification of potential conflicts in recommendations and offers an opportunity for resolution among professionals prior to discussions with patients and families.

Communication

Communication among collaborating professionals results in more efficient health care. Professionals who work with each other in a coordinated manner are more likely to identify problems early as a consequence of shared information. In addition, effective communication permits physicians and other members of the health-care team to avoid the escalation of tension that occurs in many medical situations and settings. Professionals tend to focus on their own areas of expertise in providing patient care, but a mutual flow of information increases opportunities for learning of potential areas of difficulty for patients that any one professional alone may not be likely to identify. Similarly, coordinating care among various providers helps to reduce the likelihood of service duplication, allowing for more efficient patient care.

Increased Job Satisfaction

Collaborating effectively with colleagues and other professionals contributes to personal job satisfaction. Rather than

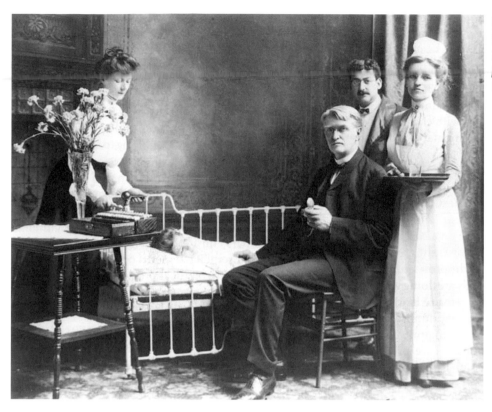

Courtesy of the Library of Congress, Washington, D.C. *Professional and gender roles were once firmly established in the healing professions, and physicians tended to be white, male, and clearly in charge.*

feeling isolated, frustrated, and adversarial in the work setting, professionals who collaborate enjoy the pleasure associated with working as a part of a larger group. People who work effectively as team members are likely to feel appreciated for their work and supported by those around them, and it is intensely gratifying to witness the high quality of care that collaboration and coordination offers patients and families.

MULTIDISCIPLINARY, INTERDISCIPLINARY, AND TRANSDISCIPLINARY MODELS OF COLLABORATION

There are several models by which professionals work together in patient care. The choice of model depends on several elements, including organizational culture, staff structure, type of care being provided and the needs of the patient. These models of care may occur among professionals who work together infrequently or occasionally, or among professionals who function as an ongoing team. The team approach has a formal or structured relationship among its members, such as a team on a hospital ward or a specialty group such as the "oncology team." Infrequent collaboration with specific individuals often means the professionals know little about each other and

may have limited opportunity for developing a working relationship. By contrast, other teams have repeated contact among their members which allows greater familiarity among professionals, more opportunity for developing working relationships and trust, but also more opportunities for conflict within the team.

Multidisciplinary Teams

Multidisciplinary care is the provision of patient care by a set of professionals from multiple disciplines. Most often the team includes several professions, such as nursing and respiratory therapy, but it can also be comprised of a set of physicians from varied specialties. For example, a patient receiving medical care from a primary physician, a cardiologist, and an oncologist is receiving multidisciplinary care. Both meanings of the term "multidisciplinary" reflect a model of care that has the strength of involving professionals with differing perspectives and expertise to care for varied patient needs. However, sometimes each professional or specialist draws on his or her unique expertise with little knowledge of or regard for the interventions of the other disciplines. That is, each professional may be working in a "silo" alongside other professionals, but with little or no interaction with the other members of the team providing care. Needless to say, patients suffer when this occurs.

than on individuals' opinions. Skillful negotiation among professionals can lead to compromise that achieves everyone's goals without diminishing any person's sense of participation. A well-known resource for negotiation skills is Fisher, Ury, and Patton's (1991) book *Getting to Yes: Negotiating Agreement Without Giving In*.

> The physician can bury his mistakes, but the architect can only advise his client to plant vines.
>
> FRANK LLOYD WRIGHT

Power Dynamics

Hierarchy and Power

All relationships have a power dynamic that affects how people relate to one another. In medical care, physicians typically hold positions of power and are awarded the greatest respect among all health professionals. Physicians, literally, give "orders," and the word regimen derives from a Latin phrase that means "to rule." However, even within medicine, structured hierarchies exist among the ranks of interns, residents, fellows, and attending physicians. Regardless of whether one occupies a power position or not, it is important to recognize that power and the perception of power affects collaboration across professions. Members of less powerful professions may expect hierarchical interactions with physicians, while others may deliberately disregard power differences. Still others may resent the power dynamic and inadvertently or deliberately work to sabotage what would otherwise be a collaborative relationship.

Physicians and Power

Although the structure of health care has shifted over the years, significantly changing the structure of decision making in medicine, the physician continues to be the primary decision maker on the health-care team. In fact, *it is imperative for the physician to recognize his or her organizing role, the limitations of this role, and the need for involving other professionals in a patient's care.* No one person can be "all things to all people." In order to best serve patients, it is often essential to collaborate with other professionals who can provide expert advice and intervention in specific areas of specialization. As a team leader, the physician needs to be able to recognize when to involve others and how to best orchestrate care for patients.

Shared Leadership

Among colleagues who work as a team on a regular basis, it may be most effective to neutralize the power dynamic by having shared leadership. This approach recognizes each

professional in the collaboration as equally powerful and responsible for the team's functioning and professional practice.

Conflict Anticipation and Management

Conflict Anticipation

Although most people are uncomfortable with conflict, disagreement is inevitable in the medical setting. Whether it is a difference in professional recommendations for treatment, disagreement about how a situation should be handled, or a conflict between providers, it is important to realize that conflict is often unavoidable. *Viewing conflict as a normal and expected element of professional life enables the clinician to prepare for it and approach it more calmly.* Conflict among professionals should be handled in a manner that maintains respect and preserves positive relations (even if the parties involved do not feel very positive at the time). After all, many times conflict takes place with people with whom one has to work on a regular basis or with people one may encounter again. People who manage conflict effectively are highly valued by their colleagues, even those with whom there have been disagreements.

> This is where the strength of the physician lies, be he a quack, a homeopath or an allopath. He supplies the perennial demand for comfort, the craving for sympathy that every human sufferer feels.
>
> LEO TOLSTOY
> *War and Peace*

Conflict Management

Many people prefer to avoid or ignore conflict rather than address it. Although this approach may be justified in some situations, *managing conflict is advisable for most professional relationships.* Techniques such as negotiation and compromise can often eliminate the conflict or at least bring the parties closer to agreement. Respectful listening and avoidance of reactive behaviors, such as angry outbursts and defensiveness, also help manage conflict. In many cases, candid discussion that clarifies perspectives and reasoning will address conflictual situations. Problem-solving approaches similar to those used for patient care situations can be applied to other professional disagreements. However, even when the parties do not reach agreement, respectful interaction can have important long-lasting effects on working relationships and the potential for future positive interaction with colleagues. It is worthwhile to invest in building familiarity and relationships with colleagues with whom there is frequent interaction, as conflict resolution may occur more quickly and smoothly among professionals with established relationships.

> I can remember when older physicians refused to recognize socially a man who devoted himself to the eye alone.
>
> S. WEIR MITCHELL
> American neurologist and author
> *Bulletin of the New York Academy of Medicine*

ATTITUDES FOR SUCCESSFUL COLLABORATION

Any relationship with another professional, representative of an organization, or member of the community is more effective when professionals exhibit positive attitudes and behaviors. Although this is common sense, it involves an awareness and thoughtfulness in practice that is easily neglected when people are rushed, stressed, or distracted. The following discussion will address several elements that can influence the quality of interpersonal relations.

Respect and Patience

Any interaction with another person, new or familiar, should begin with an attitude of respect. People are more likely to cooperate and work collaboratively if they feel respected and valued for their contribution, whether large or small. *Conveying respect to people with whom one works, regardless of their title or profession, will lead to relationships that are likely to be positive and gratifying for both parties.* Demonstrating respect may occur through behaviors such as courteousness and graciousness, acknowledging the value of others' time and effort, and showing appreciation for others' work. These behaviors do not require one to "like" every person; rather, they set a tone for professional interaction.

Demonstrating patience with colleagues is an important component of respect and an essential behavior in the medical setting. Some medical situations, such as emergencies, require quick decision making and immediate responses. However, the majority of interactions among professionals need to be reasonably paced but not pressured. Working with other professionals requires people to realize that everyone is juggling competing priorities, stressful demands, and multiple responsibilities. Colleagues may not be able to respond as quickly as one would like, but it is important to demonstrate patience that conveys respect for another person's other work. The same patience that is offered to patients and families as part of compassionate care should be extended to colleagues.

Appreciation of Professional Differences and Diversity

The value of working with other professionals lies in the diverse set of perspectives and expertise that colleagues may offer. However, diverse opinions may at times be threatening, especially when they reflect disagreement among those working together. In many situations, the diversity of perspectives can broaden the understanding of a situation rather than require one person to be right while another person is wrong. The key to embracing the richness that diversity offers is to approach differences without defensiveness; in actuality, *professional differences are rarely personal attacks*. However, it is important to be aware of "turf" issues, especially the tendency for professionals to be protective of areas of practice they see as solely belonging to their profession. Like defensive behaviors, turf issues limit professionals' ability to appreciate the value of colleagues' expertise and potential contributions to patient care.

Focus on Patients and Families

Maintaining focus on patient and family care as the primary priority is a defining factor of effective collaboration. Avoiding the distraction of personal differences, personality conflicts and role competition among professionals may not be easy, but it is essential for achieving a high quality of collaboration in service of patients and families.

Compassion

Working in the field of medicine carries tremendous responsibility under circumstances of constant time limitations and heavy workloads. Like all people, medical professionals have emotional reactions to work-related stress. They also cope with the usual personal and social life stressors that other people experience such as the demands of family, friends, relationships, and finances. Recognizing one's own sources and levels of stress helps a person realize when reactions to colleagues are primarily a reflection of one's personal state of mind. Recognizing that other professionals may also be distressed for a wide variety of reasons also helps colleagues to be more understanding and effective in interacting with others. Just as one aims to provide compassionate care to patients and families, one should offer compassionate collaboration with colleagues.

> After two days in the hospital I took a turn for the nurse.
>
> W.C. FIELDS

CULTURE AND COLLABORATION

Western Biomedical Culture

Medicine is itself a culture that has established norms for behavior, numerous symbols, and elaborate rituals. Those working in the medical setting may not realize that there is a distinct culture to the setting, and that the culture reflects perspectives that may be foreign, frightening, and/or distasteful to those outside the culture. For example, hospital staff members usually do not see anything unusual about people being dressed in thin hospital gowns that offer little privacy. However, outside the setting of a hospital, such attire would be considered highly unusual and inappropriate. Similarly, views about medications and medical procedures may seem "normal" to professionals in the field of medicine but not to the general public. Since members of the general public become "patients" in the context of medical care, it is important to realize that *behaviors that medical professionals see as perfectly normal and expected in the medical setting may seem very odd to other people.* Such cultural differences may become illuminated in relationships with professionals outside of the medical setting, organizations that are not medically oriented, and communities that may have differing views on health and well-being.

Western biomedical practice reflects viewpoints that differ dramatically from those of Eastern medical practice and many other cultures in the world. For example, Western approaches focus on the individual, stress individual patient rights, and assume that patients desire treatment. Outside of Western biomedical culture, many groups emphasize the family or community, and give precedence to the needs and wishes of the larger group. It is important to recognize that Western medicine is only one model of medicine rather than a universal way of understanding health and disease.

Professional Culture

A key element to working well with professionals from varied disciplines is understanding that each profession, and even each specialty within a profession, has its own culture. *This culture defines normative behavior and provides a framework for viewing the world that shapes the way professionals understand and interpret experience.* Professions in the medical setting, such as nursing, social work, and medicine, each have dramatically different cultural norms. Each has its own system for educating its members and expectations for appropriate professional behavior. Awareness of professional culture becomes important in collaboration because it helps people understand differences in viewpoints and approaches to care. Often times these differences are assumed to be evidence of personal differences or inadequacies when in fact they simply reflect differences in professional cultures.

As an example, norms of behavior in medicine and social work are very different regarding how emotions should be handled in professional settings. Generally, medical trainees and professionals are taught to hide or minimize their emotions when providing patient care, and medical students are seldom taught to process the emotions that arise in the context of their professional work. In contrast, social work requires its professionals to practice ongoing self-awareness regarding emotional reactions to interactions and professional practice. Social work training often includes formal attention to processing of emotions as an integral component of professional preparation. These differences in professional culture, if unrecognized, may lead to misinterpretation of colleagues' behavior in the work setting.

Personal Culture

Professionals' personal cultures must also be recognized as a potential source of difference and misunderstanding, as well as an opportunity to learn and grow. Like all people, medical professionals bring a personal culture that reflects their background. Personal culture includes such elements as nationality, ethnicity, religion, geographic location, and sexual orientation. Differences in personal culture may influence how professionals interact and relate to each other, especially when colleagues do not know each other's backgrounds or have limited understanding of different cultures.

Differences in culture, on every level, require respect and dialogue. They need not be sources of conflict, but this often occurs when these differences are unrecognized in professional relations.

> The surgeon is a man of action. By temperament and by training he prefers to serve the sick by operating on them, and he inwardly commiserates with a patient so unfortunate as to have a disease not suited to surgical treatment.
>
> STANLEY O. HOERR
> *American Journal of Surgery*

ORGANIZATIONS

Health-care professionals work within organizations on a daily basis, and they often have to collaborate with exter nal organizations as well. Organizations may be public or private, for profit or nonprofit. Organizations that physicians work with regularly include insurance companies, home health-care agencies, child protective services, and hospice. Physicians also may work indirectly with certain organizations via social workers or other professionals; examples include consulates, banks, and patients' employers. Reasons to work with organizations often revolve around accessing care or services for patients, but the collaboration may also be necessary for developing policy or conducting research. For example, several medical centers may work together to develop ethical guidelines to address specific patient scenarios commonly seen across the organizations.

Organizations, though comprised of people, are themselves entities. Depending partially on the size of the organization, the impact of any one person on how the organization functions or responds may be weak or strong. In order to work most effectively within an organization or with another organization, one needs a basic understanding of organizational qualities such as structure, culture, mission, and priorities. Understanding these qualities will help you determine how best to achieve your goals with any organization.

Organizational Structure

Organizational structure determines how policies and decisions are made in that organization. For health-care providers working within an organization, familiarity with the organization's structure is essential for problem-solving and accessing resources in the work setting. Many health-care organizations are hierarchical and have multiple layers of supervision and power. Other organizations may be more lateral, with greater equality among employees with fewer levels separating staff and administration. Knowing the structure of an organization enables a person to determine whom they need to contact in order to receive information, access organizational resources, and influence change in the organization.

Organizational Culture

Like other forms of culture, organizational culture includes norms for behavior, perspectives for understanding and interpreting information and events, and mechanisms for es-

tablishing priorities. The culture will determine such things as how formally or casually staff generally dress and behave, the degree of formality that people from the organization expect when interacting with people outside the organization, and expectations of communication among staff, supervisors, and administrators. Understanding an organization's culture helps a person to determine how to behave when working with staff from that organization in order to achieve the most successful outcomes. As with individual culture, organizational culture may be important to understand to avoid offending someone from the organization.

Organizational Mission and Priorities

Every organization has a mission that drives the work of that organization, often providing the basis for determining organizational priorities. Working with organizations requires understanding that each organization has a unique set of priorities that may or may not overlap extensively with those of the organization within which one works. Understanding an organization's priorities can guide one's approach to accessing the resources of that organization or attaining the assistance and responsiveness one wants from that organization.

COMMUNITIES

All people and organizations reside within a community; this community both influences them and is influenced by them. Communities are groups that have culture, like individuals and organizations. Health-care providers may speak about the medical community when discussing all physicians as a single entity. For the purposes of health care, the term *community* usually refers (1) to a geographic cluster that defines the group, such as a neighborhood or town area (i.e., the "Los Angeles community") or (2) to ethnic, racial, or cultural groups, such as the "African-American community." Physicians work with these communities in the context of providing medical care, health education, or health services research.

An important part of working with communities involves understanding that relations occur in the setting of the community rather than in the medical setting. Physicians sometimes have to work in a setting outside the medical culture and within the culture of the community, be it a physical or conceptual community. *This distinction is significant because of the shift it creates in the power dynamics of the relationship between medical providers and those they serve.* People in the context of the community are not necessarily "patients"; they may not be or feel vulnerable; they may not experience a need for involvement of medical providers; and they operate under their own cultural norms and expectations, not the norms of the medical setting. Consequently, hierarchies and power relationships that apply to the medical setting may not be relevant in working with communities.

It is essential to have some understanding of a community in order to work successfully with its members. The community, whether a neighborhood or a population group, has cultural patterns that reflect the members' world views. For example, an African-American community, as a whole, may place great importance on spirituality and religion and explanatory sources for understanding physical problems and healing. Without knowing about a community perspective such as this one, a medical provider will not know (1) who in the community to contact, or (2) how to approach the topic of illness and healing in a way that is relevant and nonoffensive to the community. *When working with communities, it is critically important to determine who is best qualified to serve as liaison between the medical world and the community.* These liaisons, sometimes called **community contacts**, are resources for information and connection with the community. They often educate medical providers about the community and they may broker the relationship between the two. They are people whom the community trusts, and thus are an indispensable component of working with communities. Community contacts can assist in answering important questions about the community such as

- Who are the community leaders, if they are different from the liaisons?
- How does communication within the community occur?
- Who are the decision makers in the community and within the community's families?
- What are the defining ideas underlying the functioning and priorities of the community?

Medical providers and health-care centers may or may not be in the same physical location as the population community with whom they hope to work or serve. Providers working in the same geographic location as the community they hope to serve may have the advantage of familiarity with the community and opportunities to observe the functioning of the community group. Those who are geographically apart from the community of interest have the physical separation as a concrete representation of the symbolic gap that members of the community may feel. *Whether one's goals are to provide care, educate, or conduct research, familiarity with the community, on the community's terms and turf, is central to the relationship.* Attempting to impose one's own viewpoint and ways of working on a community is ineffective for achieving one's goals and is likely to offend and distance the community from further interactions with the medical world.

> There are five duties in surgery: to remove what is superfluous, to restore what has been dislocated, to separate what has grown together, to reunite what has been divided and to redress the defects of nature.
>
> AMBROISE PARE

SUMMARY

Patient and family care often involves interaction with other professionals, organizations, and at times, communities. The ability to work effectively with others is an important part of medical care, though perhaps more difficult to quantify than one's ability to perform a procedure. Skills and attitudes one exercises in interacting with others contribute to the success of each interaction. Ideally, one should model the behaviors and attitudes one would like to experience from others. Working with other professionals, organizations, and communities is essentially about relationships and communication. Both are central to the human experience, both require thoughtful attention and skill to be effective and gratifying, and both benefit from ongoing efforts toward improvement. The outcome of successful collaboration with other professionals, organizations and communities will be visible in the quality of patient and family care.

CASE STUDY

Ms. Smith is a 28-year-old woman recently diagnosed with breast cancer. She lives alone in a third floor apartment on the edge of town but visits her elderly mother daily to assist her with activities of daily living such as cooking and bathing. Prior to this diagnosis, Ms. Smith felt healthy and strong, reporting no serious illnesses or conditions. She was independent, athletic, and working full-time as an architect in a highly respected firm. She was shocked to learn that she had cancer and continues to have difficulty understanding the implications of the diagnosis. Despite this, Ms. Smith is heeding recommendations from her community-based primary care physician (PCP) not to delay pursuit of treatment.

Ms. Smith was referred for treatment by her PCP to a medical oncologist at a large medical center in town. At the medical center, she met with the medical oncologist, a surgeon, and a radiation oncologist. In an effort to provide Ms. Smith with a cohesive treatment plan that will best serve her, Ms. Smith's situation was discussed at a weekly interdisciplinary oncology team meeting. The three physicians provided suggestions for use of each of their treatment modalities in caring for Ms. Smith. They reviewed several possible treatment scenarios and combinations, respectfully offering expertise while maintaining Ms. Smith's needs as the focus of discussion. Other members of the interdisciplinary team, including the nutritionist, the social worker, and the physical therapist each asked specific questions regarding Ms. Smith's situation. Based on the discussion and questions raised during the meeting, a care plan and set of recommendations were chosen by the team.

The medical oncologist then contacted Ms. Smith to convey the agreed-upon recommendations. In addition to discussing the course of treatment the team has chosen, the medical oncologist informed Ms. Smith that the social worker and the nutritionist from the team would be contacting her. The nutritionist would assess Ms. Smith's current dietary habits, offer assistance and recommendations on maintaining an optimal diet while receiving treatment, and offer assistance with managing nutritional needs during treatment when one lives alone. The social worker would conduct a thorough biopsychosocial-spiritual assessment to determine Ms. Smith's needs for psychosocial support (such as supportive psychotherapy, psychoeducation, and social support), potential future needs for practical assistance (including transportation to treatment, finding a wig prior to treatment-related hair loss, and arranging time off from work) and assistance with community resources of care for Ms. Smith's mother. Ms. Smith is informed that if she chooses to pursue the team's recommendations, the team will review her progress weekly to ensure that all team members are apprised of her situation and can share information. The medical oncologist indicates that he will serve as liaison between the team and Ms. Smith to minimize mixed-messages from the multiple providers, and that he will maintain monthly contact with her community-based PCP.

After speaking with the medical oncologist, Ms. Smith decides to pursue care with this team of health-care providers. She appreciates receiving clear information that is a product of discussion among several colleagues from varied professions. She is relieved to hear that considerations beyond her treatment plan, such as her nutrition and emotional/social needs, will receive expert attention in collaboration with her medical care providers. Finally, she is reassured by knowing that her PCP, a physician she trusts and plans to continue seeing, will be apprised of her progress by the oncology team that will be providing her breast cancer care.

SUGGESTED READINGS

Castro, R.M., & Julia, M.C. (Eds.). (1994). *Interprofessional care and collaborative practice*. Pacific Grove, CA: Brooks/Cole.
   The book provides a framework for collaboration among health-care professionals using both conceptual and case-based information. Included are such topics as professionalization and socialization in collaboration, group process and dynamics, and professional ethics.

Fisher, R., William, U., & Patton, B. (1991). *Getting to yes: Negotiating agreement without giving in* (2nd ed.). New York: Penguin Books.
   The book, based on the work of the Harvard Negotiation Project, provides a clear, straightforward method for negotiating personal and professional disputes. The strategy is intended to achieve conflict resolution that is mutually acceptable to all parties, promoting a "win-win" outcome to those engaged in the negotiation.

Hayward, K.S. (2005). Facilitating interdisciplinary practice through mobile service provision to the rural older adult. *Geriatric Nursing, 26*(1), 29–33.
   The article offers an example of interdisciplinary team collaboration and community collaboration by discussing a program for rural older adults.

Journal of Interprofessional Care. Published by Taylor & Francis.
   This is a journal entirely dedicated to the topic of interprofessional care in health and mental health.

Martin, D.R., O'Brien, J.L., Heyworth, J.A., & Meyer, N.R. (2005). The collaborative health-care team: Tensive issues warranting ongoing consideration. *Journal of the American Academy of Nurse Practitioners, 17*, 325–330.
   An examination of verbatim transcripts of interviews with physicians and advanced practice nurses identifies five categories of tensive issues that influence quality of collaboration.

PART 4
PHYSICIAN-PATIENT INTERACTIONS

WHAT THE DOCTOR SAID

He said it doesn't look good
he said it looks bad in fact real bad
he said I counted thirty-two of them on one lung before
I quit counting them
I said I'm glad I wouldn't want to know
about any more being there than that
he said are you a religious man do you kneel down
in forest groves and let yourself ask for help
when you come to a waterfall
mist blowing against your face and arms
do you stop and ask for understanding at those moments
I said not yet but I intend to start today
he said I'm real sorry he said
I wish I had some other kind of news to give you
I said Amen and he said something else
I didn't catch and not knowing what else to do
and not wanting him to have to repeat it
and me to have to fully digest it
I just looked at him
for a minute and he looked back it was then
I jumped up and shook hands with this man who'd
just given me
something no one else on earth had ever given me
I may even have thanked him habit being so strong

RAYMOND CARVER

15 The Physician-Patient Relationship

Howard Brody

> There, I think, is the oldest and most effective act of doctors, the touching. Some people don't like being handled by others, but not, or almost never, sick people. They need being touched, and part of the dismay in being very sick is the lack of close human contact.
>
> LEWIS THOMAS
>
> How is it that Sassall is acknowledged as a good doctor? By his cures?... No, he is acknowledged as a good doctor because he meets the deep but unformulated expectation of the sick for a sense of fraternity. He recognizes them. Sometimes he fails—often because he has missed a critical opportunity and the patient's suppressed resentment becomes too hard to break through—but there is about him the constant will of a man trying to recognize.
>
> JOHN BERGER
> *A Fortunate Man*

THE PHYSICIAN'S WORDS AND THE PATIENT'S BRAIN

In 2002, **Fabrizio Benedetti,** a neuroscientist at the medical school of the University of Turin, wrote a review called, "How the Doctor's Words Affect the Patient's Brain" (Benedetti, 2002). The theme he addressed has an ancient lineage, which the Spanish medical historian, **Pedro Lain-Entralgo,** addressed in a book called *The Therapy of the Word in Classical Antiquity* (Lain-Entralgo, 1970). Yet there was nothing antiquated about Benedetti's review—he summarized recent investigations of his neuroscience group at Turin and referred to other studies using neuroimaging techniques to explore brain chemistry.

One research finding from Turin was particularly intriguing. Benedetti and his colleagues studied a group of patients who had recently had major surgery and were receiving heavy-duty pain medications, such as morphine, intravenously. The medication, however, was administered under two different conditions. In one, the patient witnessed a health worker injecting the medication into the intravenous line, and was told that this was a potent analgesic and would soon take effect. In the other condition, the patient was hooked to an intravenous pump that was programmed at give the same dose of the medication at specified times, but with no way for the patient to know when the medication was being infused. All patients had their pain levels continuously monitored.

The analgesic medication administered with the patient's knowledge and awareness had just about twice the pain-killing effect as the same chemical compound administered blindly (Amanzio et al., 2001).

It is worth taking a minute to think about this. The vast majority of studies of drugs look only at the first type of situation—the patient takes a medicine, and knows that she is taking the medicine, and what it is supposed to be for. Virtually no such study has a control group in which patients have the medication slipped into their morning cups of coffee without their knowledge. (There is good reason why we do not do such studies; they would, as a rule, be unethical.) But suppose such studies were routinely done. And suppose the findings mirrored those of the Turin investigators—that *fully half of the effects of most drugs rely on the patient's awareness of taking the medication, and the expectation that it will do them good, and only half of the efficacy of the drug depends solely on its chemical properties.* This is only an intriguing hypothesis at present. But imagine how this finding would change the way we think about medical practice—and the importance of the **physician-patient relationship.**

Benedetti pointed out in his review that it is not merely the case, today, that we can observe these effects. It is now also true that we have a much better idea of how to account for such results. We'll talk more later about a key finding from the Turin research group's work—that when patients experience pain relief because they expect to, the effect appears to be mediated by **endorphins**, opiate-like neurochemicals manufactured by the brain that bind to the same receptor sites as do morphine and other exogenous opiates. As part of the larger study that included the work with postoperative pain relief, the group conducted some laboratory studies on experimentally-induced pain. They used a different drug, **ketorolac** (a nonsteroidal antiinflammatory drug chemically unrelated to opiates) as a pain-reliever, and again compared the effect size of open vs. hidden administration. In an especially elegant twist, they added an injection of **naloxone** to the open injection of ketorolac. Naloxone is an **opiate antagonist**. It blocks the effects of both exogenous opiates such as morphine, and the brain's naturally occurring endorphins. Since ketorolac is not an opiate, naloxone will not reverse the pain-relief effect of that drug. But when given along with the open injection of ketorolac, the naloxone reduced the effectiveness of the injection to the same level as the hidden injection of ketorolac.

The Turin group interpreted these results as sorting out **two separable healing effects**. The first is the purely chemical analgesic effect of ketorolac. This is not reversed by naloxone, and is the same whether the patient knows he is getting the medication or not. The second is the extra boost, as it were, that the patient gets from *knowing* that the drug is being given and *expecting* that it will help. This extra boost, Benedetti and colleagues concluded, is mediated by endorphins in the brain, therefore, it is subject to reversal by naloxone. And, again, *this "extra boost" was responsible for about half of the total analgesic response.*

LISTENING TO THE PATIENT AND LATER HEALTH OUTCOMES

The ketorolac-naloxone study, by its nature, could be done only in an artificial laboratory setting, and so one should use caution in extrapolating those results to clinical work with real patients. That caution need not be applied to an older study done by family physicians at the University of Western Ontario. They asked a disarmingly simple question. Suppose that you have a group of patients, all coming to the family physician's office with a wide variety of common complaints. *What characteristic of the physician visit best predicts that, 1 month later, the patients will report that they feel better?*

The research group looked at a number of such visits and carefully analyzed what went on. Most of the variables

PATIENTS

Not the official ones, who have been
Diagnosed and made tidy. They are
The better sort of patient.

They know the answers to the difficult
Questions on the admission sheet
About religion, next of kin, sex.

They know the rules. The printed ones
In the Guide for Patients, about why we prefer
No smoking, the correct postal address;

Also the real ones, like the precise quota
Of servility each doctor expects,
When to have fits, and where to die.

These are not true patients. They know
Their way around, they present the right
Symptoms. But what can be done for us,

The undiagnosed? What drugs
Will help our Matron, whose cats are
Her old black husband and her young black son?

Who will prescribe for our nurses, fatally
Addicted to idleness and tea? What therapy
Will relieve our Psychiatrist of his lust

For young slim girls, who prudently
Pretend to his excitement, though age
Has freckled his hands and his breath smells
old?

How to comfort our Director through his
Terminal distress, as he babbles of
Football and virility, trembling in sunlight?

There is no cure for us. O, if only
We could cherish our bizarre behaviour
With accurate clinical pity. But there are no

Notes to chart our journey, no one
Has even stamped CONFIDENTIAL or Not to be
Taken out of the hospital on our lives.

U.A. FANTHORPE

they studied had no correlation with the patient's later outcome. The thoroughness of the history and physical, what laboratory and x-ray tests were done, what treatment was prescribed, how complete a note was written in the chart—none correlated well with later improvement. It seemed that virtually everything we try to teach in medical school and residency made little difference.

One factor, however, was highly associated with later improvement. This was the patient's perception that *the physician had listened carefully enough so that both physician and patient agreed on the nature of the problem* (Bass, Buck et al., 1986). This result was actually not surprising, since a study done a few years earlier at Johns Hopkins University had similarly shown that *the patient's sense of being carefully listened to was the crucial variable in later improvement* (Starfield et al., 1981).

The Western Ontario physicians, however, were not fully satisfied. They took one group of patients—those coming in for the first time complaining of headache—and followed them for a full year. What would predict that the headache was improved one year later? Once again the answer was: the patients' perception that at the first visit, they had the chance to discuss the headache problem fully with the physician (Bass, McWhinney et al., 1986).

> Those who have learned by experience what physical pain and bodily anguish mean, belong together all the world over; they are united by a secret bond. One and all they know the horrors of suffering to which man can be exposed, and one and all they know the longing to be free from pain.
>
> ALBERT SCHWEITZER

THE PLACEBO EFFECT IN EVERYDAY PRACTICE

Bass and colleagues at Western Ontario did not have a special name for what they were studying in 1986. Later they summarized their research findings into what they came to call the **patient-centered clinical method** (Stewart et al, 1995). Benedetti and his group at Turin, on the other hand, believed that their studies of open vs. hidden injections were part of their larger inquiry into the **placebo effect**.

As historians have noted, the idea that the quality of the physician-patient relationship—or what words the physician utters to the patient—can have an important effect on health and disease goes back to the time of **Hippocrates**. At

---

BOX 15.1 Summary of research into the placebo effect

1. On average, about one third of research subjects given a placebo will demonstrate improvement. This rate varies considerably among studies and the reasons for the variation may be of greater scientific interest than the overall average.
2. Placebos can be powerful agents in relieving pain or anxiety, but their effectiveness is not restricted to those conditions. Virtually every potentially reversible symptom has been shown at one time or another to respond to placebos.
3. Placebos can affect both "organic" and **"psychogenic" symptoms**, and response to placebo does not provide any help in distinguishing which is which. Indeed, as we come to find out more about the neurophysiology and neurochemistry of symptoms like pain, it is increasingly questionable whether the so-called organic/psychogenic distinction makes any sense.
4. Placebos can alter physiologically measurable variables such as blood sugar, and not merely the individual's subjective state.
5. The application of **neuroimaging** techniques to the study of the placebo effect is still in its infancy. What has been learned so far suggests that when a placebo effect occurs, it involves the same neural structures and pathways as would pharmacologic treatment of the same disease. There is also strong scientific support for the hypothesis that expectancy-related placebo pain relief is endorphin-mediated.
6. Placebo effects can be as striking, and occasionally as long-lasting, as any effect produced by drugs. Some studies have indicated a powerful placebo effect from a sham surgical procedure.
7. Placebos can also mimic many of the side effects seen with pharmacologic therapy.

8. As a general rule, research aimed at identifying a **"placebo personality type"** has been fruitless. Most people seem to be potential placebo responders given the right set of circumstances.
9. Older research often overestimated the size and frequency of the placebo effect because other effects were confused with it—most notably, the natural tendency of the human body to heal itself (natural history of illness). Even when these other effects are controlled for, however, a placebo effect can still be demonstrated in many instances.
10. Placebo effects can be triggered by two different sorts of psychological processes. In one, people can experience a placebo effect because they expect a positive outcome to occur (**expectancy**). In the other, people can experience a placebo effect because they are placed in similar circumstances where healing has occurred in the past (**conditioning**).

REFERENCES

Brody, H. (2000). The placebo response: Recent research and implications for family medicine. *Journal of Family Practice, 49,* 649–654.

Fisher, S., & Greenberg, R.P. (1997). The curse of the placebo: Fanciful pursuit of a pure biologic therapy. In S. Fisher & R.P. Greenberg (Eds.), *From placebo to panacea: Putting psychiatric drugs to the test* (pp. 3–56). New York: Wiley.

Guess, H.A., Kleinman, A., Kusek, J.W., & Engel, L.W. (Eds.). (2002). *The science of the placebo: Toward an interdisciplinary research agenda.* London: BMJ Books.

Harrington, A. (Ed.). (1997). *The placebo effect: An interdisciplinary exploration.* Cambridge, MA: Harvard University Press.

Moerman, D.E. (2002). *Meaning, medicine, and the "placebo effect."* New York: Cambridge University Press.

BOX 15.2 Possible biochemical pathways for placebo effects (the "inner pharmacy")

Endorphins. Endorphins were among the first neuropeptides studied in relation to the placebo effect; early research showed that the placebo effect could be reversed by naloxone, an endorphin antagonist. Subsequent research, particularly studies by Benedetti and colleagues (see text), has demonstrated consistently that endorphins play an important role in placebo pain relief (so long as expectancy is an important psychological mechanism) and probably in a number of other symptoms. Neuroimaging studies confirm that the brain nuclei involved in placebo effects for pain include centers known to be responsible for endorphin secretion.

Catecholamines and **serotonin.** Catecholamines were the first hormones shown to be highly responsive to stress and emotional state. Besides their effects on heart rate, blood pressure, and other manifestations of the "fight or flight" response, adrenocortical hormones have also been shown to be linked to altered immune responses. This suggests that, ultimately, catecholamine and psychoneuroimmune pathways (see below) may come to be viewed as a single complex pathway.

Psychoneuroimmune responses. Immune function can be altered experimentally through changes in stress or relaxation. Neuropeptide receptor sites have been identified on immune cells, illustrating how catecholamines and endorphins may all "talk" to each other and to the immune system. While psychoneuroimmunology remains a promising route for future placebo research, to date there have been few studies directly linking placebo effects with immune system function and with measurable health outcomes in human disease.

REFERENCES

Amanzio, M., & Benedetti, F. (1999). Neuropharmacological dissection of placebo analgesia: Expectation-activated opioid systems vs. conditioning-activated specific subsystems. *Journal of Neuroscience, 19,* 484–494.

Hafen, B.Q., Karren, K.J., Frandsen, K.J., & Smith, N.L. (1996). *Mind/body health: The effects of attitudes, emotions, and relationships.* Needham Heights, MA: Allyn and Bacon.

BOX 15.3 The **meaning model**

A positive placebo effect is most likely to occur when the patient's meaning of the experience of illness is altered in a positive direction.

A positive change in meaning is most likely to result when the following elements are present:
• Patients feel listened to.
• Patients are provided with a satisfactory explanation for their symptoms.
• Patients sense care and concern in those around them.
• Patients are helped to achieve a sense of mastery or control over the illness.

REFERENCE

Brody, H. (2000). The placebo response: Recent research and implications for family medicine. *Journal of Family Practice, 49,* 649–654.

scious patient. Nor need the physician necessarily be present—it is very likely that if patients who strongly believe in the power of alternative medicine order such a product from an Internet site, they will have an equally powerful placebo effect when they take it. In other words, *the placebo effect is a much more widespread and important phenomenon than the administration of placebos,—which, again for ethical reasons, is hardly ever justified in clinical practice.* Box 15.1 summarizes what is now known about the placebo effect.

Thanks to the work of groups such as Benedetti and colleagues in Turin, we also know a good deal more today about the biochemical pathways (including the endorphin system) that appear to be responsible for the placebo effect (Box 15.2). It seems not too far-fetched to say that the human body is supplied with its own **inner pharmacy**, capable of dispensing its own healing medications when persons find themselves in the right sort of environment and are presented with the right stimuli (Bulger, 1990). For centuries people have talked about the mannerisms of the ideal physician, using vague terms such as "the art of medicine," "bedside manner," and so forth. We are now in a position to place the inquiry on a more scientific footing. We can ask in what ways the physician needs to behave—what sort of relationship with the patient needs to be created—in order for the physician to best turn on that inner pharmacy.

The available research suggests that the inner pharmacy, or placebo effect, is likely to be turned on optimally when *the patient's meaning of the experience of illness is altered in a positive direction.* What counts as a positive alteration in the "meaning of the experience of illness"? Thanks to the research at Western Ontario and elsewhere, we can say with some confidence that *the patient's sense of being fully listened to* is one such "turn-on." Adding the results of other studies, we can expand this list into what we may call the **Meaning Model** (Box 15.3; Brody, 2000).

least as long ago as the Renaissance, physicians had become used to using dummy or imitation medicines in some circumstances, observing that the unknowing patient often responded just as if he had received the actual drug. Eventually such treatments came to be called **placebos** and the resulting impact on the patient, the **placebo effect.**

Modern research into the placebo effect demonstrates that the power of words, and of the patient's expectations, to alter the course of a symptom or illness is not confined to situations in which a fake medicine is administered. (Recall that in the open vs. hidden injection study, all the patients received "real" morphine.) So it is reasonable to regard the placebo effect as occurring throughout most of medicine, at least whenever a physician encounters a con-

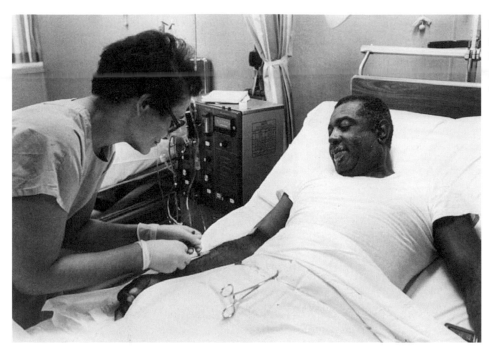

Expectations help determine outcome in any clinical setting. Copyright © National Kidney Foundation, Inc. *Learning how to shape patient expectations will help you become "a healing sort of person."*

It would be nice if we could say that everywhere medicine is practiced, these "positive meaning" elements are fully present. Sadly, we know that in our complex and often impersonal medical care system, this is not true. All too often patients have the opposite experience. The problem may remain mysterious and no one may offer a suitable explanation. No one may listen. The patient might feel coldness and distance instead of care and concern from the treating personnel. The end result might be a patient who feels even more helpless and victimized. When these negative-meaning elements are present, we would expect that the patient would suffer worse outcomes. Some investigators refer to this unfortunate result as the **nocebo effect**, the harmful opposite of a positive placebo effect (Hahn, 1997).

AN EXAMPLE OF POSITIVE MEANING: "WOMEN'S COMPLAINTS"

Here's a practical example in which one physician saw a serious nocebo effect occurring, and worked to change it to a positive placebo effect.

At about the same time that the Western Ontario family physicians were puzzling over what made patients better, **Kirsti Malterud** was starting out as a general practitioner in Bergen, Norway. She soon found in her office a number of patients suffering from "**women's complaints.**" They had symptoms relating to the genital tract or pelvic area. In some cases the symptoms were crippling in their impact on the women's lives. The gynecologists and internists in Bergen had performed numerous investigations on these

women, but had been unable to make any firm diagnosis. Eventually they told many of them that their pains were "all in their head" or in one way or another signaled to them that they should not come back.

These desperate women hoped that a woman physician would somehow be able to care for them. At first, however, Malterud had no better idea as to what to do. She had after all been trained in the same tradition, that if you did not have a diagnosis, you could not offer treatment. Besides, when the women were given medications in a shotgun fashion, they hardly ever got better and kept coming back with the same symptoms.

Eventually Malterud scored a breakthrough in her thinking when she came to view what her colleagues had been doing as creating a nocebo effect. *The sort of care these other physicians had given, with all the best of intentions, had the net result of making these women feel powerless.* They suffered from these symptoms and were told, in effect, that only by letting the physicians work on them could they ever get better. The physicians undressed them, poked and prodded at their private parts, and subjected them to a variety of uncomfortable procedures. After all was done, the women were told that they were even more defective than had first been thought. Not only did they have these severe symptoms, but they did not even have the good sense to have a diagnosable disease. Obviously, if they were so uncooperative, the problem was theirs, not the physicians'. So of course they left the office empty-handed, with the clear message that nothing could be done for them, and that nothing would ever get any better.

Armed with this insight, Malterud asked how she could alter these women's experience of their illness. She eventually found that she obtained the best results if she made sure that at each visit, she asked these women four questions (Malterud, 1994):

- What would you most of all want me to do for you today?
- What do you yourself think is causing your problem?
- What do you think that I should do about your problem?
- What have you found so far to be the best way of managing your problem?

This list of questions happens to match well with the recommendations from a classic paper on how to apply knowledge from the social sciences to everyday medical practice (Kleinman, Eisenberg, & Good, 1978).

Malterud's way of approaching the patient gradually started to turn the nocebo effect into a positive placebo effect. Suddenly the patients found themselves looked to as experts, instead of as defective bodies. Somebody actually wanted to know what they thought, and somebody actually was turning to them for guidance as to what should be done about their own problems. Somebody, it seemed, was finally willing to listen to them. And, if something they themselves had done might hold the clue to how to better manage their problems, maybe they were not powerless after all. Maybe, if they put their minds to it, they could come up with even better ways of taking care of themselves in the future. *Malterud found that treating her patients as thoughtful and creative problem-solvers, rather than as bundles of defective tissue, produced the best outcomes.*

MEANING AND THE IMPORTANCE OF STORY

We've seen that ideally, a positive placebo effect could be a part of every physician-patient encounter, even if placebos are never administered. This has led some commentators to argue that the term **placebo effect** is too misleading to be useful any more. One systematic review of the literature suggested the term **context effects**, since the entire healing context, and not merely the chemical content of the pill, is responsible (Di Blasi et al., 2001). Other authors, using a model very similar to ours, proposed instead calling these responses **meaning effects** (Moerman & Jonas, 2002).

We might next ask how patients attach meaning to the experience of illness in the first place. The most basic human way we can assign meaning to any set of events in the world is to tell a **story** about it (Brody, 2003). A story organizes events into both a chronologic and a cause-effect sequence. A story situates events within the context of the life of the individual and of the larger community or society. When patients tell the story of an illness, they take a

> **The Wisdom of HIPPOCRATES, 460–375 BCE**
> **Greek physician**
>
> Sleep and watchfulness, both of them, when immoderate, constitute disease.
> *(Aphorisms II)*
>
> Persons who are naturally very fat are apt to die earlier than those who are slender.
> *(Aphorisms II)*
>
> He who desires to practice surgery must go to war.
> *(Corpus Hippocraticum)*
>
> I will not use the knife, not even on the sufferers from stone, but will withdraw in favour of such men as are engaged in this work.
> *(Corpus Hippocraticum)*
>
> The art has three factors, the disease, the patient, and the physician. The physician is the servant of the art. The patient must co-operate with the physician in combating the disease.
> *(Epidemics I)*
>
> I will neither give a deadly drug to anybody if asked for it, nor will I make a suggestion to this effect.
> *(The Oath)*
>
> So do not concentrate your attention on fixing what your fee is to be. A worry of this nature is likely to harm the patient, particularly if the disease can be an acute one. Hold fast to reputation rather than profit.
> *(Precepts I)*
>
> Sometimes give your services for nothing. And if there be an opportunity of serving one who is a stranger in financial straits, give full assistance to all such. For where there is love of man, there is also love of the art.
> *(The Art VI)*
>
> The physician must have a worthy appearance; he should look healthy and be well-nourished, appropriate to his physique: for most people are of the opinion that those physicians who are not tidy in their own persons cannot look after others well.
> *(Attributed)*

stab at explaining what caused the illness; what future results will arise from it; and what impact all of this has on their past, present, and future lives and activities. Experts in medical interviewing have suggested that we ought to think of the process of "taking a medical history" as being better characterized as *eliciting the patient's story* (Smith & Hoppe, 1991).

Patients go to physicians for many reasons. Obviously, they want something they can take or do that will resolve their

> What happens when my body breaks down happens not just to that body but also to my life, which is lived in that body. When the body breaks down, so does the life.
>
> ARTHUR FRANK

ailments. Some want something as simple as a piece of paper saying it is okay for them to go back to work. But many patients seek a physician's care while laboring under some degree of distress or anguish. A way of characterizing this distress is: "Something is happening to me. I have constructed a story to try to make some sense of it. But my own story either doesn't make much sense, or else it has really scary implications for my future. Can you help me tell a better story, which will make sense and also provide me with some comfort and reassurance?" We could summarize this succinctly as, "My story is broken; can you help me fix it?" (Brody, 1994).

The notion of "fixing stories" brings us back to the **patient-centered clinical method**, the proposal that emerged from the research begun by the family physicians at the University of Western Ontario (Stewart, 1995). This method assumes that two stories of the illness will eventually be told. The patient will describe the illness in terms of the symptoms he has felt and the impact these have had on his life. The physician, after the appropriate investigations, will tell a medical story of the illness. Often this medical story will be in terms of diseases and tissue damage, such as, "you have a strep throat," or, "it sounds as if you may be having gastroesophageal reflux; I may have to suggest some further tests to be sure." Both the patients' and the physicians' stories are valuable and are essential to a good outcome. *What makes the method "patient-centered" is that the physician's job is not done until she has worked with the patient to reconcile the two stories. The patient, in the end, is the "expert" in whether or not the reconciliation has occurred.* If the physician's story of the illness or disease is not acceptable or meaningful to the patient, more work remains to be done, no matter how elegant a diagnosis the physician may have made, or no matter how scientifically sound the treatment plan.

Let's look at the patient-centered clinical method from the vantage point of "fixing a broken story" and making optimal use of the **Meaning Model**. How should the reconciliation occur? What would count as the ideal coopera-

> Physicians of the Utmost Fame
> Were called at once; but when they came
> They answered, as they took the Fees.
> "There is no cure for this disease."
>
> HILAIRE BELLOC
> *Cautionary Tales for Children*

tion between physician and patient in *constructing a better story?*

CONSTRUCTING BETTER STORIES— A CASE ILLUSTRATION

Here's a case that could be almost a daily occurrence in the office of a primary care physician during the winter season (see Case Example below). How would we analyze this physician-patient encounter, given our goals of utilizing the Meaning Model and constructing a better story?

CASE EXAMPLE

The patient complains of a cough that has persisted for several days. The physician's careful interview elicits, along with the usual description of symptoms, the absence of fever and the presence of nasal congestion. When the physician asks the patient what he is most worried about, the patient says that his aunt recently nearly died of pneumonia and he is worried that this disease might be present in his case also. Examination reveals no fever, nasal congestion, some irritation of the posterior pharynx, and clear lung fields. The physician reassures the patient that he has no signs of pneumonia and that the cough is probably related to postnasal drainage. She recommends a vaporizer and other simple home measures to try to relieve the nasal congestion. She also lists danger signs of possible pneumonia for the patient to watch for "just in case."

First, let's recall that our *overall objective is an effective and healing physician-patient* **relationship**, *not merely a satisfactory* **encounter**. This suggests that the physician has two agendas. First, the disease, if one is present, should be satisfactorily identified and treated; and the patient should feel listened to, cared for, and more in control of events. Second, all of those things should happen in a way that lays a positive groundwork for future collaboration and cooperation. The physician should be looking ahead to the sorts of problems this patient might encounter in the future. This visit, ideally, should set the stage for the physician and patient to work together as a team to address those problems.

Now let's return to addressing what happens in the visit itself. For the physician's reassurance to be satisfying to the patient, and for the patient to feel adequately listened to, **the new story** ("post-nasal drip" instead of "pneumonia") *must emerge from a true therapeutic collaboration.* The physician must indicate to the patient, both verbally and nonverbally, that she is fully attentive to the history and physical and that she carefully considered alternative possibilities before coming up with her final explanation. (Even if this is the tenth case of post-nasal-drip-cough the physician has seen today, the patient wishes to believe that he

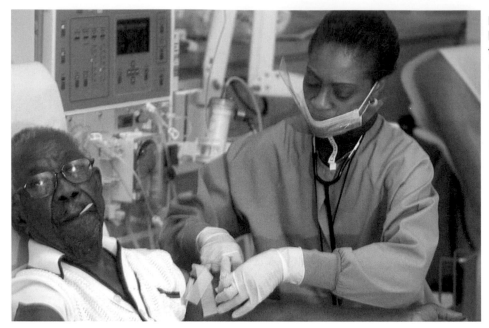

Health-care providers sometimes forget how alien and strange it feels for a patient to be in the hospital © National Kidney Foundation, photo by Erica Berger. Reprinted with permission.

has received the same attention as if he had walked in with a rare complaint previously unknown to medical science.) The physician must be alert during this entire process to the patient's verbal and nonverbal feedback. If the patient looks relieved and nods his head, the physician can proceed to conclude the visit. If the patient raises an eyebrow or looks more worried, the physician must stop and explore more carefully what the patient is thinking.

If the patient feels that he has been a full collaborator in constructing the new story, he will perceive the story as *meaningful from his point of view*. That is, he must be able to imagine what was said actually going on in his own body. The explanation offered by the physician must square with the patient's previous life experience. If, for instance, he has had allergies in the past, and had a tickle in his throat that made him cough, he may readily accept the idea that the cough is caused by a nasal process. If, by contrast, the patient feels wheezy and tight in his chest, he may resist any explanation of his cough that attributes the symptom to upper respiratory problems. In any case, the time and care that the physician took in eliciting the history and offering the explanation will help determine whether the patient ends up feeling that the new story is about *his* cough, or is a stock explanation that the physician is handing out to all patients that day.

Patients come to physicians for *medical* care, not mere emotional reassurance. To be worthy of the trust the patient places in the physician, the latter must help to create a story that is *biomedically sound*. It must be scientifically correct that post-nasal drainage can cause a cough. If the physician actually fears that this patient is developing lung cancer, she must not offer the post-nasal drip explanation merely to make the patient feel better. In our case, the patient might be immensely relieved if the physician were to prescribe an antibiotic. But if no antibiotic is truly indicated, the physi-

cian ought not send the patient out of the office with an inappropriate story, "I must have needed an antibiotic." If the biomedically sound story is "post-nasal drip not requiring an antibiotic," *the physician must negotiate that correct story with the patient even if it takes some extra time.* Later in an ongoing relationship, that extra time will pay dividends. By contrast, prescribing an unnecessary antibiotic now just to save time will come back to haunt the relationship later.

Another feature of the best sort of healing story is that it will *promote the right sorts of healthy behaviors*. If the physician has recommended a vaporizer and perhaps a saline nasal spray, with an over-the-counter decongestant if those do not work, then the patient must imagine himself actually doing these things, and must imagine that doing them will produce the desired outcome. In other words, the story mutually constructed by physician and patient must end (in the patient's version) with, "And I went home and did what the doctor recommended, and in just a few days my symptoms were gone." This part of constructing a new healing story is relatively easy when the measures required are simple and the disease is self-limited. As patients increasingly face multiple chronic illnesses demanding major lifestyle changes, this aspect of constructing a new story becomes much more challenging.

The final requirement of the ideal healing story is also made more challenging by serious or chronic illness. This requirement is that the new story *facilitates the patient in getting on with his life*, either after the illness has resolved (for acute illnesses) or with the illness as a constant presence (chronic illness). **Eric Cassell**, in his classic study of the dangers of highly technological and impersonal medical practice, describes what happens when physicians adequately diagnose and treat the patient's disease, but fail to relieve the patient's **suffering** (Cassell, 1991). *Suffering, as Cassell re-*

lates, is often caused by a basic sense of being split apart where one was formerly whole. When healthy, the patient viewed herself as one with her own body, and as a functioning member of her community within her network of assigned roles and relationships. When chronically ill, this patient may see herself as now alienated from her body, which will no longer do what she wants it to, and which now places new demands on her for its care. The patient may also see herself as alienated from her family and community, as the illness makes it impossible for her to perform some of her role responsibilities, and as she feels that others around her simply cannot understand what is happening to her.

> Drug therapy involves a great deal more than matching the name of the drug to the name of a disease; it requires knowledge, judgement, skill and wisdom, but above all a sense of responsibility.
>
> DESMOND ROGER LAURENCE
> Professor of pharmacology

In the face of this sort of suffering, the physician's care and compassion, and willingness to listen, may be the first time that the patient senses that a lifeline has been tossed to her, drawing her back into a whole relationship with the human community. The ultimate relief of the suffering will probably require that the patient constructs a new story of the rest of her life. She will have to give up the old "healthy" life story in which she could simply do what she wanted to without thinking. She will have to construct a new story in which she lives a life that is still satisfying in terms of her core values and relationships, and that permits her to carry on with her most cherished life projects. In this new story, the illness will be a sort of companion as she lives her new life. She will have to follow her new diet, get the right sorts of exercise, take the correct medications, and subject herself to more types of medical care more often. The physician who works carefully and consistently with the patient over a number of visits to help in the construction of this new healing story is doing some of the most important work that can be done in medicine.

> The ultimate indignity is to be given a bedpan by a stranger who calls you by your first name.
>
> MAGGIE KUHN
> *Observer*

AN EVIDENCE-BASED PHYSICIAN-PATIENT RELATIONSHIP

So far, we have seen that a number of general principles can effectively guide us in creating the sort of physician-patient relationship that is most likely to assure positive healing outcomes:

- The **Meaning Model**: ways to promote a positive placebo effect as part of each patient encounter
- **Collaborative construction of stories**: working with patients to tell better stories about their illnesses, realizing that story is the major way we have of assigning meaning to our lives
- **Patient-centered care**: incorporates both the Meaning Model and collaborative story construction, reminding us that we should approach medical diagnosis and treatment *through* our relationship with patients, rather than seeing diagnosis and treatment as somehow separable from those relationships

Today medicine is under increasing pressure to become more **evidence-based**. Some fear that this trend will undermine humanism in medicine. According to the old adage, they fear "the measurable driving out the important." They imagine that since we can more easily measure whether (for example) a drug lowers blood pressure or whether a spiral CT scan can effectively detect appendicitis, we will refocus solely on technique and ignore medicine's human relationships.

Admittedly it is hard to study the physician-patient relationship in the same rigorous way we evaluate new pharmaceuticals. Imagine trying to do a study in which you randomly assigned thousands of patients to either good or poor relationships with their physicians, and then came back in 10 years to see what outcomes had occurred. Or imagine that you tried to do a randomized controlled trial in which you kept all other elements of the physician-patient relationship constant, only in half the cases the patient received a meaningful explanation for their illnesses, while in the other half they received a confusing explanation. In some ways, our understanding of the physician-patient relationship is destined to fall short of "the best" evidence.

Yet this need not mean that we cannot pursue two important goals. First, we can continue as best as we can to document what happens to our patients' health when they experience different sorts of encounters and relationships. Second, we can try further to refine our understanding of what works and what doesn't, so that ultimately our teaching of ourselves and of future physicians will be better grounded scientifically.

Let's look at just a few examples. We have already seen how the family physicians at the University of Western Ontario based their patient-centered clinical method on measurable patient outcomes. Later, a massive study in the United States called the **Medical Outcomes Study** documented repeatedly how *certain ways of interacting with patients produced better health outcomes in a variety of chronic conditions.* Patients who were encouraged to become active participants in their own care, using a patient-centered approach, had better results, while their medical care generally cost less (Safran et al., 1994; Kaplan et al., 1996). Surveying this literature, a group of primary care experts concluded that "sustained partnerships" with patients had been proven to produce better health outcomes in a wide variety of diseases and conditions (Leopold, Cooper, & Clancy, 1996). When in 2001 the **Institute of Medicine** of the **National Academy of Sciences** issued its influential report, called *Crossing the Quality Chasm*, it included *patient-centered* as one of six essential criteria for the quality of medical care (Institute of Medicine, 2001). Similarly, a task force describing the "**Future of Family Medicine**" singled out patient-centered care as the key element for the future development of that primary care specialty (Future of Family Medicine, 2004).

SUMMARY

We have solid evidence today on which to argue that the sort of physician-patient relationship we have described in this chapter is:

- Humane and compassionate
- Ethically respectful of patients' rights
- Well-grounded in a scientific understanding of the human brain
- Effective in producing superior health outcomes
- Efficient in holding down the costs of medical care

There is, therefore, every possible reason to proceed in making this sort of relationship the norm rather than the exception, even as we await further intriguing scientific evidence from groups like Benedetti and colleagues at Turin.

SUGGESTED READINGS

Amanzio, M., Pollo, A., Maggi, G., & Benedetti, A. (2001). Response variability to analgesics: A role for nonspecific activation of endogenous opioids. *Pain, 90,* 205–215.

Bass, M.J., Buck, C., Turner, L., Dickie, G., Pratt, G., & Robinson, H.C. (1986). The physician's actions and the outcome of illness in family practice. *Journal of Family Practice, 23,* 43–47.
An excellent, pioneering study showing that the patient's and physician's agreement on the nature of the problem (which in turn requires that the physician listen carefully to the patient) predicts later resolution of common symptoms.

Bass, M.J., McWhinney, I.R., Dempsey, J.B., and the Headache Study Group of the University of Western Ontario (1986). Predictors of outcomes in headache patients presenting to family physicians—1 year prospective study. *Headache Journal, 26,* 285–294.

Benedetti, F. (2002). How the doctor's words affect the patient's brain.

Evaluation and the Health Professions, 25, 369–386.
A review of much recent research on the placebo effect, and on how the medical setting and context (including the physician-patient relationship) affects neural systems.

Brody, H. (1994). "My story is broken, can you help me fix it?" Medical ethics and the joint construction of narrative. *Literature and Medicine, 13,* 79–92.

Brody, H. (2000). The placebo response: Recent research and implications for family medicine. *Journal of Family Practice, 49,* 649–654.
Elaborates the Meaning Model and evidence supporting it, and recommends actions to implement the model in primary care practice.

Brody, H. (2003). *Stories of sickness* (2nd ed.). New York: Oxford University Press.
Explores the importance of story and narrative in medicine and in medical ethics.

Bulger, R.J. (1990). The demise of the placebo effect in the practice of scientific medicine—a natural progression or an undesirable aberration? *Transactions of the American Clinical and Climatological Association, 102,* 285–293.

Cassell, E.J. (1991). *The nature of suffering and the goals of medicine.* New York: Oxford University Press.
An important book on the nature of suffering as it involves the whole person and the person's social relationships, and how medicine can both ameliorate and exacerbate suffering.

Di Blasi, Z., Harkness, E., Ernst, E., Georgiou, A., & Kleijnen, J. (2001). Influence of context effects on health outcomes: A systematic review. *Lancet, 357,* 757–762.

Future of Family Medicine Project Leadership Committee. (2004). The future of family medicine. *Annals of Family Medicine, 2,* S1–S32.
A report on the future of family medicine that stresses the importance of patient-centered care.

Hahn, R.A. (1997). The nocebo phenomenon: Scope and foundations. In A. Harrington (Ed.), *The placebo effect: An interdisciplinary exploration* (pp. 56–76). Cambridge, MA: Harvard University Press.

Institute of Medicine. Committee on Quality of Health Care in America. (2001). *Crossing the quality chasm: A new health system for the 21st century.* Washington, DC: National Academy Press.
A major report on quality care, arguing that "patient-centered" is one of six essential elements of good quality.

Kaplan, S.H., Greenfield, S., Gandek, B., Rogers, W.H.& Ware, J.E. (1996) Characteristics of physicians with participatory decision-making styles. *Annals of Internal Medicine, 124,* 497–504.
One of a series of publications from the Medical Outcomes Study, describing a style of physician-patient communication associated with health improvements.

Kleinman, A.F., Eisenberg, L., & Good, B. (1978). Culture, illness, and care: Clinical lessons from anthropological and cross-cultural research. *Annals of Internal Medicine, 88,* 251–258.
A classic study of the application of social-science insights to everyday physician-patient encounters.

Lain-Entralgo, P. (1970). *The therapy of the word in classical antiquity* (trans. L.J. Rather & J.M. Sharp). New Haven, CT: Yale University Press.

Leopold, N., Cooper, J., & Clancy, C. (1996). Sustained partnership in primary care. *Journal of Family Practice, 42,* 129–137.

Describes the model of "sustained partnership" and assesses evidence that it produces superior health outcomes.

Malterud, K. (1994). Key questions—a strategy for modifying clinical communication: Transforming tacit skills into a clinical method. *Scandinavian Journal of Primary Health Care, 12,* 121–127.
Malterud describes her method of asking key questions that empower female patients as part of the routine office visit.

Moerman, D.E., & Jonas, W.B. (2002). Deconstructing the placebo effect and finding the meaning response. *Annals of Internal Medicine, 136,* 471–476.

Safran, D.G., Tarlov, A.R., & Rogers, W.H. (1994). Primary-care performance in fee-for-service and prepaid health systems. *Journal of the American Medical Association, 271,* 1579–1586.

Other results from the Medical Outcomes Study, with special focus on the cost-effectiveness of good physician-patient relationships in primary care practice.

Smith, R.C., & Hoppe, R.B. (1991). The patient's story: Integrating the patient- and physician-centered approaches to interviewing. *Annals of Internal Medicine, 115,* 470–477.

Starfield, B., Wray, C., Hess, K., Gross, R., Birk, P.S., & D'Lugoff, B.C. (1981). The influence of patient-practitioner agreement on outcome of care. *American Journal of Public Health, 71,* 127–132.

Stewart, M., Brown, J.B., Weston, W.W., McWhinney, I.R., McWilliam, C.L., & Freeman, T.R. (1995). *Patient-centered medicine: Transforming the clinical method.* Thousand Oaks, CA: Sage.

An eighty-four-year-old woman living in Maine has never had a complete medical exam. Her kids insist that she go to the doctor, and although she's never been sick, she goes. She's not a very sophisticated woman, and the young doctor is amazed she's in such good shape.

After the exam he tells her, "Everything seems to be in good order, but there are additional tests I'd like to run. Come back next week and bring a specimen."

The old woman doesn't know what he is talking about.

He says, "What I need is a urinary sample. Would you bring that in and we'll run some additional tests." She still doesn't understand. The doctor says, "Before you come in, void in a jar." The woman responds quizzically, "What?"

The doctor finally gets exasperated and says, "Look, lady, go piss in a pot." She gets red in the face, smacks him over the head with her pocketbook, replies, "And you go shit in your hat," and promptly walks out.

RICHARD S. WURMAN
Information Anxiety

THE PATIENT

The first thing to remember about the patient is that he or she is anxious. This may or may not be apparent but can safely be assumed to be true for several reasons. The patient is ill or subjectively distressed and may have already developed theories about what is actually wrong. The possibility of having disease evokes fear of death and disability, fear of bodily harm, and fear of separation from loved ones (e.g., through hospitalization). In addition, physicians often intimidate patients. No matter how kind and eager to help the physician may be, the patient's reaction to the physician's *presence* cannot be controlled. Patients expect great things from their physician and feel a strong sense of dependence on the physician to meet their physical and emotional needs. It is critical for the physician to realize that these anxieties can complicate the interview, making it difficult to elicit information and essential to check that the information provided to patients was heard and understood as intended. The physician cannot simply ask questions and assume that the desired answers will be returned. *Patient anxiety and the emotion-laden nature of the physician-patient relationship for the patient require putting the patient at ease, establishing a trusting relationship, and monitoring the words spoken and the phraseology of questions.*

A second important point is that patients and physicians have different agendas during the interview. Typically patients are seeking relief from subjective complaints (symptoms) and speak the **language of illness**. Physicians are seeking to elicit the objective signs that aid in diagnosis and speak the **language of disease**. Although the physician

might prefer that the patient present his or her complaint and history in precisely the sequence required for write-up, this rarely happens and need not be encouraged. With increased experience, the interviewer gradually becomes more comfortable taking the naturally emitted, occasionally vague and disorganized words of the patient and transforming them into a comprehensive, meaningful, and orderly medical history. While this medical history will be useful for the health-care team, team members need to subsequently translate clinical information and options into terms that patients and families can understand.

THE PHYSICIAN

The role of the physician entitles him or her to inquire into private and intimate details of the patient's life and to conduct a physical examination on a relative stranger. It also obliges the physician to be professionally competent, to put the patient's interests ahead of personal interests, and to provide help and comfort whenever possible.

Although the primary purpose of the interview from the physician's perspective may be diagnostic, *an interview can and should also be therapeutic for the patient*. Depending on the physician's conduct, the patient can potentially come away from every physician encounter feeling better understood, better informed, and reassured of the physician's interest and availability. Alternatively, he or she can come away feeling misunderstood, confused, and alienated.

The following vignette exemplifies an exchange with little therapeutic content:

The interviewer failed to knock at the patient's door. He introduced himself in a hasty mumble so that the patient never had his name clearly in mind. He mispronounced the patient's name once and never used it again. The physician conducted the interview while seated in a chair about 7 feet from the patient. There was no physical contact during the interview. On several occasions the patient expressed her emotional distress. On each occasion the interviewer ignored the emotional content of her statements:

- *Doctor:* Exactly where is this pain?
- *Patient:* It's so hard for me to explain. I'm trying to do as well as I can. (Turning to husband:) Aren't I doing as well as I can?
- *Doctor:* Well, is the pain up high in your belly, or down low? (Platt & McMath, 1979.)

Several aspects of this vignette are worthy of comment. The failure to knock and to learn the patient's name and the hasty introduction indicate a neglect of the most basic amenities. *The physical distance between physician and patient may also have been excessive, paralleling the emotional distance created by the physician's failure to pursue the emo-*

tional content of the patient's statement. Most of all, notice the physician's insistence on eliciting the site of the pain. This is certainly a necessary aspect of the interview, but at this moment the patient is incapable of answering. *If the physician had been more willing to explore the patient's difficulty in explaining, he might have learned something of critical importance about the symptom and about the patient.* The patient would be more likely to experience the physician as a person who has patience and pays attention, which could only enhance the patient's future confidence in the ability to describe her symptoms. Instead, the physician has learned very little, and the patient is no better off than before this exchange. These are the consequences when a physician is narrowly devoted to eliciting disease-related information at the expense of learning about the patient who hosts the disease.

Physician anxiety can also be an obstacle to effective interviewing (and may have played a role in the vignette). Although anxiety on the part of the patient should always be assumed, somehow a clinical encounter is supposed to be a routine and entirely rational interaction for the physician. This is simply not true. Insecurity with the role of a physician, discomfort with sudden access to the bodies of patients, concerns about age and sex differences, and anxiety about exploring certain topics may be perfectly natural at early stages of professional development. The danger arises when such anxieties lead the physician to avoid asking necessary questions or pursuing important leads.

BUT HER EYES SPOKE ANOTHER LANGUAGE

The door opened.
She walked towards the waiting seat.
She sat.
Her hands wrestled in her lap.
She crooked her fingers to conceal the nicotine stains and bitten nails.
She chewed the inner side of her lower lip.
She plucked at the clasp of her handbag.
"I have a cold," she said
but her eyes spoke another language.

"No, no trouble at home."
She flinched before the subtle onslaught.
She danced and weaved through the questions.
She fell.
Tears welled and filled her eyes.
The comforting arm went unnoticed.
The hell she lived erupted from her lips.
She discharged herself and her shoulders crumpled.
She sobbed to a halt and dried her eyes upon a paper handkerchief.
"Thank you," she whispered and left by the back door.

DUNCAN DARBISHIRE

THE SETTING

The setting for an interview can either facilitate or inhibit the spontaneous and open transmission of information. *Privacy, comfort, and sufficient time are three desirable aspects of setting that may be difficult to achieve.* In a hospital setting, privacy is threatened by the presence of roommates and by the intrusions of visitors and other health-care professionals. In a busy outpatient clinic an interview conducted in a cubicle may be hampered by limited privacy, physical discomfort (including extraneous noise), and time limitations. These factors are not completely under the physician's control. However, being aware of their potential to affect the interview, the physician should exercise control when possible. For example, if the interview is being conducted in an austere office with uncomfortable chairs, the physician can briefly acknowledge the problem and at least offer the more comfortable of the two chairs to the patient. If the problem is a noxious level of noise, it may

> The sad truth is that our trillion-dollar medical care system seems to feel that time spent with patients is a luxury it simply can't afford.
>
> FRANK DAVIDOFF
> *Annals of Internal Medicine*

> Touching with the naked ear was one of the great advances in the history of medicine. Once it was learned that the heart and lungs made sounds of their own, and that the sounds were sometimes useful for diagnosis, physicians placed an ear over the heart, and over areas on the front and back of the chest, and listened. It is hard to imagine a friendlier human gesture, a more intimate signal of personal concern and affection, than these close bowed heads affixed to the skin.
>
> LEWIS THOMAS
> *House Calls*

have to be endured, but perhaps the effort to give the patient undivided attention can be doubled and freedom from other intrusions can be provided. Privacy and comfort are important, but the physician can compensate for their absence with a combination of consideration and attentive listening.

A physician's time is valuable. In some practices, financial success is predicated on a policy of limiting office visits to 12 minutes. It is difficult to believe that the needs of patients can be handled adequately when physicians are encouraged to focus on the clock. *However rushed the physician may feel and whatever the reason, he or she must be aware that the sense of time urgency is antithetical to professional obligations.* Patients know when they are being hurried along and can recognize when the practitioner's mind is not entirely on them. Some react with resentment and others react by trying to extricate the physician from the situation. This may take the form of omitting critical symptoms from their statement of the problem, failing to ask questions that could clarify an instruction, or canceling a future appointment out of a genuine, albeit somewhat masochistic, desire not to overburden the physician. None of these reactions is acceptable, and all can be avoided if the Type A impatience and irritability that medical environments often impose is controlled. While the physician is with the patient, full attention and unhurried participation in the interview must be practiced. Having command of the interviewing techniques to be discussed helps make efficient use of the time spent with patients.

The best interview is a collaborative process between two people of equal status, no matter how different their roles. It is better not to sit behind a desk during an interview because the desk imposes a barrier between the participants that is both real and symbolic. Similarly, it is better to sit at the same level as the patient rather than to stand, which makes the patient feel dominated. Finally, interviewing a patient who is unclothed, partially dressed, or dressed in a hospital gown contributes to the patient's sense of unequal status. It is usually best to keep the interview portion of an examination separate from the physical examination as another means of emphasizing equal status. It may sound paradoxical, but *the more a patient perceives himself or herself to be an equal partner in this health-care venture, the more likely he or she will be to accept the physician's influence.* Along these lines, it is useful to recognize that you may be the relative expert in terms of medicine, but patients are the experts on their lives.

THE SEGUE FRAMEWORK: INTEGRATING COMMUNICATION AND CLINICAL TASKS

At this point, it is important to provide a very tangible sense of how effective communication can be integrated into clinical work. The SEGUE Framework, a research-based checklist developed by one of us (GM), has become the most widely used model for teaching and assessing communication skills in North America. In addition to serving as a reminder of the general areas on which to focus (i.e., Set the Stage, Elicit Information, Give Information, Understand the Patient's Perspective, End the Encounter), the SEGUE acronym connotes the transition or flow of the medical encounter: from beginning to end, and from problems to solutions. The SEGUE Framework provides a common vocabulary for teaching, learning, assessing, and studying communication in medical encounters.

The checklist highlights a set of essential communication tasks (i.e., things that are important to do during a medical encounter). Since the tasks themselves can be accomplished in a variety of ways, it is important to develop a repertoire of communication skills and strategies that will work for you and your patients. This built-in flexibility with respect to the skills and strategies required to accomplish relevant tasks reflects the reality and individuality of human communication. In other words, *SEGUE offers a flexible framework, not a script.* While things might not progress in the order presented, the brief explanations and examples offered below are intended to provide a better understanding of each SEGUE task.

Set the Stage (S)

1. Greet the patient appropriately.

The key is to decide upfront what "appropriately" means, and then stick to that definition. Here are examples of the criteria for this task:

If you and the patient have not met

You should confirm (i.e., ask or say) the patient's name and introduce yourself using your first and last name. For instance, if Dr. Robert Franklin is meeting Ms. Jane Smith, it is often better to walk into the room and say: "Jane Smith? Hi, I'm Dr. Bob Franklin," rather than assuming that she prefers to be called Jane. A medical student or resident should provide both his/her name and role (e.g., "I'm Ellie Brown, a first-year medical student working with Dr. Franklin.").

If you and the patient have met previously

You should acknowledge this in greeting ("Hi Ms. Smith; good to see you again" or "I don't know if you remember me from last time; I'm Dr. Janet Jones, a resident working with Dr. Franklin.").

2. Establish the reason for the visit.

You can accomplish this task in a number of ways by asking such questions as: "What brings you in today?," "What can I do for you today?," or "So this is your 6-month recheck?"

3. Outline an agenda for the visit (e.g., issues, sequence).

Oftentimes, the patient has different priorities than you do. *The key to this task is to ask the patient if there is anything he or she would like to discuss beyond the stated reason for the visit* ("Anything else?"). This negotiation should occur before you begin exploring specific issues in detail. Providing an outline of how the encounter will flow is also helpful. Outlining an agenda lets both parties know that their issues will be addressed.

4. Make a personal connection during visit (e.g., go beyond medical issues at hand).

This task focuses on treating/acknowledging the patient as a person. While it is probably best if this happens early in the visit, it can occur at anytime during the visit, as long as it is sincere. This is something patients notice, and appreciate. Example:

Patient: "I'm in college"
Doctor: "Oh, what are you studying?"

→ *5. Maintain the patient's privacy (e.g., knock, close door).*

Self-explanatory: If there is no door, you can maintain the patient's privacy by standing or sitting nearby. This is also a consideration in physical exam situations (e.g., draping).

Elicit Information (E)

6. Elicit the patient's view of health problem and/or progress.

Since patients have their own ideas about health and their own hypotheses about what might be causing and/or exacerbating a health problem, it is important to elicit their perspectives.

You can accomplish this task by asking the patient an open-ended question such as "Can you tell me how you're doing?," "How have things been going?," or "How are you doing now that you've started the treatment?" The patient's ideas, worries, and concerns can often be elicited if you remain silent after asking the "What brought you in today?" question.

7. Explore physical/physiological factors.

You can accomplish this task by asking about signs or symptoms regarding the health problem (e.g., duration, location, intensity, etc.).

8. Explore psychosocial/emotional factors (e.g., living situation, family relations, stress, work).

The key here is learning about relevant factors in the patient's life that might influence his or her health problem and health status.

9. Discuss antecedent treatments (e.g., self-care, last visit, other medical care).

The point of this task is to find out what the patient has done for the health problem before coming to see you for this visit.

10. Discuss how the health problem affects the patient's life (e.g., quality of life).

Quality of life is subjective and is best assessed by discussion. Here, instead of exploring how the patient's life affects the health problem, you are trying to learn how the health problem affects the patient's life. This task can be accomplished by asking general questions like "How has the problem affected your life?," "How has this affected your daily life?," "Tell me about a typical day," "Is this preventing you from doing things you like to do?," or more specific questions (e.g., about activities of daily living).

11. Discuss lifestyle issues/prevention strategies (e.g., health risks)

The idea here is that you identify health risks, as well as the extent to which the patient is managing them. Diet, exercise, alcohol or drug use, smoking, and safe sex are examples of the topics that could be discussed. This task is often facilitated when you provide the patient with a preface such as "I'm going to ask some questions to get a better picture of your overall health."

→ 12. *Avoid directive/leading questions.*

"You're not having chest pain, are you?" is an example of a directive, or leading, question. This kind of question sometimes sounds like a statement ("No problems with your chest?"). *The problem with these questions is that they put words in the patient's mouth, and it is often very difficult for patients to correct their provider.* Similarly, if a physician asks a directive question about an uncomfortable topic (e.g., "So, no drugs?"), patients might take the opportunity to let the topic slide. Directive/leading questions are distinct from closed-ended questions like "When did it start?," "Is the pain sharp, dull, burning, squeezing, or does it feel like something else?" that are very helpful when asked at appropriate junctures.

→ 13. *Give the patient the opportunity/time to talk (e.g., don't interrupt).*

We are all familiar with explicit interruptions and their effect on conversations. It is also important that you avoid "jumping" on the patient's last word, which sometimes cuts patients off before they are really finished talking. If patients go off on a tangent, try to let them know that you are interested, but need to focus on their main concerns.

→ 14. *Listen. Give the patient your undivided attention (e.g., face patient, give feedback).*

As Sir William Osler said about 100 years ago: "Listen to the patient, for he [or she] is telling you the diagnosis." Facing the patient, giving verbal acknowledgment, and providing nonverbal feedback (e.g., nodding, "uh huh") are examples of ways you can show you are paying attention.

Patients notice, and tend to become less forthcoming, when a clinician is not facing them, rarely looks up from taking notes, is reading the chart while the patient is talking, or is otherwise distracted from what the patient is saying.

→ 15. *Check/clarify information (e.g., recap, ask "How much is not much?").*

At issue here is the accuracy of information. Checking means that you recap what the patient has said to ensure that you interpreted it correctly ("OK, so swelling tends to be worse in the morning, is that right?"). Clarifying means

that you ask the patient to be more specific about vague information. Example:

Doctor: "How much do you smoke?"
Patient: "Not much."
Doctor: "How much is not much?"

Give Information (G)

16. *Explain the rationale for diagnostic procedures (e.g., exam, tests).*

You should let the patient know why you are conducting procedures. Examples include: "I'm going to listen to your lungs" before using a stethoscope, "Let's check the range of motion in your leg" before moving a patient's leg, and "I think we should check for strep" before swabbing the patient's throat.

17. *Teach patient about his or her own body and situation (e.g., provide feedback and explanations).*

The medical encounter provides an excellent opportunity for giving information that can help the patient learn about his or her body or situation. You can accomplish this task by telling the patient what you found in a physical exam ("You seem a bit weaker on this side") or laboratory test ("Your strep test came back negative—that means you don't have strep throat"). You can also accomplish this task by explaining relevant anatomy ("The rotator cuff is really a set of muscles ..."), the diagnosis ("It looks like you're having tension headaches—they're often related to stress and it sounds as if your new job is pretty stressful ..."), or treatment ("This kind of antibiotic works on a wide variety of bacteria, but has a few side-effects ...").

18. *Encourage patient to ask questions/Check his or her understanding.*

It is useful to actively solicit questions from the patient ("Do you have any questions?," "Is that clear?," or "Does that make sense?"). This is a very effective way to check the patient's understanding. NOTE: Asking "Is there anything else?" is *not* the same as encouraging the patient to ask questions.

→ 19. *Adapt to patient's level of understanding (e.g., avoid or explain jargon).*

Self-explanatory: There is no need to say "ambulate" when you mean "walk."

Understand the Patient's Perspective (U)

20. Acknowledge the patient's accomplishments/progress/challenges.

At issue here is whether or not you respond to a patient's overt statement about something perceived as very positive or very difficult, or to an expression of emotion. Your response (or lack thereof) very clearly suggests to the patient the degree to which you are listening and the extent to which you care.

21. Acknowledge waiting time.

If the patient has been waiting (or will have to wait) for a long period of time, you can accomplish this task by letting the patient know that you are aware of the wait.

→ *22. Express caring, concern, empathy.*

The focus here is on attention to the patient's subjective experience. You can accomplish this task by letting the patient know that you understand—or at least appreciate—the patient's perspective. This can be accomplished either verbally or nonverbally; the key is to respond. Patients tend to become less forthcoming when you appear detached, aloof, or overly businesslike.

→ *23. Maintain a respectful tone.*

Whether or not you agree with or like the patient, it is most inappropriate and unprofessional to be condescending, patronizing, or rude.

End the Encounter (E)

24. Ask if there is anything else patient would like to discuss.

Sometimes patients feel they need permission to bring up issues beyond the "chief concern" or the main reason they've been hospitalized. Even if you do this as part of outlining the agenda toward the beginning of the encounter, you should explicitly ask the patient about this at the end of the encounter as well. In order for the patient to feel that it is actually permissible to raise another issue, you should ask this question before getting up to leave. If time is a factor—and it often is—you can always suggest discussing new issues that come up in a subsequent visit.

25. Review next steps with patient.

You can accomplish this task by saying either what you will do for the patient *or* what the patient should do once the visit is over. Examples include:

"I will check on the test results for you."

"Please make an appointment to come back in 6 months."
"You can get dressed now."
"The nurse will be in to show you how to do that."
"Don't forget to pick up your prescription at the pharmacy."

If You Suggested a New or Modified Treatment/Prevention Plan

26. Discuss the patient's interest/expectation/goal for the plan.

Does the patient see and/or agree with the need for this plan?

27. Involve the patient in deciding upon a plan (e.g., options, rationale, values, preferences, concerns).

Not all patients want to be involved in decision making, but all should be involved to the extent they are comfortable. In addition to providing options and discussing rationale, it is especially important to explore the patient's values, preferences, and concerns.

28. Explain likely benefits of the option(s) discussed.

Do the specific benefits relate to the goal for this plan?

29. Explain likely side-effects and risks of the option(s) discussed.

In addition to providing the information, let the patient know what to do if he or she experiences a problem.

30. Provide complete instructions for the plan.

Make sure that the patient understands your instructions.

31. Discuss the patient's ability to follow the plan (e.g., attitude, time, resources).

This is an essential, and often neglected, component of the process. A patient is unlikely to follow—or even start—a treatment plan unless he or she thinks it is do-able. At the same time, many patients are unlikely to spontaneously offer their views on this subject.

32. Discuss the importance of the patient's role in treatment/prevention.

It certainly helps if patients understand that they are partners in the process. Talk about what they can do to facilitate improvement (e.g., monitoring details of their situation and letting you know how things progress).

The SEGUE Framework

Patient: _____   Physician or Student: _____

Set the Stage		Yes	No
1.	Greet patient appropriately		
2.	Establish reason for visit:		
3.	Outline agenda for visit (e.g., "anything else?," issues, sequence)		
4.	Make a personal connection during visit (e.g., go beyond medical issues at hand)		
→ 5.	Maintain patient's privacy (e.g., close door)		

Elicit Information		n/a	Yes	No
6.	Elicit patient's view of health problem and/or progress			
7.	Explore physical/physiological factors			
8.	Explore psychosocial/emotional factors (e.g., living situation, family relations, stress)			
9.	Discuss antecedent treatments (e.g., self-care, last visit, other medical care)			
10.	Discuss how health problem affects patient's life (e.g., quality-of-life)			
11.	Discuss lifestyle issues/prevention strategies (e.g., health risks)			
→ 12.	Avoid directive/leading questions			
→ 13.	Give patient opportunity/time to talk (e.g., don't interrupt)			
→ 14.	Listen. Give patient undivided attention (e.g., face patient, verbal acknowledgement, nonverbal feedback)			
→ 15.	Check/clarify information (e.g., recap, ask "how much")			

Give Information		n/a	Yes	No
16.	Explain rationale for diagnostic procedures (e.g., exam, tests)			
17.	Teach patient about his/her own body & situation (e.g., provide feedback from exam/tests, explain rationale, anatomy/diagnosis)			
18.	Encourage patient to ask questions/Check understanding			
→ 19.	Adapt to patient's level of understanding (e.g., avoid/explain jargon)			

The SEGUE Framework continued

Understand the Patient's Perspective	n/a	Yes	No
20. Acknowledge patient's accomplishments/progress/challenges			
21. Acknowledge waiting time			
→ 22. Express caring, concern, empathy			
→ 23. Maintain a respectful tone			

End the Encounter	Yes	No
24. Ask if there is anything else patient would like to discuss		
25. Review next steps with patient		

If suggested a new or modified treatment/prevention plan:	n/a	Yes	No
26. Discuss patient's expectation/goal for treatment/prevention			
27. Involve patient in deciding upon a plan (e.g., options, rationale, values, preferences, concerns)			
28. Explain likely benefits of the option(s) discussed			
29. Explain likely side-effects and risks of the option(s) discussed			
30. Provide complete instructions for plan			
31. Discuss patient's ability to follow plan			
32. Discuss importance of patient's role in treatment/prevention			

Comments:

Items without an arrow focus on *content*; mark "Yes" if done *at least one time* during the encounter.

Items with an arrow (→) focus on *process* and should be maintained throughout the encounter; mark "No" if at least one relevant instance when not done (e.g., just one use of jargon).

SHARING INFORMATION

A primary purpose of the clinical interview is to share information, an activity that takes two forms: (1) eliciting information from patients to diagnose their condition and understand them, and (2) providing patients with information such as diagnoses, prognoses, prescriptions, and treatment recommendations. The interview also helps establish a positive relationship with the patient that can be the foundation of the eventual therapeutic relationship.

Information about patient symptoms is necessary before a diagnosis is made, but it is not sufficient for effective treatment. *A broader aim of the interview is to understand the patient more fully and to develop hypotheses about personality, life experiences, assets and liabilities, and reactions to illness.* If a physician cannot anticipate that a patient will have difficulty adhering to a treatment regimen or will be at risk to develop psychiatric complications, an accurate diagnosis by itself hardly guarantees successful treatment.

A physician seeking diagnostic and psychosocial information from a patient should make every effort to elicit information that is as *full-bodied* and *spontaneous* as pos-

> Doctors don't get paid for talking to patients. In a medical economy dominated by third-party paymasters—insurance companies, the government, health plans, etc.—the harsh reality is that doctors get paid mostly for tests and procedures. It is not surprising, therefore, that patients should be subjected to a multitude of encounters with expensive medical technology, not all of which is essential or without risk ... Even more serious, of course, is the reduced time for the careful questioning by the physician that has held such a high place in medical tradition.
>
> NORMAN COUSINS
> *Head First: The Biology of Hope*

sible. Patient descriptions that are full-bodied have a live and organic quality to them that is unmistakable. The physician can sense the effort that has gone into making the description accurate and elaborate. Patient descriptions that lack this quality tend to be brief, flat, unidimensional, and stereotyped, and they make it more difficult to diagnose the condition or understand the patient. Similarly, spontaneity in patient verbalizations indicates that the patient is speaking freely, without hesitancy and without editing his or her remarks. This is the ideal to which an interviewer should aspire because it means that the broadest range of information is being elicited. Patients who edit their responses to inquiries are withholding information and depriving the physician of the opportunity to do what he or she is trained to do—to separate essential from irrelevant details. The creation of such full-bodied and spontaneously offered information is a joint product of the physician and the patient. It may be impossible to change a patient's innate descriptive abilities, but it should also be evident that *how questions are posed and how the physician listens profoundly influence the quality of the information the patient provides.* Information giving is the second way in which information is shared during a clinical interview; it will be considered in more detail later in this chapter.

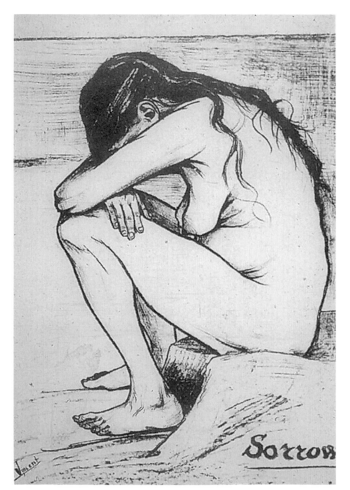

Sorrow *Vincent van Gogh (1882).* Drawing, 38.5 × 29 cm. van Gogh Museum Foundation, Amsterdam.

INTERVIEWING TECHNIQUES: FOCUS ON ELICITING INFORMATION

The interviewing techniques discussed in this section form a continuum of interviewer control. At one end of the spectrum is the use of silence, which imposes minimal interviewer control over the patient and affords the patient a wide range of response alternatives. At the other end of the spectrum is the kind of direct question that affords the patient the opportunity to answer only yes or no. *Both of these techniques have their place in the clinical interview* (although not at the beginning), along with facilitation, confrontation, and a variety of other clinical tools. Because the physician is seeking a full-bodied and spontaneous account of the patient's difficulties, the best use of these techniques often involves moving through a cycle of information seeking that begins with modest control and proceeds to progressively greater use of authority. Whichever technique you choose, the key to successful interviewing lies in remembering to *listen* to the information elicited.

Open-Ended Questions

Starting the interview with questions such as "What brings you in today?," "How are you?," "How can I help you?" and "What kind of problems have you been having?" communicate to the patient that he or she can begin anywhere, without restriction. They also put the momentary burden of responsibility on the patient (which is perfectly appropriate), and they minimize bias. To begin an interview with more specific or direct questions ("Tell me about your headaches.") restricts the field of discourse prematurely and may suggest to the patient that other topics are inappropriate or not medically relevant.

Starting an interview with an open-ended question facilitates the diagnostic process because the answer that the patient chooses to give in response to the open-ended question has a special significance. However, two observational studies indicate that few physicians give patients the opportunity to make a complete opening statement of their concern. In only about 25% of office visits studied did physicians allow patients to complete their opening statement. *Most of the time, physicians interrupted and redirected patients to discuss the first concern expressed.* As the authors of one of these studies noted, physicians "frequently and perhaps unwittingly inhibit or interrupt their patients' initial expression of concerns."

Medical students sometimes justify their avoidance of open-ended questions by claiming they take up too much time. (Presumably the students are referring not to the questions themselves but to the time patients take to answer them.) This is a rationalization based on a misunderstanding of interviewing technique and purpose. An interview that employs open-ended questions is using those questions to elicit a free flow of information in the service of making a diagnosis and understanding the patient. It is the interviewer's responsibility to guide the patient's discourse if needed. Open-ended questions are recommended because they are often the most efficient means to this end. However, physicians should not think of an open-ended interview as one that employs open-ended questions exclusively.

Students and physicians sometimes come away from an interview in which they used open-ended questions but were not impressed with their yield. However, *an open-ended question does not guarantee an elaborate answer; it merely increases its likelihood.* Children, adolescents, and even some adults may not be able to respond to such questions with elaborate accounts. For example, some very literal minded patients (as well as those with organic mental disorders) respond to a question such as "What brought you to the clinic?" with an answer such as "I drove my Toyota." Physicians should not be discouraged by their early efforts to use a new skill and should not be seduced into asking only direct questions when some open-ended questions fail.

Silence

If a patient responds to an open-ended inquiry with a minimal response, consider using silence to signal that you want to hear more. Silence imposes minimal control on the patient. It communicates to the tight-lipped patient that the physician wants to hear more and is willing to wait. Sometimes patients are guarded in responding to open-ended questions simply because they imagine that a brief response is required or because that has been their experience with physicians in the past. An expectant and attentive silence on the part of the interviewer is often all that is needed to get the patient to elaborate on his or her problems.

When a patient is talking in a full-bodied and spontaneous way, silence is the most appropriate response. When the patient becomes silent, a brief silence on the interviewer's part is again appropriate, because the patient may have stopped speaking to collect his or her thoughts or to find the right word to describe a concern. Interruptions or interjections would likely be premature. The patient whose pause signals the end of a train of thought often turns his or her gaze on the physician, indicating a willingness to give him or her a chance to speak. Whether the physician decides to do so or remain silent depends on his or her assessment of the situation. Early in the interview, the physician may deem it essential to pursue what the patient said. Or the physician may decide that he or she wishes to give the patient more time to talk. Silences are less likely later in the interview after a full account of the patient's difficulties has been gathered. At such times, the physician may more confidently proceed with direct questions with very specific aims.

When a patient is overwhelmed with emotion, often the best thing to do is to remain silent. To say something at such a juncture is to run the risk of inhibiting the expression of the emotion that is almost always therapeutic or cathartic. To say nothing, to simply *be* with the patient while he or she weeps, for example, gives the patient control over how much or how little emotion to display.

In certain situations the use of silence is not advised. Patients with neurological disorders, for example, often need a fair amount of structure to permit them to respond adequately and may become confused and disoriented if silence is used where guidance is needed. Adolescents may be intolerant of ambiguity for other reasons and find an interviewer's silence discomforting. Occasionally a patient is overly talkative, although paradoxically such patients never seem to be very informative. Here is a clear case in which silent indulgence of the patient does little good, and the physician may have to interrupt the patient to gain control of the interview and guide it in more meaningful directions.

Facilitation

"Encouraging communication by manner, gesture, or words that do not specify the kind of information sought is called facilitation" (Enelow & Swisher, 1986). Facilitation involves slightly more control than silence and subsumes a wide variety of interventions that require little expenditure of energy on the part of the interviewer. *Despite their seeming simplicity, facilitating techniques play a powerful role in both eliciting information and guiding the interview to desired topics.* An attentive facial expression, a raised eyebrow, a shrug of the shoulders, and a nod all are mannerisms or gestures that can encourage a patient to continue with his or her associations. The physician does not speak a word, yet the patient knows that the interviewer is interested in what is being said and is curious to hear more. Words such as "yes," "okay," "go on," and "I see" serve essentially the same function, as does the utterance "mmm-hhh." Such vocalizations serve as reinforcers and increase the probability that the patient will talk more freely about the subject that has been reinforced in this way. However, interviewers must guard against employing such easy-to-use and potent techniques mechanically or in stereotyped ways that may have the unintended effect of distracting and inhibiting the patient. Listening to interviews on audiotape and watching them on videotape provide safeguards against abuse of these techniques.

Another set of facilitating techniques that involves a bit more control on the interviewer's part is any intervention, verbal or nonverbal, that conveys to the patient that "I don't understand" or "I am puzzled by what you are telling me." This communication can be made directly or indirectly, for example, via a quizzical look.

A very *powerful facilitating technique, if used appropriately and in moderation, involves the judicious repetition of key words spoken by the patient.* Words condense and summarize patient experiences. They can sometimes be taken at face value; in other situations they need to be explored in greater depth for what they connote. An economical and effective way of inviting patients to elaborate on the meaning of their words is simply to repeat words that are of interest, with a slight interrogative vocal inflection.

The following are the responses of three physicians with a patient whose initial complaint is expressed by the words, "My head is killing me." Physician A asks, "Have you had headaches before?" This is a reasonable question, but it is likely that the answer will emerge naturally if the patient is given the opportunity to give an account of his or her difficulties without physician interference. By asking this question at this time, the physician is interrupting the patient's flow of ideas and narrowing the range of response alternatives.

Physician B responds by saying, "Tell me more about how your head is killing you." This is a legitimate request, but it is 10 words long and may be too formal and professional sounding to facilitate good rapport.

Physician C responds by noticing the violent imagery in the patient's brief description of her headache. She decides that such an emotion-filled word deserves to be articulated at greater length (**"unpacked"**), and she replies, "Killing you?" This imposes only modest control over the patient's next response and follows the patient's lead as closely as possible. It increases the probability that the patient's responses will provide a fuller account of this symptom, one that spontaneously includes the information about site, onset, duration, and history that any physician desires. It may also elicit significant material concerning the patient's fears and fantasies regarding what is wrong, fears legitimately assumed to exist if the patient's description is taken at face value.

Two additional facilitating remarks are "How do you mean?" and "How so?" They serve the same function as the repetition of key words and phrases, can be used in the same situations, and put a little more variety into the interviewing repertoire. Variety is important because as soon as a patient becomes conscious that the physician is employing these techniques, the interview suffers.

> If your news must be bad, tell it soberly and promptly.
>
> SIR HENRY HOWARTH BASHFORD
> *The Corner of Harley Street*

Confrontation

Confrontation involves pointing out to patients aspects of their behavior of which they were unaware. It represents a moderately high degree of control on the part of the interviewer. *It is a technique to be used sparingly.*

Confrontation can be appropriate in several circumstances. If a patient continues to offer only brief, unelaborated responses to open-ended questions, silences, and facilitations, and if this seems related to some distress that the patient is experiencing, a comment along the lines of "You seem uncomfortable talking about this" makes the patient aware that the discomfort has been noted and somewhat lengthier responses are expected. The comment is made in the form of an observation by the interviewer. This allows the patient more latitude in responding. By using the tentative phrase "you seem," rather than the more presumptuous "you are," the interviewer avoids coming across as all knowing and can retreat from the observation more gracefully if it proves to be wrong.

Once the confrontation has been made, the patient can either admit or deny it. If the confrontation is acknowledged, the patient can proceed to elaborate on the nature of the difficulty. A patient might say, for example, "Yes, I am uncomfortable; I really don't know how much detail to go into." Or, "Yes, I am uncomfortable; I haven't told you something that I think you need to know." Whatever the reason for the patient's reticence, confrontations of this sort help to clear the air and set the stage for the resumption of more open discussion. Should the patient be genuinely confused by the confrontation, he or she can simply ask for clarification. If this happens, the interviewer should describe the patient behaviors that led to the inference of patient discomfort to clarify the situation and promote greater understanding, and the patient can easily deny the observation if he or she desires. The observation may be correct, but the patient does not trust the interviewer sufficiently to admit such private concerns. Even in this case, the fact that the interviewer made the appropriate inquiry, used the appropriate technique, and did not insist on a certain answer signals to the patient that this is an observant physician interested in removing obstacles to a better physician-patient relationship and not afraid to tread (gently) into potentially delicate areas. This augurs well for the future of the relationship.

Other circumstances in which confrontation is useful occur when a disparity is observed in different aspects of the patient's behavior. For example, the disparity may be a contradiction between two of the patient's remarks, and the confrontation could take the following form: "You say your foot doesn't bother you, but just a moment ago you said you can't put any weight on it." Notice how gentle such a confrontation can be. It is not accusatory; the physician is simply juxtaposing two of the patient's statements. *Implicit in this statement is the same exhortation that underlies all the other interventions just discussed: "Tell me more."* The only difference is that in the case of confrontation, the interviewer is exerting more control over the nature of the material to be elicited.

Often the disparity to be confronted is between what the patient says and does. A patient may blandly discuss suicidal thoughts or may discuss the most seemingly insignificant matters with great trepidation. These discrepancies between verbal and nonverbal aspects of behavior must be investigated. The physician might confront the suicidal patient by saying, "You seem so nonchalant." To the nervous patient, the physician might say, "You're shaking" or "I hear such fear in your voice." Many other situations exist in which the patient's nonverbal behavior communicates something that is not being addressed. Confrontation gives the patient both permission and the opportunity to express emotions verbally.

Direct Questions

The highest level of control among all the interviewing techniques is found in closed, or direct, questions. An entreaty phrased as "Tell me how you're doing" is broader in focus and less controlling than "Tell me what is wrong," which, in turn, is broader in focus than "Tell me when the nausea began." For some patients and in some situations, interviewers may have to rely more heavily on direct questions. A question such as "How would you describe the pain?" may yield only an equivocal response. In this case it would be appropriate to give the patient a question with a multiple-choice format: "It is a burning, aching, or pricking type of pain?" Direct questions are very helpful when used appropriately: they serve to fill in missing details, tie up loose ends, and sharpen the focus of the interview. They are also associated with a number of potential pitfalls.

One problem is the possibility that *a direct question can bias the patient's answer through the inadvertent use of an emotion-laden word or through poor phrasing.* For example, asking patients if they have a history of mental illness has a more pejorative quality than asking if they have ever seen a mental health professional (and following an affirmative response with a request for more detailed information). Asking married patients whether they have had any affairs is judgmental and may evoke a less honest answer than a question about other sexual partners. Similarly, asking about "illicit drugs" or "illegal drugs" is unlikely to yield an honest response; it is more appropriate to ask about "any drugs like marijuana or cocaine, that sort of thing." Similarly, it is often difficult for patients to provide honest answers to a common form of direct questions—leading questions—such as "So, no drugs?" or "You're not having chest pain, are you?" either because patients are reluctant to correct the physician or might prefer not to discuss the topic at all.

The other major problem with direct questions is the chilling effect they can have on patient spontaneity. The following exchange demonstrates how the excessive use of direct questions deprives the patient of the chance to develop a more full-bodied account of her problem:

Doctor: What sorts of troubles have you been having?
Patient: I've been going downhill for 2 years. Nothing seems to be working right.
Doctor: What is the worst part?

Patient: My legs. I have constant pain in my legs. It's got-
            ten so bad I can't sleep.
Doctor: What about your breathing?
Patient: Oh, that's all right. I can breathe fine. I just hurt
            so bad in my legs.
Doctor: Are you still smoking?
Patient: Yes, with this pain I've gone back to cigarettes for
            relief. But I'm down to half a pack or so a day.
Doctor: Are you having pains in your chest?
Patient: No.
Doctor: How about cough?
Patient: No, I hardly ever cough.
Doctor: How much are you actually able to do?
Patient: Well, I was able to do everything until about 2
            years ago, but now I can hardly walk half a block.
Doctor: Why is that?
Patient: My legs. They hurt.
Doctor: Do they swell up?
Patient: Well, they've been a bit swollen the last 2 or 3
            weeks but the pain is there whether they swell or
            not.
Doctor: All right, I want to ask you some things about
            your medical history now. (Platt & McMath,
            1979)

The physician's first question is fairly open ended. By following up with "What is the worst part?" he allows the patient an opportunity to describe the chief complaint. But
his next four comments are all symptom-oriented questions imposed on the patient. They do not follow the patient's lead. She clearly wants to discuss her legs, and he
clearly has an agenda of his own. By the end of this exchange he still knows little about her leg pain and is forced
to endure a second round of description of the leg pain that
is no more detailed than the first round. (Compare "I have
constant pain in my legs" with "My legs. They hurt," six
responses later.) The physician is working hard, but this
interview has not gone anywhere. This encounter is an example of an interview style known as **high physician con-
trol-low patient control**. *According to empirical research this
style is highly prevalent in clinical settings.* During such interviews the physician tends to talk more and the patient
less as time goes on. This is in direct contradiction to good
interviewing technique. After the preceding interview, the
physician described the patient as "not wanting to talk." In
fact, the interviewer's use of direct questions to control and
limit the interview had forced her to this point.

Direct questions are an absolutely essential component
of a clinical interview: Physicians and other health-care
professionals cannot do without them. The problem is that
they are easily misused and frequently used to the exclusion
of other techniques that do a better job of eliciting unbiased information and developing a sense of productive collaboration.

> The doctor may also learn more about the illness from the way the
> patient tells the story than from the story itself.
>
> JAMES B. HERRICK, M.D.
> *Memoirs of Eighty Years*

STRATEGIES FOR GIVING INFORMATION: FOCUS ON CHECKING UNDERSTANDING

Physicians approach the interview with a primary interest
in gathering information. Patients have a slightly different
interest: they want to know what the physician thinks
about their complaint and what course of treatment will
be recommended. They want an explanation of their illness
and a statement about the benefits and risks of treatment.
*More often than not, patients leave the interview disappoin-
ted with the information received.* In the best study available
on this topic, physicians spent little more than 1 minute
(on average) of a 20-minute interview giving information.
Yet they perceived themselves to spend more than 9 minutes informing their patients. This is a gross distortion of
what actually takes place, and *this misperception is a major
factor in both patient dissatisfaction with physicians and poor
patient adherence to treatment regimens.* The problem was
particularly acute when the patient was poorly educated or
from a lower-class background, when the physician had a
busy practice (defined as more than 20 outpatients per
day), and when the physician was from a lower-middle-
class or lower-class background. Male patients tended to
receive less attention and fewer explanations than female
patients, perhaps because female patients ask more questions and are more verbally active during an interview.

Even if the amount of time spent in explanations and
other forms of information giving were increased, the
problem of the quality of the information given would remain. *Instructions should be as simple, brief, and jargon-free
as possible.* Telling a patient to take medication on an as-
needed basis is not a good idea. Even telling a patient to
take medication every 6 hours is subject to misunderstanding, unless it is made clear that the patient should take it
four times through the day and night.

It can be difficult to anticipate all the potential misunderstandings that can occur when an already anxious patient is
trying to assimilate your instructions. One colleague interviewed a longshoreman who had sought treatment at a clinic for patients with chronic pain. As he told his story about
his earlier experiences with physicians, he suddenly began to
cry. It seems that he had been told, 3 months earlier, that he
had degenerative arthritis, and he had been depressed ever
since. For this man, degenerative arthritis meant that his
spinal cord was degenerating, or crumbling, and that he

would soon be totally disabled, unable to walk, work, or support his family. His anguish could have been avoided if his physician had taken the time to explain the meaning of this diagnosis in terms that the patient could readily understand, and checked to make sure he understood.

Hospitalized patients are often particularly deprived of information concerning their condition and future treatment. This only imposes additional uncertainty in a situation that is already stressful and anxiety provoking. Several years ago, one of us (PBZ) was at the bedside of a cancer patient who was complaining about how his physicians were keeping him in the dark about their plans for him. As we spoke, the surgical resident entered, introduced himself, and announced that the patient would have surgery in the morning. He then turned and left the room. Such conduct is not only unprofessional, it is countertherapeutic.

Studies that compare the medical outcomes of patients with and without adequate information about their treatment frequently show that *provision of information is advantageous for both the physician and the patient.* In one such study, anesthesiologists visited patients in the experimental group preoperatively to describe what the patients would experience when they awoke after surgery. The physicians indicated that the patients would experience pain, told them where it would hurt, and how it would feel, emphasized that this was normal and would be self-limiting, and urged the patients to ask for analgesics if the pain became too great. When compared with a control group, these patients were judged ready for discharge 2.7 days earlier and made 50% *fewer* requests for pain medication.

Patients almost invariably have a different frame-of-reference than that of their physicians. Moreover, there is a limit to the amount and complexity of information that humans can absorb in a short time span. Accordingly, checking understanding of explanations and recommendations is absolutely essential. We recommend the following technique to ensure that each patient has heard what was intended. *After an explanation or recommendation, ask the patient to repeat what has just been said in his or her own words, not verbatim.* Physicians will be surprised at what they hear and at the frequency with which explanations and instructions are distorted and misconstrued. More importantly, this exercise gives the opportunity to correct any misunderstandings and to clarify any earlier ambiguities. In addition, physicians can be more secure in the knowledge that patients understand the medical advice on their own terms.

HANDLING PATIENT EMOTIONS

Illness is frequently accompanied by negative psychological states. When patients are anxious, angry, or depressed, it can be difficult to elicit a full and spontaneous account of their difficulties. On many occasions the patient's psychological state *is* the primary problem. The ability to handle such situations smoothly and therapeutically takes time and practice, but a number of general guidelines can be considered.

Anxiety

If a patient is fidgety, restless, or easily startled, seems nervous, or has a tremor in his or her voice, the patient may be anxious. Proceeding with the interview may be difficult until the anxiety is discussed. The technique of confrontation is most useful in these circumstances, with the physician simply saying to the patient, "You seem upset," or nervous, or whatever descriptor is most appropriate. Usually the patient seizes on this opportunity to speak about his or her anxiety. This sharing helps diminish anxiety and restore the alliance between physician and patient.

Some patients may be chronically anxious, but many others may be anxious as a function of the situation in which they find themselves. For some, the prospect of submitting to a physical examination with a relative stranger is anxiety arousing. For others, the passivity and loss of independence associated with being ill (and hospitalized) can be threatening. For still others, anxiety may be associated with earlier, unpleasant experiences with a physician or a procedure. In any of these instances, and in any other instance of patient anxiety, the prescription is the same: the physician's responsibility is to elicit the source of the patient's concern, understand it, and take appropriate measures to diminish it.

We spoke of diminishing and not eliminating the patient's anxiety. Anxiety cannot be completely eliminated, and its elimination is not necessary for a successful interview. Once anxiety has diminished to a point at which the interview can proceed, the interviewer can conclude that he or she has handled the problem satisfactorily. With a patient who is anxious about being exposed during a physical examination, it might be best, once the nature of the anxiety has been established, simply to defer the physical examination until better rapport has been achieved with the patient. With a highly active patient, threatened by the enforced passivity and dependency of illness, the physician might acknowledge the discomfort that the situation entails, review why it is necessary, and promise to take the necessary steps to increase the patient's activity and sense of personal control. With a patient who anticipates an unpleasant procedure, accurate information is often enough to reduce anxiety. If the procedure is a painful one, and if anxiety is so high as to threaten patient participation, hypnosis, modeling, or medication might be helpful. In refractory cases, referral to a psychologist or psychiatrist may be necessary.

Anxiety often presents itself in subtle ways. For example, patient questions may actually be veiled expressions of anxiety. *When a middle-aged patient asks a resident how old he or she is, it is fairly certain that the patient doubts that someone so young, and presumably inexperienced, can be helpful.* When a mother of five beset by her children's behavioral problems asks a student on a pediatric rotation if he or she has children of his or her own, we can assume again that the question is not being asked out of idle curiosity. In ordinary social conversation it is considered rude not to answer a direct question. However, in a clinical context, to take such a question at face value and to answer it immediately and directly is to fail to address the underlying concern of the patient.

Such expressions of anxiety and concern masquerading as direct questions take many different forms. "Should I marry my girlfriend?" "Is a 20-pound weight loss anything to be concerned about?" "Should I accept chemotherapy?" "Can jogging cause a heart attack?" These may be perfectly legitimate questions, and they may even be within the expertise of a physician. But it is never appropriate simply to give an affirmative or negative answer and leave it at that. Instead, the clinician's responsibility is to clarify the precise nature of the question and, if appropriate, to provide the information needed by the patient to make an informed decision. For direct questions such as these, a response that puts the responsibility for clarification back on the patient (e.g., "You seem unsure" or "You seem concerned") is the most appropriate first step. Only when it is understood why the patient asks and how the patient intends to use the answer is it proper to respond. Even at this juncture *a distinction should be made between advice and information.* If a 40-year-old woman asks whether she should attempt to have a baby, it is one thing to provide her with information about the risks and something else entirely to advise or direct her in one direction or another.

Another response to patient anxiety that ought to be avoided is the falsely reassuring response that says to the patient that everything will be all right. **Reassurance** that is based on the facts of the case and does not raise unreasonable expectations is a useful way to allay patient anxiety. *Too often, however, reassurance is used to protect the feelings of the physician and does nothing to reassure the patient.* If the patient senses that the clinician's efforts at reassurance are not genuine, the clinician becomes still another person from whom the patient must conceal intimate feelings.

The following vignette demonstrates that responses to a patient that acknowledge his or her concerns and reflect true understanding are the most reassuring responses of all. Imagine how differently this encounter would have been if the physician responded with reassuring platitudes of the "Of course you're not going to die" or "I'm sure you don't have cancer" variety.

Patient: I'm worried about these headaches. I know what headaches can mean.

Doctor: What they mean?
Patient: Brain tumors. Cancer. Deep down I think I'm already convinced I have an inoperable tumor.
Doctor: It must be a frightening thought to live with.
Patient: Well, I've probably lived with it most of my life. My father died of a brain tumor when I was 5.
Doctor: (after a brief silence) And now you're worried that it's your turn.
Patient: Mmm-mmm. Yes and no. I realize I'm jumping the gun. What my father died from was not a hereditary disease. And my symptoms could be the result of a million things. It's just hard not to think like this with my family history. If I were going to bet on what's wrong, I wouldn't really bet on cancer. I'd bet this whole thing is stress related.
Doctor: How so?

Depression

Depressed mood is another common response to physical illness, one expressed in terms of hopelessness, guilt, low self-esteem, and fatigue. Interviews with depressed patients can be laboriously slow and unproductive. Here, too, confrontation can be a useful technique. Commenting on the slow process of the interview ("You seem to be having trouble keeping pace with me") or on the patient's mood itself ("You seem tired" or "You seem kind of blue") gives the patient a chance to discuss his or her difficulty with the interviewer if he or she so wishes. *Acknowledging that the patient appears to be on the verge of crying ("You look like you're about to cry") effectively grants the patient permission to cry or not to cry and can open the door to important emotional material.*

If the physician is concerned about the magnitude of depressive affect, the patient's **suicide potential** should be assessed. Usually it is best to begin indirectly, asking if the patient feels hopeless, derives any meaning from life, or has ever wished he or she were dead. Broaching the subject in a progressive or gradual fashion is not the same as being evasive. *If the patient senses that the physician is timid about asking about suicidal intent, he or she is more likely to give an evasive answer.* Eventually, if the answers convince the physician that the patient is contemplating suicide, direct inquiry must be made: "Have you thought about taking your life?," "Have you thought about how you would do it?," or "Have you thought about how other people would feel?" *Clear expressions of suicidal intent must always be taken seriously. The more lethal the method contemplated, the easier the patient's access to the method, and the more vivid his or her fantasies about how others would be affected, the greater the risk.* At this point the clinician must be frank with the patient, declaring the intention to plan for the patient's protection and recovery by involving family members and a mental health professional. Patients may object strongly, but as a rule they are grateful that the practitioner has assumed responsibility for the burden of the immediate future.

Anger

If a patient is covertly angry, the appropriate response of the physician is to use the technique of confrontation, just as a physician would respond in the case of the patient's unacknowledged anxiety or depression. One of the authors once interviewed a patient who was giving brief and unelaborate responses to his questions. All the while his face was reddening, his fists were clenched, and his voice was becoming more hostile. It was not difficult to sense his anger, and the interviewer braced himself for his response. It developed that he thought that his interviewer was in his hospital room to give him a spinal tap, and he believed the extensive questions and leisurely pace were part of an effort to delay the inevitable. The patient wanted to get on with the procedure. Had the interviewer not been willing to confront the patient, an altercation would have been likely. This encounter demonstrates the need for an interviewer to clarify the purpose of the interview at the outset as part of his or her introductory remarks.

Perhaps more common in clinical practice is the overtly angry patient for whom the use of confrontation may be redundant. Patients get angry for numerous reasons, but these reasons can be conveniently grouped into two categories. First, a patient may be angry because of something said or not said, or done or not done. The possibilities are legion and include the physician failing to introduce himself or herself, making the patient wait a long time, failing to remember some critical fact about the patient, hurting the patient, making accusatory or moralistic-sounding remarks, withholding information, or failing to allow the patient to think he or she has given a full account of the illness. If the physician is the source of the anger, whether or not by design, no alternative exists other than owning up to this responsibility, taking appropriate remedial measures, and, if necessary, apologizing.

The second possibility is that the patient is the source of the anger and would be angry whether or not the physician did something provocative. *Anger is often a comparatively safe way for a patient to express fear.* Patients are often frightened by their illnesses or by the proposed treatments and may use anger as a means of both discharging and denying such anxiety. In addition, some patients are frightened by the loss of control that assumption of the sick role entails and respond with anger as a means of reasserting their authority. The sensitive clinician learns to listen for the feelings of powerlessness that underlie such overt anger

and does not respond reflexively or in a way that merely engenders the same feelings of powerlessness that made the patient angry at the outset. In addition, the physician must appreciate that *anger is often displaced from another person who has frustrated the patient.* If the receptionist offended the patient or if the patient has been disappointed by physicians in the past, the clinician may well be the innocent recipient of unwarranted hostility.

In each of these cases the natural tendency is to become defensive and want to retaliate. Such responses might be momentarily cathartic but are generally ill advised because they are not in the patient's best interest. The ideal way to handle an angry patient is to make a concerted effort to understand the nature of the anger. If the anger is justified, the acknowledgment of responsibility is often enough to restore the physician-patient alliance to a productive level of functioning. If the anger is not justified by the physician's behavior, accepting the patient's anger and permitting its full expression are cathartic for the patient and give him or her greater insight into its actual source.

REFERRAL TO A PSYCHOTHERAPIST

Making referrals is a neglected but important aspect of patient care, and perhaps the most difficult referral is one to a psychiatrist or another mental health professional. *It is relatively certain that if the physician does nothing but say to the patient that consultation with a psychiatrist is recommended, that recommendation will not be followed.* Most patients find this threatening, and 20% to 40% of patients reject psychotherapy when it is offered. Such referrals are most successful when they are discussed over several sessions, when the physician is able to provide a straightforward and nonthreatening rationale, and when the patient is encouraged to express reservations.

Three common misconceptions about psychotherapy should be routinely addressed whenever the issue of a referral arises. *The first misconception is the notion that only crazy people need to see psychotherapists.* Whether or not the patients voice this concern, it is generally useful for the interviewer to say that he or she does not think they are crazy, does not believe their problems are all in their head, and *does* believe their complaints are real. Then, a nontechnical explanation of the recommendation should be offered: for example, that most illnesses have an emotional component and that even greater concern would be raised if the patient were displaying no psychological effects. Or the physician might say that almost anybody undergoing the same physical difficulties or stresses would be likely to experience psychological symptoms. At any rate, an expression of concern coupled with a statement to the effect that a mental health professional is better equipped to help with the problem ought to make the idea of a referral more palatable.

A second common misconception is the notion that psychotherapy is equal to psychoanalysis. The patient must be assured that referral does not mean a 5 day/week treatment of long duration in which he or she is asked to lie on a couch and free associate to a silent individual sitting out of view. Only a fraction of patients in need of psychotherapy are interested in and suited for this form of treatment.

A third misconception is the idea that the psychiatric referral is being used to get rid of the patient. This misconception is common among chronically ill patients who are especially dependent on their physicians and among patients whose relationships with their physicians have been characterized by disagreement and strain. *Such patients must know that the physician is not giving up on them and that this is not the end of the relationship.* It simply means that certain aspects of their lives are beyond the physician's competence and could be better handled by someone else.

Once the physician has given the explanation for the referral and discussed these common misconceptions, the patient needs an opportunity to ask questions and express additional concerns. Patients who characteristically deny emotional difficulties and patients who lack insight into the inappropriateness of their behavior are particularly resistant to referral for psychological evaluation or treatment. Therefore the physician must not feel compelled to complete discussion of a referral in a single session. Some physicians routinely mention the possibility of future referrals in their first contact with a patient if they have any reason to suspect that a referral may be necessary. If a referral to a psychiatrist or psychologist is mentioned in passing at this point, in conjunction with the possibility of referral to a neurologist, cardiologist, or other specialist, it becomes easier to reintroduce the idea.

SUMMARY

Attention to interpersonal and communication skills can facilitate effective and efficient clinical encounters. This chapter provides useful approaches, but *practice, reflection and feedback are the keys to developing and improving your interactions with patients.* The notion that patients and providers have different – but equally valuable – perspectives and roles in clinical encounters was captured in the title of a book by Tuckett et al. published 20 years ago: *Meetings between Experts.* Keeping this deceptively simple idea in mind as you progress in your training will help you and the patients you serve.

CASE STUDY

This is an excerpt from the second clinic visit of a 38-year-old plant foreman with intermittent chest pain. Extensive testing has not revealed any abnormality. All results were within normal limits.

Dr. Jones: How are you today, Mr. Smith?

Mr. Smith: Things are pretty bad at work. This is our busy time and everyone's stressed out. I'm doing okay, though.

Dr. Jones: Well, I've reviewed your tests with our cardiologist, and we agree that there really isn't anything wrong. Chances are it's just a combination of things, maybe stress or indigestion.

Mr. Smith: Okay, but I don't see it getting any better. Sooner or later, I'll have a blowout.

Dr. Jones: I don't think that's likely. You're young and in good health; you don't smoke or have a family history of heart disease. Some people get chest pain when they're under stress.

Mr. Smith: You say it's not likely, but I don't know. I've got a lot of problems, and all I hear from everyone is that it's in my head.

Dr. Jones: It's not in your head. The pain is real, but you're not having a heart attack. We can order more tests, but they're not going to show anything.

Mr. Smith: I don't know how you can be so sure. I've been having trouble catching my breath lately too. And my brother-in-law ran 10 miles a day and never smoked or drank, and he dropped dead of a heart attack just 1 month before I came to see you.

This is *not* an example of a good interview. Dr. Jones has a nice manner and was trying very hard in this instance, but the physician and patient were largely talking at cross-purposes. *Review this interview line by line, and see if you can improve on Dr. Jones' interviewing technique. Can you find examples of open-ended questions or facilitation? How might the interview have been different if Dr. Jones had used these techniques and tried to follow the patient's lead rather than convince Mr. Smith that he does not have heart disease? How might the patient feel when the physician is willing to order more tests despite his skepticism?*

SUGGESTED READINGS

Billings, J.A., & Stoeckle, J.D. (1999). *The clinical encounter: A guide to the medical interview and case presentation* (2nd ed.). Chicago: Year Book Medical Publishers.
  An introduction to the medical interview and to oral and written case presentation. The second half of the book considers more advanced topics such as the mental status examination, functional assessment, and various difficult relationships.

Platt, F.W. & Gordon, G.H. (2004). *Field guide to the difficult patient interview* (2nd ed.). New York: Lippincott, Williams, & Wilkins.
  Short chapters that cover topics that are relevant for medical trainees and practitioners at all levels. Each chapter offers principles and tangible procedures for dealing with difficult topics and situations.

17 Diagnostic Reasoning in Medicine

Barry Nurcombe

> Time after time I have gone out into my office in the evening feeling as if I couldn't keep my eyes open a moment longer. I would start out on my morning calls after only a few hours sleep, sit in front of some house waiting to get the courage to climb the steps and push the front-door bell. But once I saw the patient all that would disappear. In a flash the details of the case would begin to formulate themselves into a recognizable outline, the diagnosis would unravel itself, or would refuse to make itself plain, and the hunt was on.
>
> WILLIAM CARLOS WILLIAMS
> *The Doctor Stories*

Clinical reasoning is a risky business. In a sense, the patient is on an uncertain journey. The beginning of the journey must be ascertained, its route chosen, and the destination selected. The physician's task is to collaborate with the patient to elicit the clinical problem, design a plan of investigation, collect pertinent information, and reach a diagnostic conclusion that has implications for treatment. This chapter describes the reasoning of the experienced clinician, discusses its natural strengths and weaknesses, and considers how it could be aided. In essence, we will be talking about clues, interpretations, patterns, hunches, evidence, and the reaching of conclusions, and about a number of flaws that can impede or derail the process.

THE TACTICS OF DIAGNOSTIC REASONING

Salient Clues

From the very beginning of the clinical encounter, the physician scans the patient for clues. Referral information, physique, gait, handshake, dress, facies, and eyes all convey potentially useful information. After identificatory information is obtained, the patient is encouraged to tell her story, as far as possible spontaneously, the clinician operating as an attentive listener. Next, the clinician seeks detailed information, organizing the inquiry according to functional systems. Following this, physical examination is conducted.

Every patient presents a plethora of information. The experienced clinician, however, is alert for those salient clues that are likely to be of importance. Blue lips are more salient than blue eyes, for example (though, sometimes, blue sclerae can be very interesting). It is through training and experience that salient clues are recognized.

Clinical Inferences

Some salient clues (e.g., "tall") are recorded with little transformation, close to the original perception. Other clues, simply or in combination, must be interpreted. For example, a patient may complain of swelling of the ankles. The physician inquires how long it has been noticed, whether it varies during the day or day to day, and whether the patient has other symptoms (e.g., varicose veins, pains in the legs, breathlessness, chest pain). The physician weighs the evidence from history and examination before inferring that the patient has edema of the ankles, for example, and whether the edema is of peripheral or central origin. The experienced clinician does not rush to inference before weighing the evidence.

Patterns

Single clues or inferences are seldom enough. As history-taking and physical examination proceed, salient clues and inferences are combined to form patterns. *Research demonstrates that, less than a minute from the beginning of the interview, clinicians begin to form patterns.* Initially, the patterns are incomplete —like jigsaw puzzles from which key pieces are missing. *Aha, says the clinician, this is a sick-looking, febrile young woman who has cramping, lower abdominal pain, sweating, and urinary frequency.* This pattern forms the "problem space" from which clinical hypotheses—diagnostic hunches—are derived.

Hypotheses

From the incomplete jigsaw of symptoms and signs, the clinician generates a number of hypotheses. These hunches begin to emerge early in the interview, and are progressively refined, expanded, or dropped as the encounter proceeds. Diagnostic hypotheses may be in the form of anatomical locations (e.g., pelvic), pathophysiology (e.g., pulmonary edema), disease processes (e.g., infection), or disease categories (e.g., bronchopneumonia). The array of hypotheses may be at a single horizontal level or hierarchically arranged (see Figures 17.1 and 17.2).

Sometimes the pattern is so clear that an immediate or "spot" diagnosis jumps out. However, even in apparently obvious cases, in order not to leap to a premature conclusion, the wise clinician will entertain at least one other possibility. In fact, the disciplined generation of hypotheses keeps the mind open for new information that does not fit one's preconception. Many physicians pride themselves at being able to diagnose rare diseases. Typically, they do so

by adding to their array of hypotheses a rarity, a canary at the end of a line of sparrows. The main function of the canary is to prevent "routine" thinking. (It is that last case on a Friday afternoon with the "garden-variety" earache that turns out to have a mastoid abscess.)

Ordinarily, the clinician generates three to five hypotheses. However, *hierarchical arrays enable the clinician to entertain even more hunches than would otherwise be the case.* Expert diagnosticians generate accurate hypotheses early in the clinical process, forming "small worlds" consisting of small subsets of diseases and their distinguishing characteristics, leading to a series of limited comparisons of related diagnostic hypotheses.

> More is missed by not looking than by not knowing.
>
> THOMAS MCCRAE
> *Aphorism*

Evidence

The inquiry process is twofold. The clinician collects information that screens for problems prevalent in the demographic group to which the patient belongs (**standard inquiry**). For example, given the prevalence of suicidal ideation among adolescents and its potential seriousness, it is essential to ask an emotionally disturbed adolescent if he or she has thought of suicide. In addition, evidence is collected for or against the hypotheses in question (**discretionary inquiry**). For example, if bronchopneumonia is suspected, the clinician will examine the chest for symmetrical movement,

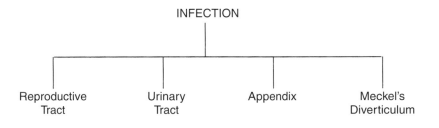

FIGURE 17.1 A horizontal array of anatomical hypotheses.

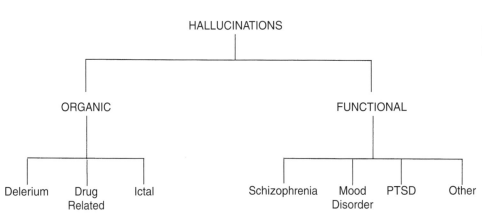

FIGURE 17.2 A hierarchical array of categorical disorders.

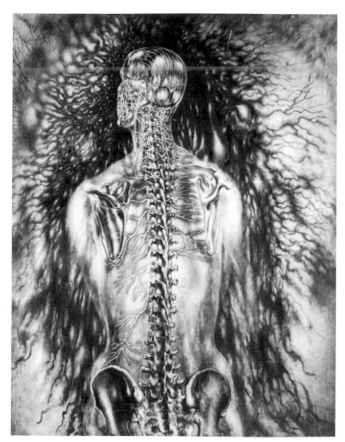

Anatomical Painting (1946) *Pavel Tchelitchev (1898–1957). Oil on canvas. Collection of the Whitney Museum of American Art, New York. Gift of Lincoln Kirstein. This painting captures both the beauty and the complexity of the central nervous system and suggests the diagnostic challenges facing the physician.*

resonance, and lung sounds, examine the sputum (and perhaps attempt to culture bacteria from it), and order chest X-rays. In particular circumstances (e.g., if a bronchial foreign body or tumor is suspected), special investigations such as bronchoscopy will be conducted. The most telling inquiries yield evidence that is incompatible with a particular hypothesis, thus eliminating it. Think of hypotheses (and especially of your pet hunches) as pins at which you launch the bowling balls of your inquiry, until only one remains. Apply **Occam's razor** and try to integrate diverse clinical features under the one diagnosis. However, be aware that it is not always possible to do so. Many patients, particularly elderly ones, have more than one disorder.

Revision

Inquiry processes generate evidence that tests the hypotheses and allows them to be retained, dropped, or revised. Sometimes, new hypotheses emerge if fresh information

becomes available. The entire process is a sophisticated mixture of feed-forward (the hypotheses direct the inquiry) and feed-back (the evidence tests the hypotheses).

Conclusion

Eventually, the evidence allows the clinician to drop particular hypotheses, while others both withstand critical inquiry and are supported by corroborative evidence. The surviving hypothesis (or hypotheses) then becomes the working diagnosis. However, the expert clinician is always alert for new information arising later in the clinical process (for example, during treatment) that might provoke a review of the working diagnosis.

> I rolled a quire of paper into a kind of cylinder and applied one end of it to the region of the heart and the other to my ear, and was not a little surprised and pleased to find that I could thereby perceive the action of the heart in a manner much more clear and distinct than I had ever been able to do by the immediate application of the ear. I saw at once that this means might become a useful method for studying, not only the beating of the heart, but likewise all movements capable of producing sound in the thoracic cavity.
>
> RENE LAENNEC
> *Auscultation Medicine*

THE STRATEGY OF DIAGNOSTIC REASONING

The diagnostic process is a form of hypothetico-deductive reasoning. In order to pursue it effectively, the clinician must adhere to the following guidelines:

1. Tolerate uncertainty, consider alternatives, and avoid premature closure.
2. Separate observation from inference, clue from interpretation.
3. Give adequate weight to negative evidence and to fresh evidence appearing later in the clinical encounter.
4. Revise interpretations, hypotheses, and working diagnoses if secondary evidence does not support them or if the evidence requires that fresh hypotheses be considered.
5. Don't go on interminably. Reach a reasonable conclusion when enough information has been gathered. Commit yourself to a diagnosis and treatment plan, but keep your eyes and ears open for fresh information.
6. Be aware of your personal reactions to the patient. Avoid stereotyping and other "routine" forms of thinking.

Examples of *inefficient* styles of reasoning are:

- Premature closure on a "spot" diagnosis
- The generation of an overinclusive profusion of unsystematic inquiries not directed by hypotheses
- Leaving no inquiry "stone" unturned in case something turns up
- A slavish reliance on "cookie-cutter" protocols
- The reluctance to come to a conclusion, for fear of having missed something, leading to interminable inquiry.

Symptoms are the body's mother tongue; signs are in a foreign language.

JOHN BROWN
Horae Subsecivae

THE DIAGNOSTIC FORMULATION

Although the diagnostic process appears to converge upon a conclusion (e.g., subacute bacterial endocarditis), it is not an end in itself. The clinician expands the conclusion into a dynamic formulation (e.g., subacute bacterial endocarditis caused by streptococcus viridans infection of the mitral valve previously scarred by rheumatic fever, the bacterial infection emanating from abscessed teeth, leading to progressive incompetence of the mitral valve with pulmonary congestion and edema).

The expanded formulation describes an interplay between **predisposition** (a heart valve scarred by previous rheumatic fever), **precipitation** (bacteraemia from infected teeth), the current dynamic **pattern** (a heart valve eroded by streptococcal infection, failing, leading to progressive failure of the left side of the heart, with the pooling of blood and fluid in the lungs), and **prognosis** (e.g., the progressive heart failure with acute pulmonary edema).

A dynamic formulation, therefore, is more than a static tag. It is stated in such a way as to guide the clinician's treatment planning (e.g., antibiotic to prevent bacterial growth and allow treatment of the dental abscess; inotropic drug to augment the force and velocity of ventricular contraction; diuretic to reduce lung congestion; possible later surgical intervention to repair an incompetent heart valve).

When medicine is practiced in the tropics, with little or no aid from laboratory tests, clinical acumen is the most important tool used in arriving at the correct diagnosis.

MICHAEL BROOK
Manson's Tropical Diseases

RESEARCH INTO DIAGNOSTIC REASONING

Diagnostic reasoning is "bounded" by the absolute limits of working memory. In order to cope with these constraints, the clinician transforms an "open" problem (one with no clear end point) into a number of "closed" problems or "small worlds" (each with an end point), by generating hypotheses and collecting data accordingly.

Medical problem-solving involves pattern recognition, probability estimation, and decision making. An incomplete pattern or "problem space" is matched against a number of complete syndrome possibilities. The hypothetical complete patterns are retrieved from long-term memory, presumably by associating the incomplete perceived patterns with the key features of stored prototypical symptom configurations. The hypotheses, then, act as "small worlds" that organize the gathering of information. The entire process depends upon general cognitive ability and specific experience with the kind of problem space at hand.

Medical reasoning is a risky business, and diagnoses and prognoses are often made in the context of uncertainty. Decisions must often be made before all the information is available; and the data (e.g., clinical findings, laboratory tests, X-rays, psychological tests) are subject to varying degrees of error because they are conceptually distant from the pathology that is the origin of medical problems. It is not surprising, therefore, that medical reasoning is subject to flaws ("**heuristic errors** and **biases**"). Among these flaws, the following have been described:

- Ignorance of base-rates
- Stereotypic reasoning
- Preference for positive evidence
- Limits on hypothesis generation
- Failure to control for the placebo effect
- The difficulty of evaluating utility
- Overconfidence.

Inadequate Knowledge of Base-Rates

Clinicians unfamiliar with Bayes' Theorem fail to take base-rates into account. **Bayes' Theorem** can be stated as follows: the probability that a disease is present, given a particular finding $P(D|F)$—is a function of the probability of that finding given the disease $P(F|D)$ multiplied by the probability of the disease $P(D)$, divided by the probability of the finding in that population $P(F)$:

$$P(D|F) = \frac{P(F|D) \times P(D)}{P(F)}$$

However, medicine is seldom taught in these terms. If a set

of clinical features resembles the text book pattern, the clinician may overestimate $P(D|F)$, without adequately taking $P(F|D)$, $P(D)$, or $P(F)$ into account. Moreover, *clinicians often rely upon subjective but erroneous estimates of base rates.* Clinicians tend to overestimate $P(D)$ as a result of past **salient experience**, for example a memorable encounter with a rare disease. Finally, clinicians tend to be conservative thinkers, slow to correct subjective base-rates in the light of new information.

Stereotypic Reasoning

Preconceptions, particularly stereotypes, can bias the recall of information and the collection of new evidence. *This is particularly likely when communication between doctor and patient is affected by differences in social class, ethnicity, sex, or age.*

Preference for Positive Evidence

There is a natural tendency to prefer the corroboration of a pet hypothesis to its testing by critical inquiry. As Francis Bacon said:

> "It is the peculiar and perpetual error of the human intellect to be more moved and excited by affirmatives than by negatives; whereas it ought properly to hold itself indifferently disposed toward both alike. Indeed, in the establishment of a true axiom, the negative instance is the more forcible."

> Physicians should define their diagnostic and therapeutic goals in terms of the everyday life and function of individual patients ... Unfortunately, that ideal is seldom met ... In part the problem arises because physicians are trained from the first days of medical school to disregard the knowledge they bring with them of everyday life and human function as irrelevant to medicine ... Doctors are not trained to include in their decision making the kind of "soft" and often subjective information that is relevant to the everyday life and function of sick persons.
>
> Eric J. Cassell

Natural Limits on Hypothesis Generation

The accuracy of diagnosis is limited by the number of hypotheses generated. As a rule, the human computer is limited to about three to five hunches. However, the efficiency of short-term memory can be augmented if diagnostic hypotheses are organized hierarchically (see Figure 21.2).

Failure to Control for The Placebo Effect

In regard to treatment planning, clinicians sometimes forget that clinical experience does not control for the placebo effect, hence the longevity of some unproven (and possibly baseless) remedies. **Evidence-based medicine** attempts to counter flawed reasoning of this type.

The Evaluation of Utility

In evaluating the desirability of an outcome, clinicians often have trouble with utility, the subjective value of an outcome. The question is, whose utility? The patient's or the doctor's? Considerations of this type are involved, for example, in the choice between radical and limited mastectomy for breast cancer.

> The most valuable diagnostic instrument is the passage of time.
>
> Henry George Miller

Overconfidence

Despite the limitations of medical reasoning, *clinicians tend to be overconfident in the correctness of their decisions.* Their overconfidence possibly reflects a way of coping with the difficulty of risky decision making when life and death are at stake. Overconfidence is preferable to paralysis.

> In the practice of medicine more mistakes are made from lack of accurate observation and deduction than from lack of knowledge.
>
> George Howard Bell
> *Experimental Physiology*

AIDS TO CLINICAL DECISION MAKING

The human mind is unparalleled in its capacity for eliciting and weighing salient clues, making interpretations, and recognizing patterns. However, it is relatively limited in its capacity to generate hypotheses, take base-rates into account, or test hypotheses consistently (particularly by collecting negative evidence). As already described, there are other biases that could impede accurate diagnosis.

The digital computer could supplement the limitations of short-term memory by generating larger arrays of hypothetical competitors, taking base-rates into account in estimating relative probabilities, and suggesting reliable inquiry plans for each hypothesis. Computers are more likely to complement clinicians rather than to supplant them. *An imaginative and flexible use of computer power, therefore, could relieve clinicians from overtaxing their limited memory and free them to do what they do best: elicit clues, weigh them, and combine them into the working patterns that are the grist of diagnostic reasoning.*

When additional information cannot possibly alter the decision, but only gives rise to a greater sense of comfort on the part of the physician, such additional information is of no benefit to the patient. Its only benefit is in reducing the discomfort of the physician.

HAROLD M. SCHOOLMAN

SUMMARY

Beginning with a clinical problem, this chapter analyzes the tactics of diagnostic reasoning into the following sequential elements: salient cues, clinical inferences, diagnostic patterns, diagnostic hypotheses, the gathering of evidence, the progressive revision of hypotheses, and the arrival at a diagnostic conclusion. The strategy of diagnostic reasoning is also discussed. The concept of diagnostic formulation is introduced. The **"heuristic fallacies"** that commonly impede logical decision making are described: premature closure, failure to consider alternatives, confirmatory bias, inadequate knowledge of base-rates, stereotypic reasoning, and the natural limits of working memory. Finally, the way in which computers could augment natural diagnostic reasoning is discussed.

CASE STUDY

Susan, a young college student, enters your office. Susan is dressed in sweatshirt, jeans, and sneakers. You do not recognize her. Your records indicate that she is 18 years old, the daughter of one of your patients, and a student at the local community college. Ten years ago, your partner treated her for a urinary tract infection. Susan looks ill. Cheeks flushed, eyes clouded, and facial expression strained. She tells you that, for two days, she has had "cramps" in her lower abdomen, much worse for the last 6 hours. She feels hot and sweaty. She has to urinate frequently.

Sounds like an infection, you think, but it could be inflammation or the obstruction or overaction of a hollow viscus.

Possibly urinary tract or pelvic in origin. Could be systemic. Better check for diabetes. Must exclude pregnancy.
You ask some questions. Susan answers that the pain has always been located in the central lower abdomen. It is mostly constant, but it's getting worse. It is not aggravated or relieved by anything.

Her bowel motions have been loose over the past 2 days. She did not feel like eating breakfast today. She feels nauseated. Although she passes urine frequently, it does not hurt to do so, and the color of her urine is unremarkable. For a few days she has had increased vaginal discharge, creamy in color, without blood. Her last menstrual period was 3 weeks ago. Her periods are regular and not excessive. She takes oral contraceptive medication (triphasil) regularly. She had sexual intercourse last week. You check her other systems, but there are no symptoms referable to them.

Susan's past history is unremarkable: general health good, an attack of cystitis when she was about 10 years old, mild asthma as a child, no surgical history, no significant obstetric or gynecological history. She smokes 10 cigarettes per day. No alcohol or drugs. She is a student commuting to the local community college. She has a steady boyfriend.

Central lower abdominal pain, constant and getting worse, loose bowels, urinary urgency and frequency (but no dysuria), anorexia, nausea, vaginal discharge, and past urinary tract infection. Pregnancy seems unlikely but must be checked. Still sounds like an infection, possibly of the urinary tract or pelvic organs. Loose motions could indicate a primary bowel condition, but could be secondary. General systemic causes (e.g., diabetic ketosis, uremia) must be excluded. Physical examination will focus on the urinary tract, pelvic organs, and lower bowel.
A well-nourished young woman. Temperature 39.0°, BP $^{110}/_{75}$, PR 105, RR 15. Warm, sweaty palms. Heavy breath. Chest clear. Mild systolic murmur over the base of the heart. Tender and guarded in lower abdomen, without rigidity or rebound tenderness. Rectal examination normal apart from discomfort on palpating cervix through the rectal wall. Vaginal speculum reveals mucopurulent discharge from cervix. Endocervical and high vaginal swabs are taken. Bimanual examination reveals tenderness in both fornices, but no masses.

Her fever and vital signs indicate inflammation. Physical examination suggests a pelvic site. Possibly reproductive tract, infected appendix, or Meckel's diverticulum. Heart murmur probably caused by rapid heart action. Urinary tract infection must be excluded. Could it be an ectopic pregnancy or a septic abortion? Must check for pregnancy and exclude systemic disease. Blood, urine, endocervical and high vaginal swab examinations are ordered.

You tell Susan that she should be admitted to hospital for further investigations and that gynecological consultation is in-

dicated. She asks you what you think is wrong. You tell her that it could be an infection in her reproductive tract, but that other possibilities need to be checked out.

Full blood count reveals neutrophilia with toxic granulation but no other abnormalities. Urine microscopy reveals a slight increase in leucocytes and red blood cells. Serum creatinine normal. No glycosuria or ketonuria. Gram stains of the endocervical and high vaginal swabs reveal leucocytes and mixed bacteria. Urine and serum LCG tests negative.

Good. She's either not pregnant or less than 2 weeks pregnant. Not likely to be an ectopic pregnancy. Urine findings nonspecific. Blood findings suggest inflammation. Swabs consistent with genital tract infection. Physical examination is consistent with a pelvic infection.

The gynecological consultant confirms your findings and recommends immediate laparoscopy. Laparoscopy reveals bilateral swollen, reddened fallopian tubes. There is pus in the Pouch of Douglas. Appendix normal. Antibiotic treatment is commenced. The endocervical and high vaginal swabs grow Bactcrioids and Gardnerella. The endocervical swab is positive for Chlamydia. The final diagnosis is chronic pelvic tract infection.

How did Susan contract this infection? How can further attacks be prevented? What are the implications and complications of chronic salpingitis? What does Susan need to know?

> Nor bring to see me cease to live.
> Some doctor full of phrase and fame.
> To shake his sapient head, and give
> The ill he cannot cure a name.
>
> MATTHEW ARNOLD
> *A Wish*

SUGGESTED READINGS

Cox, K. (2002). Perceiving clinical evidence. *Medical Education, 36,*, 1189–1195.
An explanation of clinical perception in terms of rapid recognition (using the nonverbal brain) followed by guided search (using the slower, verbal reasoning brain). Experiential cognition is achieved by integrating the two modes of knowing.

Elstein, A.S., Shulman, L.S., & Sprafka, S.A. (1979). *Medical problem solving: An analysis of clinical reasoning.* Boston: Harvard University Press.
This classic text describes the theory and outcome of a series of experiments (with medical students, internists, and neurologists) on hypothetico-deductive reasoning, conducted at Michigan State University.

Eva, L.W. (2004). What every teacher needs to know about clinical reasoning. *Medical Education, 39,* 98–106.
A pertinent article that describes analytic (conscious) and nonanalytic (rapid pattern-matching) strategies of diagnostic reasoning, suggesting that a combination of the two approaches is the most effective.

Groves, M., O'Rourke, P., & Alexander, H. (2003). Clinical reasoning: The relative contribution of identification, interpretation, and hypothesis errors to misdiagnosis. *Medical Teaching, 25,* 621–625.
An analysis of the stage in the clinical process at which errors of reasoning are most likely to occur: cue identification, cue interpretation, pattern recognition, or hypothesis generation.

Kahneman, D., Slovic, P., & Tversky, A. (1982). *Judgment under uncertainty: Heuristics and biases.* New York: Cambridge University Press.
This often-quoted text introduced the concept of "heuristic errors and biases," the flaws in intuitive reasoning that can impede good judgment.

Kushmiruk, A.W., Patel, V.L., & Marley, A.A. (1998). Small worlds and medical expertise: Implications for medical cognition and knowledge engineering. *International Journal of Medical Informatics, 49,* 255–271.
An article focusing on the early generation of plausible diagnostic hypotheses ("small worlds") and the stepwise strategic process that discriminates between hypotheses.

18 Patient Assessment

John C. Linton & Steve Cody

> Scientific medicine has hitherto paid much attention to disease and almost none to health, to causative agents rather than to the person or host, that is, to the seed rather than to the soil; and to the sick rather than to the people who become sick.
>
> J. AUDY

Evaluating a patient's personality, behavioral characteristics, and capabilities is an important part of effective care. Sometimes these findings will apply directly to the determination of a diagnosis and treatment, as in cases of psychiatric disorder and mental retardation. At other times, factors such as intelligence and personality may place some patients at increased risk for certain medical conditions, or complicate effective treatment. Much can be learned about a patient through careful interviewing, but there are also formal techniques that are more focused and objective. These techniques range from the semistructured mental status examination, to highly structured and standardized tests of intelligence and neurocognitive functioning. Some techniques such as the mental status exam will be a routine part of an interview, while others such as personality inventories or intelligence tests will have to be administered and interpreted by a psychologist.

All of these techniques involve *sampling behaviors* in a more or less systematic fashion. Patients are presented with questions, tasks, or stimuli, selected to reflect a broader aspect of functioning, such as intelligence. Such procedures are useful because they allow one to predict how a patient will function outside the context of the assessment.

An attentive and observant physician will be aware of things patients are communicating that are not limited to the *content* of what they say. There is often much to be learned from the *process* aspects of communication; in other words, *how* patients express the things they share. Pa-

tients reveal a great deal of themselves in the demeanor they adopt toward the physician, the kind of information they provide and when they provide it, and the tone of their responses to advice and information. Subtleties of attitude, emotion, and nonverbal behavior can be critical to psychiatric diagnosis, but are also important in understanding the unique patient with whom the physician is trying to establish and cultivate trust and cooperation. Attending to all this can seem overwhelming to the new physician, who may be struggling to remember all the important questions to ask, but these skills can be developed with practice.

Of course, the astute physician will also know the importance of being thoughtful about what the patient actually says. Some conditions directly affect the ability of the patient to comprehend what is happening and communicate effectively with an interviewer. In some situations, patients will be ambivalent about the information they share. More generally, one can be misled by assumptions that prevent the physician from understanding the specific situation of that person. For example, *it may be a mistake to assume that the patient means the same thing the physician meant by the word "depressed."* It is often better to ask for data than for conclusions (e.g., "How much do you drink?" rather than "Do you have a drinking problem?")

MENTAL STATUS EXAMINATION

For patients in psychiatric and some nonpsychiatric medical settings, it is necessary to conduct a psychiatric interview, which includes a comprehensive psychiatric history. The psychiatric history is an account of events from the past as recalled by the patient. As such, the history is highly subjective; the recounted *events* were not witnessed by the interviewer. Therefore, the clinician must also conduct a mental status examination, which is an objective report on the patient's current mental functioning as witnessed by the interviewer. In a sense the mental status examination is to the mental health clinician what the physical examination is to the internist. Just as the findings from the physical examination allow an objective appraisal of current physical status, *the mental status examination is an objective assessment of the quantitative and qualitative range of the patient's mental functioning at a specific point in time.*

Technically the mental status examination is conducted and reported on as a separate part of the clinical psychiatric interview. In fact, however, this separation is artificial because information gathered throughout the entire interview may be applicable to the psychiatric examination; conversely, specific mental status findings may prompt the clinician to reevaluate the medical or psychiatric history already obtained or to return to previous portions of the interview to re-examine specific details. The clinician often switches back and forth a number of times from one aspect of an interview to another while gathering information about a patient.

Importance of the Mental Status Examination

The mental status examination provides a system for organizing information, allowing diagnosis of different psychiatric disorders. Individuals with psychiatric problems who come to a psychiatric setting are the most clearly in need of such an assessment; however, patients with ostensibly nonpsychiatric medical problems sometimes have subtle psychiatric disorders that emerge only during such a structured examination.

In addition, *patients frequently change with time, and the mental status examination establishes a baseline against which to measure this change.* An individual may be treated by different clinicians in different places at different times, and the findings from his or her mental status examination offer a standard and widely accepted form of communication between professionals regarding the mental functioning of that patient. Thus, the mental status examination assists in understanding, diagnosing, and measuring the progress or deterioration of patients, and it facilitates communication among professionals.

Conducting and Interpreting The Mental Status Examination

Conducting a mental status examination requires the clinician to listen empathically to a person's description of his

or her subjective experiences while remaining aware of speech patterns and observing often subtle behavior. In emergency department settings and on medical floors the clinician is often required to gather complex information quickly and organize it into a cogent, accurate mental status evaluation. At the same time the clinician must develop a rapport with the individual, assist the individual to feel secure and understood, and maintain the confidentiality of the relationship. The clinician must cover a variety of specific examination areas through observation and questioning yet must not appear to be checking off items on a prepared list.

Weighty decisions often are made on the basis of mental status examination results, such as whether patients are capable of self-care, are competent to manage their financial affairs, are currently psychotic or at risk for psychosis, or are prone to commit suicide or some other violent act. It is important to gather information that is as accurate as possible and to consider variables that might reduce this accuracy. For instance, patients are sometimes emotionally upset and difficult to follow; they may be unable to attend to or concentrate on questions or tasks; or they may have perceptual difficulties, such as impaired hearing or eyesight, or expressive or receptive language disorders. Sometimes patients may not comply with the examination and may resist revealing information about themselves. Such noncompliance may result from a patient's particular personality or it may result from the nature of the evaluation, particularly if it involves legal issues or financial compensation.

Many mental status examinations are performed informally. A patient who is seeking only medical attention or outpatient counseling for adjustment problems may be evaluated quickly and show no need for further assessment. If a person shows symptoms of substantial disturbance or mood, perception, memory, or thinking, however, a formal mental status examination is required. An overview of the major parts of the mental status examination follows.

Presentation

General Appearance. The examiner's report should create a picture of the subject, so that anyone reading the report will be able to visualize the patient's unique appearance. The overall physical impression is recorded, including gait, posture, body shape, scars or tattoos, facial features and expression, grooming, and cleanliness. It is helpful to estimate how old the patient looks relative to his or her chronological age. Clothes, cosmetics, and jewelry often indicate how the subject wants to be perceived by others. The clothing's condition and appropriateness to the occasion and the weather should be noted.

And Man Created God in His Own Image, (1930–1931) *Ivan Le Lorraine Albright, 1897–1983.* Oil on canvas 121.9 × 66 cm. Gift of Ivan Albright. Copyright © The Art Institute of Chicago. All rights reserved. *Simply looking closely at your patients is the beginning of an effective mental status examination. What hypotheses would you have about this man?*

Level of Consciousness. It is important to describe how alert the patient was when he or she was interviewed. This is especially important when mental status examinations are conducted on hospitalized medical and psychiatric patients and on emergency department referrals. Clearly the presentation of the patient's mental functioning will be influenced by level of consciousness.

The examiner should be as descriptive as possible, stating in detail how the patient responded to questions, requests, prompts, and so forth. Level of consciousness is usually described on a continuum from comatose to alert.

In a **coma**, neither verbal nor motor responses occur in response to noxious stimuli. Patients in a stuporous state require repeated energetic stimulation to be aroused. Lethargic patients are sleepy, inactive, and indifferent, responding to input from others in a fashion that is incomplete and delayed. The **drowsy** individual is sleepy but can be aroused by aversive stimuli. **Alert** wakefulness is the state in which the individual responds promptly and appropriately to all perceptual input.

Attitude Toward Interviewer. How the patient relates to the examiner and the interview situation affects the quality and quantity of information obtained. The examiner should give a descriptive summary of how the patient interacted during the session, commenting on both general attitude and changes in the patient's style of responding.

Sometimes in the course of an interview the examiner may discuss certain topics that affect the patient's attitude; the patient may show sudden resistance to further discussion or, conversely, show evidence of greater involvement in the process at that point. It is wise for the examiner to note what content areas caused which reactions because this can provide clues to the patient's mental status for further investigation. The examiner should also note his or her reaction to the patient. Awareness of personal reactions may help the examiner predict how others will respond to the patient.

Motor Behavior. The motor behavior section of the mental status report describes the specifics of patient behavior during the interview. The patient's gait, gestures, and firmness of handshake are noted, along with involuntary or abnormal movements such as tremors, tics, hand wringing, **akathisia**, or stereotyped mannerisms. The examiner should note if the patient mimics his or her movements (**echopraxia**) or if the patient's limbs remain in positions that are unnatural or uncomfortable once placed there (**waxy flexibility**). The clinician should also report on the pace of movements. Psychomotor restlessness or **agitation** is seen in the patient who has difficulty sitting still and who must constantly move about, scratching, biting his or her nails, or rising from the chair or bed and wandering around the room. At the other extreme, **psychomotor retardation** is indicated by a significant slowing of movement and speech. The patient sits quietly and seldom moves, and facial expression is flat. It is important to record specific behavior rather than merely summarizing global impressions. The behavior of most patients can be described as "normal;" however, evidence of any of the previously mentioned suggests significant emotional disturbance.

Speech. The speech section is devoted to describing *manner;* not content. The examiner listens for the rate of speech and notes characteristics such as rapid, slowed, pressured, slurred, or loud or soft speech. Speech problems such as stammering or stuttering are indicated, as are any symptoms of aphasia.

Emotional State: Mood and Affect

The description of emotion is typically divided between **mood**, *a subjectively experienced feeling that is fairly persistent, and* **affect**, *the emotional tone of the interview or the overt manifestation of mood as directly observed by the interviewer.* In other words, patients feel and complain of problems with mood, and their mood influences how they view the world. Patients do not complain about their affect. Clinicians see and evaluate affect, and it can change frequently during the course of an examination.

In addition to patient reports regarding emotion, the interviewer pays special attention to many cues, including facial expression, speech, and nonverbal cues such as gestures and body language. Here again, specific descriptions of the patient's emotional expressions are likely to be more valuable than summary impressions.

Range of Emotional Expression. The examiner should describe the predominant emotion as reported by the patient, such as sadness, depression, anger, guilt, or fear. It is wise to question patients further to determine what personal meanings are attached to these descriptors rather than assume their meaning.

Moods can vary in intensity. Normally happy individuals are known as **euthymic**; however, this positive mood can become exaggerated along a continuum in which the individual's mood first becomes elevated, then euphoric, then expansive. At the other end of the spectrum, unpleasant moods are dysphoric and can include **dysthymia**, anxiety, and irritability. Dysphoric patients commonly come to the interview with complaints about mood. Those who are euphoric or expansive seldom complain about their moods, but others do!

The range of the person's affect is important to indicate. A "normal" individual has a *broad* range of affect; he or she appears sad when discussing unhappy topics and laughs when things are funny. If affect is **blunted**, the patient has a significantly diminished and narrowed range of emotional responsiveness. With a **flat affect** the patient relates little or no feeling, seems devoid of emotion, and shows little or no change in facial expression, regardless of what is discussed. *This is a symptom classically associated with schizophrenia.* **Constricted affect** is commonly seen in depression. Emotions are present, but the patient is too depressed to act on them. **Labile affect** refers to emotion that shifts rapidly from one expression to another with the slightest provocation. Such individuals can be happy one minute, angry the next, and depressed the next. Labile affect is found in certain personality disorders and is prominent in

Worn out *Vincent van Gogh (1882).* van Gogh Museum Foundation, Amsterdam. *The signs of clinical depression are not always this obvious.*

organic brain disease. Finally, clinicians are increasingly recognizing patients who are **alexithymic**, or seemingly incapable of discussing their emotions. Discussion of emotions and connections between their physical symptoms and feelings seem to elude them completely. Such patients are most often found in general medical settings, and they can be very frustrating for those caring for them.

> It is useful to remember that *affect* is to *mood* as *weather* is to *climate*.

Appropriateness of Emotions. The examiner should determine and note whether the affect and presentation are appropriate to the subject matter being discussed. At times there may be a wide discrepancy between the subject being discussed and the patient's facial expressions and projected emotional tone. A person who discusses problems for which the appropriate response would be sadness, anxiety, or anger, yet acts cheerful or silly, and smiles, shows inappropriate affect. Some patients feign this behavior, but if the finding of inappropriate affect is sustained, it usually reflects significant psychopathology.

Biological Indicators of Affect. The examiner should inquire about psychophysiological changes that may accompany the patient's emotional state. This is perhaps most salient with depression. It is important to determine whether the patient has **diurnal variation** in mood, that is, whether the person's spirits are worse in the morning and improved during the day or vice versa. *The examiner should note characteristics of the patient's sleep, paying special attention to problems with getting to sleep, waking too early and not being able to get back to sleep, or sleeping more or less than is usual* (however, the examiner should be careful not to use his or her personal standards for adequate sleep for comparison).

Changes in the patient's appetite, such as a reduction in frequency and amount from what is customary, should be noted. Significant recent weight changes should also be recorded. The examiner should determine whether the patient's **libido**, or sex drive, has changed and, whether there has been an increase or decrease in sexual activity. Changes in the patient's interest in everyday activities such as work, family, and hobbies should be noted, as should the patient's ability and motivation to carry out daily living activities.

Some clinicians also address **suicide** and **homicide** at this time. *No mental status examination is adequate without a statement about the patient's thinking with regard to suicide or homicide.* The clinician must always determine whether the patient is likely to harm or kill himself or herself or others. This is best assessed by asking *directly* about the history of such thoughts, or plans. The final report should state clearly that these issues have been explored and the nature of the findings. If they are positive, the examiner should offer some evaluation of the situation's urgency. A patient who "might tell my wife to ask a pharmacist for some pills that are poison" is probably less at risk than one who seems hopeless, lives alone, and has "a loaded pistol in the bedside drawer." However, *all suicidal ideation should be treated with clinical respect and appropriately evaluated.*

> The thought of suicide is a great consolation: with the help of it one got through many a bad night.
>
> FRIEDRICH NIETZSCHE

Perceptual Disturbances

Abnormal sensory functioning is described in the perceptual disturbances section of the report. At one time or another, most people have brief experiences with "dream states," a sense of depersonalization or **déja vu**, or the experience of falsely hearing someone call their name. This happens infrequently in "normal" individuals, most often during times of stress. However, this category also includes more significant perceptual disorders.

Hallucinations and Illusions. A **hallucination** is a sensory impression that exists in the absence of a real external stimulus. Patients may report hearing voices that no one else can hear, seeing objects that are not there, feeling sensations without tactile stimulation, and tasting or smelling things that are not present. Hallucinations involving the **vestibular sense**, in which the patient feels as if he or she is flying, occur occasionally. Some patients admit having hallucinations but many do not, and the examiner must infer their existence when patients seem preoccupied, as if listening to voices or sounds, or stare at something that seems real to them, sometimes moving their eyes around to follow it. When observing such behavior, the examiner should tactfully inquire about the experience.

Auditory hallucinations can include sounds, complete words and sentences, or commands to act. The voices can be strange or familiar. *A useful rule is that auditory hallucinations are most often found in functional disorders, typically schizophrenia, but also in affective (manic or depressive) psychoses.* Such hallucinations tend to be more consistent in schizophrenics and more transient in patients with affective disorders. They can also be found in organic mental disorders, such as **alcoholic hallucinosis**.

Hallucinations can be mood incongruent or mood congruent. The former hallucinations do not match the patient's mood; the latter hallucinations do. *Schizophrenic patients tend to have mood-incongruent hallucinations, whereas patients with affective disorders have more mood-congruent hallucinations.* Depressed patients may hear voices telling them that they deserve punishment, whereas withdrawn, frightened schizophrenics may hear that they are destined to rule the world with Jesus. *The clinician should determine whether the voices are telling the patient to harm himself or herself or others and whether this command can be resisted.*

Visual hallucinations are most common in organic mental disorders such as delirium but can also be found in a variety of other conditions such as brief reactive psychoses or severe grief reactions. Visual hallucinations can also result from the effects of drugs or sensory deprivation. They occur infrequently in schizophrenia and are often described as frightening. Patients with some forms of personality disorder describe experiences that sound like hallucinations, when in fact their imaginations are active and they relish the attention that comes with such discussions.

Illusions are misperceptions of real stimuli, such as thinking that a stranger is a familiar acquaintance until he or she gets closer. Such experiences are most common in states of anxiety or extreme fatigue. Persons without demonstrable mental disorder may have them; they can also accompany functional psychoses because such patients may be emotionally upset and exhausted as part of their clinical syndrome. Patients sometimes think that illusions are hallucinations, and the examiner should attempt to differentiate between the two.

Depersonalization and DerealizationIDerealization. **Depersonalization** refers to a strange feeling of change or loss of reality of the self and the accompanying feeling that there is something different about the self or the emotions that cannot be explained. *With depersonalization the individual feels that he or she is different; with derealization the person feels that the environment has changed somehow and that external reality is no longer familiar.* These conditions are best assessed by asking patients whether they feel natural, if they or their bodies feel different or unusual, or if their environment seems strange. Both of these conditions can occur in "normal" individuals under certain circumstances, but they most often accompany panic disorder, agoraphobia, or depression.

Thought Processes

The examiner cannot directly assess a patient's thoughts and so must depend on behavior and speech to evaluate how well a person's mental associations are organized and expressed and what they are about.

Stream of Thought. When assessing stream of thought, the examiner is interested in the quantity and rate of thought, again as measured by speech. At one extreme the patient produces little or no speech, perhaps saying only a few words. Unless there is reason to suspect that he or she is being purposefully resistive, such poverty of speech suggests a retardation or slowing of thoughts. At the other extreme the patient's speech is overabundant and accelerated or racing so that it is difficult to follow. This is usually referred to as **pressured speech** and is often seen in persons with acute anxiety or agitated depression who feel pressed to talk; it sometimes suggests the presence of flight of ideas, which is a diagnostic sign of mania.

Continuity of Thought. *Continuity of thought is assessed by determining to what extent the patient's thoughts are goal directed, as well as the nature of the associations between the patient's ideas.* Some abnormalities of thought continuity are extremely pathological, whereas others, although usually pathological, may also result from limited intelligence, cultural differences, or a severe reaction to overwhelming dysphoria. The abnormalities of thought that are always pathological include **clang associations**, in which thoughts are connected illogically by rhyming or puns; **echolalia**, a

condition in which the patient repeats exactly what the clinician says; use of **neologisms**, which are invented or condensed words that have meaning only to the patient; **perseveration**, which is the apparently involuntary responding to all questions in the same way; and the presence of **word salad**, a nonsensical mix of words and phrases. Usually pathological, and certainly noteworthy, are **looseness of associations**, a condition in which the person jumps from one topic to another and the connection between thoughts is lost; **blocking**, which is the sudden cessation of thought in the middle of a sentence and the inability to continue or recover what was being said; **circumstantiality**, which is characterized by the absence of direction toward a goal in language and thought and the inclusion of details that are unnecessary and eventually tedious and which is common in obsessional individuals who do not want to leave anything out, no matter how trivial; and **tangentiality**, which is a severe form of circumstantiality, in which the patient strays completely from the topic and includes thoughts that seem to be totally unrelated and irrelevant. Tangentiality is most often seen in schizophrenia.

Because patients are often upset, they may present their thoughts poorly, and at first the thought process might seem to be disordered. Rather than assuming that this is the case, the examiner should ask the patient, "What does that mean to you?" or "Could you explain to me what you just said?" A patient's thoughts should be clear to an unbiased observer; if they are not, the examiner should be comfortable enough to ask about them.

Content of Thought. The content of thought section of the mental status examination assesses the integrity of the patient's thoughts. Most of this material will have already been developed during the general psychiatric interview or elsewhere in the mental status examination. However, a number of specific abnormalities of thought content must be investigated before certain diagnoses can be ruled out.

A **delusion** is a belief that is false and unique to the individual. It cannot be adequately explained by reference to the patient's cultural or subcultural background and in fact would be rejected by others with the same cultural background. Delusions can appear in many different guises. For example, a person with **delusions of reference** has a feeling of being watched, discussed, or ridiculed by others; **delusions of persecution** most commonly involve the belief that the person has been singled out to be plotted against or harmed in some way; **delusions of grandiosity** refer to the belief that the individual has assumed the identity of a famous person, living or dead, or has special talents or unique powers; **delusions of jealousy** result from false beliefs that a spouse or lover has been unfaithful; **delusions of guilt** refer to the feeling of having committed an unforgivable deed; and **erotomania** refers to the delusion that a stranger or a celebrity loves the person but cannot make it public. The examiner should ask patients objectively about delusional thoughts without attempting to dissuade them from or agreeing with their notions. The examiner should also determine the level of organization of the delusional system and assess whether it is a passing idea or a systematized way of viewing the world. *It is critical that the examiner ascertain whether the patient intends to act on a delusional belief.* For example, the examiner should determine whether the patient intends to retaliate in some form against others for their perceived persecution.

> If a patient is poor he is committed to a public hospital as "psychotic"; if he can afford the luxury of a private sanitarium, he is put there with the diagnosis of "neuroasthenia"; if he is wealthy enough to be isolated in his own home under constant watch of nurses and physicians he is simply an indisposed "eccentric."
>
> PIERRE MARIE JANET
> *Strength and Psychological Debility*

Obsessions are repetitive irrational thoughts. Patients dislike these thoughts and realize that they are not normal; they wish to be rid of the thoughts but are unable to stop the intrusion into their thinking. Obsessions are usually accompanied by a sense of anxiety or morbid dread, which patients find painful but irresistible. **Compulsions** are related to obsessions except that they involve behaviors instead of thoughts. Compulsions are stereotyped and repetitious rituals the individual is driven to perform even though the person knows the actions are senseless. Performing the ritualistic deeds is not enjoyable *per se*, but it reduces anxiety, thereby reinforcing the action; if compulsions are resisted, the patient becomes exceedingly anxious.

The clinician should try to determine the degree to which both obsessions and compulsions interfere with the patient's life. Is it a minor irritation, or is the patient in danger of losing a job because checking and rechecking the locks in the house dozens of times before leaving makes the patient chronically late for work? Finally, preoccupations involve the degree to which a patient is absorbed in his or her thoughts to the exclusion of reality. Brilliant but eccentric individuals are noted for absentmindedness when focusing on certain ideas. At the other end of the continuum is the person who can think about nothing but homicide or suicide or who has autistic fantasies. When present, preoccupations and their intensity should always be noted.

A **phobia** is a morbid fear of an object, animal, or situation that would not frighten the average person. The phobic individual goes to great lengths to avoid contact with the feared stimulus. If it is easily avoided (e.g., snakes in a large city), the patient's phobia should cause little disruption of daily activity, but if the phobic stimulus is regularly encountered (e.g., elevators in a large city), it is more problematic. Patients are seldom seen primarily for phobias, which often

coexist with other syndromes. The examiner may have to question the patient about specific phobic anxiety because this information is seldom offered spontaneously.

Cognitive State

Some examiners choose to assess cognitive abilities early in the examination before determining emotional state and thought processes to ensure that what is observed *as* thought or mood disorder is not really an impaired cognitive state. However, this area is more commonly focused on at the end of the examination, when the information can be used in interpreting what was observed earlier.

Orientation. Orientation refers to the patient's ability to understand the nature of his or her current environment relative to time, place, person, and situation. For most patients this part of the examination is unnecessary, particularly if earlier in the interview the quality of the material communicated to the examiner indicates that the individual is well oriented. Disorientation can exist in functional psychoses such as schizophrenia and major affective disorders but is most common in organic disorders.

Orientation to time is assessed by asking the patient about the year, season, month, day of the week, and date. Occasionally someone who appears to be functioning well surprises an examiner with a time response that is incorrect by decades. Some believe that this is the most sensitive indicator of disorientation because time changes constantly, whereas the other spheres change less often or not at all. **Orientation to place** is determined by asking the patient to name his or her location by country, state, county, city, type of building, and location in the building. Clinicians should use common sense and caution here, asking about easier locations such as country only after the patient cannot respond to the type of building or the city. One should also take into account the person's intelligence. **Orientation to person** involves the patient's awareness of his or her own name and the names and roles of those in the immediate environment. In some cases this is the last area to show deficit, and it is the first to reappear in reversible organic states. The patient who is oriented to situation is aware that he or she is a patient and that a clinical examination is taking place, rather than a social visit or job interview. If no deficits are noted in any of the previously mentioned areas, the individual is said to exhibit a clear **sensorium**.

Attention and Concentration. Attention refers to the patient's capacity to focus on one activity or task at a time. The clinician usually gets a sense of the patient's ability to attend during the other phases of the interview. Lack of attention is sometimes volitional. Patients may be purposely noncompliant and oppositional and may ignore the clinician or engage in some other behavior designed to compete with the interview process. However, patients may also be distracted by anxiety or psychotic preoccupations. In such cases the patient cannot distinguish between relevant and irrelevant stimuli and may attend to sounds outside the room or internal voices rather than to the examiner.

Although the interview can never actually take place with a person who has serious attentional deficits, a patient with deficits in **concentration** *is able to attend for short periods* and the examination may get off to a good start. However, he or she soon becomes distracted and must be guided back on track with repeated questions and restructuring of the interview task.

When a patient has a significant problem with attention or concentration, more formal testing is required. The most common test, known as **"serial sevens,"** asks the patient to subtract 7 from 100, then 7 from that answer, and so on as far as possible. However, some clinicians believe that this requires too much mathematical ability and instead suggest the use of "serial ones," a task that requires the patient to count backward by ones from any number (e.g., 62), and stop at another number (e.g., 19). This task provides a relatively pure measure of concentration.

Memory. Memory can be clinically assessed in five basic dimensions: *Immediate memory refers to the ability to recall what a person has just been told;* **short-term memory** *involves retrieving information received about 5 minutes earlier;* **recent memory** *involves recognizing material from the past several days to several months;* **long-term memory** *involves recalling data from the past few years; and* **remote memory** *involves recalling events from the distant past.* When an individual's memory fails, immediate memory typically fails first, remote memory last. Recent, long-term, and remote memory can usually be assessed by evaluating how well the patient remembers personal history and current happenings. However, some patients with organic mental disturbances **confabulate,** or invent plausible but false stories that mask their memory problem. Therefore, a patient's recollections should be independently verified by other sources, such as family members, if there is any doubt as to the veracity of the patient's statements.

Immediate and short-term memory can be assessed by formal testing. The most common method is to ask the patient to remember five neutral objects, such as a car, shoe, umbrella, teacup, and flashlight. The patient is asked to repeat them and, if correct, is then told that he or she will be asked about them again in 5 minutes. The examination continues for another 5 minutes, and then the patient is asked to repeat the items. Most patients remember four or five items. A score of three is borderline performance, and recall of less than three items suggests a need for further evaluation of organicity.

Finally, the examiner must not forget to record the items he or she asked the patient to recall or should use a standard list. More than one busy examiner has forgotten what the patient was asked to remember!

Intelligence.. The only true measure of **intelligence** is derived from intelligence testing, which is seldom available at the time of the mental status examination. However, an examiner can at least estimate a patient's level of intellectual functioning by his or her comments during the interview. *The person's use of vocabulary is probably the best estimate of overall intelligence,* particularly if one considers level of education as well. A good vocabulary in a patient with limited schooling suggests that he or she is an academic underachiever, whereas a weak vocabulary in a college graduate suggests that the person's intellectual functioning may be declining.

The patient's **fund of information** encompasses general knowledge that can be assessed by asking questions about a wide range of subjects such as geography, history, and current events. It is important to remember that educational and cultural limitations can play a significant role in the patient's educational and knowledge base.

Testing **abstraction** is an additional measure of the patient's intelligence and is accomplished by asking the individual to find commonalties among apparently dissimilar objects, such as asking how a drum, guitar, and violin are alike. The patient who responds that they are all musical instruments shows good skill in abstraction; the patient who says simply that they all make noise is responding concretely. It is also useful to ask the patient to interpret proverbs, again controlling the test for the person's age and cultural background by avoiding dated or colloquial stimuli. Finally, if the examiner suspects significant intellectual impairment, a formal intelligence assessment should be requested.

Reliability. The examiner should give some estimate of the reliability of the patient as an informant or historian. Several factors must be considered, such as the individual's intelligence, contact with reality, and personality style and the purpose of the evaluation. For example, if the patient is being evaluated because of pressure from family or the court system, he or she is likely to tell a different story from someone who is seeking symptom relief. Patients with poor memories may wish to cooperate but be unable to recall vital information and confabulate stories that are quite believable. The clinician's notion as to the reliability of the data should temper and qualify all of the information gathered from the interview.

Insight and Judgment. *Insight is the capacity to understand that one has a problem, to conceptualize how it came about, and to think about how it might be solved.* The degree of a patient's insight is a general predictor of how well the individual will cooperate with treatment, especially if treatment is at all insight oriented.

The clinician can determine the patient's **judgment** by assessing the history gleaned from the interview and by directly assessing interview behavior. Judgment refers to the individual's ability to deal with social situations and to understand and adhere to reasonable social conventions. Obviously, the psychotic patient who goes without eating for days shows poor judgment. However, even individuals with normal intelligence and no major psychopathology can have notoriously bad judgment, repeatedly making disastrous romantic, vocational, and economic decisions. This finding should be noted and reported, because it has clear implications for treatment.

Summary

Conducting a comprehensive mental status examination is a mixture of art, social persuasion, and science. Knowing how, when, and at what level to conduct this examination is an invaluable clinical skill and is critical to superior patient care. Although the examination may appear complex and difficult, in reality it is relatively brief and easily learned by most physicians.

Unfortunately the mental status examination can also become perfunctory, cursory, and truncated to the point that it yields little information of value. However, *master clinicians routinely include a full mental status examination in their assessments of patients*, using a structured format such as the one outlined in this chapter. The few extra minutes it adds to the patient interview is a small price to pay for information that is structured, systematic, and easily communicated to other professionals.

PSYCHOLOGIC AND NEUROPSYCHOLOGIC TESTING

Testing offers the most structured and systematic approach to sampling behavior for learning about a patient's personality, abilities, and functioning. In some cases, formal testing is essential to a diagnosis, as is the case with intellectual assessment in the course of diagnosing mental retardation or learning disorders. In other cases, testing can be useful in differential diagnosis, illuminating the personality factors that contribute to a patient's situation, determining whether patients' capacities fit a given demand (e.g., driving), or establishing how an illness or injury has affected the patient. For purposes of discussion, it can be useful to consider three broad areas of psychological assessment: (1) measures of personality and psychopathology, (2) mea-

sures of intellect and academic functioning, and (3) neuropsychological assessment.

Criteria for Evaluating Testing Techniques

Just as medical tests are expected to meet scientific standards to be accepted for clinical decision making, so too must psychological tests meet basic standards. In order to be useful, tests must be **standardized**, **reliable**, and **valid**.

Standardization refers to the idea that the stimuli and materials, instructions and procedures, the way in which responses are scored, and interpretation of the results are consistent from one administration of a test to another. Holding all these things constant from one person to another allows the test results to reflect only the differences among people. Standardization permits the establishment of norms, much as normal ranges are defined for various medical tests. The clinician is able to identify behaviors and characteristics that deviate from the norm, and quantify the extent of deviation.

Reliability refers to the stability of test findings over time and repeated administration. Just as blood pressure readings should be essentially the same if taken twice or if taken by different clinicians, tests should yield stable findings in a stable characteristic, and yield essentially the same findings when given by different examiners. Establishing that a measure is reliable allows the clinician to conclude that a change in scores reflects some change in the person, rather than irrelevant variability.

Although reliability ensures a consistent valuation of what the test is claimed to measure, it does not ensure that the test, in fact, measures what is claimed. **Validity** is established by demonstrating that the test accurately relates to other measures of the construct, accurately predicts a person's status now or in the future, and differentiates among people accurately. In practice, a test is only considered valid for certain uses and for certain populations, and understanding these limitations is critical to using a test correctly. The ultimate criterion for evaluating a psychological test is utility, but a test that is not valid, reliable, and appropriately standardized is unlikely to be useful.

Assessment of Personality and Psychopathology

A broad range of measures exists for evaluating personality characteristics, emotional state, and symptoms of psychiatric disorder. These measures vary widely in focus, extensiveness, and method. They may evaluate many different

Title Page of Anatomy Text *Vesalius (1543).* Courtesy of the National Library of Medicine. *Most physicians perform in the superior to very superior range of intellectual ability.*

aspects of personality functioning, or focus on symptoms in a specific area of interest; some are aimed at evaluating "normal" aspects of personality functioning, while many others are used for clinical purposes.

Most currently used instruments are considered *objective* in that they ask for specific answers to specific questions that have a given meaning and significance. For example, respondents read a statement (e.g., *I am often depressed*) and decide if it is true or false as applied to them. In **projective testing**, the stimuli are much more ambiguous and the range of responses is more diverse. Perhaps the best known example of a projective personality test is the **Rorschach Ink Blot Test**, where the designs are not intended to look like anything in particular and persons can theoretically see all manner of things in the patterns made by the blot. Because the stimuli have no obvious meaning and the possible responses are so diverse, it is thought that responses are a *projection* of a person's inner feelings and ways of thinking. Other projective tests ask the subject to generate stories in response to pictures of persons in ambiguous situations, to complete the stems of sentences such as "I am most afraid of ..." with a personally relevant answer.

The best known and most widely used of the objective tests of personality and psychopathology is the **Minnesota Multiphasic Personality Inventory** (MMPI), currently in its second edition. The 567 statements, identified as true or false by the subject, load onto 10 primary clinical scales, many more supplemental and content scales, and several *validity* scales. The purpose of the validity scales is to provide information about the person's approach to taking the test, and they can help determine if the person is exaggerating, minimizing, or responding inconsistently. The scores a person obtains on various scales quantify the extent to which the person deviates from expected norms.

Intellectual and Academic Skills

Formal assessment of intellect began just about 100 years ago with a test introduced in France in 1905 by Alfred Binet. Currently, the most widely used tests of intelligence are the measures originally devised by David Wechsler. These include the **Wechsler Adult Intelligence Scale** (WAIS-III, for subjects 16-years old and older), the **Wechsler Intelligence Scale for Children** (WISC-IV, for subjects 6-16), and the **Wechsler Preschool and Primary Scale of Intelligence** (WPPSI, for ages 4–6).

Intelligence tests yield a score called an *IQ* (intelligence quotient). The idea of an intelligence quotient originated with early formulations of IQ as a ratio of chronological age and a "mental age" exhibited in test performance. Students may have seen a description of this *ratio IQ* as Mental Age/Chronological Age × 100. For a variety of reasons, the ratio IQ has been superseded by the *deviation IQ*, in which scores can be directly interpreted in terms of departure from an average level. IQ scores, which are a type of *standard score*, have a mean of 100, and a standard deviation of 15. The scores compare a person with others in his or her age group; a score of 115, for example, places a person one standard deviation above the mean, at the eighty-fourth percentile for persons of a similar age. The use of age-group norms corrects for normal age-related change in different areas of functioning.

A global score called a Full Scale IQ provides a statement about overall functioning, but sometimes conceals significant underlying variability. The Wechsler tests traditionally included two broad groups of specific measurements. Verbal tests, yielding a **Verbal IQ**, included such things as vocabulary, general information, and social reasoning. Another group of tests emphasizing visual abilities and speed generated a **Performance IQ**. Current editions provide four index scores representing more specific domains of ability. These deal with verbal abilities, visual and visuospatial abilities, speed of processing, and working memory.

One situation in which formal intellectual assessment will figure prominently is in diagnosis of mental retarda-

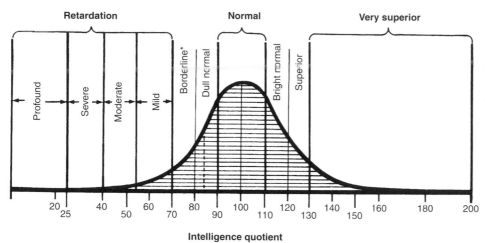

FIGURE 18.1 The distribution of IQ scores in the general population. Both the American Association on Mental Deficiency and the American Psychiatric Association use the range 71 to 84 to define borderline intellectual functioning.

tion and learning disorders. One essential criterion for diagnosis of mental retardation is a finding of subnormal intellectual functioning, typically defined as an IQ score of 70 or below (which falls at least two standard deviations below the norm, or in the bottom 2% of the age group). An essential criterion for diagnosing learning disorders is a finding of approximately normal intelligence, combined with failure to achieve at an expected level in one or more areas of academic ability.

A variety of standardized tests exist for evaluating academic skills. Some are best used for screening, some focus on a narrow area, and others offer an entire battery of tests examining a wide range of abilities. Scores are commonly expressed as standard scores with mean of 100 and a standard deviation of 15, and will have norms for age and education.

Neuropsychological Assessment

Clinical neuropsychology is an established specialty area in clinical psychology. The neuropsychologist assesses intellectual, cognitive, social, and emotional functioning and makes inferences about the integrity of cerebral functioning, and about the ability of the patient to perform in a variety of social, interpersonal, and vocational roles. The value of assessment rests in identifying the functional significance of brain impairment (how a lesion affects a person's behavior and capabilities), and in the assessment of disorders in which behavioral manifestations precede structural change in the brain (e.g., dementia) or involve no structural evidence of impairment (e.g., mild head trauma).

Evaluation will typically include interviews with the patient and perhaps with family members or other significant others, review of records, and formal testing of various dimensions of neurocognitive functioning (summarized in Box 20.8). Testing may involve the use of standardized batteries of tests; the ones most likely to be encountered in practice are the **Halstead-Reitan Neuropsychological Bat-**

tery and the **Luria-Nebraska Neuropsychological Battery**. The former is more widely used and better known; the latter is somewhat briefer and the required equipment is more portable and less expensive.

SUMMARY

Understanding patients thoroughly underlies all efforts to diagnose and plan treatment. The techniques described in this chapter can be of invaluable assistance as clinicians work to comprehend the nature of the patients in their charge.

CASE STUDY

William H. is a 59-year-old man who comes in at the urging of his wife with problems including recurrent gastrointestinal distress, diarrhea, and headaches. Workup does not reveal any evident medical condition, but it comes out in conversation that his symptoms have stymied three attempts at taking the admission test for law school. He is eligible for retirement, and his wife is encouraging him to pursue a long-expressed dream of becoming a lawyer. He presents himself as exceptionally intelligent, but his grades were unspectacular in college. He has an engineering degree, and has worked in the same technical capacity for a state agency for over 30 years but he has never been promoted or received merit pay. He has had periods of depression for many years but never sought treatment. He lived with his mother for most of his adult life, marrying after her death 4 years earlier.

The physician makes a referral for evaluation, recognizing the possibility that anxiety, depression, and personality issues may contribute to this man's presenting problems. What factors lead the physician to think this?

The patient's academic and work history do not suggest a person of exceptional intellect. An objective appraisal of intellectual functioning may help the physician respond to the situation. Assessment of the patient's emotional status and personality can help clarify the extent to which his symptoms might represent anxiety over the prospect of actually following through on his dream, manifestations of underlying depression, or conflicts about dependency.

Intellectual assessment indicates that Mr. H. is a person of superior ability, with a Full Scale IQ of 128, which places him at the 97th percentile for persons in his age group. He has exceptional verbal abilities and excellent working memory, which involves mental manipulation of information in immediate memory. His visual and visuospatial abilities are above average. Simple speed of processing is average.

Mr. H.'s MMPI validity indices suggested that he might underestimate his problems, looking to appear more healthy than he is, but not to an extent that would invalidate the profile. The dominant features suggest depression and somatization. Persons with similar profiles are more likely than others to react to stress with physical symptoms and tend to present physical symptoms that medical findings will not adequately explain. They tend to be passive and dependent in relationships and have trouble expressing aggressive feelings overtly. They are often emotionally immature and rely excessively on denial and repression as defenses. The psychologist also administered the Millon Clinical Multiaxial Inventory (MCMI-III), which indicated dependent personality features.

The physician now knows that Mr. H. has the intellectual capacity to be successful in law school, but there are significant indications that he may be conflicted and stressed by the prospect of actually pursuing a law degree. He might be counseled about the natural stress that would be associated with such a drastic change in his life and the idea that some people react to this kind of stress with physical symptoms. These symptoms are no less genuine for being a reaction to stress. Referral to a therapist can help this patient address his conflicts and clarify what he wants, and can help him deal with the stressors if he wants to proceed with enrolling in law school.

SUGGESTED READINGS

Leon, R.L. (1989). *Psychiatric interviewing: A primer.* New York: Elsevier North-Holland.
This is an older but still valuable little book for students and residents. It covers the mental status examination in nonpsychiatric primary care, difficult situations such as taking sexual histories, and use of collateral family interviews. Common pitfalls to avoid when learning to interview are also covered.

Health and Psychosocial Instruments (HaPI) Database, PO Box 110287, Pittsburgh, PA, 15232–0787.
This is a comprehensive CD-ROM database allowing health professionals to access thousands of psychosocial instruments used in health care settings. These include questionnaires, interview schedules, coding schemes, rating scales, tests, projective techniques, and measures using vignettes. HaPI uses *Medical Subject Headings (MeSH)* to key the medical literature, and *Thesaurus of Psychological Index Terms* for the behavioral literature.

Rozensky, R.H., Sweet, J.J., & Tovian, S.M. (1997). *Psychological assessment in medical settings.* New York: Plenum.
This book discusses how a well-organized psychological assessment service should operate in a medical setting. Special emphasis is given to referral questions, efficiency, and quality control.

Zimmerman, M. (1993). A 5-minute psychiatric screening interview. *Journal of Family Practice, 37,* 479–482.
This is a remarkably clever paper, which presents a very brief screening tool to be used by busy primary care physicians to identify patients who require further evaluation. This interview is concise and quickly covers the gamut of functioning using down-to-earth questions that are unlikely to offend the patient.

19 Recognizing and Treating Psychopathology in Primary Care

Debra Bendell Estroff & Pilar Bernal

> In my father's time, talking with the patient was the biggest part of medicine, for it was almost all there was to do. The doctor-patient relationship was, for better or worse, a long conversation in which the patient was at the epicenter of concern and knew it.
>
> LEWIS THOMAS

In the context of today's rapidly changing health care, appropriate allocation of medical resources to both improve quality of care and increase efficiency of services has become a priority. Traditionally, medical education focused on organ systems. Medical specialties evolved from the expertise clinicians developed treating specific organs or illnesses. However, the presence of **comorbidity** (e.g., depression exacerbating diabetes or anxiety contributing to mitral valve prolapse) made diagnosis and treatment more complex. In addition, the influence of a patient's level of functioning and social support systems often altered the outcomes for patients with the same diagnosis and given the same treatment.

In a landmark study, clinical researchers documented that *women with breast cancer who participated in group therapy had longer survival rates than women in matched control groups who did not participate in therapy groups*. It is critical for primary care physicians to be aware of studies like this one documenting the power of social support. It has become increasingly clear that good doctors treat whole patients and not simply diseased organs.

THE PRESENTATION OF MENTAL ILLNESS IN PRIMARY CARE SETTINGS

The focus of treatment in medicine has shifted from treatment for acute conditions to treatment of chronic illness.

The central problems that concerned early physicians included infection, nutrition, high infant mortality, and limited life expectancy; these problems have not disappeared, but significant advances have been made in each of these areas. Physicians increasingly confront the serious morbidity associated with psychosocial problems, and their practice often centers on the treatment of chronic illness and mental health problems.

More than 30 years ago it was shown that psychiatric illness was one of the most common reasons for consulting a medical practitioner, and of psychiatric disorders 95% were treated without specialist involvement. This trend has persisted through the years and psychiatric illnesses are still among the most common disorders presenting in primary care medical settings. The term *"de facto mental health services system" refers to the fact that 50% of the nation's mentally ill receive treatment solely from primary care practitioners and not from psychiatrists or other mental health providers*. Recent epidemiological surveys confirm this trend, showing that psychiatric disorders, particularly *depressive disorders, substance use disorders, and anxiety disorders are routinely treated in primary medical care settings*.

Psychiatric illnesses such as depression, anxiety, posttraumatic stress disorder (PTSD), and substance abuse have been shown to be associated with significant psychosocial morbidity, excess mortality, and increased cost to society, yet these disorders frequently go undetected and untreated. Only a minority of patients with psychiatric disorders will ever receive treatment, whether from a generalist or specialist.

Posttraumatic Stress Disorder

It is important for every primary care physician to be able to recognize and treat PTSD. Recent studies indicate that as many as 60% of men and 51% of women in the general population report at least one traumatic event at some time in their lives, and 17% of men and 13% of women experience more than three such events. The most common traumatic events include witnessing someone injured or killed; being involved in a fire, flood, or natural disaster; being involved in a life-threatening accident; robbery; or the sudden tragic death or injury of a close relative or friend. Less common, but some times more traumatic, events included molestation, physical attack, rape, combat, and physical abuse. Despite these high rates of trauma, only 10.4% of women and 5% of men actually report experiencing PTSD.

PTSD is a chronic and highly comorbid condition. When a person recovers spontaneously, this most often occurs within 3 months of the trauma. About one third of PSTD cases are better after a year, but two thirds are not. *After 10 years, over a third of patients with PTSD still experience symptoms several times a week.* Individuals with any PTSD symptoms are at a higher risk for health problems and more likely to experience chronic illnesses. Studies of combat veterans, rape victims, refugees, hostages, disaster victims, and women with a history of physical and sexual abuse have found that *the physical complaints of trauma victims are numerous and serious, resulting in a disproportionate use of the health-care system and outpatient expenses up to two times as great as those of other health-care users.* In many cases, the patient feels that the trauma has no bearing on the present physical complaint. Individuals with PTSD symptoms are no more likely to seek treatment through the mental health system than nonvictims and, in fact, appear to be even more reluctant than others with emotional problems to seek professional help.

People with PTSD have a high degree of **comorbidity**. Sixteen percent of patients with PTSD have one other psychiatric diagnosis, 17% have two other psychiatric diagnoses, and nearly 50% have three or more additional psychiatric diagnoses. Even the most conservative studies show that those with PTSD are two to four times more likely to

have other psychiatric diagnosis including depressive disorders, anxiety disorders, phobias, substance abuse, or somatization disorders. *Somatization was found to be 90 times more likely in those with PTSD than those without it, suggesting an important, but often overlooked, connection between PTSD and physical complaints.*

TABLE 19.1 Symptoms of PTSD

Post-traumatic stress disorder
- intrusive images, thoughts, perceptions, dreams of trauma
- avoidance of thoughts, feelings, conversations, places, people associated with trauma
- difficulty falling or staying asleep
- diminished interest or participation in significant activities
- difficulty concentrating
- inability to recall important aspects of trauma
- sense of foreshortened future
- restricted range of affect
- irritability or outbursts of anger
- feeling of detachment or estrangement from others
- hyper-vigilance
- exaggerated startle response

Depression and Anxiety

Depressive disorders, substance abuse disorders, and anxiety disorders are common in primary medical care settings and constitute a major source of disability. *Depression is without question the most common psychiatric problem that primary care clinicians encounter.* Major depressive disorders develop in 15% of the population (with a higher incidence for women) during their lifetime, and an estimated 70% to 80% of these patients will seek treatment from their primary care physician. In addition, *almost a third of all patients seeing their primary care physician have a diagnosable anxiety disorder.*

TABLE 19.2 Symptoms of depression and anxiety

Depression	Anxiety
• feelings of hopelessness	• excessive anxiety and worry, more days than not for at least 6 months
• poor appetite or overeating	• difficulty controlling the worry
• insomnia or hypersomnia	• sleep disturbance
• low energy or fatigue	• easily fatigued; restlessness or feeling keyed up or on edge
• poor concentration or difficulty making decisions	• difficulty concentrating or mind going blank
• low self-esteem	• anxiety causes significant distress or impairment in daily functioning
• suicidal ideation or attempts	• muscle tension
• in children/adolescents can manifest as irritability or angry outbursts	• irritability

Refer to *DSM-IV* for further symptomatology

Substance Abuse

Abuse of both legal and illegal substances is common and debilitating in both adults and adolescents. Between 17–27% of Americans are affected by substance abuse and dependence over their lifetime. Even higher rates are found in hospitalized patients and in emergency departments. As with other psychiatric problems, *substance abuse remains largely undetected and underdiagnosed* and is accompanied by stigma and shame.

Substance abuse is linked with multiple health complications, as well as psychosocial problems. For example, smoking has been linked with cancer, cardiovascular disease, and pulmonary disease of various types. In addition, smoking causes complications in conditions such as peptic ulcers and pregnancy, and increased mortality.

Alcoholism, another common substance abuse problem, is the third leading cause of death in this nation. Alcohol is an important contributing factor in half of the motor vehicle accidents, half of homicides, a quarter of suicides, and in a substantial majority of deaths from drowning, fires, poisonings, and falls. Alcohol is also responsible for widespread toxicity of multiple organ systems, including the brain, heart, liver, endocrine system, gastrointestinal system, skeletal muscle, and skin systems. Neurotoxicity is another consequence of alcoholism. Seven organic mental disorders are associated with alcohol, including intoxication, uncomplicated withdrawal, withdrawal delirium, idiosyncratic intoxication, alcohol hallucinosis, alcohol amnestic disorder, and dementia associated with alcoholism. In addition alcohol, often in association with other drugs, is a major contributing factor in cases of domestic violence, child abuse and neglect, homelessness, and a broad range of criminal acts.

Fetal Alcohol Spectrum Disorder (FASD) refers to a range of mental and physical defects that develop in an unborn fetus when the mother drinks alcohol during pregnancy. This alcohol in the bloodstream crosses the placenta and interferes with the ability of the fetus to receive nutrients and oxygen. Some babies born with FASD have distinctive facial characteristics including **short palpebral fissures**, an **indistinct philtrum**, and a **thin upper lip**. With or without these facial characteristics, children with FASD are often seriously handicapped with symptoms that include growth deficiencies, skeletal deformities, facial abnormalities, organ deformities, and

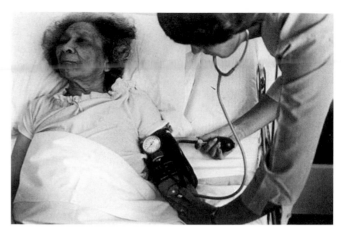

Woman with Depressed Affect Courtesy of the National Institute on Aging. *Learning to recognize depressed affect is a critical clinical skill.*

central nervous system handicaps. *Primary care physicians are often the first health-care providers to identify the symptoms of FASD*, and they can play an important role in educating women of child-bearing age at risk for becoming pregnant about the importance of avoiding all alcohol exposure during pregnancy.

PRIMARY CARE DETECTION

Even though most patients with mental disorders are seen only in primary care settings, *these disorders frequently go unrecognized by primary care practitioners.* Mental health specialists provide services to only a very small percentage of those with mental health difficulties such as depression, anxiety, PTSD, and substance abuse. Between 15% and 40% of adult primary care patients have diagnosable mental disorders, yet fewer than 20% of these are treated by mental health specialists. Since primary care physicians are those most likely to see patients with psychiatric disorders, it is imperative that they ask patients about traumatic exposure and changes in their home, work, or social life. *All competent primary care providers have to be familiar with the symptoms of psychiatric disorders*, and they must continually decide whether to refer those patients to mental health professionals.

Adolescents

Adolescents are generally healthy. Few adolescents are hospitalized, and outpatient care typically focuses on relatively minor problems such as colds, sore throats, ear infections, skin and vision problems, and allergies. While adolescents have the lowest utilization of health-care services of any age group and are the group least likely to seek care in tradi-

TABLE 19.3 Likelihood of birth defects	
Down syndrome	1/800 births
Cleft lip ± palate	1/800 births
Spina bifida	1/1000 births
Fetal alcohol syndrome	1–2/1000 births

tional office-based settings, they are also more likely to be uninsured than any other age group. This is especially true for ethnic minorities and the economically impoverished. Ironically, uninsured adolescents tend to have the most significant health problems, as poverty is associated with increased risk of disease and chronic illness.

> In my experience of anorexia nervosa it is exclusively a disease of private patients.
>
> SIR ADOLF ABRAMS
> British physician

About 6% of the adolescent population between the ages of 10 and 18 years have a chronic condition that limits their daily activities. The major physical disabilities for this group include chronic respiratory conditions such as asthma and diseases of the muscle and skeletal system.

The single leading cause of disability among adolescents is not physical disabilities, but mental disorders, which make up 32% of all disabilities for this age group. Between 17%–22% of youth under age 18 suffer from developmental, behavioral, or emotional problems. The former U.S. Office of Technology Assessment (OTA) estimates that at least 7.5 million youth under the age of 18 are in need of mental health services, but less than one third of these children receive services.

The suicide rate has increased more rapidly among adolescents than in the rest of the population. Most adolescents who commit **suicide** have suffered from a psychiatric disorder including affective disorders (especially depression), conduct disorders, substance abuse, anxiety disorders, eating disorders, and schizophrenia. In the past 60 years, the leading cause of death for adolescents has changed from natural causes to injury and violence. Overall mortality rates for young people rise by 239% when they reach ages 15 to 19, with violence responsible for this dramatic increase. Approximately 80% of the deaths in this age group are from accidents, homicide, or suicide. With such a high mortality rate among adolescents, it is imperative for primary care providers to be acutely aware of symptoms that may indicate a need for mental health treatment.

Children

The American Academy of Pediatrics has called for physicians to be more involved with the identification and treatment of chronic psychosocial morbidity in children. As with adults, the rate of identification of mental health problems in children is shockingly low. *Primary care physicians vary widely in their ability to correctly identify children as behaviorally or psychiatrically disordered*, identifying between .6% to 16% in different medical settings. Although

TABLE 19.4 Internalizing and externalizing symptoms	
2- to 5-year-olds	6- to 19-year-olds
Internalizing Items	**Internalizing Items**
Tires easily, little energy	Is afraid of new situations
Feels sad, unhappy	Feels sad, unhappy
Feels hopeless	Feels hopeless
Is down on him or herself	Is down on him or herself
Worries a lot	Worries a lot
Seems to have less fun	Seems to have less fun
Externalizing Items	**Externalizing Items**
Is irritable, angry	Fights with other children
Fights with other children	Takes unnecessary risks
Teases others	Does not listen to rules
Refuses to share	Does not understand other's feelings
Gets upset easily	Teases others
Hits others	Blames others for troubles
Hard to control	Refuses to share
Jellinek & Murphy (1989)	

psychosocial problems are both common and disabling, fewer than 2% of children and adolescents receive care from mental health specialists in any given year. This lack of mental health services for children creates a burden on other service sectors, including schools, child welfare services, correctional facilities, and nonpsychiatric health-care providers, particularly primary care physicians.

Many children experience difficulties with emotional regulation. Emotional regulation is the ability to direct and modify intense feelings. The central focus of emotional regulation is impulse control. One aspect of lack of control is externalizing problems with emotions displayed in impulsive anger and attacks on other people or things. Examples of externalizing behaviors include: fighting with others, taking unnecessary risks, and not understanding other's feelings. Others display internalizing problems with inhibition or fear being the primary response. Examples of internalizing behaviors include worrying a lot, feeling hopeless, and feeling sad and unhappy.

The relationship between childhood mental disorders and parental mental disorders has been well established, with research demonstrating that 25–50% of the children of mentally ill parents also have psychiatric disorders that require evaluation and follow up. Several studies have suggested that psychological disturbance in children is more closely related to the degree of parental *functional impairment* than to the presence of a parental psychiatric diagnosis. High levels of stress and low levels of cohesion and social support have been associated with psychiatric illness in both children and their parents.

As with the adult population, relatively few children are

seen by mental health specialists. It is estimated that between 5–15% of all children under the age of 18 have significant mental health problems, yet only 2% of children with mental health difficulties are seen by specialists, while primary care physicians see about 75% of children with psychiatric disabilities. Pediatricians often play a central role in the detection and management of mental disorders in children.

IDENTIFICATION AND DIAGNOSIS

Some of the obstacles to the diagnosis and treatment of mental disorders in primary care medical settings include inadequate training, incompetent diagnosis and treatment, economic pressures, and physician discomfort with discussions of patients' emotional problems. One significant barrier to effective detection of mental disorders is the idea that psychiatry is somehow separate from the rest of medicine. There is a **mind-body split** built into the language of medicine that dates back to the time of Descartes and separates mental and physical causes of illness. In addition, physicians are often not trained to recognize and manage psychiatric problems. Additional demands made on physicians have increased steadily over the years, while the fundamental demands of practice (health monitoring and supervision, preventive care, management of acute medical problems, and preventive guidance for parents) have remained constant. In addition to core medical tasks, *physicians are now expected to recognize and manage developmental and behavioral problems such as depression or learning and attention-deficit disorders, as well as environmental threats such as family violence, child abuse and neglect, and parenting and family relationship problems.* Preventive services including a wide range of screenings, parent counseling, and immunization services are routinely expected of primary care physicians.

Identifying mental illness is often more difficult in primary care settings than in psychiatric settings. Patients in primary care clinics often present with ill-defined or somatic complaints that are not acknowledged or recognized as mental health problems. Patient resistance to psychiatric disorders and treatment is also common in primary care. Primary care patients often do not expect or desire psychosocial assistance for unrecognized mental health problems.

The process of care is very different in psychiatric and primary care settings, which may also contribute to the difficulty in detecting psychiatric problems. In psychiatric settings, the mental health problem is the sole focus of care, whereas in primary care, clinicians often manage multiple problems simultaneously and almost never address mental health difficulties apart from other health problems.

One response to the increasing recognition by physicians of the need to treat psychosocial problems has been

TABLE 19.5 Most frequent principal reasons for family physician office visits
1. Cough
2. Symptoms referable to throat
3. General medical examination
4. Back symptoms
5. Hypertension
6. Ear ache or ear infection
7. Headache, pain in head
8. Blood pressure
9. Stomach pain or cramps
10. Head cold, upper respiratory infection
11. Prenatal examination, routine
12. Physical examination required for employment
13. Skin rash
14. Chest pain, fever
15. Fever
16. Diabetes mellitus
17. Neck symptoms
18. Well-baby examination
19. Nasal congestion
20. Low back symptoms
Adapted from Ostergaard, D. & Schmittling, G. (1994).

screening within primary care settings. **Screening** for mental health problems has been popular since 1985 when 46% of physicians reported using questionnaires in their practice. *Screening may be especially important because primary care physicians range so widely in their ability to recognize children with behavioral or psychiatric problems.* Since the majority of disordered children are seen by primary care providers, researchers across the country have focused on screening in pediatric practices as a way to assist in proper identification of this population. For the adult population, screening for depression, anxiety, and substance abuse is critical in primary care settings.

Several studies have evaluated the ability of physicians to accurately assess psychiatric disability among their patients. *These studies consistently report underrecognition of mental health problems.* For example, in a study of 2–18-year-olds, using an objective measurement of psychopathology, underrecognition by primary care providers was closely documented, and pediatricians routinely failed to identify those patients who needed mental health services. These pediatricians had **low sensitivity** and **high specificity** in their identification of psychiatric disorders; in other words, *they failed to detect many positive cases but seldom misidentified negative cases.*

In a similar study, multiple regression analyses measured utilization and the cost of health and psychiatric care. The average cost of health care per child was $393 for one year of medical services within an HMO. The average health-care cost for children with symptoms of anxiety and de-

Home Health and Institutional Placement

Family members confronting the difficult decision of whether to place a relative in an institution often turn to their family physician for advice. Explicit criteria for the physician to use in counseling a family include regular incontinence of bladder and bowel, inability of the relative to cooperate in their care, inability of the relative to realize that a home with familiar caregivers is stable and secure, risk to the health or mental stability of others in the home, and primary caregiver burnout. Options available to families include assisted living facilities, general nursing homes, and nursing homes with locked units and mental health expertise. A mid-level alternative might be mental health services in the home setting provided by a mental health nurse who has a sophisticated understanding of assessment tools and treatment protocols such as clinical pathways.

Rehabilitation Strategies

Chronic psychiatric disorders limit an individual's ability to function in multiple spheres. Traditional psychotherapy does not address practical aspects of daily living and coping strategies. For the more impaired psychotic and depressed patients, socialization, activities of daily living, time management, and organization are important areas of treatment. When integrated into a comprehensive treatment plan that includes psychotropic medication, psychotherapy, and other treatment modalities, psychosocial rehabilitation offers the patient and their families important assistance with these practical matters.

SUMMARY

It is essential to train physicians to recognize mental illness. Psychosocial and psychiatric conditions affect a large number of patients, and their pain goes unrecognized and untreated. Medical science illuminates the delicate balance between mind and body. Learning to recognize and treat the whole human being is an essential skill for tomorrow's primary care physicians.

> We disparage labeling of all kinds in psychiatry insofar as these labels apply to supposed diseases or conditions of specific etiological determination. We deplore the tendency of psychiatry to retain its old perjorative name-calling function. Patients who consult us because of their suffering and their distress and their disability have every right to resent being plastered with a damning index tab. Our function is to help these people, not to further afflict them.
>
> KARL MENNINGER (1963)

CASE STUDY

A 17-year-old female college student is brought to the emergency department of your hospital when she goes into a coma, apparently as a result of noncompliance with her insulin treatments. She was diagnosed 2 years ago with diabetes mellitus. Several candy bar wrappers were found in her backpack at the time of her hospitalization as well as some writings in her notebook expressing suicidal thoughts. When she wakes up she refuses to speak to anyone. Her roommates report that lately she has been keeping to herself and hiding out in her room. She sleeps a lot, but still has trouble getting up for class. She is irritable and becomes angry easily, and her grades are slipping. She doesn't go out as much with friends anymore and seems to have gained weight in the last few months.

How would you manage this patient? Would behavior modification programs such as self-monitoring be appropriate? Should the patient be referred to psychiatry for evaluation of her depression and her potential risk for suicide? Are the patient's problems primarily psychiatric or medical? Do you need this young woman's permission to discuss her case with her parents?

Depression is very common and primary care physicians need to be aware of the symptoms in adolescents and young adults. Suicide is one of the leading causes of death for young adults, further underscoring the importance of vigilance on the part of physicians for the development of depression. In general, studies have shown that *between 1 to 2 years after the initial diagnosis of a chronic illness, patients go through a second adjustment, realizing "this is for life."* In cases of chronic illness, anticipatory guidance for families to understand that this period of adjustment may occur in the second year after diagnosis is helpful. Noncompliance with treatment is a very common issue during adolescence and may extend into young adulthood. Interventions that enable children and adolescents to deal realistically with the "this is for life" response are important, as well as education on the short- and long-term consequences of noncompliance with treatment. Young adults and their families should be referred to psychiatry to deal with depression and for help adjusting to the realities of life with a chronic illness. At 17 the patient is still a minor even though she is attending college.

Your patient is discharged after a brief psychiatric consultation suggests she is not acutely suicidal. However, you schedule an appointment with her for the following week and discover she has continued to lose weight. Her vital signs and EKG are within normal limits.

Would a patient like this benefit from antidepressant medication? Is bed rest and a restricted diet advisable? Will you want this young woman and her parents and siblings to be in family therapy? Should she be hospitalized?

Your patient was able to recover from her acute symptoms and does not require a more intensive level of psychiatric care at this time. However, her progress should be monitored from both a physical and psychological perspective.

After 6 months you note that your patient has been only partially compliant with treatment and she continues to gain weight. She returns for her weekly medical appointment and discloses to the RN who is weighing her that she knows how to access her father's gun and has been thinking about killing herself. She begs the nurse not to tell you about her suicidal thoughts, but the nurse feels you must be informed that your patient has a plan for killing herself and she has selected a method that is clearly lethal.

Is a suicide threat a medical problem or a legal issue? Should you call 911 or the police? Will you want this patient on antidepressant medication at this point? How long will you have to wait for the medication to take effect? Should she be hospitalized or simply seen the following day? Is this a case that a primary care doctor should handle or would it be advisable to ask for a psychiatrist, clinical psychologist, or social worker to consult on this case? What is your responsibility if you are convinced the patient should be in the hospital but her insurance company disagrees and refuses to accept your recommendation?

Suicidality is a common psychiatric emergency among patients with eating disorders. As such, it should be assessed and evaluated by a mental health professional. It is probably most prudent to consult with a psychiatrist in this case because of the likelihood that antidepressant medication will need to be prescribed. The psychiatrist in turn may elect to work with a social work or psychology colleague.

It is your obligation to make the best medical decisions possible, and your patient will have to negotiate with her insurance company to ensure she receives appropriate coverage for her medical expenses. You can work as her advocate in these negotiations, however, your psychiatry colleague may be in a better position to argue that inpatient psychiatric care is essential for this young woman.

SUGGESTED READINGS

American Psychiatric Association. (2000). *Diagnostic and statistical manual of mental disorders* (4th ed., text revision). Washington, DC: Author.

The classic diagnostic manual in psychiatry, and a book that is used frequently by almost all mental health professionals.

Barlow, D. (2002). *Anxiety and its disorders (2nd ed.).* New York: Guilford.

Bernal, P., Bendell-Estroff, D., Abdouraham, J.F., Murphy, M., Keller, A., & Jellinek, M.S. (2000). Psychosocial morbidity. *Archives of Pediatrics, 154,* 261–266.

This journal article evaluates the efficacy and utility of screening in primary pediatric settings.

Kashikar-Zuck, S., Goldschneider, K., Powers, S., Vaught, M., & Hershey, A. (2004). Depression and functional disability in chronic pediatric pain. *The Clinical Journal of Pain, 34,* 341–349.

This article defines succinctly for physicians the quality of life issues associated with depression for children.

Lord, C, & Mcgee, J. (2001). *Educating children with autism.* Washington, DC: National Academics Press.

This book will aid pediatricians as well as parents to cope with a complicated and often confusing array of educational options for autistic children.

20 Managing Difficult Patients

Brenda Bursch

> It is not a case we are treating; it is a living, palpitating, alas, too often suffering fellow creature.
>
> JOHN BROWN
> Edinburgh physician and author

Most health-care providers have a desire and feel a responsibility to be helpful to their patients. It is typically assumed that the patients have a similar desire; they want to be cured, and they can and will act in their own best interests. It takes very little time and experience for most physicians to recognize that the practice of medicine is far more complex than this idealistic formula. *No matter how caring and tolerant you are as a physician, it is likely that you will have patients that you find yourself dreading*, patients with whom you feel frustrated or confused or angry. You might feel guilty about such feelings, or you might feel that it is not within your power to help these patients. The purpose of this chapter is to describe management strategies you can use to help challenging patients more effectively obtain the care they need from you.

WHO ARE THE "DIFFICULT" PATIENTS?

Approximately 15% of patient encounters are perceived as "difficult" by physicians. Physicians report they are most frustrated by patients who require much of their time and do not follow medical recommendations. Contrary to what might be expected, it is not the medically complex patients who are considered difficult, but patients who are seen as demanding, aggressive, rude, seeking secondary gain, or having multiple nonspecific psychosomatic complaints. Patients seen as "difficult" frequently have a depressive or anx-

iety disorder, alcohol abuse or dependence, a personality disorder, unexplained somatic symptoms, or more severe symptoms. They also have poorer functional status, more unmet expectations related to their appointment, less satisfaction with their medical care, and higher use of health services. Perhaps equally important, clinicians with poorer psychosocial attitudes rate more patients as difficult.

In 1978 Grove proposed four categories to describe patients who are seen by physicians as difficult: dependent clingers, entitled demanders, manipulative help-rejecters, and self-destructive deniers. Although these category terms may be unnecessarily pejorative, the accompanying descriptions are useful. **Dependent clingers** exhaust their doctors and caregivers with requests and needs—for explanation, affection, analgesics, sedatives, and attention. It is not uncommon for clinicians to feel aversion in response to a patient they view as highly needy. It is helpful to remember that individuals who have an insatiable need for attention are not happy and have no intention of provoking feelings of aversion in their clinicians. Regardless of the medical problems present in highly needy patients, *the most effective and helpful intervention can be to arrange predictable, limited, and appropriate types of attention for them.*

Entitled demanders often use guilt, intimidation, or threats to manipulate clinicians. Not surprisingly, such patients' threats are ultimately self-defeating since clinicians become fearful of them and often respond with anger, sometimes striking back at the patient. Surprisingly, *patients who appear angry or threatening are often quite frightened.* They may be extremely fearful of abandonment by the medical team, loss of control, receiving suboptimal care, or numerous other possible consequences of their situation. It is especially important that clinicians remain nondefensive and agree with angry and demanding patients that they have a right to a high quality of care. It can be very helpful to remember that these patients are fundamentally fearful and potentially in need of guidance regarding how to more effectively communicate with the treatment team.

Manipulative help-rejecters, sometimes called "crocks" by frustrated clinicians, have symptoms that seemingly can never be relieved or that continually change over time. Some even appear to derive satisfaction from the failures of the clinicians, perhaps pleased that they can maintain their relationship with the clinician as long as they have symptoms. *Common emotional reactions experienced by physicians to this type of patient include worry about overlooking a treatable illness, irritation with the patient, helplessness, and self-doubt.* Not surprisingly, patients often have the same feelings. They are worried about a potentially lethal disease being missed, they worry that they will not be believed, they worry that they really are crazy, they become frustrated with clinicians who can not explain or fix their symptoms, and they feel helpless. It is essential that the clinician communicate with

these patients using language which conveys a biopsychosocial model, and *avoid the temptation to dichotomize problems as either physical or mental*. If rapport is established, a focus on functioning with a rehabilitation approach can be effective.

Self-destructive deniers deny the need for self-care to the point of being self-destructive; they could be considered chronically suicidal, though they would more likely admit to hopelessness than acknowledge suicidal ideation. Some may appear to find meaning in observing their own demise. Clinicians may feel a desire to save these patients or they may sometimes covertly wish the patient would die. Because it is hard for these patients to see that they are potentially contributing to their own deterioration, it is important to gently confront their denial by being supportively explicit about the choices they have, by acknowledging any healthy decisions or actions they take, and by pointing out any unhealthy decisions they are making.

THE PHYSICIAN'S FRAME OF REFERENCE

It can be extremely rewarding to successfully treat, or minimize **iatrogenic harm** in, a patient that other clinicians have deemed untreatable. As might be clear from the previous section, *it is possible to use your reactions to patients as a diagnostic tool to help you discern what your patient is feeling and what he or she needs*. Not surprisingly, you may have some patients with elements of several of the emotions and actions described above.

The first essential frame of reference to adopt is that *anyone can be difficult*. This includes you. It is far more useful to think of the appointment as difficult, while refraining from labeling a person as difficult. After all, few people feel good about being angry, needy, or self-destructive. It is possible to learn how to manage difficult patient encounters in a manner that will help both you and your patient. Once you adopt this frame of reference and develop good management skills, you might even find yourself fascinated by difficult patient encounters.

The next step is to recognize that *you will see patients under unusual times of stress*. You have chosen a career that will require you to be in contact with highly distressed individuals. People are more vulnerable to illness and injury when extremely stressed. Additionally, *injury and illness is stressful to most people under the best of circumstances*. Most clinicians are not born with the intuitive knowledge about how to best

TABLE 20.1 Common scenarios

Patient Behavior	Common Physician Reaction	What a Patient Might Be Feeling	Potentially Helpful Physician Responses	Caution
Unending requests for explanations, medications or other forms of attention.	Aversion Exhaustion	Anxiety	Arrange predictable, limited, and appropriate types of attention for them.	Avoid being 100% accessible to patient.
Attempts to use guilt, intimidation, or threats to alter physician behavior.	Fear Anger	*Fear* of: • abandonment by the medical team, • loss of control, • receiving suboptimal care, or • other consequences of their situation.	• Remain nondefensive. • Agree with angry/demanding patients that they have a right to a high quality of care. • Provide guidance about how to more effectively communicate with the treatment team.	Avoid potentially dangerous situations and document well.
Complaints of symptoms that are not associated with identifiable disease, are never relieved, or continually change over time.	• Worry about overlooking a treatable illness. • Irritation with patient. • Helplessness. Self-doubt.	• Worry about a potentially lethal disease being missed. • Worry that they will not be believed. • Worry that they really are crazy. • Frustration with clinicians who can not explain or fix symptoms. • Helplessness.	• Inform patient that you believe them and do not think they are crazy. • Explain problem using biopsychosocial language. • If rapport is established, a focus on functioning with a rehabilitation approach. • Emphasize need for active self-care.	Avoid the temptation to dichotomize problems as either physical or mental.
Denies the need for self-care or does not engage in self-care.	• Desire to save patient. • Wish that the patient would die.	• No anxiety about health. • Confusion regarding concern of clinician. • Possible depression.	Gently confront denial by being supportively explicit about the choices they have, by acknowledging any healthy decisions or actions they take, and by pointing out any unhealthy decisions they are making.	
Excessive flattery, frequent gifts, or efforts to establish a personal relationship with the physician.	Aversion Attraction	*Fear* of: • abandonment by the medical team, • loss of control, • receiving suboptimal care, or • other consequences of their situation.	Politely refuse requests for social contacts, offers of personal favors, or excessive clinical contacts.	Avoid boundary violations.

CASE EXAMPLE

Mr. Eastman is the father of a 4-year-old girl undergoing a bone marrow transplant. The Director of the hospital calls you to let you know that Mr. Eastman complained that you did not sufficiently wash your hands before examining his daughter. When you get to the hospital room, Mr. Eastman starts to loudly complain about a stain on the floor. You are angry that he complained about you and feel he is being extremely unreasonable. You can respond in several ways; here are two options:

You can ask Mr. Eastman to refrain from complaining and inform him that he is being unreasonable in his expectations.	You can sincerely acknowledge Mr. Eastman's fear for his daughter's life and discuss the rationale behind and reasonable goals for contagion precautions.

While either approach might stop Mr. Eastman from complaining so loudly for the moment, the second approach is more likely to facilitate a beneficial (and perhaps enjoyable) discussion that will strengthen the trust in your relationship and help your patient's father cope with the stress and tension he is experiencing in this frightening situation.

CASE EXAMPLE

Mrs. Robinson, who is somewhat shy, comes in with flu-like symptoms. An appointment can take two directions from the start depending on your assessment of patient expectations.

APPROACH 1

"Good morning Mrs. Robinson, I see from the nurse's note that you aren't feeling well. What symptoms are you having today?" *Note: This question assumes she wants a diagnosis and treatment plan.*	You learn she is having flu-like symptoms. You are annoyed that so many people with the flu come in for antibiotics. You explain to her that she probably has the flu but does not need antibiotics.

APPROACH 2

"Good morning Mrs. Robinson, I see from the nurse's note that you aren't feeling well. What can I do for you today?" *Note: This question lets her set the agenda.*	You learn she is worried that she might have HIV and wants to learn more about how it is transmitted. You then do some patient education, take a risk history, and decide if an HIV test is indicated.

The second approach is far more likely to meet Mrs. Robinson's real needs, and she will be much more satisfied with both the physician and the encounter.

---

handle these situations. Consequently, it is essential that you obtain training in managing difficult situations with a focus on behavioral responses when under stress.

It can be important to separate what is being said from how it is being said. It is normal to respond to both *what* your patient is telling you as well as *how* your patient is communicating with you. It is also normal to have a harder time hearing what is being said if you are disturbed by how it is being communicated to you. While much can be learned by how your patient is communicating, it is important to remember that important information can easily be lost if communicated poorly. Making a conscious decision to consider the content of a message and the patient's communication style separately can be very helpful during difficult patient encounters. This simple technique can help you better understand your patient as well as the experiences of other involved clinicians. You can then decide, and discuss with your team members, which aspects of the communication are most relevant and require your response, and which aspects are best ignored.

You can respond in ways that improve the situation or make it worse. There will be days that challenge your patience and endurance. There will be patients that you feel are unaffected by your recommendations or concerns. There will be situations over which you have no control. Nevertheless, the choices you make in difficult patient encounters can significantly alter the course of the exchange, your day in general, and your relationship with your patient. Even with the most challenging patient encounter,

you have choices in your responses that can potentially create a positive experience.

MANAGING PATIENT EXPECTATIONS

Unmet patient expectations can lead to difficult patient encounters, as well as decreased patient satisfaction and increased health-care utilization. *Dissatisfied patients are less likely to adhere to medical recommendations, follow up with appointments, or enjoy symptom improvement, and they are far more likely to change health-care providers.*

Primary care patients frequently expect to obtain information during a medical appointment, and do not necessarily expect medical tests or referrals. However, physicians often fail to accurately perceive patients' expectations, and *an estimated 15% to 25% of primary care patients do not have their expectations met during a medical appointment.* Consequently, assessing patient expectations is an important first step to improving patient satisfaction and possibly other health outcomes. Patient expectations can include being examined, having medical tests ordered, being referred to another clinician, being given a prescription, receiving education about a problem (including the normal trajectory and available treatments for an illness), receiving education about a treatment (including administration instructions, expected effects/side effects, expected improvements, and related timelines), and/or ways to self-manage a problem. *Although simple, the best way to ensure you are meeting your patients' expectations is by asking them what they are hoping to get out of their appointment rather than simply assuming that they want what you have offered.*

It is also important to help your patient develop appropriate expectations about his or her health, illness, treatment, and/or need for self-care. Having expectations that are too high or too low can lead to less than optimal health and functioning. Written patient educational materials can be of great assistance in helping patients set realistic and appropriate expectations. Consider the following patients' expectations after hip replacement surgery:

CASE EXAMPLE

Expectations Too Low	Expectations Too High
Mr. Hart had heard that most people die within 1 year of hip replacement surgery. Therefore, he decided there was no need to put himself through physical therapy and it was pointless to try to walk again. He requested a wheelchair and started to get his affairs in order.	Mrs. McKinney had heard that hip replacement surgery was wonderful. However, she became very upset when her physical therapist asked her to engage in therapeutic exercises that caused pain. In addition, she was surprised that her recovery took so long. She knew some people took longer to improve, but had expected she would complete her recovery in no more than 2 weeks.

MANAGING DIFFICULT PATIENT ENCOUNTERS

The Angry Patient

Anger is almost always a secondary emotion, and a protective response to another emotion. It can be effective at blocking the physical or emotional pain associated with fear, criticism, or perceived injustice. *Anger can also be a symptom of numerous emotional and neurological disorders.* Regardless of the etiology of the anger, it is helpful to remember that your angry patient might be feeling very vulnerable. Because an angry patient can create much distress for all clinicians involved, it is especially important to remember to check your frame of reference.

CASE EXAMPLE

Mr. Martellino is a 53-year-old man who has been in the waiting room for over 2 hours. This is partly because he was 45 minutes early, but it is also true that your last patient required considerable time and had to be hospitalized. Mr. Martellino is furious and yells loudly at you for wasting his time. He threatens to change health plans and wants to file a complaint. You have been on call all night and feel like walking out of the room.

Issues to consider:

- Safety. Is Mr. Martellino simply blowing off steam or is he being physically threatening too?
- Most people do not yell in this type of situation, and there likely is more to the story of Mr. Martellino's anger. For example, there might be something else he is angry or scared about; the delay may have seriously upset his schedule for the day; and/or Mr. Martellino's neurological functioning may be impaired.
- Most people would be angry and frustrated in a similar situation.

Communication tips:

- Avoid responding in an angry manner. This rarely improves a situation.
- Apologize and explain that an urgent patient issue delayed you.
- If the patient continues to yell, allow him to complete the outburst. Again, apologize and acknowledge the frustration. Respectfully ask the patient if he wishes to continue with his appointment or if he feels too upset or behind schedule to proceed.
- Help the patient switch topics by talking about the reason he came in today.
- Carefully document the exchange. While the outburst may have been situational, it is also helpful to track the episodes as part of your assessment. Additionally, it is helpful to have documented the event if a complaint is filed.

Consider the anger as potentially part of the clinical presentation, and do not allow it to trigger an angry response from you. The exchange will go best if you can remain calm, consider the message content and the communication style of your patient separately, and treat your patient respectfully.

Regardless of the reason for the anger, it is important to first consider your safety. Do you need to have someone else in the room with you, have an escape route, or call security? If it appears there is no physical danger present, attempt to de-escalate the anger as quickly as possible. Potentially helpful interventions include remaining nondefensive; determining what the patient is angry about, apologizing for any errors or inconveniences, even if they were not your fault (apologies can prevent lawsuits); agreeing that all patients have a right to a high quality of care; smiling and maintaining a soft voice; asking what the patient would like at this time; and attempting to refocus the patient in a productive direction.

The Pain Patient

Clinicians often dread seeing patients with chronic pain or other symptoms that do not conform to an identifiable disease or do not respond as expected to treatment. Such patients often trigger worry in clinicians about having missed a diagnosis on the one hand or contributing to an addiction on the other hand. *You should assume that the symptoms are genuine and explainable, regardless of the presence of tissue pathology or inflammation.* Persistent physical symptoms that are not fully explained by medical illness or tissue pathology are common and are often referred to as functional symptoms and disorders. These symptoms are caused by altered physiological function (the way the body works) rather than by structural abnormality.

Functional disorders are not diagnosed with x-rays or laboratory tests, but with symptom-based criteria. Examples of functional disorders include headaches, irritable bowel syndrome (IBS), and nonepileptic seizures. There is a growing research interest in identifying the biological mechanisms contributing to persistent somatic symptoms (for example, hypersensitivity in the gastrointestinal tract associated with IBS).

The key to working effectively with patients with functional disorders is to *avoid the temptation to dichotomize problems as either physical or mental*, and become highly adept at understanding all illness within a **biopsychosocial context**. The biopsychosocial model posits that illness is the product of biological, psychological, and social subsystems interacting at multiple levels. For example, biological factors contributing to functional abdominal pain include changes in intestinal wall sensory receptors, modulation of sensory transmissions in the nervous system, cortical perceptions, and pain memories. Psychological factors that might contribute include temperament, increased focus on pain-related stimuli, emotional responses to pain, pain memories, and efforts to cope with and manage pain. Relevant social factors can include family history of pain, family member responses to pain, and stressful life events. Other correlates of functional somatic symptoms include substance use, comorbid anxiety disorders, prior medical illness, physical injury, hospitalization, and a history of trauma.

A multimodal rehabilitation approach is recommended over a single sequential treatment approach. Interventions should address possible underlying symptom mechanisms, specific symptoms, and disability. In general, treatment goals should focus on increasing independent functioning (activities of daily living, vocational, social, and physical); remediation of specific symptoms, deficits, or problems revealed in the assessment; enhancing communication, especially of distress, with peers and family members; and facilitating more adaptive problem-solving skills. Treatment techniques designed to address possible

> Beware of the young doctor and the old barber.
>
> BENJAMIN FRANKLIN

underlying symptom mechanisms and specific symptoms include cognitive-behavioral strategies (e.g., cognitive behavioral psychotherapy, self-hypnosis, or biofeedback), behavioral techniques, family interventions, physical interventions (e.g., massage, acupuncture, transcutaneous electrical nerve stimulation (TENS), physical therapy, occupational therapy), and pharmacological interventions. In general, *interventions that promote active coping are preferred over those that require passive dependence.* Evidence-based treatments should be recommended whenever possible.

The Seductive Patient

Seductive patients exhibit excessive admiration, affection, and flattery, and these behaviors can initially seem comforting and benign to a clinician. The desire for a safe, supportive relationship is probably the most common motivation for patients to act seductively toward their physicians. However, clinicians can easily become overinvolved with patients who make them feel skilled, smart, attractive, or powerful, especially when the clinician is personally stressed, such as by a death or divorce, an ill family member, or excessive work. *It is important to remember that seductive patients may have a history of emotional problems and often have been victims of abuse, including incest, rape, and physical abuse.*

The ethics codes of the American Medical Association (1995–2005) and the American Osteopathic Association (2003–2005) outline the physician's duty to act in the best interests of patients, including refraining from exploiting the doctor-patient relationship. *This duty includes "key third parties," such as those who may accompany your patients to medical visits or hospitalizations.* This stance is based on two basic premises: (1) the patient-doctor relationship is nonreciprocal and the physician has more power than patients, and (2) professional medical objectivity is often lost when a physician enters into a personal intimate relationship with a patient. Research clearly documents that when physicians become intimate with patients, the patients often suffer lasting emotional harm.

Warning signs that you may be becoming overly involved include telling your favorite patient about your personal problems, spending more time with the patient than is allotted for a minor problem, scheduling him or her for the end of the day, offering free or substantially discounted care, exchanging gifts, making plans to see the patient out-

---

CASE EXAMPLE

Mrs. Rockwood is a 35-year-old woman who experienced a severed Achilles tendon while playing tennis. She had an unremarkable surgery and appears to be healing well, but now complains of severe pain. There is no indication of an infection or other explanation for her pain. She requests a higher dose of pain medication than is normally prescribed at this point in time for such surgeries. You are worried about providing the higher dose of the medication.

Issues to consider:
- Did she over-use her limb, sustain another injury, or develop a complication?
- Does she have risk factors for development of a chronic pain disorder or for opioid intolerance (for example, past injuries, comorbid anxiety, or past opioid use)?
- Does she or another family member have a substance use problem?
- Does she recognize that physical therapy is normally painful?

Communication tips:
- Accept that the patient is experiencing more pain than is typical.
- Determine specific concerns and situations that elicit greater pain.
- Evaluate for complications, comorbid problems, and exacerbating factors.
- Evaluate past injury, surgery, and opioid use behavior. Patients who previously developed tolerance for opioids often require higher doses, even years later.
- Describe a rehabilitation approach to recovery. If indicated, *encourage a focus on functioning rather than pain*. Set expectations: Physical therapy may not improve pain while functioning is still improving.
- Provide recommendations that include medications and non-medication approaches to pain management.

CASE EXAMPLE

Ms. Cooke is a 26-year-old unmarried woman who is new in town and comes in for her annual physical exam. She is highly attractive and very friendly. She brings you cookies and asks if you need any help in your office. She recently went through a difficult break-up and would like to take her mind off of it by doing some volunteer work for you. She found your name on the Internet and is impressed by your work. You are very flattered and feel tempted to take her up on the offer to organize your office.

Issues to consider:
- Safety. Is Ms. Cooke simply friendly and helpful, or could she be stalking you?
- Most people do not offer to volunteer to work for their physician, especially a new one; there is likely more to Ms. Cooke's offer. For example, she might be experiencing a personal crisis, have a history of becoming overly close to professionals, have a family member with the disease you are studying, and/or come from a very small town where this is normal behavior.
- What are some potential complications from working with your patient?

Communication tips:
- Avoid responding in an overtly rejecting manner. This rarely improves a situation.
- Thank the patient for her kind offer and state your policy on the topic (for example, not using patient volunteers, not using volunteers of any type, or not needing someone at the moment).
- Encourage volunteering through established community or hospital volunteer programs.
- Avoid sending conflicting messages to the patient. Maintain friendly, but professional communication and contact at all times.
- Carefully document the exchange. While the offer may have been perfectly innocent, it is also helpful to track the behavior as part of your assessment. Additionally, it is helpful to have the documentation if it ever becomes necessary to terminate treatment or in the event a complaint is filed.

---

side the office, and/or spending considerable time on the telephone with your patient.

It is important to understand what it is that the seductive patient is attempting to gain by his or her behaviors, to communicate clearly with the patient about your role as a physician, to avoid sending mixed messages, to discourage the seductive behavior, to document in the medical record any seductive behavior exhibited by your patient, to encourage your patient to obtain support from a mental health professional if indicated, to obtain consultation for a colleague if you are unsure if a patient is being seductive, and to refer to another clinician if needed. Never ignore seductive behavior, even if you think it is likely to be harmless. Likewise, *failing to document your patient's unusual behavior is like failing to document a fever. Not only is it clinically pertinent, but it will also be important to have the information in the medical record if the situation escalates into a legal problem.*

While some patients might be obviously inappropriate, it might be less clear in other situations.

In situations with clearly inappropriate attempts to seduce you, a more aggressive response can sometimes be necessary.

The Noncompliant Patient

Clinicians are often frustrated when they discover that a patient has not adhered to medical recommendations, perhaps not recognizing that *roughly 75% of patients do not follow all medical recommendations all of the time.* On average, adherence has been found to be best among patients with HIV, arthritis, gastrointestinal disorders, and cancer, and worst among patients with pulmonary disease, diabetes, and sleep disorders. Better adherence is associated with

CASE EXAMPLE

Mr. Finley, a 42-year-old man, who is new to your clinic, presents for a routine annual checkup. You perform the examination with your female medical assistant present. Two weeks later the patient returns and says, "I just had to see you again." During the office visit, he talks about a current difficult relationship and indicates that he is looking for someone new to care for him. He asks if you are interested in going out to dinner. You inform him that you are flattered, but not interested, and that you do not date patients. You document the behavior in the medical record. The next day, flowers and a card are delivered to you from the patient, again asking for a date and teasing that he won't take "no" for an answer since he feels you are meant to be together.

Issues to consider:
- Safety. Is Mr. Finley simply being friendly, or could he be stalking you?
- Do you need to obtain consultation from risk management, a colleague, or a mental health professional?

Communication tips:
- Do not meet alone with the patient.
- Avoid responding in an overtly rejecting manner; however, your message must be clear and definite. Restate your policy on the topic (not dating any patients *or former patients*).
- Remind your patient that it can sometimes be helpful to see a therapist when having painful and difficult relationship problems. Provide referrals.
- Inform the patient in writing that you wish to terminate care and that you recommend he see a physician of the other gender; provide referrals and offer to have records transferred.
- Carefully document the exchange in the medical record.
- Do not respond to future cards, flowers, or other gifts.

Age and eyesight may be two factors affecting adherence Courtesy of the National Institute on Aging.

- disagrees with the physician;
- meets emotional needs by visits to the doctor: nonadherence increases contact;
- has treatment goals that differ from those of the physician.

The medical recommendations:

- cause unacceptable side effects;
- are too complex or time consuming;
- are too frightening or anxiety provoking;
- are too expensive, and/or transportation to obtain the treatment is too expensive;
- are not consistent with patient beliefs.

As with many of the problem encounters discussed in this chapter, careful planning pays off and prevention is always the best cure.

To enhance adherence, during the initial evaluation and treatment planning and during subsequent points of treatment planning:

- Determine your patient's understanding of the problem or disease.
- Ask about religious or cultural factors that might influence thoughts about the problem and treatment.

less complex recommendations (taking medication vs. changing health behaviors). Reasons for not adhering to medical recommendations vary and the patient is not always aware of the fact that he or she did not follow their physician's recommendations.

Some reasons for patient nonadherence include the following factors.

The patient:

- does not understand the seriousness of the condition and/or the instructions provided. This can occur because of language problems, comprehension difficulties, a physician's desire to maintain a positive attitude or protect a patient from bad news, inadequate patient education, and/or a patient feeling overwhelmed and, thus, being unable to absorb the information.
- forgets the recommendation or instruction;
- is angry, depressed, guilty, worn out, frightened, or embarrassed by the condition;
- is uncomfortable with the physician;

CASE EXAMPLE

Mr. Golden is a 68-year-old man recovering from hip replacement surgery. He indicates that he no longer has the strength to ambulate and is requesting a wheelchair. The physical therapist reports to you that Mr. Golden is simply not interested in rehabilitation. Mr. Golden states that he is old enough to have wheelchair and it is wrong to push him into physical therapy. Mr. Golden is otherwise quite healthy; he is married, has several grandchildren living nearby, and he previously played golf 3 days per week. You are extremely frustrated by his reluctance to engage in physical therapy and understand that he is risking his MediCare coverage if he does not make progress.

Issues to consider:
- Does Mr. Golden have a comorbid medical condition interfering with adherence?
- Is he depressed, scared, angry, frustrated, in pain, embarrassed, or guilty?
- Have there been changes in his psychosocial situation?
- What does he believe about his prognosis? Does he believe that he will not live much longer?

Communication tips:
- Avoid responding in an angry manner. This rarely improves a situation.
- Attempt to engage him in conversation about his emotional response to his situation.
- Normalize his feelings (for example, it is normal to be fearful of falling again, angry at his physical therapist, or sad about his decline in health).
- Correct any information that is likely to be incorrect (for example, he might believe that all people die shortly after hip replacements, that physical therapy is not normally as frightening as he is experiencing it to be, or that he will die at age 70, just like his father did).
- Provide education regarding the normal course of recovery, the self-care requirements for optimal recovery, and the risks of not making progress.
- Point out the healthy decisions made by the patient (for example, making the decision to proceed with the surgery, completing all the postsurgical medications).
- Gently point out the unhealthy decisions made by the patient (for example, skipping physical therapy sessions and avoiding particular exercises).
- Assess his life goals and treatment priorities.
- Have a problem-solving discussion about what would help him engage in physical therapy.

CASE EXAMPLE

Miss Gracie is a 44-year-old woman with recurrent urinary tract infections. She is highly concerned about this problem and spends much of her time researching her disorder. She makes frequent telephone calls to you to discuss her hypotheses about her medical problem (for example, a primary immune deficiency) and alternate treatment approaches (for example, herbs and acupuncture). You find yourself dreading these calls and even start to wonder if she really has recurrent UTIs. You want her to feel less anxious, but it seems nothing helps her anxiety. You really wish she would find another doctor.

Issues to consider:
- Why are you dreading her calls?
- Does Miss Gracie have good ideas?
- Do you need to do your own literature search or consult a colleague?
- Does she take your advice?
- Have there been changes in her psychosocial situation?
- Does she have any comorbid medical or psychiatric problems?

Communication tips:
- Be sure to take her questions seriously; it will not help the situation to train her that physicians are unhelpful.
- Do your research; a seemingly unconventional idea might have an evidence base to support trying it.
- Attempt to understand what you dread about this patient so that you can directly address the problem.
- Avoid responding in an angry or rejecting manner. This rarely improves a situation.
- Attempt to engage her in conversation about her emotional response to his situation. How is she coping with this recurrent problem?
- Make an agreement with her regarding when and how she can contact you. For example, you might ask her to make weekly appointments with you, but to restrain from calling with questions between appointments.

- Ask the patient if they think the plan will work for them.
- Provide your patient with specific, clear, and printed instructions.
- Review how you will communicate with your patient (appointments, calls, email).
- Document all instructions given to the patient and all discussions about the treatment regimen.

Once you have detected nonadherence, the following approaches may be useful:

- Consider the nonadherence a symptom and develop a differential diagnosis to determine the underlying explanation.
- Ask the patient why they are engaging in a specific behavior. "Why are you skipping your evening medication?"

- Assess the interest and ability of your patient, or the caregiver, to participate in decisions and self-care.
- Educate your patient and family (when indicated) about the medical condition.
- Develop treatment goals jointly with your patient.
- Include the patient and family (when indicated) in planning the treatment.

- Do not criticize your patient.
- Be willing to compromise.
- Prioritize the treatment goals.
- Simplify the treatment.
- Engage your patient in problem-solving to increase investment in adherence.
- Document observations and discussions.
- Consider terminating your relationship with the patient if you feel they would be better served elsewhere.

The Needy/Demanding Patient

Needy patients generally want frequent contact with you. They may have endless questions or concerns; they may have frequent requests for further assessments or specific treatments; they may expect that rules and schedules will be altered to accommodate them. In some cases, multiple family members want contact with you. For clinicians who attempt to avoid disappointing patients and families at all costs, these patients can be enormously draining. *The best way to ensure quality care and reasonable burden is to develop and adhere to **practice guidelines**.* These guidelines should be shared with every patient at the initial visit and should be repeated for those who ignore them. If multiple family members are involved, either have one designated family spokesperson or meet with the family as a group.

TERMINATING A PATIENT RELATIONSHIP

Once you have accepted a patient into your care, you have an ethical and legal obligation to provide services as long as the patient requires them. However, as discussed in this chapter, *there are times when is it acceptable to terminate a patient relationship, as long as you do so in a conscientious manner.* You may consider terminating a patient relationship when the patient is unmanageably noncompliant, unreasonably demanding, or threatening, or when it is simply not possible to develop a good rapport. There are also times you may have to end the relationship because you are moving, retiring, or changing jobs.

Patient abandonment is a legal term referring to the termination of a physician-patient relationship at a critical stage of treatment, without good reason, and without giving the patient adequate time to find another comparably qualified physician. The AMA's Council on Ethical and Judicial Affairs considers patient abandonment, as described above, to be unethical and explicitly states that *the patient's failure to pay a bill is itself not sufficient justification for terminating a therapeutic relationship.* To avoid the legal and ethical

problems associated with patient abandonment, in 1998 the American Medical Association, Office of the General Counsel, summarized appropriate steps that should be taken to terminate a patient-physician relationship. They include:

1. Giving the patient *written notification* by certified mail, return receipt requested;
2. Providing the patient with a *reason for the termination* (e.g., inability to achieve/maintain rapport, noncompliance, or failure to keep appointments);
3. Agreeing to provide *ongoing care for a reasonable period of time* (typically 30 days; your letter should include an anticipated date of termination) to allow a patient to find another physician;
4. Providing *general referrals* (such as local medical societies, hospital medical staffs, or community resources) to help a patient locate another comparable physician; and
5. Offering to *transfer records* to the new physician (with signed consent to do so).

Particularly risky times to attempt a patient termination include when the patient is in an acute phase of treatment, such as immediately postoperatively or during the diagnostic workup, or when you are the only specialist available or the only source of medical care in the area. Additionally, if the patient is part of a capitated insurance plan, you might need to speak with the third party payor to request a transfer of the patient to another physician.

SUMMARY

No matter how caring and tolerant you are as a physician, it is likely that you will have patients that you find yourself dreading, patients with whom you feel frustrated or confused or angry. However, this is not necessary bad; in fact, *your reactions to patients can be used as a diagnostic tool to help you discern what your patient thinks, feels and needs.*

It is important to learn how to manage difficult patient encounters in a manner that will help both you and your patient. Once you accept this as part of your role as a physician and develop effective patient management skills, you might find yourself fascinated by the challenges and drawn to the rewards associated with difficult patient encounters.

CASE STUDY

Ms. Jetter, a 29-year-old woman with a 10-year history of intractable chronic pain of her lower extremities, was referred for evaluation and treatment after failing numerous previous rehabilitation programs aimed at helping her learn how to walk again. She was described as highly uncooperative and difficult. On one occasion, her behavior had escalated to the point of a physical altercation with a physical therapist.

On initial exam, Ms. Jetter appeared alert, oriented, cooperative, intelligent and verbal. She made good eye contact and was well groomed. She endorsed being irritable and a worrier. She indicated that she worries about her health, the health of her parents, and "everything else." When describing her previous physical rehabilitation programs, she reported that she was extremely traumatized because she had no sense of control and she didn't trust her clinicians. Because her fear and anxiety led to greatly increased arousal in the central nervous system, her pain was exacerbated and became more centralized.

It was unclear why Ms. Jetter seemed to be in more pain and have a more difficult time than other patients. The increase in pain caused by her extreme arousal impeded her recovery and caused others to view her as difficult. Naturally, this situation was quite confusing to both the treatment team and to Ms. Jetter (and her family).

After much investigation, cognitive testing conducted as part of a psychological evaluation of Ms. Jetter identified a specific deficit that made it difficult for her to anticipate the intentions of others. While this is a common deficit among autistic individuals, Ms. Jetter was not autistic and this deficit had not previously been identified. Once this deficit was defined for her, she gained an important insight and was quickly and easily able to recount numerous episodes in which her deficit contributed to her difficulty in relating to others.

When she thought back to the altercation with the physical therapist, Ms. Jetter realized that she experienced the normal behaviors of the physical therapist as assaultive because she could not understand that he was trying to help her and trust that he would demonstrate restraint and not exacerbate her pain. The repeated exposures to this inac-

curately perceived assaultive behavior led to the development of clinical Post Traumatic Stress Disorder (PTSD).

Effective interventions included treating Ms. Jetter's PTSD, educating the physical therapist about her cognitive deficit, clearly communicating intentions to Ms. Jetter before touching her, and allowing Ms. Jetter to set the pace of her rehabilitation. While she had been thought of as a "difficult patient" for years, Ms. Jetter's story demonstrates how curious clinicians can solve a long-standing and perplexing mystery. The treatment team was able to enjoy the satisfaction associated with helping a patient previously labeled as "difficult," and Ms. Jetter was finally able to work with a rehabilitation team to once again learn to walk.

SUGGESTED READINGS AND WEBSITES

American Medical Association, Office of the General Counsel, Division of Health Law Copyright 1998; Available at *http://www.ama-assn.org/ama/pub/category/4609.html*; retrieved on August 10, 2005.
This website provides a list of appropriate steps that should be taken to terminate a patient-physician relationship.

American Medical Association, Medical Ethics Code (1995–2005). Available at: *http://www.ama-assn.org/*; retrieved on August 12, 2005.

American Osteopathic Association, Medical Ethics Code (2003–2005). Available at: *http://www.osteopathic.org/*; retrieved on August 12, 2005.
These websites contain the Ethics Codes for doctors.

DiMatteo, M.R. (2004). Variations in patients' adherence to medical recommendations: A quantitative review of 50 years of research. *Medical Care, 42*, 200–209.
This review offers insights into the literature on patient adherence and provides direction for future research.

Men's Bath *Albrecht Dürer (1496).* The German National Museum, Nuremberg. *This work is an example of Dürer's preoccupation with the four temperaments. The man at the pump typifies the melancholic humor (and may be a portrait of Dürer himself). The man with the flower represents the sanguine temperament, whereas the choleric type is seen in the man with the scraper. Finally, the phlegmatic personality is represented by the man with the stein of beer.*

the study of how individuals and cultures express themselves as human beings.

The pursuit of the humanities is a uniquely human endeavor. We are the only species that represents its experiences through metaphor and simile. This distinction is remarkably similar to Osler's famous distinction of humans from the rest of the animal kingdom as the only species for which medicines are desired and pursued. In other words, *the human desire for poetry is akin to the human desire for understanding sickness and health.* Both are elements that are unique to the fundamental experience of being human.

Where, then, does this leave the modern physician with regard to the role of the humanities in medical education and practice? Virtually no practicing or aspiring physician would doubt the utility of an appreciation and understanding of the expression of human experience in order to be a good doctor. However, how students and physicians pursue this goal, how much time is devoted to these principles, and to what extent these principles can effect change in the growing perception that doctors and patients float further and further apart remains to be seen. Fortunately, there is enormous interest in asking exactly these questions in current medical debate. This chapter will, therefore, focus on how the study of the humanities can positively influence modern medicine, and on some of the more promising resources and curricula that are addressing these complicated issues. Finally, a list of resources that can aid the physician in the integration of the principles of the liberal arts with the practice of medicine will be outlined and explored.

> Know then thyself, presume not God to scan.
> The proper study of mankind is man.
>
> ALEXANDER POPE
> *An Essay on Man*

one carefully wade through these various definitions and arrive at some consensus about what is most useful to our patients and to ourselves.

WHAT ARE THE HUMANITIES? WHAT IS THEIR RELATIONSHIP TO THE PRACTICE OF MEDICINE?

Turning again to antiquity, one should note that the formal study of humanities is essentially a renaissance phenomenon, referred to as the *studia humanitatis*. The roots of this academic pursuit were classical in nature, encompassing fields as diverse as literature, drama, poetry, law, theology, philosophy, and ethics. This is similar to current definitions, and this chapter will more or less adhere to this definition. In short, the study of the humanities here refers to

THE CONTRIBUTIONS OF THE HUMANITIES TO THE ART OF MEDICINE

A great deal of enthusiasm and energy is currently being devoted to the rediscovery of the humanities as part of medical training. It is beyond the scope of this chapter to discuss these efforts in detail, but one should note that a genuine renaissance of interest in the humanities is currently successfully fighting for space in diverse medical curricula. The reasons for these changes are many, but in general there is a sense that a better grasp of the principles of critical inquiry into the arts and literature will lead to an overall improvement in fundamental issues such as the doctor-patient relationship, the appreciation and mastery of empathic skills, and the universality that the study of humanities contributes to one's own capacity to withstand powerful and sometimes uncomfortable feelings.

Doctors deal on a daily basis with the existential and experiential issues that are represented in the fine arts. To this end, many have suggested that doctors themselves will be better able to withstand the emotional assaults that can accompany routine exposures to human suffering if they have a better grasp of the ways powerful experiences in general have been represented throughout artistic expressions. To the extent that such explorations can lead to better self-awareness, many have postulated that the capacity to heal will be similarly improved through the honing of empathic skills in the displaced space that study of the humanities engenders. Consider, for example, the following passage from William Shakespeare's Richard II:

> Let's talk of graves, of worms, and epitaphs;
> Make dust our paper and with rainy eyes
> Write sorrow on the bosom of the earth,
> Let's choose executors and talk of wills:
> And yet not so, for what can we bequeath
> Save our deposed bodies to the ground?
> Our lands, our lives and all are Bolingbroke's,
> And nothing can we call our own but death
> And that small model of the barren earth
> Which serves as paste and cover to our bones.
> For God's sake, let us sit upon the ground
> And tell sad stories of the death of kings;
> How some have been deposed; some slain in war,
> Some haunted by the ghosts they have deposed;
> Some poison'd by their wives: some sleeping kill'd;
> All murder'd: for within the hollow crown
> That rounds the mortal temples of a king
> Keeps Death his court and there the antic sits,
> Scoffing his state and grinning at his pomp,
> Allowing him a breath, a little scene,
> To monarchize, be fear'd and kill with looks,
> Infusing him with self and vain conceit,
> As if this flesh which walls about our life,
> Were brass impregnable, and humour'd thus
> Comes at the last and with a little pin
> Bores through his castle wall, and farewell king!
> Cover your heads and mock not flesh and blood
> With solemn reverence: throw away respect,
> Tradition, form and ceremonious duty,
> For you have but mistook me all this while:
> I live with bread like you, feel want,
> Taste grief, need friends: subjected thus,
> How can you say to me, I am a king?
>
> *Act III, Scene II*

Within this extremely evocative passage, one senses the very questions that are central to the nuances of medicine. Without question, Richard is suffering greatly. At the same time, the passage can also be read as ripe with self-pity and narcissism, making it difficult to empathize with Richard's plight. Indeed, a major theme of the play involves the tragic difficulties Richard encounters as he attempts to align his own court with his suffering in the setting of his persistent hubris and self-aggrandizing. And yet, does his suffering constitute signs and symptoms of a medical problem? What might be an appropriate intervention to alleviate Richard's clear thoughts of death, isolation, and fatalism? If medical students are taught to adhere strictly to medical nosology, they will note that his suffering exhibits narcissistic features and potential suicidality, but they will be hard pressed to identify clear symptoms of a mood disorder that would more accurately direct treatment However, the passage cries out for analysis and empathy, and it is the rare individual who is not gripped with a desire to help in some way with the desperation that Richard experiences. Similarly, one hopes that the visceral nature of Richard's suffering is experienced at least somewhat by whoever reads the passage. In this way, the analysis of the work itself engenders both a sense of self-awareness (what some clinicians have called **autognosis**) and a desire to act to alleviate suffering.

Thus, whether a reader determines that Richard is suffering pathologically or normally becomes less important. What takes precedence is a need to alleviate the suffering as much and as effectively as possible. To undertake this task, one must first examine one's own reactions to Richard's anguish, decide the extent to which these personal reactions are valid guides to how best to proceed and provide care, and then implement this care.

Many medical students have noted that the very act of reading such works is in and of itself therapeutic. This is not to say that physicians ought to prescribe literature for their patients in the same manner that they prescribe other therapeutics. However, the realization of the universality of feeling that art and literature engender can greatly help medical students recognize that *simply being with a patient can prove enormously therapeutic*. Indeed, it is this kind of empathic presence that many critics of modern medicine feel is most grievously lacking in current medical practice. If medical educators can help aspiring physicians understand that the act of carefully and viscerally reading a passage from literature or examining a painting can generate genuine emotion and cathartic healing, one moves much closer to helping those same aspiring healers appreciate the powers of empathy and connection in the doctor-patient relationship.

> I realize I have two professions, not one. Medicine is my lawful wife and literature my mistress. When I grow weary of one, I pass the night with the other. Neither of them suffers because of my infidelity.
>
> ANTON CHEKHOV
> Letter

> *Stupidity* ... seeps like a corrosive poison through every level of society, and lays it blighting hand on every aspect of social, professional, political and cultural life ... What can you—what, as humanist physicians, must you do—to fight stupidity? First, you must asure your own complete inoculation against this plague by massive daily applications of art, music, and literature. Then you must do the most difficult thing of all: you must be wholly honest with your patients.
>
> ROBERTSON DAVIES
> *Can a Doctor Be a Humanist?*

THE REBIRTH OF THE HUMANITIES IN THE MEDICAL CANON

In fact, many physicians recently have eloquently discussed the importance of incorporating the humanities into medical training and practice. For example, an innovative program directed by Abraham Verghese and Therese Jones at the University of Texas in San Antonio provides longitudinal and mandatory exposure to the humanities for all medical students. The directors of this program note that their goals are nothing less than to "create the kind of doctor one would be proud to have for one's self and one's family," by using the humanities as integral to a "new curriculum" that protects, nurtures and respects the "innate humanity, dynamic imagination, and precious individuality of students." In other words, students individually and dynamically pursue topics usually reserved for the liberal arts, and in so doing generalize what they learn to their overall capacity as complete healers.

> My "medicine" was the thing that gained me entrance to these secret gardens of the self. It lay there, another world, in the self. I was permitted by my medical badge to follow the poor, defeated body into these gulfs and grottos.
>
> WILLIAM CARLOS WILLIAMS
> *Autobiography*

Similar sentiments can be found in a wonderful essay written by Brian Hurwitz, a distinguished professor of medicine at Kings College in London and published by the Royal College of Physicians. Dr. Hurwitz notes that "productive clinical encounters depend on diverse sorts of communications: spontaneous and staged, verbal and nonverbal, intimate and detached interchanges, observations and interpretations." While much of these encounters demands the guidance of scientific and evidence-based principles, Dr. Hurwitz argues as well that attention to "arts and humanities" makes equal contributions to medical practice to the extent that such attention helps doctors to emphasize

ROCK OF AGES

This miner comes in
with hardly a story for anything
serious. A little pain
back where he busted his back,
sick to the stomach
since Easter, not enough
not to eat. Man's got to eat,
right? When he takes a smoke
his stomach rolls like a room
in Noah's ark. He's plain
apologetic. It's nothing,
it's the wife, she's always
looking for the worst.

Blue-black roots around his arms,
he stumbles, coughing,
from the elevator cage
covered with coal from head to foot,
clanging his lunch bucket.
He pulls off his black boots.
His feet are porcelain.
Crystals glisten
at the base of his neck.

I put my hands on his chest.
The skin, granite-like at first,
cracks and crumbles.
Shale! I listen
to his stony breathing,
and hear a man
scrambling the lip of an open mine
and kicking showers of shale
at the ominous figure
that follows him. The man
is running for his life. He's not
fast enough. It's nothing,
it's the dampness. . . . His skin
is translucent, revealing
cold, hard lumps of coal
that endure—I tell him, Yes,
you need some tests—

when the rest is gone.

JACK COULEHAN

"meaning and interpretation." He goes on to argue that "educationally, the arts and humanities develop a range of skills and capacities: from observation, argument, and analysis, to self-awareness; capabilities that are insufficiently nurtured by school science courses and conventional medical curricula. Caring for sick people frequently confronts nurses and doctors with intense questions about the meaning of life and exposes them to human tragedies and comic absurdities, sometimes simultaneously. The arts can tackle such issues with an immediacy and range of response often lacking in medicine." In this sense, the passage from Shakespeare offered above contributes greatly where a more analytic and scientific approach often falls short.

Finally, one must be wary of limiting attention to the humanities in medical training and practice to discussion and analysis of only so-called "fine arts and literature." Popular culture, from music to film to television to video games, are all expressions of the human condition. There is growing interest among medical educators to pursue a better understanding of both the risks to and benefits for our patients of increasingly pervasive media that bombard our daily lives. Patients and physicians express themselves through their feelings engendered not only by established poets, but also by pop music, the satisfaction of winning a virtual reality game, or the feelings inspired by very real identification with fictional television characters. Many patients cried when Buffy called off her relationship with Angel in *Buffy the Vampire Slayer*. Just as the *The Bell Jar* can prove both therapeutic or detrimental to a patient's health, so too can identification with the real or fictional stories that pervade popular culture. Ignoring these phenomena deprives physicians of a means by which they might better connect with and understand their patients as well as themselves.

> If I had to live my life again, I would have made a rule to read some poetry and listen to some music at least once a week; for perhaps the parts of my brain now atrophied would thus have been kept alive through use.
>
> CHARLES DARWIN

THE FUTURE OF THE HUMANITIES AND MEDICINE

The arguments for including the humanities in medical school curricula are growing in scope and volume. Nevertheless, what exactly one does with these ideas on a more systemic scale remains unclear. Rafael Campo, a poet and internist based at Harvard Medical School, has noted that those who advocate for a greater humanities presence in medical education and practice often seem somewhat conflicted about the role that humanities should play in med-

icine. Should humanities be taught alongside all medical courses, with relevant readings and experiences similar to the San Antonio model, or should emphasis on humanities inform more traditional questions in medicine such as ethical considerations around advanced directives and neonatal care? Are these agendas necessarily exclusive? Perhaps, as some have suggested, all medical schools should have separate departments of "medical humanities" with faculty from the liberal arts as well as physicians and allied professionals. These are issues that are evolving in a piecemeal way with little centralization of goals and agendas. However, both the public and those who are applying to medical school seem universally to favor increased integration of humanities within medical institutional practices. What remains to be seen is the extent to which these strongly held beliefs will manifest a cultural change within the practice of medicine itself.

SUGGESTIONS FOR APPLICATIONS OF THE HUMANITIES TO THE PRACTICE OF MEDICINE

There are many avenues through which medicine as a discipline can embrace an appreciation of the humanities as a means of improving the delivery of care. A few of these methods are suggested above, but it is useful to outline the central ways in which humanities can be utilized.

Encourage medical students to have greater exposure to the study of humanities as a condition for acceptance to medical school.

This notion is potentially controversial. The growing breadth of medical information often necessitates increased attention to scientific study even before medical school starts. As these needs grow, there will be inevitable and understandable tension between the desire that students master more and more science before starting their studies vs. the desire that they also demonstrate more proficiency in the study of liberal arts. The few studies that have examined those students applying for medical school with primarily humanities majors have found slightly worse performance among these candidates on standardized assessments, but improved performance on interpersonal assessments and a greater willingness to discuss abstract and complicated issues. Students in this group, perhaps not surprisingly, were also found to have a slightly increased likelihood of choosing psychiatry over other medical disciplines.

> The greatest enterprise of the mind always has been and always will be the attempt to link the sciences and the humanities.
>
> EDWARD O. WILSON

Humanities Training Throughout Pre- and Postgraduate Medical Curricula

Many of the references mentioned above and listed at the end of this chapter make passionate pleas for active implementation of humanities training for medical students. Scholars have argued that training in humanities can be helpful in areas as wide ranging as pattern recognition to the therapeutic nature of improved empathic connections. While students on the whole have received these additions to the medical canon favorably, there are few studies examining whether or not these changes effect real professional change. The new live-patient interview that is now part of the United States Medical Licensing Examination (USMLE) offers an opportunity to study whether or not medical programs that actively combine the study of the humanities with medical training create more empathic, connected, and effective physicians. Similarly, the growing practice of the 360-degree evaluation of medical professionals might help to clarify whether postgraduate humanities curricula accomplish the goals of better, empathic doctor-patient relations. However, the qualities that are being sought by pursuing appreciation of arts and literature within medical practice are difficult to measure. Improvements in doctor-patient relations are to some extent qualitative changes, not always suited to the outcomes measures that characterize the standards for medical evidence.

These issues are not new, and much can be learned from experience.

The challenge of making objective observations concerning the subjective nature of the experience of illness has always been a central paradox in the practice of medicine. Patients have historically felt misunderstood, and it would be foolish to suggest that the current divide between doctors and their patients, which is often lamented, is purely a product of modernity. While technology and deemphasizing more abstract analyses certainly play some role, there are fascinating examples of misunderstood patients dating back hundreds of years. For example, the French physician and philosopher, Jean Marc Gaspard Itard, apparently realized this divide when he suggested that the misunderstanding of the plight of contemporary women was the primary genesis for an epidemic of hysteria in nineteenth century Paris. Similarly, examination of letters to the celebrated eighteenth century Swiss physician Samuel Tissot demonstrate remarkable similarities to the complaints of the modern patient. One patient wrote that the consulting physician "found me very well indeed; for me, I was still feeling sick." Frustrated sentiments such as these are present throughout medical history, and it would, therefore, be disingenuous to bemoan a completely lost era of patient-doctor understanding. Instead, these examples provide potent arguments for the

use of the humanities as a means of reshaping a very ingrained culture. The subjective nature of illness is by definition reconceptualized as objective when one discusses characteristics such as natural history, prognosis, and treatment. However, the melding of universal and deeply personal responses to inquiries into arts and literature holds real promise as a means of helping physicians to reconcile these competing forces. Humans experience art both internally and as it relates to their prevailing culture. To this end, the experience of art can help physicians to understand the unique perspectives of the individual with regard to the global conclusions that the study of illness and experience entails. As always, history is the most efficient teacher.

> Make it a point not to let your intellectual life atrophy through non-use. Be familiar with the classics of English literature in prose and verse; read the lives of the great men (sic) of the past, and keep pace with modern thought in books of travel, history, fiction, science. A varied intellectual life will give zest to your medical studies ... Let music and art shed their radiance upon your too often weary life and find in the sweet cadences of sound or the rich emotions of form and color a refinement which adds polish to the scientific man (sic).
>
> WILLIAM WILLIAMS KEEN
> The ideal physician. *JAMA* (1900), 34:1592–1594.

SUMMARY

Many physicians relish the opportunity to contemplate art, literature, and other aspects of human expression. Columns such as the very popular "A Piece of My Mind," published in the *Journal of the American Medical Association*, and now anthologized by the AMA press, clearly demonstrate the need that doctors feel to both express themselves artistically and to look to cultural expression as a means of understanding their own sense of purpose. In fact a huge number of these essays discuss poems, painting, plays, and books. Journals as esteemed as the *Lancet* review art exhibits, and the *American Journal of Psychiatry* has long reviewed books only loosely connected to the practice of medicine. Nevertheless, medical training and practice is increasingly crowded and burdened. Rather than considering a turn to the humanities as yet another hurdle for already beleaguered students and practitioners to endure, it makes sense to reconceptualize this endeavor as a rejuvenating and affirming experience. In this sense, attention to the humanities is synergistic and not at all burdensome. The study of the humanities can instead remind physicians of the essential humanity of their patients that is central to the doctor's calling.

SUGGESTED READINGS

Jones T., & Verghese, A. (2003). On becoming a humanities curriculum: the Center for Medical Humanities and Ethics at the University of Texas Health Science Center at San Antonio. *Academic Medicine, 78*, 1010–1014.

A wonderful summary of a very successful medical humanities curriculum integrated throughout all 4 years of a traditional medical education.

Campo, R. (2005). A piece of my mind. "The medical humanities," for lack of a better term. *JAMA, 294*, 1009–1011.

A thoughtful and provocative essay on the many variations of medical humanities that are possible throughout medical training.

Hurwitz B. (2003). Medicine, the arts, and humanities. *Clinical Medicine, 3*, 497–498.

A great historical perspective on the humanities and medicine and a passionate plea for the reintegration of humanities into medical practice.

Louis-Courvoisier, M., & Mauron, A. (2002). "He found me very well; for me, I was still feeling sick": The strange worlds of physicians and patients in the 18th and 21st centuries. *Medical Humanities, 28*(1), 9–13.

A summary of the ways that physicians often and historically fall short of accurately understanding their patients, and suggestions for ways that attention to a humanities curriculum might help to alleviate this problem.

Dolev, J.C., Friedlaender, L.K., & Braverman, I.M. (2001). Use of fine art to enhance visual diagnostic skills. *JAMA, 286*, 1020–1021.

An innovative approach to the use of fine art and paintings in teaching pattern recognition to medical students for disciplines such as dermatology and radiology.

Schlozman, S.C. (2000). Vampires and those who slay them: Using the television program *Buffy the Vampire Slayer* in adolescent therapy and psychodynamic education. *Academic Psychiatry, 24*, 49–54.

An example of the ways in which popular culture can be utilized to better understand important medical and psychiatric concepts.

PART 5
SOCIAL AND CULTURAL
ISSUES IN HEALTH CARE

THE HANDS

The Emergency Department is usually quiet early Saturday mornings. Things that hurt too badly have caused the owners of such pain to come in earlier—and the accidents haven't as yet had time to happen. But the early morning is a favorite time for the elephant-on-the-chest discomfort of a heart attack: it may come on during the rapid eye movement portion of sleep, that part of sleep associated with dreaming. With a thumping dream, good or bad, the eyes roll under the lids like marbles in oil. It can be as though you're running while lying down, your body tense, heart pumping wildly to no purpose, blood pressure up. Perhaps that's when it happened to him.

What we know is that he sat up on the side of the bed, still, as when he went to sleep, 39 years old. And complained of pain. An ambulance was called and got to him quickly: no question what he had or what must be done. Lying there, hurtling there under the siren, he stopped breathing. Resuscitation was begun: pump, breathe, pump, breathe. Two minutes from the hospital. Radio the Emergency Department: *Roger. Man with chest pain. Just arrested. ETA 1 minute. Get the doors open.*

Galvanized is the word for what happens then in the Emergency Department: a flurry of white coats, hands, legs, linen. Drugs, EKG ready. The whip of the siren. *They're on the ramp.*

39, I keep thinking. *Damn!*

As the EKG machine is hooked up, the tube for breathing pure oxygen is put down. *He's pinker. Keep pumping on the chest.* Nothing on the EKG. Not a thing, just the mechanical jumps of the needle as the Resident pumps a perfect 60 times a minute. Nothing to shock. Flat line. Drugs—that's what we need: *epinephrine, bicarb. Hurry. Keep pumping!*

The Resident is sweating heavily and is relieved when someone offers to take over for him. Nothing works. No drug is helping. Try another. *Try calcium.*

I swear his hand moved—no, his *arm* moved. *Both* arms are moving! His heart still dead, but he's moving his arms! *God. Never Saw That Happen Before.*

The hands come up on his chest to the hands of the pumping Resident and *push* them away. He's making a sound around the tube in his mouth.

Check the EKG. Stop pumping. Check it.

Nothing.

The hands fall down lifeless again. Pump.

Pump! Try some more epinephrine. Nothing. Straight line. Nothing on his own.

Get me a pacemaker.

The hands come up again, pushing away the doctor's hands.

Stop pumping so I can see the EKG. Nothing. The man's hands fall down again as the pumping is interrupted momentarily. We're keeping him alive but he won't let us.

Here's the pacemaker. Keep pumping. Check the blood gases.

The pacemaker doesn't help. He has no pump left. His heart muscle is gone. We keep trying, pumping. The hands come up and fall back down. Death is fighting off life and the living.

We work for hours. The hands are weaker; they do not rise as often; they do not rise at all; they do not move. We have lost in spite of everything. The something that waits inside us all for the first falter and stumble of the heart has won.

I hope his wife is a strong spirit. I'd like to tell her about the hands. About how he struggled. How we hurt with him in that purgatory until we were all rendered innocent of everything we might have been guilty of, then and tomorrow.

JOHN STONE

22 Culturally Competent Health Care

David M. Snyder & Peter Kunstadter

> [R]educing racially or culturally based inequity in medical care is a moral imperative. As is the case for most tasks of this nature, the first steps, at both the individual and societal levels, are honest self-examination and the acknowledgment of need. That process, which is now well underway, will enrich physicians and patients alike.
>
> H. JACK GEIGER

Human behavior in health and illness is shaped by physical, social, and cultural influences. It is often necessary to consider each of these "levels of analysis" in order to achieve a complete understanding of a patient's illness and his or her responses to medical advice and treatment regimens. Failure to do so can lead to incorrect diagnoses, ineffective or harmful treatments and patient nonadherence with medical advice. This chapter focuses on the contributions of culture to patients' health status, their concepts of health and illness, and their behavioral expectations for themselves as patients and for health professionals.

Culture and Health Care

"Culture" refers to the beliefs, values, social structures, situational behavioral expectations, language, and technology shared by a group of people. These attributes endure over time, but are not homogeneously held by all members of the group. Each group has formal and informal ways of passing its culture on to new members. Culture also changes over time and across generations as a result of technological and environmental change and contact with other cultures. When members of differing cultures encounter each other, they must negotiate their differences in order to achieve a mutual satisfying interaction. This is true whether the interaction is in the economic, political, or health-care domain.

The impact of an individual's life experience is filtered through his or her values, beliefs, and knowledge. These provide meaning for those experiences and become causal models that explain the rules governing how one should respond to changing circumstances. For example, the first contact some Hmong (refugees from Southeast Asia who now live in the United States) had with modern care was in refugee camps in Thailand. Health care in one of the camps was run by a fundamentalist religious organization. This organization discouraged traditional diagnostic and treatment methods, and carried out forced child immunization programs without adequate health education or consent of the parents. Some refugees came to believe that modern medical care represents an attack on their culture and when they saw that some children became febrile after they received immunizations they thought that immunizations were administered in order to make their children sick.

Attitudes toward health care are also shaped by the experiences of others with whom we identify. For example, if we hear that another person we perceive as being like us has had a bad experience at a particular hospital, we are less likely to seek care at that hospital.

Culture is usually thought of as an attribute of ethnic, religious, or national groups, but other social groups, including professional groups such as physicians, also have distinct cultures. For example, physicians must negotiate a mutual understanding—a common set of behavioral expectations—with patients. This can be a challenge, even when patients share the physician's culture. It is an even greater challenge when the doctor and patient come from significantly different backgrounds. **Culturally competent**

health care is health care that successfully accommodates such cultural differences, allowing effective communication between doctor and patient, a shared understanding of each other's behavioral expectations and, above all, mutual trust and respect.

Aside from the interests of physicians in providing the best possible care for their patients, increasingly *federal and state laws mandate culturally appropriate or competent care.* For example, "cultural and linguistic competence" is a requirement of California's Medicaid Managed Care program. The legal basis for this requirement is Civil Rights legislation and the **Americans with Disabilities Act.** Other laws mandate equal access and participation in federally funded programs through the provision of bilingual services. How these requirements should be operationalized, implemented, and evaluated is currently being actively debated by representatives of departments of health services, health-care providers, third party payers, ethnic minority organizations, and academics throughout the country.

> Doctors are men who prescribe medicines of which they know little, to cure diseases of which they know less in human beings of whom they know nothing.
>
> VOLTAIRE

THE CULTURE OF THE MEDICAL PROFESSION IN AMERICA

Values

The ethical foundations of modern medical practice have roots as old as western civilization itself. The earliest written statements of the moral obligations of the physician such as the **Hippocratic Oath** (500 BC) reveal values to which we still adhere in the twenty-first century—e.g., the requirement that physicians do no harm to their patients, an emphasis on the confidentiality of clinical information and a ban on sexual relationships between doctor and patient. The core values we consider in making medical decisions today reflect changes in our society over the centuries, but they also demonstrate the conservatism inherent in value systems. This is clearly demonstrated in the current debates over abortion and euthanasia.

Some of the core values of modern medical practice are:

- *Autonomy:* The right of the patient to decide whether or not to accept recommended medical procedures or treatments. This value is embodied in our informed consent procedures. It assumes that a competent individual is best able to determine whether accepting a medical recommendation is in his or her best interest.

- *The value of human life:* The obligation to preserve life and to avoid actions that shorten life.
- *Honesty:* The obligation to be truthful with patients regarding diagnosis, prognosis, and the advantages and disadvantages of alternative treatments.
- *Confidentiality:* The obligation not to reveal information about patients to others not participating in their medical care.

Ethical dilemmas arise when a medical decision brings one or more of those values into conflict. For instance, our obligation to preserve life may conflict with the value we place on patient autonomy when a patient refuses a treatment we regard as essential to prevent his or her death. The value we place on honesty may conflict with the obligation to avoid actions that harm the patient, as occurs when the patient's culture interprets a fatal prognosis as a curse that will *cause* the patient to die.

The process of resolving ethical dilemmas entails three steps:

1. Establishing the facts regarding
   - The patient's clinical condition
   - The alternative clinical actions, the likely consequences of each, and the recommendations of the clinicians involved in the patient's care
   - The wishes of the patient and/or others who must consent to any recommended clinical actions
2. Identifying the ethical issues and associated values
   - The patient's values
   - The values of the health-care providers
3. Reconciling the facts and the values and identification of a preferred action

This process works well when the facts are clear, those who must consent to the recommended action are identified and participate in the decision-making process, and all participants know and share values and prioritize those values similarly. The strong Western value placed on the individual (as contrasted with other cultures that value the group over the individual) is pervasive in Western medicine and in the ethics (such as autonomy) which are stressed in Western medical practice. Cultural differences in values complicate ethical decision making, and they may also obscure assessment of the patient's clinical condition. In addition, *specific symptoms may be valued differently in different cultures.* For example, in many cultures, pain may be denied or minimized because of the value placed on "toughness," particularly in men. In Islamic patients, pain may be valued as a way of expiating sin. For many, fear of addiction to analgesics may be greater than fear of pain. Culture also influences how specific pathologic processes present symptomatically. For example, *depression may be experienced and expressed as feelings of sadness (in Northern*

Europeans), chest pain (in the Hmong), or denied in other cultures because of the shame associated with mental illness.

Patients' health-care decisions reflect the values and behavioral expectations governing relationships and social roles. For example, a patient or his or her family may weigh the economic impact of various treatment alternatives and the effect of these costs on the family before making a decision about a particular treatment. Because a sick person is expected to decrease normal activities, lose some autonomy, and increase their dependency, some patients may delay admitting they are sick because of professional or family obligations that the patient believes take precedence over accepting the role of a sick person.

Beliefs

The culture of medicine shares many values with the culture of science. For example, most physicians believe that symptoms have causes that are amenable to discovery through the gathering and analysis of objective data and they often distrust that which they cannot measure. They strive to explain illnesses in terms of what they know about normal and disordered anatomy and physiology. They make distinctions between "objective" and "subjective" data and tend to devalue the latter. They follow a **dualism** first articulated by Descartes, the seventeenth century French philosopher, that distinguishes between body and mind. They believe in "progress" and contend that medical science is continuously advancing. The latest (drugs, scanners, operative techniques) is assumed to be the best. As individuals, physicians may have strong religious and spiritual beliefs, but they clearly separate the spiritual aspects of their patients' well-being from their physical health and tend to concern themselves exclusively with the physical.

Most non-Western and preliterate societies have very different beliefs regarding the causes of illness and their treatment. They may define symptoms that are not recognized by Western medicine as indications of disease and may not recognize symptoms as abnormal that Western doctors believe are critically important. For example, some Hmong traditionally think that childhood diarrhea is "normal," not a symptom of illness. Non-Western and preliterate societies may have different explanations for some of the diseases known to medical science and may believe in diseases that have no known pathophysiology. These **folk illnesses** require specific treatments determined by the symptoms, often involving rituals conducted by a folk healer. The distinctions Western patients and physicians make between physical illness and the spiritual world is often less clear or even absent in these cultures. The Hmong, a Southeast Asian ethnic minority group, believe that many illnesses are caused by loss of one of several souls, and the diagnosis and treatment of such disorders requires that a **sha-**

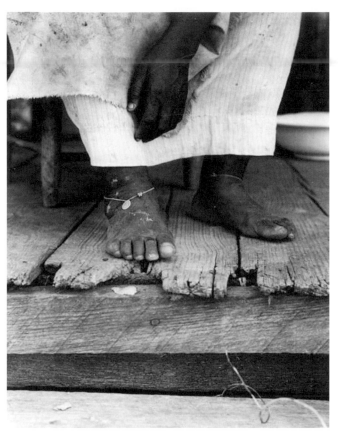

An amulet worn by a Mississippi sharecropper to ward off arthritis Courtesy of the Collections of the Library of Congress, Washington, D.C. *Belief systems are powerful determinants of behavior, and patients can experience considerable relief from symptoms from their expectation that relief is forthcoming.*

man visit the spirit world to find the lost soul and convince it to return to the patient's body. Many cultures have a belief in an "evil eye" and the power of curses to cause disease. Latino ethnic groups have a number of folk illnesses including *mal ojo* (the evil eye), *empacho* (GI obstruction caused by food or other substances getting stuck to the wall of the stomach or intestines), *golpe de aire* (an illness caused by being struck by the wind), and *susto* (an illness caused by a frightening or other emotionally traumatic experience). Similar concepts are known by different names in many other cultures. *The history of the patient who believes he or she is suffering from what we label as a folk illness often clearly indicates that a particular belief system is present, but only if the physician is aware that belief in such illnesses exists in the patient's culture.*

Patients' behavior is impacted by their knowledge and beliefs regarding their symptoms and diagnoses. It is also impacted by the social meanings those symptoms and diagnoses have for them. The physician should be aware of the different social values attributed to specific symptoms and specific diseases by different groups. In most cultures today, the diagnosis of HIV/AIDS is heavily burdened with social values that may adversely impact a patient's seeking of needed medical diagnosis and treatment. In the past, leprosy was regarded as a shameful condition in Western societies, as it still is to some non-Western cultures such as the Hmong. The physician's ignorance of the patient's culture and its health beliefs will often lead to communication problems and mutual frustration.

> Some white man's hospitals don't cure the Navajos. They treat the illness, not the person. After an operation, a Navajo often goes to his medicine man to be purified, to be treated psychologically as well as physically.
>
> JOHN NOBLE WILFORD

Social Structure

The social structure of medicine is extremely complex and includes informal relationships among physicians and other health professionals, formal organizations such as hospital medical staffs, medical associations, and specialty societies. In addition, nonmedical organizations have tremendous impact on medical practice. These include groups representing other health professionals, governmental regulatory agencies, medical equipment and pharmaceutical manufacturers, and health insurance companies. Relationships between physicians and these organizations involve complex and dynamic issues of control over decision making and resource allocation. These complex power conflicts are tempered by equally complex mutual dependencies. Many patients, particularly those with different cultural origins, have little understanding of the constraints that health-care organizations place on physicians.

The physician's role within the health-care system has expanded greatly over the past 200 years, largely as a result of expanding scientific medical knowledge and technology. Antibiotics, vaccines, anesthesia, and surgical and obstetrical antisepsis have greatly increased the likelihood that a visit to the doctor will improve rather than worsen a patient's health status. In previous centuries, much more health care was provided within the family itself and by others such as midwives, apothecaries, barbers, or people with special knowledge of herbal remedies.

Advances in medical science have changed the scope of problems we regard as "illness." It was not that long ago that most mental illnesses were regarded as signs of possession by the devil or of moral rather than physical infirmity. The "medicalization" of an increasing number of conditions has not been without controversy—e.g., consider the changes in how differences in sexual orientation have been regarded over the past 20 years.

There are numerous health professions and facilities in our society, each with its particular capabilities and relationships with the others. We attempt to make this complex system more rational and approachable through the concept of the "primary care physician." **Primary care** has three principal characteristics: It is *first contact care*—the source of care patients are supposed to seek first when feeling ill. It is also *comprehensive care*. The primary physician is supposed to meet most of the patient's health-care needs himself or herself and to be the one who advises the patient as to when other health-care services, e.g., a specialty consultation or a hospital stay, are necessary. Finally, it is *longitudinal care*, and the primary physician has a long-term relationship with the patient, which is not limited to a particular episode of illness.

Societies with few scientifically trained medical personnel tend to rely on family, knowledgeable laypersons, and traditional healers as sources of health care and there is often little differentiation between healers and those concerned with spiritual well-being. In those cultures in which spiritual causes of illness are believed to be important, the authority of the healer may rest more on a "calling"—e.g., being "chosen" through supernatural means—than on education and training. In less highly differentiated societies, the healer's role may not be his or her primary occupation, but rather a secondary role.

Many cultures do have a degree of specialization among healers. They may have shamans who deal with illnesses caused by spiritual issues, herbalists who have expertise in treating illnesses amenable to herbal remedies, and others with expertise in treating traumatic injuries. Members of these cultural groups may be accustomed to seeking treatment from one or another of these healers according to their own best judgment or seeking treatment from more than one type of healer until one of them provides a coherent assessment and clear treatment plan. Paradoxically, even though our own health-care system is more complex than any other, with a wider array of specialists, *patients from other cultures with less highly differentiated medical systems may have a greater difficulty understanding the role of the primary care provider*. Their propensity to seek care from multiple providers may be perceived as "doctor shopping." They also may experience a primary physician's reluctance to refer to a specialist as a discriminatory decision to withhold optimal care.

> As it takes two to make a quarrel, so it takes two to make a disease, the microbe and its host.
>
> CHARLES V. CHAPIN

Language

Medicine has a language of its own, and **medical jargon,** *while essential for effective communication between colleagues, can be a substantial barrier to effective communica-*

tion with patients. Even when doctor and patient speak the same language, the quality of their communication depends on the patient's level of education and medical sophistication as well as the physician's ability to use terms known to the patient. When the physician and the patient do not share a language, Federal law as well as competent practice requires that an interpreter be utilized. Except in an emergent situation, when waiting for a medical interpreter would endanger the patient, it is not advisable to employ a family member, especially a child, as an interpreter. When communication with a patient requires translation, the potential for misunderstanding increases dramatically. Likewise, if a patient's native language does not even have its own words for common Western medical concepts, communication is even more challenging. (For example, some languages do not have words for illnesses we commonly diagnose, like cancer.) In addition, patients raised in less technologically advanced societies may not be at all familiar with common treatment modalities, e.g., radiation therapy. A skillful **medical interpreter** is of tremendous value in such circumstances, and *skill in working with medical interpreters is a core skill for physicians serving a culturally and linguistically diverse patient population.* In such settings, the interpreter must do much more than translate words from one language to another. He or she must also translate concepts regarding anatomy, disease causation, the diagnostic process, treatment modalities, prognosis, and the consequences of delayed treatment. The interpreter is not just a translation machine. The physician should consider the interpreter as an expert member of the team who can help in interpreting the patient's views of his or her illness and the patient's nonverbal as well as verbal responses to the physician's recommendations. The interpreter can also guide the physician with regard to the decision-making processes associated with seeking and accepting diagnosis and treatment. This will often require consultation between physician and interpreter both before and after the physician sees the patient.

Behavioral Expectations

The place of the health-care system within the larger society is influenced by that society's definition of illness. *Illness is generally defined by social scientists (as well as by most cultures) as an inability to perform customary tasks and/or social role obligations.* The person who is sick is excused from these obligations until he or she is again well. Simple refusal to perform one's duties is not illness and is not excusable. Voluntary nonperformance of social obligations may be defined as a crime (when laws are broken) or as a sin (when core values are rejected or taboos are violated). Cultures vary in how each of these forms of "deviant behavior"—illness, crime, and sin—is delineated, and an act

> Quit your pills and learn from Osteopathy the principle that governs you. Learn that you are a machine, your heart and engine, your lungs a fanning machine and a sieve, your brain with its two lobes an electric battery.
>
> ANDREW T. STILL
> Rural Missouri doctor and founder of osteopathy
> *The Autobiography of A.T. Still*

that one society attributes to illness may be regarded as criminal in another cultural context. In fact, the differentiation of illness, crime, and sin is often difficult, even within a given society.

The sick individual is excused from the performance of customary obligations. A child with a fever does not have to go to school and he or she will be given an "excused absence." Likewise, an injured worker does not have to work, and he or she will be given "sick leave." However, these allowances are predicated on the person who has taken the sick role fulfilling the special obligations of that role. These include making appropriate efforts to regain health, usually by seeking medical care for the illness, and complying with the treatments prescribed by the health-care providers. In return, patients expect the doctor to take their complaints seriously, to treat them with respect, to take responsibility for their health care, to demonstrate competence in diagnosing and treating illness, and to provide them with information regarding their illness and its treatment. A doctor who is not competent or knowledgeable regarding the patient's illness is expected to admit his or her limitations and seek consultation from other physicians.

The relationship between healer and sick individual and the expectations each has for the other share many characteristics across cultures. The healer is expected to have expertise in determining the cause of the patient's illness and providing treatment for it. He or she is expected to act according to the best interest of the patient at all times. The patient is expected to answer the healer's questions honestly and provide the healer with pertinent information regarding current symptoms, past health problems, and other circumstances that might assist the diagnostic and treatment process.

In the United States, mature and mentally competent individuals are expected to decide for themselves if they are sick. Often, this basic decision is made after discussion with family members, and it is predicated on the recognition of symptoms as signs of illness. Symptoms that are believed to be the natural consequences of a recognized event and those that resolve spontaneously or with self-care and are not felt to threaten prolonged or permanent disability do not generally lead people to regard themselves as "sick."

In our culture, decisions about health care, including

when to seek medical advice and whether or not to accept medical treatment, generally are made by the patient or, in the case of a child, by the parents. In many other cultures, such decisions are made only after consultation with the head of the family or another authority figure such as a community leader. This often results in a more prolonged decision-making process than physicians can readily accept, particularly when there is some urgency about initiating treatment. In addition, whom the family must consult before consenting to treatment may not be explicitly communicated to the physician who may not even know that the patient or family is delaying consent for treatment in order to consult others. Even if this *is* known, the physician may not have the opportunity to talk to the "real" decision makers. The decision makers may have the authority to make medical decisions for a patient, yet still be woefully ignorant of modern medical practice. *When a patient or family expresses a wish to delay consenting to diagnostic procedures or treatment, the physician should enquire whether there are others who should be consulted.* If there are, the physician should offer to meet with those individuals to directly explain the medical issues and recommendations. Familiarity with the customs regarding medical decision-making in the groups residing in the physician's community is extremely important for all physicians and especially for primary care providers.

All cultures have cultural beliefs about avoiding illness and injury, but they do not necessarily share our belief in preventative medicine. On the other hand, they often have beliefs regarding illness prevention and health promotion that we do not share. For example, many Asian cultures have beliefs regarding what foods are appropriate for persons with specific health conditions, e.g., pregnancy or fever. Hospital diets in this country usually do not take these beliefs into account. Our practices such as periodic physical examinations for apparently healthy adults, prenatal care in medical settings, or well-child visits for healthy children have no counterpart in most non-Western cultures. In most cultures, and in our own until relatively recently, responsibility for health promotion resided entirely within the family.

Adherence to recommendations regarding health promotion and illness prevention is often challenging because of differences between patients' and physicians' understanding of disease processes and their respective behavioral expectations of each other. For example, there may be major differences in their values, e.g., regarding short- vs. long-term benefits and risks of various types of behavior. There are also likely to be differences in expectations regarding the responsibilities of the patient or of the patient's relatives for actions to retard the progression of chronic diseases such as diabetes. The culturally competent physician must be familiar with the family structure of the patient and the patterns of authority and responsibility within the family.

THE PRACTICE OF CULTURALLY COMPETENT HEALTH CARE

It is frequently useful to initiate a clinical encounter with some questions that establish the patient's expectations for the encounter. For example:

"Why are you seeking medical care at this time?"
"What do you think the nature of your problem is?"
"What do you think the cause of your problem is?"
"What do you expect of me?"
"How can I help you?"

Establishing these basic facts can facilitate any patient visit and enhance the likelihood that the encounter's outcome will be mutually satisfactory to both physician and patient. It is important to realize, however, that the patient's feelings about the presenting problem may distort his or her responses. The patient may not easily reveal this fear that their symptoms are caused by a life-threatening disease.

A man from a culture that values stoicism in men may not readily admit to fear or pain. Many cultures have taboos against discussing sexual functioning, particularly with members of the other gender. Sensitivity to the emotional impact of specific symptoms or diagnoses is vitally important for the physician.

The importance of practicing culturally competent health care derives both from pragmatism and from the core values of our medical culture. Recognition that cultural factors influence our patients' health behavior, knowledge of health beliefs and practices within the groups to which we provide health care, and respect for these differences is absolutely necessary for the effective diagnosis and treatment of patients in a culturally diverse community.

We enter into encounters with patients with certain expectations regarding their behavior and our own. When these expectations are violated, we consciously or unconsciously seek to explain the discrepancy between what we

---

CASE EXAMPLE

A 16-year-old African-American male presented to the Children's Clinic complaining of a 5 by 3 cm mass on the lateral surface of his left forearm. History and examination suggested that this was almost certainly a benign lipoma. This diagnosis was explained to the patient, and he was advised that surgical excision was not necessary unless the mass interfered with function or its appearance bothered him. The physician noticed that the young man still appeared rather anxious and didn't respond to the implied question regarding the surgical option. Suspecting that the patient had an unspoken question, he asked, "Are you afraid that lump might be cancer?" The patient looked up, making eye contact for the first time, and nodded his head. "It's not cancer," the physician said. The patient smiled broadly and said, "Thanks, Doc."

CASE EXAMPLE

A 7-year-old Hmong boy was referred to the orthopedics clinic with bilateral club feet. The surgeon recommended surgical correction, but, to his surprise, the parents refused treatment. This was seen as an irrational decision and contrary to the best interest of the child. In the face of the parents' adamant refusal to consider surgery, Child Protective Services was called, and a court order mandating surgery was sought. As part of the court's inquiry, a child psychiatrist was asked to evaluate the child and his parents. The psychiatrist determined that the Hmong believe that congenital deformities such as the patient's club feet represent retribution for some wrong doing by an ancestor, such as an unpaid debt. If the congenital deformity were repaired, the family would inevitably have another child with some equally serious handicap. The child whose deformity was repaired would suffer a greater social burden within his family than the burden that resulted from his untreated club feet. The court decided to permit the parents to refuse treatment, believing that within this particular cultural context the best interests of the child were served best by respecting the family's belief system.

CASE EXAMPLE

A 10-year-old Mexican-American boy was referred to a behavioral pediatrician for learning problems. Although the boy had been healthy throughout his life, his mother saw him as a vulnerable child and she had always been somewhat overprotective. Perinatal history was significant in that his mother had been in a motor vehicle accident during her pregnancy with the patient. While she had not been seriously injured, she appeared to connect the accident with the young man's subsequent learning difficulties. Being familiar with Mexican folk diseases, the doctor inquired whether the mother believed she had suffered from **"Susto."** She readily affirmed that she was convinced this was, indeed, the cause of her son's problem. The pediatrician recommended the child have psychological and language evaluations to determine how the boy's learning problem could be remediated most effectively, However, he also asked the mother whether she had consulted a **curandera** (a Mexican folk healer). He did not actually recommend she do so, but by asking the question, he "gave the mother permission" to seek traditional treatment for her folk disease at the same time more conventional diagnostic procedures were pursued.

expected and the observed behavior. If we are unaware of the role of cultural differences in shaping patient behavior, we tend to view the unanticipated behavior as deviant. We regard the patient who does not meet our expectations as "sick," "bad," or "evil," and see their symptoms as manifestations of illness, crime, or sin. If we are aware that cultural differences influence doctor-patient interactions, we can add "cultural differences" to our "differential diagnosis" of unexpected patient behaviors. The medical dictum, *"If you don't think of it, you won't see it,"* generally applies to the process of differential diagnosis; it also applies to the recognition of cultural factors in illness.

Knowledge of the patient's culture and the beliefs about illness and appropriate behavior for patients and healers held by the groups with which the patient is affiliated often can provide a shortcut to accurate assessment of unexpected behavior in clinical settings.

While knowledge of the common health beliefs and practices of an ethnic group can be of great value, it is important to realize that stereotyping the health beliefs and behaviors of ethnic or religious minorities can also lead one astray. To appreciate this, one need only reflect on the diversity of behavior in clinical situations seen among members of one's own cultural group.

ATTRIBUTES OF THE CULTURALLY COMPETENT PHYSICIAN

The practice of culturally competent health care requires that health-care providers and health-care organizations

possess certain attitudes, knowledge, and skills. These are achieved through a developmental process that begins with the realization that cultural differences influence patients' responses to illness and to health-care providers. The culturally competent physician is alert to the influences of culture on patient behavior and, rather than seeing these influences as an inconvenience, accepts them as an intrinsic part of the challenge of medical practice. Moving beyond acceptance, the culturally competent physician recognizes the importance of the patient's culture to his or her sense of identity and self-esteem and avoids actions and words that demean the patient's values and beliefs. The culturally competent physician values his or her ability to communicate well with patients of diverse backgrounds, recognizing this ability as a core element in overall clinical competence. *The culturally competent physician actively seeks knowledge about each patient's culture, believing such knowledge to be central to the practice of medicine.*

Physicians who work well with culturally diverse patients are skillful in recognizing when their lack of knowledge of a patient's culture is compromising their ability to provide optimal care. Information about the health beliefs and practices of patients is actively sought and utilized by the culturally competent physician. Such information can be obtained from the medical and social science literature, from medical colleagues and other health professionals with experience in providing cross-cultural health care, and from patients themselves. **Community agencies** serving ethnic minority and immigrant groups are usually eager to assist physicians who wish to understand their patients better and to mediate the conflicts and misunderstandings that arise in health-care settings out of lack of cultural knowledge.

The attitudes, knowledge, and skills of the culturally competent physician are summarized in Boxes 22.1, 22.2 and 22.3.

BOX 22.1 Attitudes of the culturally competent physician

- Appreciates cultural diversity as a positive attribute of his or her community
- Is interested in and attempts to learn the contributions of cultural beliefs and practices to patient health and illness behavior
- Demonstrates respect for patients regardless of ethnicity, religion, language, educational level and economic status
- Values skill in providing culturally competent health care

BOX 22.2 Knowledge of the culturally competent physician

For each culture served:
- The epidemiology, physiology, prevention, diagnosis, and treatment of high incidence, culturally specific causes of morbidity and mortality
- Community and family social structures
- Cultural values of the patients he or she serves, with particular emphasis on values relevant to health, illness and care for the ill
- Patterns of health services utilization
  - Use of traditional healers
  - Use of medical services
  - Traditional health beliefs
  - Recognition of illness
  - Classifications of disease
  - Knowledge of risk factors and preventability of disease
- Criteria for severity of illness and urgency of seeking treatment
  - When should help be sought
  - Who should be consulted for which type of illness
  - How to tell when a treatment is effective
  - Expectations for patient behavior
  - Expectations for practitioner behavior
- Family members' roles in caring for the ill and in making care decisions
  - Traditional health practices
  - Prevention
  - Diagnosis
  - Treatment
  - Rehabilitation
  - Traditional health practitioners
  - Categories of practitioners
  - Scope of practice
- Methods of diagnosis
  - Methods of treatment
  - Methods of prognostication
  - Patterns of referral and collaboration among practitioners
  - Practitioner/patient/family communication

BOX 22.3 Skills of the culturally competent physician

- Identify communication difficulties based on cultural differences between patient and provider
- Use cross-cultural knowledge in
  - determining the beliefs of the patient regarding his or her illness and teaching the patient about modern concepts of that illness
  - teaching patients about modern medical services and how to make best use of them
  - averting conflict
  - providing information that is comprehensible and acceptable
  - utilizing family and community social structures in decision making and patient care
  - utilizing traditional health practices and practitioners appropriately
- Use appropriate resources to enhance culturally appropriate care
  - Hospital social services
  - Medical staff expertise
  - Behavioral science faculty expertise
  - Medical interpreters

SUMMARY

Medical education tends to emphasize the statistically normal in the study of human anatomy, physiology, and behavior, and exceptions tend to be viewed as abnormal. However, the competent physician recognizes the difference between pathological conditions and normal variation in patients. Culture is a major source of variation in response to illness and to health-care interventions.

This chapter has discussed the role of culture in patients' efforts to maintain health and respond to illness. Awareness of our patients' culturally determined health beliefs and practices is essential for the competent practice of medicine in our culturally diverse society. Achieving culturally competence in medical practice is certainly a challenge, but it is necessary for the effective provision of health care to patients whose cultural background differs from our own.

CASE STUDY

Pluralistic Health Care and Kidney Failure

Mr. Yang is a 60-year-old Hmong man who has specialized knowledge as a Hmong spiritual healer. After the defeat of the U.S.-backed Hmong forces, he and his family fled to Thailand in 1987 and came to the U.S. a few years later.

Traditional Hmong religious services are often accompanied by consumption of alcohol, and Mr. Yang's services were in heavy demand in the refugee camp in Thailand. It was there, where he was drinking frequently, that he first noticed what the camp's Western medical doctor diagnosed as hives, attributed to an allergy to alcohol. The doctor told him he would die if he continued drinking, so after thinking about it Mr. Yang decided to stop.

When Mr. Yang came to the U.S. for the first 2 years he did not drink a lot of beer or wine, only Pepsi. At a feast in 1995, Mr. Yang said that he and some other people don't drink beer and wine now that they live in the U.S., but his host urged them to drink saying "that's why you guys have been 'female' since coming here, and now that I'm here all of us are 'male' and we will all drink beer." That started Mr. Yang drinking again. He participated in more ceremonies and drank and became ill again. Then he was invited by his in-laws to another town to perform a ceremony. "My in-laws bought wine and mixed it with *Krating Daeng* (Red Bull).* This made me feel like I was getting hives again and I thought that I was allergic to the *Krating Daeng.*"

Mr. Yang asked his wife for some traditional medicine and felt better after taking it. On his way home from the ceremony he ate some mushrooms and suddenly his feet were swollen. He went to see the doctor right away and got some medicine and the swelling improved.

Mr. Yang was invited to a funeral ceremony, and he initially tried to refuse because his feet were swelling. However, Mr. Yang played the mouth organ and he was a gifted musician. He finally capitulated after his friends insisted that he attend the ceremony and perform. At Hmong funerals, the mouth organ is played while dancing as part of a traditional ceremony, and the exercise seemed to help Mr. Yang. His swelling diminished and he felt much better after the funeral.

A relative came to see him one day and told Mr. Yang that he also had swelling that was helped by some medicine from Mexico. Mr. Yang took a shot and his swelling improved. He wanted another shot, but the medicine was all used up. One of his friends contacted someone in a town near the Mexican border who sent him five vials.

After the second shot Mr. Yang's swelling came back, and this time it went up past his knees and his face was peeling. He drove to Mexico and showed the medicine bottle to many pharmacists until he found the medicine. The pharmacist refused to sell it to him without a prescription from a doctor. Five other places told him the same thing. He then went to see a non-English-speaking Mexican doctor to get a prescription. She gave him a shot and charged him $61 and wrote him a prescription for oral medicine. The doctor said "Whoever gave you this medicine is your enemy, not your friend. It is not for your swelling, it is a steroid to help you make muscles." Mr. Yang said "It doesn't matter, I am adjusted to it, and it helps me. I came all this way just to buy this. I have plenty of oral medication, I am searching for just this medicine." The Mexican doctor still refused, so Mr. Yang bought the medicine the physician prescribed.

The medicines the Mexican doctor prescribed had many side effects. Mr. Yang's ears were ringing, but he took the medicine for 7 days and the swelling got better.** Then his wife made an appointment for him at a local clinic. Mr. Yang got another kind of medicine and stopped taking the medicine from Mexico but he did not get better so he was referred to another doctor who specializes in kidneys. Mr. Yang took the new medicine and seemed to improve.

After a family picnic at which he ate a lot of fruit and many other kinds of food the swelling returned and he was hospitalized for 5 days and began dialysis. "I thought I was going to die with such a big needle going into me." His swelling improved and he continued on dialysis, which required frequent changes of sites for the needles. "In the beginning I was having it four times a day: 6 in the morning, 12 noon, 6 in the evening, and midnight. Then they wanted to do it five times a day. I could not go to work. You cannot do it outside or anywhere. You have to be in a room where there is no air conditioning and all the windows are closed. It is important that no air goes into my body ... You have to wash your hands very clean before you put it on and off."

When asked why he thought he had his illness Mr. Yang said "I think it is not the food that caused this, I think it was the drinking ... I told my friends, my in-laws, we eat a lot of beef ... I don't think we would be ill like this naturally, there have to be people who were trying to get rid of us ... It is not so much the drinking. When we came to the departure camp in Thailand I was taking about 100 pills.*** I could feel my male strength weaken. After taking the pills I was always sleeping. I did not take the pills anymore. Whenever I watched someone do a shaman ceremony I would always be sleepy. Before, I was not like this. Wherever I sit, I would just fall asleep. After these pills, I feel my kidneys died. I feel I have become mentally disabled having taken so many medications. Now I'm waiting for a kidney."

When asked about his health care Mr. Yang replied "I think the U.S. health care really tries to help me. I have always been an easy person, so I never had any problem with any nurses or doctor. I use traditional healing. I have acquired knowledge of shamanism, but herbal medicine does not seem to help me."

---

* A popular canned nonalcoholic tonic with high caffeine content that is now sold widely in the U.S., and is also sold in Thailand where it is sometimes mixed with alcoholic drinks.

** In traditional Hmong treatment it is common for a shaman to predict the cause and proper treatment (e.g., animal sacrifice to a specific spirit) and pledge to make the sacrifice if the patient improves after a certain number of days. If the patient does not improve after, say, 7 days, the diagnosis and prescription were incorrect and the shaman either repeats the ceremony or the patient may try another diagnostician.

***Apparently these were amoxicillin pills.

Comments

This case illustrates more or less simultaneous acceptance and use of traditional medicine plus many sources of modern medicine. Despite the ideal of continuity of care there were great discontinuities (as well as pluralities) in Mr. Yang's care: use of herbal medicines and traditional spiritual treatments as first choices in a sequence of health-seeking, use of modern medicines obtained from friends and in Mexico, and medicines and other treatments obtained from several modern physicians in the U.S.

Cultural factors involved in this case include use of traditional medications and healing methods and traditional beliefs (e.g., Hmong believe that participation in traditional ceremonies, such as funerals, may help the performer of the ceremony; using a medication that was probably prescribed for continuous use for a period of several days, then evaluating and rejecting it).

Hmong in Southeast Asia often report that peer pressure (applied to Mr. Yang to persuade him to drink alcohol) is the reason for starting or continuing to drink, smoke, or use narcotics. Shaming (accusing Mr. Yang of being "female"), and feelings of loss of maleness is another important theme in this case.

The case also illustrates doubts in Mr. Yang's mind as to the ultimate cause of the illness: food, alcoholic beverages, *Krating Daeng* tonic, modern medicine, poisoning, or sorcery. Even at the end of this case history, when Mr. Yang was waiting for a kidney transplant, it seems that he was not told, or did not understand, the modern medical etiology of his kidney failure.

- What would you do if you encountered a patient like Mr. Yang who is actively seeking health care for a potentially life-threatening situation from a variety of traditional and modern sources?

- How much difference would it make in your treatment of Mr. Yang if you knew this much background?
- How much of Mr. Yang's story do you think you would get from your usual medical history taking techniques?

SUGGESTED READINGS

Barker, J.C., & Clark, M.M. (Eds.). (1992). Cross-cultural medicine a decade later. *Western Journal of Medicine, 157*, 247–374.
This special edition of the *Western Journal of Medicine* was devoted to the current challenges to providing cross-cultural medical care. Some of the articles address specific health-care issues that require particular sensitivity to cultural variables, e.g., "The effects of values and culture on life-support decisions." Others focus on a specific ethnic group, e.g., "Older Russian emigrés and medical care."

Cross, T.L., Bazron, B.J., Dennis, K.W., & Isaacs, M.R. (Eds.) (1989). *Toward a culturally competent system of care*. Washington, DC: CASSP Technical Assistance Center, Georgetown University Child Development Center.
This monograph includes a lucid description of the continuum of cultural competence and a discussion of its implications for health care. While focusing on the special needs of "minority children who are severely emotionally disturbed," the monograph is a valuable resource for any provider of human services to culturally diverse populations.

Lipson, J.G., Dibble, S.L., & Minarik, P.A. (Eds.). (1996). *Culture & nursing care: A pocket guide*. San Francisco, CA: UCSF Nursing Press.
Culture and nursing care is a handbook which addresses the health beliefs and practices of 24 ethnic minority groups. Each chapter includes practical information regarding group-specific considerations for diet, symptom management, diagnostic and therapeutic procedures, and many other topics. The handbook was written for nurses, but it is a valuable reference for all health professionals.

23 Complementary and Alternative Medicine

Marc Brodsky & Ka-Kit Hui

> There is much that we can learn from complementary medicine to make our patients feel better while our science attempts to make them get better ... However, to encourage the terminally ill to spend the last few precious months of life chasing the false promise of a cure is as cruel as it is intellectually dishonest.
>
> MICHAEL BAUM
>
> The art of medicine consists in amusing the patient while nature cures the disease.
>
> VOLTAIRE
>
> If you are genuinely skeptical about a particular treatment, voice that skepticism during the period that the person is trying to decide whether or not to do the treatment. That's being honest and helpful. But if the person decides to do the treatment, then shelve your skepticism and get behind them 100%. At that point your skepticism is cruel and unfair and undermining.
>
> KEN WILBER
> *Grace and Grit*

A number of different terms have been introduced over the years to describe the group of diverse medical and health-care systems, practices, and products that are not presently considered to be part of conventional medicine. Complementary and Alternative Medicine, or CAM, the term currently in fashion, includes the worldviews, theories, modalities, products, and practices associated with these systems and their use to treat illness and promote health and well-being, according to the White House Commission on Complementary and Alternative Medicine Policy (WHCCAMP) report. The **National Center for Complementary and Alternative Medicine** (NCCAM) of the Na-

tional Institutes of Health (NIH) classifies CAM therapies into five categories, or domains:

1. alternative medical systems built on complete systems of theory and practice,
2. mind-body interventions,
3. biologically based therapies,
4. manipulative and body-based methods, and
5. energy therapies that are classified as biofield therapies and bioelectromagnetic therapies.

Recognizing some of the limitations of modern medicine, Americans are increasingly turning to medical systems and therapies outside the conventional health-care system to meet their needs and optimize their quality of life. As public interest in CAM grows, the body of knowledge on the mechanism of action and clinical efficacy of CAM therapies is also rapidly expanding. Stakeholders in the medical, political, business, and legal sectors are incorporating CAM into an emerging model of integrative and collaborative care. Physicians, to be effective problem-solvers in this evolving health-care system, must be able to inform their patients on the safe and effective use of different CAM systems and modalities.

HISTORY OF CAM

Historically, the health-care system in the United States was made up of a mix of different medical systems, according to the WHCCAMP report. The diverse practitioners of past centuries included botanical healers, midwives, chiropractors, homeopaths, and an assortment of other lay healers offering herbs, physical manipulation, and other treatments for a range of illnesses. With the advent of germ theory and significant scientific advances in antiseptic techniques, anesthesia, and surgery, these healing systems became marginalized, as scientific medicine evolved into the dominant system. This was reflected in the revolution in medical education which began around the turn of the twentieth century. William Osler (1847–1919) wrote *The Principles and Practice of Medicine* in 1892, which became the primary medical textbook in the vast majority of medical schools in the United States. After a report by Abraham Flexner in 1910, medical institutions that did not meet the standards of what was considered to be a "scientifically-based" curriculum found it difficult to survive. With the introduction of life-saving hormones and antibiotics in the early and middle part of the twentieth century, what is now considered conventional medicine secured its dominant status. Although most of the other health-care systems and their therapies did not disappear, they were considered outside the conventional health-care system and were not highly regarded by medical professionals and the public.

As a result of the success of public health interventions and advances in the treatment of infectious diseases and other acute illnesses, people began living longer and new health challenges are emerging. Previously fatal illnesses, such as heart disease and cancer, are now chronic conditions. The aging population is also affected by other chronic conditions such as arthritis, back pain, diabetes, and hypertension. With increasing need for chronic care, failure of the acute care model to adequately address these conditions, and escalating conventional health-care costs, Americans are increasingly seeking therapies outside conventional medicine for their health care.

CURRENT STATUS OF CAM

Although heterogeneous, the major CAM systems have many common characteristics, according to the WHCCAMP report. *These similarities include an emphasis on whole systems, the promotion of self-care and the stimulation of self-healing processes, the integration of mind and body, the spiritual nature of illness and healing, and the prevention of illness by enhancing the vital energy, or subtle forces, in the body.* People of varied backgrounds are attracted to these characteristics of CAM and incorporate these theories and practices into their health care. However,

> There is no disease, bodily or mental, which adoption of vegetable diet and pure water has not infallibly mitigated, wherever the experiment has been fairly tried.
>
> PERCY BYSSHE SHELLEY
> *Queen Mab*

some patients are more likely to use CAM: women, people with higher educational levels, people who have been hospitalized in the past year, and former smokers.

According to a 2002 NCCAM survey, *approximately 62% of Americans in 2002 reported using some form of CAM over the previous 12 months.* People use CAM for a wide variety of problems, most commonly to prevent and treat musculoskeletal conditions or other conditions involving chronic or recurring pain. Patients with these conditions use CAM as they search for therapies with fewer side effects, more time with health-care professionals, attention to emotional and spiritual concerns as well as their disease, and an opportunity to participate in their own care as well as follow doctors' orders.

> Similar diseases are cured by similar things.
>
> CHRISTIAN FRIEDRICH SAMUEL HAHNEMANN
> German physician and founder of homeopathy

REGULATION OF CAM

Until recently, the primary response of Federal, state, and local health-care regulatory agencies was to restrict access to CAM services to protect the public from unproven and potentially dangerous treatments. Since the early 1990s, however, scientific evidence has supported the benefit of some CAM approaches and products, when used appropriately, in treating illness and promoting health. State licensure laws, precedents regarding malpractice liability and professional discipline, and statutes on health-care fraud have been introduced to protect patients by enhancing quality assurance, improving access to therapies, and honoring **medical pluralism** in creating models of integrative care.

State and federal food and drug laws govern the regulation of herbal medicines and dietary supplements under the provisions of the Dietary Supplement Health and Education Act of 1994 (DSHEA). In that legislation, the **Food and Drug Administration** (FDA) was authorized to establish good-manufacturing-practice regulations for dietary supplements. *The Act, however, designated that supplements be regulated as foods.* This decision exempted manufacturers from conducting safety and efficacy testing that are required for prescription and over-the-counter medications. In addition, the FDA's regulatory-approval process was eliminated, limiting the agency to a reactive, postmarketing role if products were found to be harmful. *The Federal Trade Commission, instead of the FDA, has primary responsibility for monitoring dietary supplements for truth in advertising.* A 2005 Institute of Medicine (IOM) report on CAM in the United States recommends a framework for cost-effective and science-based evaluation of dietary supplements by the FDA.

> Homeopathy waged a war of radicalism against the profession. Very different would have been the profession's attitude toward homeopathy if it had aimed, like other doctrines advanced by physicians, to gain a foothold among medical men alone or chiefly, instead of making its appeal to the popular favour and against the profession.
>
> *Report to the Connecticut Medical Society* (1852), quoted by COULTER in *Dividend Legacy*

RESEARCH ON CAM

Unlike the evidence base that, in general, characterizes conventional medicine, CAM has often lacked or had only limited experimental and clinical study. A wave of scientific research, however, is beginning to address this knowledge gap. As an example of the scientific focus on CAM, the *National Center for Complementary and Alternative Medicine* (NCCAM) was established by Congress in 1999 as one of 27 institutes and centers at the National Institutes of Health (NIH). NCCAM is dedicated to exploring CAM healing practices in the context of rigorous science, training CAM researchers, and disseminating their findings to the public and professional communities. NCCAM has funded more than 1,000 research projects at over 200 institutions. Much of this research is clinically oriented, including studies of herbal/botanical products, acupuncture, Reiki, chiropractic manipulation, acupuncture, and a variety of mind-body practices. Findings from these studies have been published widely in peer reviewed medical journals.

The strategic plan of NCCAM outlines a set of broad goals and objectives in four areas: investing in research, training CAM investigators, expanding outreach, and facilitating integration. To achieve these goals, NCCAM is recruiting researchers to design the necessary tools, technologies, equipment, models, databases, and other resources.

The randomized controlled trial (RCT) is the experimental design most commonly funded by the National Institutes of Health, including NCCAM, and remains the "gold standard" of evidence for treatment efficacy. One of the main challenges to evaluate CAM therapies is the limitation of the RCT to evaluate the complexity of factors that determine the impact of a treatment on a person's health, according to the IOM report on CAM in the United States. These factors can include such things as the philosophical context of a CAM system, simultaneous use of CAM and conventional treatments, individual preferences, and the doctor-patient relationship. Other study designs have been applied to provide information about effectiveness when RCTs cannot be done or when their results cannot be generalized to the real world of CAM practice.

With the growing evidence-base of CAM treatments, boundaries between CAM and mainstream medicine are constantly changing. As this evidence is collected and disseminated to the wider health-care community and the public, it should provide a reliable basis for making policy decisions that will facilitate the public's access to safe and effective CAM approaches and products.

> Did you ever see the customers in health-food stores? They are pale, skinny people who look half dead. In a steak house, you see robust, ruddy people. They're dying, of course, but they look terrific.
>
> BILL COSBY

BEYOND CAM TO INTEGRATIVE MEDICINE

The call to change the practice of medicine to better meet society's needs and expectations is growing. The 2001 IOM report, *Crossing the Quality Chasm*, described a gap between the current quality of care in the United States and what is currently possible. *The IOM recommended designing delivery systems of care that are safe, effective, patient-centered, timely, efficient, and equitable.* Goals of the proposed system would be to have patients who are fully informed, retain control and participate in care delivery whenever possible, and receive care that is respectful of their values and preferences.

In an attempt to narrow this gap in the health-care system, Americans frequently do not limit themselves to a single medical system for their care. Therefore, it is important for physicians to understand how CAM and conventional medical treatments interact with each other and to orchestrate different traditions of medicine in a coordinated way. Recognizing the evolving health-care system and changing patient preferences, 27 academic medical institutions collaborate in the **Consortium of Academic Health Centers for Integrative Medicine** (CAHCIM), with the goal of achieving some consensus on practice, research, and education concerning Integrative Medicine. *Integrative Medicine was defined as an approach to the practice of medicine that makes use of the best available evidence, taking into account the whole person (body, mind, and spirit), including all aspects of lifestyle.* It emphasizes the therapeutic relationship and makes use of the rich diversity of therapeutic systems, incorporating both conventional and CAM approaches. Implicit to Integrative Medicine is the belief that physicians should value and cultivate a whole person approach in their own lives and engage in life-supporting activities that will foster their own health so as to serve as effective role models for their patients.

> **BOX 23.1 Definition of Integrative Medicine**
>
> Integrative Medicine is the practice of medicine that reaffirms the importance of the relationship between practitioner and patient, focuses on the whole person, is informed by evidence, and makes use of all appropriate therapeutic approaches, health-care professionals, and disciplines to achieve optimal health and healing.
>
> *Developed and adopted by The Consortium of Academic Health Centers for Integrative Medicine, May 2004; Edited May 2005*

To prepare medical students to meet society's expectations of them as physicians, CAHCIM developed a set of competencies for undergraduate medical education that can serve as a template for schools across the nation as they move to develop curricula in this area. The consortium also developed a "user's guide" to provide specific examples and illustrations of how medical schools can approach the implementation of the recommended competencies.

AN EXAMPLE OF A SPECIFIC CAM APPROACH: ACUPUNCTURE

Acupuncture describes a family of procedures involving stimulation of anatomical locations on the body by a variety of techniques. The traditional theory of acupuncture is based on the premise that there are patterns of energy flow *(qi)* through the body that are essential for health. Disruptions of this flow are believed to be responsible for disease. Acupuncture may correct imbalances of flow at identifiable points close to the skin. The most studied mechanism of stimulation of acupuncture points employs penetration of the skin by thin, solid, metallic needles that are manipulated manually or by electrical stimulation. *Acupuncture has been shown to activate endogenous opioid mechanisms and modulate the limbic system and subcortical structures and may stimulate gene expression of neuropeptides.* The growing body of science of the mechanism of acupuncture prompted the Food and Drug Administration in 1996 to reclassify acupuncture needles from the category of "experimental medical devices" to surgical devices regulated under good manufacturing practices and single-use standards of sterility.

> The results in Japan which I will relate surpass even miracles. For chronic pains of the head, for obstruction of liver and spleen, and also for pleurisy, they bore through [the flesh] with a stylus made of silver or bronze.
>
> JACOB DE BONDT
> describing acupuncture (1658)

The following year, in 1997, NIH convened a group of experts and published a consensus statement on acupuncture. *The experts concluded that acupuncture was efficacious in the treatment of adult postoperative and chemotherapy nausea and vomiting, and in postoperative dental pain.* The group also suggested that acupuncture may be useful as an adjunct treatment or an acceptable alternative in other conditions such as addiction, stroke rehabilitation, headache, menstrual cramps, tennis elbow, fibromyalgia, myofascial pain, osteoarthritis, low back pain, carpal tunnel syndrome, and asthma. Subsequent systematic reviews of the efficacy of acupuncture for a variety of conditions generally recommend more studies with improved methodologies.

> The Lord hath created medicines out of the earth; and he that is wise will not abhor them.
>
> ECCLESIASTICS 38:4

SUMMARY

The full context of CAM goes beyond individual representative systems and modalities. CAM, with its widespread use by the public, is inextricably linked to a new way of looking at the full continuum of health to meet the needs and expectations of our society. The formation of this new health system will include rigorous scientific studies, new models of clinical care, and innovative educational programs that integrate biomedicine, the complexity of human beings, the intrinsic nature of healing and the rich diversity of therapeutic systems. A new generation of leaders in medicine, research, education, politics, business, information technology, and the media are being groomed to tackle the scientific, educational, regulatory, and political obstacles to integration of different medical systems and therapies.

CASE STUDY

A 24-year-old Vietnamese American female medical student presented with an 11-month history of pain in the neck, shoulders, and upper back, decreased range of motion of the neck, and periodic swelling overlying the area of the left trapezius muscle. She first noted her symptoms during a time of intense stress while she was visiting her parents. At that time, she frequently argued with her mother, struggled with her parents' marital problems, and ended her relationship with her boyfriend. Since the onset of her symptoms, she has had worsening pain, exacerbated by stress. She has had some relief with professional massage, self-massage, and application of local heat. She has not taken any medications for her symptoms, but regularly takes birth control pills, multivitamins, over the counter antacids, metamucil, ginseng, ginkgo, and chrysanthemum tea. Her only significant medical history is a left anterior cruciate ligament reconstruction following a skiing accident at age 21. She denies any use of tobacco and recreational drugs, and consumes an average of four alcoholic drinks per week and a cup of coffee every morning. Her diet includes frequent sweets and red meat, with a craving for chocolate around the time of her menses. She has difficulty falling asleep and finds that using earplugs and focusing on her breathing are helpful. She has no early awakening or disturbed sleep. She exercises twice a week on the treadmill for 30 minutes, and lifts 8-pound weights overhead. She lives with 2 roommates in an undesirable living situation.

Specific questions reveal that the patient's energy level is sometimes decreased in the late afternoon. She has had no recent weight changes, but reports cold intolerance and frequent cold extremities. She reports chronic dry and red eyes but does not wear contact lenses. She experiences dyspepsia twice a week, which is relieved with an antacid. She also reports abdominal bloating and cramping if she does not take Metamucil regularly. She has regular and heavy menses with clots, with a duration of 9 days. On physical examination she has a prominent left trapezius, and cervical and thoracic muscles are tender to palpation bilaterally. She has multiple trigger points for pain and decreased range of motion of her neck.

An Integrative Medicine analysis of this case: The patient's problem list included myofascial neck pain, dyspepsia, cold intolerance, dry eyes, and insomnia. Review of the clinical information and previous laboratory evaluation led to the conclusion that the patient's symptoms did not represent a serious disease process. Usual Western paradigms could not offer a diagnosis for her seemingly disparate collection of functional symptoms. There was no evidence-based approach to managing the patient with this myriad of conditions that are often seen in clinical practice, apart from the symptomatic approach she was already taking.

Chinese medicine concepts helped to explain how stress, sleep problems, and physical trauma from overloading exercises depleted her resiliency and her ability to maintain homeostasis of her mind-body-spirit system. Anger in this patient led to intense muscle spasm that affected the neck, shoulders, and upper back, which may have contributed to her other symptoms. A hands-on approach to the physical exam identified myofascial trigger points that were recognized as a source of her pain and may have represented an early warning sign of depletion of her functional reserve.

The treatment approach incorporated biomedicine and Chinese medicine to address this patient's problems. The plan consisted of trigger point injections, massage, and acupuncture treatments. A care plan was devised for the patient that included self-massage of acupressure points, appropriate exercise without overloading, proper diet, good sleeping habits, and yoga. The treatment plan included consideration of a low-dose muscle relaxant or Chinese herbal formula at bedtime if symptoms persisted. The patient made a number of life-style changes in response to this plan, and had significant relief of symptoms as well as an increase in general well-being.

SUGGESTED WEB SITES

http://nccam.nih.gov/
This site provides information about the National Center on Complementary and Alternative Medicine and includes current research updates, educational materials for patients, and information about ongoing clinical trials.

http://www.whccamp.hhs.gov/finalreport.html
This site provides the *White House Commission on Complementary and Alternative Medicine Policy* (WHCCAMP) report that addresses issues related to access and delivery of CAM, priorities for research, and the need for better education of consumers and health-care professionals about CAM.

http://www.imconsortium.org/html/about.php
This site provides information about conferences and collaboration available for students and faculty of academic medical centers interested in the work of the Consortium of Academic Health Centers for Integrative Medicine.

http://www.iom.edu/reports.asp
This site provides all of the reports from the Institute of Medicine, including *Crossing the Quality Chasm* and *Complementary and Alternative Medicine in the United States,* that were used as primary source documents for this chapter.

24 The Impact of Social Inequalities on Health Care

Russell F. Lim, Francis G. Lu, & Donald M. Hilty

Despite major steps forward in the fight against cardiovascular disease, there is compelling evidence in the United States that we have not been fully effective in translating, disseminating, and expediting the adoption of scientific advances to improve outcomes for our society. We have failed to develop public health infrastructures and health-care systems in parallel with the scientific progress to implement effective, evidence-based prevention and treatment strategies.

ROBERT BONOW et al.
Circulation, 2002;106:1602.

Disparities result in part from differences in income, wealth, employment and educational opportunities. These differences are large and unfavorable for African-Americans and other minorities.

JAMES S. JACKSON

There have been numerous reports over the last 10 years describing the impact of sociocultural factors on health-care disparities, but two reports are especially important. The Institute of Medicine's (IOM) report, *Unequal Treatment*, stated that after controlling for socioeconomic factors, ethnic minorities received different, and often outdated, treatments compared with majority patients with the same diagnoses. Likewise, a supplement to the Surgeon General's report on *Mental Health*, entitled *Mental Health: Culture, Race, and Ethnicity*, stated that ethnic minorities have reduced access to care when compared to the majority population. Worse yet, other reports have documented that African-Americans and Hispanic-Americans are disproportionately diagnosed with schizophrenia when bipolar disorder would be a more appropriate diagnosis. Still other studies have shown that African-Americans have been given more dangerous "typical" oral and depot antipsychotics in higher doses, when they should have received the standard of care: atypical antipsychotics and lower doses (although at least one other study saw no difference in use of atypical antipsychotics). Other reports have shown that Latinos as more likely to be diagnosed with an affective disorder, despite the presence of psychotic symptoms that would suggest another psychiatric disorder is present.

Racial and ethnic health-care disparities are important for many reasons. Ethically, physicians are obligated to provide high quality care, and they should be concerned if this level of care is not available to everyone. There are important public health implications as well, as disparities in health care are likely to result in a higher prevalence of infectious disease. Economically, disparities that cause higher morbidity, whether caused by an inability to pay for costly procedures or by misdiagnosis, result in higher overall health-care expenditures that affect all taxpayers because many ethnic minorities participate in Medicaid or other public insurance programs. Finally, the existence of racial and ethnically related health-care disparities are evidence of continued racial discrimination, indicating that as a nation we have far to go before we realize our founding fathers' assertion that all men were created equal and have equal rights.

The **Liaison Committee on Medical Education** (LCME) has recognized the importance of diversity in health care, and has added the following objective to its list of standards and objectives for the accreditation of American medical schools:

Medical students must learn to recognize and appropriately address gender and cultural biases in themselves and others, and in the process of health-care delivery.

The objectives for clinical instruction should include student understanding of demographic influences on health-care quality and effectiveness, such as racial and ethnic disparities in the diagnosis and treatment of diseases. The objectives should also address the need for self-awareness among students regarding any personal biases in their approach to health-care delivery.

In this chapter, we will present the evidence for health-care disparities for ethnic minorities, discuss some of the biases and barriers that create these disparities, and suggest individual, educational, and institutional strategies to reduce them.

> The Wisdom of IVAN ILLICH, 1926–2002
> Social philosopher and activist
>
> The medicalization of early diagnosis not only hampers and discourages preventative health-care but it also trains the patient-to-be to function in the meantime as an acolyte to his doctor. He learns to depend on the physician in sickness and in health. He turns into a life-long patient.
> *Medical Nemesis*
>
> Healthy people need no bureaucratic interference to mate, give birth, share the human condition and die.
> *Medical Nemesis*
>
> The medical establishment has become a major threat to health.
> *Limits to Medicine*

> The health status of all U.S. racial and ethnic groups has improved steadily over the last century. Disparities in major health indicators between White and non-White groups, however, are growing. In general, African-American, American-Indian, and Hispanic ethnic and racial groups are disadvantaged relative to Whites on most health indices, whereas Asian-Americans appear to be as healthy, if not healthier, than Whites on most indicators. These overall group comparisons, however, mask important differences in the health status of ethnic subgroups.
>
> NATIONAL INSTITUTE ON AGING

HISTORICAL BACKGROUND

There have been health-care disparities based on race, culture, ethnicity, and social status throughout history, but we will focus on recent American history, starting with Native-Americans who were almost wiped out by diseases brought from Europe, such as smallpox and tuberculosis, in the early 1600s through 1700s. The U.S. Government thought Native-American health beliefs were odd, and the Office of Indian Affairs provided almost no medical services until the creation of the Indian Health Service in 1954. Many Native-American children sent to boarding schools became ill and died from tuberculosis. Others who became sick on the reservations were removed and treated in mainstream hospitals that were ill equipped to meet their needs. There was a widespread and systematic destruction of Indian culture: Native Americans were not allowed to speak their own languages, the elders (culture bearers) died prematurely from infectious diseases, and many Native Americans were driven from land their ancestors had lived on for centuries.

African-Americans experienced forced emigration and enslavement in the 1600–1800s, and they were denied basic rights such as suffrage and freedom. African-Americans brought their own folk health system with them from Africa; however, these practices were not adequate to deal with the health challenges associated with poverty, slavery, and abuse. After the Union's victory in the Civil War, all slaves were emancipated; however, they were almost wiped out by disease, and former slaves had no formal health care until **Freedman's Hospitals** were opened in the late nineteenth century.

It was not until the **Civil Rights Act of 1965** that the most blatant forms of segregation in health care were ended. Since that time, affirmative action programs have begun to increase the numbers of African-American physicians. However, African-American physicians are still dramatically underrepresented in the physician workforce (i.e., African-Americans represent about 12% of the U.S. population, but only about 3% of physicians in the United States are African-American).

Other immigrant groups came to this country more willingly, although these groups also suffered discrimination and marginalization. The Chinese came in the 1850s, but they were prohibited by U.S. law from becoming citizens until 1943. It was illegal for Chinese workers to bring their wives to the United States until the **War Brides Act** was passed in 1945. Even then their numbers were limited by strict immigration quotas until 1965. The "Model Minority" myth has led many people to think of Asian-Americans as successful and high achieving, but the percentage of Asian-Americans living in poverty is twice as high as the percentage of Caucasians living in poverty. Similarly, many Hispanic-Americans have been exploited and marginalized, limited to menial labor or farm work, and denied health benefits or access to health care because of their undocumented status. Other White immigrant groups were discriminated against when they first arrived in this country, such as the Germans, Irish, Italians, Jews, and Poles, but have since joined mainstream American society.

Birth of a Sharecropper (1939) *James Turnbull (1909–1976). Watercolor on paper, 53 × 73 cm. Collection of the Whitney Museum of American Art, New York; Purchase 43.16. Lay midwives have delivered most of the world's babies.*

Definitions

The National Institute of Health (NIH) defines **health disparities** as "differences in the incidence, prevalence, mortality, and burden of diseases and other adverse health conditions that exist among specific population groups in the United States." These health disparities include differences in overall life expectancy and higher rates of cardiovascular disease, cancer, infant mortality, birth defects, asthma, diabetes, stroke, sexually transmitted diseases, oral diseases and disorders, mental illness, and other disorders. Contributing factors include "reduced access to health care, increased risk of disease and disability due to occupation or exposure, [and] increased risk of illness due to underlying biological, socioeconomic, ethnic, or familial factors, cultural values, and education."

The IOM report, *Unequal Treatment*, defined health-care disparities as "racial or ethnic differences in the quality of health care that are not due to access-related factors or clinical needs, preferences, and appropriateness of intervention." The NIH definition is broader and includes both disease and health care, while the IOM definition is specifically targeted at health-care delivery. If one compares the NIH definition to the IOM's, it becomes clear that there are other factors that influence access to health care, such as **socioeconomic status** (SES), the availability of health insurance, health literacy, geography, gender, sexual orientation, age, and generational and immigrant status. Indeed, the report states that "racial and ethnic minorities are less likely than Whites to possess health insurance" as a result of larger numbers living in poverty; even when poor members of minority groups have health insurance, it is often

publicly funded. Other barriers to care are often present, such as high co-payments and inadequate access to transportation. In 2005, 45.8 million Americans lacked health insurance, and this number included 21 million fulltime workers.

SES is related to health literacy, and patients with low SES tend to have lower levels of education and know less about how to maintain health and prevent disease. Geography also plays an important role in the quality of health care; because ethnic minorities tend to live in different areas than the Caucasian majority, they often do not have access to the same health-care opportunities.

> One reason why medical history is not much taught in medical schools is that so much of it is an embarrassment.
>
> LEWIS THOMAS

Health is also affected by **gender**. For example, Hispanic and African-American women have higher risks of developing cardiovascular disease than Caucasian women. One study showed that more than one in four women was uninsured at some time during the past year, and half of the uninsured women had no coverage for more than a year. However, women were more likely than men (32% vs. 24%) to have a health condition that needed ongoing medical treatment. Fifty percent of the women in the study regularly needed prescription drugs, but half of these women reported not filling a prescription in the past year because it was too expensive. Sixty percent of women without health insurance delayed getting medical care be-

explanation—demographic data showed that the African-American physicians in the study were internists, while the Caucasian physicians were cardiologists. At the time of the study, 1994–1995, there were only 316 African-American cardiologists out of almost 20,000 practicing cardiologists, or about 1.5%.

Convincing data document that many patients experience racial discrimination in clinical encounters, which understandably results in **mistrust of Caucasian doctors**. For example, one study of African-American, Asian-American, and Hispanic-American patients in King's County, WA, showed that nearly one third of the African-American respondents experienced incidents of differential treatment, including rude behavior and racial slurs, during their lifetime, while 16% reported such incidents within the past year. These experiences resulted in patients delaying treatment or avoiding the individual or institution responsible, but less than half of the respondents had made a verbal complaint. Patients made comments like "I vowed never to take my child to [that] hospital," or "it was the last time my son would ever see [that] doctor." Such interactions obviously have a powerful impact upon the treatment (or lack thereof) that African-Americans receive. The same study showed that one fifth of all Hispanic patients experienced discrimination at some time in their lives, and between 7% and 19% of Asian-Americans did as well.

> They have no physicians, but when a man is ill they lay him in the public square, and the passersby come up to him, and if they have ever had his disease themselves or have known anyone who has suffered from it, they give him advice, recommending to do whatever they found good in their own case, or in the case known to them. And no-one is allowed to pass the sick man in silence without asking him what his ailment is.
>
> HERODOTUS

Refusal of Treatment

Patients refuse treatment for any number of reasons, including fear of needles, distrust of physician, and differing health beliefs. These patients can be especially frustrating for physicians, but appreciating and understanding a patient's ethnic and cultural background may help the doctor understand the patient's reticence to do what the doctor believes is in the patient's best interest. The IOM report concluded that patient refusal was only part of the reason that ethnic minorities lacked equal access to treatment.

Language Differences

According to the 2000 census, there are over 11 million people in the United States who are linguistically isolated, an increase of 54% over the 1990 census. Without the ability to speak English, these individuals often cannot access health care without the help of an interpreter. In addition, the physician's inability to communicate in the native language of a patient limits his or her ability to form an empathic connection with patients.

BOX 24.2 Some Health Insurance, Health, and Treatment Differences Between Population Subgroups

- Hispanics were least likely to have health insurance, least likely to receive flu or pneumonia vaccinations, and had the highest prevalence of poor or fair health.
- Cigarette smoking was common in American-Indian communities with a median of 42.2% for men and 36.7% for women. According to the Centers for Disease Control and Prevention Behavioral Risk Factor Surveillance System (BRFSS), Black men without a high school diploma have the next highest smoking prevalence at 41.8%
- Blacks had the highest prevalence of hypertension, the highest self-reported prevalence of diagnosed diabetes, and the highest rate of hospitalizations for stroke.
- Ischemic heart disease and stroke were inversely related to education, income and poverty status.
- Among Medicare enrollees, congestive heart failure hospitalization was higher in Blacks, Hispanics and American-Indians/Alaska-Natives than among Whites.

There are three less than optimal substitutes for a trained interpreter when a patient doesn't speak English fluently: (1) Patients and providers themselves, who may possess partial communication skills; (2) family and friends; and (3) nonclinical personnel, such as housekeeping staff or bilingual bystanders. The last two methods compromise patient confidentiality, and are likely to result in less accurate translations. The **Office of Civil Rights** (OCR) has issued guidelines for patients with Limited English Proficiency (LEP) that are currently being reviewed for implementation. These guidelines state:

> [E]very federal agency that provides financial assistance to nonfederal entities must publish guidance on how their recipients can provide meaningful access to LEP persons and, thus, comply with Title VI regulations forbidding funding recipients from "restrict[ing] an individual in any way in the enjoyment of any advantage or privilege enjoyed by others receiving any service, financial aid, or other benefit under the program" or from "utiliz[ing] criteria or methods of administration which have the effect of subjecting individuals to discrimination because of their race, color, or national origin, or have the effect of defeating or substantially impairing accomplish-

ment of the objectives of the program as respects individuals of a particular race, color, or national origin."

Prejudice and Bias

Prejudice is defined as "an antipathy, felt or expressed, based upon a faulty generalization and directed toward a group as a whole or toward individual members of a group," whereas bias is "a preference or an inclination, especially one that inhibits impartial judgment," or "an unfair act or policy stemming from prejudice." Thus, prejudice can result in bias, or bias can be less stereotypical, but still result in a nonimpartial judgment. Most physicians are quick to deny prejudice or bias, and fail to recognize subtle prejudicial attitudes that may be reflected in their behavior.

Several studies have had clinicians evaluate vignettes describing patients suffering from pain, altering only their racial designation. In one of these studies, male physicians gave the Caucasian patients twice as much hydrocodone (Vicodin) compared to African-American patients, whereas the women physicians did the opposite.

Other research has evaluated the influence of race and sex on medical students' perceptions of patients' symptoms to determine if subtle bias exists early in medical training. In one of these studies, 164 medical students were randomly assigned to view a video of a Black female or White male actor portraying patients presenting with identical symptoms of angina. The medical students felt that the Black woman had a less desirable health state than the White man with identical symptoms, and students were less likely to identify the Black female patient's symptoms as angina. Nonminority students reported higher health states for the White male patient, whereas minority students' assessments did not differ by patient. Male students assigned a slightly lower health status value to the Black female patient. The researchers concluded that there were significant differences in the ways the students evaluated patients based on their own ethnicity and gender and the patient's ethnicity and gender.

> The task of medicine is to promote health, to prevent disease, to treat the sick when prevention has broken down and to rehabilitate the people after they have been cured. These are highly social functions and we must look at medicine as basically a social science.
>
> HENRY E. SIGERIST
> *Civilisation and Disease*

Stereotypes

Stereotypes are a way of using social categories, such as skin color, age, and gender, to simplify complex situations; ste-

reotypes develop from our need to predict, understand, and control situations. Unfortunately, they also tend to suppress an individual's personal characteristics that do not conform to the general profile created by the stereotype. In addition, there are "in" groups, for which we have positive feelings, and "out" groups, for which we have negative feelings. Stereotypes can also be implicit, and often the person who stereotypes others is not consciously aware of the influence of stereotyping. Stereotypes are profoundly important in health care; for example, *stereotypes influence physicians' beliefs about whether or not patients will follow treatment recommendations.* In one study, physicians were shown to believe that African-Americans patients were less likely to follow-through with treatment recommendations, and this belief clearly influenced the treatment decisions the physicians made.

Clinical Uncertainty

Most clinical decisions are made in the context of uncertainty, but diagnostic accuracy depends on reducing the amount of uncertainty as much as possible. Beliefs about culture are sometimes used to reduce the amount of uncertainty in a clinical encounter; however, these beliefs have to be grounded in cultural competence and genuine cultural sophistication if they are going to be useful. For example, a physician may misinterpret the severity of the patient's symptoms because he or she is unaware of differing cultural norms for the expression of symptoms. Physicians are most familiar with their own cultural group, and they are likely to use their cultural background as a basis from which to understand the implicit messages being sent by body language, eye contact, tone of voice, inflection, etc. However, these nuances of communication may be expressed in different ways or mean different things in other cultural groups, and their meaning may be influenced by age, SES, gender, or ethnicity.

INTERVENTIONS

Health-care disparities can be addressed at many levels: (1) at the level of the individual provider, through education and recruitment of minority physicians and medical students; (2) at the level of the office, clinic or hospital, by creating structures that are more accessible to ethnic minorities; and (3) at the level of legal and regulatory policy. Truly effective interventions will have to target all three—individuals, groups, and systems. In addition, health-care providers, administrators, and staff will all require more training and sophistication in treating minority populations if we are ever going to successfully eliminate the profound health-care disparities that currently exist in our society.

TABLE 24.1 The DSM-IV-TR outline for cultural formulation

1. Cultural identity of the individual
   An individual's cultural identity includes the individual's cultural reference group(s), languages spoken, cultural factors in development, etc.
2. Cultural explanations of the illness
   The cultural explanations of the illness refer to predominant idioms of distress and local illness categories. This includes meaning and severity of symptoms in relation to cultural norms, as well as perceived causes and explanatory models, and help-seeking experiences and plans.
3. Cultural factors related to psychosocial environment and levels of functioning
   These include social stressors and supports such as family or religious groups, as well as levels of functioning and disability.
4. Cultural elements of the clinician-patient relationship
   This includes ethno-cultural transference and counter transference, as well as the use of an interpreter, and psychological testing.
5. Overall Cultural Assessment
   The overall cultural assessment is a summary of all of the above factors, and how they affect the treatment plan.

Adapted from Manson (1996).

Clinical Interventions

The **American Psychiatric Association** (APA) focused on culture and its effects in developing the fourth edition of the *Diagnostic and Statistical Manual* (DSM-IV), and its subsequent revision, DSM-IV-TR (Text Revision). The DSM-IV and DSM-IV-TR includes the Outline for Cultural Formulation (OCF) in Appendix I, as well as a Glossary of Culture Bound Syndromes. The OCF provides a framework for the incorporation of the patient's cultural identity, health beliefs, supports, and stressors, and takes into account the effect of culture on the patient-clinician relationship. The DSM-IV-TR also identifies culturally specific diagnoses such as acculturation problem or spiritual crisis. Finally, there are sections in the narrative introductions for each of the major diagnostic categories for age, gender, and culture that will guide the reader to assess a person with a different or unfamiliar ethnic background. In addition to the DSM-IV-TR, there are many excellent books and articles on assessing the culturally different; several of these are described in the Suggested Readings at the end of this chapter.

Many disciplines have developed **mnemonics** to help clinicians remember the importance of culture when working with patients. The **BELIEF** mnemonic emphasizes exploring the patient's health Beliefs, eliciting an Explanation, helping the clinician to Learn from the patient, discovering the Impact on the patient, showing Empathy,

and asking about Feelings. The **ETHNIC** framework, designed for use by medical students during their clinical assessments, reminds students to ask patients to Explain their illness and Treatment, and to ask about whether they have sought help from folk Healers. They also have to Negotiate with the patient and plan an Intervention, Collaborating with the patient, family, and folk healers. The **LEARN** framework is similar, as it encourages clinicians to Listen, but put emphasis on the clinician's role as a cultural broker in Explaining the problem, as well as Acknowledging cultural differences, and then Recommending and Negotiating treatment. Each framework has its strengths and weaknesses, and the authors recommend combining parts from each one into daily clinical practice. These mnemonic devices are encapsulated in Table 24.2.

TABLE 24.2 Mnemonics for taking a cultural history

BELIEF
Beliefs about health (What caused your illness/problem?)
Explanation (Why did it happen at this time?)
Learn (Help me to understand your belief/opinion.)
Impact (How is this illness/problem impacting your life?)
Empathy (This must be very difficult for you.)
Feelings (How are you feeling about it?)

ETHNIC
Explanation (How do you explain your illness?)
Treatment (What treatment have you tried?)
Healers (Have you sought any advice from folk healers?)
Negotiate (mutually acceptable options)
Intervention (agreed on)
Collaboration (with patient, family, and healers)

LEARN
Listen with sympathy and understanding to the patient's perception of the problem
Explain your perceptions of the problem
Acknowledge and discuss the differences and similarities
Recommend treatment
Negotiate treatment

Sources: Doobie et al. (2003); Levin, Like, and Gottlieb (2000); Berlin and Fowkes (1983).

Educational Interventions

All of the health sciences are now teaching students about culture and diversity, hoping that students will develop the knowledge, attitudes, and skills necessary to facilitate the assessment and treatment of ethnic minority patients. Some of the most successful methods include cultural awareness exercises for attitudes, lectures to promote awareness about particular ethnic groups, and case-based learning to teach cultural case formulation skills. Other approaches have included teaching health-care students how to work with an interpreter and various ways to elicit patient's cultural health beliefs. Specifically, *Unequal Treatment* included two recommendations related to education:

> Recommendation 5–3: Increase the proportion of underrepresented U.S. racial and ethnic minorities among health professionals. "The benefits of diversity in health professions fields are significant, and illustrate that a continued commitment to affirmative action is necessary for graduate health professions education programs, residency recruitment, and other professional opportunities."
>
> Recommendation 6–1: Integrate cross-cultural education into the training of all current and future health professionals.

Policy Interventions

Cultural and Linguistic Appropriate Services (CLAS) Standards

In 1998, the U.S. Department of Health and Human Services **Office of Minority Health** (OMH) requested a review and comparison of existing cultural and linguistic competence standards and measures on a national level, and proposed draft national standards language. An analytical review of key legislation, regulations, contracts, and standards currently in use by federal and state agencies and other national organizations was conducted. Proposed standards were then developed with input from a national advisory committee of policy administrators, health-care providers, and health services researchers. Fourteen standards were created, defining culturally competent care, how to provide services in the appropriate languages for the client, and supporting cultural compe-

---

TABLE 24.3 National standards for culturally and linguistically appropriate services (CLAS) culturally competent care

Culturally Competent Care

1. Health-care organizations should ensure that patients/consumers receive from all staff members effective, understandable, and respectful care that is provided in a manner compatible with their cultural health beliefs and practices, and preferred language.
2. Health-care organizations should implement strategies to recruit, retain, and promote at all levels of the organization a diverse staff and leadership that are representative of the demographic characteristics of the service area.
3. Health-care organizations should ensure that staff at all levels and across all disciplines receive ongoing education and training in culturally and linguistically appropriate service delivery.

Language Access Services

4. Health-care organizations must offer and provide language assistance services, including bilingual staff and interpreter services, at no cost to each patient/consumer with limited English proficiency at all points of contact, in a timely manner during all hours of operation.
5. Health-care organizations must provide to patients/consumers in their preferred language both verbal offers and written notices informing them of their right to receive language assistance services.
6. Health-care organizations must assure the competence of language assistance provided to limited English proficient patients/consumers by interpreters and bilingual staff. Family and friends should not be used to provide interpretation services (except on request by the patient/consumer).
7. Health-care organizations must make available easily understood patient-related materials and post signage in the languages of the commonly encountered groups and/or groups represented in the service area.

Organizational Supports for Cultural Competence

8. Health-care organizations should develop, implement, and promote a written strategic plan that outlines clear goals, policies, operational plans, and management accountability/oversight mechanisms to provide culturally and linguistically appropriate services.
9. Health-care organizations should conduct initial and ongoing organizational self-assessments of CLAS-related activities and are encouraged to integrate cultural and linguistic competence-related measures into their internal audits, performance improvement programs, patient satisfaction assessments, and outcomes-based evaluations.
10. Health-care organizations should ensure that data on the individual patient's/consumer's race, ethnicity, and spoken and written language are collected in health records, integrated into the organization's management information systems, and periodically updated.
11. Health-care organizations should maintain a current demographic, cultural, and epidemiological profile of the community as well as a needs assessment to accurately plan for and implement services that respond to the cultural and linguistic characteristics of the service area.
12. Health-care organizations should develop participatory, collaborative partnerships with communities and utilize a variety of formal and informal mechanisms to facilitate community and patient/consumer involvement in designing and implementing CLAS-related activities.
13. Health-care organizations should ensure that conflict and grievance resolution processes are culturally and linguistically sensitive and capable of identifying, preventing, and resolving cross-cultural conflicts or complaints by patients/consumers.
14. Health-care organizations are encouraged to regularly make available to the public information about their progress and successful innovations in implementing the CLAS standards and to provide public notice in their communities about the availability of this information.

tence in the organization. These standards are presented in Table 24.3.

Recruitment and Retention Policies

One approach to diversity is to recruit staff who are similar to the patients they treat and the community they serve. However, this approach has met with only limited success, and increasingly clinicians are being trained to work with clients from many different cultures. Common interventions include training in cultural competence in residency/fellowship programs, subcontracting with minority providers to train majority staff, and tying executive promotion to demonstrations of success in providing culturally competent services.

Coordination with traditional healers and collaboration with community workers is becoming increasingly common in health-care settings. Traditional healers are powerful symbols of their culture who can serve as partners in delivering culturally sensitive and appropriate services. Likewise, community workers have important links to the communities they serve and can guide patients who are baffled and confused by the complexities of contemporary and bureaucracies associated with health care in the United States in the twenty-first century.

Administration or Organizational Accommodations

Common administrative interventions to reduce health-care disparities include providing care in settings close to where patients live and work, provision of transportation, and, in some settings, home visits. The clinic milieu needs to mesh with patients' cultural values, and health-care directives and instructions have to be available in the language of the patient. The problems associated with providing culturally competent services can be especially acute in rural areas, where few providers may possess the cultural competence necessary to provide appropriate services. However, the telecommunications revolution offers some solutions, such as telepsychiatry, and both patients and providers are turning to technology to ensure access to culturally competent care.

> The real public health problem, of course, is poverty.
>
> WENDELL L. WILKIE
> *One World*

The President's New Freedom Commission Report-Federal Guidelines for Mental Health Care

In July 2003, the **President's New Freedom Commission on Mental Health** issued a report titled *Achieving the Promise: Transforming Mental Health Care in America*. Of the six overall goals that were discussed as a means to transform

the mental health system, two are especially relevant to this chapter: (1) Mental Health Care is Consumer and Family Driven, and (2) Disparities in Mental Health Services are Eliminated. Some of the report's specific recommendations concerning racial and ethnic disparities that affect health-care delivery include the following:

Recommendation 3.1: Improve access to quality care that is culturally competent. "The Commission recommends making strong efforts to recruit, retain, and enhance an ethnically, culturally, and linguistically competent mental health workforce ... These efforts could include: (1) recruiting and retaining racial and ethnic minority and bilingual professionals, (2) developing and including curricula that address the impact of culture, race, and ethnicity on mental health ... (3) training and research programs targeting services to multicultural populations, (4) engaging minority consumers and families in workforce development, training, and advocacy ... All Federally funded health and mental health training programs should explicitly include cultural competence in their curricula and training experiences."

Recommendation 3.2: Improve access to quality care in rural and geographically remote areas.

Recommendation 4.4: Screen for mental disorders in primary health care, across the life span, and connect treatment and supports.

Recommendation 5.3: Improve and expand the workforce providing evidence-based mental health services and supports. "Every mental health education and training program in the nation should voluntarily assess the extent to which it ... emphasizes developing cultural competence in clinical practice and ensures that the diversity of the community is reflected among trainees and in the training experience."

Recommendation 5.4: Develop the knowledge base in four understudied areas: mental health disparities, long-term effects of medications, trauma, and acute care.

Diversity in Health-Care Professionals Increases Access to Care

Diversity among professionals will help reduce health-care disparities. The 2004 Institute of Medicine report, titled *In the Nation's Compelling Interest: Ensuring Diversity in the Health-Care Workforce*, summarized the evidence documenting that greater diversity among health professionals is associated with improved access to care for racial and ethnic minority patients, greater patient choice and satisfaction, better patient-provider communication, and better educational experiences for students while in training. The report made 25 recommendations addressing six specific areas: (1) improving admission policies and practices; (2) reducing financial barriers to health professions training; (3) encouraging diversity efforts through accreditation; (4) improving the institutional climate for diversity; (5) applying community benefit principles to diversity efforts; and (6) other mechanisms to encourage support for diversity efforts. The recommendations in Sections 1, 4 and 5 specifically addressed health professions educational institutions (HPEIs). They included the following:

- HPEIs should develop, disseminate, and utilize a clear statement of mission that recognizes the value of diversity.
- HPEIs should establish explicit policies regarding the value and importance of culturally competent care and the role of institutional diversity in achieving this goal.
- HPEIs should develop and regularly evaluate comprehensive strategies to improve the institutional climate for diversity.
- HPEIs should proactively and regularly engage and train students, house staff, and faculty regarding institutional diversity-related policies, expectations, and the importance of diversity.

Interventions for Improving Mental Health-Care Disparities

The Surgeon General's Supplement to the Report on Mental Health, titled *Mental Health: Culture, Race and Ethnicity*, concluded with "A Vision for the Future" in which recommendations were grouped in areas according to six aspirational goals: (1) continue to expand the science base, (2) improve access to treatment, (3) reduce barriers to treatment, (4) improve quality of care, (5) support capacity development, and (6) promote mental health. The recommendation most relevant to education follows:

> Minorities are underrepresented among mental health providers, researchers, administrators, policymakers, and consumer and family organizations. Furthermore, many providers and researchers of all backgrounds are not fully aware of the impact of culture on mental health, mental illness, and mental health services. All mental health professionals are encouraged to develop their understanding of the roles of age, gender, race, ethnicity, and culture in research and treatment. Therefore, mental health training programs and funding sources that work toward equitable representation and a culturally informed training curriculum will contribute to reducing disparities.

SUMMARY

It is clear that health-care disparities are affected by expectations, beliefs, and attitudes that in turn are shaped by culture and influenced by gender, skin color, and age. Recent reports such as *Unequal Treatment* have highlighted the inequities based on race and ethnicity that are still inherent in modern medical practice. These inequities result in poor health outcomes for ethnic and cultural minorities that result in higher costs for all, increase the disease burden on society, and are a major public health concern that should trouble all medical students. Unfortunately, the Civil Rights Act of 1965, and the civil rights movement have not been sufficient to provide adequate health care for all Americans. There is still much work to be done in the area of cultural competence that would help address these health-care disparities in minority populations. We have discussed interventions for the problem of disparities that can occur on a personal, educational or policy level. Psychiatry is particularly well positioned to look at the impact of these issues and to teach cultural competence, which in turn should reduce health disparities. Perhaps a new generation of physicians—those reading this book—will be able to make a difference and help solve the vexing, intractable and clearly linked problems of social inequalities and health-care disparities.

CASE STUDIES

We present three cases that illustrate challenges in providing culturally appropriate care in ethnic and cultural minorities.

1. M.V. is a 45-year-old Hmong woman with complaints of headaches, backaches, dizziness, and tiredness. She came to the United States from a refugee camp in Thailand 10 years ago. Ms. V. has 8 children, aged 15, 13, 11, 9, 8, 6, 4, and 2. The patient speaks no English, and lives in a poor part of town. She receives Medicaid, and is poorly educated. In order to get to her appointment at the Mental Health Clinic, she has to take several buses, and an interpreter has to be arranged for her. She believes her illness is caused by "bad spirits," and has already seen a shaman for treatment. She witnessed her father and mother being shot by the communists during their escape from Laos. Ms. V. is unemployed and has no job skills. She has nightmares and flashbacks, and hears the voices of her dead family calling to her. The patient has already tried to hang herself, and was hospitalized at the local mental hospital for 72 hours; however, she currently states that she would never attempt suicide again because of her children.

The case of M.V. is a common one in Sacramento. She has many barriers to health care, including language, health beliefs, geography, low socioeconomic status, public insurance, and poor education. Patients such as these are often seen in the primary care setting, and their health beliefs and traumatic experiences are frequently ignored. Often it is difficult to get a trained interpreter for the Hmong language, and mental health issues are not often recognized when the presenting complaints are somatic. The patient needs a referral from the primary care provider to mental health services. The county's mental health system is required to provide services in the patient's language, including intake, assessment, treatment, and access to patient rights advocates. Providers are required to provide a culturally sensitive assessment and treatment plan that includes an assessment of the patient's health beliefs, as well as a collaborative approach that involves family and community members. In the refugee population, it is also very important to assess for traumatic events prior to coming to the United States, as the diagnosis of posttraumatic stress disorder could be missed. She also has come for mental health services at a late stage in her illness, typical of many non-Western patients.

2. H.G. is a 37-year-old monolingual Spanish-speaking woman from Mexico with diabetes. She works as a migrant farm worker in the Central Valley of California. She comes every harvesting season to help with the crops. Her blood sugar is never very well controlled, as she has no regular doctor in the United States, but she can get her medications in Mexico. She presents to the emergency room at the University Hospital with a foot ulcer that refuses to heal, and blood tests reveal that her blood sugar is alarmingly high.

This patient's situation presents some challenges, as H.G. is an undocumented worker who does not speak English, and does not live in the United States full-time. Important policy decisions will determine if she is seen, because of her undocumented status, and a culturally sensitive treatment plan would have to be created for her care here in the United States, as well as after her return to Mexico.

3. F.J. is 31-year-old African-American man with a long history of substance abuse including alcohol and marijuana. He was just released from prison after serving time for assault. Prior to his incarceration, he drank two six-packs of beer per day, along with daily use of marijuana. He comes in to the mental health clinic complaining of mood swings, depression, irritability, and insomnia. He was given Haldol, a typical antipsychotic medication, while incarcerated, as he was diagnosed with schizophrenia while in prison.

Mr. J.'s case is similar to many African-American males who find themselves in the criminal justice system, rather than a mental health clinic, and who often present for treatment after many encounters with jail and prison. Substance use is very common, and must be addressed in the overall treatment plan. Many African-Americans are involved in a church community, and can be referred to their church for support and counseling. Mr. J. was misdiagnosed as having schizophrenia, instead of bipolar disorder and alcohol dependence, and put on older medications that exposed him to the risk of tardive dyskinesia. His mood swings were never treated or assessed properly, as a result of diagnostic biases about African-Americans.

SUGGESTED READINGS

Brach, C., & Fraserirector, I. (2000). Can cultural competency reduce racial and ethnic health disparities? A review and conceptual model. *Medical Care Research Review, 57*(Suppl), 181–217.
  This article demonstrates how cultural competency can help us understand the importance of proper interpreting skills, as well as systems-level interventions.

Hays, P.A. (2001). *Addressing cultural complexities in practice.* Washington, DC: American Psychological Association.
  This book is an excellent resource for learning how to do a culturally competent assessment in a mental health setting.

Lu, F.G., Lim, R.F., & Mezzich, J.E. (1995). Issues in the assessment and diagnosis of culturally diverse individuals. In J. Oldham & M. Riba (Eds.), *American Psychiatric Press annual review of psychiatry, volume 14.*(pp. 477–510). Washington, DC: American Psychiatric Press.
  An excellent introduction to the use of the DSM-IV-TR Cultural Formulation. Also available online at http://www.fanlight.com/downloads/Culture_Guide.pdf

New Freedom Commission on Mental Health. (2003). *Achieving the promise: Transforming mental health care in America. Final report.* DHHS Pub. No. SMA-03–3832. Rockville, MD: Department of Health and Human Services.
  This is the report from the New Freedom Commission which will guide much of the U.S. mental health policy in the next decade.

Office of Minority Health. (2000). *Assuring cultural competence in health care: Recommendations for national standards and an outcomes-focused research agenda.* Accessed August 28, 2005, http://www.omhrc.gov/clas/
  Important background information on the CLAS standards.

Smedley, B.D., Butler, A.S., & Bristow, L.R. (2004). (Eds.). *In the nation's compelling interest: Ensuring diversity in the health-care workforce.* Institute of Medicine (IOM). Washington, DC: National Academies Press.
  A companion to *Unequal Treatment,* this report highlights the importance of a diverse workforce.

Smedley, B.D., Stith, A.Y., & Nelson, A.R. (2003). (Eds.). *Unequal treatment: Confronting racial and ethnic disparities in health care.* Washington, DC: National Academy Press.
  This book is a ground-breaking study of the influence of race and ethnicity on medical treatment and controls for socioeconomic sta-

tus. The accompanying CD-ROM contains important background articles, such as one by Byrd and Clayton on "Racial and Ethnic Disparities in Health Care: A Background and History," which is a brief history of ethnic disparities over the history of the United States.

United States Department of Health and Human Services (USDHHS). (2001). *Mental health: Culture, race, and ethnicity: A Supplement to mental health: A report of the Surgeon General.* Rockville, MD: US Dept of Health and Human Services, Public Health Service, Office of the Surgeon General.

Groundbreaking report that supplements the Surgeon General's Report on Mental Health and acknowledges the importance of race, ethnicity, and culture on mental health at a federal level.

PART 6
HEALTH POLICY
AND ECONOMICS

CODA

He spoke of boyhood days in France
and walks with comrades on the plage,
of wine and spicy bouillabaise
and timorous visits to the whores
of cities like Marseille where he
had once acquired the clap and felt
himself both man and idiot.

He came here in the twenties, found
a wife and lived as most men do.
He smoked too much and later coughed
away his life in flecks of blood,
at first with bronchiectasis
and then with cancer of the lung.

I faithfully examined him
each weekend afternoon. We'd sit
and talk then of his younger days
and all the fun he'd had in France,
how onion soup had once been made
(not from a can), and how the whores
had pirouetted en chemise.

His wife would pour us each a drink
and we would sip our scotch or rye
in studied ritual. She sat
or stood in shadow, casual
and smiling, but with frightened eyes
which screamed in silence.

          He and I
would toss around the paper mouse
with which the kitten he had bought
would play ferociously.

We often spent an hour that way;
musing, he would reminisce,
his wife would smile her unwept tears,
and I would comfort wordlessly.

The cat would pounce upon the mouse,
and we would sip our drinks and wait.

SAMUEL STEARNS

25 Health Services in the United States

E. Andrew Balas

> Once the formal teaching rounds were over, they talked only about the problems they faced. For some, the talk was about the malpractice crisis, the freeze on Medicare fees, the impact of diagnosis-related groups, and shrinking incomes. For others, it was the endless paperwork in applying for research funding ... Medicine, they said, was no fun anymore ... the faculty reminisced about the good old days, which neither they nor the students would ever see.
>
> CAROLA EISENBERG
> *It Is Still a Privilege to Be a Doctor*

Those who practice medicine are obligated to serve both individuals through one-on-one medical care and the public through high quality and cost-effective health services. In practice, it is often difficult to balance these obligations. The growing contrasts between impressive technological virtuosity, skyrocketing costs, and flawed access bring issues of the health-care system into prominence. The impressive achievements of American medicine are dramatically illustrated by those cured from diseases that would have been fatal just a few years ago, by the unparalleled positive changes in the lifestyles of many Americans, by the thousands who come to receive high quality care in the United States, and by the 60% of **Nobel prizes** in medicine awarded to U.S. physicians and scientists after World War II.

On the other hand, the challenges facing society and the medical community are numerous: Rising health-care costs threaten to bankrupt businesses, millions of Americans have inadequate access to health care, the preponderance of specialists in the workforce limits the availability of much-needed primary care physicians, and the fragmentation of medical services causes duplication and forces many patients to seek care from multiple and nonintegrated providers. The public and also many large corporations that cover increasingly expensive health benefits are noticeably unhappy with the status quo. While preserving their traditional role as caregivers and advocates of patients, health-care professionals have to broaden their perspective by understanding the social context and organizational environment in which they provide care.

In spite of investing great resources, studies show major unmet needs in community health, including preventive care, professional workforce allocation, and collaborative public health efforts nationally. Comparisons of total health expenditure per capita and life expectancy at birth show that the United States spends $4,499 per capita and now has 67.6 years of life expectancy at birth. According to the World Health Report 2002, the comparable numbers are $2,754 and 70.2 years for Germany, $2,213 and 71.6 years for Australia, and $2,009 and 73.6 years for Japan. It is apparent that a significant and growing gap exists between the investment in U.S. health care and its measurable outcomes in community health.

The interaction between clinical decisions and societal incentives is becoming a recognized and critical issue for health services. Through their recommendations and clinical decisions, physicians, nurses, and other health-care professionals have a tremendous influence, not only on the outcome of care, but also on the use of health-care resources. Individual variations in clinical behavior demonstrate the influence of practice style. For example, some physicians tend to recommend immediate surgery while others suggest only watchful waiting for similar patients with prostate cancer. These differences in clinical practice cannot be fully explained by education, age, time in practice, or similar variables. Instead of trying to come up with explanations, newer pragmatic studies have focused on the methods necessary to change practice style. Simple approaches (e.g., traditional education methods or close supervision) seem to have very limited value in quality improvement and cost control of health services.

In recent years, concerns over chronic diseases and disparities in health care have become increasingly salient. For example, over 18.2 million people suffer from **diabetes**, including 5.2 million who are undiagnosed. Diabetes and its complications resulted in $132 billion of directly attributable excess U.S. cost in 2002. Among African-Americans, the incidence of diabetes is 1.6 times greater than in Caucasian population. The disease disproportionately affects African-American women. The rates of long-term complications of diabetes, including retinopathy, neuropathy, nephropathy, and diabetic end-stage renal disease are significantly higher in adult African-Americans. Lower extremity amputations are more prevalent in African-Americans, more costly, and require longer hospital stays than those required for Caucasians.

In addition to the inherent stress of patient care caused by unexpected changes or complications, practitioners often face stress and frustration created by health-care organizations and the third-party payors who are supposed to assist them. Fear of malpractice litigation, long resident hours, or the continuing demand for explanation, justification, and documentation are examples of such situations. The days of independent practitioners making independent decisions are unlikely to come back in an era of technical sophistication, risk sharing, and teamwork. *Physicians, trained to treat sick people, often find themselves in the role of a part-time business executive who is responsible for administration, marketing, and streamlining the care of certain types of patients.* In addition, physicians are often asked for their opinions about new health policy proposals. Because of the need for medical students to understand these issues, this chapter focuses on three critical areas: the provision and financing of health services, methods to improve quality and control costs, and reform proposals to change the system of health care.

> Nothing can be more important to a State than its public health; the State's paramount concern should be the health of its people.
>
> FRANKLIN D. ROOSEVELT
> US President
> *Report of the Special Health Commission*

OVERVIEW OF THE HEALTH CARE SYSTEM

America's pluralistic and competitive health-care system is a reflection of the social and cultural values of society. In the United States, choice and diversity are widely accepted values and, correspondingly, the health-care system consists of a large variety of providers, payors, and financing mechanisms. Obviously, this system is quite different from the monolithic, often bureaucratic, and fully government controlled health-care systems of many countries. This overview describes the major players and components of health services in the United States. First, the various inpatient and outpatient care providers are discussed. This is followed by a list of the most important financing mechanisms. Finally, the major categories of payors are described. The reason for this separate discussion is that financing mechanisms should never be identified or confused with payors. The same payor can use various payment mechanisms, while different payors often use similar or identical reimbursement mechanisms.

> The new medical-industrial complex is now a fact of American life. It is still growing and is likely to be with us for a long time. Any conclusions about its ultimate impact on our health-care system would be premature, but it is safe to say that the effect will be profound ... We should not allow the medical-industrial complex to distort our health-care system to its own entrepreneurial ends.
>
> ARNOLD S. RELMAN
> *New England Journal of Medicine*

Providers of Health Services

Medical practice has always been the cornerstone of health services in the United States. Historically, general practitioners worked in their offices, made house calls, and performed various procedures. Today, house calls are rare, and most outpatient services are provided in solo and group practices, both in office-based settings. Currently, *the place of contact for 60% of ambulatory care is the doctor's office.* The solo practitioner is the sole owner of an unincorporated business. Many primary care physicians, and also subspecialists, prefer solo practices and the potentially stronger patient-clinician relationship this arrangement allows. Certainly, **solo practices** represent the lowest level of bureaucracy and organizational complexity, although long term financial viability is often challenged as evidenced by a decline in the number of such practices. On the other hand, *group practices represent a growing sector of the health-care sector economy.* According to the definition of the American Medical Association, a **group practice** is an organization formed by three or more physicians to provide medical care, consultation, diagnosis, and/or treatment through the joint use of equipment and personnel, and with the income distributed in accordance with methods previously determined by members of the group. Today, over 206,000 physicians in the United States are working in single specialty, multispecialty, or family practice medical groups. The average size of group practices is about nine physicians. One of the earliest and best examples of a group practice is the **Mayo Clinic**, organized in 1887.

The traditional focus of **hospitals** is the care of patients who need special attention for a few days, or longer, in a place where trained personnel, necessary supplies, and equipment are available. In addition to inpatient care, hospitals often provide specialized diagnostic and therapeutic services for outpatients. These specialists, the structures of their collaboration, and housing of advanced technology made the modern hospital the hub of the health-care delivery system. The medical staff of community hospitals consists mostly of private practitioners who have admitting privileges. These practitioners can admit their patients, decide how long a patient will stay, and order hospital services. **House staff** is a term used to describe interns and residents who are employees of the hospital and function under the supervision of the attending physician. Hospital care is provided by a large variety of professionals including nurses, technicians, and therapists. Public hospitals are owned by the federal, state, or local government. Community hospitals are not-for-profit organizations, owned and operated by community associations or religious organizations. *The emergency room of the community hospital is now not only an urgent care center, but also a setting for free medical care for the poor and uninsured who cannot afford care anywhere else.* Unlike not-for-profit (or tax exempt) hospitals, for-profit (or investor owned) hospitals are owned by private investors. About half of the nation's hospitals are operated by nonfederal, multihospital systems that own, lease, or manage more than one acute care hospital. Interestingly, in many other countries outpatient and inpatient care are strictly separated and hospitals employ salaried physicians who accept referrals from ambulatory care physicians.

Health care is also provided by various freestanding and institutionally based **outpatient facilities**. To meet the needs of local communities, many hospitals maintain primary care and specialty clinics. Free-standing emergency and urgent care centers provide care for patients requiring immediate medical attention. Community mental health centers provide outpatient mental health care. These centers are often financed by state mental health departments and local communities, or they can be independent not-for-profit entities. **Ambulatory surgery centers** provide one-day surgical care, where patients are admitted on the day of surgery and usually discharged after recovery from anesthesia. Specialized dialysis clinics provide in-center and home hemodialysis therapy for patients with end-stage renal disease. **Home health care**, a rapidly changing type of health service, includes skilled nursing care, physical therapy, counseling, respiratory therapy, and medical social service provided to patients in the home setting. Poison control centers offer emergency advice and referral in cases of poisoning. Institutional and community pharmacies not only dispense drugs, but are also valuable resources of pa-

tient education. In addition to laboratories in hospitals and physicians' offices, there are many independent, privately owned clinical laboratories providing high volume, complex, or esoteric testing.

Long-term residential care encompasses a range of services addressing the health, social, and custodial needs of people who lack some capacity for self-care. Rehabilitation hospitals and units serve the temporary needs of patients discharged from acute care and help them to make the transition to self-care. According to the generally accepted definition, *conditions lasting 90 days or more are considered chronic.* **Nursing homes** provide extended inpatient or residential care for people having chronic health, mental health, and/or social problems (e.g., the elderly or the functionally disabled). People reside at a nursing home for an extended period of time and are usually called residents rather than patients. Recent data indicate that *U.S. hospitals had an average occupancy rate of 63% while most nursing homes had to maintain 90% or higher occupancy rates in order to remain financially viable.* Most patients in **state or county mental hospitals**, where another major type of long-term care is provided, are people diagnosed as schizophrenic and patients with organic brain syndromes. As a result of deinstitutionalization, care of the mentally ill has shifted to home- and community-based care.

The health facilities operated by the federal government represent a sector of health care where the government is involved both in the financing and the provision of services. The **Department of Veterans Affairs** (VA) operates the largest, integrated health-care system in this country. Health care is provided primarily for veterans who served 90 days or more in an armed service and received an honorable discharge. The VA system includes 173 hospitals, 238 ambulatory care clinics, and numerous other facilities. After World War II, an extensive partnership between medical schools and the Veterans Administration provided physicians for the veterans and allowed residents to complete graduate medical education in VA facilities. The quality of VA sponsored research is highly regarded in many clinical areas. The **Department of Defense** operates clinics and hospitals to provide health care for members of the seven uniformed services and their dependents. The basic mission of the military health-care delivery system is to support military operations. The armed forces have developed extensive regionalized health services throughout the world. Men and women on active duty are entitled to health care; dependents, survivors, and retirees may qualify for care, depending on availability. The Department of Health and Human Services operates the **Indian Health Service**. This service was created to provide medical care for American Indians and Alaskan Natives. The largely rural system includes facilities on Indian reservations and in certain other locations.

Health maintenance organizations (HMOs) represent a changing segment of the U.S. health-care system. One of the first, largest, and best-known HMOs is the **Kaiser-Permanente Medical Care Program**. HMOs provide **managed health care**, i.e., the integration of the financing and delivery of patient care. A typical HMO contracts with employers to provide comprehensive health services for their employees in exchange for a monthly premium per enrollee (**capitation**). Obviously, HMOs have a major financial interest in controlling the cost of care while maintaining or improving quality. Therefore, strong incentives and barriers influence enrollees to use clinicians of the plan (e.g., services of nonplan physicians are not reimbursed without referral by an HMO primary care provider), incentives and barriers for clinicians are used to contain costs (e.g., only drugs in the **formulary** of the HMO can be prescribed), and active utilization and quality control programs exist. For example, several HMOs started to encourage 24-hour hospital stays for uncomplicated vaginal delivery. While lower cost makes managed care attractive, the multiple restrictions on care have proved to be unpopular and markedly limit interest in enrollment.

There are several **types of health maintenance organizations**: (1) **staff models** use salaried staff physicians, (2) **group models** contract with one or more large multi-specialty group practices, (3) network models contract with individual physicians and many different group practices, and (4) **independent practice associations** (IPAs) of physicians are formed to contract with HMOs. With the exception of the staff model, HMOs can compensate their clinicians on either a fee-for-service basis or capitation basis under which a percent of the per member income is forwarded to the physician or physician group. In the latter case, *physicians assume financial risk for any over-utilization of services.* Most HMOs provide a wide range of patient care, including primary, specialty, and inpatient care. Some managed health-care organizations specialize in the treatment of a specific group of diseases for a capitated payment (e.g., mental health care, management of diabetes). *There are twice as many for-profit as not-for-profit HMOs.* Point of service plans also offer reimbursement for services provided by out of network physicians but at a lower rate.

> The legislature is clearly accountable not just for what is funded in the health care budget, but for what is not funded. Accountability is inescapable ...
>
> JOHN KITZHABER
> Physician and former Governor of Oregon

Financing Mechanisms

It is widely acknowledged that health-care financing shapes the delivery of health service, and methods of reimbursement provide powerful incentives and disincentives. Many physicians state that they treat the patient and not the patient's pocket, and some research studies support these claims. However, *financing and reimbursement repeatedly have been shown to influence both the type and frequency of many patient care activities.* People are often confused by the fact that different payors use different reimbursement methods and the mix of these components is changing continuously. Overall, *there is no other area where the pluralistic nature of American health care is more visible than in the field of financing and reimbursement.*

Fee-for-service is the classic method of reimbursement for health services. Under this method, specific services (procedures) are defined as units for reimbursement and patient bills list the units of services provided. The most widely used coding system is the **Current Procedural Terminology** (CPT), published and updated annually by the American Medical Association. The **Resource-Based Relative-Value Scale** (RBRVS), a new method of calculating fees based on CPT procedures, takes into account **three components: physician work, practice expenses, and malpractice insurance.** Fee-for-service practice is very effective in demonstrating the relationship between provided services and charges. Patients can control the accuracy of billing and third party payors can get valuable information about the appropriateness of the services provided. On the other hand, keeping track of small and multiple line-items of services increases paperwork and contributes to administrative overhead. *Fee-for-service payment is often perceived as a financial incentive to increase the use of profitable procedures.*

Prospective payment systems (PPS) assign predefined reimbursement amounts to the treatment of each of the nearly 500 diagnosis related groups. *Under PPS, clinicians keep the difference if their actual costs are lower than the payment rate and have to absorb the difference if their actual costs are higher.* **Diagnosis Related Groups** (DRGs) are units of reimbursement in the most widely used PPS for inpatient care (e.g., DRG 254 is Fractures, Sprains, Strains, and Dislocations of Upper Arm and Lower Leg Except Foot, Age Greater than 17 without Complications or Co-morbid Conditions; the corresponding average length of stay is 3.4 days). In a DRG-based prospective payment system, additional days of hospitalization or treatments for some complications require special consideration and *hospitals have a financial interest in limiting the use of resources.* Many studies indicate that the DRG-based prospective payment has not jeopardized quality of care, and has only been partially successful in limiting cost.

Global budgeting is a mechanism for financing health-care organizations with a fixed annual amount in exchange for negotiated health services. Advantages of global budgeting include simplicity of administration and effectiveness in limiting health-care expenditures. On the other hand, this reimbursement method separates the service delivered to a patient and the global payment received from a third party (usually the government). Analysts note that strict limits on expenditures often results in withholding of needed health-care benefits. Revenues depend on nego tiations in government offices and not on meeting the needs and expectations of patients. National and institutional global budgeting were the financial foundations for socialist health care. Today, many former socialist countries are rapidly moving away from the inefficiencies and inequities of this reimbursement method. On the other hand, *Canada and the United Kingdom are countries where global budgets have been used with more success.*

Capitation refers to prepayment of a fixed monthly fee on behalf of an enrolled person for a comprehensive package of health-care benefits regardless of services actually rendered. Obviously, some enrollees will get expensive treatments, including major surgery or hospitalization, while others will never contact their physician. *Under capitation, the clinician assumes a significant financial risk by charging the same monthly premium to all members regardless of health status or actual utilization of services.* Usually strong incentives and barriers are applied to encourage enrollees to use the clinicians of the capitated plan. Capitation integrates the financial and clinical sides of care. The usual advantages of capitation include comprehensive health-care benefits and powerful incentives to control costs, prevent disease, and lower administrative costs. On the other hand, capitated plans limit choice of physician and self-referral.

Out-of-pocket expenses represent the share of the costs incurred by the patient. Most private insurance plans specify a **deductible** amount that has to be reached before insurance payments become available. The **copayment** is the amount that has to be paid by the patient per unit of service (e.g., $10 per prescription) and **coinsurance** is the fraction of expenses (e.g., 25%) paid by the patient. Deductibles, copayments, and coinsurance maintain the responsibility of individuals and help ensure financial accountability between patient and doctors. These are important considerations in a situation in which most health-care bills are paid by third-party payors. The **annual or lifetime maximum** defines an upper limit for expenses reimbursable by third-party payors. Anything above that limit has to be paid by the patient or someone else. Finally, monthly premiums paid for continuous health insurance coverage also represent a type of out-of-pocket expenses. *It is estimated that approximately one third of medical expenses are paid by individuals.*

Grants and gifts have always been significant sources of funding for health care. Historically, philanthropic gifts by individual benefactors or organizations have been essential for the expansion of health services. (e.g., donations by wealthy individuals and development grants from foundations or businesses). Many religious organizations have played an important role in arranging health care for the poor. Government grants are redistributions of federal tax revenues to supplement local and state taxes in financing various public health services and programs (e.g., cancer control or community health centers). Formula grants are allocated to states based on such factors as state population or magnitude of specific health problems. Matching grants have to be matched up to a certain percentage by the agency or institution receiving the grant. Project grant awards are usually made to one of several competing applicants to help carry out a particular federal program. Usually, grants are used to improve and expand health services rather than cover existing operating expenses.

Cost-shifting is a strategy for managing lack of payment. It is frequently used to recover the expenses of nonreimbursed or underreimbursed care by shifting the cost to other payors. Currently, a significant percent of care provided by some hospitals is not reimbursed and some mechanism is necessary to maintain financial viability for the institutions. Usually, *patients with private insurance are charged substantially higher amounts to cover the expenses of those who cannot afford care.* Internal cost shifting is also used to recover expenses of unprofitable but needed services (e.g., emergency rooms) from the revenues generated by profitable services (e.g., specialized surgery).

> Health care companies are not in business to heal people or save lives; they provide health care to make profits. In effect, in the necessary effort to control health care costs through the market mechanism, power has shifted from physicians and patients to insurance companies and other purchasers of services.
>
> GEORGE SOROS
> *The New York Times*

Third-Party Payors

The extremely high costs of health care and the unpredictability of the need for medical care led to the development of various **third-party payors**. In spite of the misleading terminology used in some countries, free health care does not exist. Someone has to pay the cost of care and the differences among various health-care systems are found in the routes that money takes as it moves from consumers to providers of care. The payor is the person or organization paying for the provided health service. To ease the burden of paying health-care bills, third-party payors, such as insurance carriers, have evolved. *Insurance carriers pool the resources of many individuals and then distribute the resources to cover very large and unexpected expenses of the few.* By paying a fixed monthly or annual premium, people share the costs and thereby lower the individual risk of a large unpredictable health-care expense. For obvious reasons, the pooling and sharing role of health insurance is particularly important for low income people.

The **employer-based health insurance system** is a characteristic feature of American health care. During World War II, the War Labor Board set restrictions on wage increases, but ruled that fringe benefits up to 5% would not be considered inflationary. To compete for skilled labor, employers began to increase benefits and this seemingly insignificant ruling led to an employer-based health insurance system in the United States. A series of legal and tax developments also encouraged both employers and employees to want comprehensive health insurance benefits. *Today, about 70% of the population under age 65 is insured through employer benefit programs.* Usually, employers offer two to five health insurance plans, and one of them is often a managed care plan. Most frequently, health insurance plans are arranged with one or more commercial insurers. However, not all employers offer health insurance plans, and *employees of small businesses may have particular difficulty affording health insurance.*

For-profit and not-for-profit **insurance companies** offer a variety of health insurance policies. In the middle of the 19th century, the Franklin Health Insurance Company of Massachusetts started to offer insurance to help their customers cope with medical expenses resulting from bodily injuries. The first large health insurers appeared on the market before the Great Depression (Blue Cross in Dallas). Traditionally, *Blue Cross provided hospitalization insurance and Blue Shield covered physician services.* In addition to the not-for-profit Blues, a large number of for-profit insurance companies offered insurance against the cost of illness. *Currently, about one-third of all medical care costs are covered by private health insurance and employee benefit programs.* There are about 800 commercial insurance carriers and 70 Blue Cross and Blue Shield plans. In addition, 650 HMOs, a rapidly growing number, offer a combination of health insurance and health-care delivery through capitation. Some large corporations and unions self-insure or partially self-insure employee benefit programs. Most of these organizations offer a variety of products and use different financial mechanisms to reimburse care.

Medical and dental insurance policies are contracts that provide specified health-care benefits in return for monthly or annual premium payments. Policies range from comprehensive health insurance to specialized products like long-term care insurance or coverage for expenses not reimbursed by Medicare (**Medigap policies**). **Indemnity plans** offer cash payment for health services regardless of the expenses actually incurred. **Service benefit plans** pay a percentage of usual, customary, and reasonable (UCR) fees (most frequently 80%). **Hybrid plans** offer indemnity coverage for certain services and percentage reimbursement for others. However, no benefit package can be unlimited, and there are important restrictions in all health insurance policies: certain procedures are not reimbursable (e.g., experimental treatments, plastic surgery); limits are imposed on the use of selected resources (e.g., a maximum 30 hospital days); and maximum benefit restrictions (caps) limit the financial responsibility of the insurance carrier (e.g., a $1,000,000 lifetime maximum).

Preferred Provider Organizations (PPOs), are loosely controlled versions of managed health care, and often play a broker role between employers and providers. There are about 1,016 PPO plans, and half of these are operated by insurance companies. Participating physicians are asked to provide services for negotiated discounted prices in order to preserve or increase their market share. *The average physician discount is about 17%; however, the depth of discounting is usually much more for surgical specialties and subspecialties than for family physicians.* In addition to the negotiated fee schedules, PPOs also are characterized by consumer choice of providers (with incentives for consumers to use PPO providers), utilization review, and expedient settlement of claims. The utilization control methods of PPOs usually include preadmission approval before hospitalization and **mandatory second opinions** before elective surgeries. PPOs often combine various financial mechanisms for reimbursement. For example, *the use of DRGs has become less common, while per diem rates are used more frequently in determining hospital reimbursement.*

Social health insurance is managed by the federal government and states. In Europe, the German government was among the first to mandate health insurance for workers below a certain income level (*sickness funds*). Today, the government of most countries is involved in the financing of health care. With social health insurance, the tax corresponds to premium and entitlement corresponds to benefits. In the United States, members of the armed forces, veterans, and American Indians are entitled to medical care financed by the federal government. Persons 65 and over, disabled individuals, and patients with chronic renal failure are entitled to benefits of the federal Medicare program. **Medicare Part A** finances hospital care, posthospitalization care, and home health agency visits. **Medicare Part B** provides supplementary medical insurance covering physician services, physician ordered supplies and services, and various outpatient services. The Medicare program is financed through a payroll tax, with beneficiaries of the Part B plan paying a monthly premium. There are also deductibles, and other out-of-pocket expenses. The **Medicaid** program (*a state-federal partnership program*) finances health care provided to low income individuals and families. In the sense that income is being redistributed from the rich to the poor through this government funded system, it is considered welfare medicine, a special type of cost-shifting. Medicaid is financed partly by the federal government and partly by the participating states. The Social Security Act mandates that every state must finance certain basic health services, but the exact scope of services and income standards vary considerably among states. *The financing mechanisms used by the federal government and states include prospective payment (DRGs), fee-for-service (Medicare Part B), global budgeting (Veterans Administration), and capitation (Medicaid HMO contracts).*

> The increasing ability of physicians to disentangle specific disease entities ... was an intellectual achievement of the first magnitude and not unrelated to the increasingly scientific and prestigious public image of the medical profession. Yet, we have see a complex and inexorably bureaucratic reimbursement system grow up around these diagnostic entities; disease does not exist if it cannot be coded.
>
> CHARLES E. ROSENBERG
> *The Care of Strangers: The Rise of America's Hospital System*

Information Systems and Health Care

Communication processes are essential for the coordination of care. As a result, information systems represent a critical component of health services. According to some estimates, *30% of the patient information needed by physicians is missing during a typical visit.* This results in part because communication among various clinicians is often slow and insufficient. Physicians must assimilate an overwhelming amount of data on patients' history, condition, treatment, and functional status, and it is often difficult to know which data are critical for making clinical decisions. Paper-based communication is especially slow and difficult to integrate across providers and services. For example, conflicts between laboratory data and medication often remain undetected. *Hospitals spend only about 2% of their operating budget on information systems. The corresponding numbers are 10% for banking and 6 to 7% for insurance.* As health-care organizations feel increasing pressure to improve efficiency, they will want data to guide their decisions and information systems to enhance communications.

Computer-stored medical record systems can remedy many of the shortcomings of traditional paper-based documentation: physicians can access data in seconds; records are more legible and better organized; and simultaneous and remote access are also supported. More importantly, **electronic medical records** make the patient data readily available for further processing that can include medical decision-support systems and quality evaluations. For example, the HELP integrated information system of the Later Day Saints Hospital in Salt Lake City checks the electronic patient records daily and sends reminder messages to ensure the proper use of antibiotic prophylaxis 2 hours before surgery This information intervention reduced the postoperative wound infection rate by 50%, and resulted in significant cost savings because the average postoperative infection adds $14,000 to the hospital bill. **Nursing systems** provide computer-based support for the formulation and execution of nursing care plans. **Laboratory systems** support the extralaboratory communication cycle (test ordering, reporting the results to requesting physician) and intralaboratory cycle (labeling specimens, data processing, record keeping, quality control, and reporting results). **Pharmacy systems** print labels, drug-dispensing reports,

and drug-use review reports. There are numerous other successful clinical computer applications (e.g., radiology systems, intensive care monitoring, and systems for office practice). *Integration of the disconnected patchwork of systems is one of the most important challenges in the quest for effective and fast processes of patient care.*

The advent of powerful, low-cost computers has dramatically improved the efficiency of health-care administration. Computers assist in scheduling appointments, print encounter forms, call patients to reduce no-show rates, and customize correspondence. Financial management systems record the number and types of services provided and accounts receivable. Computers have automated the billing process, which involves the application of multiple reimbursement methods and fee schedules. Computer systems also help to detect and collect outstanding receivables. Marketing and strategic business planning can be assisted by the computerized analyses of procedures, revenues, and patient demographics. Finally, computers have altered the way physicians and other health-care providers search for information. For example, the **MEDLINE** database of the **National Library of Medicine** is an unparalleled and popular source of medical information. The system contains references to the recent journal literature and offers support for sophisticated comprehensive searches. In addition to the most frequently used MEDLINE database, several other bibliographic and full-text databases are available through the Internet.

PROCESS AND QUALITY OF HEALTH SERVICES

To provide good quality care for more people, physicians and other health-care professionals have to look at the chain of activities in which they participate from a different perspective. Physicians take care of persons seeking help, and, for the overwhelming majority of physicians, patient care is not only providing services and a source of living, but also a matter of moral obligation and compassion. It is often difficult to think and act in terms of a patient population. When you see a sick person, you want to provide the best and everything you possibly can. Indeed, *research studies document that physicians make different decisions when they focus on the needs of a group of patients and not on the needs of a particular individual.* To serve more patients better, the process of health care has to be analyzed. Usually, professionals are thoroughly familiar with the activities they perform and have a general understanding of what others do. However, this level of understanding is rarely enough to achieve coordination from the patient's perspective, improve performance, and achieve a convincing and measurable change in the outcome of services.

Concepts of Quality in Health Care

Analyses of health services require adequate measurement of the quality of care. Analyses of quality can separate the **quality of design** (e.g., appropriateness of a surgical procedure to treat a particular medical condition) and the **quality of delivery** (e.g., success rate of a selected surgeon). However, most quality evaluations focus on one of the following three aspects of health services: resources, processes, and outcomes.

Quality of structure refers to attempts to measure and influence the quality of care by testing and approving (or disapproving) specific resources of care. Clearly, the quality of resources is a necessary foundation of good patient care and is likely to remain a mainstream concept. However, its obvious limitation is that the coordinated process of cost-effective patient care cannot be fully evaluated by testing the components of care alone. Currently, the main categories of routinely tested structural characteristics include:

1. **Human resources.** In the United States, only persons who have appropriate graduate education and who have passed the required licensure exams can practice medicine (e.g., the **United States Medical Licensing Examination**IUnited States Medical Licensing Examination). Licensure is needed to begin lawful practice. Additional training and examination are required to become a **board-certified specialist** (e.g., a radiologist, general surgeon, or ophthalmologist). Similarly, nurses can become registered nurses (R. N.) after 2 to 4 years of education and passing a state board licensing examination. In most states, Nurse Practice Acts define different scopes of practice for registered and nonregistered nurses (e.g., usually medication cannot be administered by unregistered nurses). With advanced training and education, nurses can also be certified as specialists (e.g., nurse anesthetists).

2. **Facilities.** Hospitals, managed health-care organizations, or nursing homes have to be licensed to operate. Furthermore, medical facilities have to be inspected before they qualify for Medicare or Medicaid reimbursement. In addition, facilities cannot become accredited until they meet clearly defined standards for equipment, housekeeping, regulations, and certain procedures (e.g., adequate review of all blood orders). For the purposes of accreditation, the **Joint Commission on Accreditation of Health-Care Organizations (JCAHO)** was established in 1952 by the American Medical Association, the Colleges of Surgeons and Physicians, and the American Hospital Association.

3. **Drugs and equipment.** In the beginning of this century, the claims of many patent medicine companies were both misleading and dangerous. For example, medicines often contained opium derivatives and many people be-

> **The Wisdom of PAUL STARR, 1949–**
> **Professor of Sociology, Harvard University**
> *The Social Transformation of American Medicine*
>
> The medical profession has had an especially persuasive claim to authority. Unlike the law and the clergy, it enjoys close bonds with modern science, and at least for most of the last century, scientific knowledge has held a privileged status in the hierarchy of belief.
>
> In America, no one group has held so dominant a position in this new world of rationality and power as has the medical profession.
>
> If the medical profession were merely a monopolistic guild, it's position would be much less secure than it is. The basis of its high income and status, as I have argued all along, is its authority, which arises from lay deference and institutionalized forms of dependence.
>
> Probably no event in American history testifies more graphically to public acceptance of scientific methods than the voluntary participation of millions of American families in the 1954 trials of the Salk vaccine.
>
> A corporate sector in health care is also likely to aggravate inequalities in access to health care. Profit-making enterprises are not interested in treating those who cannot pay. The voluntary hospital may not treat the poor the same as the rich, but they do treat them and often treat them well.
>
> The development of medical care, like other institutions, takes place within larger fields of power and social structure. These external forces are particularly visible in conflicts over the politics and economics of health and medical care.
>
> The organizational culture of medicine used to be dominated by the ideals of professionalism and volunteerism which softened the underlying acquisitive activity. The restraint exercised by these ideals now grows weaker, the health center of one era is the profit center of the next.
>
> From a relatively weak, traditional profession of minor economic significance, medicine has become a sprawling system of hospitals, clinics, health plans, insurance companies, and myriad other organizations employing a vast labor force.
>
> Physicians in training or engaged in research do not require their patients' good will for future business. Their professional rewards depend on the opinion of colleagues.

came addicted to them. In 1906, Congress responded by passing the Food and Drug Act. Today, the federal **Food and Drug Administration (FDA)** has a wide range of responsibilities. All new drugs must be proved not only safe, but also effective before being approved for marketing. Similar but less stringent approval is needed before

> The irony is that the healthier Western society becomes, the more medicine it craves.
>
> ROY PORTER
> *The Greatest Benefit to Mankind*

marketing any medical device affecting the structure or function of the human body.

Quality of process focuses on the activities of clinicians and assumes that there is a causal relationship between specific clinical procedures and the outcome of care. **Utilization**, the most frequently applied statistic, is the number of procedures performed divided by the number of potentially eligible cases. It is a condition-specific, easily interpreted measure. However, the relationship between process and outcome is often unclear (e.g., electronic fetal heart rate monitoring and the health status of the newborn from an uncomplicated pregnancy). *There are two fundamental approaches to analyzing the process of patient care:*

1. Analyses of clinical **practice variation** focus on the consistency of health-care delivery. In Maine, *Wennberg observed that by the time women reached 70 years of age, in one hospital market the likelihood they had undergone a hysterectomy was 20%, while in another market, it was 70%.* In Vermont, the probability that children would undergo a tonsillectomy ranged from 8 to 70%. On the other hand, procedures with less ambiguous indications showed much smaller variation of practice pattern (e.g., surgical repair of inguinal hernia, hospitalization for hip fractures). Subsequent small area analyses confirmed the existence of random (unexplained) practice variations in many clinical areas and in many countries. Based on these studies, the American Medical Association concluded that *drastic variations in how patient care is provided can be an indicator of either the provision of inappropriate care or failure to provide appropriate care.*

The effect of nonmedical factors on the use of health services has been extensively investigated to explain major variations in clinical practice patterns. In these analyses, anything other than the health status of the patient is considered to be a nonmedical factor. The list of analyzed nonmedical factors is very long (e.g., education and specialty of the physician, insurance status of the patient, size of the hospital, and financial interest of the clinician). Many of these factors predict the frequency of certain medical procedures. However, none of the nonmedical factors seems to have a general and consistent influence on variation. An analysis of data from 23 counties in California by the RAND corporation used an expert panel to re-evaluate the appropriateness of three clinical procedures (coronary angiography, carotid end-

arterectomy, and upper gastrointestinal endoscopy). The study documented significant variations in the appropriateness of these procedures, but the variations in appropriateness could not explain the overall variation in utilization rates.

2. Analysis of **compliance with recommendations** compares actual practice patterns to established clinical standards. In such analyses, quality is perceived as a utilization rate within the recommended range. Such standards are available in various clinical areas. For example, the U.S. Preventive Services Task Force developed recommendations for a variety of clinical services (e.g., increase pneumococcal pneumonia and influenza immunization among institutionalized chronically ill or older people to at least 80%). The **Healthy People 2010** document recommends that the average number of cesarean deliveries should not exceed 15.5 per 100 deliveries (the current national average is about 17.8%). **Case-mix adjustment** is a controversial technique to create global quality measures and adjust them to differences in the severity of patient conditions. It is believed to be often inaccurate and certainly hard to interpret. Condition-specific process measures are powerful when controlled evidence from randomized clinical trials links the process to the outcome of care. For example, annual eye examination in an experimental group successfully reduced the rate of vision loss among diabetic patients in comparison to a randomly selected control group. The **HEDIS quality scorecard** of the National Committee on Quality Assurance (NCQA) includes several clinical parameters, mostly process measures.

Several studies indicate the slow effect of scientific evidence on clinical practice patterns. For example, between 1980 and 1987, intermittent positive pressure breathing was clearly demonstrated to be an outmoded treatment for chronic obstructive pulmonary disease. However, a study from the Agency for Health Care Policy and Research documented that, despite a lack of scientific evidence verifying its efficacy, this procedure attained widespread use. Hospitals with a shorter case-mix-adjusted length of stay and private non-profit or investor-owned hospitals were more likely to abandon this procedure before 1980. In Canada, a widely distributed and nationally endorsed consensus statement on the indications for cesarean sections was released in 1986. The statement recommended a decrease in the use of this procedure. Data on actual practice following the publication of the guidelines showed only minimal change from the previous upward trend. Other studies also confirmed that *traditional publication and education methods frequently have only a temporary effect, and utilization rates quickly revert to their earlier level.* Clearly, new approaches are needed to accelerate implementation of current and scientifically validated clinical recommendations.

Quality of outcome is probably the most attractive quality concept, because it attempts to assess the real result of health services; i.e., the change in the health status of the patient or populations. There are two levels in the description of health status and they use different measuring techniques.

On the **national level**, annual reports on vital and health statistics of the population in the United States are published by the **Centers for Disease Control and Prevention (CDC)**. Vital and health statistics are also published by states. These reports combine total population-based sources (e.g., U.S. Standard Live Birth and Death Certificates, and Fetal Death Reports) and randomly selected, representative sample-based information sources (e.g., National Health Interview Surveys and National Hospital Discharge Surveys). For example, in 1996, the overall life expectancy at birth was 76.1 years. At the same time, the infant mortality rate, another critical health status indicator, was 7.2 deaths per 1,000 live births. This infant mortality rate was more than twice as high as that of Japan. *International comparisons, such as these, are often hampered by differences in culture and lifestyle, which exert a more profound effect than the health-care system* (e.g., in the United States, between 1974 and 1991, the prevalence of smoking declined from 37% of persons 25 years of age and over to 26%, an unparalleled change in international comparisons). Although national statistics provide valuable information, more specific data are needed for quality improvement purposes.

On the **organizational level**, it is extremely valuable, but difficult, to measure clinician-specific outcomes of care. The paramount interest of patients and third-party payors is to select the most effective clinicians based on outcome results. In addition, cases with adverse outcomes cost dramatically more than routine cases. Therefore, linking reimbursement for health services to patient outcomes is a very attractive concept. Finally, clinicians would also like to see fair comparisons of the outcomes of the patient care they provide. However, most health-care organizations have short episodic contacts with their patients. This fact limits the availability of data and the relevance of overall health status measures to the particular care provided.

The concept of **evidence-based medicine** means preferring clinical procedures that have been linked to improved health status in randomized clinical trials. Such measures are increasingly recommended (e.g., Misoprostol prophylaxis for chronic NSAID users, annual diabetic eye exam, mammography for patients over 50 years of age). Other, frequently used clinician-specific indicators are inpatient or 30-day mortality, nosocomial infection rate, unanticipated readmissions, surgical complication rates by the type of surgery, unplanned returns, and emergency room visits.

Patient satisfaction is an increasingly accepted outcome indicator of quality. Many physicians and health-care organizations realize the influence of patient satisfaction on functional status and the financial consequences of leaving a patient unsatisfied. Patient satisfaction is the product of the patient's comparison of his or her expectations with the service actually received. Surveys can measure satisfaction with the resulting functional status, specific elements of care processes, and communication with clinicians.

Quality cannot be interpreted as merely the absence of malpractice or major and harmful deviation from the accepted standards of medicine. Traditionally, professionals have been liable for injuries and other damages caused by their incompetent actions. A Babylonian text defined malpractice and the corresponding punishment in 2000 B.C.E.: "If the doctor shall open an abscess with a blunt knife and shall kill the patient or shall destroy the sight of the eye, his hand shall be cut off." Current **tort standards** hold physicians as individuals responsible for damages caused by malpractice, and this responsibility is primarily financial. Obviously, malpractice lawsuits are heavily influenced by social and cultural values, and *there are major differences in the frequency of lawsuits among various specialties and various areas of the country. The typical physician can expect to be sued once every 10 years, but three times as often in high-risk specialties or particular regions of the country.* However, nobody would conclude that obstetricians (a high risk specialty) provide lower quality care than radiologists (a low risk specialty).

The practice of **defensive medicine** arises from the fact that physicians have been primarily sued for not using rather than using certain diagnostic tests or treatments. Therefore, the fear of malpractice litigation has resulted primarily in the ordering of additional clinical procedures. This is considered one of the significant components of health-care inflation. *It is estimated that in the United States defensive medicine adds $10 to $15 billion in unnecessary expenditures.* There is also evidence that physicians are spending more time on paperwork and that many physicians have reduced the scope of their practice (e.g., primary care physicians who will not provide prenatal care). The total cost of the tort system is more than $230 billion a year and the expenses are growing. **Tort reform** is a recurrent issue of many health-care reform proposals.

Specifications of Ideal Patient Care

The fundamental mission of clinical research, including original studies and reviews, is to find and recommend efficient diagnostic and therapeutic procedures. However, the variety of clinical research methods is very large and there are substantial differences among studies in the practical applicability of results. This description will focus on techniques that are used to obtain or summarize evidence for direct clinical implementation.

Randomized controlled clinical trials are increasingly recognized as the top quality source of scientific evidence

MURMUR

They cut open his chest
and split the ribs, stitched
bits of leg veins
to the outside of his heart,
patched it all together
and stapled him shut,
sent him home.

Now he feels a turbulence
like a bird fluttering inside him.
As if his heart's old house
has a bad door that won't close,
shudders in the wind.

I place the cold, hard coin
of my stethoscope on his bare chest,
touching down on each of the four places,
medical's school's rote lessons a thing of habit
as I listen for the Tennessee ...
Tennessee ... of a stiffened ventricle,
the Kentucky ... Kentucky ...
of congestive failure.

Systole, diastole ... lub—
dub ... lub—dub ...,
I count ten healthy beats,
watch him breathe.

Perhaps it was the two hours on bypass,
the six weeks he missed work
for the first time in his life, or
how like an infant he needed others
to help him rise from a chair,
take his first steps around the unit.

I fold away my stethoscope.
He traces the pink zipper of a scar
down the front of his chest,
tells me he's been married to the same woman
almost fifty years, has a son
who sells life insurance,
a daughter in Topeka, three grandkids.

And now I hear it, too.
How his heart that once said ... today
... today ... now seems to say
remember me ... remember me ...

PETER PEREIRA

on the practical difference made by a clinical procedure or intervention. The clinical trial is a well-defined research design which has been known and used for decades. In a classic parallel group drug trial, a randomly selected half of all eligible subjects are assigned to the intervention group (they take the new drug) and the remaining eligible subjects serve as control (they take the **placebo**, an identically looking and tasting but neutral drug). *As a result of proper randomization, the two groups are assumed to be fully comparable and any differences in outcome are attributed to the intervention.* There are many types of clinical trials (e.g., factorial designs, cross-over trials), but the basic principles are the same: prospective and contemporaneous monitoring of the effect of a randomly allocated intervention. *Since the 1930s, no drug has been marketed without demonstration of the beneficial effects in randomized controlled clinical trials.*

Today, clinical trials are increasingly used to test all kinds of clinical interventions. These include surgical procedures (e.g., carotid endarterectomy), diagnostic techniques (e.g., electronic fetal heart rate monitoring), computerized information services (e.g., improving preventive care through computer generated prompting), health insurance plans (e.g., fee-for-service vs. capitation). It is widely accepted that **clinical trials** represent a design superior to **before-and-after studies** (vulnerable to changes over time that are unrelated to the effect of intervention) or **matched control studies** (a much less reliable method of obtaining comparable groups of subjects). Reflecting the growing significance of clinical trials, there are several registries of trial reports in various areas of medicine and the federal **Agency for Healthcare Research and Quality (AHRQ)** funds evidence centers to process the results of the best controlled clinical studies. For example, the pioneering Oxford registry of randomized controlled clinical trials of Chalmers and his colleagues systematically collects trial results in the area of perinatal care.

To provide good quality care, a cost-effective, consistent, and seamless continuum of services is needed. As a result of its immense complexity and high degree of specialization, this important continuum is often missing in the delivery of health services and *patients complain that their clinicians do not communicate with one another.* To establish a continuum of services, coordination among various clinicians, departments, and ancillary services is needed. This is often difficult in medium-sized or larger health-care organizations. The difficulties are even greater when the activities of different health-care organizations need to be coordinated to serve the same patient with a chronic health-care problem.

Disease management is an increasingly applied concept to coordinate the care for the chronically ill patients who represent a particularly demanding segment of services. Evidence-based disease management is built on clinical procedures that have been linked to improved outcome in randomized clinical trials. Such substantiated procedures are recommended for widespread use, promoted through various organizational techniques like physician reminders, and used as indicators of care in quality scorecards. Regardless of the size of the health-care organizations, bounded and frequently repeated sets of interrelated activities can usually be identified, analyzed, and improved in solo medical practices, as well as in large managed health-care organizations. *The controlled evidence is particularly compelling on the value of patient education and more active patient participation in the management of chronic disease.*

Although it is only recently that patient care and related activities have been viewed as a service process, the notions of work flow, sequential operations, and their control have been already explored and have helped to create efficient processes in many service industries. Today, service process is defined as a bounded and repeatable set of interrelated activities leading from a well-defined beginning to a specific outcome. For example, management of acute myocardial infarction starts with the reporting of the first signs and ends when the patient recovers or dies. Among others, the usual activities include transportation, admission, diagnostic testing, pain relief, development of nursing care plans, documentation, thrombolytic therapy, discharge, and a cardiac rehabilitation program. The nine simple steps summarized in Box 25.1 are recommended to manage any process, regardless of complexity. **Flowcharting**, also known as logic or diagramming, is the basis for analyzing and improving any process. Flowcharts graphically represent the activities that make up a process. Flowcharts can be supplemented with tables listing activities, associated direct costs (personnel and other), and times (actual processing time and cycle time, which is the usual waiting time for the activity) for further analysis and definition of the ideal process.

Clinical practice guidelines and clinical pathways are two illustrations of the use of process management techniques in health care. **Clinical practice guidelines** are specifications for efficient and effective medical care. Guidelines are developed through the synthesis of published scientific evidence, particularly clinical trial results, supplemented by expert opinion when research results are not available. Usually, guidelines recommend specific clinical actions for patients with a particular condition (e.g., measurement of postvoid residual volume for patients with urinary incontinence). Many guidelines have been developed and published by various professional societies and expert panels sponsored by government agencies. *The Agency for Healthcare Research and Quality compiles, and regularly updates, a comprehensive database of published clinical practice guidelines* (**www.guidelines.gov**).

Clinical pathways represent another systematic approach to identify key (primarily hospital nursing) activities necessary to obtain desired patient outcomes in the management of frequently occurring clinical problems

---

BOX 25.1 Steps of clinical process management and continuous quality improvement

1. Determine process ownership
2. Identify issues and process boundaries
3. Specify all activities of the process
4. Determine outcome and patient expectations
5. Develop clinical practice recommendation
6. Specify measurable quality objectives
7. Disseminate and implement recommendation
8. Measure performance based on objectives
9. Obtain feedback and perform corrective action

(e.g., major depression in adolescents). The clinical pathway is a list of recommended activities for the first, second, and all subsequent days of hospitalization. In spite of their rapidly growing popularity, currently available clinical practice guidelines and critical pathways have limitations. Usually, medical and nursing activities are defined separately, and measurable quality improvement objectives are rarely specified.

Managing the Process of Patient Care

The ultimate test of any effort to re-engineer the process of care is its effect on actual practice patterns. Most quality improvement and cost control opportunities reside in the usual process of patient care, and data on clinical practice patterns can help to redesign these processes. However, the process of redesign has to continue in dissemination of information and implementation. Several techniques have been used very effectively to manage the process of patient care.

Continuous quality improvement (CQI) is a systematic management approach designed to improve product performance, customer satisfaction, and profitability. The concept has already been applied in many health-care organizations. Traditional quality assurance efforts fail because they try to separate good and bad clinicians and to effect change through discipline and termination of the contracts of selected clinicians. Since nobody likes to be identified as a "bad apple," the concept and the corresponding disciplinary actions alienate clinicians. This focus on the evaluation of individual mistakes is also very expensive. Finally, clinicians quickly learn to beat the system that was designed to catch and punish them. In contrast, *continuous quality improvement focuses on processes instead of individuals, evaluates through measurement and data, and interprets detected defects as opportunities for improvement* (Box 25.1). Because most people would like to perform more effectively, the nonjudgmental and quantitative approach of CQI is gaining acceptance in the health-care industry. After refocusing its peer-review organizations, the **Center for Medicare and Medicaid Services** (CMS) began using CQI to evaluate providers participating in the Medicare program. This is a major shift away from the earlier focus on individual case reviews. Identification of measurable quality improvement objectives and subsequent tracking are critical components of any CQI program (e.g., reduction of the infection rate after surgery). Interestingly, *clinical quality improvement often results not only in outcome improvement, but also in cost savings* (e.g., an average postoperative infection can add more than $14,000 to the cost of care).

Utilization management aims to influence the use of selected clinical procedures by physicians and other health-care providers. Traditionally, utilization control has focused only on preventing the use of selected procedures. On the other hand, utilization management also promotes cost-effective alternatives and increased use of recommended procedures (e.g., cancer screening or immunization). Utilization management often starts with the exploration of more cost-effective alternatives. Use of less expensive **generic drugs** instead of brand name drugs is the preferred alternative in many health-care plans. **Preadmission testing** saves cost by having all routine preoperative tests done as an outpatient with the patient admitted the same day surgery is to be performed. The list of procedures that can be adequately performed on an outpatient basis is rapidly increasing, and **outpatient surgery** has become an important tool for cost saving (e.g., hernia surgery, breast biopsy, laparoscopic cholecystectomy, vaginal hysterectomy). Four other tools have been applied in utilization management:

1. **Authorization** refers to the requirement that approval has to be obtained before using certain services. The authorization is usually based on the documentation of need by a physician. Preadmission authorization is required by many third-party payors. In cases of nonemergency or elective surgical procedures, a second opinion from another physician can be required to avoid unnecessary use of clinical procedures. Specification of **Max-LOS** (maximum allowable length of hospital stay) is another way to limit the use of an expensive service. **Gatekeeper systems** are authorization programs that require approval or referral by the primary care physician before patients use certain services (e.g., specialists, hospitalization). The gatekeeper concept is extensively used in several countries, including HMOs in the U.S. and the National Health Service in the U.K.

2. **Concurrent reviews** represent a continuous, but less standardized, approach to the control of utilization. In managed health-care plans, utilization-review nurses coordinate hospital discharge planning and facilitate all activities of utilization control. Information is gathered by telephone or through personal interviews. Based on the collected information and manuals of care standards, utilization-review nurses control the use of certain procedures and plan discharge. *Peer review is considered to be the most threatening quality assurance technique and the most difficult to perform meaningfully.* Interestingly, daily review of the decisions of board certified specialists by higher ranking physicians is a routine activity in the hospitals of many European countries.

3. **Financial incentives** are frequently highlighted, but not always effective, tools of utilization management. Obviously, reimbursement has an effect on utilization in any type of health-care system, including fee-for-service care and global budgeting. In addition, reimbursement influences the availability and cost-effectiveness of procedures. However, health services research has documented that the effect of financial incentives on practice is much less significant than expected. For example, *one study indicated an inverse relationship between the frequency of cesarean sections and hospital charges.* In combination with other utilization management tools, managed health-care plans often use **withholds** (a percentage of the primary care capitation is withheld and used to pay for cost overruns) and **risk/bonus arrangements** (e.g., achieving a 2% reduction in length of stay yields a 1% bonus).

4. **Formal actions** represent the most intrusive approach in utilization management. **Credentialing** is a formal action that involves the screening of clinicians before they are allowed to practice with a group. **Screening** normally involves review of training, certification, hospital privileges, malpractice insurance, and history. **Economic credentialing** evaluates the utilization of expensive procedures by a particular clinician. **Sanctions**, or threat of sanctions, represent the most serious form of behavior modification (e.g., verbal reprimands about specific behaviors, warning letters, or termination of contracts with physicians). **Formal actions** are last resorts, and their efficiency is very limited in achieving actual improvement.

Information interventions are probably the most important and dynamically developing tools of utilization management. Communication and information are necessary for the cohesion of organizations and health care is an information intensive service. Information is important not only as a source of knowledge, but increasingly is viewed as a clinical intervention. Therefore, the value of information can be measured in randomized controlled clinical trials. Several clinical trials documented the beneficial effects of the following three types of information interventions:

1. **Education** represents the most frequently applied method of disseminating clinical practice recommendations. Obviously, educational methods can be valuable in gen-

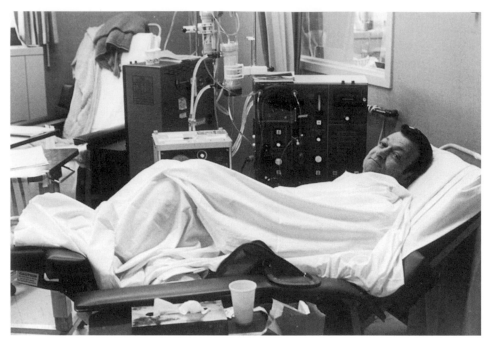

Used with permission from the National Kidney Foundation, Inc., New York. *Renal dialysis has provided tremendous health benefits but at considerable cost. Deciding if expensive benefits such as dialysis should be available to everyone who needs them is one of the major challenges of health politicy.*

erating more appropriate care. A review of several experiments concluded that *group educational interventions may change physician attitudes and knowledge; however, whether these effects result in improved practice patterns remains unclear.* Numerous studies indicate that the effect of education on clinical practice patterns is often short and small. Therefore, it is recommended that educational methods be combined with other techniques. The most frequent and successful combinations include the sustained and recurring approaches.

2. **Reminder messages** recommend specific clinical actions. For example, a message that a patient is eligible for influenza vaccine can be printed on the encounter form by a computer. Several controlled experiments have demonstrated that physicians respond to computer generated reminders by performing the recommended interventions (e.g., influenza immunization, and mammography). Computer's can scan each patient's record to identify tests and other procedures that are due. Furthermore, reminders are also very effective in changing patient behavior (e.g., reducing no-show rates). Although reminders represent the most effective utilization management intervention, their implementation may require computerization (e.g., electronic patient records, integration of various departmental systems).

3. **Information feedback,** an increasingly popular methodology, uses periodic evaluation of past patient care activities to influence future decision-making. Unlike reminder methods, feedback reports do not recommend specific diagnostic tests or treatments for a particular patient. Instead, *these reports provide information about a physician's behavior vis-à-vis other physicians.* Several studies have indicated that health-care providers will

change their practice patterns when confronted with credible information about how they compare to the practice styles of their colleagues. Several randomized controlled clinical trials have documented the modest effectiveness of peer-comparison feedback (profiling) methods. For example, a series of interventions at a general hospital provided physicians with feedback at regular intervals concerning the number of lab services employed in treating their patients. Rates of lab tests allowed each physician to compare his or her use of lab tests with that of peers in the same department at the same hospital. The intervention resulted in a reduction of 1.8 tests per patient.

HEALTH CARE REFORM

Many people in the United States feel that they need better health care, but lack of money and scarcity of resources limit access. The dynamic tension between growing public expectations and limited resources periodically erupts in public debates. Between eruptions, the tension appears mostly in academic discussions and substantive reform proposals are developed in periods when health care is not in the headlines. Certainly, continuing changes in the U.S. health-care system are necessary if the country is going to move toward better and more equitable services. The debate about reform revolves around three basic concepts:

1. **Quality of care** should always be a primary concern, and crises often emerge from discontent with the quality of health care. Sometimes, the discontent arises from the

lack of scientific progress in certain areas (e.g., prevention and treatment of AIDS). However, most frequently, international comparisons lead to the recognition of crisis and the development of reform proposals. In recent years, the growing number of uninsured people and the pressures to control costs raised concerns regarding health-care quality and consumer protection. Considering that quality is a subjective value, the answer appears to be more competition and consumer choice in the health-care market. For example, it is unlikely that legislating the minimum length of stay can give the same sense of quality as an open discussion of various options based on the latest scientific advancements.

2. **Access** is not just an important issue but sometimes it is put ahead of quality in securing health services. Access can be limited by the scarcity of clinicians and facilities (e.g., underserved rural areas) or by lack of insurance. Historically, insurance companies have often refused to insure people with **preexisting conditions**, i.e., diseases that require expensive treatment. Indigent care, or uncompensated charity care, remains the only resort of these uninsured people. With the emergence of new employment trends, particularly the growing role of small businesses, a declining rate of private health insurance has been observed. The traditional dominance of large employers and their health benefit plans is increasingly challenged. Apparently, changes in the system of private health insurance are needed to meet the changing needs. Furthermore, widespread use of advanced technologies like **telemedicine** is expected to improve access to quality care in rural areas. Several telemedicine techniques have been successfully tested in controlled clinical trials.

3. **Cost** is the third issue, *especially in the United States where health-care expenditures exceed 15.3% of the GDP.* The cost of health care is rising all over the world, and the introduction of new technologies offers only a partial explanation. High costs create financial hardships for many families and, eventually, limit access to much needed health care. While the skyrocketing costs of health care demand new approaches, many Americans fear that cost containment will lead to decreasing quality of care. Indeed, international statistics confirm that when countries spend less, their citizens usually get less care. For example, several countries could spend more on health care and provide life-saving renal dialysis and transplantation for more people. However, the relationship between cost and quality is not simple and straightforward. It is widely believed that there are many opportunities to improve the health status of the population while at the same time saving costs.

The public expects that structural changes of the health-care system will lead toward a better balance among quality, access, and cost. Many middle-class Americans enjoy a high quality of care and this care could be made more available

> The steeply rising heal-care costs remind me of what Jack Kent Cooke, the owner of the Washington Redskins, supposedly said when he was asked why he fired George Allen as his football coach: Cooke is quoted as saying, "I gave Allen an unlimited budget and he exceeded it."
>
> MARK SIEGLER

and more affordable. For example, in a little over a decade there was a 27% drop in death from heart disease, a similar decrease in infant mortality rates, and 72% drop in mumps cases. Cigarette consumption fell by 25%, and alcohol consumption fell by 4%. Despite these impressive gains, surveys indicate *that these health benefits are distributed very unevenly among various layers of the society, and the percent of Americans satisfied with their health and physical condition has fallen.*

There are several signs of major structural shifts in health-care delivery, and reform proposals need to consider these changes. For example, there has been a significant shift from inpatient care toward outpatient care. Hospitals have always been very expensive, and the search for less costly alternatives has been continuous. Today, many diseases that have been traditionally treated in hospitals are treated in outpatient settings or at home. Consequently, *the average length of hospital stay and rate of hospitalization have gone down dramatically.* Managed health-care plans transform the hospital from a revenue center into a cost center, and further shrink the need for acute care hospitalization. The trend is also apparent in the area of mental health care, where it is called **deinstitutionalization**, i.e., discharging people who are mentally ill or retarded from state and county mental health hospitals to care in the community. The emergence of managed health care is causing another structural shift from specialty care toward primary care. Traditionally, *specialists have dominated the American health workforce (50.7%) and the interest in generalists' careers among medical school graduates has been declining for many years.* On the other hand, family practice is the medical specialty that provides continuing and comprehensive health care for the individual and the family. This is exactly the coordinating role needed by most managed health-care plans.

One critically important legislative change affecting the health-care system was the **Health Insurance Portability and Accountability Act of 1996 (HIPAA).** This legislation was designed to improve administrative efficiency by standardizing the exchange of data and protect security and privacy of transmitted information. *HIPAA covers individually identifiable health information in any form or medium.* In actual patient care and also in clinical research, HIPAA compliance is an important compliance issue. Particular attention must be paid to protecting the privacy and confidentiality of individually identifiable health information or any other form of protected health information (e.g., prior authorization by participating patients, de-identified health information for research, use of a "minimum necessary" principle that ensures only limited data sets are transferred from the clinical environment to outside entities for reimbursement or research).

In recent years, the **Institute of Medicine** of the National Academies has been particularly influential in reshaping the health policy debate, including improvement of mental health services. In 2001, the Institute of Medicine released an important report, *Crossing the Quality Chasm: A New Health System for the 21st Century*. This report concluded that the U.S. health-care system is in need of fundamental change and recommended a framework for improving health care: care based on continuous healing relationships, customization based on patient needs and values, the patient as the source of control, shared knowledge and the free-flow of information, evidence-based decision-making, safety as a system property, the need for transparency, anticipation of needs, continuous decrease in waste, and cooperation among clinicians. A follow-up report by the Committee on Crossing the Quality Chasm, *Adaptation to Mental Health and Addictive Disorders*, explored the implications of the original chasm report for the field of mental health and addictive disorders.

> Many acknowledge their deep concern about the system privately but publicly remain silent. Compromising care to control cost is a vexing social issue in which the integrity of the profession is at stake, and medicine must have a clear, strong voice in these public decisions. Before we face far more odious choices, we must come to grips with these difficult trade-offs. So far ... the air is filled with a strained silence.
>
> JEROME P. KASSIRER
> *New England Journal of Medicine*

Many people believe that Medicare's benefit structure has not kept pace with the rate of medical innovation. The skyrocketing costs of prescription drugs has became a major financial challenges for seniors, and many of them have not been able to afford vitally important treatments. The **Medicare Prescription Drug, Improvement, and Modernization Act of 2003** created a new prescription drug benefit, and seniors with no drug coverage or average drug expenses will see drug costs cut in half. Under this plan, low-income seniors pay minimal amounts for prescription drugs. However, these new benefits raised new concerns regarding the future of the Medicare program. This new federal entitlement is estimated to cost $311 billion over a 10-year period. Furthermore, innovation in health sciences is much broader than just new drugs, and the new program does not capitalize on those accomplishments.

The underlying dilemma for society is whether to provide high-cost benefits to relatively few people (e.g., soft tissue trans-plants) and deny low cost services to many people (e.g., prenatal maternal care), or whether to guarantee universal access to a basic level of health care and deny those services with excessive costs. Generally, **rationing** is unavoidable when health-care needs exceed available resources (e.g., approved budget, capacity of diagnostic equipment, or volume of surgeries in a tertiary care center). *Rationing can exclude low-priority services (e.g., surgical treatment of chronic pancreatitis) or certain groups of people (e.g., the poor, uninsured, elderly, or disabled).* Rationing groups of people is the most controversial approach, for nobody likes to be rationed out of the system. In addition, exclusion raises a series of ethical issues and objections, and rationing can be interpreted as a deprivation of the equal protection rights guaranteed to all citizens by the fourteenth amendment of the Constitution. The mechanisms of rationing usually include waiting lists and ranking by physicians, i.e., selection of the most deserving candidates for the rationed services. In spite of the strong opposition, serious ethical controversies, and negative publicity, *some form of rationing is found in the health-care system of almost all developed countries.*

SUMMARY

Striking the right balance between competition and regulation has always been one of the most significant dilemmas for health policy. Proponents of the regulatory approach and increased government intervention highlight the responsibility of society for ensuring that quality health services are available for everyone, and often describe health care as a fundamental human right. On the other hand, proponents of the market-based approach believe that free market and competition are better able to meet social needs as well as being the most effective mechanism for restraining health costs. The future of the pluralistic health-care system is likely to be a continuing search for the right balance between respect for the individual and responsibility of the society.

CASE STUDY

Mr. Jones is a 35-year-old technician living in a village near a major city. He is married, has no children, and lives in an apartment. Mr. Jones has polycystic renal disease, which has led to a progressive and irreversible deterioration of renal function. Conservative therapy with diet and medication is no longer effective and his renal function has dropped to less than 10% of normal. Transplantation is a therapeutic option but the limited supply of cadaver kidneys can result in a wait of 1–2 years. Mr. Jones has no relatives who could donate a kidney to him. Therefore, dialysis is needed until a transplant becomes available. During the last year, Mr. Jones' disease has rapidly progressed. As a result of repeated infections, changes in energy, and other symptoms, dietary restrictions, concerns about keeping employment, plus worries about treatment, Mr. Jones has been depressed and the quality of his life has deteriorated.

Two types of treatment are supported by the closest dialysis clinic, 30 miles away: **in-center hemodialysis** (HD) and **continuous ambulatory peritoneal dialysis** (CAPD). HD requires trip to the clinic 3 times a week. The treatment is provided in a recently built and well-equipped center. However, the 3-hour dialysis and related traveling prevent daytime working during those days. To find another job in his area seems impossible. On the other hand, CAPD can be performed by the patient at home or work. It might allow Mr. Jones to keep his current job, but it presents a demanding schedule of four sterile fluid changes a day, 7 days a week, and must be done carefully to avoid infection. Mr. Jones heard rumors about the possibility of painful and potentially dangerous peritonitis episodes. He would like to keep his job but is very concerned about his health and survival. He wants to get the best professional help and have the best possible quality of life until a matching cadaver kidney becomes available.

Financially, Mr. Jones has health insurance through his employer. Insurance plus Medicare, which is available to patients of any age who need dialysis or transplant, would provide coverage for the costs of his treatment. Mr Jones has good coverage and should have similar costs and coverage with either in-center hemodialysis or CAPD. If he should lose his employment, he could qualify for social security disability benefits. Medicaid and state kidney program could also be used to help pay for treatments, travel, and medication.

Questions

1. Studies show that the social costs of CAPD are much less in comparison to in-center hemodialysis. CAPD is more demanding for the patient and there are certain risks involved but the treatment is less costly and often compatible with employment. *How would you consider these social factors in your clinical decision?*

2. Recent data indicate that the outcome of chronic peritoneal dialysis has improved and it is now close to the outcome of hemodialysis. However, some people believe that it is a second-class treatment. *Illustrate the issues of quality, utilization, rationing, and continuity of care with the example of dialysis.*

3. Patients are increasingly considered as active participants of care. Therefore, decision-making is often shared between patient and physician. Mr. Jones has some difficulties in understanding the complex issues related to his new treatment. *How would you share information regarding the process, outcome, and cost of dialysis treatment?*

SUGGESTED READINGS

American Diabetes Association Standards of Medical Care in Diabetes. (2005). *Diabetes Care, 28,* S4–36.
 This is an annual update of one of the best clinical practice guidelines for the management of a frequent chronic disease.

Balas, E.A., Jaffrey, F., Kuperman, G.J., Austin Boren, S., Brown, G.D., Pinciroli, F., & Mitchell, J. (1997). Electronic communication with patients: Evaluation of distance medicine technologies. *Journal of the American Medical Association, 278,* 152–159.
 This systematic review summarizes the results of randomized controlled clinical trials testing various distance technologies. It also illustrates the concept of evidence-based medicine as it is applied to an emerging new area.

Berwick, D.M., Godfrey, A.B., & Roessner, J. (1991). *Curing health care: New strategies for quality improvement.* San Francisco, CA: Jossey-Bass.
 This book is a detailed description of the National Demonstration Project on Quality Improvement in Health Care. It gives several clinical examples illustrating application of the methods of total quality management to control costs and change quality in health care.

Committee on Quality Health Care in America, Institute of Medicine. (2001). *Crossing the quality chasm: A new health system for the 21st century.* Washington, DC: National Academy Press.
 A landmark report on ways to improve the quality and efficiency of the U.S. health system.

Evans, R.S., Larsen, R.A., & Burke, J.P. (1986). Computer surveillance of hospital-acquired infection and antibiotic use. *Journal of the American Medical Association, 256,* 1007–1011.
 This article covers improved perioperative antibiotic use and reduced surgical wound infections through use of computer decision analysis.

Iglehart, J.K. (1992). The American health care system: Introduction. *New England Journal of Medicine, 326,* 962–967.
 Iglehart published several excellent articles describing the American health care system in the *New England Journal of Medicine.* This article is the first in that series and all articles are recommended readings.

Tierney, W.M., Miller, M.E., & McDonald, C.J. (1990). The effect on test ordering of informing physicians of the charges for outpatient diagnostic tests. *New England Journal of Medicine, 322,* 1499–1504.
 This randomized controlled clinical trial indicates that displaying the charges for diagnostic tests significantly reduces the number and cost of tests ordered, especially for patients with scheduled visits.

U.S. Preventive Services Task Force. (1997). *Guide to clinical preventive services: An assessment of the effectiveness of 169 interventions.* Baltimore, MD: Williams and Wilkins.
 The majority of deaths among Americans under age 65 are preventable and this book provides scientifically sound and specific recommendations for disease prevention and health promotion. The Guide is the result of an unprecedented cooperation between the government and private sector in the United States and Canada.

Wennberg, J. (1984). Dealing with medical practice variations: A proposal for action. *Health Affairs, 3,* 6–32.
 Wennberg ranks among the leaders of the nation's medical care epidemiologists. In this article, he describes the phenomenon of variations in the use of medical care and the possible reasons for dramatic variations.

26 American Medicine Is Sick

David T. Feinberg

> Like many other observers, I look at the U.S. health care system and see an administrative monstrosity, a truly bizarre mélange of thousands of payers with payment systems that differ for no socially beneficial reason, as well as staggeringly complex public systems with mind-boggling administered prices and other rules expressing distinctions that can only be regarded as weird.
>
> HENRY AARON

Most stakeholders of American medicine agree that the system is in bad shape; many argue it is in the death throes. Some argue for a complete reform of the health-care system, while others argue for incremental change. Yet *everyone agrees that our system is too costly, doesn't emphasize prevention, and doesn't provide sufficient insurance coverage for enough of our citizens.* The extant health-care system is heavily bureaucratic, and much of its value is lost on needless paperwork, unnecessary layers of administration, an excessive number of administrators and a host of other problems. Employers and employees alike complain that the cost of health insurance is excessive. Doctors are filing claims for medical disability—for themselves—in record numbers.

What would you do if "American Medicine" came to you as a patient? What would be the chief complaint? What would the history of present illness tell us? What would be the diagnosis and, most important, what would be the treatment? Let's examine American medicine as if it were a patient. Let's see if using the patient model we can figure out not only what is wrong but also what the treatment should be.

IDENTIFYING DATA: American Medicine over the Last Century

CHIEF COMPLAINTS

- Costly
- Millions of uninsured and underinsured Americans
- Huge financial burden on American companies trying to compete globally
- Lacks true integration
- Bureaucratic
- Outcomes unclear or poor

HISTORY OF PRESENT ILLNESS

In 1910 two physicians turned their Tacoma, WA medical clinic into a prepaid group plan. Mill workers got health coverage for fifty cents per month. This was the first example of "managed care" in the U.S. While this attempt to cover all the workers' health needs in one area may have worked, costs got out of control in other parts of the U.S. In 1927 Congress met to form the Committee on Costs of Medical Care. This committee was charged with finding out why health-care costs had become "excessive." At that time, hospital stays cost about $4 per day.

Two years later a group of 1500 school teachers in Baylor, TX created a group health insurance plan that would later become known as **Blue Cross**. For $6 per year, each teacher was covered for up to 21 hospital days annually.

National health insurance was initially included in the original Social Security Act; however, it was removed from the legislation in 1935. Three years later, Dr. Sidney Garfield contracted with Kaiser Corporation, then a construction company, to provide prepaid health care to 5000 workers building the California Aqueduct. Within a decade, Kaiser Corporation gave up on the construction business and became a health-care company. Kaiser now has millions of members and spends over $10 billion on health care every year.

Throughout the nineteenth century, trade unions had been fighting for health benefits, but in 1940 only 12 million Americans had health insurance through their jobs. It took a World War to get many employers to offer this expensive benefit. During the Second World War, the government froze wages to keep inflation under control. Employers faced a labor shortage, but they couldn't offer higher salaries to attract workers. The War Labor Board, however, permitted them to compete for employees with benefits packages. Before long, offering health insurance was standard practice for companies. After the war, the now-established practice continued, and by 1950, 77 million workers had health insurance through their employers. *No one planned this system, and it evolved with almost no deliberation or forethought.*

> The American health system is confronting a crisis. The cost of private health insurance is now increasing at an annual rate in excess of 12 percent, while at the same time individual are paying more out of pocket and receiving fewer benefits ... One in seven Americans is uninsured, and the number of uninsured is on the rise. ... The health care delivery system is incapable of meeting the present, let alone the future needs of the American public.
>
> *Institute of Medicine* (2002)

Up until about 10 years ago, most private insurance plans offered by employers to employees were what are to referred to as **indemnity plans**. Patients and their families could see any doctor they wanted, and physicians could admit patients to any hospital in which the doctor was privileged. All testing was covered regardless of its necessity, and no questions were asked. The only cost to families was their annual deductible. *Under this fee-for-service system, every advance in medical science (CT scans, new medications, etc.) drove up the cost of care.* The sicker the patient, the more money the doctor could charge and the more money the hospital would make. Routine physicals, the cornerstone of primary prevention, often were excluded from coverage in traditional indemnity plans.

The government once again got involved, and in 1965, Medicare and Medicaid were added to Social Security. Health care for the disabled and the elderly (**Medicare**) and for the poor (**Medicaid**) became an American right. Since this time, the federal and state governments have been America's biggest purchasers of health care.

During the same period, Dr. Paul Ellwood developed the concept of a **Health Maintenance Organization** (HMO). These were to be private health companies operating in open markets with government oversight. Prevention was a key concept in Dr. Ellwood's vision of an HMO. In 1973, President Nixon signed into law the "HMO Act," which allowed new HMOs to receive government grants to help defer the start up costs involved with setting up a new HMO. HMO enrollment in the 1970s and 1980s was minimal.

> Some services, like cataract surgery, are financial "winners" because they pay much more than they cost to produce, while other services, like talking to a patient, are "losers" because they pay less than they cost.
>
> PAUL STARR

In 1983 the Federal Government attempted to set limits on escalating medical costs. Five hundred **diagnosis-related groups** (**DRGs**) were developed for which the government fixed prices. Although DRGs were designed to control costs, the number of diagnoses for more expensive medical problems actually rose by 10 to 13%.

In the 1980s, health care made up 10% of everything the U.S. was producing. By 2005, health-care costs exceeded 15% of gross domestic product (GDP). This means that *Americans spend over two billion dollars a day on health care, and health care consumes one out of every seven dollars Americans produce.* That is more than four thousand dollars per person per year.

Many would argue that spending on health care is not necessarily problematic. Health is undoubtedly one of the most important aspects of life. However, those American businesses that pay for much of our health care fought back. In 1988, for example, AlliedSignal, a Fortune 500 aerospace company, offered its 80,000 employees coverage by an HMO for a lower payroll deduction. Many workers signed up and the company saved millions in health-care costs. Other companies were attracted to HMOs as one way to curtail run-away health-care costs. These efficiencies became increasingly important because, as more American businesses began competing in the global market place, they were at a marked disadvantage when competing with many countries in which workers had national health insurance.

> The social cost of sickness is incalculable. The prevention of disease is for the most part a matter of education, the cost is moderate, the results certain and easily demonstrated.
>
> HAVEN EMERSON
> *The Social Cost of Sickness*

In 1992 General Motors announced a $23.5 billion loss, which it attributed to an employee benefit package that added more than $1,400 to the cost of a car. In contrast, a similar car made in Japan had only about $200 of "health care" in it. GM actually was spending more on health insurance than on steel. American businesses clearly needed some mechanism to curb the yearly increases they faced with health expenditures.

Managed care, an approach to health care that emphasizes utilization review, prior approval for procedures, and limiting outpatient visits and hospital stays, appeared to be the answer to the dilemma of ever increasing health-care costs. For example, in 1993, health-care premiums were rising 10% nationwide, but the **California Public Employees Retirement System** (CALPERS) was able to secure a 0.7% *decrease* by contracting with a managed care firm.

Over the 1990s American businesses performed beautifully and stock prices soared. Many Americans saw their mutual funds and pension plans increase; these gains were partially the result of managed care, and this approach to the management of health-care benefits helped American businesses reward their investors.

In 1993, President Bill Clinton and First Lady Hillary Clinton developed an approach to health care reform designed to cover the uninsured and streamline medicine's daunting bureaucracy. However, *the Health-Care Security Act they proposed failed as a result of insurance company lobbying and public apathy.* In the meantime, managed care continued to grow. By 1994, so many Americans were covered by HMOs that for the first time ever the average health benefit paid by employers actually decreased.

Managed care introduced many new, and sometimes troubling, practices for American medicine. By limiting access to only contracted providers, managed care companies could pay doctors less in return for sending them more patients. They could do the same with hospitals and pharmacies, and **drug formularies** became a familiar part of American medicine. By only including certain covered (and low cost) medications, managed care companies could limit pharmaceutical costs. However, this only worked for few years. American medicine kept advancing and the cost of care kept increasing.

> Is there no hope? The sick Man said.
> The silent doctor shook his head,
> And took his leave, with signs of sorrow,
> Despairing of his fee tomorrow.
>
> JOHN GAY
> *The Sick Man and the Angel*

Managed care companies then turned to **preauthorization** and **utilization management** in their attempts to constrain costs. When insured by plans that incorporated these practices, patients could only be admitted to a hospital or undergo surgery if a managed care representative approved such care.

These approaches initially worked. For example, simply requiring prior authorization was shown to decrease utilization. Likewise, when hospital stays were only approved for a certain amount of days, the insurance company made money. After the allowable number of days expired, the hospital was required to discharge the patient or directly absorb the cost of further care. This is a classic example of **cost shifting**. Again, these tactics only lasted a few years. Both consumers and providers figured out how to "work the system" to decrease managed care denials.

Since managed care started with American business, most of those covered were relatively young workers and their families. One of the biggest health-care expenses for young healthy women is childbirth, and managed care companies saw coverage of childbirth as one of their most costly benefits, so insurers worked hard to limit this benefit. Prior to managed care, women stayed in the hospital for up to 5 days following a noncomplicated vaginal delivery and up to 2 weeks following a caesarian section. In contrast, managed care companies set standards that required new mothers to leave the hospital in less than 24 hours. Even though research did not indicate that this practice was harmful to mother or child, the public revolted. In 1996, the **Newborns' and Mothers' Health Protection Act** was signed into law. *This legislation prohibits insurers from restricting benefits for a hospital stay in connection with childbirth to less than 48 hours following a vaginal delivery or 96 hours following a cesarean section.*

Still determined to limit health-care spending, managed care companies turned to **capitation plans**, in which providers (doctors) and facilities (hospitals) were prepaid for caring for a defined population. Do you remember the mill workers in Tacoma who received health care for fifty cents a month? American medicine had returned to the same model. In the new capitation plans that were developed, a managed care company would receive money from an employer to provide health care for all of a company's employees, with rates usually set at about $100 per month per employee. As its first priority, the managed care company would pay itself about $15–$25 for administration and profit. It would then transfer the risk of caring for its members to those health systems that had contracted with the managed care firm. With only about $80 to deal with, the monies were divided. Hospitals took about $30, primary care providers took another $30, and the remainder was used to run large doctor groups with some money set aside to cover the costs of specialty care if it was needed. Under this plan, doctors were paid $30 every month for every member for whom they were the primary care provider. If a doctor had 1,000 patients signed up, every month the doctor would get $30,000, regardless of whether these patients come in or not. Doctors received bonuses if they kept referrals to specialists to a minimum because this left more money in the risk pool. *This practice set up an obvious conflict of interest for those physicians who would lose money by making too many referrals to specialists and profit from limiting the referrals they made.* If too many of the doctor's patients became sick (e.g., during a flu epidemic), the doctor lost money because his or her patients needed frequent attention, more nurses, and specialty care.

The managed care industry became more and more competitive as the 1990s were ending, and managed care companies needed greater market share, more enrollees, and greater clout if they were to continue to earn the record profits that Wall Street was demanding. In response, these companies turned their attention from signing up members from the private sector (employees) to recruiting patients from the public sector—specifically those covered by Medicaid and Medicare. However, these patients (the poor, elderly, and disabled) have different health-care needs than employees who are generally healthy.

Companies have met with mixed success in applying the managed care model to public insurance programs like Medicare and Medicaid, and many managed care companies found that these new populations were more costly than anticipated. In 1999, 440,000 Medicare patients were dropped by their HMOs because the companies were shutting down or turning to other, more profitable, activities. *It soon became clear that the excess fat that had been cut from the health-care system during the 1990s was now all gone.* Medical costs continued to rise as new medicines and technologies were developed. In 1999, average health-care premiums rose 5–9%. It became clear that managed care was no longer able to achieve the cost savings that the business sector demanded.

American businesses needed to find a way to keep health-care cost down and quality up. Managed care was becoming less useful, and it increasingly was clear that managed care was not going to solve America's health-care cost crisis.

What happened next was that American businesses leaped over managed care and went right to providers, effectively cutting out the middleman. This not only saved money, in part because the managed care companies had been very profitable, but, more importantly, it enabled purchasers of care (American businesses) to work closely with providers of health care. One of the best examples of this model is a group called the **Leapfrog Group**. The group's mission follows:

The Leapfrog Group is an initiative driven by organizations that buy health care who are working to initiate breakthrough improvements in the safety, quality, and affordability of health care for Americans. It is a voluntary program aimed at mobilizing employer purchasing power to alert America's health industry that big leaps in health-care safety, quality, and customer value will be

recognized and rewarded. (http://www.leapfroggroup.org/about_us)

Hospitals across the U.S. are busily following leapfrog recommendations because these recommendations are linked to reimbursement. Examples of leapfrog initiatives include computerized physician orders and board certified intensive care providers.

One way to get patients concerned about the cost of care is to make them more responsible for payment. Remember that health benefits come from our employers because of a wage freeze during WWII? This creates what economists call **moral hazard**. Moral hazard occurs when the purchasers of health insurance (employers) are not the users of health care (employees). This sets medicine apart from most other economic activities. Indeed, *health insurance is almost unique in American business because core economic principles don't seem to apply.* For example, few people genuinely shop for their health insurance, making cost comparisons and prudent purchases. Instead, most employees are covered by employer-sponsored plans that offer only one plan. Because employers historically have covered our health-care costs, most U.S. citizens don't recognize the true cost of health care. However, all of this is changing.

More and more insurance companies are shifting the costs of care to patients and introducing a variety of mechanisms to contain costs. For example, **generic medicines** and formulary medicines have lower copayments for patients than branded or nonformulary medications. Likewise, managed care plans are now offering a greater selection of choices for enrollees. Less expensive plans are more restrictive while more expensive plans allow greater freedom in choosing doctors and hospitals.

Although these plans work for many people, the core problem is that many working families can't afford *any* of their health insurance options. Not only does America have millions of uninsured citizens, every day an ever increasing number of full-time workers are becoming uninsured because the employee contribution for their health insurance through their jobs is too high or because they aren't even offered health insurance. *It is striking to note that America's most successful retail company, Walmart, insures less than half its workers.*

> The marginal value of one or one billion-dollars spent on medical care will be close to zero in improving health.
>
> AARON WILDAVSKY
> *Collected Papers*

Meanwhile, for those still able to afford health insurance, a new era in American medicine is arriving: **Consumer Driven Health Care** (CDHC). In its purest form, CDHC is a market-based system. In such a system, consumers can tailor insurance to their own needs; families can purchase insurance with various benefits, prices, and coverage. For example, a well-to-do, healthy family might choose a plan that had a high monthly premium, a high deductible, and full benefits. In contrast, a poor, single, working mother might choose a policy with a low premium, no deductible, and very limited benefits (e.g., very limited access to care and a tightly managed provider network). The well-to-do family would pay out-of-pocket for many of the services until their annual deductible was met, at which time their insurance would cover all remaining costs for the year. The members of this family would have an **open network** and be able to see any health-care provider they choose. Providers in a consumer-driven system could be innovative and set their own prices. *Consumer-driven supply and demand with transparency is the cornerstone of CDHC.* The federal government would play an active role in overseeing CDHC plans.

FAMILY HISTORY

The American Medical Association (AMA) has a surprisingly low percentage of members. This mission of the AMA, in part, follows:

> *Together we are stronger. The American Medical Association helps doctors help patients by uniting physicians nationwide to work on the most important professional and public health issues.* (http://www.ama-assn.org/ama/pub/category/1815.html)

If this is what the AMA is supposed to do, then why are physicians so reluctant to join this organization? One of the reasons is that *medicine is a variegated, heterogeneous profession.* For example, many doctors in high-income urban centers no longer accept insurance. These physicians have transitioned to a strictly cash-pay practice and subsequently only serve patients who are affluent. (This practice is sometimes referred to as **boutique medicine**.) Other doctors are still working in heavily penetrated managed-care environments. These doctors spend seemingly endless hours filling out forms and rushing through patient encounters, all the while seeing their incomes decrease. Still other doctors are working in county or state-run institutions. These doctors care for the poor, underinsured, and uninsured, dealing with a population that is mired in a system that does not provide for basic human needs. Other doctors work in academia; others are working in the pharmaceutical industry, and still others in the prison system. Representing such a diverse group is a challenge for organized medicine.

> Medical men do not know the drugs they use, nor their prices.
>
> SIR FRANCIS BACON
> *De Erroribus Medicorum*

MEDICATIONS

American medicine is clearly using drugs, and *the relationship of the U.S. medical system with the pharmaceutical industry is cozy at best and unethical at worst.* The pharmaceutical industry has higher profits than almost any other American industry. These profits are justified by claims that their business models require profits to support heavy investments in research and development (R & D). However, over the last decade most new drugs marketed by pharmaceutical companies have been **"me too"** (**copycat**) **drugs** rather than true new discoveries. In fact, most pharmaceutical companies spend more on sales and marketing than on R & D. In addition, the pharmaceutical industry has the largest lobby in Washington, and *the number of lobbyists working for "big Pharma" actually exceeds the number of lawmakers elected to Congress* (i.e., 535 Senators and Representatives).

Drug companies also have enormous power with physicians, and they spend thousands of dollars every year to send representatives into doctors' offices. The companies sponsor research and conferences, with tremendous control over company-sponsored clinical trials. *Some critics have even charged that these companies invent conditions so that they can market their products;* for example, few physicians saw patients asking about erectile dysfunction (ED) before Pfizer made the condition a household word in a multimillion dollar marketing campaign for Viagra (sildenafil citrate).

Finally, the unhealthy relationship between the U.S. health-care system and the pharmaceutical industry is reflected in the fact that *the cost of medications in the U.S. is dramatically higher than the cost of identical drugs in most other industrialized countries.* In response to these inequities, many Americans now purchase medicine from Canadian pharmacies over the Internet as a way to limit family spending on medications, and there is growing political pressure to permit importation of medicine from Canada and other developed countries where the costs of drugs are often dramatically lower.

SOCIAL HISTORY

The open secret of the medical profession is that *almost all of the premature deaths by disease in this county can be prevented by lifestyle changes.* Why most Americans and most

PEAU D'ORANGE

We barter the difference
between black and gray.
"Surgery, radiation or
death," you say and leave
the decision to me,

while I insist you are the gods
I believed in as a child.
I prayed you to pull magic
out of your black leather bags
to wave away the rattling
in my bones.

I accept your calling
my breast an orange peel,
let you lay hands on this fruit
my mother said no man
must touch. In this disease
there is no sin.

If you lift the chill
that unravels my spine,
I will send you stars
from the Milky Way,
send them spinning down,
dancing a thousand-fold. Please
let me grow old.

MARCIA LYNCH

- *Millions of Americans are uninsured and underinsured.* These are not just the very poor. Many middle-class, working families have no insurance because their companies don't offer it, or they are self-employed and the cost of coverage is just too high.
- *American businesses are once again seeing their profits erode* as the cost of providing health benefits continues to rise faster than any other cost. They are passing more of the cost of care directly to their employees.
- *Our system lacks any type of integration.* Many medical errors are made because our information systems are paper based and not shared among all providers.
- *The system is heavily bureaucratic.* Cost of providing care in the U.S. is higher than Canada because of the increased cost we incur as a result of the large payer mix.
- *Our health outcomes are not where they should be,* especially considering the vast sums of money we spend on health care.
- *The pharmaceutical industry and drug company advertising is heavily influencing physicians' practice patterns.*
- *Americans are loath to change their unhealthy lifestyles.*
- *Organized medicine in America does not have the membership or clout necessary to actually effect reform.*
- *Preventive medicine takes a back seat to technology and tertiary care in America.*

> The problem of the uninsured continues to grow quietly; in the long run, its effects will be so pervasive that it is bound to re-emerge as a major national issue. If it does not, then we will find ourselves living in a much meaner America than many of us who entered the healing professions ever imagined.
>
> STEVEN A. SCHROEDER
> *New England Journal of Medicine*

DIAGNOSIS

This patient is *very* sick

PLAN

There are two rather different approaches to fixing America's sick health-care system. On one hand, many policy experts advocate for a **single-payer system** in which *everyone* is insured. It is likely that this kind of universal health insurance system would be either federally or state run (e.g., individual states like Vermont might elect to implement state-run single payer systems). Under a single-payer system, a Government program would insure all Americans irrespective of their income or ability to pay. *The administrative savings associated with such an approach likely would be sufficient to offset the additional costs associated*

American doctors ignore this fact is no mystery. Lifestyle changes require vision, technique, and commitment. These are far more complicated than simply "take this pill and lose 30 pounds in 30 days." Americans seem to want the quick fix.

PHYSICAL EXAM

Physical exams focus on the actual current state of the patient. The current state of American medicine follows:

- *It is very costly.* Even though managed care kept costs down in the early 1990s, now costs are rising at a rate higher than inflation.

with insuring the 45 million Americans who currently lack health insurance. Critics of such a system point to the typical inefficiencies that one sees in a government-run system: bureaucracy, inefficiency, poor customer service, excessive costs, and lack of innovation. Physicians and medical students who are proponents of a single payer system frequently join *Physicians for a National Health Program* (PNHP; www.pnhp.org).

> Behind false claims of efficiency lies a much uglier truth. Investor-owned care embodies a new value system that severs the community roots and Samaritan traditions of hospitals, makes physicians and nurses into instruments of investors, and views patients as commodities. Investor ownership marks the triumph of greed.
>
> STEFFIE WOOLHANDLER and DAVID HIMMELSTEIN
> *Canadian Medical Association Journal* (2004)

On the other end of the spectrum, there is **CDHC** (consumer-driven health care). This is a system in which health care intersects with true market economics. A concern for supply and demand defines this approach, and the only role for federal or state government is to review and regulate the practices of private insurers. In such a system innovation is rewarded, customer service is high and theoretically market forces cause price to fall. Opponents of this type of system claim that health care is not a commodity, but rather a unique set of products and services that shouldn't be, and never will be, entirely subject to market forces.

If we look back over the last decade, we most likely will end up with a hybrid of these two extremes. However, regardless of the system or systems that the next decades bring, we need to answer the following questions:

- How can we cover the uninsured and underinsured?
- How can we decrease the bureaucracy in medicine?
- How can we incorporate more information technology into American medicine?

- How can we get Americans to embrace healthy lifestyles?
- How can we limit the pharmaceutical industry's influence on doctors?
- How can we better measure outcomes of the care that we provide?
- How can we better decide what care to give and when to give it?

Perhaps a new generation of physicians will help us solve these vexing, long-standing, and recalcitrant problems.

SUGGESTED READINGS

Angell, M. (2004). *The truth about the drug companies: How they deceive us and what to do about it.* New York: Random House.
This hard-hitting exposé, written by a former editor-in-chief for the *New England Journal of Medicine*, is likely to change forever the way you look at the pharmaceutical industry.

Herzlinger, R.E. (Ed.). (2004). *Consumer-driven health care.* San Francisco: Jossey-Bass.
This volume, edited by a Harvard Business School professor, documents the growth of consumer-driven health care and argues that it will profoundly change the U.S. health-care system.

Himmelstein, D., & Woolhandler, S. (2001). *Bleeding the patient: The consequences of corporate health care.* Monroe, ME: Common Courage Press.
This book is written by two Harvard physicians who argue that the savings associated with adoption of a single-payer health-care system in the U.S. would be more than enough to offset the cost of providing care for 45 million currently uninsured.

Theodasakis, J., & Feinberg, D.T. (2000). *Don't let your HMO kill you.* New York: Routledge.
This book, written by two physicians, documents the fact that many of the patients enrolled in HMOs are unhappy, and provides survival strategies for both providers and patients coping with the bureaucratic red tape associated with managed care.

Appendix A

Behavioral and Social Science Topics of High and Medium Priority for Inclusion in Medical School Curricula

From the Institute of Medicine Report on *Improving Medical Education: Enhancing the Behavioral and Social Science Content of Medical School Curricula*

Domain	High Priority	Medium Priority
Mind–Body Interactions in Health and Disease	• Biological mediators between psychological and social factors and health (1, 8, 15, 19)	• Psychosocial, biological, and management issues in somatization (17, 19, 20)
	• Psychological, social, and behavioral factors in chronic disease (2, 7, 8, 15, 19)	• Interaction among illness, family dynamics, and culture (2, 15, 21, 22)
	• Psychological and social aspects of human development that influence disease and illness (3–6, 10–14)	
	• Psychosocial aspects of pain (7)	
Patient Behavior	• Health risk behaviors (11)	
	• Principles of behavior change (10, 11, 20)	
	• Impact of psychosocial stressors and psychiatric disorders on manifestations of other illnesses and on health behavior (8, 10, 19, 20)	
Physician Role and Behavior	• Ethical guidelines for professional behavior (13–15, 20)	
	• Personal values, attitudes, and biases as they influence patient care (10, 13–15, 17, 18, 21)	
	• Physician well-being (13)	
	• Social accountability and responsibility (14, 15, 24, 25, 26)	

Domain	High Priority	Medium Priority
	• Work in health-care teams and organizations (14)	
	• Use of and linkage with community resources to enhance patient care (14, 24)	
Physician–Patient Interactions	• Basic communication skills (11, 15, 16)	• Context of patient's social and economic situation, capacity for self-care, and ability to participate in shared decision making (15, 16, 20, 22)
	• Complex communication skills (11, 16, 18, 19, 20)	• Management of difficult or problematic physician–patient interactions (16, 20)
Social and Cultural Issues in Health Care	• Impact of social inequalities in health care and the social factors that are determinants of health outcomes (2, 22, 24)	• Role of complementary and alternative medicine (23)
	• Cultural competency (22)	
Health Policy and Economics	• Overview of U.S. health-care system (25, 26)	• Variations in care (24, 25)
	• Economic incentives affecting patients' health-related behaviors (25)	
	• Costs, cost-effectiveness, and physician responses to financial incentives (15, 25, 26)	

Reprinted with permission from *Improving Medical Education: Enhancing the Behavioral and Social Science Content of Medical School Curricula*, © (2004) by the National Academy of Sciences, courtesy of the National Academies Press, Washington, DC.
(The numbers in parentheses refer to the relevant chapters in *Behavior and Medicine*.)

Appendix B
Medical Statistics and Research Design

Fredric M. Wolf

Statistics for medical practitioners is important not only for the understanding of medical research but also in the diagnosis, prognosis, and treatment of patients. Diagnostic categories that are currently in use are accepted because they have repeatedly been shown to be statistically accurate (i. e., valid). A similar diagnosis may provide dissimilar prognoses for patients with varying characteristics, such as sex, age, weight, height, or other physical characteristics. Studies have consistently shown that both diagnosis and prognosis can be significantly improved by practitioners who rely on statistical and probability data, as well as their own experience. The following review is intended to provide a brief summary of the more basic biostatistical and research design concepts and their uses.

PROPERTIES OF DISTRIBUTIONS

A **frequency distribution** is the number of occurrences for each possible value (or score) of a **variable** (something that varies). For example, the number of people having different levels of serum uric acid in their blood would form a frequency distribution that might look like this:

Serum uric acid (mg/dl)	Number of people
3.0–3.9	1
4.0–4.9	2
5.0–5.9	4
6.0–6.9	2
7.0–7.9	1
TOTAL	10

The variable of interest here is serum uric acid content of blood. The 10 people represent a **sample** of a larger group of people called the **population**. This frequency distribu-

tion represents descriptive information about these 10 people (**descriptive statistics**). We can only generalize what we find for these 10 people to larger groups of people (i. e., the population) similar to these 10 (**inferential statistics**).

Central Tendency

Various measures of central tendency exist. The most frequently occurring number in the distribution is called the **mode**. In the example previously given, more people (four) have a serum uric acid level of 5.0 to 5.9 mg/dl than any other level, and 5.4 mg/dl (the midpoint of the interval 5.0 to 5.9 mg/dl) is therefore the mode of this distribution.

The average serum uric acid level for our sample of 10 people is called the **mean**. If the levels were single numbers (and not a range of numbers, e. g., 3.0–3.9 mg/dl), every person's serum uric acid level would simply be added and then the total would be divided by the number of people to obtain the mean. Because uric acid levels are presented as intervals and not as single numbers here, the midpoint of each interval is used. The mean is represented by x (the symbol for a variable, which is serum uric acid in this example) with a bar over it, or $\bar{x}$. The formula for calculating $\bar{x}$ is:

$$\bar{x} = \frac{\Sigma x}{n}$$

where Σ = summation, x = variable, $\bar{x}$ = mean, n = number of people.

For our example,

$$\bar{x} = \frac{3.4 + 4.4 + 4.4 + 5.4 + 5.4 + 5.4 + 5.4 + 6.4 + 6.4 + 7.4}{10}$$

$$\bar{x} = 5.4$$

The last of the three measures of central tendency is the **median**, which represents the middle number of a distribution when all the numbers are arranged in order from smallest to largest. In our example, the interval 5.0 to 5.9 is the interval in the middle of our distribution, and its midpoint, 5.4, is therefore the median. The median divides a distribution into two equal parts, each containing half (50%) of the numbers in the distribution.

SHAPE

When the mean, mode, and median all are the same number and the distribution is shaped like a bell, the distribution is symmetrical and is said to be a **normal distribution**. To graph the distribution, the various levels of the variable are placed along the X-axis (the **abscissa**) and the frequencies of occurrence along the Y-axis (the **ordinate**). We then plot the frequency for each level of the variable. For example:

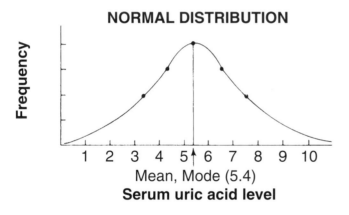

If, however, the mode is greater or less than the mean, it is a **skewed distribution**. The serum uric acid example is listed in Table B.1.

TABLE B.1

Serum uric acid level	Positively skewed	Normal	Negatively skewed
3.0–3.9	1	1	1
4.0–4.9	4	2	2
5.0–5.9	2	4	2
6.0–6.9	2	2	4
7.0–7.9	1	1	1
Total n	10	10	10
Mean ($\bar{x}$)	5.2	5.4	5.6
Median	4.4	5.4	6.4

When the median is less than the mean, it is a **positively skewed distribution** (the "tail" of the distribution is on the right side). That means there are fewer high values than low values in the distribution. When the median is greater than

the mean, it is **negatively skewed distribution** (the "tail" of the distribution is on the left side). That means there are fewer low values than high values in the distribution. When these skewed distributions are graphed, they look like this:

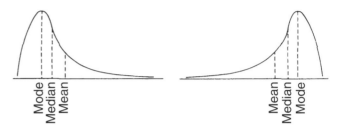

If it is a distribution with two modes, it is a **bimodal distribution**. This suggests that there are two distinct populations (e. g., sick and well people) represented on the variable being measured. It might look like this:

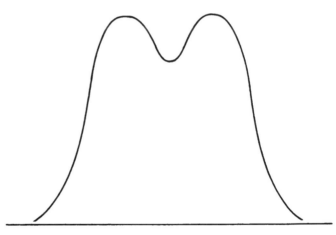

BIMODAL DISTRIBUTION

Serum uric acid (mg/dl)	Number of people
3.0–3.9	1
4.0–4.9	4
5.0–5.9	1
6.0–6.9	4
7.0–7.9	1

Although normal distributions are always symmetrical, the converse is not always true. That is, a symmetrical distribution is not necessarily normal. Normal distributions are generally considered to be bell shaped and are called **mesokurtic**. Symmetrical distributions that are not normal take one of two forms: those that are pulled straight up and become narrow or peaked are called leptokurtic, and symmetrical distributions that are pushed down or flatter are called **platykurtic**. For example:

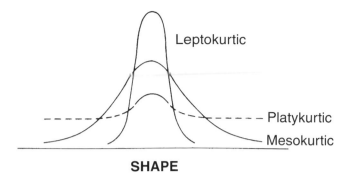

SHAPE

Variability

From the previous example, it is apparent that any difference in the shape of our distribution is *not* caused by differences in measures of central tendency among the three distributions, because their means, modes, and medians are identical. Differences in shape result from differences in **variability** around these measures of central tendency. If the frequencies for each level of serum tend to cluster around the mean, a peaked, leptokurtic-shaped distribution results. On the other hand, if the frequencies tend to spread out away from the mean, a flatter, platykurtic-shaped distribution results.

There are generally three measures of variability: range, variance, and standard deviation.

The **range** is the difference between the largest and smallest numbers in a distribution ($4 - 1 = 3$ in our serum uric acid example). Because the range is made up of the two most extreme scores, it tends to be unreliable and is infrequently used.

The **variance** of a set of numbers in a distribution is the average of the squares of the difference of each number from the mean. The formula for calculating the variance is:

$$\sigma^2 = \frac{\Sigma(x - \bar{x})^2}{n - 1}$$

where
$\sigma^2 = s^2 =$ Variance
$x \;\; = \;\;$ Score
$\bar{x} \;\; = \;\;$ Mean
$n \;\; = \;\;$ Number of subjects

The three-step process is as follows:

1. Calculate the mean
2. Subtract the mean from each number (x) and square the result
3. Find the average of these squares

Note that in the preceding formula we divide by $n - 1$ instead of just n. This is done when dealing with relatively small samples, usually less than 30 (i. e., when $n < 30$). This compensation is made to adjust for the tendency of the

variance to be somewhat biased for small samples, generally being smaller than the variance for the entire population. For the example on page 337, the variance is calculated in the following manner, using the midpoint of the serum uric acid intervals as our scores:

x	$\bar{x}$	$(x - \bar{x})$	$(x - \bar{x})^2$
3.4	5.4	−2	4
4.4	5.4	−1	1
4.4	5.4	−1	1
5.4	5.4	0	0
5.4	5.4	0	0
5.4	5.4	0	0
5.4	5.4	0	0
6.4	5.4	1	1
6.4	5.4	1	1
7.4	5.4	2	4
			$\Sigma(x - \bar{x})^2 = 12$

$$\sigma^2 = \frac{\Sigma(x - \bar{x})^2}{n - 1} = \frac{12}{9} = 1.33$$

The **standard deviation** is the positive square root of the variance.

$$\sigma = \sqrt{\frac{(x - \bar{x})^2}{n - 1}} = \sqrt{1.33} = 1.15$$

where $\sigma = s =$ standard deviation.

The standard deviation is one of the most useful measures of variability around the mean for a distribution of numbers. An extremely important use of the standard deviation is in the transformation of raw numbers into **standard scores**. Among the most commonly used standard scores are **z-scores**, which represent the position of a number in the distribution relative to the mean. Z-scores are expressed in terms of standard deviations. The following is the formula for calculating a *z*-score:

$$z = \frac{x - \bar{x}}{s}$$

where
$x \;\; = \;\;$ A score in the distribution
$\bar{x} \;\; = \;\;$ The mean of the distribution
$s \;\; = \;\;$ The standard deviation of the distribution
$z \;\; = \;\;$ The standard score of equivalent x

Using the previous example, we would calculate the *z*-score for a raw score of 7.4 in the following manner:

$$z = \frac{7.4 - 5.4}{1.15} = \frac{2.0}{1.15} = 1.74$$

z-scores are desirable because for any distribution of numbers, the mean *z*-score is 0, whereas the standard deviation is 1. Thus, a raw score of 7.4 (i. e., a person with a serum uric acid level of 7.4) is equivalent to a serum uric acid level 1.74 standard deviations above the mean for this sample of 10 people.

When there is a normal distribution of scores for any given variable, z-scores are helpful in another way. The following is a **standardized normal distribution** with a mean z-score of 0 ($z = 0$) and standard deviation of 1 (SD = 1):

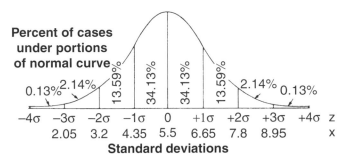

NORMAL DISTRIBUTION

An interesting property of **normal distributions** is that 68% of the population falls within ± 1 standard deviation of the mean on the measured variable (i. e., serum uric acid level). Thus, 68% of people should have serum uric acid levels between 4.35 and 6.65. Approximately 95% of people have serum uric acid levels within ± 2 standard deviations of the mean, or between 3.2 and 7.8. If we go out 3 standard deviations, approximately 99% of people's serum uric acid levels are encompassed.

SCALES OF MEASUREMENT

A number of statistical tests are appropriate for exploring medically related questions. These tests tell whether certain findings are likely to be the result of chance or whether a real systematic relationship is occurring. Before the various statistical tests are summarized, some background understanding of scales of measurement and sampling is necessary.

There are essentially four different ways of measuring phenomena. The simplest scale of measurement is called a **nominal scale**. This scale is used when we want to categorize data into various groups. The only restriction is that all of the objects put into one group must have something in common with each other and must be different from objects in other groups. If the variable of interest is gender of patients, males and females would represent two independent categories (or levels) of the variable "gender."

Using an **ordinal scale** provides a somewhat more complex way of measuring a variable. Here the concern is with measuring a person having more than or less than another person on the variable in question. For example, a person with gout may show considerable improvement, slight im-

provement, no change, slight deterioration, considerable deterioration, or death after treatment. An ordinal scale thus makes use of the idea of grouping used for nominal scales but also orders people from more to less.

An **interval scale** makes use of both the ideas of grouping and order but also requires the use of equal units of measurement. For example, a thermometer is marked off in equal units, and Centigrade and Fahrenheit scales are interval scales. The difference between 20°F and 21°F is equal to the difference between, for example, 55°F and 56°F. Thus, thermometers use equal units of measurement and are interval scales.

A **ratio scale** has all the properties of an interval scale (that is, grouping, order, and equal units) with the addition of a true or absolute zero point. This means that zero represents the complete absence of the variable being measured. For example, 0°F (or 0°C) does not mean the absence of temperature and therefore does not represent an absolute zero point. If, on the other hand, the height or weight of an object is measured, zero height or weight does represent a complete absence of these characteristics.

SAMPLING

A **random sample** is one in which every element in (or member of) the population has an equal and independent chance of being selected for the sample, and each possible sample representing the population has an equal chance of being selected. If findings are to be generalized with a particular sample to the entire population, it is important that the sample be random so that it accurately reflects the composition of the population, thereby minimizing bias.

A **stratified random sample** is a sample that contains proportional representation on one or more selected characteristics similar to the proportional representation in the population. In medicine it is often important to stratify random samples on the basis of age, sex, disease severity, and similar variables to reflect the proportion of persons of varying age and sex groups in the whole population.

We rely on the **central limit theorem** to generalize what is found with a particular sample to the larger population. If a distribution of all possible samples representing a particular population were formed, the central limit theorem holds the following:

1. The distribution of means of these samples would be approximately a normal distribution.
2. The mean of this sampling distribution would be equal to the population mean.
3. The standard deviation of this sampling distribution would be equal to the standard deviation of the population (s) divided by the square root of the number of

subjects (n) in each sample. This is called the **standard error of the mean** ($\sigma_{\bar{x}}$).

Symbolically,

$$\sigma_{\bar{x}} = \frac{\sigma}{\sqrt{N}} = \sqrt{\frac{(x - \bar{x})^2/n - 1}{n}}$$

STATISTICAL TESTS

The test of significance of any statistic is always the statistic itself divided by its own standard error. Selection of an appropriate statistical test is determined by the scale of measurement (i. e., nominal, ordinal, interval, or ratio) used to measure the **independent variable** (the predictor) and the **dependent variable** (the outcome, or what we want to predict).

Each of the five statistical methods summarized in Table B.2 is briefly illustrated. All the examples that are used are hypothetical and for illustrative purposes only.

Chi-Squared (χ^2)

If both variables of interest are measured on nominal scales (i. e., if both variables are formed on the basis of group membership alone), the **chi squared** (χ^2) is the appropriate test to see whether the observed pattern of occurrence significantly differs from that expected by chance alone. The occurrence of gout, which results from excessive serum uric acid levels in blood, could be tested to discover whether it is related to place of residence. Suppose 50 people who live in the city and 50 who live in the country are sampled and it is discovered that 30 city people have gout, whereas only 15 country people do. The following table can be set up by filling in the appropriate cells (the underlined numbers were previously given, and the others can be obtained by simple addition or subtraction):

	No Gout	Gout	
Country	35	_15_	_50_
City	20	_30_	_50_
Total	55	45	100

The first thing to do is calculate the number of people expected in each of the cells on the basis of chance alone.

The numbers for "total" are called marginals, since they

Expected values	$\frac{(55)\,(50)}{100} = 27.5$	$\frac{(45)\,(50)}{100} = 22.5$
	$\frac{(55)\,(50)}{100} = 27.5$	$\frac{(45)\,(50)}{100} = 22.5$

If O = observed value and E = expected value, then:

O – E	$(O - E)^2$	$(O - E)^2/E$
35 – 27.5 = 7.5	56.25	56.25/27.5 = 2.05
15 – 22.5 = –7.5	56.25	56.25/22.5 = 2.50
20 – 27.5 = –7.5	56.25	56.25/27.5 = 2.05
30 – 22.5 = 7.5	56.25	56.25/22.5 = 2.50

df = (r – 1) (c – 1) r = number of rows = 2 $\chi^2 = \Sigma\,[(O - E)^2/E] = 9.10$
df = (2 – 1) (2 – 1) = 1 c = number of columns = 2

are in the margins outside the four cells. These expected values are found by multiplying the two marginals associated with each cell and then dividing this by the total number of cases (n). For the cell in the upper left corner, 50×55 is multiplied and then divided by 100 (the total number of subjects) to obtain an expected value of 27.5. Thus, it would be expected on the basis of chance alone that 27.5 people in our sample would be from the country and not have gout, whereas 35 people have been observed to exhibit both of these characteristics.

To determine whether place of residence is significantly associated with prevalence of gout, the following four-step procedure is followed:

1. Calculate the expected value for each cell and subtract it from the observed value in our sample.
2. Square this difference.
3. Divide this squared difference by the expected value for that cell.
4. Sum the values obtained in step 3 and compare it with the value necessary for significance in a chi-squared table, using degrees of freedom = $(r - 1)(c - 1)$, where r equals the number of rows in our table and c equals the number of columns.

χ^2 Example

The χ^2 value of 9.1 with 1 degree of freedom is now compared with the value in a χ^2 table necessary to reach statistical significance at the alpha (α) = 0.05 level (i. e., that only a 5% probability exists that a value this large or larger is because of chance and not because of significant systematic effect). The table value is 3.84, and χ^2 = 9.1. Because the χ^2 value is higher, a statistically significant association exists between place of residence and incidence of gout in this sample.

t-Test

As summarized in Table B.2, a t-test is used when determining whether there is a significant difference on a variable of interest between two distinct groups of subjects (e. g., sick and well). The dependent variable must be measured on either an interval or a ratio scale.

Suppose we want to determine whether the serum uric acid level for people with gout is significantly higher than the level for people without gout. If random samples of 50 people with gout and another 50 people without gout are selected, the hypothesis that the serum uric acid level will be significantly higher for the gout group can be tested. Suppose when the uric acid level for the gout group is tested, an average of 7.5 mg/dl with a standard deviation of 1.5 is obtained; the non-gout group has a mean of 4.5, with a standard deviation of 1. The t-test formula for answering the question is:

$$t = \frac{\bar{x}_1 - \bar{x}_2}{\sqrt{\dfrac{s_1^2}{n_1} + \dfrac{s_2^2}{n_2}}}$$

$$t = \frac{7.5 - 4.5}{\sqrt{\dfrac{(1.5)^2}{50} + \dfrac{(1)^2}{50}}} = \frac{3.0}{0.25} = 11.77$$

where
$\bar{x}_1$ = Mean for gout group
$\bar{x}_2$ = Mean for non-gout group
s_1^2 = Variance for gout group
s_2^2 = Variance for non-gout group
n_1 = Sample size for gout group
n_2 = Sample size for non-gout group

Because we are interested in determining whether the level is higher for the gout group, the test of this hypothesis is directional (i. e., **one tailed**). We are not concerned with whether the level for the gout group is either greater than or less than the non-gout group (in which case we would have a nondirectional, or **two-tailed hypothesis test**). First the t-value of 11.77 is compared with the t-table value required to reach statistical significance at the α = 0.5 level (one-tailed test) with degrees of freedom = $n_1 + n_2 - 2$ (or $50 + 50 - 2 = 98$). Because 11.77 is greater than 1.66 (the tabled value for t with 98 degrees of freedom), our hypothesis that people with gout have higher levels of uric acid than people without gout is supported.

Because the people in the two groups in the previous example are different, this t-test is called an **independent** t-**test**. Suppose, however, that we have a random sample of 100 patients with gout, who have a mean uric acid level of 7.5 with a standard deviation of 1.5. Suppose that after 1

TABLE B.2 Various scales of measurement for independent and dependent variables with appropriate statistical tests

Independent variable (IV)	Dependent variable (DV)	Statistical test
Nominal	Nominal	Chi-squared (χ^2)
Nominal (2 groups only)	Interval or ratio	t-test
Nominal (2 or more groups, 1 IV only)	Interval or ratio	One-way analysis of variance (F-test)
Nominal (2 or more groups, 2 or more IVs)	Interval or ratio	Factorial design analysis of variance (F-test)
Ordinal, interval, or ratio	Ordinal, interval, or ratio	Pearson correlation coefficient (r_{xy})

month of treatment, the group's mean uric acid level drops to 6.0 with a standard deviation of 1.25. Is this decrease statistically significant? Because there is one group of people measured on the same thing (i. e., uric acid level) at two points in time, a **dependent or paired** t-**test** is used to answer this question. This formula varies slightly from the one previously presented and can be found in most statistics books.

One-Way Analysis of Variance

If we have only two groups, we can use a t-test to answer the question posed earlier of whether a group's mean uric acid level drop from 7.5 to 6.0 is significant. However, if we have more than two groups, we must use a **one-way analysis of variance** (ANOVA). The result of an ANOVA with only two groups is mathematically equal to the result of a t-test.

Suppose we have a random sample containing three groups. Group 1 does not have gout, group 2 has gout and has been treated, but group 3 has gout and has not yet received treatment. To answer the question of whether these three groups' serum uric acid levels differ significantly, a ratio (called an F-**test**) of the variation among the groups to the variation within the groups (called a within or **error term**) is formed. A table similar to Table B.3 can be developed.

For the sake of simplicity, the example is limited to two people in each of the three groups or a total $N = 6$, as in Table B.4. The sum of squares, degrees of freedom, and mean squares are calculated as follows:

The sum of squares within each group is calculated in the following manner (Table B.5):

TABLE B.3

Source of variation	Sum of squares (SS)	df	Mean squares (MS)
Between		$k-1$	$SS_{between}/df_{between}$
Within		$N-k$	SS_{within}/df_{within}
Total		$N-1$	

N = Total size of the sample; k = number of groups; df = degrees of freedom

TABLE B.4

	Group 1 Uric acid level	Group 2 Uric acid level	Group 3 Uric acid level
Person 1	1	3	5
Person 2	3	5	7
$\bar{x}$	2	4	6

The grand mean $= \dfrac{\bar{x}_1 + \bar{x}_2 + \bar{x}_3}{k} = \dfrac{2 + 4 + 6}{3} = 4$

1. Subtract the mean for each group from the uric acid level for each person in that group.
2. Square these differences and sum them (note: this procedure is analogous to calculating the variance).
3. Next the total variance or total sum of squares in Table B.6 is calculated. The same procedure is followed as in Table B.5, except the grand mean for everyone is subtracted from each person's score, and then this difference is squared and then summed (Table B.6).
4. To calculate the sum of squares between groups, the sum of squares within is simply subtracted from the total sum of squares:

TABLE B.5

Groups

No gout $(x - \bar{x})$	$(x - \bar{x})^2$	Gout with treatment $(x - \bar{x})$	$(x - \bar{x})^2$	Gout without treatment $(x - \bar{x})$	$(x - \bar{x})^2$
$1 - 2 = -1$	1	$3 - 4 = -1$	1	$5 - 6 = -1$	1
$3 - 2 = 1$	1	$5 - 4 = 1$	1	$7 - 6 = 1$	1
Sum of squares (SS)	2		2		2

Total SS within = 2 + 2 + 2 = 6

TABLE B.6

Groups

No gout $(x - \text{Grand mean})$	Squared	Gout with treatment $(x - \text{Grand mean})$	Squared	Gout without treatment $(x - \text{Grand mean})$	Squared
$1 - 4 = -3$	9	$3 - 4 = -1$	1	$5 - 4 = 1$	1
$3 - 4 = -1$	1	$5 - 4 = 1$	1	$7 - 4 = 3$	9
Sum of squares (SS)	10		2		10

Total SS = 10 + 2 + 10 = 22

$$SS_{between} = SS_{total} - SS_{within}$$
$$SS_{between} = 22 - 6 = 16$$

The table can now be completed (Table B.7).

TABLE B.7

Source of variation	SS	df	MS
Between groups	16	2	8
Within groups	6	3	2
Total	22	5	

The following F-test is then used to determine whether the difference among the groups is significant:

$$F = \frac{MS_{between}}{MS_{within}} = \frac{8}{2} = 4.0$$

Once again, this value is compared with the value in an F-table for 2 and 3 degrees of freedom (i. e., the df associated with the $MS_{between}$ and the MS_{within}). Because 4.0 is less than 9.55 (the tabled value for an F-test with 2 and 3 degrees of freedom), these differences are not statistically significant. Note, however, that if the sample size had been 30 (i. e., 10 people in each group), the df for the MS_{within} would have been $30 - 3 = 27$ (the number of subjects minus the number of groups). With 2 and 27 df, the F value of 4.0 would be statistically significant. For this reason it is important to be careful when you are interpreting the results of statistical tests, because larger samples increase the likelihood that a difference between groups will reach statistical significance, whereas smaller samples decrease the likelihood of statistical significance.

If our F-test had been significant, we would then compare the means of each of our three groups to see which of them are different from the others. Because a straight t-test would increase the likelihood of making an error, we use a **posteriori** or **post-hoc** test such as the Newman-Kuels, the Scheffe, the Tukey, the Duncan, or the HSD (honestly significant difference) test.

This one-way ANOVA example was similar to our independent t-test example, because each group comprised different people. However, just as a dependent (or paired) t-test was used when the uric acid level was measured for the same people on two occasions, if the same people were measured on three or more occasions (gout before treatment, gout with treatment, and after cure), **repeated measures analysis of variance** would be used.

Factorial Design

A **factorial analysis of variance design** is appropriate when there are two or more independent variables with one dependent variable. These independent variables are called **factors,** whereas the groups into which each factor is divid-

ed are called **levels.** For example, suppose one independent variable or factor is the level of gout the subjects have-no gout, gout with treatment, or gout without treatment. This independent variable, called factor A, has three levels. If we want to also know whether place of residence simultaneously influences serum uric acid levels, this can be called factor B with two levels-city or country residence. Thus, we have a 3 × 2 (three by two) factorial design, with serum uric acid level still the dependent variable. Not only can we assess the main effects of degree of gout (factor A) and place of residence (factor B), but we can also assess the interaction (AB) of gout × residence ("×" is read as "by"). The design would look like this:

		B	
		b₁	b₂
		City	Country
a₁	No gout		
A a₂	Gout with treatment		
a₃	Gout without treatment		

For illustrative purposes let's change our example to simplify the calculations. Suppose there are two different interventions for treating gout and we want to determine which one is superior. In addition, there might be reason to believe that place of residence (city vs. country) may influence serum uric acid levels and possibly that one treatment may be better for city dwellers, whereas the other may be better for country dwellers (this is the interaction hypothesis). Our 2 × 2 factorial design looks like this:

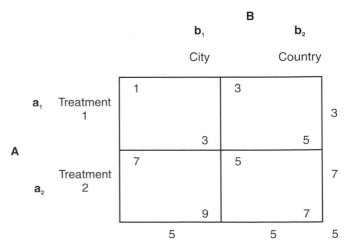

Suppose there is a total of 8 subjects in our sample, with two people from the city given treatment 1, two people

TABLE B.8

Source of variation	SS	df	MS	F
A (treatment)		$(r-1)$		MS_A/MS_{within}
B (residence)		$(c-1)$		MS_B/MS_{within}
AB (treatment × residence)		$(r-1)(c-1)$		MS_{AB}/MS_{within}
Within (error)		$(r)(c)(n-1)$		
Total		$N-1$		

r = number of rows; c = number of columns; n = number of subjects in each cell; N = total number of subjects

from the city given treatment 2, two people from the country given treatment 1, and two people from the country given treatment 2. The numbers in the cells just illustrated represent their uric acid levels, whereas the numbers outside the cells in the marginals represent the averages (means) of the columns and rows. The 5 in the lowest right corner is the grand mean, or the average of all the scores in the cells. Our factorial ANOVA table looks like Table B.8.

To determine our sum of squares from treatment group (SS_A), the grand mean (5) is subtracted from the means for level a_1 (3) and a_2 (7); this difference is then squared, summed, and multiplied by the number of observations for each level of A (i. e., 4). For example,

$$3 - 5 = -2, (-2)^2 = 4$$
$$7 - 5 = -2, -(2)^2 = 4$$
$$\Sigma = 8$$
$$SS_A = (8)(4) = 32$$

The mean squared term (MS_A) is simply SS_A/df_A, or 32/1 = 32.

The following similar procedure is used to calculate SS for the residence factor (B):

$$5 - 5 = 0, (0)^2 = 0$$

$$5 - 5 = 0, (0)^2 = 0$$

$$\Sigma = 0$$

$$SS_B = (0)(4) = 0$$

$$MS_B = \frac{SS_B}{df_B} = \frac{0}{1} = 0$$

The sum of squares within the cells is calculated just as in the one-way ANOVA example, that is, subtract the cell mean (underlined in the figure above) from each score in each cell, square these differences, sum them, and multiply this sum by the number of people in each cell (which is 2 in the figure at the right):

$$\text{Our } MS_{within} = \frac{SS_{within}}{df_{within}}$$

With $df_{within} = (r-1)(c-1) = (2-1)(2-1) = 1$

Thus, $MS_{within} = \frac{8}{1} = 8$

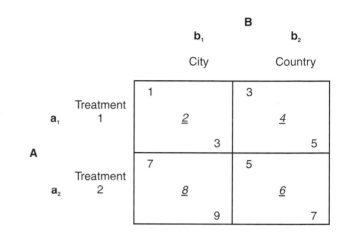

$$1 - 2 = -1, \quad (-1)^2 = 1$$
$$3 - 2 = 1, \quad (1)^2 = 1$$
$$7 - 8 = -1, \quad (-1)^2 = 1$$
$$9 - 8 = 1, \quad (1)^2 = 1$$
$$3 - 4 = -1, \quad (-1)^2 = 1$$
$$5 - 4 = 1, \quad (1)^2 = 1$$
$$5 - 6 = -1, \quad (-1)^2 = 1$$
$$7 - 6 = 1, \quad (1)^2 = 1$$
$$SS_{within} = 8$$

The total sum of squares (SS_T) can also be calculated as in the one-way ANOVA example by simply subtracting the mean of all the scores (i. e., grand mean) from each score, squaring these differences, and then summing them. For example:

$$1 - 5 = -4, \quad (-4)^2 = 16$$
$$3 - 5 = -2, \quad (-2)^2 = 4$$
$$7 - 5 = 2, \quad (2)^2 = 4$$
$$9 - 5 = 4, \quad (4)^2 = 16$$
$$3 - 5 = -2, \quad (-2)^2 = 4$$
$$5 - 5 = 0, \quad (0)^2 = 0$$
$$5 - 5 = 0, \quad (0)^2 = 0$$
$$7 - 5 = 2, \quad (2)^2 = 4$$
$$SS_T = 48$$

The interaction sum of squares (SS_{AB}) is found by subtracting SS_A, SS_B, and SS_{within} from SS_T. For example:

$$SS_{AB} = SS_T - SS_A - SS_B - SS_{within}$$
$$SS_{AB} = 48 - 32 - 0 - 8 = 8$$

Table B.9 is the completed ANOVA table.

TABLE B.9

Source of variation	SS	df	MS	F
A (treatment)	32	1	32	16
B (residence)	0	1	0	0
AB (treatment × residence)	8	1	8	4
Within (error)	8	4	2	
Total	48	7		

Our obtained *F* values for A, B, and AB are now compared with the *F*-table value necessary to reach statistical significance (using df's associated with the MS's used in each *F*-ratio in the previous table; i. e., df = 1 and 4 in each instance in the example). The *F*-table value with df = 1 and 4 necessary to obtain statistical significance is 7.71. Thus only the effects of factor A, the different treatments, are statistically significant, whereas the effects of place of residence (factor B) and the interaction of treatment by residence (AB) are not statistically different.

Interaction

Suppose for illustrative purposes that the interaction term (AB) was significant. This would mean that the cells in our design have significant differences. To better understand the nature of this interaction, it is helpful to graph the cell means, as in the following figures:

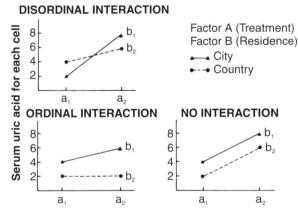

The interaction just described is called **disordinal,** because the two lines cross. This means that treatment a_1 is superior for country residents (b_2), whereas treatment a_2 is superior for city residents (b_1). If there is a significant interaction but the lines do *not* cross, then it is an **ordinal** interaction. This means that although one treatment may be more effective for people residing in one place than the other, the same treatment may still be superior to the other for both residencies. It is possible, however, that in the ordinal interaction graphed in the figure, the effect of treatment a_1 is not significantly different for city (b_1) or country (b_2) dwellers but that treatment a_2 is significantly superior for city dwellers. The situation in which there is no interaction is illustrated graphically by parallel lines.

Pearson Correlation Coefficient (r_{xy})

To determine whether two things measured on ordinal, interval, or ratio scales are significantly related to each other, we can calculate the correlation between them. The following is a formula for calculating the correlation between two variables:

$$r_{xy} = \frac{\Sigma(x-\bar{x})(y-\bar{y})/n}{\sqrt{\frac{\Sigma(x-\bar{x})^2}{n} \times \frac{\Sigma(y-\bar{y})^2}{n}}} \quad .$$

The denominator of this formula comprises the standard deviation of variable x:

$$\sqrt{\frac{\Sigma(x-\bar{x})^2}{n}}$$

multiplied by the standard deviation of variable *y*:

$$\sqrt{\frac{\Sigma(y-\bar{y})^2}{n}}$$

TABLE B.10

Person	No. of cigarettes/week (x)			Serum uric acid level (y)			
	x	$(x-\bar{x})$	$(x-\bar{x})^2$	y	$(y-\bar{y})$	$(y-\bar{y})^2$	$(x-\bar{x})(y-\bar{y})$
1	2	−1	1	1	−4	16	4
2	4	1	1	3	−2	4	−2
3	3	0	0	5	0	0	0
4	5	2	4	7	2	4	4
5	1	−2	4	9	4	16	−8
	$\bar{x}=3$		$\Sigma(x-\bar{x})^2=10$	$\bar{y}=5$		$\Sigma(y-\bar{y})^2=40$	$\Sigma(x-\bar{x})(y-\bar{y})=-2$

$$r_{xy} = \frac{-2/5}{\sqrt{\frac{10}{5} \times \frac{40}{5}}} = \frac{-2}{\sqrt{(10)(10)(4)}} = \frac{-2}{(10)(2)} = -0.10$$

The numerator is called the average of the cross products of the two variables. Suppose we want to see whether a relationship exists between the serum uric acid level and the number of cigarettes smoked per week by a random sample of five people. In Table B.10 the number of cigarettes each person smokes per week is symbolized by x and their serum uric acid level is symbolized by y.

In this example, the correlation is –0.10. This is a negative relationship, that is, as the values of one variable increase (e. g., the number of cigarettes smoked), the values of the other variable decrease. Again, we compare our obtained value, $r_{xy} = -0.10$, with the value necessary to reach statistical significance in a correlation table for $p = 0.05$, two-tailed test, with df = $n - 2$ or $5 - 2 = 3$. The value necessary to reach statistical significance must be less than –0.878 or greater than 0.878. Because –0.10 falls between these two values, it is not significant (note that a positive or negative r or t value does not influence whether the value is statistically significant). Thus, the number of cigarettes smoked per week is not significantly related to serum uric acid levels.

Once the correlation coefficient between two variables is calculated, it is possible to use this information in several ways. First, if r is squared, the amount of variance shared between the two variables is found. Thus, in our example any variation in one of these two variables would be accompanied by approximately a 1% variation in the other; this is the amount of variance shared by the two variables. It is important to remember that correlations or relationships between two variables do not indicate that one has caused the other. In fact, it is uncertain which caused which, and all that is known is the amount of variance they share in common.

A second use of a correlation coefficient is in a regression equation used for prediction when a person's score for one of the variables is known but is not known for the second. Suppose we know only that someone smokes 10 packs of cigarettes per week. What can we predict his or her serum uric acid level to be? The following regression equation is used to answer this question:

$$\hat{y} \text{ predicted} = \bar{y} + b(x - \bar{x})$$

where
$\hat{y}$ = Predicted serum uric acid level
$\bar{y}$ = Average serum uric acid level for the sample
x = This person's number of cigarettes/week
$\bar{x}$ = Average number of cigarettes/week for the sample
b = $r_{xy}(s_y/s_x)$

$$\hat{y} = 3 + b(10 - 5)$$
$$\hat{y} = 3 + (-0.2)(5)$$
$$\hat{y} = 3 - 1 = 2$$

where

$$b = (-0.10)\sqrt{\frac{40/5}{10/5}} = (-0.10)(2) = -0.20\}\}$$

Thus, we would predict that someone who smokes 10 packs of cigarettes per week would have a serum uric acid level of 2.

TEST CHARACTERISTICS

It is important to recognize that no piece of diagnostic information, whether obtained from the history, physical examination, or laboratory, is 100% accurate or valid for all patients all of the time. It is always possible for errors to occur, so it is important to recognize the strengths and limitations of diagnostic information to try to minimize error. The term **false positive** is used to indicate patients who in reality do not have a particular disease but are incorrectly classified as having the disease. On the other hand, **false negative** is used to indicate patients who in reality do have a particular disease but are incorrectly classified as not having the disease. It is useful to summarize this type of information in a 2 by 2 table (opposite page, top).

Sensitivity and Specificity

Sensitivity and specificity are the two indices used to evaluate the accuracy or validity of diagnostic information. Suppose we want to evaluate the accuracy of a new diagnostic test for gout and we obtain data on 1,000 patients seen in a specialty clinic in which gout is fairly common. Suppose that, of 1,000 patients examined, half (500) were ultimately found to have gout. For those who had gout, the test was positive in 400 patients. For those without gout, the test was positive in only 50 patients.

Sensitivity is the percentage of patients whose tests indicate the presence of a particular disease and who in fact do have the disease. It is calculated by dividing the number of true positives by all those who have the disease (i. e., both true positives and false negatives). Thus, the sensitivity of the test is 400/500 = 80%. **Specificity** is the percent of patients whose tests indicate the absence of a particular disease and who in fact do not have the disease. It is calculated by dividing the number of true negatives by all those who do not have the disease (that is, both true negatives and false positives). In this example (page 502) the specificity would be 450/500 = 90%.

Predictive Value

Although these test characteristics are important to know, it is also useful to determine the predictive value of a test. The **positive predictive value** of a test is the probability of a disease if a test result is positive. It is the true positives

**True outcome
(gold standard)**

Comparing a test result with the true outcome (or "gold standard")

	Patient has disease	Patient does not have disease	
Positive (patient appears to have disease)	True positive	False positive	True positives + False positives
Negative (patient appears not to have disease)	False negative	True negative	False negatives + True negatives
	All patients with disease	All patients without disease	All patients

Test result (conclusion drawn from the results of the test)

True outcome

	Patient has gout	Patient does not have gout	
Positive (patient appears to have gout)	True positive (400)	False positive (50)	True positives + False positives (450)
Negative (patient appears not to have gout)	False negative (100)	True negative (450)	False negatives + True negatives (550)
	All patients with gout (500)	All patients without gout (500)	All patients (1,000)

Test result

divided by the true positives plus the false positives, or 400/450 = 88.9% in the example. The **negative predictive value** is the probability of its not being a particular disease if a test result is negative. It is the true negatives divided by the true negatives plus the false negatives, or 450/550 = 81.8% in the example.

Although the expression "test result" is typically meant to denote a laboratory finding, the same concepts of sensitivity, specificity, and predictive value apply to all diagnostic information, including historical and physical findings.

TEST CHARACTERISTICS

Pre- and Post-test Odds and Likelihood Ratios

Another way of thinking about diagnostic testing is to consider the effect a positive or negative test result has on a patient's odds (or chances) of having a particular disease. This can be conceptualized by Bayes' theorem in which the odds of having the disease following the test result (the

	Outcome present	Outcome absent	
Treatment Group	a (20)	b (80)	$a + b$ (100)
Control Group	c (40)	d (60)	$c + d$ (100)
	$a + c$ (60)	$b + d$ (140)	$a + b + c + d$ (200)

Odds (treatment) = a/b = 20/80 = 25%

Odds (control) = c/d = 40/60 = 67%

Odds ratio = Odds (treatment)/Odds (control)
= 25%/67% = 0.37

Risk (treatment) = $a/(a + b)$ = 20/100 = 20%

Risk (control) = $c/(c + d)$ = 40/100 = 40%

Relative Risk = Risk (treatment)/Risk (control)
= 20%/40% = 0.50

Risk Difference = Risk (treatment) – Risk (control)
= 20% – 40% = –20%

NNT (Number needed to Treat) =
$$\frac{1}{\text{Risk Difference}} = \frac{1}{-0.20} = 5$$

post-test odds) is a function of the odds of having the disease before the test and the information provided by the test result, which is denoted as the **likelihood ratio**. The odds of having the disease before the test, called the pre-test odds, is directly related to the prevalence of the disease in the population group to which the patient is a member, where **prevalence** is the percentage of people with the disease in the population of interest. Thus in our gout example, the prevalence of gout in this particular population is very high, 50% (500/1000). The **pre-test odds** is simply the ratio of all the people with gout compared to all the people without gout, or stated slightly differently, the prevalence divided by one minus the prevalence, or in this instance, prevalence = 50%/50% = 1. The likelihood ratio can be either positive, i.e., for a positive test result, or negative, i.e., for a negative test result. The **positive likelihood ratio** is the ratio of true positives to false positives, or 400/50 = 20 in our example. The **negative likelihood ratio** is the ratio of false negatives to true negatives, or 100/450 = 0.22 in our example. This is expressed through Bayes' theorem by the formula:

Post-test Odds = Pre-test Odds × Likelihood Ratio (LR)

If the test result is positive, then the post-test odds equals

1 × 20 or 20, which has increased substantially over the pre-test odds of 1. If the test result is negative, then the post-test odds are 1 × 0.22 or 0.22, which is substantially less than the pre-test odds.

ASSESSING ODDS AND RISK

Odds ratios and relative risks are alternative ways of expressing the probability that a particular outcome will occur measured on dichotomous scales, such as the presence or absence of disease, relapse, recurrence, or complications. Suppose, for example, that 200 patients are randomized to either a treatment or a placebo (control) group such that there are 100 patients in each group. If we know that 20 patients in the treatment group and 40 in the control group experience a recurrence of disease, the **odds** of recurrence would be 20/80 (or 25%) for the experimental groups and 40/60 (or 67%) for the control group. The **odds ratio** would simply be the ratio of these odds, for example, 25%/67% (or 0.37).

The risk of recurrence, on the other hand, would be 20/100 (or 20%) for the treatment group and 40/100 (or

40%) for the control group. The **relative risk** of recurrence for the treatment group would therefore be 20%/40% (or 50%) less than that of the control group. The relative risk is sometimes referred to as the event rate ratio, the risk ratio, or the incidence rate ratio. The **risk difference** (or event rate difference) is the difference between the relative risks for the treatment and control groups, for example, 20% minus 40%, or −20%. The risk difference is sometimes referred to as the absolute risk reduction. If we take the reciprocal of the absolute risk reduction (i. e., divide 1 by this number), we can estimate the number of patients we would need to treat to prevent the recurrence of disease in one patient. This is called the number needed to treat (NNT). In our example, where the risk difference is −20%, we would prevent recurrence of disease in one patient for every five patients we treated (i. e., 1/0.20 = 5).

SELECTED BIOSTATISTICAL TERMS

Alpha Error (α)

See Type-I error

Alpha Level (α)

See significance level

Beta Error (β)

See Type-II error

Case-Control Study

A **case-control study** or a **case-history study** looks at events (e. g., disease and exposure) that have already occurred. In this type of study the investigator compares a group of subjects with a particular disease (called cases) with a group of subjects without disease (called controls) on the presence, absence, or level of the risk factor or factors under consideration. This type of study is also called a **retrospective study,** because the study goes back in time.

Clinical Trials

Clinical trials are experiments in which the efficacy or effectiveness of a preventive or therapeutic agent or procedure is tested in individual subjects. **Randomized clinical trials** are experiments in which subjects are randomly allocated (i. e.,

have an equally likely chance of being assigned) to the treatment (experimental) group or the control group.

Cohort

A **cohort** is a group of persons who share a common experience within a defined time period. The most common example is a birth cohort (i. e., all persons born in a given year). Other examples would be all people graduating in one class or survivors of myocardial infarction in 1 particular year. This type of study is also called a **prospective study,** because subjects are followed forward in time.

Confidence Interval

Confidence Intervals (CIs) are a useful way of expressing a range of values within which the true value of interest is likely to fall, typically 95% of the time (or 90% or 99%). It helps us to quantify the degree of uncertainty in measurement. Thus a narrower confidence interval indicates a more precise estimate of the true value, while conversely, a wider confidence interval suggests a less precise estimate of the true value. Confidence intervals can be calculated for many statistics, including Odds Ratios, Relative Risk Ratios, estimates of the Number of Patients Needed to Treat (NNT) to prevent a bad outcome or bring about a good outcome (see "Assessing Odds and Risk" above), and means (or averages). An example of how a 95% Confidence interval is calculated for a mean is provided below.

Let $\bar{x}$ be a sample mean and s be the sample standard deviation. If the lower boundary of the confidence interval is:

$$\bar{x} - 1.96 \frac{s}{\sqrt{N}}$$

and if the upper boundary of the confidence interval is:

$$\bar{x} + 1.96 \frac{s}{\sqrt{N}}$$

an interval is called a 95% **confidence interval** for μ (the population mean):

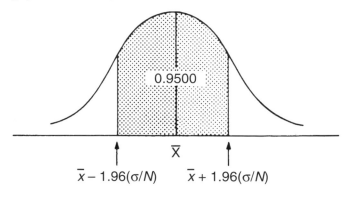

The formula above tells how to find a 95% confidence interval for μ. This means that there is a 95% probability that the population mean will fall within this interval. We must still realize that 5% of the time the population mean will fall outside this interval. This is true because the sample means are normally distributed, and 5% of the values of a random variable in a normal distribution will fall further than 2 standard deviations from the mean.

Depending on the nature of the problem, some statisticians prefer a 99% confidence interval for μ or a 90% confidence interval for μ. The boundaries for these intervals are listed in Table B.11.

TABLE B.11

	Lower boundary	Upper boundary
99% confidence interval	$\bar{x} - 2.58\frac{s}{\sqrt{N}}$	$\bar{x} + 2.58\frac{s}{\sqrt{N}}$
90% confidence interval	$\bar{x} - 1.64\frac{s}{\sqrt{N}}$	$\bar{x} + 1.64\frac{s}{\sqrt{N}}$

Cross-Sectional Study

A **cross-sectional study** is conducted at one point in time and attempts to determine how the prevalence of a condition is related to the variables measured. This is often called a **prevalence study** because it typically provides information about the distribution (rather than etiology) of a disease in the population, for example, on the basis of age, sex, race, or occupation.

Decision Analysis

Decision Analysis is an approach to making decisions under conditions of uncertainty, which often characterize medical situations and judgments. In general, there are four main steps in decision analysis: specifying the problem by identifying alternative choices that can be made, specifying the (temporal) sequences in which choices can be made, specifying the information on which decisions are based (often represented as probabilities), and making the decision among the choices. Often formal decision analyses are represented as **decision trees,** or visual diagrams, that can be useful in quantifying and understanding the various components of the decision to be made and the alternatives from which choices must be made.

Degrees of Freedom

For a series of numerical quantities, the **degrees of freedom** (df) refer to the number of independent quantities among the entire series. Alternatively, the degree of freedom may be better conceptualized by being defined as the total number of quantities in the series (n) minus the number of restrictions imposed on the quantities. For example, when the definition of variance is considered, the quantities involved are deviations about the mean, namely, the series of $x - \bar{x}$ values. There is a total of n such deviations. There is one restriction imposed on these deviations, namely, that their sum is zero. With n deviations and one restriction, this means $n - 1$ df. In other words, if numerical values were assigned for a series of n deviations about the mean, once $n - 1$ was assigned such numbers, the last number would automatically follow, since the sum of all deviations must be zero. Thus, n deviations about the mean contain $n - 1$ df.

Double-Blind Study

In a **double-blind study** neither the subjects nor the observers (experimenters) know which subjects are in the treatment (experimental) or control group. This is done to diminish the possibility of inferential bias associated with knowledge of treatment group membership.

Incidence

The **incidence** of a disease is the number of *new* cases of disease appearing in a given time period.

Inference

Statistical inference refers to the way that predictions are made about a population based on a sample drawn from that population.

Longitudinal Study

A **longitudinal study** is one in which the same subjects are followed over a certain time period. This type of study is also called a **prospective study,** because subjects are followed forward in time.

Meta-Analysis

Meta-analysis is the application of statistical procedures to collections of empirical findings from individual studies that address a common research question for the purpose of integrating and synthesizing these findings in a quantitative fashion. It is sometimes referred to as a quantitative literature review in contrast to the traditional narrative literature review. In essence, the result taken from an individual study becomes the unit of analysis (in contrast to a person, e. g., a patient, which is the common unit of analysis in a research study) and a quantitative estimate of the magnitude of the effect is obtained. This is called an **effect size.**

The practical appeal of using effect sizes to represent study outcomes is that it provides a common, standardized metric or unit of analysis for a study result that is then comparable across studies. The advantages are multifold. First, the magnitude of an effect, and not just its statistical significance, can be ascertained. Second, results from independent studies addressing a common research question can then be compared directly. Third, these results can be synthesized or aggregated by averaging the results of the collection of studies addressing this research question. Fourth, the characteristics of each study can be systematically coded (e. g., size of sample, type of study design, intensity of the intervention, and gender or age of subjects) and related to each study's effect size, typically through correlational or analysis of variance techniques. Because results from studies in the literature often contain conflicting results, a properly constructed meta-analysis enables us to empirically examine the degree to which different study characteristics (as mediating or moderating variables) influence the outcome. Fifth, it is often difficult for any one investigator or laboratory to conduct large-scale experiments with large numbers of subjects, thereby making these individual study results unstable or of low statistical power (i. e., unacceptably high probability of not finding a statistically significant effect based on the small number of subjects alone). Aggregating results from many small sample size studies, particularly if they are randomized controlled trials, takes advantage of the combined numbers of subjects and evidence from all studies, thereby generating a more stable estimate and greater power than that derived from any of the single studies. This ability to generate more generalizable results through meta-analysis is true even if there are a number of larger-scale trials in the literature, because the combined evidence speaks more powerfully than the individual parts either to unequivocally confirm and quantify the magnitude of an outcome across studies that can then guide policy or to help identify and provide explanations for conflicting results.

Nonparametric Statistics

Nonparametric statistics are used when the assumptions about a normal distribution necessary for conventional statistical tests cannot be met. They are therefore called distribution-free statistics and are often used with small samples. Some of the more commonly used nonparametric tests are the median test, the Mann-Whitney U test, the chi-square test, the Fisher exact test, and the Wilcoxon matched-pairs signed-rank test.

Null Hypothesis

A **null hypothesis,** denoted H_0, states that there is no statistically significant difference between the population parameters (e. g., means). The **alternative hypothesis,** H_a, states that there is a statistically significant difference between the population parameters. Hypotheses are never proved (because we are working with probabilities) but are supported or rejected.

Power

The statistical **Power** of a test or research study is used to calculate the minimum number of research subjects that would be needed to fairly test a research hypothesis (question) at given levels of alpha (α) and beta (β), the Type I and Type II error rates (see definitions of Type I and Type-II errors). α is typically set at .05 and β at .80 (or more stringently, .90). Once we determine what size effect is clinically important, say a reduction in blood glucose levels of one-half of a standard deviation unit (or alternatively, reducing blood glucose levels by some fixed percentage, say 10%), and set our levels for α and β, it is then possible to determine the minimum number of subjects that we would need to recruit to each group in our study to fairly test the hypothesis that the intervention would result in a significant change.

Prevalence

The **prevalence** of a disease is the number of cases (frequency) of disease in a population at a given point in time. **Prevalence rate** is equal to the frequency of disease divided by the population size.

Probability

Probability refers to the odds that an event will occur. If an event can occur in a number of equally likely ways (n) and if a number of these ways are considered favorable (f), the probability of getting a favorable outcome is:

$$\frac{\text{Number of favorable outcomes}}{\text{Total number of outcomes}} = \frac{f}{n}$$

The symbol p(A) is used for "the probability of event A." Probability is referred to as the **relative frequency** of the event, because it represents the percentage of times that the event will happen in repeated experiments.

Significance Level

The **significance level** of a test is the probability that the test statistic falls within the rejection region.

The .05 level of significance is used when the statistician decides that the risk of rejecting a true null hypothesis should not exceed .05. The .01 level of significance is used when the statistician decides that the risk of rejecting a true null hypothesis should not exceed .01.

Single Blind Study

In a **single blind study** only the experimenters and not the subjects know which subjects are receiving treatment. This is done to diminish the possibility of biasing the outcome of the study as a result of patients knowing of which study group they are a member (e. g., treatment or placebo).

Systematic Reviews

Systematic reviews are designed to provide summaries of the medical literature pertaining to a specific question (typically, but not necessarily limited to, an intervention). These reviews use explicit methods to perform a comprehensive literature search and critical appraisal of individual studies that are selected based on explicit inclusion and exclusion criteria for studies. The goal of a systematic review is to reduce potential biases in the review as much as pos-

sible. Thus these reviews are considered to be more "objective" than traditional narrative reviews, which typically are more "impressionistic." The characteristics and quality of each study in the review are typically coded and summarized in the review. Often, but not always, data are combined or pooled across studies addressing the same question using a quantitative approach called **meta-analysis** (see definition).

Type-I Error

A **Type-I error,** also called an **alpha (α) error,** is made when a true null hypothesis is rejected (i. e., a null hypothesis is rejected when it should be accepted).

Type-II Error

A **Type-II error,** also called a **beta (β) error,** is made when a false, null hypothesis is accepted (i. e., a null hypothesis is accepted when it should be rejected).

The following figure indicates how these two errors are made:

	and we claim that	
	H_0 is true	H_0 is false
H_0 is true	Correct decision (no error)	Type-I (α) error
H_0 is false	Type-II (β) error	Correct decision (no error)

If

Appendix C
Abridged Directory of Humanities Resources for Medical Education and Practice

Carol C. Donley, Martin Kohn, & Steven C. Schlozman*

The connection between literature and medicine is as ancient as the Greek god Apollo, the father of Asclepius, and the divine representation of light, order, music, poetry, and medicine. This connection is continued in the long and illustrious list of physician-writers, from Francois Rabelais of the fifteenth century to such twentieth-century authors as Somerset Maugham, William Carlos Williams, Walker Percy, and Richard Selzer. The intervening centuries provided other notable physician-writers including John Keats, Anton Chekhov, and Sir Arthur Conan Doyle.

Literature as a sanctioned element of medical education is a very recent development. In 1972, the Pennsylvania State University College of Medicine at Hershey appointed the first medical school faculty member with a degree in literature. Since that time many full- and part-time appointments have followed. In addition, in many institutions, imaginative literature has come to be included in all aspects of physician training from premedical to continuing professional education.

During the past 20 years literature and medicine in the curriculum has developed four primary expressions: images of disease, illness and suffering; images of healers; the physician-writer; and literature as a means of healing (Jones, 1990). There also has been recent interest in the ethical and aesthetic application of literature and narrative to medicine.

We believe, for many reasons, that taking the time to read imaginative literature can give us, as John Stone says, "the hard data by which our lives are lived." What follows is a listing of some of those reasons:

- *Literature broadens understanding through the presentation and appreciation of multiple perspectives of "reality."*

Literature makes us see; it opens our eyes to notice the often overlooked other(s) and their points of view. It helps us recognize our own prejudices in relation to race, gender, ethnicity, and sexual orientation.

- *Literature provides a means of improving ethical discernment and practice.* Modern medical ethics has been dominated by a reductionistic approach whereby "higher order" rules or principles are applied to specific cases or dilemmas. This problem-solving approach, although consistent with trends in medical education, gives short shrift to the rich details of the human story of health, illness, and healing that literature does give us.

- *Reading literature can increase the analytic skills of the physician.* The act of reading is an act of interpretation, whether what one reads (and interprets) exists on the printed page or as a patient in a hospital bed or waiting room. Commenting on Kafka's masterpiece, *The Metamorphosis*, Stone (1990) compares it to patients the physician sees: "[This] story resists easy explanations and invites vigorous discussion. Its subtleties, its ambiguities, are not unlike those of our patients" (p. 67).

- *Reading literature is enjoyable.* Physician-playwright Lawrence Schneiderman has explained his commitment to reading literature in the following way:

"One of my favorite stories, which is true, is that Osler, no matter how late he went to bed, would read some work of literature for 10 minutes. This was in Cushing's biography, and I remember thinking, if Osler did it for 10 minutes, I should give myself half an hour. Every night throughout my internship, my residency, no matter how late I got home at night, another half hour's lack of sleep wouldn't matter [1987, p. 85]."

* This directory was initially compiled by Carol C. Donley and Martin Kohn for the third edition of *Behavior and Medicine*. The current directory includes their extensive recommendations along with additional readings and commentary by Dr. Schlozman.

Literature is a means of correcting the foreclosing of experience. What does one give up as a physician-in-training? Too often it is experiences in the world of everyday life, and the cultural richness of the humanities and fine arts. Reading literature moves us toward becoming more complete persons and toward recognizing our patients as whole persons—not simply as the bearers of medical problems.

Literature is a means of shaping professional identity. Professional identity is not something that remains fixed throughout one's career. The timely (occasional) chance to view one's life-as-a-physician from the vantage point of literature can lead, we believe, to more reflective and fulfilling practice, especially when a habit of reading is developed during the formative medical school years.

Creating the list that follows was no simple task. We chose to annotate primarily modern works that medical students have found interesting, accessible, and challenging yet not overwhelming for persons who often feel overburdened. Longer works are not excluded, but we have included only those we believe are most worthy of your time. The dates of publication are those of currently available texts (not necessarily the original date of publication). These works have been organized into the following categories:

• Selected works by Shakespeare
• Selected works of recognized modern authors
• Selected works of physician-authors (last half of the twentieth century)
• Selected works of prominent physician-writers of the late nineteenth, early twentieth century
• A selection of contemporary anthologies
• A selection of modern and contemporary drama addressing medical issues
• Medical bildungsroman
• Resources in the field of literature and medicine
• Resources exploring the relationship of popular culture to psychiatric and medical issues.

In addition to the annotated works, we have provided resource lists pertinent to the field of literature and medicine. We hope you find these useful as well.

Any selection process will result in the exclusion of a great deal of fine work. (*The Bibliography of Literature and Medicine* and *The Online Database of Literature, Arts, and Medicine,* which we heavily relied on, have thousands of entries.) Forgive us for our omissions; let us know about the "gems" you have found. Share them with a fellow student or teacher.

REFERENCES

Hawkins, A.H., & McEntyre, M.C. (2000). *Teaching literature and medicine.* New York: Modern Language Association.

Jones, A.H. (1990). Literature and medicine: Traditions and innovations. In B. Clarke & W. Aycock (Eds), *The body and the text.* Lubbock, TX: Texas Tech University Press.

Selzer, R., Stone, J., Schneiderman, L.J., & Borgenicht, L. (1987). Physician-writers in dialogue. In D. Wear, M. Kohn, & S. Stocker (Eds.), *Literature and medicine: A claim for a discipline.* McLean, VA: Society for Health and Human Values.

Stone, J. (1990). *In the country of hearts: Journeys in the art of medicine.* New York: Delacorte Press.

SHAKESPEARE

William Shakespeare is often credited with having captured all aspects of the human condition throughout his plays and sonnets. Indeed, the British school of acting often refers to specific Shakespearean characters as a means by which actors may understand the motivations for any roles they are asked to undertake. One play with a clear medical theme is *Richard III*, in which Richard's bodily disfigurement and his corresponding feelings of impotency and insecurity lead to tragic missteps in leadership and judgment. Similarly, Hamlet's famous contemplation of existential suicidality (to be or not to be ...) often serves as a catalyst for the discussion of suicidality in general, and King Lear's hubris and disappointment in his children can provoke an equally compelling discussion of family and interpersonal dynamics. Shakespeare's sonnets often mix suffering with resiliency, and offer a mechanism by which students can explore the factors that confer strength in the setting of medical and emotional challenges. Sonnet number 29 is an excellent example.

SELECTED WORKS OF RECOGNIZED MODERN AUTHORS

Barker, Pat. *Regeneration.* (1991).
This is the first of a trilogy of semifictional accounts describing the psychiatric treatment in Great Britain of soldiers during World War I. A central character is the poet, Siegfried Sasoon, who vigorously protests the war in a well-publicized letter to the Queen, but nevertheless continues as a soldier. The novels detail the ethical and medical issues that often characterize and are sometimes in conflict in the treatment of traumatized soldiers during times of war.

Broyard, A. *Intoxicated by my illness* (1992).
In intensively personal essays, literary critic and essayist for the *New York Times,* Anatole Broyard, chronicles his experiences and thoughts during his last months of life and does so with wit, insight, irony, and intelligence.

Camus, Albert. (1948). *The Plague.*
Set in Oran, Algeria in the late 1940s, this allegorical novel tells the

story of the town's fight against bubonic plague. The narrator, Dr. Bernard Rieux, is indefatigable in his efforts to eradicate this pestilence and is carried by his belief that there is more to admire in humankind than to despise. Metaphorically this novel presents the existential dilemma we all struggle with individually and communally in confronting our death—our attempt to find meaning in the face of the absurdity of our existence.

Carver, R. *Will You Please be Quiet, Please?* (1976); *What We Talk About When We Talk About Love* (1981); *Cathedral* (1983); *Where Water Comes Together With Other Water* (1985).

These are stories that present the lives of trapped people who often struggle with economic, marital, and personal failures and losses, though sometimes, as in "A Small Good Thing" (death of a child) and "Cathedral" (blindness), a spiritual healing does occur.

Chekhov, A. (See the section on nineteenth-century physician-writers.)

Chopin, K. *The awakening and other stories* (1981).

A remarkable early feminist, she was too frank for the early twentieth-century beliefs about women and how they should act, so her works were out of print for half a century, though now she is recognized as a major artist. Her female characters are caught between their own independent spirit and the restrictions of the culture in which they live.

Erdrich, L. *Tracks* (1988); *Love Medicine* (1993).

Faulkner, W. (See later citations.)

This is a Nobel prize-winning author whose focus on his Yoknapatawpha County, Mississippi becomes universalized as the characters work through archetypal problems. The character of Dr. Peabody appears in several works, including *As I Lay Dying* (1957), where he keeps a professional but wryly sympathetic distance from the backwoods family he serves. *The Sound and the Fury* (1959) portrays a family with a mentally retarded son (who narrates the first section), alcoholic father, hypochondriac mother, a son who commits suicide in college, and two other children who both suffer in their own ways from the family's dysfunction. In addition, many of Faulkner's short stories provide extremely evocative and compact explorations of human experience. *Barn Burning* is an excellent example, in which a young boy struggles with his competing loyalty toward his father and recognition of his father's significant and sociopathic flaws.

Garcia Marquez, G. *Love in the time of cholera* (1988), *The Leaf Storm* (1972).

This Nobel Prize winning author has brought a special blend of magic and realism to his portraits of Colombian people struggling with everyday issues of living, as well as more troubling problems such as plagues, insanity, stresses from political upheavals and guerilla war, foreign dominance, etc.

Gilman, C.P.S. *The yellow wallpaper* (1973).

This is a moving account of a woman's descent into madness. Her physician-husband, with the "best" of intentions, helps propel and keep her on this frightening journey. Her mad mission takes shape while she is forced to sleep in the nursery of their country house. She tries in vain to free the woman she believes is creeping behind the yellow wallpaper of that oppressive room.

Hemingway, E. (See later citations.)

Winner of the Nobel Prize, he is known for his heroes who demonstrate "grace under pressure" whether they are up against a bull or in a battle or hunting or fishing or enduring pain. His novels include *The Sun also Rises* (1926); *A Farewell to Arms* (1929); *To Have and Have*

Not (1937); *For Whom the Bell Tolls* (1940); and *The Old Man and the Sea* (1952). His short stories are collected in *Complete Stories* (1987). See especially "Indian Camp," "A Day's Wait," and "The Doctor and the Doctor's Wife."

Hurston, Zora Neale. *Their Eyes Were Watching God* (1937).

Ibsen, Henrik. (See the section on modern and contemporary drama.)

Irving, John. *The Cider House Rules* (1985).

A novel made into a successful movie, dealing with many issues of abortion, adoption, incest, and a drug-addicted physician, but a heart-warming story, nevertheless.

Jackson, Shirley. *We Have Always Lived in the Castle*. (1962). This chilling novel is written from the point of view of a very disturbed adolescent who is somehow strangely appealing and sympathetic to readers. The story often provokes a discussion of how one understands the experience of compassion for those who commit horrific acts in the setting of significant psychiatric distress.

Kafka, Franz. *The Metamorphosis* (1961). *In the Penal Colony* (1919). Gregor Samsa awakens one morning to discover that he has become a giant insect (a dung beetle). The story follows his and his family's reaction to this transformational event. Of particular interest metaphorically is the similarity of Gregor's plight to the effects of disease, disfigurement, and chronic illness on patients' self-understanding and interpersonal relations. The stories also explore some of the existential issues associated with the growing alienation that many associate with increasing modernity.

Krysl, Marilyn. *Midwife and Other Poems on Caring* (1989).

This is a result of 1 year the poet spent serving as artist-in-residence at the Center for Human Caring, University of Colorado Health Sciences Center, School of Nursing. It "provides a new language and a new voice for nursing's quest to seek alternative ways of being in relation to human caring and healing." *Soulskin* (1996).

Lorde, Audre. *The Cancer Journals* (1980).

This is a chronicle of breast cancer from diagnosis to recovery from an African-American-lesbian perspective. It offers many insights, including those on reconstruction and prostheses.

Malamud, Bernard. (See later citations.)

Malamud is a National Book Award winner, whose stories portray elderly and often insignificant Jews who become caught up in universal spiritual struggles. He is a writer of great compassion and understanding. We especially recommend his stories "Idiots First," "The Jewbird," and "The Mourners", found in *The Magic Barrel* (1958); *Idiots First* (1963); *Rembrandt's Hat* (1973), and *The Stories of Bernard Malamud* (1983). All of these are collections of short stories.

McPhee, John. *Heirs of General Practice* (1986). McPhee, an excellent essayist, discusses the birth of family medicine as a discrete discipline. His style is almost journalistic, as he explores many young physicians and their patients in rural New England.

O'Connor, Flannery. *The Complete Stories* (1971).

This book was winner of the National Book Award. O'Connor is a brilliant writer of the precariousness of human life, portrayed often with grotesque comedy and with violence in the midst of spiritual searches. O'Connor suffered and died of lupus. We especially recommend these stories: "Everything That Rises Must Converge," A Good Man is Hard to Find, "The Lame Shall Enter First," "Good Country People," and "Revelation."

Oe, Kenzaburo. *A Personal Matter* (1969) and *"Aghwee the Sky Monster"* (1977).

Also see the *New Yorker*, February 6, 1995, for a discussion of how his son's disability has influenced his work. Nobel Prize winner.

Olds, Sharon. *The Father* (1992).

An important contemporary poet, Olds captures the human conditions that deeply move us. Of all her work, *The Father* is especially worth reading because it examines the feelings of pain and joy she experienced in response to her father's illness and death.

Olsen, Tillie. *Tell Me a Riddle* (1989).

An elderly woman finally has found peace at home. Her husband wants to move to "the Haven." Buried beneath this current conflict are years of anger, frustration, struggles, and moments of love. A diagnosis of inoperable cancer in his wife, a diagnosis not revealed to her, compels the husband to take her for final visits to their children's homes. Many months later the wife realizes her fate yet finds some peace before death through the loving care of a granddaughter. Interestingly, Ms. Olsen did not start writing until very late in life. The very existence of her work allows a discussion of what moves people at different and important developmental stages.

Ondaatje, Michael. *The English Patient* (1992).

This was a Booker Prize winner and a stunning movie, both of which explore conflicts of loyalty, love ,and betrayal.

Plath, Sylvia. *The Bell Jar* (1966); *The Colossus* (1960); *Ariel* (poetry) (1965).

Autobiographical material serves as the source for *The Bell Jar,* the story of a young woman's troubling twentieth year. This year included several hospitalizations, suicide attempts, shock treatment, and other encounters with medical personnel, one of whom is her medical student boyfriend. The *Ariel* poems are especially powerful, intense, and painful; they document her obsessive concerns with her father and her personal struggles with depression. *The Bell Jar* is particularly evocative, often mentioned by adolescent patients and featured in more than one contemporary movie.

Pomerance, Bernard. (See the section on modern and contemporary drama.)

Sarton, May. *Halfway to Silence* (1980); *Anger* (1986); *At Seventy: A Journal* (1987); *After the Stroke* (1988); and *Recovering: A Journal* (1988).

Her journals and poetry describing the experiences of growing older, suffering a stroke and recovering, and living on her own have a strength and character that richly reward the reader.

Sexton, Anne. *The Complete Poems* (1981).

This offers some of the most excruciating poetry about mental illness and suicide. See especially poems originally collected under the titles *To Bedlam and Part Way Back* (1960) and *Live or Die* (1966).

Shaw, George Bernard. (See the section on modern and contemporary drama.)

Tolstoy, Leo. *The Death of Ivan Ilych* (1958). In *Tolstoy's Tales of Courage and Conflict.*

Ivan Ilych has led a "most simple and most ordinary and therefore most terrible" life. He realizes on his deathbed that his life, although lived in a proper and fashionable way, was lacking in meaning. As the story of illness and death unfolds, we meet a family who does not care for him and physicians who are concerned only about finding the cause of his illness. Only Gerasim, a naive peasant boy who comes to nurse Ivan Ilych, seems to respect him for his humanity. Out of the nightmare of his final 3 days Ivan Ilych does come to value his family over himself and is delivered from annihilation to a peaceful death.

Updike, John. (See later citations.)

Updike is a prolific author of many novels, including the *Rabbit* series, and several collections of short stories and poems. Updike captures the domestic scenes of families, sometimes together but often breaking up. We recommend a very interesting short story, "Journal of a Leper," [*The New Yorker, 52*(22), pp. 28–33, July 19, 1976] which documents the deterioration of character that occurs as a victim of skin disease is cured; the story is a study of the relationship between health and self-image.

Walker, Alice. (See later citations.)

Winner of the Pulitzer Prize for *The Color Purple* (1982), Walker's short stories are collected in *In Love And Trouble: Stories of Black Women* (1973) and in *You Can't Keep a Good Woman Down* (1982). Note especially her stories "Strong Horse Tea," "To Hell with Dying," and "Everyday Use." Her 1992 novel *Possessing the Secret of Joy* is about female circumcision and its effects on the health and happiness of the women involved.

Welty, Eudora. *The Collected Stories of Eudora Welty* (1980).

These stories are rooted in the South but are universal in their depiction of human issues and their sense of the extraordinary and symbolic. Welty has a wonderful sense of humor and a sense of the absurd. See especially "A Visit of Charity," "Petrified Man," "A Worn Path," and "A Wide Net."

Williams, William Carlos. (See the following section on recent physician authors.)

SELECTED WORKS OF PHYSICIAN-AUTHORS
(Last Half of the Twentieth Century)

Abse, Dannie. *One Legged on Ice* (1983); *View From Row G* (1990); *White Coat, Purple Coat: Collected Poems 1948–1988* (1991); *A Poet in the Family; A Strong Dose of Myself* (plays and autobiography).

Welsh physician-poet with a keen awareness of history and the large forces that shape human life, Abse is also acutely observant of the details under the stethoscope.

Beernink, Kenneth. *Ward Rounds* (1970).

This second edition was published after the death of the author, a young multitalented physician. The poems are about the patients he cared for and are arranged by the diseases they had.

Brody, Howard, *Healer's Power* (1992); *Stories of Sickness* (1987).

Canin, Ethan. *The Emperor of the Air* (1988) (short stories); *Blue River* (1991) (novel); *The Palace Thief* (1994); *For Kings and Planets* (1998).

Ethan Canin works in California as a doctor and at the Iowa Writers' Workshop as a member of the faculty. His stories and novels are tender and wise portraits of everyday people whose lives are not so ordinary as they seem at first glance.

Coulehan, Jack. *The Knitted Glove* (1991) (poetry). *First Photographs of Heaven* (1994).

This sensitive and caring poetry is often told from the perspective of the patient, including hostility and anger, as well as a sense of humor.

el Sadaawi, Nawal. *Woman at Point Zero* (1983); *The Hidden Face of Eve: Women in the Arab World* (1980).

This Egyptian novelist-physician was once Egypt's Director of Public Health, though her active support of women's intellectual and social freedom led to her being dismissed and eventually thrown in prison. Now in the United States, she devotes her time to writing and speaking on women's issues.

Feldshuh, David. *Miss Evers' Boys.*

An award-winning play about the Public Health Service funded Tuskegee study of untreated syphilis in black men. Though the play is being performed around the country, it has not been published in its final form. It raises many issues about racism and about conflict between government-sponsored medical research and patients' well-being.

Gonzales-Crussi, Frank. *Notes of an Anatomist* (1985); *Three forms of Sudden Death and Other Reflections on the Grandeur and Misery of the Body; On the Nature of Things Erotic* (1988); *Five Senses* (1989).

Groopman, Jerome. *The Measure of Our Days: New Beginnings At Life's End (1997).*

Beautifully written medical/spiritual memoirs of several cases of critical illness, some resolving in a life-changing recovery and others ending in death but with meaningful realizations along the way. One chapter was first printed in *The New Yorker*.

Hellerstein, David. *Battles of Life and Death* (1986) (essays); *Loving Touches* (1988) (novel); *A Family of Doctors* (1994).

Hilfiker, David. *Healing The Wounds: A Physician Looks at His Work* (1985) (autobiography). *Not All of Us are Saints,* (1994).

This is a man with a deep sense of service and extraordinary compassion for the down and out, the addicted, and street people.

Klass, Perri. *Recombinations* (1985); *Other Women ''s Children* (1990) (novels); *I am Having an Adventure* (1986) (short stories); *A Not Entirely Benign Procedure* (1987) (account of her experiences in medical school); *Baby Doctor: A Pediatrician's Training* (1992) (account of 3 years as intern and resident).

These thoughtful, often funny accounts of coping with pressure and sleeplessness describe the life of a mother-writer-physician as she grows in experience.

Massad, Stuart. *Doctors and Other Casualties* (1993).

Mates, Susan Onthank. *The Good Doctor* (1994). Won the 1994 John Simmons Short Fiction Award of the University of Iowa Press.

Nuland, Sherwin. *Medicine: The Art of Healing* (1992), *How We Die: Reflections on Life's Final Chapter* (1994). The latter won the National Book Award for nonfiction.

Percy, Walker. *The Moviegoer* (1961); *Love in the Ruins* (1971); *The Second Coming* (1980); *Lancelot* (1977); *The Thanatos Syndrome* (1987) (novels); *Lost in the Cosmos: the Last Self Help Book* (1984).

Winner of the National Book Award, Percy is known for his philosophical as well as medical examinations of mental illness, chronic illness, search for meaning—an informed existential exploration of the self. Dr. Tom More, protagonist of both *Love in the Ruins* and *The Thanatos Syndrome,* is "an old-fashioned physician of the soul."

Remen, Rachael Naomi. *Kitchen Table Wisdom (1996).*

Sacks, Oliver. *The Man Who Mistook His Wife For a Hat* (1987) (on the neurologically impaired); *Seeing Voices* (1989) (on the deaf); *Migraine* (1985); *Awakenings* (1990); *A Leg to Stand on* (1984); *An Anthropologist on Mars* (1995); *The Island of the Colorblind* (1997).

Case histories are presented in humane, thoughtful essays about patients and physicians confronting unusual predicaments. *Awakenings* became a popular movie.

Sams, Ferrol. *Run With the Horsemen* (1982); *Whisper of the River* (1984) (novels); *The Widow's Mite* (1987) (short stories).

Sams is a popular speaker and master storyteller.

Schneiderman, L.J. *Sea Nymphs by the Hour* (1972) (novel).

Schneiderman has also written numerous short stories and plays, not yet collected. See especially "Sequel " in *Confrontation,* spring/summer 1980.

Selzer, Richard. *Rituals of Surgery* (1987); *Mortal Lessons: Notes on the Art of Surgery; Taking the World in for Repairs* (1987); *Letters to a Young Doctor* (1983); *Confessions of a Knife* (1987) (collections of essays and short stories about medical practice); *Imagine a Woman* (1990) (short stories); *Down from Troy* (1992) (autobiography); *Raising the Dead* (1993).

These are especially well-written accounts of the physician as human—sometimes with a temper, sometimes not knowing what to do, often with extraordinary compassion.

Stone, John. *Smell of Matches* (1972); *In All This Rain* (1980); *Renaming the Streets* (1985) (poems); *In the Country of Hearts: Journeys in the Art of Medicine* (1990) (essays).

These are heartwarming (sometimes heartbreaking), insightful pictures of everything from teenage mothers to old diabetics.

Thomas, Lewis. *The Lives of a Cell: Notes of a Biology Watcher* (1975); *The Medusa and the Snail* (articles that appeared originally in *The New England Journal of Medicine*); *The Youngest Science: Notes of a Medicine Watcher* (1983); *Late Night Thoughts on Listening to Mahler's Ninth Symphony* (1983); *The Fragile Species* (1992).

These are meditations, prophesies, and celebrations of life on earth, with special attention to humane treatment of people and other living things, including the planet itself. There is concern with universal issues, as well as contemporary problems such as drug abuse and acquired immunodeficiency syndrome (AIDS).

Verghese, Abraham. *My Own Country: A Doctor's Story of a Town and Its People in the Age of AIDS* (1994).

As he works with several different patients dying of AIDS and the families and townspeople around them, the doctor tries to understand what it is like to suffer from this disease, what it is like to be gay, what people go through to protect their privacy, how people deal not only with impending death but with redefinitions of identity.

Williams, William Carlos. *The Autobiography of William Carlos Williams* (1951); *The Collected Poems of William Carlos Williams, Vol. 1 (1909–1939) and Vol. 2 (1939–1962); Paterson* (book-length poem); *The Doctor Stories* (1984), edited by Robert Coles.

Williams is one of America's major poets, ranked with Frost and Stevens. Several of his stories have become classics in medical education (see "The Use of Force" for a physician losing control and "Old Doc Rivers" for a physician addicted to drugs). Clear unsentimental short stories and poems comprise *The Doctor Stories*. Williams has the courage to present a doctor who dares to explore his subterranean thoughts and feelings, a doctor willing to admit and face his mistakes and errors of judgment. The introduction by Coles and the afterward by Williams' physician-son, William Eric Williams, also are good reading.

SELECTED WORKS OF PROMINENT PHYSICIAN-AUTHORS
(Late Nineteenth and Early Twentieth Century)

Bulgakov, Mikhail. *A Country Doctor's Notebook* (1975). First published in 1925–27.
> After graduating in 1916, Bulgakov practiced for about 10 years before giving up medicine for a career as a writer.

Chekhov, Anton (great Russian playwright and short story writer)
> Chekhov put himself through medical school by writing. His widely published major plays include *The Seagull* (1896); *Uncle Vanya* (1899); *The Three Sisters* (1901); and *The Cherry Orchard* (1904). His hundreds of short stories appear in various collections, including *Great Stories by Chekhov*. He is one of the most brilliant and influential writers of modern times.

Conan Doyle, Sir Arthur (English creator of Sherlock Holmes)
> Bantam Classics has published *Sherlock Holmes: The Complete Novels and Stories, Vols. I and II* where detective fans can find the case-solving exploits of the masterful Holmes and his partner, Dr. Watson. A number of the stories have medical themes. See also *Round the Red Lamp; Being Facts and Fancies of Medical Life,* Doyle's collection of stories about doctors.

Maugham, W. Somerset (English playwright, novelist, short story writer)
> Maugham drew on his medical experience for his first novel *Liza of Lambeth* (1936); major works include *Of Human Bondage* (1950) and *The Razor's Edge* (1944). The short stories, which include his best writing, are found in *Collected Short Stories* (1951).

Osler, Sir William.
> Osler is a masterful medical teacher who taught students to use "the patient as a text" and to get their medical education at the bedside. His 1889 valedictory address at the University of Pennsylvania is included in *Aequanimitas and Other Addresses To Medical Students, Nurses, and Practitioners of Medicine* (1932).

A SELECTION OF CONTEMPORARY ANTHOLOGIES

Davis, Cortney; and Shaefer, Judy; (Eds.). *Between the Heartbeats: Poetry and Prose by Nurses* (1995).

Donley, Carol; and Buckley, Sheryl (Eds.). *The Tyranny of the Normal: An Anthology* (1995); *What's Normal? Narratives of Mental and Emotional Disorders* (2000).
> These anthologies collect essays and fictional work about people outside physical and mental health norms: dwarfs, the disfigured, the obese or skeletal, the mentally ill or handicapped. Following the lead essay by Leslie Fiedler, they focus on the tyrannical social pressures to normalize (diets, growth hormones, plastic surgery, medications for behavior problems). Those who cannot be sufficiently normalized are ostracized or institutionalized.

Downie, Robin S. *The Healing Arts* (1994).

> Contains representations of healing from multiple genres including prose, poetry, essays, stories, music, paintings, and cartoons.

Hawkins, Anne Hunsaker; and Ballard, James O. *Time to Go: Three Plays on Death and Dying, With Commentary on End-Of-Life Issues* (1995).
> These plays were commissioned with the intent of their being used in a reader's theater style production/discussion format. Also included in this volume is information about advance directives.

Klein, Michael (Ed.) *Poets for Life* (1989).
> Subtitled "Seventy-six poets respond to AIDS," this important volume also includes a well-written introduction by the editor and other essays. "A valuable, enduring, and *useful* cultural document. It is a cry from the heart."

Kohn, Martin; Donley, Carol; and Wear, Delese (Eds.). *Literature and Aging: An Anthology* (1992).
> This is an extensive collection of stories, poems, and plays about aging primarily by modern North American authors of diverse backgrounds. It is organized around the themes of aging and identity, aging and love, aging and family, and aging and the community.

LaCombe, Michael A. *On Being a Doctor* (1995).
> A collection of prose and poetry written primarily by doctors. Many of the pieces first appeared in the column of the same name in the journal *Annals of Internal Medicine* during the period of 1990–1994.

Mukand, Jon (Ed.). *Articulations: The Body and Illness in Poetry* (1994).
> This is an extremely useful comprehensive collection of contemporary poetry about medicine compiled by a physician-poet. The works are divided into nine sections; "The Medical Environment," "Patients' Views of Illness," "Patients' Views of Doctors," "Physicians," "Family and Friends," "Women," "Mental Illness," "Disability," and "Social Issues." Each section is proceeded by a well-written essay.

Mukand, Jon (Ed.). *Vital Lines: Contemporary Fiction About Medicine* (1990).
> This is a valuable companion to his collection of poetry organized along similar themes.

Osborn, M. Elizabeth (Ed.). *The Way We Live Now* (1990).
> This book contains 10 plays of varying length and style about AIDS and an insightful essay by Michael Feingold, *The Village Voice* theater critic. "In this volume you will find a range of human possibilities as wide and complex as the reach of the epidemic itself—as is necessary if we mean to battle it." It includes one of the early AIDS plays, *AS IS*.

Reynolds, Richard,;Stone, John; Nixon, Lois LaCivita; and Wear, Delese (Eds.). *On Doctoring* (1991).
> Commissioned by the Robert Wood Johnson Foundation, this is an extensive and highly worthwhile collection of stories, essays, and poems intended to "help you realize the breadth and wonder of your chosen profession."

Sachs, Dan (Ed.) *Emergency Room* (1996).
> Contains short stories based in the emergency room exclusively by physician-writers including John Stone, Richard Selzer, David Feldshuh, Samuel Shem, and Perri Klass.

Secundy, Marian Gray; and Nixon, Lois LaCivita (Eds.). *Trials, Tribulations, and Celebrations: African-American Perspectives on Health, Illness, Aging, and Loss* (1992).
> This excellent collection is the first and, at the moment, only anthology of African-American stories and poems about health issues. It is

important reading for all health-care givers who work with black Americans as colleagues and patients.

Walker, Sue; and Ruffman, Rosaly. *Life on the Line: Selections on Words and Healing* (1992).
Included are the experiences of 228 writers of illness, disability, suffering and death, with such division topics as AIDS, abuse, rituals, and remedies.

Wear, Delese; and Kohn, Martin (Eds.). *Poetry: A Collection of Poems Written by Medical Students, 1983–1991.* (Vols. 1–3).
These are the works of the prize-winning medical student poets from the William Carlos Williams poetry competition, sponsored by the Northeastern Ohio Universities College of Medicine. Autobiographical sketches of the authors accompany their work.

Yalom, Irving. *Love's Executioner: and Other Tales of Psychotherapy.* Irving Yalom has written a series of sometimes fictional accounts of psychotherapy in which he discusses issues such as transference and countertransference in terms relevant to the practice of all of medicine.

A SELECTION OF MODERN AND CONTEMPORARY DRAMA ADDRESSING MEDICAL ISSUES

Beckett, Samuel. *Endgame* (1957); *Krapp's Last Tape* (1969); *Rockabye* (1980), and several other plays and novels.
This Nobel prize-winning playwright's work portrays people trying to find meaning, trying to make some sense out of their lives, and trying to figure out who they are and why they are on earth. *Endgame* has the parents of the leading character kept in garbage cans, a powerful metaphor. On his birthday, Krapp makes a tape and listens to previous entries of his recorded diary; reminiscences, especially of a love scene, prevent him from finishing his final tape. *Rockabye* is a haunting movement from life into death.

Edson, Margaret. *W;t* (1995).
This play won the 1999 Pulitzer Prize. English scholar of Donne's "Holy Sonnets" finds, as she is dying of ovarian cancer, that her intellectual brilliance and aloofness dot not help her much nor does her role as research subject who must endure the full eight courses of chemotherapy, which will produce good research data but won't improve her chances to live.

Ibsen, Henrik. *An Enemy of the People* (1977).
A medical officer who has responsibility for the town's municipal baths discovers the water is contaminated. His zeal in trying to prevent harm to bathers is resented by the townspeople and local authorities, including his brother, who is mayor. They want to protect the economic interests of the town, which depends on tourists who visit their health spa. The doctor's absolutist stand to close the baths earns him the designation of an enemy of the people. Other widely published plays of particular interest include *The Wild Duck* (themes of figurative and literal blindness) and *Ghosts* (themes of the effects of venereal disease on the family).

Kopit, Arthur. *Wings* (1978).
This is a carefully researched play about a woman living through and with aphasia that was brought on by a stroke. The title is derived from the main character's early life exploits as an airplane wing-walker.

Kushner, Tony. *Angels in America* (1992, 1993).
Winner of the Tony Award and the Pulitzer Prize, *Angels in America* is recognized as a major American play, with themes of AIDS, religious and racial conflict, politics, and through it all, a compassionate moral vision.

McPherson, Scott. *Marvin's Room* (1992).
This is a sensitive and often funny portrait of a caregiver who tries to take care of a father who has had a stroke and a senile aunt, only to discover that she herself has leukemia. It has good insights into the issues of caregiving, including family avoidance of responsibility.

Nichols, Peter. *A Day in the Death of Joe Egg* (1967).
Parents of a severely handicapped daughter try to keep going and keep their marriage alive, but the hopeless, endless caregiving for their little "vegetable" breaks them apart.

Norman, Marsha. *'Night, Mother.* (1983).
This is a prize-winning play concerning an epileptic's decision to kill herself; a relentless and inevitable momentum propels her toward suicide as she and her mother face each other with honesty.

O'Neill, Eugene. *Long Day's Journey Into Night* (1956).
Drug addiction, tuberculosis, and alcoholism affect the members of the family portrayed in this drama. Their physical suffering is overlaid with the psychological suffering they inflict on one another. It is an autobiographical portrait.

Pomerance, Bernard. *The Elephant Man* (1979).
This is one of the most interesting and challenging recent plays about the inevitable mixture of harm and help physicians bring their patients. This play raises many questions about motivations for caring for patients, including questions of money and ego.

Shaffer, Peter. *Equus* (1973).
This is a prize-winning play about a psychiatrist "curing" a disturbed young man and making him "normal," or at least safe for the people and horses around him, but at a price that causes the doctor much concern. It is as much a study of the doctor as it is of the boy.

Shaw, George Bernard. *The Doctor's Dilemma* (1954).
The preface to this play is as important to read as the play itself. In it Shaw claims that all professions are conspiracies against the laity. He also proposes a public health system. The dilemma in the play, which features satiric characterizations of various types of physicians, revolves around the distribution of a limited resource, in this case a treatment for tuberculosis. Will it go to a poor but morally worthy fellow physician, or to an immoral but brilliant artist who is married to a very attractive (soon to be widowed) woman?

Vonnegut, Jr., Kurt. *Fortitude* (1968).
In this farcical play, a take-off on the novel *Frankenstein,* a plot reversal occurs: Dr. Frankenstein will *not* let his creation (a perplexed elderly billionaire's widow who is hooked up to numerous artificial organs) die. Important questions about the patient-physician relationship, quality of life, the ambition of medical researchers, and immortality are raised through off-beat humor.

West, Cheryl. *Before It Hits Home* (1993).
This play follows the life of Wendal Bailey, an African-American man who is bisexual and has contracted AIDS. The nature of his relation-

ship with his lovers and his family in light of his diagnosis is the focus of this play.

Williams, Tennessee. *The Glass Menagerie* (1945); *A Streetcar Named Desire* (1947); *Cat on a Hot Tin Roof* (1955).

Williams is a Pulitzer-Prize winner whose work portrays damaged people, often mentally disturbed or living in illusions, who cannot seem to cope with reality. *The Glass Menagerie* portrays a woman whose husband has left her; she tries to console herself through hopes of a suitor for her crippled daughter. *Streetcar Named Desire* centers around the contrasting lives of sisters Blanche and Stella Dubois. Blanche lives in a world of illusion, unable to cope with the loss of the family plantation. The seductive Blanche eventually is raped by Stella's husband Stanley. Both sisters avoid reality, Stella through denial, Blanche through insanity. Intrafamilial conflict is also at the heart of *Cat on a Hot Tin Roof*. Deception ("mendacity") is the way in which the family members operate. The family patriarch's attention and money are coveted by his wife, sons, and daughters-in-law. This becomes even more important as they (and he) discover he is dying of cancer.

MEDICAL BILDUNGSROMAN

This list of selected works includes fiction and nonfiction accounts of medical school and residency education. These "coming into the adult world" literary works vary considerably in quality. (We appreciate the contributions of Suzanne Poirier, Ph. D., University of Illinois College of Medicine, Chicago, and Anne Hudson Jones, Ph. D., The University of Texas Medical Branch at Galveston.)

Cook, Robin. *The Year of the Intern* (1972).

Crichton, Michael. *Five Patients: The Hospital Explained* (1970).

Doctor X. *Intern* (1965).

Douglas, Colin. *The Intern's Tale* (1975).

el Saadawi, Nawal. *Memoirs of a Woman Doctor* (1957).

Gordon, Richard. *Doctor in the House* (1961).

Greenbaum, Dorothy; and Larkin, Diedre S. *Lovestrong: A Woman Doctor's True Story of Marriage and Medicine* (1984).

Harrison, Michelle. *A Woman in Residence: A Doctor's Personal and Professional Battles Against an Insensitive Medical System* (1982).

Haseltineaa, Florence; and Yew, Yvonne. *Woman Doctor* (1976).

Hejinian, J. *Extreme Remedies* (1974).

Hellerstein, David. *Battles of Life and Death* (1986).

Hoffman, Stephen A. *Under the Ether Dome: A Physician's Apprenticeship at Massachusetts General Hospital* (1986).

Klass, Perri. *A Not Entirely Benign Procedure: Four Years as a Medical Student* (1987).

Klein, Kenneth. *Getting Better: A Medical Student's Story* (1981).

Konner, Melvin. *Becoming a Doctor: A Journey Through Medical School* (1987).

LeBaron, Charles. *Gentle Vengeance: An Account of the First Year at Harvard Medical School* (1981).

Marion, Robert. *The Intern Blues: The Private Ordeals of Three Young Doctors* (1989).

Massad, Stewart. *Doctors and Other Casualties* (1993).

Morgan, Elizabeth. *The Making of a Woman Surgeon* (1980).

Mullan, Fitzhugh. *White Coat, Clenched Fist: The Political Education of an American Physician* (1976).

Nolan, William. *The Making of a Surgeon* (1968).

Patterson, Jane; and Madaras, Lynda. *Women/Doctor: The Education of Jane Patterson, M. D.* (1983).

Pekkanen, John. *M.D.: Doctors Talk About Themselves* (1988).

Ravin, Neil. *M. D.* (1981).

Reilly, Philip. *To Do No Harm: A Journey Through Medical School* (1987).

Scalia, Joni. *The Cutting Edge* (1978).

Shem, Samuel. *The House of God* (1978).

RESOURCES IN THE FIELD OF LITERATURE AND MEDICINE

Database

On-line database of literature, arts, and medicine, (Felice Aull et al., Eds.), electronic editions published bi-monthly, available at a Web site: http://endeavor.med.nyu.edu/lit-med/medhum.html.

This is the fastest growing, most complete annotated bibliography for literature and medicine with nearly 1000 literature annotations representing the work of about 500 authors, searchable through more than 130 keywords. It also has the sections on art and film annotations. A wonderful resource.

Books

Brody, Howard. *Stories of Sickness* (1987).

This book is written by a physician-philosopher who stresses the importance of narrative and story in patient care, especially in regard to the ethical aspects of that care. Many literary sources are cited throughout this work.

Coles, Robert. *The Call of Stories* (1989).

A world-renowned psychiatrist and medical educator reveals how stories have shaped his life and how he uses literature in his teaching. Subtitled *Teaching and the Moral Imagination,* it includes a chapter entitled "Bringing Poems to Medical School Teaching."

Frank, Arthur W. *The Wounded Storyteller* (1995). Also the author of *At the Will of the Body* (1991).

Frank writes from his own experience of illness, which, in turn, has been influenced by his work as a sociologist, and his scholarly interest in embodiment, narrative, and postmodernism.

Hunter, Kathryn. *Doctors' Stories: The Narrative Structure of Medical Knowledge* (1991).

The emphasis here is on medicine as the art of interpreting a story, including the patient's telling of it and of the symptoms and of the physician's creation of a narrative to describe the case.

Nelson, Hilde; and James Lindemann. *The Patient in the Family: An Ethics of Medicine and Families.* (1995).

This is a thought-provoking critique of current dogmas that limit medical ethics to doctor-patient relationships. Medicine is altering the structure of families; families are challenging the autonomy of physicians and patients. The text includes many interesting cases.

Nelson, Hilde Lindemann. *Stories and Their Limits: Narrative Approaches* (1997).

This collects several thought-provoking papers given at the spring conference of the Society for Health and Human Values, held at the University of Tennessee at Knoxville (1996). Most of the papers are authored by major figures in bioethics and in literature and medicine.

Trautmann, Joanne; and Pollard, Carol. *Literature and Medicine: An Annotated Bibliography* (1982).

This is an invaluable resource for the field. Works are organized chronologically, and topical areas such as age, madness, grief, homosexuality, and women as healers are suggested for each entry.

Wear, Delese; and Nixon, Lois LaCivita. *Literary Anatomies: Women's Bodies and Health in Literature* (1993).

Journals and Organizations

Art and Understanding.

It is published six times per year by Art and Understanding, Inc., a not-for-profit organization in Albany, NY. It is an "international magazine of literature and art about AIDS."

Humane Medicine.

It is published quarterly by the Canadian Medical Association, "a journal of the art of healing."

Journal of Medical Humanities.

It is "dedicated to the multidisciplinary consideration of medicine from the perspective of the humanities and bioethics," and is published by Human Sciences Press, Inc. It includes articles pertinent to literature and medicine and occasionally imaginative literature as well.

Kaleidoscope.

This is an international magazine published semiannually (since 1979) by United Disability Services, Akron, OH. It "explores the experiences of disability through creative writing and the arts."

Literature and Medicine.

An annual volume that began in 1982, it became a semiannual publication in 1992. It is the primary scholarly journal in the field and is published by Johns Hopkins University Press.

Medical Humanities Review.

This is a semiannual review of publications in the medical humanities and is published by the Institute for the Medical Humanities, the University of Texas Medical Branch at Galveston. It includes work pertinent to literature and medicine.

Mediphors.

This is a literary journal of the health professions, publishing fiction, poetry, art, and photography pertaining to health care. It is published by *Mediphors*, Box 327, Bloomsburgh, PA, 17815.

PWAC NY NEWSLINE.

This is published by People with AIDS Coalition of New York, Inc. It regularly features literature and personal stories by and about people with AIDS.

Society for Health and Human Values. Newsletter: *Of Value.*

Now beginning its twenty-fifth year, this international interdisciplinary organization is dedicated to humanities and human values related to health care and the education of health-care professionals. Its members include practicing health-care professionals, scholars, teachers, health-care policy developers and students in these areas, as well as ministers, lawyers, and others with an interest in the society.

The *Society for Health and Human Values* (SHHV), the *Society for Bioethics Consultation* (SBC), and the *American Association of Bioethics* (AAB) voted in 1997 to consolidate into a new organization: the *American Society for Bioethics and Humanities* (ASBH). ASBH is a multidisciplinary organization of health-care professionals, teachers, consultants, and others who have an interest in clinical and academic biomedical humanities. The website is www.asbh. org.

Columns in Medical Journals

A growing number of medical journals, including *Journal of the American Medical Association* ("A Piece of My Mind," "Poetry and Medicine"), *Annals of Internal Medicine* ("On Being a Doctor"), *Annals of Emergency Medicine* ("Change of Shift"), and *The American Journal of Medicine* ("Reading for Survival"), are featuring creative work and essays by physicians and medical students. *Academic Medicine* offers commentary on literary works used in medical education through its "furthermore ..." column. The *Journal of Family Practice* has just introduced a column on "The Art of Medicine." Note that many of these essays have been anthologized as published collections.

Medical School Literary and Arts Publications

A number of medical schools publish literary and other artistic works of students, as well as those of faculty and staff. These efforts include *Wild Onions* from Pennsylvania State University College of Medicine at Hershey; *Auscult* from the University of Wisconsin College of Medicine; *Body Electric* from the University of Illinois College of Medicine, Chicago; *Medical Muse* from the University of New Mexico School of Medicine; *Tapas* from St. Louis University School of Medicine; and *Quill and Scalpel* from Johns Hopkins University School of Medicine. Northeastern Ohio Universities College of Medicine has published three volumes of medical student poetry (see the section on Contemporary Anthologies).

Resources exploring the relationship of popular culture and medical and psychiatric issues include the Media Column in *Academic Psychiatry*, in which psychiatric and social manifestations of cultural phenomena such as professional wrestling, popular music, contemporary television, and daytime talk shows are explored. Glenn Gabbard and Krin Gabbard have written a fascinating discussion of current cinema, exploring the psychodynamic aspects of different movie genres in their appropriately titled book, *Psychiatry and the Cinema*. Similarly, the recently published media issue of *Child and Adolescent Psychiatric Clinics of North America*, edited by Eugene Beresin and Cheryl Olson, discusses the interplay of internet, video, music, and television in the psychological lives of young people.

Appendix D
USMLE Practice Questions

Chapter 1: Mind, Brain, and Behavior

1. A young woman has just been told that there is a mass in one of her breasts which may be malignant. Which of the following brain processes is most likely to be impaired as she listens to the explanation of the physician?
   a. Implicit memory
   b. Encoding and storage of memory
   c. Retrieval of memory
   d. Short-term memory
   e. Long-term memory

2. The presence of mirror neurons in the brain enables people to do which of the following?
   a. Conceptualize spatial images as they would be in reverse
   b. Create empathy by feeling what another person is feeling
   c. Make maps of the internal intentional state of another person's mind
   d. Reflect back to someone else how they appear to others
   e. Connect across the two hemispheres of the brain

3. Which of the following is true about implicit memory?
   a. It does not require conscious, focal attention to be encoded
   b. It requires the hippocampus to be activated
   c. It includes autobiographical memory
   d. It becomes available in the second year of life
   e. It is remembered in narrative form

4. Talking about an overwhelming feeling is a common type of treatment for emotional distress. Which of the following best describes why this would help the patient regulate his internal state?
   a. Talking distracts the patient from the overwhelming feelings
   b. Talking activates implicit memory

   c. Talking allows the therapist to connect with the patient emotionally
   d. Talking shuts down activation of the right hemisphere
   e. Talking allows activation of the left hemisphere

Chapter 2: Families, Relationships, and Health

1. A 17-year-old unmarried girl is brought to the clinic by her older sister. They suspect the adolescent is pregnant, and are requesting a pregnancy test. Which of the following is true?
   a. The girl cannot be seen or examined because her parents are not with her to give permission
   b. The parents of the girl must be contacted immediately
   c. The girl can be seen, but abortion or contraception cannot be discussed with her
   d. The girl must give permission before anything is discussed with the sister
   e. The girl's boyfriend must be contacted before any testing is done

2. A young man who is a cancer survivor states that the cancer experience has given him a better sense of what is important in life. This is an example of
   a. Posttraumatic stress
   b. Denial
   c. Posttraumatic growth
   d. Identification with the aggressor
   e. Projection

3. Which of the following is the best statement about the proven impact on the clinical course of a person with schizophrenia of a family member who has high levels of expressed emotion, because they are deeply emotional involved and very critical of the patient?
   a. The patient needs more medication
   b. The patient has fewer relapses

c. The patient needs less medication

d. The patient is more likely to be paranoid

e. The patient is more likely to be withdrawn

4. The two distinct components of emotional support for patients which have been found to be related to religion or spirituality are best described as
   a. Inner peace and meditation
   b. Social support and personal faith
   c. Denial and rationalization
   d. Ritual and dogma
   e. Charismatic leader and social norms

4. Which of the following is the best statement about the concept of temperament?
   a. It is a set of inborn traits that organize the child's approach to the world
   b. It is the environmentally determined way a child responds to the world
   c. It is the term used to describe how a child manages aggression and anger
   d. It is the term used to describe personality in children
   e. It is the term used to describe how anxious or depressed a child is

Chapter 3: Birth, Childhood, and Adolescence

1. A three-year-old child is brought in for a screening physical examination prior to starting pre-school. Which of the following would be considered developmentally inappropriate for a child of this age?
   a. The child throws a temper tantrum when she cannot get a toy she wants
   b. The child is afraid of sitting on toilet, as she fears she will get flushed
   c. She sometimes has "accidents" with her urine and feces
   d. Her articulation makes her speech sometimes difficult to understand
   e. She has a vocabulary of about 10 words

2. Which of the following is a true statement about puberty?
   a. Puberty happens earlier in boys than girls
   b. Early puberty is more of a social problem for boys than girls
   c. Breast buds and testicular enlargement can start as early as age 9
   d. Pubertal changes occur over a period of 3 to 6 months
   e. Puberty does not start until after the growth spurt

3. A 14 month old child is hospitalized with "failure to thrive." Which of the following is the best statement as to what this diagnosis means?
   a. The child is unhappy although the family situation is good
   b. The child is small for age without any major medical diagnosis
   c. The child has multiple organ failure
   d. The child is being abused and is withdrawn
   e. The child is anxious and will cry when separated from mother

Chapter 4: Early Adulthood and the Middle Years

1. Which of the following is a true statement about sexual infidelity leading to divorce?
   a. About 60% of the husbands have been unfaithful to their wives
   b. About 60% of the wives have been unfaithful to their husbands
   c. Most of the sexual infidelity is the result of sexual dysfunction
   d. The risk of sexual infidelity is decreased by birth of a child
   e. The risk of sexual infidelity is decreased by retirement

2. Triangulation in a family relationship is best explained by which of the following descriptions?
   a. A child pitting his or her parents against each other to get his own way
   b. Use of a third person to avoid direct confrontation between two people
   c. Use of the family to avoid dealing with issues at work
   d. Use of work to avoid being with a spouse or children
   e. Struggle between two parents over who is closest to a child

3. Which of the following is true about women working outside the home compared to homemakers?
   a. Divorce rates have decreased as more women have entered the work force
   b. Career-oriented women are more likely to marry
   c. Working women report worse mental and emotional health
   d. The risk of divorce increases with the amount of the woman's income
   e. The risk of divorce decreases with the amount of the woman's income

4. According to Erikson, a key developmental issue of young adulthood is best characterized by which of the following?
   a. Making a contribution to the world
   b. Making an impression on the next generation
   c. Achieving the capacity for intimacy
   d. Becoming close to his or her family of origin
   e. Dealing with financial concerns

Chapter 5: Old Age

1. Which of the following is a true statement about changes in brain function and structure associated with "normal" aging?
   a. Decrease in cerebral spinal fluid
   b. Decrease in communication skills
   c. Decrease in brain volume
   d. Decrease in ventricular size
   e. Decrease in primary and tertiary memory

2. Living situations for older people in which housing and meals are provided along with help with everyday living activities and transportation are called which of the following?
   a. Board and care
   b. Assisted living
   c. Elder hostels
   d. Nursing homes
   e. Retirement homes

3. Which of the following best describes the responsibility of the physician regarding driving by elderly patients?
   a. Identify those persons who may be unsafe to drive
   b. Tell patients to stop driving when they are over 85
   c. Determine driving competency
   d. Keep patients independently driving as long as possible
   e. Tell patients to stop driving when they are over 75

4. Which of the following is a true statement about psychiatric illness in the elderly?
   a. New onset of schizophrenia does not happen after age 60
   b. Psychotherapy is not useful for treatment of psychiatric illness in people over 60
   c. Antipsychotic medications are the best treatment for behavioral problems in people over 60
   d. Suicide rates are very high among the elderly compared to other age groups
   e. Most people are at least mildly demented by the time they are 70

Chapter 6: Death, Dying and Grief

1. During a routine physical examination, a healthy 13-year-old boy asks his pediatrician "How likely is it for a kid my age to commit suicide?" Which of the following is the best clinical response?
   a. Answer factually that suicide is the third leading cause of death in the 10- to 14-year age range
   b. Ask if he is depressed or suicidal
   c. Ask an open-ended question to get more information about the impetus for the question
   d. Point out that this is a peculiar question for someone who is just entering adolescence
   e. Answer factually, offer to talk about the issue more if the boy wants, and then arrange to discuss you concerns with his parents

2. A 34-year-old woman recently diagnosed with an astrocytoma appears quite cheerful despite the poor prognosis of her tumor. When told the location of the tumor makes surgical resection impossible, she appears unaffected. Using the typology of Kubler-Ross's stages of dying, which of the following is the most likely stage of this patient?
   a. Anger
   b. Denial
   c. Bargaining
   d. Depression
   e. Acceptance

3. A young woman is concerned about her 68-year-old father, who recently lost his wife to lung cancer. Based on the literature on bereavement, which of the following is the most accurate statement about the implications of this stress on the father's health?
   a. He is at greater risk for psychiatric problems, but not medical illness
   b. He is at greater risk for death of all causes
   c. He is greater risk for lung cancer, given the exposure to his wife's illness
   d. He is likely to become noncompliant with treatment of his own illnesses
   e. He is at no greater risk of illness on the basis of his loss

4. A 58-year-old man with end stage liver disease states that he is not interested in pursuing a liver transplant, as he says "I have lived long enough, and others need the transplant more than me." Which of the following is the best clinical response to this statement?
   a. Treat him for depression as he is clearly suicidal
   b. Tell him he owes it to his family to have the liver transplant
   c. Have him psychiatrically evaluated for suicidality

d. Assess whether he understand the options and consequences

e. Document that he has made a decision, and take him off the list

Chapter 7: Chronic Benign Pain

1. Which of the following is true regarding behavioral approaches to treatment of chronic pain?
   a. Patients' spouses are rarely involved in the treatments
   b. These methods emphasize reductions in verbal pain behavior
   c. These methods focus on short-term benefit
   d. These methods focus on regaining function
   e. These methods ignore nonverbal pain behavior

2. Which of the following is the most accurate statement about factors contributing to chronic pain behavior?
   a. Dramatic pain behavior indicates influence of operant factors
   b. Observed behavior is consistent with 'self-report of behavior
   c. Behavior is influenced by both positive and negative reinforcement
   d. Functional disability is directly related to pain intensity
   e. Behavior is consistent with conscious motivation and goals

3. Which of the following is the best description of the usual psychological status of patients with chronic benign pain?
   a. They are exaggerating the pain to gain attention or financial rewards
   b. They have histories of sexual or physical abuse or trauma
   c. They suffer from depression before the onset of pain
   d. They have histories of aggression and perpetrators of physical abuse
   e. They are underachievers and lazy

4. Which of the following is a true statement concerning behavioral treatments for chronic pain?
   a. Treatment can be done by people with very limited training
   b. Patients are taught that pain is primarily psychological, not physical
   c. Patients are taught that pain is primarily physical, not psychological
   d. Patients are taught that pain medication is dangerous
   e. Patients are taught to return to work or school

Chapter 8: Stress and Illness

1. Homeostasis is best defined as which of the following?
   a. A state of activation in response to stress
   b. The tendency for the body to maintain an optimal state
   c. The ability of the body to convert food into energy
   d. A developmental stage in males
   e. A state of relaxation following intense exertion

2. The chronic sympathetic nervous system activation which characterizes a stress response triggers the release of glucocorticoids into the blood, resulting in which of the following?
   a. Decreased angiogenesis
   b. An autoimmune condition
   c. Suppression of the immune system
   d. Proliferation of killer T cells
   e. Increased peripheral blood glucose levels

3. A 35-year-old man has decided to quite his pack a day cigarette smoking, to help his chronic bronchial distress. Despite a nicotine patch, he finds he has cravings after each meal, during coffee breaks, and at social gatherings. Which of the following best explains these episodic cravings?
   a. A genetic predisposition to nicotine addiction
   b. Avoidance of nicotine withdrawal symptoms reinforces smoking
   c. Nicotine cravings conditioned to cue situations
   d. Culturally reinforced smoking behavior
   e. Modeling of smoking behavior by his parents when he was young

4. Which of the following characteristics of what has been called a Type A behavior pattern is most closely associated with coronary artery disease?
   a. Time urgency
   b. Competitiveness
   c. Impatience
   d. Hostility
   e. Perfectionism

Chapter 9: Addiction

1. An 18-year-old man presents to the clinic requesting treatment for cocaine abuse. Which of the following is the best evidence-based treatment for cocaine abuse?
   a. Modafinil
   b. Cognitive behavioral therapy
   c. Naltrexone
   d. Insight-oriented psychotherapy
   e. Bupropion

2. Which of the following drugs of abuse has been found to be associated with the most profound changes to dopamine and serotonin systems?
   a. Cocaine
   b. Nicotine
   c. Methamphetamine
   d. Alcohol
   e. Marijuana

3. Acute withdrawal from which of the following substances of abuse can be fatal?
   a. Alcohol
   b. Heroin
   c. Oxycodone
   d. Methamphetamine
   e. Cocaine

4. A 22-year-old married woman approaches her gynecologist about preparation for her first pregnancy. Abstinence from which of the following drugs of abuse is most important to discuss with her to prevent birth defects in her baby?
   a. Cocaine
   b. Nicotine
   c. Barbiturates
   d. Benzodiazepines
   e. Alcohol

Chapter 10: Psychodynamic Approaches to Human Behavior

1. A physician has just told a patient that he has liver cancer. In response to a question from the patient concerning his prognosis and treatment, the physician launches into a lengthy and highly technical discussion of age-corrected mortality rates and double-blind studies of chemotherapy. Which of the following is the defense mechanism this physician appears to be using?
   a. Intellectualization
   b. Displacement
   c. Projection
   d. Repression
   e. Regression

2. According to psychodynamic theory, which of the following is a superego function?
   a. Reality testing
   b. Hostile impulses
   c. Conscience
   d. Problem-solving
   e. Defense mechanisms

3. A medical student makes a conscious effort to temporarily set aside his marital difficulties to study for the next examination. This is an example of which of the following?
   a. Undoing
   b. Denial
   c. Sublimation
   d. Turning against self
   e. Suppression

4. A patient is angry at his physician for being late for an appointment, but is not comfortable confronting her directly. Instead, he tells the physician how angry he was with a colleague earlier in the day while the colleague kept him waiting while he met with another employee. This is an example of which of the following defense mechanisms?
   a. Reaction formation
   b. Repression
   c. Identification
   d. Displacement
   e. Fixation

Chapter 11: Facilitating Health Behavior Change

1. Which of the following best describes the role of physicians in relation to facilitating health behavior change in patients?
   a. Physicians diagnose and treat illness, not behavior
   b. Physicians provide information about the impact of health behavior
   c. Physicians require compliance with health behavior plans
   d. Physicians help patients find motivation to change
   e. Physicians tell patients what they need to do

2. Which of the following is the best description of the response to proposed behavior change of patients in the *preparation stage* according to the Transtheoretical Model?
   a. Tend to resist any proposed behavior change
   b. Require the most commitment to change in terms of time and energy
   c. Do not plan to change their behavior in the next 6 months
   d. Have not yet resolved their ambivalence toward changing
   e. Need the physician to tell them what to do next

3. The health-care provider's role in Motivation Interviewing is best described as which of the following?
   a. Invite the patient to consider new information and offer new perspectives
   b. Inform the patient of the best course of action
   c. Refrain from discussing health behavior change with the patient
   d. Make sure the patient knows how dangerous their current behavior is
   e. Bring in others to confront the patient with the need to change

4. Which of the following is a major goal of Motivational Interviewing?
   a. Argue with patients until they are convinced to change their behavior
   b. Increase the patient's confidence in their ability to achieve change
   c. Convince the patient the doctor is an authority and should be listened to
   d. Frighten the patients with the possible consequences of their actions
   e. Identify the people who can confront the patient with the need to change

Chapter 12: Human Sexuality

1. A 35-year-old man has come to the outpatient medicine clinic for an "executive physical" for his new job in management at a large advertising company. He was married six months ago. As part of the thorough history he states that he has been having problems with ejaculation almost immediately after vaginal penetration. His wife has been very frustrated by this, and has pleaded with him to get some help. Which of the following is a true statement to use in advising this man about his problem?
   a. Psychological issues are the primary cause in the majority of such cases
   b. This is a rare problem, occurring in less than 5% of men
   c. One useful approach to this problem is the "squeeze" technique
   d. This normal at this stage of the marriage, and needs no treatment
   e. There is nothing that can be done, so his wife needs to live with it

2. Which of the following statements is true in the assessment of an adult man with erectile dysfunction?
   a. If he has erections in the morning, the problem is purely psychological
   b. Serum prolactin and testosterone levels will help determine the etiology
   c. Viewing erections as a contest will help him achieve an erection
   d. Use of alcohol or nicotine will improve his performance
   e. There is no effective treatment for this problem

3. Which of the following is true with regard to vaginismus?
   a. Treatment is rarely effective
   b. It is caused by voluntary contraction of the pubococcygeus muscle
   c. It is the result of sexual abuse or rape
   d. More than half of the women with vaginismus have had dyspareunia
   e. It indicates that the woman really does not like her sexual partner

4. A 22-year-old woman comes to her gynecologist at her husband's urging. She has recently admitted to him that she find intercourse painful, and he thinks there must be something wrong with her. Which of the following is the best first response to this young woman?
   a. Reassure her that intercourse should not be painful, and there are things that can be done to help her
   b. Tell her that this kind of problem is almost never anatomical, and recommend that she seek marital counseling
   c. Advise her that this is usually the result of a current or past vaginal infections, and start asking about the number of past sexual partners
   d. Counsel her that pain on intercourse usually reflects experience with sexual abuse, and ask her if her father molested her as a child
   e. Assure her that intercourse should not be painful, that her husband must not be doing it right, and suggest sex therapy

Chapter 13: Medical Student and Physician Well-Being

1. A third year medical student is holding a retractor in the operating room during surgery. She observes that one of the surgical residents is repeatedly making sexual comments to a fourth year student who is also in the OR. The other student appears very uncomfortable, but is not saying anything. Which of the following is the most useful approach to this situation?
   a. Speak with the other student afterward and offer to help speak with the attending about the resident
   b. Speak with the other student afterward and commiserate about the sexualized culture of surgery
   c. Join in the sexual joking with the resident, to distract attention from the other student

d. Speak up immediately, and angrily tell the resident that this is inappropriate behavior

e. Immediately report the resident to the Chairman of Surgery

2. While on his Obstetrics and Gynecology clerkship, a third year medical student is told to help the attending with a procedure. Once in the room, the student realizes that the procedure is a second trimester surgical abortion. He is a deeply religious Catholic, and is horrified that he is expected to participate in something he views as murder. Which of the following is the best approach to this situation?

a. Participate, and then report the attending for power abuse

b. Ask to observe rather than participate

c. Ask to be excused, and briefly explain why

d. Participate and make arrangements so it does not happen again

e. Reconsider the choice to become a physician

3. A first year medical student finds himself struggling as he prepares for his first examination in medical school. He has always had trouble with multiple choice question exams, but has been able to do well in college because he spent a lot of time studying, and it was always clear what the teachers wanted you to know. Now he feels that the amount of material is overwhelming, and the sample exam questions take too long for him to read to complete a test in the time allotted. Which of the following is the best approach for this student?

a. Do the best he can, and be ready to drop out if he fails the exam

b. Do the best he can on the exam, and seek help if he fails

c. Contact the Dean's office or Office of Disabilities for help

d. Find out from the professors exactly what will be on the exam

e. Reconsider the choice to become a physician

4. Two second year medical students who are in a small learning group together notice alcohol on the breath of another student in the group. Thinking about the student together, they realize she has been late to class a lot recently, appears irritable, and has lost a lot of weight. Which of the following is the best interpretation and next step for these two students to take regarding their observations?

a. Assume she is stressed, but it is her business, and leave her alone

b. Assume she is stressed, needs support, and invite her to some social events

c. Assume she is stressed and impaired, and report her to the Dean's office

d. Assume she is stressed and ill, and start asking others if she has HIV

e. Assume she is stressed and depressed, and encourage her to seek help

Chapter 14: Working with Other Professionals, Organizations, and Communities

1. A palliative care team is trying to move from working as a multi-disciplinary team to an inter-disciplinary team. Which of the following is the best description of the new way this team will be functioning?

a. Members of the team know what the others are doing

b. All of the team members are physicians

c. All treatment decisions must be made by consensus

d. Anyone on the team can prescribe medications

e. All of the team members can do each other's jobs

2. The internist who is the attending for a hospital team disagrees with a surgeon who he had asked to consult on one of his patients. Which of the following is the most effective way for the internist to deal with this conflict?

a. Give both opinions to the patient and let the patient choose

b. Write a note of disagreement in the chart, and leave it there

c. Get another surgeon to consult

d. Stop asking that surgeon to consult on patients

e. Set up a meeting between the internist and surgeon to discuss the issues

3. A young unmarried adult woman visiting from India is hospitalized for acute appendicitis. She communicates through a translator that she cannot give consent to have surgery, but needs to have her father make this decision. Which of the following is the best approach to get her the surgery she needs?

a. Explain to her that in this country she has to make her own decisions

b. Help her to consult with her father in India and document consent

c. Have two physicians write that it is an emergency, and do the surgery

d. Get a court order to have the surgery

e. Bring in a male Indian physician to explain the surgery to her

4. The most common type of organizational structure in medical teams is

a. Shared leadership

b. Rotating leadership

c. Dictatorship

d. Hierarchical

e. Consensus

Chapters 15: The Physician-Patient Relationship

1. According to Eric Cassell, which is most important for suffering to be healed?
   a. The physician cures the disease
   b. The physician prescribes a detailed regimen to follow
   c. The physician arrives at an accurate diagnosis
   d. The physician and patient form a positive relationship
   e. The physician helps the patient reconnect to body and community

2. Which of the following statements about the placebo effect is true?
   a. Certain personality types predictably respond to placebos
   b. Once a patient knows it is a placebo, it loses all effectiveness it had
   c. Placebos work for pain, but not for objectively measurable problems
   d. Placebo responses can be long-lasting
   e. Placebos do not cause side-effects

3. Which of the following is the factor that has been shown to best predict a patient's self-report of symptom improvement?
   a. The physician's choice of the most effective drug
   b. The patient's sense of being fully listened to at the visit
   c. How long the physician has known the patient
   d. How thorough a physical exam was conducted
   e. The patient's education and income level

4. Which of the following is the best statement of why the patient's story of the illness is important for healing?
   a. Patients like to feel they are the center of attention during office visits
   b. Patients believe in anecdotal evidence, not scientific fact
   c. The story conveys the meaning of the illness, and meaning is essential to healing
   d. The story may include diagnostic clues the physician missed while taking the history
   e. Telling the story is a helpful emotional catharsis for the patient

Chapter 16: Communicating with Patients

1. Which of the following is the best approach if there is a discrepancy between a patient's description of his or her mood and what the physician observes in the patient's body language?
   a. Confrontation
   b. Silence
   c. Facilitation
   d. Direct questions
   e. Transition statement

2. Which of the following is a true statement about time in physician- patient interactions?
   a. Physicians allow patients as much time as needed for an opening statement
   b. Physicians underestimate the amount of time they spend educating patients
   c. Physicians interrupt their patients every 17 seconds, on average
   d. Physicians spend more time with their patients if they sit during the interview
   e. The more time the physician spends with the patient, the more satisfied the patient will be

3. A young physician is interviewing an elderly woman who asks him how old he is. Which of the following would be the best response to her question?
   a. "I am sorry but I do not answer personal questions."
   b. "I am 28 years old but I'm very well trained."
   c. "You seem concerned about my youth. Don't worry. You're in good hands."
   d. "Perhaps you're concerned as to whether I can be of help to you."
   e. "I just look young. I know what I am doing."

4. A patient informs the physician during an initial interview that he is having mood swings. Which of the following would be the most useful response for the physician to make?
   a. "You don't seem unusually depressed to me."
   b. "What do you mean by mood swings?"
   c. "We have some very effective treatments for bipolar disorder."
   d. "What else is troubling you?"
   e. "Have you been abusing alcohol or drugs?"

Chapter 17: Diagnostic Reasoning in Medicine

1. A healthy adolescent male presents with headaches. On further inquiry, it becomes clear that he has depressed mood and suicidal ideation. His history reveals that his mother was killed when the patient was six years old. Which of the following is the best hypothesis at this

point regarding the contribution of the mother's death to his distress?

a. A perpetuating factor
b. A prognostic factor
c. A precipitating factor
d. A predisposing factor
e. A presenting factor

2. Which of the following is an essential element of diagnostic reasoning?

a. Don't decide until all possible alternatives are explored
b. Separate observation from inference
c. Stick to established protocols
d. Aim for certainty and clarity
e. Make the differential list as inclusive as possible

3. A physician is evaluating a young woman with lower abdominal pain. Which of the following will be most helpful in the diagnostic reasoning for care of this patient?

a. Pattern recognition and probability estimation
b. Stereotypic thinking and probability estimation
c. Probability estimation and preference for positive evidence
d. Pattern recognition and salient experience
e. Limits on hypothesis generation and stereotypic thinking

4. A 47-year-old man with chronic back pain declares that he has found a wonderful new treatment which helps with his pain. His physician believes this is a placebo response, and that the patient is taking inactive drug. Which of the following heuristic errors is the physician most likely to make in this case?

a. Stereotypic reasoning
b. Limits on hypothesis generation
c. Ignorance of base-rates
d. Preference for positive evidence
e. Evaluation of utility

Chapter 18: Patient Assessment

1. Which of the following is the best description of the unique feature of projective tests of personality?

a. Use of ambiguous test stimuli to which the person responds
b. Use of objective norms against which to evaluate the person
c. Use of large numbers of true/false questions
d. Use of the results to predict behavior in the future
e. Different versions for different ages

2. A 48-year-old man with chronic alcohol abuse presents for evaluation of forgetfulness. A previous note in his chart notes that he has exhibited confabulation. Which of the following best describes what has been observed?

a. The patient deliberating feigned impairment in memory
b. The patient had no short term memory impairment
c. The patient denied impairment in memory despite obvious failures
d. The patient made a variety of implausible excuses for the memory failures
e. The patient reported events and experiences which never actually occurred

3. Which of the following best describes the meaning of an IQ score?

a. A person's genetically determined capabilities
b. How a person's mental age compares to his chronological age
c. How a person compares to others in his age group
d. A person's maximum capabilities
e. A person's educational performance level

4. A 75-year-old male widower has been admitted to the hospital, after his family reported increasing confusion. Which of the following aspect of the mental status examination is the most sensitive evaluation of his orientation?

a. Knowledge of the date
b. His name and social security number
c. Knowledge of the city he is in
d. Knowledge of the building he is in
e. Knowledge of the season

Chapter 19: Recognizing and Treating Psychopathology in Primary Care

1. A 4-year-old boy is admitted to the hospital, accompanied by his mother, for continued treatment of chronic osteomyelitis in his right leg. His medical history shows multiple hospitalizations, surgeries, blood transfusions, radiographs and several incision and drainage procedures. While there is evidence of infections, the radiographs were actually negative for osteomyelitis. Numerous courses of antibiotics have been used with poor results and the child has had frequent fevers in the 103°–105° Fahrenheit range. The child is typically treated and then released early for continued intravenous therapy at home, due to his mother's prior training as a nurse. Which of the following diagnoses should be of most concern to the attending physician?

a. Separation anxiety disorder
b. Somatization disorder
c. Maternal depression
d. Folie à Deux
e. Munchausen's Syndrome by Proxy

2. An 11-year-old boy with a history of frequent accidents is brought in for a physical exam by his mother. In the course of the exam, this boy appears very nervous, holding himself rigidly, and remaining aloof. His mother says that he has violent outbursts during which he hurts his younger sister and breaks things. He also has had a very difficult time making friends at school. As the mother tells this to the pediatrician, the boy glares at her and seems very angry. The physical examination shows several bruises on different parts of his body in various stages of healing. Which of the following is the best next step in assessment and management of the child?
a. A private interview with the child and a careful trauma examination
b. A call to ask the police to do an interview with the child
c. An interview of the child and mother together in the doctor's office
d. Call the school to see if they have evidence of abuse
e. Refer the child to a psychiatrist for the behavior problems

3. A 25-year-old male presents in the emergency room with symptoms of rapid respiration, sweating and constant worrying that he is having a heart attack. He reports that he has gone to his physician every other day for the past week, and that the doctor does not appear to take his concerns seriously, but he can't calm down. Which of the following is the best approach to this patient?
a. Explain that this is just anxiety- his heart is normal
b. Request a psychiatric consultation to rule out an anxiety disorder
c. Admit him to a cardiac unit to rule out a heart attack
d. Explain some simple relaxation techniques which can help
e. Prescribe benzodiazepines to be taken as needed

4. A 14-year-old girl is brought to her primary physician by her mother because of concerns about her diet. She has lost over 20 pounds in the last year, reportedly by exercising and eating less. The girl is currently 5'7† and weighs 87 pounds, but a year and a half ago she weighed 120 pounds. The mother reports that her daughter obsessively counts fat grams and calories and is "obsessed" with eating. She runs on the cross-country team at school and usually maintains A's and B's. She hasn't had a menstrual cycle in the last six months. Her EKG shows bradycardia with a rate of 36. Which of the following is the best next step in management?
a. Call psychiatry for an emergency consultation

b. Send the patient home on medical bed rest and a 2000-calorie a day diet
c. Request a dietary consult
d. Admit her to a medical unit for cardiac monitoring and a psychiatric consult
e. Encourage the mother to consult with an eating disorder specialist

Chapter 20: Management of Difficult Patients

1. A 32-year-old man presents to the Emergency Department requesting pain medication. The man has a swollen left knee, and gives a history consistent with an ACL tear. However, the amount of pain the patient reports is more that is usual for this type of injury. Which of the following is the best approach to this patient?
a. Give the patient as much pain medication as he wants in the ED, but nothing to take home
b. Give the patient the usual amount of pain medication given for that type of injury, to take as needed
c. Don't give any pain medication, as the patient is clearly drug-seeking
d. Titrate the pain medication and instruct the patient about a regular schedule of pain medication with a taper
e. Give the patient mild medication but tell him it is very strong

2. A 25-year-old woman with cystic breast disease has been calling the outpatient clinic almost daily, with questions about diet, herbs, acupuncture, massage, and different types of mammograms. Her grandmother died of breast cancer at age 40, so her concern is understandable, but overwhelming. Which of the following is the best approach to this patient?
a. Tell her she is only allowed to call once a week
b. Give her the nurses' pager number, so she can feel there is always someone who can answer her questions
c. Set up frequent and regular visits to the doctor and/or nurse
d. Recommend she see a surgeon about a prophylactic mastectomy
e. Tell her she clearly is psychiatrically ill, and give her benzodiazepines

3. A 48-year-old woman with a 20-year history of diabetes mellitus is seen in the outpatient diabetes clinic for her regular visit. One of the staff cringes as she sees the patient walk in, saying that the patient never follows her diet or exercise plans. Which of the following would be

the best recommendation to the staff for approaching this patient?

a. Have the patient meet another patient who is blind and has lost her leg to diabetes, to impress her with the risks

b. Assess what it is about the plan that seems too difficult to do, and how the patient could be helped to feel able to do it

c. Tell the patient that she is letting everyone in the clinic down by not taking care of herself when they are all trying to help her

d. Set up the appointments so that the patient does not come on the day that staff person works in the clinic

e. Suggest to the patient that she may be happier with another doctor

4. A 19-year-old man with sarcoma has been only intermittently coming for chemotherapy treatments. He states that he believes he is going to die anyway, so doesn't want to waste too much time being sick. The prognosis is poor even with full treatment, but the partial treatment is totally ineffective, and is causing enough immunosuppression to increase the risk of a life-threatening infection. Which of the following is the best approach to this situation?

a. Inform the patient that he must take the full treatment or you will take him to court to make him do it

b. Inform the patient that you can't stand to watch him committee suicide, and refer him to another oncologist

c. Inform the patient that you will not give him partial treatment, but could switch to a palliative approach, if that is truly his choice

d. Inform the patient of the risks he faces, and keep treating him whenever he chooses to come

e. Inform the patient that he can't committee suicide, and get a court order to force him to get treatment

Chapter 21: Humanities and the Practice of Medicine

No questions

Chapter 22: Culturally Competent Health Care

1. Illnesses like "the evil eye" (mal ojo) and susto are best understood as which of the following?
a. Primitive conceptualizations of psychiatric illness
b. A culturally defined health belief

c. Religious explanations of psychiatric illness
d. Superstitions which keep people from getting health care
e. Uneducated versions of hysterical illness

2. Which is the most appropriate response to parents who are refusing surgical correction of a child's deformity because they see the deformity as a punishment?
a. Call social services, as this is child neglect
b. Tell the parents that this is not how we do thing in the United States
c. Consult the family's religious leader, to see if this is the general belief
d. Do the surgery anyway, as the parents are clearly psychotic
e. Discharge the child and family from care, as uncooperative

3. A 60-year-old man presents with liver disease. He has failed to stop drinking alcohol despite several warnings of how dangerous this is for him. He states that drinking is a part of the healing ceremonies his culture requires, and it would be shameful for him to refuse. Which of the following is the best approach to this situation?
a. Refuse to treat him unless he stops drinking
b. Ask if there is any way for him to drink less, or a substitute
c. Tell him the alcohol does more harm than the ceremonies are doing good
d. Ask him to help you understand about the role of alcohol in his culture
e. Ask his wife to come in, and tell her he is killing himself

4. Which of the following statements by a physician best reflects cultural competence?
a. "It is fine for you to see the healer so long as you keep taking your real medications."
b. "Why do you need your father here to decide if you will let your son have surgery?"
c. "I need you to translate while I explain to your Grandma about her hysterectomy."
d. "I just want you to know that I won't take any of your soul whenever I take your blood- isn't that what you people think?"
e. "What do you think is the cause of your problem?"

Chapter 23: Complementary and Alternative Medicine

1. A 24-year-old woman comes to the internal medicine clinic requesting acupuncture for her cocaine cravings. She has recently completed a drug rehabilitation pro-

gram and has not used cocaine in over a month. However, she is experiencing severe cravings which make it difficult for her to concentrate in graduate school, and has heard from others that acupuncture can help. Which of the following is the best approach to her question?
a. Tell her there is no real evidence of the effectiveness of acupuncture
b. Refer her to a psychiatrist, as she clearly needs more help
c. Tell her it is better to stay with one modality of approach
d. Discuss acupuncture as one of the options in a full-care plan
e. Reluctantly refer her to an acupuncturist, while telling her it won't work

2. A 72-year-old man is in the intensive care unit with congestive heart failure. The nursing staff is upset when the family asks to bring a "healer" to visit in the ICU. Which of the following is the best response to this request?
a. Tell the family that this is not permitted, and try to make alternative arrangements
b. Tell the nurses that the patient is dying anyway, so they should let the family do what they want
c. Find out what type of intervention is proposed, and if this would be safe in an ICU setting
d. Ask the social worker to educate the family about hospitals in the United States
e. Make arrangements to discharge the patient to a hospice setting, where these things can be set up

3. Which of the following is true about the use of complementary and alternative medicine (CAM) in the United States?
a. Over 60% of the population reports using some CAM in the past 12 months
b. CAM is most often used for acute pain
c. Most of the evidence supporting use of CAM is from randomized, controlled trials
d. CAM is most often used by people who are not well educated
e. Most people who use CAM in the US are not citizens

4. Which of the following best describes the quality control mechanism in the United States for herbal medications and dietary supplements?
a. The Food and Drug Administration evaluates them like any other medications
b. The Federal Trade Commission monitors them for truth in advertising
c. There is no federal regulation of herbal supplements because they are considered food
d. There is no need for federal regulation, as they have no medical effect

e. There is no need for federal regulation, as they are natural and thus safe

Chapter 24: The Impact of Social Inequalities on Health Care

1. According to the Surgeon General's Supplement to the Report on Mental Health, *Mental Health: Culture, Race, and Ethnicity*, which of the following statements is true about specific ethnic groups living in the United States?
a. African-Americans are under-represented in the homeless and incarcerated populations, and the child welfare system
b. Hispanics have an 80% incidence of limited English proficiency
c. The suicide rate for American Indians is 50 percent higher than the general population
d. Asian-Americans present to the physician earlier in their illness course, with less severe symptoms, than other groups
e. American Indians are less likely to have mental health and substance abuse problems

2. Which of the following is a true example of health-care disparities in mental health?
a. Increased use of typical antipsychotic medications in Caucasians as compared to African-Americans
b. Diagnosis of bipolar disorder instead of schizophrenia in Hispanic-Americans
c. Diagnosis of bipolar disorder instead of schizophrenia in African-Americans
d. Hispanic-Americans being given the diagnosis of an affective disorder despite the presence of severe persistent psychotic symptoms
e. Overdiagnosis of schizophrenia in Caucasians of lower socioeconomic status

3. Which is of the following *has not* been found to be an illness category with significant health disparities?
a. Cardiovascular disease
b. Liver Transplantation
c. Diabetes
d. Stroke
e. Mental illness

4. Which of the following is true about health-care disparities in the United States?
a. They are a national economic problem, and cannot be addressed at the level of the individual physician and patient
b. They could be eliminated if the cultural diversity of

the United States was represented in the cultural diversity of U.S. physicians

   c. Addressing them requires training administrators as well as physicians and nursing staff

   d. They could be eliminated with an adequate and inclusive health insurance program

Chapter 25: Health Services in the United States

1. Use the following HEDIS clinical quality indicators to compare the quality performance of a specific plan to the corresponding national averages in parenthesis:
Advising smokers to quit 40% (61)
Beta-blocker treatment for heart attack patients 65% (61.9)
Mammography screening rate 60% (70.4)
Cervical cancer screening rate 58% (70.4)
Diabetic retinal exam rate 29% (38.4)
Cesarean section rate (age 15-34) 16.4% (20.6)
Childhood immunization rate 64% (65.3)
Which of the following is the most appropriate recommendation for action that is consistent with the principles of evidence-based medicine?
   a. Recalculation of rates after case-mix adjustment
   b. Rates are acceptable, no further action needed
   c. Multiple information interventions to improve preventive care
   d. Identification of responsible clinicians and disciplinary action
   e. Continuing medical education program focusing on deficiencies

2. A 24-year-old woman (gravida 1, para 0) presents to the labor and delivery floor at 39 weeks' gestation, complaining of frequent abdominal cramps and vaginal spotting. Contractions are occurring every 10 minutes and her cervix is 3 cm dilated and 80% effaced. The plan of management should include:
   a. Minimum 24 hours of hospital stay
   b. Minimum 48 hours of hospital stay
   c. Discussion of hospitalization
   d. Intravenous tocolysis
   e. Cervical cerclage

3. Which of the following best describes the level of evidence to support the recommendation made in the following abstract? "The importance of education in the management of diabetes is recognized but has rarely been assessed in children. In a longitudinal controlled study we have examined the effect of a program of education on the knowledge, diet, and concentration of HgA1c in a group of diabetics. The program took the form of two packages of education each consisting of four weekly meetings, in which small groups of parents and older children were led in a discussion of different aspects of diabetes. Only one of the 119 families who began the study failed to complete it. Family knowledge about diabetes improved as a result of the program, although this was poorly retained in the fathers. A trend to improvement in several aspects of diet was noted but did not reach significance. A significant fall in HgA1c was apparent seven months after the education in children aged 11 years and over. Those whose initial control was poor improved most. We conclude that such meetings should be considered as a useful adjunct to regular diabetic clinics."
   a. Good evidence to support the recommendation (randomized controlled trial)
   b. Fair evidence to support the recommendation (controlled trial without randomization, cohort or case-control analytic studies, multiple time series, uncontrolled experiments with dramatic results)
   c. Poor evidence to support the recommendation (respected opinions, descriptive epidemiology)
   d. Fair evidence against the recommendation
   e. Good evidence against the recommendation

4. A child with asthma is brought to the emergency room in serious respiratory distress, the latest in a series of crises that appear to characterize the disease of this patient. Beyond appropriate treatment of this episode, what medical management intervention is likely to make the biggest immediate difference in the life of this patient?
   a. Critical pathway implementation
   b. Evidence-based disease management
   c. Aggressive utilization management program
   d. Physician profiling and credentialing
   e. Continuing medical education

Chapter 26: American Medicine is Sick

No questions

Appendix B: Medical Statistics and Research Design

1. The results of a randomized clinical trial (RCT) of a new treatment regimen for people with hypertension indicate that the risk of stroke is 10% with the new treatment compared to 15% for the standard, conventional treatment. Based on this information, what is the estimate of

the number of patients that would need to be treated with the new treatment to prevent one stroke?
a. 5 patients
b. 10 patients
c. 15 patients
d. 20 patients

2. Suppose the Centers for Disease Control conducted a national survey to estimate the number of cases of avian (bird) flu in each state. When summarizing the results of the survey, the median number of cases per state was greater than the mean (average) number of cases. This suggests what type of distribution best characterizes the data?
a. Population
b. Skewed
c. Normal
d. Sample
e. Bimodal

3./4. The one-year results of a clinical trial to test a new drug in comparison to the currently used drug to prevent death for people with AIDS are shown below:

	Dead	Alive
New Drug	10	90
Old Drug	20	80

3. What is the risk of dying within one-year with the new drug?
a. 10%
b. 20%
c. 50%
d. 80%
e. 90%

4. What is the relative risk of dying within one-year with the new drug compared to the old drug?
a. 10%
b. 20%
c. 50%
d. 80%
e. 90%

5. In a poorly designed clinical trial, the investigators erroneously conclude that an intervention does not reduce recurrence of a heat attack for patients who have previously experienced a myocardial infarction when in fact the intervention does reduce recurrence. What type of error is this?
a. Incidence
b. Prevalence
c. Power
d. Type I
e. Type II

6. A new drug is being tested to determine if it will prevent the onset of AIDS for persons recently diagnosed as being infected by HIV. One half of patients recruited in this study are given the new drug, while the other half are given the most widely currently used current drug. Neither the physician caring for a patient nor the patient knows which drug a patient is receiving. This is an example of what type of study?
a. Cross-sectional
b. Longitudinal
c. Single blind
d. Double blind
e. Case-control

7. The results of a survey of 20 children treated for asthma in a school clinic during the last year recorded the number of days each child missed school because of his or her asthma, and are recorded below. What is the modal (mode) number of days these children missed school?
0, 0, 0, 1, 1, 1, 1, 1, 1, 2, 2, 2, 2, 2, 3, 3, 3, 4, 7, 12
a. 0
b. 1
c. 2
d. 3
e. 4
f. 7
g. 12

8./9. The results of a new diagnostic test to identify cancer in women who are at increased risk of early onset breast cancer based on family history are shown below:

	Cancer	No cancer
Positive Test	90	20
Negative Test	10	180

8. What is the likelihood ratio for cancer if the test result is positive?
a. 9
b. 10
c. 20
d. 45
e. 70

9. What is the specificity of this test?
a. 10%
b. 20%
c. 50%
d. 80%
e 90%

Appendix E
Answer Key to USMLE Practice Questions

Chapter 1: Mind, Brain, and Behavior

1. B is correct. High emotional stress impairs the immediate tasks of learning, encoding and storage of memory, but not retrieval. Implicit memory is the nonverbal memory, which is likely to be enhanced, not impaired, under theses high stress circumstances.
2. C is correct. Mirror neurons make maps of the internal intentional state of another person's mind, by creating in the viewer the sense that they are doing it as well. Although this has implications for empathy, it is less about emotion than intentionality.
3. A is correct. Implicit memory is among the earliest memory, and does not require focused attention or activation of the hippocampus to be encoded. It is not in narrative, nor a part of autobiographical memory.
4. E is correct. Talking activates the left hemisphere, allowing processing of the experiences by the part of the brain which is more analytic and verbal, creating narrative. This allows the patient to feel more in control, and to decrease arousal of the autonomic nervous system.

Chapter 2: Families, Relationships, and Health

1. D is correct. Personal medical information cannot be given to anyone other than the parent without the minor or the parent's permission. In matters related to sexuality, minors have even more autonomy than in other areas of medical care. Although laws vary greatly from state to state regarding parental or spousal notification having to do with abortion, information can be given to a minor.
2. C is correct. Posttraumatic growth is reported by many cancer survivors, who say that the traumatic event caused them to re-evaluate their priorities. They report finding more meaning in life, and not worrying about things that now appear trivial.
3. A is correct. High levels of expressed emotion, in the setting of emotional over-involvement and criticalness by a family member, exacerbate psychotic conditions, leading to more relapse and need for more medications. No specific type of symptoms are related to this type of family support.
4. B is correct. The social (instrumental) support of a community of believers is a separate component of support from the support of an implicit sense of meaning or faith. Inner peace and meditation are both more private components of spiritual support, while the charismatic leader and social norms, and the ritual and dogma are all more extrinsic components of religious support. Denial and rationalization are classic psychodynamic defense mechanisms, and are not valuable aspects of spirituality for support.

Chapter 3: Birth, Childhood, and Adolescence

1. E is correct. A child of 4 should be able to speak in simple sentences, so this child's language is quite delayed. She will not yet have complete control of bowel and bladder, and articulation may be still difficult. Cognitive development is such that magical thinking is quite normal.
2. C is correct. Puberty extends over a period of several years, and can start as early as age 9. It usually occurs right after a growth spurt. Early puberty is seen as a positive by boys, but can be the source of ridicule and isolation for girls.
3. B is correct. Failure to thrive refers to growth failure in a young child without obvious medical reasons. It is a description of the problem, but does not indicate the

etiology. The child is often not eating properly, and this may or may not be the result of anxiety, depression, or abuse.

4. A is correct. Temperament is genetically determined, and helps to shape the way that a child interacts with the environment. It thus has an impact on aggression, anger, anxiety and depression, but it is not any of these. It contributes to, but is not equivalent to, the development of personality.

Chapter 4: Early Adulthood and the Middle Years

1. A is correct. Surveys suggest that men are the unfaithful partner in 2/3 of the divorces due to sexual infidelity. The likelihood of sexual infidelity in increased by the birth of a child or retirement, which cause major changes in the relationship between partners in a marriage. It is not generally due to sexual dysfunction.

2. B is correct. Triangulation is the use of a third person to avoid direct confrontation between two people. This is most classically done by having a child serve as a distraction from marital problems between the parents, or having an outside sexual partner rather than confronting sexual problems in a marriage.

3. D is correct. Although it remains true that the increase in women in the work force has correlated with increased divorce rates, working women report better mental and emotional health than homemakers. Career-oriented women are still less likely to marry than those who are working in other types of jobs, and those who make more money are more likely to divorce. However, one must be careful about all of these correlates, as they do not tell the direction of the relationship. It may well be that women who have their own incomes are more able to leave unhappy marriages than those without adequate incomes, rather than that working makes women less happy in marriages. It also may be that women who are less healthy emotionally are less able to get employment, rather than that being at home leads to emotional distress. This will undoubtedly continue to be researched!

4. C is correct. Erikson saw each phase of life as having a major developmental task. For young adulthood, he described it as achieving the capacity for intimacy. This often involves some distancing from the family of origin. Dealing with financial concerns is a task of middle adulthood. Generativity, which includes making a contribution and an impression on the next generation, would be seen in mid adult life.

Chapter 5: Old Age

1. C is correct. The total brain volume is decreased with aging, which increases ventricular size and may increase or leave cerebral spinal fluid volume the same. Communication skills do not decrease with normal aging. Although some aspects of memory do decrease with aging, these do not include primary or tertiary memory.

2. B is correct. Assisted living setting provide help for those who have difficulty with instrumental activities of daily living such as shopping, cooking, laundry, cleaning, and driving by providing service similar to what would be found in a hotel: meals served in a dining room, shuttles, and housekeeping services. A board and care provides somewhat similar services, but in addition does some monitoring of the people, as they are usually there due to psychiatric rather than medical problems. Retirement communities are apartments or condominiums for older people, which have other amenities, such as shuttles and exercise facilities.

3. A is correct. Although physicians do have an obligation to determine whether it a patient is safe to drive (such as reporting those with seizure disorders), they do not have to try to stop people from driving at a certain age, nor try to determine competency.

4. D is correct. Suicide is more common in the elderly, perhaps as a result of chronic illness, combined with repeated losses of close friends and family. Surprisingly, schizophrenia can first occur after the age of 60. Some types of psychotherapy can still be quite effective with the elderly, and antipsychotic medications, which are commonly given to elderly patients, are no always the best intervention for behavioral disturbances.

Chapter 6: Death, Dying, and Grief

1. C is correct. When someone asks an unexpected question, it is generally a good idea to ask more about it before assuming the motivation for the question. Most of the other answers here will close off discussion, not allowing the boy to express his concerns, whether they are for himself or a friend.

2. B is correct. This is denial- which in this system of thinking is a phase of adjustment, and not a pathological response to dying.

3. B is correct. He is at increased risk of death from all causes. This does not appear to be solely due to nonadherence to treatment, nor to psychiatric consequences of the loss, and it is clearly not due to contagion or toxic exposure. It appears to be due to an interaction between grief and the body, probably mediated through the im-

mune system, leaving one more vulnerable to a variety of illnesses.

4. D is correct. Any adult who refuses treatment must be assessed for truly informed consent. This means they need to understand that they have a problem, that there are options for treatment, and the possible consequences of those options. His decision cannot be automatically overruled or accepted without this type of assessment. Psychiatric assessment might be indicated, but he is not clearly suicidal, simply based on this statement. Nor is it appropriate to impose one's own views about transplantation on a patient.

Chapter 7: Chronic Benign Pain

1. D is correct. The focus of behavioral treatments is function. They aim for long-term, not short-term improvement, and are based on assumptions that there is often a discrepancy between self reports and observations of others. Treatment often involves spouses, and focuses on nonverbal manifestations rather than verbal reports of pain.

2. C is correct. Pain behavior is influenced by both positive and negative reinforcement, meaning it is influenced both by the positive outcomes related to the pain, and the avoidance of negative things due to the pain. Functional disability is not closely related to the paint intensity, nor is the conscious motivation related to the pain behavior. Dramatic behavioral is rarely actually associated with operant factors, which are intrinsic rewards of the behavior such as attention.

3. B is correct. Patients with chronic pain often have a history of sexual or physical abuse or trauma. This is believed to create a super-sensitivity to pain perception. Contrary to popular belief, they don't usually suffer depression prior to the onset of pain. These patients are not malingering, lazy, or violent. They tend to be anxious overachievers, who are reporting pain as they perceive it.

4. E is correct. Behavioral treatment always focuses on increasing functional behavior. This means that for chronic pain a major goal is return to work or school. Behavioral treatments require specific training and experience to be effective. Patients are taught that pain is an interaction between physical experience and the perception of the brain, and the dichotomy between mind and body is artificial and simplistic. Behavioral therapy is often done in conjunction with pain medication.

Chapter 8: Stress and Illness

1. B is correct. Homeostasis is the tendency for a body to maintain an optimal state of balance. It applies to many aspects of body function, such as the tendency of heart and lungs to become more active with physical exertion.

2. C is correct. Chronic stress leads to depression of the immune system. This would be the opposite of increasing killer T cells, or causing an autoimmune reaction.

3. C is correct. Although cigarettes do lead to a nicotine addiction, which sustains smoking behavior, even with nicotine replacement, the behavioral cues for smoking can set off episodic cravings, as anyone who has tried to quit smoking knows. This has to do with habitual behavioral, and the environmental reminders of smoking, which lead to the craving.

4. D is correct. Although there have been many studies of Type A personality that suggest that this typology is simplistic for understanding the medical impact of different temperaments, repeated studies have found that hostility is predictive of coronary artery disease.

Chapter 9: Addiction

1. B is correct. Cognitive-behavioral approaches have more of an evidence base than any other modality, including insight-oriented therapy and medications. Modafinil can help with excessive daytime sleepiness, which may be related to use of cocaine. Naloxone blocks the opiate receptors, and so is used for treatment of some other drugs of abuse. Bupropion is helpful for treatment of nicotine cravings, and some new data suggests it may helpful for methamphetamine, but has not been shown to have much utility for cocaine abuse.

2. C is correct. Methamphetamine causes more profound changes in the norepinephrine and serotonin system than any of the other listed drugs of abuse.

3. A is correct. Although withdrawal from heroin can make someone quite sick and miserable, it is not life threatening. Cocaine and methamphetamine are short-acting, so people are frequently withdrawing from them, and craving more. However, the danger from them is primarily in overdose.

4. E is correct. Alcohol has been the drug from that list which has the most serious effects on fetal formation, particularly including impact on the brain and face. Cigarettes are associated with small for gestational age children, and there is some indication of correlations with outcomes such as attention deficient disorder. Barbiturates and benzodiazepines can lead to sedation of the fetus, and can be dangerous in reducing fetal heart rate, but have not been shown to correlate to birth defects. There are mixed data on the impact of cocaine on the brain, and size, but not as much with birth defects as alcohol.

Chapter 10: Psychodynamic Approaches to Human Behavior

1. A is correct. Intellectualization is a common defense used by physicians and researchers. It uses conceptual thinking to distance one from the emotional aspects of an emotionally charged event. Displacement would be to react to something else with the emotions appropriate to the charged event. Repression is to unconsciously avoid thinking or feeling about the charged event at all, and regression is to react as though one were in an earlier developmental level. Projection is to act as thought someone else is feeling what you are feeling.

2. C is correct. In Freudian terminology, the superego functions much as our common view of a conscience, labeling certain behaviors or feelings as wrong or right. The Ego is the reality testing component of the self, problem solving, and defense mechanisms. The Id includes the urges, including that of hostility.

3. E is correct. Suppression is a conscious attempt to keep an emotional response out of current awareness. Denial would require trying to say it was not true, and turning against self would mean a blaming. Undoing requires a symbolic way of making a reality feel untrue, and Sublimation is burying the resulting feelings in something more acceptable to the individual.

4. D is correct. This is displacement of the current feeling to another circumstance. Reaction formation would mean the anger was avoided by acting very happy with and friendly to the doctor, and identification would have the patient taking on the same behavior as the doctor. Fixation would be to perseveratively come back to that incident in future relationships with the doctor, or other similar relationships. Repression is to unconsciously avoid thinking or feeling about the incident, so the patient would not be aware of feeling any anger at all.

Chapter 11: Facilitating Health Behavior Change

1. D is correct. Although physicians do provide information on the impact of health behavior, this is with the goal of helping patients find the motivation to change. They provide guidance, but ideally do not tell patients what to do, nor require compliance.

2. D is correct. In the Preparation stage, patients are still resolving their ambivalence to make change. At all stages there is resistance to change, but this is not the most difficult stage, nor is it a stage where no behavior change is anticipated in the next 6 months.

3. A is correct. The interaction between physician and pa-

tient is one of open discussion and sharing of information, with the patient as the decision-maker.

4. B is correct. Although the emphasis on Motivation is in the title, Motivational Interviewing helps the patients feel competent to make a change, increasing what is called self-efficacy. All of the other alternatives suggest a dependence of the patient on another to allow the change to happen, which is antithetical to Motivational Interviewing.

Chapter 12: Human Sexuality

1. C is correct. Premature ejaculation is quite treatable, and the "squeeze" technique is one useful approach. This should not be accepted as something to just have to live with, nor as a phase which will be outgrown- although the latter may well be true in some cases. This is a relatively common problem, and is not entirely psychological, although excitement contributes to it.

2. B is correct. Serum prolactin and testosterone levels are useful in determining the etiology. Erectile dysfunction is treatable. Nicotine, alcohol, and performance pressure are all detrimental to erectile function. Morning erections do not indicate that the problem is entirely psychological, just that the physiology of the penis itself is intact.

3. D is correct. Vaginismus is the result of an *involuntary* contraction of the pubococcygeus muscle, and is often a conditioned response to pain on intercourse. This painful intercourse may well have been due to a sexual assault, but not necessarily. Vaginismus is quite treatable and is not related to how the woman feels about her partner.

4. A is correct. Dyspareunia, or pain with intercourse, is often due to problems which are relatively easily addressed, such as inadequate lubrication or vaginal infections or abrasions. Marital counseling, sexual counseling, or further sexual history may be useful, but would not be the first response to this presenting statement.

Chapter 13: Medical Student and Physician Well-Being

1. A is correct. The first step with someone you don't know is to speak with the other student and supportively see if something can be done jointly to address the situation. It might then be appropriate to report the resident, but it is best to make sure the other student will be ok with this approach. Joining in the banter or creating an angry confrontation may serve to distract attention from the

other student, but will not resolve the problem. Simply accepting this as a cultural problem may be the easy way, but will not make changes.

2. C is correct. It is appropriate for a student or physician to ask to be excused from participation in an activity which is inconsistent with that person's values and beliefs, within the boundaries of not abandoning the patient. A physician must be able to retain the integrity of his or her beliefs while dealing with people of many differing beliefs. This should not be a reason to drop out of medical school, but it is also not a power abuse situation- unless the attending forced the student to participate even after knowing of the problem..

3. C is correct. Medical schools want all of the students to graduate, and will offer support for students who are able to do the work, but need some accommodation or help with study skills. Not seeking or using help until after one has had multiple failures is a surprisingly common response for medical students, who are accustomed to being quite self-reliant. Finding out what is on the exam is probably an approach which worked in college, but will be less effective in medical school and beyond.

4. E is correct. The first step with a colleague who may be impaired is to let them know that you have noticed, be supportive, and encourage them to get help. Ignoring it is not a good option, not is just offering social support if the person is truly impaired. Starting rumors is obviously wrong, but reporting to the Dean's office may be the right thing to do- but only if they do not follow through after receiving encouragement to seek help themselves.

Chapter 14: Working with Other Professionals, Organizations, and Communities

1. A is correct. Working as an inter-disciplinary team implies that the team communicates extensively, rather than working in separate compartments. The roles and task are still different for each discipline, and decisions are not made by consensus, but plans are shared and coordinated.

2. E is correct. Many physician disagreements are due to lack of clarity in the communication, which is largely done through the house staff or chart notes. Face to face meetings may be time-consuming, but they avoid the frustration and delays of the other options, and are the most likely to result in good patient care.

3. B is correct. Respect for cross-cultural issues requires trying to work with the individuals, rather than around them. Extended families are a part of medical decision-

making in many countries, and should be respected for those in the United States from other cultures.

4. D is correct. Hierarchical organization for decision-making is still typical in medical care teams. Consensus, while useful for some aspects of care, is inefficient in urgent situations. Rotating leadership or shared leadership is done in some administrative positions in departments, but is difficult to manage. Dictatorships tend to end in coups, so are usually transitory when they are created in medical settings.

Chapter 15: The Physician-Patient Relationship

1. E is correct. Although the relationship between the physician and patient is important, it is the connection of the patient to his or her body and community which is healing in this perspective. Healing involves far more than the diagnosis of the illness, the specificity of the treatment, or even the cure of the illness.

2. D is correct. The effect of placebos can be long-lasting, as they make physiological changes in the body. This can happen even when patients find out it was a placebo, and because of this, there can be side-effects of placebos. There is not a specific personality that predicts response to placebos, and placebos can cause objectively measurable changes.

3. B is correct. The perception by a patient that they were really heard is not only one of the best predictors of the patient's satisfaction with the visit and treatment, but also predicts relief of symptoms. This is more important than the medication, how long the physician has known the patient, the education of the patient, and how complete a physical examination was done.

4. C is correct. Although the story may include information which is helpful, the key aspect of the story is the conveying of the meaning of the illness.

Chapter 16: Communicating with Patients

1. A is correct. Confrontation in this case means stating that one's observation is different from what has been said. It can be a very simple statement such as "you look sad." Facilitations refer to words or sounds that encourage the patient to keep talking, and transition statements help the physician to change to a new area of discussion or exploration. Both are useful, but not in this particular situation.

2. C is correct. Unfortunately, physicians are notorious for

interrupting patients. They do not spend more time with patients if they sit, but the patients perceive them to have spent more time. Physicians usually overestimate how much time they spend educating patients, but patients' satisfaction is not tied to the amount of time alone.

3. D is correct. Speaking to the concern behind the question is the best approach, and this can be in the form of a hypothesis, rather than a defense about one's competence.

4. B is correct. It is essential to know what the patient means by this term before any assumptions are made, be they about depression, alcohol, or bipolar disease. Changing the topic is not useful at this juncture.

Chapter 17: Diagnostic Reasoning in Medicine

1. D is correct. The mother's death in this case is a predisposing factor, one which places him at greater risk. It is far in the past, and precedes the symptoms, so it is not a presenting or precipitating or probably a perpetuating factor. It might be seen as a prognostic factor in the sense that his symptoms could be worse with this factor, but predisposing is the best answer.

2. B is correct. Separation of observation from inference is essential to diagnostic reasoning. Aiming for certainty and clarity, sticking to established protocols, making sure all alternatives are explored and making the differential list as exhaustive as possible are all counter to effective diagnostic reasoning.

3. A is correct. Pattern recognition, paired with probability estimation, will generate a specific set of hypotheses and differential diagnosis list. Although salient experience may be helpful, it will be of limited benefit. Preference for positive evidence, stereotypic thinking, and limits on hypothesis generation will not be helpful.

4. E is correct. Although there are a number of possible errors the physician might make in this case, the most likely is for the physician to undervalue the pain relief, believing it is due to a placebo response and is thus "not real."

Chapter 18: Patient Assessment

1. A is correct. Projective tests use vague or ambiguous stimuli to encourage people to speak about their own thoughts. They have been validated to tell some things about the test-takers personality. Although there are dif-

ferent versions for different ages, this is not unique to this type of psychological test. These tests do not have yes/no questions, are not objective, and are not predictive of future behavior any more than most psychological tests are.

2. E is correct. Confabulation is an invention of events to cover for lapses of memory. It can sometimes be quite convincing, and at other times is quite fantastic, but the goal is to fill in the missing pieces of history.

3. C is correct. The intelligence quotient gives an estimate of how a person's intellectual capability compares to the mean of others of that general age range (child, adolescent, or adult). The IQ is affected by environment, so it is not an indication of the maximum capability or the genetically determined capabilities. It is not a comparison of mental age to chronological age, although this is a common misunderstanding of it.

4. D is correct. The most sensitive indicator of orientation of the items on this list is the knowledge of the building he is in, as this is very recently learned information, and no committed to long-term memory.

Chapter 19: Recognizing and Treating Psychopathology in Primary Care Medicine

1. E is correct. The indicators for Munchausen's by Proxy are pretty classic in this case. The mother is a health-care worker, the child has repeated illnesses, but careful examination shows that most of the symptoms are either due to treatment, or could be induced or reported in accurately. There is no evidence for any of the other diagnoses listed.

2. A is correct. Given the many indicators that the child has been abused, the next step is to carefully examine the child and to speak with him apart from the mother. The mother is obviously altering the child's interaction at this point. Other steps, such as the school, can wait until a later time when it is clear the child is safe.

3. D is correct. Although it is tempting to give benzodiazepines or reassurance to this man, it seems he is not having panic attacks, just anxiety, and he needs some techniques beyond reassurance to deal with that. It would not be necessary medically to admit him, and it is not clear that this would address the anxiety either.

4. D is correct. This is a very sick young woman, who needs to be watched carefully in a hospital. Psychiatry and Dietary are both excellent consults for her longer term care, but are not the most urgent problem.

Chapter 20: Management of Difficult Patients

1. D is correct. Pain medication must be adjusted and titrated for each individual patient, with the understanding that anxiety increases the perception of pain. The physician has to be careful not to punish patient who they view as drug -seeking, and to treating the pain without overreacting to requests for medication which may speak to anxiety as much as pain.
2. C is correct. Patients who are anxious often communicate this with frequent requests for reassurance. Strict limits on office visits may backfire with emergency department visits. It is usually far better to set up regular ways to provide this reassurance, such as groups of regular visits, than to try to avoid them or to violate regular boundaries by giving out private numbers.
3. B is correct. When a patient is not adherent to treatment, there is a temptation to try to frighten the patient, avoid the patient, or shame the patient into doing what is "good for them". If the problem is seen as the patient feeling unable to do what is necessary, a different and more effective approach can be taken, to help the patient feel more able to do what is needed.
4. C is correct. This young man is an adult, and if competent to give informed consent, can choose not to continue treatment. The physician's obligation is to provide care, but it does not have to aim toward cure, and does not have to make the patient do what the doctor wants. However, the physician is not obligated to provide treatment which is ineffective or even dangerous. This is a tough situation for all concerned.

Chapter 21: Humanities and the Practice of Medicine

No questions

Chapter 22: Culturally Competent Health Care

1. B is correct. These "folk illnesses" are connected with a particular cultural set of beliefs, which are not necessarily religious. This does not necessarily reflect a primitive, hysterical, or superstitious approach in the pejorative sense in which these words are generally used. The illnesses are not all what would be considered psychiatric, although they could arguably be seen as due to mind-body interactions.

2. C is correct. Working with a religious leader is the first best approach. In this way, the physician can see if this is a usual belief of this group, or is aberrant, and represents a decision which the religious leader may be able to change, or that warrant s one of the other approaches.
3. D is correct. By gaining more information, and conveying that the physician understand that this is important and not easily set aside, one if more likely to learn what the issues are, and how best to approach them sensitively. All of the other options fail to communicate that this is a dilemma for this man, by presenting only one "correct" option.
4. E is correct. Exploring, rather than assuming, is the most culturally competent approach to the patient. Using family members to translate, particularly for sensitive issues, is not appropriate. Neither is making comment s which demean the beliefs of another, as choices A, B and D do.

Chapter 23: Complementary and Alternative Medicine

1. D is correct. The idea of acupuncture should be discussed as a part of the overall plan, with appropriate evaluation of the potential utility. Acupuncture has some evidence of utility in some situations, and a request for an exploration of this option should not trigger a psychiatric referral. However, simply making a referral is not adequate, particularly reluctantly, if you are to have the patient continue to inform you about all of the options they are exploring for care in the future.
2. C is correct, and further exploration is the appropriate next step. It is not necessary to forbid all healing efforts which are not part of Western medicine, even in the hospital. Nor is it necessary to use them only when a patient is dying. However, one must be aware that common rituals, such as those involving a lighted candle would not be safe in most hospital rooms.
3. A is correct. CAM is used by the majority of the population in the United States, most of whom are citizens. Well educated people are more likely to use CAM, as are people with chronic rather than acute conditions. Most of the evidence regarding CAM at this point is descriptive, although studies are now being done to increase the evidence base.
4. B is correct. Herbal medications and dietary supplements are considered food, but this means that they are monitored by the Federal Trade Commission for truth in adverting, and not by the Federal Drug Administration.

Chapter 24: The Impact of Social Inequalities on Health Care

1. C is correct. American Indians have a much higher rate of suicide than the rate in the dominant or Caucasian culture.
2. D is correct. Studies have found that Latinos have been diagnosed with an affective illness, despite the presence of persistent psychotic symptoms that would indicate that another diagnosis might be appropriate. .
3. B is correct. Of this list, only liver transplantation has not been found to suffer significant health disparities, possibly due to a national monitoring process.
4. C is correct. Addressing health disparities in the U.S. requires interventions at all levels of clinical care. Although economics, cultural diversity and health insurance all are components of the problem, addressing these would not eliminate the problems at the level of the physician and patient.

Chapter 25: Health Services in the United States

1. E is correct. Information interventions such as feedback, reminders, and education, have been directly linked to improved outcomes in randomized clinical trails. Multiple interventions offer greater impact than any single approach, particularly education alone.
2. C is correct. Hospitalization is an option to be discussed between physician and patient. Without controlled clinical evidence, it would be inappropriate to set minimum standards of care. The woman's pregnancy at 39 weeks is at full term, and appears to be proceeding toward delivery, so the other options are not appropriate.
3. B is correct. There is fair evidence in this case, as it is a controlled, but not randomized, trial.
4. B is correct. Evidence-based disease management, a set of interventions successfully tested in randomized controlled trials, has been shown to improve clinical outcomes through proactive provisions of the various services needed to control the course of asthma, minimizing the occurrence of exacerbations.

Chapter 26: American Medicine is Sick

No questions

Appendix B: Medical Statistics and Research Design

1. The correct answer is D. The number of patients needed to be treated (NNT) is estimated by first taking the difference between the risk with the new treatment and the risk with the old treatment. This risk difference or absolute risk reduction is then divided into one (1). Thus 15% minus 10% equals 5%, and 5% (.05) divided into 1 = 20 patients. Another way of stating this is that the NNT is the inverse of the risk difference.
2. The correct answer is B. When the mean, median and mode for a distribution are all the same (equal), then the distribution is considered to be a normally distributed. When the values are different, then the distribution is skewed. When the median is greater (less) than the mean, then the distribution is negatively (positively) skewed.
3. The correct answer is B. The risk of dying within one year with the new drug is 10/100, or 10%.
4. The correct answer is C. The risk of dying within one year with the new drug is 10%. The risk of dying within one year with the old drug is 20%. The relative risk of dying within one-year with the new drug compared to the old drug is 10%/20%, or 50%, or one-half as much.
5. The correct answer is E. It is a Type II error when the null hypothesis of no difference between interventions is accepted when in fact the null hypothesis is false and there is a difference between the interventions. This has the practical effect of withholding a promising treatment from patients who might otherwise be helped by taking it.
6. The correct answer is D. A double-blind study is one in which the treatment assigned to the patient is not known by either the physician-investigator or by the patient. A third, independent party (often a nurse) not associated with the study monitors the patient for adverse effects in the event a treatment needs to be changed for a patient because of safety concerns.
7. The correct answer is B. The mode is the most frequently occurring number in a distribution, which in this instance is 1.
8. The correct answer is A. The Likelihood Ratio for a positive test results is the number of true positives divided by the number of false positives, or 90/10 = 9 in this example.
9. The correct answer is E. The specificity of a test is the percentage of people with no disease who have a negative test result, or the true negatives divided by all negatives (true and false negatives). In this example, the specificity = 180/200 = 90%.

Index

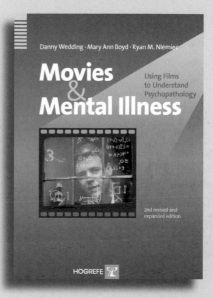 

Order Form for Examination Copies

Attention Teachers!

☐ **I would like to consider *Behavior & Medicine* for possible course adoption. Please send me a free examination copy.**
Hogrefe & Huber reserve the right to evaluate complimentary copy requests for eligibility.

Please enter the following information. All fields must be completed.

New 4th Edition!

Full Name		
Department		
School / University		
Street		
City	State	Zip
Country (if outside USA)		
Phone	Fax	E-mail
Course title / number		Course date
Number of Students	☐ per year	☐ per quarter ☐ per semester
Adoption decision date	This book will likely be	☐ optional ☐ compulsory
Book currently in use		

To obtain a complimentary examination copy of *Behavior and Medicine* by Danny Wedding and Margaret L. Stuber for possible course adoption, please send this form to:

Hogrefe & Huber Publishers • 875 Massachusetts Avenue, 7th Floor · Cambridge, MA 02319
Tel: (866) 823-4726 · Fax: (617) 354-6875 • E-Mail: info@hhpub .com

Or order your examination copy online at: **www.hhpub.com**

Order Form to Purchase

I would like to order:		Price	Total
	Copies of *Behavior & Medicine* by Danny Wedding and Margaret L. Stuber	US $39.95	
		Subtotal	
WA residents add 8.8% sales tax			
Postage & handling: USA: 1st item US $6.00, each additional item US $1.25 Canada: 1st item US $8.00, each additional item US $2.00			
		Total	

Shipping and Billing information

Order online at: www.hhpub.com

☐ Check enclosed   ☐ Please bill me
☐ Charge my: ☐ VISA   ☐ MC   ☐ AmEx

Card # _____

CVV2/CVC2/CID # _____ Exp date _____

Cardholder's Name _____

Signature _____

Shipping address:
Name _____
Address _____
_____
City, State, ZIP _____
E-mail _____
Phone / Fax _____

Order online at: **www.hhpub.com** or call toll-free **(800) 228-3749**
Hogrefe & Huber Publishers • 30 Amberwood Parkway • Ashland, OH 44805 • Tel: (800) 228-3749 • Fax: (419) 281-6883 • E-Mail: info@hhpub.com
Hogrefe & Huber Publishers • Rohnsweg 25 • D-37085 Göttingen • Germany • Tel: +49 551 49609-0 • Fax: +49 551 49609-88 • E-Mail: custserv@hogrefe.com

HOGREFE